LATIN AMERICA

A Modern History

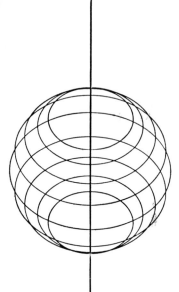

The University of Michigan History of the Modern World

Edited by Allan Nevins and Howard M. Ehrmann

LATIN AMERICA

A Modern History

BY J. FRED RIPPY

Ann Arbor : The University of Michigan Press

TO MY WIFE
Mary D. Allen Rippy

AND

MY THREE SONS
Fred, Robert, and Frazier

Preface

This book is intended both for college and university students and for the general public. It differs from some other works dealing with Latin America in several respects. I have tried, successfully I hope, to avoid producing a mere handbook or a work of reference, and with this in mind I have supplemented facts with interpretation. I have not ignored the two centuries following 1550, a long period often neglected in such surveys. I have given more than the usual emphasis to the international relations of the region from the beginning of the struggle for self-government and independence to the present day, and more than average attention to the literary lights and social critics of the National period, thus permitting the Latin Americans to reveal themselves, their merits, and their conceptions of their defects. I have also stressed the region's economic relations with the outside world, especially during the decades since independence. With the objective of simplification, I have divided the story into long chronological periods. It is likely that some critics will not approve of the time-span that I have allotted to the early National period; but let it be remembered that several of the countries did not become separate nations until 1838 or later and that two of them—Cuba and Panama—did not attain complete independence until more than thirty years after 1900. If 1900 does not seem as satisfactory as some previous year for the termination of what I have described as the early National epoch, the later date will surely become more appropriate with the passing decades. On a less important point I may disturb some of the experts. I have followed the old orthography in spelling Brazilian proper names—the one in use before 1940—in order to avoid confusing those who have read or may read the works of earlier years that have universally employed this orthography.

Convinced that reading lists should be reduced to moderate limits, I have tried to confine them to the most useful and reliable books and monographs, according to my appraisal. No doubt I have omitted not a few works of merit, but most of these can be discovered by close examination of the bibliographies in the works I have included. Absence of titles in these lists—especially Spanish and Portuguese titles, omitted because I have assumed that many readers will not be familiar with those languages—does not signify condemnation. I wish I might have added numerous sources to the lists of secondary works, but the sources are so abundant in the big libraries and so scanty in the smaller ones that I finally decided to exclude nearly all of them and to refer to such compilations as those of Cleven and Keen in the hope that readers may consult at least these two and learn to appreciate the value of eyewitness accounts and contemporary narratives and treatises. It will be observed, however, that I have mentioned several sources at various points in my survey. Those who have access to large libraries will not have difficulty in discovering many others. Those unable to make use of these libraries will have to get along without extensive examination of such sources.

This short account of the history and culture of Latin America is the result of many years of teaching and research and of the stimulating suggestions of a score of colleagues and hundreds of mature students. I shall not here mention any of them by name, but I am grateful to all of them for their inspiration and assistance, and I have identified most of the former and a few of the latter either in my reading lists or my footnotes.

Finally, I wish to point out that I have endeavored to avoid exaggerating the importance of the subject in hand, as I might well have done in the case of a region of primary professional interest to me. But I venture to add that I have no doubt that Latin America will be accorded, particularly in the United States, the attention and consideration it deserves.

Contents

MAPS

THE COLONIAL PERIOD

CHAPTER I

The Physical Environment

🐚 DEFINITION OF LATIN AMERICA

Latin America is not a geographical unit. It includes not only South America, excepting the three Guianas, but also southern North America, all of Central America save British Honduras, and several of the West Indian islands. Its area is more than 8,000,000 square miles, nearly a sixth of the earth's land surface. It was even larger until the middle of the nineteenth century, for it embraced a vast region, often described as the Spanish Borderlands of the United States, extending from California across Arizona, New Mexico, Texas, Louisiana, and the Gulf States to Florida and the Atlantic Ocean.

Neither is Latin America, often called Hispanic America, a political unit, for it is composed of twenty independent nations and Puerto Rico, the latter being a colony or "commonwealth" attached to the United States since 1898. Although half of these twenty nations are quite limited in area, most of the rest have rather extensive territorial domains, some of them among the largest in the world. All of the little nations except Ecuador and Uruguay are in Central America and the West Indies. Only Puerto Rico, El Salvador, and the island republics are densely populated. The inhabitants of the entire region numbered less than 160,000,-000 as late as the middle of the twentieth century.

The term Hispanic America suggests that the influence of Spain and Portugal—the two Hispanic countries—has been of supreme importance in this part of the world. The culture of most of the region is in fact essentially Hispanic. The official language of all but two of the twenty independent nations is Spanish; Brazil's official language is Portuguese and Haiti's French. But the region is often called Latin America because of its historical, racial, and cultural ties with France and Italy as well as with Spain and Portugal; or Ibero-America in honor of the peninsula occupied by the two Hispanic countries; or Indo-Hispanic America in order to call attention to the importance of the aboriginal people whose numbers and influence still persist. Nor should one fail to note the Negro and Negroid elements—mainly the descendants of victims brought in as slaves from Africa during the Colonial epoch—in such countries as Haiti and the Dominican Republic and in certain parts of Central America, Venezuela, Colombia, Ecuador, Peru, and Brazil. Latin America and Hispanic America will be the terms most often used to describe the region in this text.

GENERAL ASPECTS OF THE PHYSICAL ENVIRONMENT

Sixteen of the twenty independent countries of Latin America are situated entirely or mainly in the tropics, but it should not be assumed that all of these are hot countries, since many of them have large areas in high altitudes above tropical heat. Eight of the sixteen have cool highland capitals; [1] the temperature of Lima, a ninth capital, is cooled by the Humboldt Current flowing northward from the Antarctic. Mexico City is never very hot; and while a good portion of Mexico lies close to the Tropic of Cancer, mountains give much of the country a temperate climate. South America not only has vast elevated areas but extends so far toward the South Pole that all of Uruguay, nearly all of Argentina, most of Chile, and a large part of Brazil are situated in the South Temperate Zone. It is a fact, however, that somewhat more than half of Hispanic America consists of tropical lowlands characterized by depressing heat, matted jungle, and many insect pests and diseases that do not afflict the inhabitants of temperate climates.

The region also suffers from a very uneven distribution of rainfall, destructive volcanoes and earthquakes, baffling mountain barriers, scarcity of convenient natural harbors, and lack of good coking coal. A section of southern Mexico, half of Central America, and fully a fifth of South America (southern Chile and most of the basin of the Amazon) receive too much rain. Vast stretches in northern Mexico, western Peru, northern Chile, western and southern Argentina, and east central Brazil receive too little or none at all, while in many other areas the dry seasons are too arid and the wet seasons too wet.

These are grave handicaps. But Latin America has many resources in compensation. The region contains rich and varied mineral deposits, extensive and valuable forests, and a great variety of climates and soils adapted to the cultivation of numerous useful products, including wheat, barley, oats, flax, and corn as well as manioc, cacao, rice, sugar cane, coffee, cotton, bananas, pineapple, citrus fruits, tobacco, and coca. The region also contains large areas, some of them tropical plateaus and

Relief Map
of South America with Political Boundaries of 1950

MAP 1

others temperate lowlands, which are among the most favorable in the world for the raising of livestock.

The animals native to Latin America are quite different from those of Europe and Asia and largely different from those in the region later occupied by the United States. Many of the important animals familiar to the Old World were not to be found in America when the first Europeans arrived. Among those absent were elephants, camels, horses, cattle, sheep, swine, mules, and donkeys. The llamas, alpacas, and vicuñas of the mountains and plateaus of South America were poor substitutes for the domesticated livestock of Europe and Asia; nor were there in America any barnyard fowls such as chickens and geese. And although a few fur-bearing animals inhabited Latin America, these were far less numerous than in the regions that were to become the United States and Canada, so that the fur trade was comparatively unimportant in the development of the Hispanic countries of the New World. Fishing was also of minor significance; for while there were many edible fish in the streams of Latin America and in its adjacent seas, black bass and cod, salmon and mackerel, important foods of Anglo-Saxon America, were wholly or largely lacking. Hampered in these respects, Hispanic America was tortured by a multitude of venomous reptiles and pestiferous insects. The following is an incomplete list of the perils and plagues with which both men and beasts had to contend: deadly spiders and snakes; alligators, crocodiles, boas, and anacondas; jaguars, pumas, and small wolves; cannibal fish and electric eels; vampire (blood-drinking) bats, houseflies, gnats, fleas, ticks, chiggers, grasshoppers, and locusts. And, until very recently, mosquitoes bearing the germs of malaria and yellow fever infested nearly all the coastlands and some parts of the interior.

The native plants of Latin America were numerous. Many nuts, fruits, berries, and edible roots grew wild, and the American aborigines domesticated a large number of plants, as will be observed in another connection. But, until the arrival of the Europeans, many food plants familiar to Europe and Asia were lacking. Among them were barley, wheat, rye, oats, rice, sugar cane, coffee bushes, and many fruit-bearing trees that filled the orchards of the Old World.

Such, in general, are the resources and physical environment of Latin America. For the purpose of closer inspection the region may be divided into four major parts: Mexico, Central America, the West Indies, and South America.

MEXICO

Mexico has a wide variety of climates—hot, cool, and cold; wet and dry—and a rather small area of fertile arable land, but it also possesses

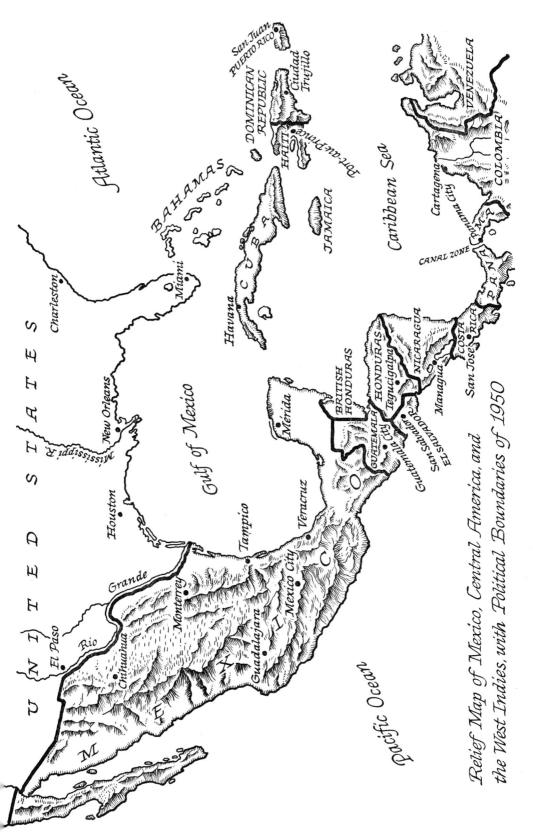

Relief Map of Mexico, Central America, and
the West Indies, with Political Boundaries of 1950

UNITED STATES

Atlantic Ocean

Charleston

Miami

BAHAMAS

San Juan
PUERTO RICO

DOMINICAN
REPUBLIC

Ciudad
Trujillo

HAITI

Port-au-Prince

CUBA

Havana

JAMAICA

Caribbean Sea

VENEZUELA

Cartagena

COLOMBIA

Panama City

PANAMA

CANAL ZONE

COSTA
RICA

San José

Managua

NICARAGUA

Tegucigalpa

HONDURAS

San Salvador
EL SALVADOR

GUATEMALA

Guatemala City

BRITISH
HONDURAS

Mérida

Gulf of Mexico

New Orleans

Mississippi R.

Houston

Tampico

Veracruz

Mexico City

Guadalajara

MEXICO

Monterrey

Chihuahua

Rio Grande

El Paso

Pacific Ocean

MAP 2

abundant minerals, some useful forests, and an isthmus of significance in world commerce and defense strategy. A land without large rivers, it is crowded with mountains: a range in the east, a higher range in the west, a third range connecting the two in the south, and still more mountains in the far south, beyond the Isthmus of Tehuantepec. Extending from the southern sierra northward between the eastern and western ranges is a great plateau which slopes down gradually until it disappears near the Río Grande or joins the highlands of New Mexico and Arizona. The southern portion of this plateau, bordered by snow-clad volcanic peaks, includes a sixth of the total area of present-day Mexico and is the heart of the country. Its altitude, running from 6,000 to 8,000 feet, affords a pleasant climate the year around. Its rainfall is sufficient to produce corn, wheat, beans, peas, and other vegetables without irrigation. Underneath much of its fertile soil are rich deposits of minerals. The larger northern portion of this great plateau, not only lower than the southern part but deficient in rainfall, is both colder in winter and hotter in summer. Poorly adapted to agriculture, although a few streams and pools provide irrigation, it is primarily a mining and grazing region.

Coastal plains make up most of the rest of Mexico. The western coastal plain is narrow. For hundreds of miles in the south there is hardly any coastal plain at all; but it widens in the north, along the Gulf of California, and although very dry here, it is crossed by several small rivers which supply water for irrigation. The long peninsula of Lower California, a plains country interrupted by a few hills, is both dry and barren. Mexico's eastern coastal plain, bordering the Gulf, is much wider than the western, but a considerable portion of it is tropical jungle or swamp. It contains a wealth of petroleum, and certain parts of it are adapted to tropical agriculture. In the southeast, it broadens out into the semiarid peninsula of Yucatán, where sisal hemp, corn, beans, peas, and other foods may be successfully cultivated. The Isthmus of Tehuantepec, also a sort of coastal plain, is suited to tropical agriculture. And with adequate means of transportation, the steep mountains farther south might be made to yield corn, potatoes, fruits, vegetables, and coffee for national and foreign markets.

CENTRAL AMERICA AND THE WEST INDIES

A backbone of highlands runs the full length of Central America, tapering off into low hills in the central part of Panama. The total area of the region is only a little more than 200,000 square miles. The highlands, much closer to the Pacific than to the Caribbean, include nests of volcanic peaks rising to heights of 12,000 to 14,000 feet which break the terrain into numerous isolated districts separated by deep gorges and dense jungle. The broad eastern lowlands suffer from excessive rainfall and perpetual humid heat, but they are capable of yielding forest products, bananas, cacao, rice, sugar cane, and many other tropical commodities. The narrow Pacific lowlands are less humid and somewhat less stifling. The chief physical assets of Central America are its fertile soils, forests, minerals, and scenery, and its location between two great oceans. Its major crops before the arrival of the Europeans were corn, beans, cacao, squash, and other vegetables, to which were later added sugar cane, coffee, bananas, and rice. Its major handicaps are high mountains, volcanoes, earthquakes, and the heavy rainfall and depressing heat of the eastern plains.

It is likely that the West Indies are the remnant of an extensive land mass that once connected Florida with the continent of South America. In historical times, however, only the islands, scores of them, have remained above water. The larger islands are known as the Greater Antilles. Other groups are the Lesser Antilles and the Bahamas. At one time or another, the Spaniards occupied the majority of them, but it will be sufficient here to mention only the most important: Cuba, Jamaica, Puerto Rico, and Española (namely, "Little Spain," sometimes called Hispaniola or Haiti). A mountain chain, now partially submerged, extends through these Greater Antilles, rising from less than 4,000 feet in Puerto Rico, to 7,000 in Jamaica, 8,000 in Cuba, and 12,000 in Española, providing relief from the tropical heat and determining the distribution of rainfall, so that the southern parts of the islands are more arid than the other sections. The main resources of the group are fertile soils, succulent grasslands, great forests, and some minerals. Cuba is best endowed with metals (copper, iron, nickel), and Cuba and Jamaica have somewhat more agreeable climates than their neighbors.

SOUTH AMERICA

South America is a continent of parched deserts, dense jungles, lofty mountains, immense plateaus, huge rivers, vast forests, spacious plains, rich minerals, suffocating heat, biting cold, and eternal spring. More than twice the size of the United States, plus Alaska, it juts far out toward Africa and lies for the most part to the east of North America. Some 4,500 miles long, its maximum width is about 3,000 miles. Its towering Andes, exceeded in height only by Asia's Himalayas, run the full length of the continent, the southern three-fifths of them almost within sight of the Pacific Ocean, and the spread of their giant ranges measures several hundred miles in some sections. The Guiana and the Brazilian Highlands on the east also cover an immense territory. Yet, in spite of these tremendous mountain masses, more than 60 per cent of the surface of South America lies less than 1,000 feet above sea level and the major parts of the continent's lowlands are within the humid and debilitating heat of the tropics. Besides the mighty Amazon, the world's largest river, South America contains three other important river systems: the Orinoco, the Magdalena, and the Río de la Plata. But not one of these big rivers flows into the Pacific; all rise in the tropics and all but one, the Plata, wind through tropical forest and jungle to the sea, so that the major parts of their great basins are unpleasant habitats for man.

Mountains and plateaus.—The three mountain systems of South America crowd the adjacent seas, reduce the width of the coastal plains, and limit the number of available natural harbors. Large sums of money and much labor have been required to make the ports safe and convenient.

The Andes almost defy description. They are composed of five rather distinct regions, which, from south to north, are as follows:

1. In the extreme south, the range is narrow and of moderate height. Rainfall is heavy; lakes, snowfields, glaciers, and timber are abundant; snow, sleet, and cold winds discourage hunters and fishermen.

2. Farther north, the mountains climb to dizzy heights, forming a single lofty range 700 miles long, with peaks rising well above 20,000 feet and with few passes. Precipitation is rather light; the temperature shifts rapidly from one extreme to the other. Deposits of precious metals are likely, but there is little attraction for permanent human habitation.

3. The Andes spread out as they approach the northern third of modern Chile, splitting into inner and outer chains, and sometimes into three cordilleras, which extend northward for more than 1,500 miles, with plateaus ranging from 6,500 to 16,000 feet running between them, and with almost no passes lower than 12,000. Most of this is an arid stretch where rain seldom falls and where snow is rarely seen except on the giant peaks. The nights are cold, and even the summer temperatures of the plateaus are so low in many sections that only the hardiest crops and grasses will grow. Salt marshes are numerous toward the north, and there are a few lakes, among them Titicaca, 13,000 feet above the sea, the world's highest navigable body of water. It it evident that this region is not well suited to agriculture and livestock. But it is exceedingly rich in minerals, including copper, vanadium, gold, silver, tin, and many others.

4. The mountains become somewhat narrower as they approach modern Ecuador, eventually forming two giant ranges that continue for 500 miles across the equator and beyond, ranges crowned by volcanoes, active or extinct, with a great plateau running between and with fertile

lands and precipitation sufficient for grass and crops. All is green now. The nights are chilly but the days are usually warm.

5. A hundred miles or so north of the equator, in the southern part of modern Colombia, the mountains spread out again into three separate cordilleras which run north or northeast toward the Caribbean, but two of them disappear before they reach the sea and the third, the easternmost, sends a branch around Lake Maracaibo and along the northern coast of modern Venezuela before it terminates. These giant ranges are drained mainly by the Cauca and the Magdalena, but from the eastern cordillera, which embraces the delightful plateau of Cundinamarca, some of the waters flow into the tributaries of the Orinoco and the Amazon. Here, again, nearly all of the landscape is green and there are perpetual warm days and cool nights. But the valleys of the Cauca and the Magdalena, especially the latter, are humid and hot and filled with pestiferous insects. (These Andean ranges have no connection with a mountain mass which rises precipitously some seventy miles east of the Magdalena River and towers above the Caribbean port of Santa Marta.)

Such are the colossal Andes. Occupying nearly a fifth of South America and forming a part of seven of its independent nations, they interpose a formidable barrier to land transportation. Although several railways and highways have been built from the Pacific coast up into the high plateaus, few have ever been pushed directly across the lofty cordilleras into the eastern lowlands and plains. Much of this vast mountain region is barren of timber and vegetation; but it is a magnificent storehouse of minerals and metals, and the two northern sections have more agreeable climates and richer vegetations than the other three.

The Guiana Highlands of northeastern South America, which form the great watershed between the basins of the Orinoco and the Amazon, are not much higher than the mountains in the eastern part of the United States, although some of their peaks reach an elevation of 10,000 to 12,000 feet. The trade winds bring heavy rains to their northern slopes, but their southern slopes are rather arid. Dense tropical forests, deep gorges, and numerous waterfalls and rapids make them almost inaccessible. Even now they are still undeveloped and almost uninhabited save by a few roving native tribes, but they are believed to be rich in minerals and forest products.

South of the Amazon Valley, the Brazilian Highlands occupy an immense area, a fourth of modern Brazil. They run along the Brazilian coast for 1,700 miles, from a few miles south of Brazil's easternmost shoulder almost to its southern boundary, and spread out hundreds of miles into the interior, sloping gently toward the west, so that, with few exceptions, the rivers that drain them flow into the tributaries of the Amazon and the Río de la Plata. Their mean elevation is about 4,000 feet, with a few peaks rising to 10,000. Their climate in the northeast is hot and dry; elsewhere it is not far from ideal: warm days, cool nights, adequate rainfall. Most of the region they occupy is excellent farming and grazing country and a good part of it contains diamonds, gold, iron, manganese, and almost every kind of mineral and metal. Falls, which interrupt navigation on nearly all of the rivers, are capable of supplying abundant hydroelectric power. Many of the slopes and valleys produce open woods or heavy forests, but broad savannas and scrubby bushes and trees are characteristic of most of the area. The southern section of these highlands, part of it still occupied by pine forests, has become the world's most famous producer of coffee.

Coastal and other plains and river basins.—Most of South America's coastal plains are narrow. On the Pacific side, from the Isthmus of Panama to the Gulf of Guayaquil, they are generally hot, rainy, and unhealthful, but the major part of them is covered with dense evergreen forests that contain valuable timbers, nuts, dyewoods, and medicinal ingredients. Included among the resources of the southern section are the leafy palms of which the finest "Panama" hats are made. The long stretch south of Guayaquil, extending nearly 2,000 miles across modern Peru and into northern Chile, is arid, much of it a desert, but the Peruvian section is traversed by numerous streams that make irrigation possible, and the extremely dry southern portion is rich in nitrates, guano, borax, iodine, and metals. Moreover, the cool Humboldt Current moderates the heat of most of the entire area. The rest of the Pacific coastal plain, running far down toward the southern end of Chile, where it is interrupted by a string of islands, is very narrow; but to the east, beyond the low coastal range, is a long valley which forms the heart of Chile and for present purposes may be considered a part of the coastal plain. With its fertile soil and most agreeable climate, this long Chilean valley is one of the garden regions of South America. Although irrigation is necessary in the northern portion, mountain streams plunging down the Andes supply considerable water for this purpose. The southern part, cooler than the northern, receives plenty of rain; in fact, rather too much in the extreme south.

The coastal plain of northern South America is mostly dense jungle until the mouth of the Atrato River is reached. East of this river, the plain tends to become wider as it extends along the Caribbean and the Gulf of Maracaibo. Here we find less rainfall, fewer trees and shrubs, and somewhat less oppressive heat. Some miles beyond Lake Maracaibo, the plain becomes narrower as it skirts northern Venezuela until it bends southeastward and finally merges with the broad delta of the Orinoco. Then, shrinking in width once more, it runs along the Atlantic, furnishing wet land for rice and bauxite for industry, and eventually merges with the huge delta of the Amazon. Beyond this delta, it continues in disconnected strips, some fairly wide and others very narrow, until it reaches the Plata Estuary and the great Argentine pampas. Appearing again in southern Argentina, it borders the uplands of Patagonia and finally approaches the Strait of Magellan. More than half of this 6,000-mile coastal plain bordering the Caribbean and the Atlantic is soggy and covered with dense forests and swamps. Some of it, however, is good farm land and some sections grow ample grass for livestock. The bays and inlets that break it here and there form South America's best harbors.

Compared with South America's other great plains, these lengthy coastal areas are of minor significance. The most extensive plains regions on the continent are closely connected with its great rivers and may be conveniently described along with the rivers themselves.

The main stream of the mighty Amazon is 4,000 miles long. The distance across its mouths averages about fifty miles, and for more than 200 miles along its lower reaches, its width is from eight to ten miles, and even twenty miles in periods of flood. Its depth in some places runs from 300 to 400 feet. Together with its tributaries, it drains a basin of 2,000,-000 square miles, more than a fourth of the continent, and provides inland transportation for a total distance of 20,000 miles. (Ocean steamers ascend the main channel for several hundred miles.) The great valley supports a huge equatorial forest, the crowning glory of the vegetable world, which contains valuable trees, oils, nuts, gums, and medicines, but its most esteemed product for more than a century was rubber. Here and there within this huge basin are a number of pleasant open plains and savannas; but, on the whole, it is hot and very humid, much of it covered by swamps, especially during the flood season. Its population was still very scanty as late as 1950. The difficulties of human habitation in this spacious region should not be exaggerated, but they seem to have been almost insurmountable.

The Brazilian campos occupy the vast space between the middle Amazon Basin and the Brazilian Highlands. They are an almost endless succession of gently rolling plains dotted now and then by clumps of trees. Each year witnesses a wet and a dry season, without great variation in temperature, the annual average being around 75°F. Although some sections occasionally suffer from drought, the campos are mostly good range country.

The Orinoco and its tributaries drain an area of 600,000 square miles and provide more than 3,000 miles of navigable waters. In seasons of flood, the river is connected by means of the Casiquiare with the great Amazonian system.The llanos (plains) of Venezuela and the less-known llanos of southeastern Colombia lie to the north and west of the main stream; on the south and east, jungles, forests, and mountains stretch away from its banks, and the major natural resources are forest products, gold, and iron. Although the plains on the north and west are a fairly good livestock region, seasonal floods and droughts, along with intense heat and plagues of insects, make life rather difficult for both man and beast.

The Magdalena Basin is only half as large as that of the Orinoco. The main river is only 1,000 miles long; and although four-fifths of it is navigable, navigation is interrupted by rapids at three different points. A considerable part of the basin, narrow except in the area within 200 miles of the river's mouth, is covered with swamps and forests, but it includes some good farming and grazing land. The climate is hot throughout the year and stifling during the rainy periods.

The valley of the Cauca, the Magdalena's largest tributary, rising in the south and flowing into it from the west, enjoys, in general, a better climate and more extensive areas suited to agriculture and stock raising. In fact, if the valley were not quite so hot, it would be ideal for these purposes. Compensating its handicaps are the gold veins and gold-bearing sands of the main stream and its tributaries.

Second in size among the great river basins of South America, the Río de la Plata is first in importance. A broad estuary and not a river, it receives the waters of the Uruguay, the Paraná, and the Paraguay, all of which have their origin in modern Brazil. The Plata Basin covers an area of over 1,000,000 square miles, almost half of it lying within the South Temperate Zone. It furnishes around 2,000 miles of water transportation and nearly 500 miles for ocean-going steamers. Rainfall is plentiful and satisfactorily distributed throughout most of the basin, which is well adapted to farming and grazing. Although timber is not plentiful, there are many clumps of pines and other trees, and, in the north, an abundance of quebracho, which supplies excellent material for tanning leather. Along the Paraná River, near the borders of Argentina, Paraguay, and Brazil, yerba maté furnishes a tea much esteemed in these countries and Uruguay. Toward the east, from the lower part of the basin, grassy and partially forested plains roll away to the Atlantic, across southern Brazil and Uruguay; stretching far away to the west, are the immense level and treeless pampas of modern Argentina, a resource more valuable, except along the arid western edge, than the campos of Brazil or the llanos of Venezuela and Colombia and, because of their proximity to the sea, their milder climate, and their more dependable rainfall, probably more valuable than much of the great plains of the United States.

From the mouth of the Plata Estuary the pampas extend toward the southwest and eventually merge with the rolling plains of Patagonia, which are temperate and rather arid in the north but moist and much colder in the south, especially the far south. Mainly a sheep country, Patagonia contains a number of waterfalls and some minerals.

This immense, varied, and complex physical setting must be kept constantly in mind if the history of Hispanic America is to be properly understood. Man's destiny depends not alone on his genius; it is also shaped by his geographical environment.

CHAPTER II

The First Americans

The coming of white men to America in 1492 and afterward was but a recent episode in the long life of the New World. The first members of the human race began to arrive 15,000 to 20,000 years before.

FIRST OCCUPANTS OF THE NEW WORLD

The earliest human occupants of America came in successive groups, perhaps century after century, from northeastern Asia, crossing over to Alaska by way of Bering Strait or the Aleutian Islands. Later they ceased to come and those in America lost contact with the home country. They were yellowish-brown people known as Mongoloids, kinsmen of the inhabitants of China and Japan; before them lay two continents, a virgin area of 16,000,000 square miles.

They were primitive people of the Stone Age, nomads who obtained their food by hunting and fishing and gathering wild fruits, grasses, and roots. They knew nothing about agriculture, and the dog was the only domestic animal they possessed. But they knew how to chip and polish stone, to twist bark or twigs into a string, to contrive simple baskets and nets, to make vessels of wood, bark, and skin; and for weapons they had throwing sticks, harpoons, and bows and arrows.

The occupation of the Americas by these Mongoloids, whom the Spaniards later called Indians, required many centuries. They probably reached the central plateau of Mexico around 8000 or 9000 B.C., and began their long trek into South America a thousand years or so later. By the time the first white men arrived, the Mongoloids had spread out over both continents. Many areas had few inhabitants; others were fairly thickly settled. The total native population of the New World in 1500 may have been 25,000,000 or more.

The progress of the Indians from hunting, fishing, and food-collecting was slow. It was in northern Central America or southern Mexico that they first learned to cultivate the most useful plants for food and other supplies. Maize, or Indian corn, was perhaps the first plant that they domesticated. They developed it from a wild grass, perhaps as early as 4000 B.C. Through the centuries, the natives of this and other regions gradually domesticated and cultivated many other plants for food, drink, clothing, and various purposes. Among these were: beans, squash, gourds, melons, peanuts, peppers, white and sweet potatoes, tomatoes, manioc (cassava and tapioca), cacao, quinoa (a kind of buckwheat), guava, pineapple, avocado, tobacco, cotton, sisal hemp (*henequén*), and agave (maguey, or the century plant). Apparently potatoes, manioc, guava, quinoa, and a few others were first cultivated in South America. Only the natives of Peru became drovers and herders, domesticating and developing there two animals of great importance to them, the llama and alpaca.

When the white men first reached the New World the majority of its inhabitants were engaged in agriculture either as a primary or as a secondary means of obtaining their food supply. Three or four millions of them, however, were still pure nomads, roaming over immense regions, hunting, fishing, and collecting wild fruits, berries, roots, and grasses just as their ancestors had done thousands of years before. This was true of the Indians of Alaska and most of Canada, of the Pacific coast and the western plains of the United States, and of southern South America. The natives of eastern North America, of the West Indies, and of northern and eastern South America engaged to some extent in agriculture, but were mainly hunters, fishermen, and food collectors. Elsewhere—largely in the mountains and plateaus from Arizona and New Mexico to northern Chile and northwestern Argentina—the American Indians depended mostly upon cultivated crops for their sustenance. These sedentary Indians composed the vast majority, although the areas they occupied were small compared with the spacious regions over which their nomadic kinsmen wandered.

Wherever agriculture was fully developed, the habits, religions, customs, and political organizations of the Indians were transformed. Their way of life, their culture, became complex. With more abundant food close at hand, population grew, economic activities became more varied, and specialization occurred. Villages became towns and cities. There were not only hunters and farmers now but artisans, merchants, porters, rulers, administrators, professional soldiers, and more medicine men and priests. Metal-working, architecture, sculpture, mathematics, engineering, astronomy, and medical science developed. Records were kept. Schools were established, at least for the upper classes. Leagues, confederacies, and empires made their appearance, welding larger areas

Principal Cultural Areas
of Primitive America

1 Arctic or Eskimo
2 Northwest or North Pacific Coast
3 California Great Basin
4 Plateau
5 Mackenzie-Yukon
6 Plains
7 Northeast or Northern Woodland
8 Southeast or Southern Woodland
9 Southwest
10 Nahua-Maya
11 Colombia or Chibcha
12 Andean or Incan
13 Patagonia
14 Tropical Forest
15 Antillean

MAP 3

into political units. Only these more sedentary natives will be considered in this discussion. The others were of minor importance, although they gave the whites considerable trouble and sometimes much-needed assistance, both in times of war and in times of peace.

At least five civilizations, or semicivilizations, had been developed in the New World by the time the Spaniards arrived. Three of these were in North and Central America. The other two were in South America.

⚜ THE CRADLE OF NATIVE CIVILIZATION

The earliest of the advanced cultures in native America was perhaps that of the Mayas (no. 10 on Map 3), from whom some of the others borrowed extensively. The home of the Mayas was southeastern Mexico (mainly Yucatán) and the northern part of Central America. Many scholars think the Mayas reached the highest development ever attained by the first Americans. They started their cultural advance in northern Central America about 100 B.C., but they suffered reversals. They reached the first zenith of their civilization between 600 and 700 A.D. Then there was a decline; between 800 and 1000 A.D. they went through their Dark Age. During this period they shifted northward into Yucatán, where their civilization flowered again between the years 1000 and 1200. But before the Europeans arrived, this civilization had also collapsed. The Mayas were no longer living in pretentious cities and towns; most of them were dwelling in straw-covered wooden huts clustered together in villages. They were not united; they were divided into numerous tribal groups at war with one another and unprepared for common defense. But they were still industrious farmers, craftsmen, and traders. The causes of their reverses and final decline are not fully known. Probably the most important were changes in climate, exhaustion of the soil, inability to live together in harmony, and perhaps some sort of plague.

The civilization of the Mayas was rather remarkable when at its height. Their learned men knew more about astronomy than was known at the time anywhere else in the world. Their calendar was very accurate, their year containing 365 days, with an extra day for every fourth year. They invented a system of numbers in which the zero was used as we use it, except that they counted by multiples of twenty instead of ten. Their system of writing was less brilliant. They did not invent an alphabet, but they reduced picture writing to a convenient abbreviated form. They recorded important dates in their history on stone shafts erected on the streets of their cities. They built huge temples and palaces in their towns, using stone and stucco as materials. Their temples were usually constructed on a broad, high platform shaped like a pyramid with the top cut off (a "truncated" pyramid). The palaces were larger than the temples, but their foundations were lower. These buildings, some of which are still standing in the jungles for scholars to examine, were adorned with beautiful statues and a riot of carvings. The Mayas were also skilled in pottery, and they made gorgeous ornaments of gold, silver, copper, and bronze, but seldom used metal for tools or weapons. They were expert weavers; some of their cotton textiles were so fine that the Spaniards thought they were silk. They made large canoes and equipped them with oars and sails. Maya merchants, who also traveled widely by land, used these canoes for coastal trade, and it is said that they navigated as far away as Cuba.

Religion was a mighty influence in Mayan life. All of their affairs were thought to depend upon the pleasure or anger of numerous gods, who were believed to control everything: disease, health, rain, winds, fertility, the sun, the moon, and all the heavenly bodies. Nothing was so important as the avoidance of the displeasure and the cultivation of the approval of these divinities. That was the main purpose of all their studies of the earth and astronomy. That was the main function of their many priests and religious ceremonies, of their temples and sacrifices, which, in the later period, included human beings. The bleeding hearts of prisoners of war were torn from their bodies and thrown upon the images of the gods in the hope of winning their favor. Young men and women of the Mayas were also sacrificed. Sometimes the young women were thrown into the sacred wells (*cenotes*) of Yucatán, perhaps in the hope of inducing the rain god to send rain.

The great mass of the Mayas worked very hard in order to gain a living and support the nobles (warriors) and priests. The majority were farmers, who cultivated maize, beans, squash, peppers, cacao, cotton, sisal hemp, and century plant. Plots of ground were distributed by the rulers to heads of families for cultivation, but the people did not own the land. There were also many artisans—spinners, weavers, carpenters, painters, masons, sculptors, and so on—and numerous merchants. Slaves were bought or captured from neighboring tribes, and the Mayas themselves were conscripted to work on the temples, palaces, and roads. For meat the Mayas depended on deer, some rabbit-like animals, and fish; and they domesticated bees for their honey and wax. Dyes, pigments, and paints were obtained from crushed insects (cochineal), forests, and the soil.

During most of the long period before their final decline, the Mayas were composed of a group of independent city states. But during the two great epochs when they reached the height of their cultural achievements their warriors and priests organized rather stable confederations, often referred to as empires. The last of these was dominated by a league of three cities in northern Yucatán which managed to keep the peace in Mayaland for nearly two centuries. Then the rulers of two of the cities became violent enemies, and shortly before 1200 one of them called in military assistance from the outside. The alien invaders—they were probably the Toltecs, who were neighbors on the west—soon got the upper hand, and held the Mayas in subjection for more than two centuries. It was not until the year 1450, after a decade of struggle, that they regained their independence. The war had left their northern towns in ruins, however, and they abandoned some of them, migrating southward toward the scene of their earlier accomplishments. They never rose to cultural greatness again.

THE SUBJECTS OF MONTEZUMA

The southern part of Mexico's great central plateau, often called the Valley of Mexico, was the seat of another civilization of the first Americans (no. 10 on Map 3). It is generally known as the civilization of the Aztecs because the rulers of the region at the time of the Spanish invasion belonged to the Aztec tribe. The Aztecs, however, did not create this civilization. They simply took over what others had created, organized it, and made certain modifications and expansions. The Aztecs were newcomers and merely one of the many Nahua-speaking tribes who had been migrating into the region from the north over a period of centuries. The earliest of the Nahua immigrants may have been the Toltecs, the Zapotecs, and the Mixtecs, who probably arrived in the Valley of Mexico between 500 and 600 A.D. It was these and other Nahua tribes who built the earliest civilization in the heart of Mexico, and even they were not altogether originators. They acquired the rudiments of agriculture from other Indians who had been sowing and reaping in this delightful region for centuries, and they also learned even more from the Mayas.

The Aztecs did not appear upon the scene until the middle of the eleventh century; and for many years after they arrived, they wandered about unwelcome among the Nahua "oldtimers." Finally, about the year 1324, they settled in the swamps of Lake Tezcoco, where they established a village of miserable grass huts, but through the years they improved their home until it became a substantial island. Their village grew into a city of 200,000 or more and was named Tenochtitlán. Meantime, from their fortified base, they raided the neighboring towns; and before the middle of the fifteenth century—probably in 1437—they formed an alliance with two Nahua cities on the borders of the lake, the cities of Tezcoco and Tlacopán. The Aztecs soon dominated the league and extended their sway over an expanding "empire," which, at its height, may have included a third of the territory of modern Mexico and may have contained a population of 11,000,000. The so-called empires of the Mayas were tiny in comparison with this Mexican state. At their zenith, the Mayas perhaps never numbered more than 1,000,000 or so.

The empire of the Aztecs, or the triple alliance, was not a closely-knit unit. The "emperor" at Tenochtitlán left the kings, or chiefs, of the other two cities of the league largely free to manage their local affairs; other towns, tribes, and districts might also have their own chiefs, provided Aztec merchants were well treated and taxes promptly paid. Heavy tribute was exacted from these tribes in every kind of produce and in human beings for sacrifice to the gods.

The Aztec monarchy was hereditary. The ruler was selected from the royal family by a group of family headmen and was advised by a council which included two high priests. The best known of the Aztec rulers, whom the Spaniards called emperors, were Montezuma I, or Moctezuma I, and his grand-nephew, Montezuma II.

The civilization developed in the Valley of Mexico by the Aztecs and the other Nahua-speaking tribes was in many ways similar to that of the Mayas, from whom they borrowed extensively. Like the Mayas, the Aztecs and their Nahua contemporaries and predecessors constructed many magnificent palaces and pyramidal temples for the worship of their numerous gods. They had more abundant food plants and a greater variety of meats than the Mayas possessed, and their tools, weapons, and building materials were superior. The Nahuas, particularly the Aztecs, were also more capable organizers. Their law courts and their schools were more elaborate; their temples and palaces were more massive and spacious, though less gracefully embellished. Their gods were more abundant, more grotesque, and believed to be more difficult to placate, and their shrines and priests were accordingly more numerous. Their altars were saturated with blood; sacrifices were offered constantly to a multitude of gods deemed more hostile than benevolent. Quail, rabbits, and thousands of human victims were offered up, especially to the terrible war god.

Among their deities was Quetzalcoatl (the "Fair God"), presumed to be far more kindly than many others but destined to a fatal role in the relations of the Aztecs with the Spaniards. He was a sort of cultural hero, who was believed once to have instructed the Nahuas in agriculture and the arts, and was expected to return some day and impart further knowledge and skill in these practical occupations.

Regarding mathematics and astronomy the Aztecs and their Nahua kinsmen probably knew less than the Mayas did. Their calendar was less accurate, although their great calendar stone was intricate and artistic; and their system of writing was somewhat less advanced.

The nobility of the Aztec state was composed of priests, war chiefs and high officials of the government, and a number of leading merchants. The monarch and many of the nobility lived in large stone mansions, luxuriously furnished, equipped with fountains and baths, and surrounded by beautiful gardens. The common people dwelt in hovels of stalks, branches, bamboo, or sun-dried brick, covered with maguey, palm leaves, or grass. They owned no farm lands. They led a laborious existence—the women and children as well as the men. They not only tilled the soil; they carried on household industries, built roads, temples, palaces, and fortifications, and served as soldiers and beasts of burden. Slaves were numerous, and included not only captives from the unrelated frontier tribes but also Nahua kinsmen of the Aztecs and some of the Aztecs as well.

The crowning achievement of the Aztecs was their capital, Tenochtitlán, which later became Mexico City. Built out in a lake, it was connected with the shore by broad roadways of stone and cement, with drawbridges that could be raised to prevent the approach of an enemy. It contained one wide avenue running through the center; elsewhere streets alternated with canals for boatmen. The streets were watered and cleaned daily. On making the rounds of the capital, the observer might see large stone dwellings, several palaces, a score or more of temple pyramids, wooden houses built on poles driven into the marshes, floating gardens of vegetables and flowers, and a busy market place filled with thousands of traders.

Besides the three cities of the Aztec league, there were a number of other towns; but they were less magnificent than Tenochtitlán. Cholula, however, seventy-five miles to the southeast, was famous for its shrines. It was a religious center for the surrounding tribes and is said to have contained 200 temples. Most of these were perhaps rather modest structures; but one, dedicated to the worship of Quetzalcoatl, was built on the top of a huge truncated pyramid larger at its base than the Egyptian pyramid of Cheops. The ruins of several of the temples of the Aztec empire may still be seen in Mexico; some of them have been rebuilt, or "restored," so as to resemble as nearly as possible their original form.

APARTMENT DWELLERS OF THE SOUTHWEST

Present-day New Mexico, Arizona, and Chihuahua (a Mexican state) were the home of the Pueblos (no. 9 on Map 3), another group of semicivilized Indians. Their culture, largely borrowed from Mexico and Central America, was less complex than that of the Nahuas and the Mayas. For centuries they dwelt in villages on top of cliffs along the edges of canyons, the whole village living in a single large dwelling containing many rooms. These locations could easily be defended, while corn and cotton and other plants could be cultivated in the fertile valleys below. Around 1100 or 1200 A.D. the Pueblos moved out onto the plains, where they established their villages on the flat tops of the mesas (small tablelands); but still each village continued to live in one large house—a rectangular, terraced, apartment-like building, made of adobe or stone and covered with poles or wickerwork and a layer of clay, an edifice sometimes rising to the height of five or six stories and housing hundreds of people. The Pueblos were good farmers; they knew how to irrigate their land. They were also skilled in weaving and pottery, and they domesticated the turkey. Like the Aztecs and Mayas, they gave much attention to the worship and appeasement of their gods; priests and medicine men were numerous and influential. But the Pueblos built no stately temples and sacrificed no human beings; nor did they possess a calendar or any system of writing.

Neither were the Pueblos remarkable for their political capacity. Each of the seventy villages in existence when the Spaniards first invaded their country seems to have been independent. Every village had its governor and its war chief, as well as a powerful religious officer. The total population at that time was some 70,000. Because of their prevailing localism, their lack of a central political organization, the Pueblos would not be difficult to subdue. Yet the influence of their religious leaders would make them restive under Roman Catholic priests, and a few decades after their conquest, a number of their villages would band together in revolt against the Spanish authorities.

The descendants of the Pueblos and their neighbors were still living in Arizona and New Mexico at the middle of the twentieth century, and their style of architecture was partly adopted in some of the towns of these states. The influence of Pueblo culture, especially before their subjugation, extended to the tribes on their western and southern borders, raising them to a higher level of civilization.

THE CHIBCHAS OF CUNDINAMARCA

Far away in northern South America, on the central plateau of modern Colombia in a region called Cundinamarca, a semicivilization had been constructed by the Chibchas before the Europeans came to the New World (no. 11 on Map 3). More advanced than that of the Pueblos, it fell considerably short of the achievements of the Mayas and the Aztecs. The Chibcha homeland embraced a region of about 6,000 square miles, which was rather densely occupied, for its population probably numbered at least 1,000,000 in 1500. How long the Chibchas had lived in this area is not definitely known; perhaps for several centuries.

The Chibchas were industrious farmers, cultivating maize, potatoes, beans, manioc, squash, quinoa, and some cotton, and irrigating their lands when necessary. They were experts in dyeing and weaving. They were skilled in goldwork and pottery, but they had no copper. They mined salt and emeralds, but apparently obtained their gold from other Indians. They engaged in brisk trade with their neighbors, improving communications by means of roads and suspension bridges, and exchanging salt, jewels, and other products for fruits, skins, timber, bamboo, cane, gold, silver, and coca leaves (from which cocaine is extracted), which they were fond of chewing. They possessed a system of numbers and a fairly accurate calendar. They made use of pictographs in writing, somewhat as the Mayas did, but they had no books. They worshipped the sun and the moon and a number of other deities. Their temples were few, but they had a multitude of sacred places, including lakes in which their rulers took ceremonial baths after anointing themselves and covering their bodies with gold dust. Along with frequent sacrifices of birds, deer, and other animals, they sometimes made offerings of human beings to the sun.

The Chibcha state was in turmoil when the Spaniards arrived. It was ruled by two supreme chiefs who divided the country between them. A number of subordinate chiefs had charge of the provinces and districts. A religious potentate, a sort of high priest, tried to preserve the peace, but frequently was unable to do so because the two supreme chiefs were such bitter rivals. If the Spaniards had not seized the country, one or the other of these native rulers might have consolidated the state and expanded it into an empire. The two sovereigns, called Zipa and Zaque, were despotic. They issued decrees, administered justice, commanded the armies, presided over the festivals.

The common people lived in huts built of wood, cane, or thatch and roofed with branches, grass, and clay. The ruling group dwelt in houses so large that the Spaniards called them castles. Although covered with thatch, they were constructed of solid wood and adobe. The walls were lined with cane and bamboo of various colors, held together by cords. The furniture and the thrones were also made of wood. Within the buildings the ground served as a floor, but it was carpeted with matting. The palaces of the supreme chiefs, and the temples as well, contained many ornaments of gold and silver and large quantities of emeralds.

🐚 EMPIRE-BUILDERS OF THE ANDES

The largest of the Indian states in the New World at the time when the Europeans arrived was the empire of the Incas (no. 12 on Map 3). It extended from central Ecuador to central Chile and eastward from the Pacific Ocean to the eastern slopes of the Andes. Its population, now believed to have been less dense than that of the Aztec empire, may have exceeded 7,000,000 shortly after 1500.

The Incas did not create the civilization which bears their name. Like the Aztecs, they took over what others had created, organizing, expanding, and developing it; and, like the Aztecs, they were late arrivals in the domain which they controlled.

The Incas did not enter the region which they were eventually to rule until 1000 or 1050 A.D. Other Indians had been dwelling in these highlands and coastal plains for many centuries, cultivating food plants, domesticating the llama and the alpaca, spinning, weaving, making pottery, working metals, and building great stone temples, palaces, and fortresses. In short, numerous Indians of the area were already semicivilized when the Incas arrived.

The Incas, like the Aztecs, were merely a tribe. Apparently they wandered about for a time before they finally settled down among other tribes in Cuzco, which became their capital. They were ruled at first by a chief elected by the leading men of the tribe. Under the leadership of such chiefs they raided and conquered in every direction until they finally controlled this extensive empire. The prestige and power of the rulers increased with their conquests, so that eventually they became hereditary monarchs who were believed by their subjects to be gods and sons of the sun-god. Cuzco, their capital, grew until it became a city inhabited by some 200,000 people, containing a large number of stone palaces and temples and protected by great stone fortifications.

These and other buildings scattered about the empire—some new and others ancient—show that the Indians of the region were skilful architects. They were also gifted engineers. The empire was covered by a vast net of roads along which were series of fortifications, posthouses, and inns. Rivers and streams were spanned by remarkable stone or suspension bridges. The latter were made of cables of woven willow rods—three supporting the floor and two serving as hand rails—and layers of branches and twigs, the cables fastened at each end to rocks or stone pillars, while boughs or cords connected the floor-cables and hand-rails. These bridges were strong enough to support several thousand pounds. In building the roads through the mountains, it was necessary to hew away the solid rock, construct embankments, and, in steeper places, to cut long flights of steps. And besides roads and bridges, the engineers and workmen constructed irrigation canals, ditches, and terraces to increase or improve the arable land.

The subjects of the Incas made good use of the soil. It was intensively cultivated wherever the climate and fertility were adapted to agriculture: the river valleys of the arid coastal area, the plateaus, and the mountain valleys and slopes, both fish and guano being used as fertilizer. The principal crops were maize, potatoes, peanuts, beans, squash, melons, manioc, quinoa, peppers, and tomatoes, as well as cotton, coca, and various fruits. The food supply was increased by fish and the meat of such animals as the llama, the alpaca, the guinea pig, and the deer.

In addition to farming and the construction of roads, bridges, temples, palaces, aqueducts, and homes for the common people, the inhabitants of Incaland worked at numerous other tasks. They had to weave many garments and blankets, for much of their country was cold. In making their textiles, they used cotton, alpaca hair, and the fleece of the llama and the vicuña. They also made sandals and various weapons, tools, and household utensils, as well as numerous images, decorations, and ornaments for religious and other purposes. In the working of metals, the fashioning of pottery, and the manufacture of jewelry set with precious stones, they displayed great skill and appreciation for grace and beauty. Like the Mayas and the Nahuas, they were very industrious.

One of the most remarkable features of the Inca empire was its organization. For purposes of administration it was divided into many units based upon territory and population. At the head of the empire was the monarch, almost absolute. An exalted and sacred personage, into whose presence no one came without humility and abasement, he was called the Inca, or Sapa Inca. Under him were four high officials who may be described as viceroys. Each was a member of the royal council and ruler of a broad section of the empire. Immediately under the viceroys were officials who governed 40,000 families. Below them were other officials ruling 10,000 and so on down to minor officials who had charge of fifty and ten families respectively. All these were mainly administrative agents of the Inca, who also utilized a number of military officials, inspectors, and spies, and perhaps other agents who served as judges.

The administrative officials of the two lowest ranks, those in charge of ten families and of fifty families, were selected from the people. The rest belonged to the nobility. Officials of the the two highest ranks usually were members of the Inca family, so that there was an Inca caste as well as a lesser nobility. Next below the nobility came the bulk of the population, the common people. Below them were the *yanaconas,* doomed to a perpetual status almost equivalent to slavery. Perhaps they had been captured in warfare on the frontiers or in revolt against the Inca. They worked in the royal household or on the estates of the monarch and the priests.

The agricultural lands of the empire were divided into three parts: one for the Incas, who also owned the minerals, the precious stones, and the llama and alpaca herds; another for the religious organizations; and a third for the people. The relative areas of each are uncertain, but the people's portion must have been much larger than that of the other two.

The people, however, did not own any land; plots were allotted to each family in proportion to its size merely for cultivation. Besides working their plots, the people had to help till the lands of the Incas and the religious organizations as well as the lands of those who for any reason were unable to cultivate them. They also had to labor on the various public works and in the mines and to serve in the armies and as royal messengers. In addition, each family had to pay tribute in the form of products of the farm and of household industry. Labor of practically every kind was done under the supervision of state officials, but age and health were considered in the assignment of tasks. The products the family had left after paying the share demanded by the Inca could be traded freely in the local markets.

Some of the commodities produced for Church and State or paid as tribute were sent directly to Cuzco. The rest were taken to warehouses of the numerous towns and villages of the empire. The royal officials obtained their supplies from these stores, and from them were distributed food, clothing, and other articles to the poor, the incapacitated, and the victims of such misfortunes as flood, drought, and earthquake. Thus it seems that the people had security; they were fairly sure of obtaining the simple necessities of life. No one save the royal family and the lesser nobility had much more; and even the royalty and the nobility, with few exceptions, did not live in great luxury. The dwellings of the common people were little better than hovels. Built of adobe, wood, perhaps sometimes of stone, and covered with thatch, they rarely contained more than one room, and the ground served as a floor.

The schools, which were established in the capital and perhaps in some of the larger towns, were not for the people. The Incas feared that too much knowledge and thought might make the masses restless and disobedient. The schools were therefore only for the children of the royal family and the other nobility. The main purpose of education was to train the youth for public offices and the professions. They received instruction in religion, law, science, administration, accounting, language, and the history and traditions of the empire. The numerous priests, who were headed by a high priest belonging to the Inca family, had charge of the schools and of higher learning in general. In mathematics, the decimal system was used and the chief instrument for accounting was the *quipu,* a device consisting of knotted strings of various colors and lengths which may have been employed also to keep other records, since the Incas had no system of writing. Although the religious sages knew less about astronomy than the Mayas did, they had a fairly accurate calendar, and they also knew a good deal about medicine and surgery.

The religion of Incaland was not cruel like that of the Aztecs. Human sacrifices were rare. The people worshipped and sought to appease many deities, but the state religion centered about the worship of the sun and of a god of creation and culture called Viracocha. In Cuzco and in many other leading settlements of the empire were temples to the sun-god. Connected with these temples were houses of "chosen women" whose duties are not fully known. Apparently they were maidens, mainly from the upper class, who cleaned and adorned the temples and made garments for the royal family and the religious leaders, thus reminding one of the virgins who served in the temples of ancient Rome. They eventually became the wives of members of the ruling classes, who practiced polygamy.

The Inca empire was thus highly organized, regimented, immobile. There was little or no movement from one class to another and, for the masses, very limited movement even from place to place, unless the Inca desired to establish a new colony. In that case, a group of families was uprooted rather remorselessly and shifted to another region for strategic reasons or in order to increase production in a more fertile section. Only the nobility traveled freely over the empire. Yet, within each class, the administrative and judicial agents seem to have tried to be impartial. Crimes and misdemeanors were severely punished, but the welfare of the people apparently was kept in mind. The Inca despotism seems, on the whole, to have been fairly benevolent as well as efficient. Too much labor, perhaps, was devoted to the building of palaces, temples, and religious houses. In general, however, it may be concluded that the masses were poor because they were too numerous for the techniques and resources available in the empire.

The Inca state possessed unusual stability. It lasted for four centuries. For most of that period it was engaged in warfare, but the wars were wars of expansion and conquest or wars of defense. Revolts and civil wars were not frequent. Only one monarch was overthrown in two centuries (1330–1530), and he was displaced by his far more able son. Eldest son followed eldest son without a break; army officers never seized the government. Insubordination, conspiracy, and struggles over the succession seldom occurred. Disobedience and conspiracy, when they occurred, were firmly dealt with. Individuals guilty of crimes against the state were executed, imprisoned, or enslaved. News from all parts of the empire was brought speedily to the capital by swift messengers and signal fires. Organization of revolt was very difficult.

But the empire was in the midst of civil war when the Spanish conquerors arrived. It was a fatal conflict caused by special circumstances. The empire had been divided by the Inca Huayna Capac in 1525 in order to make a place for an illegitimate son. This son ruled in the north with his capital at Quito; his half-brother, the legitimate Inca, governed the rest of the empire from his capital at Cuzco. The two were bitter rivals, and civil war was the result.

CULTURAL ACHIEVEMENTS OF THE FIRST AMERICANS

The achievements of the first Americans were not insignificant. Their shortcomings and cruelties can be viewed with sympathetic tolerance. They had a hard struggle to tame a vast wilderness and themselves. Industrious, inventive, skillful, they often made good use of the resources at hand. They domesticated many valuable plants that are still cultivated in the Americas and in other parts of the world. They discovered a number of drugs and made considerable progress in medicine and surgery. They domesticated the turkey, the llama, and the alpaca. They learned how to irrigate, drain, terrace, and fertilize the soil. They manufactured numerous weapons, tools, garments, utensils, and implements. They created a number of attractive decorative designs for pottery and textiles which are still used and appreciated. Their best architecture displayed great determination, skill, and power to mobilize labor. Some of their engineering feats were magnificent. They were talented in carving and sculpture and metal work, producing a multitude of decorations and implements of gold, silver, copper, and platinum, and some bronze. They devised clever methods of writing and accounting, but failed to invent an alphabet and thus advance to the phonetic system. They learned to use the decimal system in calculations, but only the Mayas learned to utilize the zero. In their religion there was much superstition, oppression, and cruelty. The governments of the larger Indian states were marred by despotism and tyranny. The masses of the people had little liberty or opportunity for individual initiative. Private property in lands and natural resources was rare.

The progress of these earliest Americans might have been much more startling if they had possessed such food plants as wheat, oats, rice, and barley and such domestic animals as horses, cattle, sheep, goats, swine, and barnyard fowls. But it was not their fault that they did not have these most useful plants and animals, for the New World seems to have contained no wild species that might have been tamed, domesticated, and transformed into such cereals and livestock. Limitations in food supply and beasts of burden made their struggle for existence very severe. Some of their shortcomings, however, are surprising. They failed to make tools and weapons of iron and to contrive such useful inventions as the plow, the arch, and the wheel. Their progress probably was retarded by lack of association with peoples and civilizations decidedly different from themselves and their own.

Whatever culture they possessed they had developed by virtue of their own talents. They borrowed almost nothing from the Old World, because all communication with it had ceased before any civilizations were developed there. What further advances they might have made if left to themselves for a few more centuries will never be known. They were subjugated shortly after the arrival of the Europeans in America and their way of life was violently changed. But these first Americans were not exterminated. Many of them lived on, worked for their masters, and mingled their blood with that of the conquerors. Four centuries after the conquest, the Indians of Hispanic America numbered 20,000,-000 to 25,000,000 and the mixbloods numbered between 50,000,000 and 60,000,000 more. Their survival makes it important to weigh their achievements and their capacity for development.

CHAPTER III

Old World Backgrounds

The first Europeans, like the first Americans, were probably immigrants from the Orient. Mankind's original home appears to have been in Central Asia. Although a part of the human race had been living in Europe for thousands of years before the Mongoloids migrated to America, no civilizations had been developed in either Europe or Asia before these Mongoloids left the Orient for the New World. To point out where the earliest civilizations sprang up and how they spread westward until some of their beneficiaries finally crossed the Atlantic and encountered the first Americans is the purpose of this chapter. For the most part, it will summarize well-known history. But this seems necessary in order to provide an appropriate perspective.

THE EARLIEST CIVILIZATIONS AND THEIR EXPANSION

It will be recalled that the first civilizations were achieved in fertile river valleys—in the valleys of the Indus of India and the Yellow River of China as well as in those of the Nile of Africa and the Tigris and the Euphrates of the Near East. From these centers civilization gradually spread to most of Eurasia and to northern Africa, so that most of the Old World became civilized before any civilizations appeared in the New.

The earliest of all civilizations developed in lands bordering the eastern Mediterranean Sea, in the Nile and Tigris-Euphrates basins, where their rise began around 3,000 years before the birth of Jesus Christ. The people of this region were the first to tame and domesticate animals for food, clothing, and beasts of burden: oxen, herds of cattle, flocks of sheep, donkeys, chickens, ducks, and geese, and eventually the horse, which they obtained from their neighbors to the northeast. In these borderlands of the Mediterranean men first invented the wheel, the arch, and the plow and engaged in intensive agriculture, irrigating and draining the soil and cultivating wheat, barley, rye, cotton, flax, fruits, and vegetables. Here they first used stone and sun-dried brick, constructing huge palaces, temples, and pyramids. Here they learned for the first time to make use of metals: gold, perhaps some silver, certainly copper and bronze, and finally iron, which the American Indians had never learned to utilize. Here they invented the first systems of writing by means of symbols more convenient than any ever employed by the first Americans. Here they investigated astronomy and mathematics, devised calendars, drafted codes of morality, and (before 1600 B.C.) invented an alphabet from which all European alphabets were later derived.

They carried the culture of these fertile river valleys along the northern and southern borders of the Mediterranean, where it was modified and taken by merchants and seamen to more distant peoples. The Phoenicians, industrious traders of Syria, carried it to the northern coast of Africa, where they founded Carthage in the ninth century B.C. They also spread it along the southern coast of Europe as far as Spain, and notably to the island of Crete, whence the Minoans transferred it to Greece. By the Greeks and the Romans, who borrowed extensively from the adjacent East but made many original contributions themselves, a civilized mode of life was eventually transmitted to most of Europe; the process was completed near the beginning of the first century of the Christian era. Thus the majority of the Europeans became civilized before any Indian civilizations sprang up in the New World, although the Mayas of Central America were already starting their rapid advance by this time.

The story of Greek achievements is a familiar story. Excelling in architecture, sculpture, painting, literature, science, and philosophy, Greek civilization reached its zenith four or five centuries before the birth of Christ. Athens, the most highly developed of the Greek communities, experimented with a democratic system of government and emphasized the dignity and freedom of the individual. But the ancient Greeks were never able to unite and live together in peace. They remained a group of warring city-states like those of the Mayas, and were finally conquered by the Macedonians under the leadership of Philip and his son Alexander. These Macedonian warriors admired Greek civilization, however, and preserved it; and Alexander extended his conquests and Greek culture, 333–323 B.C., into Egypt and the Near East.

It will be remembered that the Romans began their career of expansion about the time that the Macedonians subjugated the Greeks. Appropriating many elements of Greek culture, they eventually established a vast empire, which, at its maximum, embraced the entire Mediterranean world, including Greece, and a good part of the rest of Europe, including England. Especially noted as lawgivers, organizers, and administrators, the Romans were also gifted engineers, architects, orators, and poets.

These two great empires, the Alexandrian and the Roman, were the earliest to be organized by the Europeans. Within them occurred a fusion of cultures, with contributions flowing back and forth between Europe and Asia. From the Orient came various religions, including the Christian religion, which finally became the major religious faith of Europe and the entire Western World. During 200 years of Roman peace—the first two centuries of the Christian Era—Europe as far north as the Danube and the Rhine became both civilized and prosperous. Cities and towns grew up, connected by excellent roads. Merchants moved freely through imperial domains as large as present-day United States, inhabited by some 50,000,000 people.

Perhaps the reader will recall that shortly before 200 A.D.—approximately three centuries after the Mayas started to develop their civilization—the Roman Empire began to weaken and crumble. The probable causes of its slow decline and final collapse were a dissolute ruling class, political disorders, heavy taxes, soil exhaustion, concentration of landownership, religious beliefs that ignored the importance of things of this world and fixed attention upon the world beyond the grave, and the pressure of barbarians upon the frontiers. During the early part of the fourth century, the great empire split into two parts, and before the end of the sixth century, the western, or European portion, fell into the hands of Germanic tribes whose cultural status— except for the fact that they possessed iron weapons, wheeled vehicles, and the horse—was similar to that of the seminomadic Indians encountered by the Europeans when they arrived in America. The eastern, or Byzantine, empire, which controlled the Balkan Peninsula and the Near East, continued a much-harassed and shrinking existence until its capital, Constantinople, was captured by the Ottoman Turks in 1453.

It will also be remembered that with the breakup of the Roman Empire Western Europe entered a long period of cultural decline. Cities and towns gradually disappeared. The diminishing population became rural and agricultural. Big landlords slowly became dominant and a feudal system was established. Contacts with the more advanced cultures of the Orient almost ceased. It was a long era of disorder, violence, and ignorance, called the Dark Ages. A host of petty rulers sprang up, assuming various titles. Some were called kings, although the dominions of most hardly justified the title. On several occasions—800, 962, and more frequently thereafter—German kings had themselves crowned as Roman emperors, thus trying to revive the Roman Empire. But the effort failed; the new empire never became more than a shadow. Consolidation of Western Europe proved impossible. Only the Roman Catholic Church, with the pope at its head, maintained a semblance of unity, converting the Germanic peoples to Christianity through the efforts of its missionaries.

THE RENAISSANCE AND THE AGE OF DISCOVERY

The eleventh, twelfth, and thirteen centuries were a period of economic and cultural revival in Europe. They witnessed the growth of industry, trade, towns, and cities and the awakening of the spirit of inquiry. In its later stages, the awakening became known as the Renaissance, or Revival of Learning, which was characterized by a growing interest both in the wisdom of the ancients and in the physical world. While aboriginal Americans were struggling upward through the successive stages of barbarism toward a civilized way of life, the Europeans were emerging from their long era of darkness and chaos. Each group was probably ignorant of the other's existence (the Norsemen were an ephemeral exception) but the quickened curiosity of the Europeans, their religious zeal, their fondness for luxuries, were finally to bring them into contact with their remote kinsmen across the Atlantic. And Western Europe's renaissance was in considerable measure the product of the activities of the Asiatic relatives of the American Mongoloids!

In the year 1073 the Seljuk Turks, Moslems (Mohammedans) with Mongolian blood in their veins, destroyed the Holy Sepulcher in Jerusalem. By this wanton act they lighted up nearly two centuries of crusading zeal, which snapped the fetters of Europe's provincialism, banished many of the terrors of the unknown, and gave the Europeans a taste for the learning and luxuries of the East: its spices, silks, porcelains, and jewels. Those "half military, half migratory movements" called Crusades, "strangely compounded of religious enthusiasm and political ambition, of . . . the spirit of knight-errant and the cool calculation of the commercial bandit," marked the "beginning of that return of the West upon the East which is so persistent a factor in all modern history. Christendom, so long isolated, now first broke the barriers that had closed it in, and once more extended its frontier into western Asia." [1]

At the opening of the thirteenth century the Mongols, under their leader Genghis Khan, rode out from their original home in Central Asia upon one of the most remarkable careers of conquest in all history.

In less than fifty years they conquered most of China and swept across western Asia to the Black Sea. They seized and destroyed Kiev in 1240 and dominated nearly all of Russia. A year later they overran Poland and defeated an army of Poles and Germans at Liegnitz, in Lower Silesia. The mounted hordes then turned southward into Hungary and Rumania, but were recalled in 1242 by troubles over the succession. Dynastic disputes soon split the great empire into pieces, but Mongol supremacy nevertheless lasted through most of the thirteenth century. At the death of Kublai Khan, grandson of Genghis, in 1294, there existed a main Mongol empire embracing China and Mongolia, with its capital in Peking, an empire of Kipchak in Russia, another called Il-Khan in Persia (to which the Seljuk Turks were tributary), and two other states, one in Turkestan and one in Siberia between Kipchak and Mongolia. The Mongols had not been able to enter Africa, however; nor had they invaded India beyond the Punjab.

Strange as it may seem, these Mongols soon exhibited a rather tolerant attitude toward Europe. For a time, the barriers which the feud between Islam and Christianity had set up between East and West were lowered. Intercourse between Europe and the Orient was not seriously hampered. Many European representatives appeared at the capitals of the Great Khan (Karakorum and Peking). Indeed, for a brief period, the conversion of the Mongols to Christianity did not seem impossible. In 1269 Kublai Khan sent a mission to the pope with the view of arriving at a common understanding. He asked that the pope send to him one hundred "intelligent men acquainted with the Seven Arts, able to enter into controversy and able clearly to prove to idolaters and other kinds of folk that the Law of Christ was best." The mission, however, found the Western World popeless and engaged in a bitter controversy over the papal succession. After two years' delay, two faint-hearted Dominican friars were sent out, but they soon abandoned the expedition. The zeal of early Christendom had cooled. "All Asia was white unto the harvest, but there was no effort to reap it." [2]

Yet missionaries, royal envoys, and merchants had preceded the Dominicans; and missionaries, royal and papal envoys, and merchants would follow them, advancing far beyond the point where the Dominican friars had turned back. Already, between 1245 and 1253, John de Plano de Carpini, Neapolitan Franciscan and legate of Innocent III, and William of Rubruquis, agent of Saint Louis of France, had penetrated Central Asia to Karakorum. Between the years 1255 and 1265 Nicolo and Matteo Polo, two Venetians, traded in Mongolian Russia and eventually made their way to the court of Kublai Khan; seven years later, they again visited the Far East, accompanied by the young Marco Polo, whose account of his travels immortalized the Polos. From 1275 to 1353 John of Monte Corvino, Oderic of Pordenone, and John of Marignolli, as friars and papal legates, visited Il-Khan (Persia), Mongol China, Tibet, and the Malay Archipelago. These are only a few whom chance has rescued from oblivion.

Marvelous tales were brought back from the East by these travelers: tales of Cathay (northern China) with "ports thronged with ships and wharves glutted with costly wares"; of the "city of Kinsay ('stretched like Paradise through the breadth of Heaven') with lakes, canals, bridges, pleasure barges, baths . . ."; of imperial Cambulac (Peking) "with its Palace of the Great Kaan, its multitude of crowned barons in silken robes, its magic golden flagons, its troops of splendid white mares, its astrologers, leachers, conjurers," and "sweet-singing" chorus girls; of India with its rubies, sapphires, and diamonds; of the Moluccas, "drowsy with perfumes and rich with drugs and spices," filled with "golden temples and uncouth gods," beasts, serpents, ivory, and brilliant birds.[3]

Western Europe probably would have heard little of all these marvels if the Mongols had not tolerated and even invited commercial and cultural relations. Nor would the European response have been so eager if the Crusades had not emancipated Europeans from their provincialism and created a desire for the wisdom and wares of the Orient. Once curiosity had been thoroughly aroused and the appetite for luxuries fully developed, they became almost overwhelming. Credulous imaginations filled the unknown seas with islands and the islands with rich commodities, weird animals, strange men, or kingdoms of exiled Christians. Men's bold curiosity sent them in search of new paths and "new lands," a quest that was greatly facilitated by such opportune inventions as the compass, the astrolabe, and mariners' charts. It was mainly this eagerness to learn more of the world and to acquire more of its goods that led to the European discovery of America.

The influence of the Ottoman Turks upon the voyages of discovery along the African coast and across the Atlantic may have been slightly exaggerated by historians. Perhaps the Portuguese, led by Prince Henry and his school of navigators, were mainly in search of African commodities, such as gold, ivory, and slaves, or under the influence of a crusading spirit which impelled them to seek the Christian Kingdom of "Prester John" and dream of expelling the Moslems from the African continent. A new route to the Orient may not have been thought of until later. In like manner, it is possible that Christopher Columbus was not exclusively motivated in 1492 by the desire to reach the Far East, but was as much interested in searching for "islands and mainlands," or the dwelling places of Spanish and Portuguese Christians thought to have been sent into exile by the Moors. (Moslems were often called "Moors" in Spain.) It is true that Columbus carried a letter from the Spanish sovereigns to the "Most Serene Prince," who may have been the Great Khan of Mongolia, but this could have been for the purpose of assuring him a more cordial reception in case chance should waft him thus far. It is also true that he called the lands he discovered the "Indies" and their inhabitants "Indians," but this might be explained by the resemblance of these lands to certain portions of the East as represented by the maps with which he was familiar. The desire to find a new route to the Orient may not have been the sole motive for the voyages of discovery until after 1500.

The expeditions of Vasco da Gama (1497–98) and his successors around Africa to India and adjacent regions, however, soon revealed the advantages of an all-water route to the Far East; and the conquest of Damascus (1516) and Egypt (1517) by the Turks, followed by their policy of laying heavy tribute upon the trade passing through their dominions, made the overland routes far more expensive and hazardous. Soon after the opening of the sixteenth century, therefore, mariners serving as agents of merchants and governments irritated by the Portuguese monopoly of the route around Africa and exasperated by the Turks, did begin eagerly to search for a western water passage to the Orient; but to assign such a motive to the earlier explorers may be to attribute the objectives of men of one decade to those of another.

The fact that needs to be emphasized is that Europe—Latin Europe, at least—was ripe for an epoch of discovery and expansion. Without any disposition to disparage the achievements of the great Italian who sailed westward to America under the Spanish flag, one may observe that Columbus could have perished in mid-ocean in 1492 without long delaying the discovery of the New World. For less than eight years after that historic voyage, the Portuguese sailor Pedro Alvares Cabral, blown from his course while on his way around Africa to India, sighted the coast of Brazil (April 22, 1500).[4]

Soon after Columbus' return to Spain, the lands newly discovered and still to be discovered throughout a large portion of the earth were divided between the two Hispanic powers. The division was effected by papal bulls (1493) and the Treaty of Tordesillas (1494). Spain and Portugal forthwith set up monopolistic claims and launched an epoch of colonization which profoundly influenced the course of modern history.

⬢ SPAIN: ITS PEOPLE AND ITS RULERS

Spaniards of the late fifteenth century were a mixture of many peoples, Oriental and North African as well as European, who had come to the peninsula in successive waves during prehistoric and historic times. Civilization was brought to their country by the Phoenicians, the Greeks, the Carthaginians, and the Romans. Spain was a part of the Roman Empire for several centuries, and it was during the Roman period that the inhabitants of the country became Christians. Next, shortly after the year 500, the peninsula was overrun by Germanic tribes, especially the Visigoths, who set up a kingdom there, adopted Christianity themselves, and continued to dominate the country until shortly after the Moslem invasion, which began in 711.

During the seventh century the followers of Mohammed, a religious leader of Arabia, had established a vast empire, which included Egypt and northern Africa, from which they entered Spain and conquered most of its inhabitants within a few years. The invaders, mostly Berbers but a good many Arabs, were people of rather high culture, who developed the resources of the country with great skill. They built irrigation systems, fertilized the soil, and imported rice, cotton, sugar cane, citrus fruits, silkworms, and mulberry trees. They worked the silver, copper, lead, and iron mines. They manufactured pottery, glassware, jewelry, and leather goods. Their Toledo swords and their carved leather and ivory were famous. They also introduced the Arabic system of numbers and built the first paper factory in all Europe. Moreover, the Moslem period in Spain is especially noted for its magnificent architecture, its schools, and its science. At a time when nearly all the rest of Europe was just beginning to dispel the darkness of the Dark Ages, the Moorish capital at Córdoba was an impressive cultural center.

But the older inhabitants of Spain, especially those in the mountains of the north who had avoided subjugation, were bitterly opposed to the Moslems both because they were invaders and because they were not Christians. Aided for a time by Frankish neighbors across the Pyrenees, these northern people began a revolt shortly before the year 800, and the uprising soon became a sort of crusade, which continued intermittently for nearly seven centuries! As the invaders were slowly driven back toward Africa, Christian kingdoms and provinces came into existence: the Basque Provinces, Asturias, Catalonia, León, Castile, Navarre, Aragón, Barcelona, and others. The last stronghold held by the Moslems in Spain was Granada, from which they were finally expelled in 1492. By that time, Spanish national unity had practically been achieved. But the Moslems had left a deep impression. Spaniards thereafter were less

European than Asiatic, full of mysticism, dignified, proud, sometimes arrogant, and often capable of great self-abnegation.

It was during the reign of Ferdinand of Aragón and Isabella of Castile (1479–1516) that Spanish territorial unity was virtually achieved, that Spanish institutions were crystallized into definite and durable form, and that Spanish nationalism came into being. It was at this time also that Spanish character became so definitely fixed that subsequent centuries did not greatly modify it.

Ferdinand and Isabella, *Los Reyes Católicos,* as they are called in Spain, were sovereigns of extraordinary ability, recognized as such even by their foreign contemporaries. Ferdinand drew forth the admiration of Machiavelli, who praised him in his *Prince.* Another Italian, Guicciardini, who knew the king personally, describes him at great length: [5]

> The feats that Ferdinand has accomplished, his words, his ways, and his general reputation prove that he is an extremely sagacious man. He is very secret, and unless obliged to, does not communicate important matters; he could not be more patient. He leads a very regular life, assigning times for this and that. He likes to know all about the affairs of the kingdom, great and little, and has them go through his hands; and though he exhibits a willingness to hear everybody's opinion, he makes up his own mind, and directs everything himself. . . . He is good at knightly exercises and keeps them up; he makes a show of great piety, speaks of holy things with great reverence, and ascribes everything to God. . . . In short, he is a very notable king and has many talents; and the only criticisms upon him are that he is not generous and that he does not keep his promise.

The same observer remarked that Isabella was even superior to her husband. "It is said," he wrote, "that she was a great lover of justice, and a lady of the best breeding, and made herself greatly beloved and feared by her subjects. She was generous, of a high spirit, and very ambitious of renown, as much so as any woman of the time, no matter who." Out of deference to her imperial will or excellent judgment, the king often followed her advice. A German visitor once observed that "the Queen is king, and the King is her servant." [6] Her very strenuous life is supposed to have had a fatal effect upon her children; several of them died in infancy; one became insane.

Ferdinand and Isabella founded an absolutism which continued until the opening of the nineteenth century. Turbulent nobles were either attracted to the court or suppressed; the local brotherhoods for defense against highwaymen (the *hermandades*) were organized into royal police; the grand masterships of the great military orders which had been organized during the long struggle against the Moslems, and which not only numbered a million vassals and members but enjoyed a large annual revenue, were taken over by the crown; royal councils were set up; royal judiciaries (*audiencias*) were established; and the old parliaments (called *Cortes* in Spanish) of Castile, Aragón, Valencia, and Catalonia were often ignored or defied. *Visitadores* traveled through the kingdoms and examined the administration of justice and finance, and officials of the crown began to be subjected to the *residencia* (a judicial investigation of their conduct while in office). The captains general, who in earlier times had exercised both military and civil authority in extensive Castilian territory, had been superseded by the *adelantados* (governors), the most important of whom was probably the *adelantado* of the Canaries; but the former office could be resurrected if need should arise. Viceroys (vice-kings) were in charge of Sardinia, Sicily, and Naples. Even the ancient privileges and immunities of the municipalities began to be infringed, for the crown acquired a measure of control over *ayuntamientos* and *cabildos* (town councils) and sent out *corregidores* to inspect the town governments. Finally, the Catholic monarchs reorganized the Inquisition, conquered Granada, recovered Naples (1504), and began those negotiations with the papacy which culminated in the acquisiton of royal patronage over the church in Spanish dominions. During the next 200 years, surprisingly few additions were made to the institutional structure which they had set up. Subsequent monarchs modified, perfected, or abused it, but originated little save in the realm of taxation.

Economic conditions in Spain around 1500 were fairly good. Agriculture and stockraising were moderately prosperous and manufacturing industries were spreading to nearly all of the towns, turning out swords, woolens, silks, leather goods, ships, and many other products. A respectable navy and merchant marine were developing, and foreign commerce, encouraged by the crown, was on the increase.

The population, approximately 7,000,000 at this time, was divided into the familiar three classes, upper, middle, and lower, although the middle class, composed of emancipated peasantry and of such members of the lesser nobility as were attracted into business and industry, was rather small. The nobility, higher and lower, and the clergy constituted the upper class. The clergy were wealthy. Spain's seven archbishoprics and forty bishoprics received an income of around $7,000,000, and the annual rents of the secular clergy amounted to about $60,000,000. The regular clergy—there were approximately 9,000 religious houses in the country—were equally rich and perhaps more numerous. At the head of the nobility were the grandees, who either held public office or lived upon the income from the vast estates which they and their ancestors had seized from the retreating Moslems. The lesser nobility—hidalgos and *caballeros*—were neither so wealthy nor so fortunate; but higher and lower alike enjoyed many exemptions and privileges, disdained manual labor, and drew their sustenance mostly from the toil of peasants and others in a semiservile condition. The bottom class was composed of agricultural workers and tenants who were gradually being transformed into a free peasantry, personal servants, industrial laborers in the towns, and a rather large number of beggars. Although serfdom was on its way to extinction, a semifeudal institution called encomienda still persisted in some quarters, where free peasants and smaller landowners "commended" themselves to powerful nobles in the community and rendered them certain services in return for protection.

Of conditions shortly after 1500 Guicciardini gives a vivid, if somewhat unfriendly, description: [7]

The kingdom is thinly populated; there are some fine cities, Barcelona, Saragossa, Valencia, Granada, and Seville, but they are few for so large a country, and the other towns for the most part are of little account. The southern regions are far the most fertile, but only the land in the neighborhood of the cities is cultivated. Wool, silk, wine, and oil are exported in large quantities. There is sufficient wheat for the home market, and, if the nation were only industrious and given to trade, their iron, steel, copper, hides, and other products would make them rich. But as it is, the country is very poor . . . from the laziness of the people. They are proud, and think that no other nation compares with theirs. . . . They dislike foreigners, and are discourteous toward them. They are more warlike, perhaps, than any other Christian nation; agile, quick, and good at the management of arms, they make a great point of honor, and prefer to die rather than submit to shame. Their light cavalry is excellent, their horses very good; and the Castilian infantry enjoys a great reputation. . . .

Spaniards are thought to be shrewd and intelligent, but they are not good in liberal and mechanical arts; all the artisans at the king's court are French, or foreigners of some sort. All Spaniards look down on trade and put on airs as hidalgos and prefer to be soldiers or (before Ferdinand's time) highwaymen rather than to engage in trade or any other such occupation. It is true that in some parts of Spain they weave and make rich stuffs, as in Valencia, Toledo, and Seville; but the nation as a whole is opposed to industrial life. The country people . . . till the ground much less than they might. Spaniards are fond of show; wear fine clothes abroad; ride a stylish horse; but at home, in the house, they live in a beggarly fashion hard to believe. . . . In outward appearance they are very religious, but not so really. They are very ceremonious, full of fine words and hand-kissings, and everybody is their 'lord' and they are 'at his disposition': but their fair words are not to be taken literally. They are avaricious and great dissemblers.

In short, Spain at the beginning of the sixteenth century had "much of the reality as well as the appearance of greatness," but revealed some symptoms of ill health which, if not remedied, might lead to decline and decrepitude. Political and religious unity had been achieved, an elaborate political organization had been perfected, and the nation was becoming more prosperous. Triumph in a long series of Moslem wars had produced an energetic and optimistic people and a soldiery glowing with crusading zeal, admirably fitted by training and temperament to carve out new dominions across the sea. And intellectually and artistically, Spain was at the threshold of a Golden Age of literature, painting, architecture, and all the fine arts. Yet the very power of the monarchy would become a menace when turned toward unwise policies or when the character of the royal family declined. The intolerance which had deprived the country of the financial and commercial talent of the Jews in 1492 was not to be satisfied until it caused Spain to lose the agricultural and industrial talent of the Moors (1501) and the Moriscos (presumably converted Moors, expelled in 1609) and set up barriers against future immigrants. Disdain for manual labor would result in stagnation when there were no more dominions to subdue. Then an idle nobility would become a pest, fomenting political disorders, living upon administrative graft, and infesting the streets and highways as robbers and beggars. Huge landed estates, held together by mortmain and primogeniture, would retard the growth of the middle class and hamper economic development. The increasing wealth of the church would attract a too numerous clergy, who would succumb to luxury, idleness, and corruption and become a heavy social liability.

Within a single century Spain passed through her Golden Age and entered a long period of moral and material decline. Of the many possible causes to which the decline might be attributed—idle churchmen and nobility; religious absorption and superstition and intolerance; false pride; neglect of science, industry, and public health; vast colonies; exhausting wars; political folly—two need to be emphasized: bad government and the attempt to play an imperialistic role in Europe.

The Spanish monarchy was to blame for both of these. Four of the nine kings who ruled Spain between 1517 and 1808 were corrupt weaklings, and the four who can be described as rather able and energetic—Charles I and Philip II, who reigned during the sixteenth century, and Ferdinand VI and Charles III, who governed during the eighteenth—were stanch exponents of an intolerant absolutism or the devotees of an exhausting imperialism that looked to Europe and the strength of armies rather than to America and the efficacy of industry and sea power. All of Spain's monarchs expended Spanish blood and treasure upon European wars designed mainly to impose Roman Catholicism, or lavished wealth and favors upon an idle and often corrupt nobility. The consequences may be seen in burdensome taxes and economic restraints which contributed to the ruin of commerce and industry, to shrinkage in population, and to the general backwardness and poverty of the nation.

The population of Spain, which had stood at 7,000,000 in 1594, was hardly more than 4,000,000 in 1723. Taking no account of rogues and beggars, who probably numbered no less than 200,000, one Spaniard out of three was now an ecclesiastic, a noble, or a personal servant. Thanks to the attempted reforms of Ferdinand VI (1746–59) and Charles III (1759–88), conditions had somewhat improved before the end of the eighteenth century, but they were still sufficiently bad. Population had increased to a little more than 10,000,000, but the nobility and the clergy still outnumbered the manufacturers, artisans, and merchants, and there were fewer than 2,000,000 farmers and farm laborers. The church and the nobility owned more than half of the arable lands; only one Spaniard in forty was a landed proprietor. Government employees and the army numbered nearly 200,000, and there were still some 140,000 beggars.

These conditions, patterns of value, and concepts of government and the social order will be reflected in that portion of the New World assigned to Spain. (1) An absolute monarchy will claim that the American dominions are the personal possessions of the crown and not of the Spanish nation, and will use them for the benefit of the monarchs and their favorites. (2) Spanish officials and institutions, such as the viceroyalty, the captaincy general, the *adelantado,* the *audiencia,* the *visitador,* the *residencia,* the *cabildo,* and the *corregidor,* will be transferred to the colonies. In the presence of an inferior group of people, even the disappearing encomienda will be revived in a somewhat different form. (3) To the religious orders will be entrusted the main task of converting and taming the natives and making them "useful subjects." (4) Farming and grazing lands in America will be concentrated in a few hands as in Spain, and the common people will be hampered by the system of latifundia (large landed estates). (5) Intolerance and hatred of foreigners will close the colonies to heretics and non-Spaniards, destroy priceless relics of aboriginal culture, and retard intellectual and economic progress. (6) A tendency toward municipal autonomy, struggling against monarchal centralization, will reappear, suffer repression, and still persist until the chains of royal despotism are finally broken. (7) Spanish contempt for manual toil, Spanish love of display and fondness for military adventure and official position, will profoundly influence the character and history of the colonies. (8) Spain's monopolistic pretensions with respect to her colonies and her ambition to champion the cause of Roman Catholicism in Europe will not only hamper the progress of Spanish America, but will make it the object of attack by other European nations and even at times the prize in the contest. (9) Although the colonies will feel the heavy hand of the tax farmer and the grafting bureaucrat and suffer the consequences of the decrepitude of the mother country, they will also share the benefits of Spanish higher culture, which was at the dawn of its *Siglo de Oro* (Golden Century) in 1500.

PORTUGUESE BACKGROUND

The people of Portugal are not very different from the people of Spain. Their histories were quite similar for many centuries. The inhabitants of both are compounded of virtually the same racial stocks, except that the Portuguese, as a result of their fifteenth-century relations with Africa, received a larger infiltration of Negro blood. The two kingdoms are not separated by any effective barriers. Closely associated for many years, they were again united from 1580 to 1640. Their languages are not radically different. Both peoples went through centuries of racial and religious war on native soil against the Moors. This long struggle, together with almost a hundred years of conflict with the ambitious rulers of the Christian states of Spain, engendered in Portugal, as in Spain, a martial spirit, a national unity, and a religious zeal so intolerant and fanatical that it led to the introduction of the Inquisition and the persecution and expulsion of aliens and nonconformists. Each country developed a strong monarchy at a comparatively early period, Portugal even earlier than Spain. Each was characterized by a system of land tenure based upon large estates cultivated by a semiservile peasantry, and the upper classes of each held manual labor in contempt. The church in both countries was wealthy and powerful, the Jesuits being particularly strong in Portugal. In Spain, however, the Church was usually the subordinate agent of the State, while in Portugal it sometimes dominated the State. The vigorous municipal life that characterized each nation at the beginning of the imperial era was gradually subordinated to the central government. The commodities of each were similar, wool, silk, olives, and wine being important among them. Lastly, each had its golden age, although Portugal's was less brilliant than Spain's, and each had its royal weaklings and corrupt court, its period of decline, and its reforming rulers of the eighteenth century.

Accordingly, the colonial policies and achievements of the two countries may be expected to be rather similar. It should be recalled, however, that Portugal began its career of overseas expansion nearly a century before Spaniards ventured far out on the high seas and that Portugal scattered its efforts more widely, attempting to dominate parts of Africa, India, and the Far East as well as the eastern portion of South America that was finally called Brazil. It should also be remembered that Portugal was a much smaller nation than Spain, both in area and in population. Hardly 2,000,000 in 1500, the inhabitants of Portugal numbered scarcely more than 1,000,000 a century later and barely in excess of 3,000,000 in 1800. Perhaps largely for these reasons, the Portuguese monarchs never attempted to take an important part in European affairs. Nevertheless, the very position of their kingdom made involvement in European dynastic and power rivalries unavoidable, and Portuguese kings were often forced to form alliances with England or France. English influence became predominant by 1642; and this had significance for Brazil, since British influence tended to induce the mother country to relax the rigor of its colonial policy. Long absorption in Africa and the Orient, resulting in a mild indifference toward the American colony, had the same effect. Brazil, like the thirteen English settlements in North America, seems to have experienced in some measure that "salutary neglect" to which Edmund Burke referred.

COLONIAL ASSISTANTS AND RIVALS

Incidental reference has already been made to the Spanish and Portuguese clergy. Since the regular clergy were to be very influential in the Hispanic colonization of America, a brief reference to the foundation and ideals of the great Catholic religious orders seems appropriate at this point. The most powerful of these religious orders were the Franciscans, the Dominicans, the Augustinians, the Carmelites, the Mercedarians, and the Jesuits. All except the Jesuits were organized before the middle of the thirteenth century; the Society of Jesus was founded in 1540 by Ignatius Loyola and other Spaniards. The main purpose of the earlier brotherhoods was to protest against the corruption and wickedness of the times and advocate a return to the simple and affectionate life of Christ and the Apostles. One of the principal objectives of the Jesuits was to counteract the spread of Protestantism. But members of all the religious orders—called regular clergy because they were supposed to live in accordance with strict rules of poverty, chastity, and obedience—went forth as missionaries to convert disbelievers and heathen. Their membership was not confined to any single principality, kingdom, or nation; it was drawn from every part of Christendom. Spain and Portugal would thus receive, especially in the seventeenth and eighteenth centuries, able assistance from the outside—from Italians, Germans, Austrians, Czechs, Irishmen, and others—in the conversion and control of the American Indians. But the efforts of the monarchs and clergymen of Spain to counteract the Lutheran Reformation tended to embitter the religious sentiments of the time and to arouse the ire of the Protestants, who often sought revenge, along with plunder, in attacks upon the Hispanic colonies overseas.

The leading rivals of Spain and Portugal were, of course, France, England, and the Dutch Netherlands. Achieving national unity and strength and appearing upon the American scene somewhat later than the Iberian nations, they not only raided Hispanic commerce but founded colonies in unoccupied areas and at times even attempted, occasionally with success, to conquer some of the Iberian settlements themselves. Both France and England became menaces during the sixteenth century; the Dutch, during the early seventeenth. Owing to political decline and concentration in the Orient, the Dutch Protestants discontinued their attacks shortly after 1650, but Frenchmen and Englishmen, especially the latter, continued to be a grave threat, at least to the Spanish colonies, until the end of the Colonial period. The three rivals were dangerous mainly because of their industrial capacity, their commercial enterprise, their growing sea power, and their ability to play upon the religious motive.

CHAPTER IV

Spanish Achievements in America During the Sixteenth Century

Spain's achievements in the New World during the first century following the discovery were truly remarkable. Spaniards and others sailing under Spanish authority explored most of the long coastlines of the Americas and nearly all of their important rivers, conquered all of the semicivilized Indians except the Pueblos, and subdued many of the more primitive tribes. They also founded numerous towns, discovered and worked rich deposits of gold and silver, and introduced their food plants, their domestic animals, their institutions, and their culture into almost half of the New World.

⚜ DISCOVERY OF THE SHAPE AND LOCATION OF THE AMERICAS

The Spaniards explored the Atlantic coastline of the New World from the northern boundary of modern Maine to the southern end of South America during the first quarter of the century; by 1550 they had examined the Pacific coastline from the northern boundary of modern California to the southern tip of modern Chile, in spite of the fact that they were unaware of the existence of the Pacific Ocean until 1513, when it was discovered by Vasco Núñez de Balboa. Moreover, between 1519 and 1522 the expedition of Ferdinand Magellan, sailing under the Spanish flag and discovering the strait that bears his name, circumnavigated the earth, although Magellan himself lost his life on the way (in the Philippines). Before the end of the century the Spaniards had made several other voyages across the broad Pacific, conquered the Filipinos, discovered a convenient route of return to America, and established regular communications between the Orient and the New World.

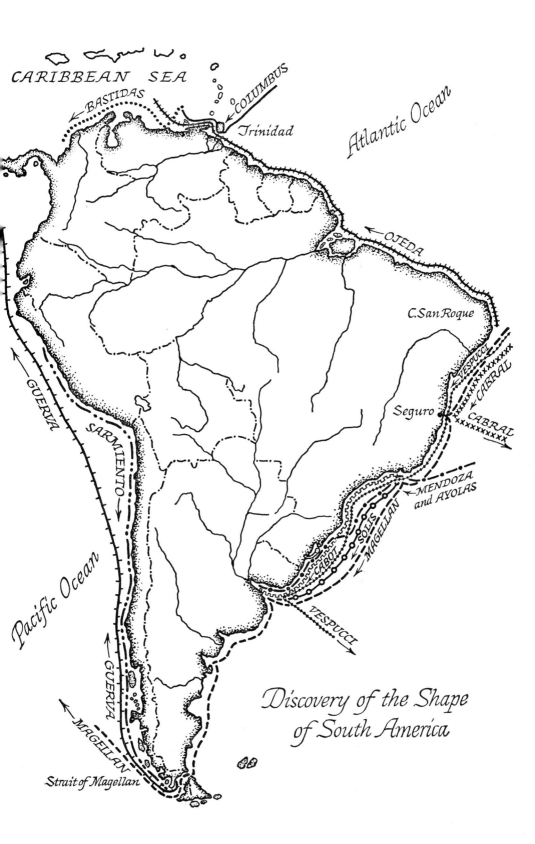

CARIBBEAN SEA

BASTIDAS

COLUMBUS

Trinidad

Atlantic Ocean

OJEDA

C. San Roque

VESPUCCI

CABRAL

Seguro

CABRAL

MENDOZA
and AYOLAS

GUERVA

SARMIENTO

Pacific Ocean

CABOT

SOLIS

MAGELLAN

VESPUCCI

GUERVA

MAGELLAN

Strait of Magellan

*Discovery of the Shape
of South America*

MAP 4

Italians and Portuguese as well as Spaniards participated in these great discoveries; but most of the expeditions were made under Spanish auspices. A few set out from Spain; the majority either used the West Indies as a base or obtained a part of their supplies and equipment there. The main objectives of the explorers were gold, silver, pearls, Indian slaves, and a strait through which they might find their way to the markets of the Far East.

The poverty of their equipment makes their achievements all the more striking. Many set out hastily from Europe in frail vessels built only for the coastwise trade; some departed without charts, nautical instruments, or adequate supplies. Not a few starved to death or lost their property or their lives by shipwreck. Their vessels were surprisingly small. The flagship *Santa María,* on which Columbus sailed in 1492, had a capacity of around 100 tons and the tonnage of his smallest no more than 75. Propelled by both sails and oars, the craft of those days had a speed of only eight to thirteen miles an hour. Conditions on board were wretched even for officers and chance passengers: tiny cabins, filthy decks, swarms of cockroaches, droves of rats, and after a time stale food and foul water. For the crews who managed the sails and worked at the oars, accommodations were much worse. Sickness was not unusual and death not infrequent. Insubordination and mutiny were common occurrences.

Most of these explorations were privately financed and nearly all were led by comparatively young men. Columbus was only forty-one when he discovered America. Balboa was thirty-eight when he first saw the Pacific Ocean. Cabral was hardly more than forty when he discovered Brazil. Magellan was still under forty when he set out on his voyage around the world, and so, when he first embarked for America, was Amerigo Vespucci, the Florentine banker and explorer after whom the New World was finally named.

CHRONOLOGY OF THE CONQUEST

The West Indies were naturally the first region in the Americas to be conquered and occupied by the Spaniards. Christopher Columbus and his associates subdued the Indians of the island of Española and established settlements there. Military leaders sent out from Española by Diego Columbus, son of Christopher, and by other governors began the subjugation and occupation of Puerto Rico, Jamaica, and Cuba. The natives of these islands were compelled to work for the Spaniards and furnish them gold and supplies. Rather gentle and delicate tribes, they were soon exterminated by hard labor, war, and epidemics of smallpox and other diseases.

The conquest and early settlement of northern South America and the

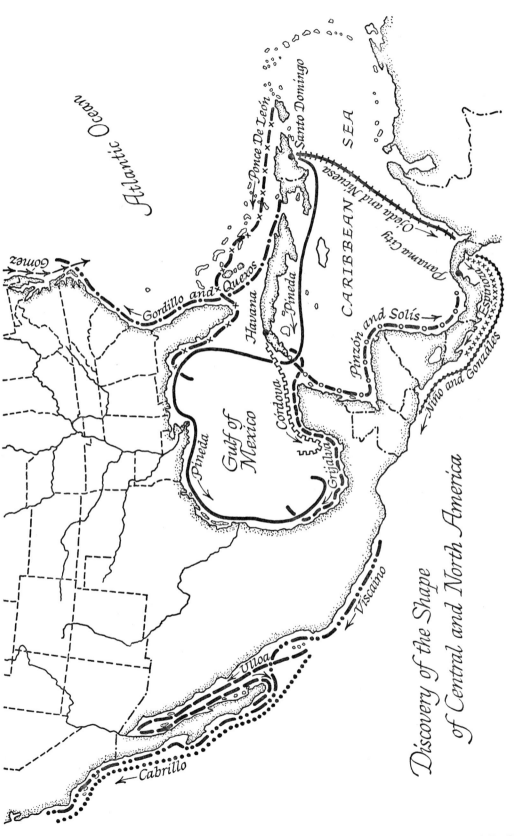

Discovery of the Shape
of Central and North America

MAP 5

southern part of Central America proceeded from the West Indian base. Starting as early as 1509, Spaniards occupied the lower part of the American Isthmus, which they called Darién or Panama. Here likewise the natives were subjected to slavery or other forms of compulsory labor, but more of them survived than in the West Indies. It was in this region that Balboa, the discoverer of the Pacific, first came into prominence. Northern South America was harassed for several years by slave raiders before any permanent Spanish settlements were made there.

It was not until 1517 or 1518 that the Spaniards began to receive definite news of the semicivilized Indian societies. Once their existence and location were ascertained, however, they were speedily invaded and conquered. The Aztecs, the Mayas, the Incas, and the Chibchas were subjugated before the middle of the century. The conquest of the Pueblos was not completed before 1600 only because the Pueblos were not deemed worthy of the effort. Their villages had been inspected by the Spaniards as early as the 1540's.[1]

FALL OF THE AZTEC CONFEDERACY

The Aztec empire was conquered by Hernando Cortés, a shrewd, bold, and ruthless young man of only thirty-four when he began his exploit. A native of southern Spain and a member of the lesser nobility, he had studied for two years at the University of Salamanca and then disappointed his parents by running away to America at the age of nineteen. He became a planter in Española and later took part in the conquest of Cuba, which served as the base for his invasion of the mainland. The governor of Cuba first gave him his commission and then tried to revoke it; but Cortés defied him and sailed from the island with a small army in February, 1519.

Reaching the coast of Mexico, Cortés effected a number of landings and rescued an Aztec slave girl and a marooned Spaniard who made themselves useful as interpreters. Continuing northward along the coast, he put his entire force ashore and founded a town which he named Veracruz. From the new town council, appointed by himself, he received a commission to proceed with the invasion of the Aztec confederacy. His purpose was to evade the authority of the Cuban governor and give his activities a legal foundation.

After winning over a number of Indian allies and burning his ships in order to prevent the less courageous of his followers from deserting and returning to Cuba, Cortés advanced into the interior in August, 1519. Traversing the coastal plain and winding his way up into the mountains, he finally emerged on the great plateau, where he engaged in several battles with the natives, mostly Montezuma's subjects, who, despite their bravery, were no match for Europeans with guns, armor, steel swords, and horses. Collecting still more Indian allies, he soon descended upon the great Aztec capital, which he entered in November without further hostilities. Badly frightened by news of Spanish prowess and half convinced that the invaders were the Fair God (Quetzalcoatl) and his attendants, Montezuma II allowed himself to be "persuaded" to reside in the quarters he had assigned to the Spaniards (a large royal palace), where he was held as puppet and prisoner.

The conquest might have been completed without further difficulty if Cortés had not been compelled to return to the coast in order to deal with an agent sent by the governor of Cuba to supervise Cortés' activities and limit his power. While Cortés was engaged in crushing this emissary and enticing away his troops, young Pedro de Alvarado, a member of the Spanish lesser nobility left in command of the densely populated Tenochtitlán, provoked the Aztecs to the point of revolt by his ruthless and injudicious conduct. Returning to the Aztec capital in June, 1520, Cortés had only enough time to rescue a part of his army by organizing a desperate flight from the city.

The subjugation of the Aztec capital now required months of preparation and a bloody war. Ammunition and boats had to be manufactured and Indian allies rallied. It was August 13, 1521, before the Spaniards were able to capture the city in the middle of the lake. The great leader of the Aztec warriors was Guatémoc, who in later years became one of Mexico's national heroes. A good part of Tenochtitlán was destroyed before the fighting ceased.[2]

Nor did the fall of the Aztec capital mean the completion of the conquest of the Aztec confederacy. Although some of the natives of the outlying districts promptly sent in their delegations to pledge submission, it was necessary to dispatch numerous companies of soldiers to demand and enforce the submission of others. More than a decade was required to build the foundations of New Spain upon the ruins of Montezuma's confederation. The old Aztec capital, largely rebuilt by the conquerors, became the capital of the new Spanish kingdom. The booty collected from the Aztecs amounted to many millions of dollars, and news of Cortés' rich haul sent hundreds of Spaniards out in search of "other Mexicos."

SUBJUGATION OF THE MAYAS

The Mayas of northern Central America and Yucatán were soon invaded. From the town of Panama, founded in 1519, Spaniards were already raiding northwestward toward the Maya country and arousing the anxiety of Cortés, who was determined to have the honor of conquering these Indians himself. The first agent he selected for the task was none other than Pedro de Alvarado, who was about the age of Cortés.

Setting out late in 1523, Alvarado advanced toward the southeast through mountain and jungle into Guatemala and a region beyond later called El Salvador. A scourge of smallpox swept the country before him and weakened the resistance of the natives, but much hard fighting was necessary both before and after the Spaniards reached the lands of the Mayas, whose subjugation required more than five years in spite of their lack of unity and co-operation. In 1524 Alvarado founded the town of Santiago de Guatemala, which eventually became the capital of a captaincy general that included most of Central America.

Still uneasy regarding the activities of the Spaniards thrusting up the Isthmus from Panama, Cortés sent out other lieutenants to invade the Mayas inhabiting a region called Honduras. In fact, he did more. When one of his agents revealed signs of insubordination, the great conqueror himself led an army through mountains, swamps, and jungles into Honduras. When he arrived there, however, he found that his disloyal officer had already been defeated and executed and his own difficult expedition rendered unnecessary.

The Mayas of Yucatán were subdued by the Montejos, father, son, and nephew, all of whom bore the name Francisco. But they received their commission from Emperor Charles V, who had decided to curtail the power of Cortés. The elder Montejo, still in his early forties when he began his efforts to conquer the Yucatecan Mayas, had spent some years in Cuba and Panama and had been an officer in the expedition against the Aztecs, but had returned to Spain with a share of the Aztec booty for the Spanish monarch. He had also married a rich Spanish widow and was therefore able to finance his new enterprise. After repeated failures, he delegated the task to the two younger men. A proud and handsome people, the Yucatecan Mayas fought with great skill and stubbornness and avoided subjugation until 1545.

CONQUEST OF THE INCA EMPIRE

Meantime Spaniards down on the Isthmus of Panama had heard of the Incas. Francisco Pizarro and Diego de Almagro, the leaders in the conquest of the vast Inca dominions, were illiterate men of humble birth, who had resided in the New World for a good many years before they began to invade Incaland. More than fifty years old, both of them, they were veterans in comparison with Cortés and Alvarado. Although quite poor, they managed with the aid of a priest to raise funds in Panama for their enterprise. After months spent in the sweltering heat of the tropics, two of their expeditions were forced to turn back to their point of departure without reaching their objective.

The third expedition left the port of Panama in January, 1531, and as the Spaniards approached the northern confines of the Inca empire, they heard of the civil war between the two half-brothers Atahualpa and Huáscar. Advancing slowly, some by sea and others by land, Pizarro and his small army soon penetrated the Inca domain, captured a number of Indian villages, and founded a Spanish town which they named San Miguel. With a detachment of soldiers and a few cannon Pizarro then scaled the lofty eastern range of the Andes and entered the Inca city of Cajamarca. Atahualpa, who was encamped with his troops a few miles away, was induced by a young lieutenant named Hernando de Soto to come to Cajamarca for a parley, and was treacherously seized by Pizarro a short time afterward. Already Atahualpa had captured Huáscar, who was promptly executed, perhaps at the command of his deadly rival. Thus one of the Inca rulers was now dead and the other a prisoner of the Spaniards.

The main body of the Spanish troops remained at Cajamarca for several months collecting plunder. Late in August, 1533, in spite of the millions of dollars (a room full of golden utensils and ornaments and another full of silver artifacts) which the Inca monarch had paid for his ransom, Pizarro strangled Atahualpa and then advanced southward along the Andes to Cuzco, the great Inca capital, which the Spaniards entered without resistance in November, 1533. The civil war between the Inca monarchs and their deaths, together with European horses, steel swords, plated armor, and firearms and Spanish intrigue, confused, terrified, and paralyzed the Inca warriors.

While Pizarro was transforming Cuzco into a Spanish city and plundering its gold-filled temples, young Sebastián Benalcázar was sent with a small detachment to capture Quito, the northern capital of Incaland. This he succeeded in doing just in time to prevent the city's seizure by Pedro de Alvarado, who had set out on his own initiative from Guatemala in the hope of acquiring further riches. Shortly afterward, on January 6, 1535, Pizarro founded the town of Lima on the banks of the Rimac River near the Pacific coast. A few months later Diego de Almagro, to whom the Spanish monarch had assigned the southern part of the Inca dominions, decided to explore his grant and headed an expedition which finally arrived in a distant region called Chile.

Thus far, the Spaniards had found the subjugation of the Inca empire comparatively easy. They had been compelled to fight only a few skirmishes. But now the situation suddenly changed. While Pizarro, Benal-

cázar, and Almagro were absent with the major part of the Spanish soldiers, the puppet Inca monarch set up by Pizarro escaped from Cuzco,
which had been left in charge of Pizarro's brother Hernando, and organized a formidable revolt. A desperate struggle for the control of the city
and the adjacent region followed, and months were required to suppress
the revolt. Manco Inca, the rebel puppet, fled to the mountains and
continued to harass the invaders until his death in 1545.

While the conquest was being extended toward the southeast, into a
region later known as Charcas and Bolivia, the Spanish warriors fell to
fighting over the spoils. Almagro, after terrible hardships suffered during
his long journey over the mountains to the far south, found no gold—
only hostile Indians living in relative poverty. He and his followers returned over the coastal desert and along the high plateau to Cuzco full
of resentment that exploded in civil war. Incaland was not fully subdued
and pacified until after the middle of the century, and by that time nearly
all of the original conquerors had encountered violent deaths. The Inca
empire became the center of the Spanish Viceroyalty of Peru, with its
capital in Lima.

🐚 SUBJUGATION OF THE CHIBCHAS

The Andean plateau of Cundinamarca, the home of the Chibchas, was
more than 400 miles beyond the northern frontier of Incaland, and much
farther from the Caribbean coasts of what later became New Granada
(Colombia) and Venezuela. Efforts to invade the land of the Chibchas
were made from one of the Venezuelan settlements by a German named
Nicholas Federmann and from Quito by Benalcázar, but the inhabitants of Cundinamarca were subdued by Gonzalo Jiménez de Quesada
and his intrepid captains and soldiers before these two adventurers arrived.

A talented young lawyer from southern Spain, Quesada belonged to
the lesser nobility and was barely forty years old when he completed his
conquest. He did not embark for the New World until the occupation
of the Spanish Main was well under way. Santa Marta (1525) and Cartagena (1533) had already been founded in the region soon named New
Granada, and two or three other Spanish settlements, Coro (1527)
among them, had been established to the east in Venezuela. But the vast
interior of the continent was still unfamiliar, and Spaniards supposed
that it might contain Indian societies as rich as those of New Spain and
Peru.

Authorized by the governor of Santa Marta to penetrate South America, Quesada left this coastal town in April, 1536. The long journey across the jungle to the Magdalena and up the hot river valley and over the rugged ridges of the Andes to the high plateau of Cundinamarca, some 800 miles from Santa Marta, required nearly nine months. The expedition suffered incredible hardships: swamps and sandbanks filled with alligators; jungles crowded with jaguars and huge snakes; humid heat, hunger, swarms of insects, Indians in canoes assaulting the Spanish detachment as it went up the Magdalena in boats; and then, after hundreds of miles of slow and enormously difficult advance, the exhausting climb up the steep mountains. But once they reached the fertile plateau, the worst of their sufferings was over. The subjugation of the Chibchas involved no great hazard. Weakened by civil war and by hostilities with their neighbors on the west, they offered no more than feeble resistance. Drawing Indian allies to their side and playing tribe against tribe, the Spaniards themselves had to fight only a few skirmishes, in which their losses were never serious. A good many natives were slaughtered and all of their war chiefs were tortured and killed, but the majority of the Chibchas survived and became slaves and serfs of their masters. The booty obtained by the commander and his cohorts was much smaller than the plunder garnered in New Spain and Peru, but it was probably worth not less than $1,000,000. On August 6, 1538, Quesada laid the foundations of the Spanish town of Santa Fé de Bogotá, which became the capital of another Spanish colony called the New Kingdom of Granada.

The conquest of some 20,000,000 semicivilized Indians was now almost complete. Swift and terrible, it was effected by surprisingly small military forces. Cortés left Cuba with less than 700 men, entered the Aztec capital with about 600; and after his flight, regained the city by assault with no more than 1,300 Spaniards, although many Indian allies fought on his side from the outset. Alvarado set out for Guatemala and El Salvador with 420 Spanish soldiers. Pizarro confronted Atahualpa with only 168 and subdued a good portion of the Inca empire with no more than 1,000 or 1,200. Quesada conquered the Chibchas with only 166 Spanish warriors!

The success of the invaders cannot be attributed entirely to their use of cannon, muskets, plated armor, steel swords, crossbows, and horses. Many other factors helped to account for their triumphs: the enfeebling superstitions and bitter feuds of the Indians; their desire in some instances to take the Europeans alive in order to sacrifice them to their war gods; and the ruthless treachery and intrigue of the Spaniards, which enabled them to capture Indian leaders and win Indian allies.

🐚 CONQUEST OF THE LESS CIVILIZED TRIBES

The subjugation of the semicivilized natives is only a part of the story of the sixteenth-century conquests of the Spaniards in America. They also subdued many of the primitive tribes—nomadic and seminomadic Indians like those familiar to the people of the United States—and the habitats of most of these were regions that became fairly important Spanish colonies and eventually important nations of Latin America.

The conquest and virtual extermination of the more primitive inhabitants of the West Indian Islands and Panama already have been noted. The conquest and occupation of southern Central America—the area south of Mayaland, which was added to the captaincy general of Guatemala and finally transformed into the modern nations of Costa Rica and Nicaragua—were achieved in part by the subordinates of Pedrarias Dávila, the first governor of Panama. Other Spaniards continued their work, but only the more pleasant highland and lake regions were subdued and occupied by the end of the century.

The conquerors of the fertile central valley of Chile, those remembered by the Chileans as the founders of their country, were Pedro de Valdivia and García Hurtado de Mendoza, and both have been honored by towns that bear their names. The natives of northern Chile, who had been tamed by the Incas, were not hard to conquer; but the fierce Araucanians, the "Apaches of the Far South," fought with great skill and courage, and some of them were not subdued until around 1880. Hurtado de Mendoza, after heroic exploits in Chile, crossed the Andes, occupied a region called Cuyo, and founded the town of Mendoza (1561) in present-day Argentina.

Among those who took a conspicuous part in the conquest of the natives of the vast central and southern basin of the Río de la Plata, were Domingo Martínez de Irala and Juan de Ayolas in Paraguay and Pedro de Mendoza and Juan de Garay in Argentina. The first region to be occupied was Paraguay, inhabited by the semisedentary Guaraní, where a Spanish settlement that soon became the town of Asunción was established in 1537. The taming of the wilder tribes to the south and southwest was a slow and difficult process. The town of Buenos Aires, shortly after it was founded by Pedro de Mendoza in 1536, had to be abandoned because of Indian attacks. It was not occupied again until 1580, when Juan de Garay arrived with colonists from Asunción. Already, in 1573, Garay had established the town of Santa Fé, and before the end of the century several other settlements were founded, mainly by colonists coming from Peru or Chile. The nomadic Charrua Indians in the area that later formed the domain of Uruguay were not subdued until after 1700, and a portion of the great plains south and southwest of Buenos Aires remained the haunt of roving Indians until the late 1870's.

At the other extreme of the South American continent, in Venezuela, only the seacoast and the adjacent highlands were occupied by the Spaniards during the sixteenth century. Many leaders participated in the conquest and settlement of this region, even including some agents of the Welzers (German bankers of Augsburg and creditors of the Spanish monarch). Juan de Ampués was the founder of Coro, the first permanent settlement. Caracas, which became the capital of the province, was not established until 1567, under the leadership of Diego Lozada. Among the primitive inhabitants of the region were the fierce Caribs, for whom the Caribbean Sea was named, and some of these tribes were not subjugated until after 1800.

Rodrigo Bastidas, founder of Santa Marta, Pedro Heredia, founder of Cartagena, Pedro's brother Alonso, and Francisco César were the outstanding conquerors of the primitive Indians in northern New Granada. The natives of the Cartagena region had a rich accumulation of golden ornaments and artifacts in their temples and graves, treasures worth several million dollars, which the Spaniards seized as booty. Benalcázar of Peruvian fame and Jorge Robledo subdued the bellicose hordes of the fertile Cauca valley, in which they established Pasto, Popayán, Cali, and other towns.

Far away in the north, Spanish rule was imposed in Florida, after numerous costly failures, during the second half of the century. Many adventurers and missionaries lost their lives in the effort to subdue and occupy this area. One of the best known victims was Juan Ponce de León, an old conqueror from the West Indies—he had subdued Puerto Rico—who is said to have gone to Florida in search of a Fountain of Youth. Beginning as early as 1512, unsuccessful efforts to seize and colonize the country extended over a period of fifty years. The main obstacles confronted were hurricanes, floods, swamps, and very hostile Indians. The occupation might have been further delayed if news of French activities had not stirred the Spanish king to more vigorous action. Philip II granted Florida to a powerful nobleman named Pedro Menéndez de Avilés, who founded San Augustín (St. Augustine) on September 6, 1565, and with the aid of Catholic missionaries established other settlements which turned out to be permanent. Menéndez captured the French Huguenots and executed 300 or 400 of them in a nationalistic and religious frenzy. A French expedition came out to retaliate and exacted a measure of vengeance, but the Spaniards remained in possession of Florida. Menéndez died in Spain in 1574, perhaps without realizing that his work in America would endure.

In New Spain, during the last seventy-five years of the century, the Spaniards subdued many wild tribes beyond the frontiers of the old Aztec dominions. With the fall of Tenochtitlán and the establishment of Spanish control over Montezuma's grand confederacy, the conquest of immense New Spain was hardly more than initiated. The captains and successors of Cortés subjugated tens of thousands of roving Indians who had never acknowledged Aztec rule, and thus added to New Spain thousands of square miles to the west, north, and northeast of Montezuma's dominions. Toward the end of the century Catholic missionaries began to play a leading role in this expansion.

ᶓᶝᶦ THE SEARCH FOR OTHER MEXICOS AND OTHER PERUS

Meantime, the Spaniards had explored a good part of the interior of the two Americas. Belief in the fabulous, inculcated by the reading of the literature of romance and by the extraordinary treasures found in Mexico, Peru, and New Granada, was an important cause of this rapid exploration. In 1536 Alvar Núñez Cabeza de Vaca, who had been shipwrecked on the coast of Texas, arrived in Culiacán, a Spanish settlement on the northwestern frontier of New Spain. He had tramped all the way across the continent, and he brought rumors of wealthy kingdoms to the north, which soon started men on quests for the Seven Cities of the Buffalo, Grand Quivira, and the Northern Mystery; by 1603 Spaniards had crossed the Great Plains of Oklahoma and Kansas to the South Platte River. In 1539 Hernando de Soto, brother-in-law of Balboa, former lieutenant of Pedrarias Dávila in Nicaragua, and companion of Pizarro in Incaland, set sail for the coast of Florida in search of another Peru. The quest led him through the hunting grounds of most of the Indians of the southeastern portion of the United States, and eventually to the discovery of the Mississippi River and its Arkansas tributary.

In South America even more amazing feats were accomplished. Here the Spaniards were dazzled by tall tales of the Gilded Man (*El Dorado*), the rich kingdoms of Meta and Omagua, the wonder-city of Manoa, and the land of the "Amazons." The stories indicated that these were to be found in the great river valleys or somewhere within the vast interior of the continent, and daring leaders set forth through tropical heat, flood, pest, and jungle. The suffering was terrific, and the cost was heavy in both men and money; but the explorers gave to the world considerable knowledge of the heart of South America.

At least a score of long expeditions were made by the end of the century, perhaps the majority of them from the coast of Venezuela. Others, however, started from Peru, from New Granada, and from Paraguay.

Some adventurers descended the mountains of northern Venezuela, crossed its llanos to the Orinoco, and explored hundreds of miles of that river and its tributaries. Others entered one of the mouths of the Orinoco and followed the great river and its affluents into the plains and forests of New Granada. Still others traveled southeast from Bogotá until they reached the junction of the Guaviare and the Orinoco, or advanced farther toward the equator to explore some of the tributaries of the Amazon. From New Granada the most extensive expeditions were made by Jiménez de Quesada, the conqueror, and his brother Hernán Pérez de Quesada.

But the most daring of all these exploits proceeded from the land of the Incas. Francisco de Orellano, companion of the Pizarros, embarked (1540) with a small party upon one of the upper tributaries of the Amazon, entered that great river, and followed it across the continent to the sea. Lope de Aguirre, a desperate character who had seized the command of a Peruvian expedition after having murdered its leader, floated down the Amazon to the vicinity of one of the tributaries of the Orinoco and by this tributary and the Orinoco made his way to the Atlantic and the Caribbean (1560–61).

While these bold adventurers were searching for fabled kingdoms, important explorations were made from Asunción. Ayolas ascended the Paraguay River for nearly 300 miles and then went across the forested plains and high mountains to Cuzco. Irala went up the Paraguay almost to its source and opened a permanent line of communication to Peru. Cabeza de Vaca, after having walked across North America from the Gulf of Mexico to the Gulf of California, rode with his companions across southwestern Brazil to Asunción, where he served a short time as colonial governor.

ESTABLISHMENT OF SPANISH INSTITUTIONS AND TRANSFER OF SPANISH CULTURE

It has often been said that the Spaniards were a cruel and greedy people, robbers and plunderers who came to America in the hope of returning home with enough loot to enable them to spend the rest of their lives in luxury. To a large extent, this is the truth. But it is not the whole truth. Not a few did plunder and rob and return to Spain to display their ill-gotten wealth. But many others were actuated by patriotic, religious, and humanitarian motives, and these came to the New World to convert and civilize the natives and to build permanent homes for themselves. The Spanish kings were ardent Roman Catholics, eager to spread their faith. If they exploited rather than developed their overseas possessions, this was because their zeal in defending and expanding Roman Catholicism in Europe made them feel that they were entitled to draw some of the sinews of royal power from America.

Even during the sixteenth century, the Spaniards did not by any means restrict their efforts in America to exploration, conquest, and seizure of the persons and possessions of its aboriginal inhabitants. They evangelized the natives, taught them new skills and new methods of production, and brought in Negro slaves from Africa to ease their burdens. They searched diligently for precious metals and jewels, but they also urged that the cultivation of native crops be continued, introduced their own familiar food plants and domestic animals, and applied themselves to the management of farms, plantations, and ranches. They founded towns, built homes, and established workshops and centers of trade. In short, during the sixteenth century and the two that followed they transplanted their institutions and culture so successfully that more than a third of the Americas is still Hispanic.

Intelligent consideration of Spanish colonial institutions must begin with emphasis upon the relationship of the New World to the Spanish crown. That this New World belonged to the Spanish monarchs and not to the Spanish nation was fundamental. They successfully asserted not only their sovereign rights in America but their property rights as well. Every privilege, office, and position, whether political, administrative, judicial, economic, or religious, must come from them. It was from this basis that the exploration, conquest, occupation, and government of the New World proceeded. The entire enterprise was undertaken by and for the royal authorities, under the direction of individuals appointed by them and directly responsible to them. A modern writer has described the system as follows:

When a leader went forth to add new dominions to the crown he sought first the royal license [usually under a contract called a *capitulación*]. To obtain it, he had to show sufficient financial backing to insure probable success. His profits were to be taken from the area subdued. He was to have the right to exact labor from the Indians, to appoint municipal officers for the first year, to possess a tract of land . . . and to bestow lands upon his followers according to their merits or services. He might recruit companies of soldiers or settlers, offering them such inducements from the conquest and taking from them such pledges of loyalty as he himself gave the king or . . . [the king's] representative. Sometimes royal funds were invested if the venture were of strategic importance. There were judicially chosen missionaries, in large numbers usually, to effect a spiritual conquest. And there were never lacking royal officials, or treasury representatives, who kept account of all treasure-trove, gold mines discovered, or any visible sources of wealth, of which the king and the leader were each to have a fifth. Never varying greatly in plan, all the expeditions of discovery and conquest closely followed this system.[3]

It was an excellent system—for the monarch. "Financial responsibility was shifted by enlisting private capital; thus, losses from shipwreck, uncompleted voyages, and unsuccessful establishments were largely borne by the unhappy victims of misadventure," not only the leaders but the humble participants as well.

According to his contract the leader might become an *adelantado,* a lieutenant, a governor, or even a captain general. "Always he had to be a man of daring and resource, for he possessed potential enemies within the expedition, in the missionaries, who sought the temporal as well as the spiritual advantage of the church, in the royal officials, who were intended as checks upon profits on behalf of the crown, and in his captains, who were all likely to . . . watch eagerly for mistakes or missteps in his management" and try to displace him.

As the monarch's overseas dominions grew, he set up in the homeland two institutions to assist him in governing them. As early as 1503, he established in Seville the *Casa de Contratación,* or House of Trade, whose duties were the supervision of commerce, navigation, and emigration and the training of pilots. By 1524, he had set up a permanent Council of the Indies, to which he entrusted supreme legislative and judicial control, under the king, of all the colonies in the New World, as well as the functions of nominating all colonial civil and ecclesiastical officials and giving advice with respect to their conduct.

The principal executive officials within the Indies themselves have already been noted. The *adelantado* gradually disappeared, his functions being connected exclusively with frontier regions. To the governor and the captain general were soon added the viceroy,[4] the most exalted and powerful of all colonial officials. Within the area under his control, he was not only civil governor but commander-in-chief of the army, vice-patron of the church, presiding officer of the supreme—or perhaps circuit—court which sat in his capital city, and superintendent of finances. During the sixteenth century two viceroyalties were established, one in New Spain, or Mexico (1535), and the other in Peru (1544), and two captaincies general: Guatemala, embracing Central America north of Panama and a part of southern Mexico, and Chile; the first set up before the middle of the century and the second near its end. Within his less important jurisdiction, the captain general exercised about the same functions as did the viceroy. Smaller administrative units were in charge of governors, *corregidores,* and *alcaldes-mayores.*

Always eager for profits and jealous of its prerogatives, the Spanish monarchy not only sent its treasury officials to America but also extended to the Indies its system of investigations and its corps of investigators (*residencia, pesquisadores,* and *visitadores*). Officials were carefully watched, often judicially investigated before the expiration of their tenure, and nearly always subjected to the *residencia* at its end. Perhaps the most effective check upon royal officials in the colonies, however, and one of the most important colonial institutions, was the *audiencia,* seven of which were established by the middle of the century and nine by 1600.[5] Composed of from four to twelve judges and one or two prosecuting attorneys, they had many functions, judicial, advisory, and even administrative. They were the highest court within the boundaries of their jurisdictions, and there was no appeal save in very important cases, which might be referred to the Council of the Indies. They also served as an advisory body to the chief executive, sat in judgment upon his acts, and communicated over his head to the Council; and in the absence of the executive, on account of death or for any other reason, the *audiencia* acted as an ad interim administrative authority.

A conspicuous feature of Spanish colonization was the planting of towns and municipal institutions. Spaniards disliked the isolation of rural life and preferred to live in urban communities. There were some 200 towns in Spanish America by 1574 and perhaps 250 by 1600. Among them were fourteen [6] destined to be the capitals of as many independent nations of a later period. Hardly a score of the important towns [7] of the nineteenth century were unfounded in the sixteenth. Herbert Priestley has vividly described these communities:

> The Spanish towns, which must be distinguished from the Indian towns, were legally established by groups of settlers numbering from ten to one hundred heads of families. . . . The grants to the towns were almost uniformly four square leagues (about eighteen thousand acres). . . . As in the New England towns, the land was divided among the colonies in proportion to their merits, capacity, or number of family dependents. The small husbandman received, inside the building area of the town, which was laid out foursquare about a public plaza, a house lot measuring fifty by one hundred feet. Outside the building area he received enough land to sow one hundred quintals (ten thousand pounds) of wheat or barley and ten of corn. He was also given a measured plot of ground for a garden and an orchard, besides pasture ground for ten sows, five mares, one hundred sheep, and twenty goats, in return for which he must provide the beginning of these herds. . . . A pioneer who had the status of a mounted soldier might receive . . . a house lot one hundred by two hundred feet and cultivable [and] pasture lands five times as extensive [as those given to a small husbandman]. The town was established by a leader, or by the group acting as a unit; the officers were generally elected, though when a leader had taken the initiative he was permitted to appoint them for the first year. From this type of grant

sprang the Spanish pueblo or town. . . . All the cities of Spanish America had such origin.[8]

The essential officers of the municipalities were the *regidores* (councilmen), sometimes only three or four, sometimes ten or twelve. From their number were chosen two *alcaldes ordinarios* (municipal judges) and an *alférez* (ensign or herald). During the sixteenth century two or three treasury officials of the crown resided in each of the towns and sat in their councils (*cabildos* or *ayuntamientos*) with voice and vote. For a time, the municipalities were centers of local self-government, but their autonomy was largely or completely abolished by the sale of offices and the encroachments of the royal governors, *corregidores,* and *alcaldes mayores.*

These towns were units of Spanish culture anchored in the New World. They had their plazas and parks, their imposing churches, monasteries, and municipal buildings, and their schools and hospitals.[9] In them were living at the end of the century more than 200,000 people of pure Spanish descent, besides many Negroes, mulattoes, mestizos (inhabitants of mixed Spanish and Indian blood), and Indians, who either resided in the rear of the Spanish homes or in municipal wards set aside for them.

Toward the end of the century, most of the subjugated Indians were dwelling, willingly or unwillingly, in separate towns and villages scattered about over the various colonies. For the most part, they were ruled by Spanish encomenderos and crown officials (*corregidores* and *alcaldes mayores*) who directed their work and largely dominated their trade, and were supposed to educate them and promote their material and moral development with the assistance of the clergy, who were also in charge of the frontier mission villages. In many instances, however, encomenderos, crown officials, and clergymen used Indian chiefs (caciques) as agents of social control, although such Indian officials were seldom more than puppets. In theory, the welfare of the natives was safeguarded by their right to appeal to royal protectors (*protectores*), to *audiencias,* and even to the Council of the Indies itself; but this right often had little practical value.

The violence of the conquest, epidemics of European diseases, compulsory labor, and the seizure of Indian lands and hunting grounds for Spanish farms, plantations, and pastures greatly reduced the native population, and racial amalgamation caused further decline in the pure Indian stocks. The natives of the West Indies, northern Venezuela, and certain parts of Central America and other colonies were practically destroyed by 1600. Father Bartolomé Las Casas asserted that 12,000,000 to 15,000,000 had been exterminated by 1541, but many other writers contend that his denunciatory estimates were the preposterous guesses of a fanatic. Las Casas probably exaggerated the cruelties of the conquerors and misinterpreted their motives, but his statistics may not be far from correct. The later estimates of Juan López de Velasco (1574), geographer of the crown, seem to indicate that there were only 7,000,000 to 8,000,000 Indians living in subjection to the Spaniards at the end of the third quarter of the century. Perhaps there were at that time no more than 2,000,000 to 3,000,000 still unsubdued. If these figures are reasonably accurate, and if the total Indian population in 1500 was in the neighborhood of 25,000,000, it would appear that more than half of the aboriginal inhabitants had been exterminated by war, disease, hard labor, mental depression, starvation, and other maladies.

In earlier decades hundreds of thousands of Indians had been reduced to slavery, but comparatively few of the some 8,000,000 under Spanish rule in 1600 were actual slaves. Their status, however, was not very different from slavery, since they were forced to work at a meager wage fixed by Spanish authorities, since their wages were sometimes withheld, and since all able-bodied adult male Indians, and occasionally even some of the adult females, were compelled to pay tribute to the encomenderos or the crown.

In some respects, the condition of those who survived may have improved after the arrival of their white masters. Their tribal feuds and their religious oppressions and cruelties were suppressed. Some of their gross superstitions had vanished or been displaced by others of a somewhat less evil nature. They had been taught, at least to some extent, the principles and comforts of a more salutary gospel. They were supplied with better tools, implements, and techniques, with additional food plants, and with far more useful domestic animals.[10] All of these transformations and resources must have conferred some benefits, in spite of the fact that they were partly offset by hard labor in the mines, the pearl fisheries, the textile factories, the workshops, and on the farms, ranches, and plantations, toil that may have been more strenuous than most of the Indians had ever experienced before the conquest.

By the close of the century their social position had been fixed. The remainder of the Colonial period would bring about little change in their status. Of the 2,000,000 to 3,000,000 still in the primitive state, many were subsequently reclaimed by the frontier missions and reduced to a settled mode of life. Of the millions under encomenderos, nearly all were slowly transferred to the supervision of royal officials, but this was of slight consequence, for they were cheated and abused by these, and eventually they were bound in peonage (forced labor to pay off debts, often contracted in times of stress or imprudence). Village life, Christianization, civilization, grinding toil, racial fusion—these were the results, if not the objectives, of Spain's Indian policy. There was much exploitation and cruelty despite many humane decrees. But after all the excesses and oppressions have been taken into account, it must be admitted that the fate of the aborigines of Spanish America was probably not less fortunate than that of the backward races subdued by other colonizing powers during the two or three centuries that followed.

There was no more important institution in the Spanish colonies than the Roman Catholic Church. To it early Spanish American society owed much that was beneficial and a little that was harmful. The clergy, both regular and secular, came over with the first explorers, conquerors, and settlers, and continued to come in increasing numbers until by the closing decades of the century the civil officials complained of a superabundance. By 1600, the church was organized into five archbishoprics [11] and twenty-seven bishoprics, and there were scores of other ecclesiastical dignitaries as well as many hundreds of priests. At the same time, the monasteries numbered more than 400, with probably 2,000 Jesuits and members of the mendicant orders. There were also three Tribunals of the Inquisition, one at Lima, another in Mexico City, and a third at Cartagena, designed to prevent any deviations from the dogma of the church.

The clergy had made large contributions to sixteenth-century achievement. If the intolerant zeal of a few had sometimes abetted the cruelties of the conquerors, if eagerness to enlarge the wealth of the church had led some to make use of compulsory Indian labor, the tender human sympathy of others had often restrained ruthless laymen and softened the hard lot of the natives. If too large a number of padres and priests exploited the Indians, many more undertook the task of Christianizing and civilizing them with a devotion seldom surpassed in the annals of the faith. If there was just ground for complaint at the accumulation of ecclesiastical wealth, it must be admitted that the colonial inhabitants owed to the church nearly all that they received in education, hospitalization, and charity. The earnest preaching and propaganda of many such men as Padre Las Casas aroused the Spanish monarchs to a realization of the miserable condition of their native wards and led to considerable humane, if largely ineffective, legislation. The failure of such legislation, notably the famous laws of 1542 designed to abolish Indian slavery and serfdom and exempt the natives from the heaviest types of work, was caused mainly by the opposition of the colonial officials and the laity, although a few clergymen were to blame; nor is it likely that these humane laws would have been issued if they had not been demanded by Las Casas [12] and his associates. The Spanish monarchy that deliberately used the state church as an agency of colonial enterprise could not entirely ignore its views.

The sixteenth century was, of course, characterized by important mining development. But beyond the early decades of the period, this did not signify neglect of agriculture and stock raising. The mining enterprises found it necessary to obtain supplies from farm, plantation, and ranch, and from the workshops and other handicraft industries as well. The first thirty years after the discovery witnessed the despoiling of the areas rich in gold accumulated by the Indians. Cortés, Pizarro, Quesada, the Heredias, and César were the most fortunate of the gold-mad conquerors, but practically all of the conquerors eagerly searched for this precious metal and even tortured the natives in the hope of compelling them to find it. The explorers who made long expeditions into the depths of the mainlands were likewise in pursuit of gold. But the widespread contagion vanished before the middle of the century, and men turned their attention to the more prosaic business of working the mines. The mines of Tasco, some eighty miles south of Mexico City, began to be worked in the 1530's, and those of Zacatecas, Guanajuato, Fresnillo, Santa Bárbara, San Luís Potosí, and many other districts of New Spain were brought under exploitation long before the close of the century. In Peru, the rich silver mines of Potosí were discovered in 1545 and the mercury mines of Huancavelica began to be worked twenty years later. Placer and other mines of precious metal were also found and exploited in New Granada, Venezuela, and Central America. The annual value of the exports of gold and silver to Spain from the colonies seldom rose above 1,000,000 pesos before 1530; but exports of these metals then began to expand rapidly. Between 1546 and 1550, the annual average was valued at more than 5,500,000 pesos, and for the last decade of the century the annual average was equivalent to 35,000,000 pesos. From 1541 through 1575, North America, mainly Mexico, sent the bulk of the two precious metals from the colonies; but South America, especially Peru, supplied about two-thirds of the treasure during the next twenty-five years. And these figures make no allowance for the gold and silver retained in the colonies or smuggled out to other countries.

It should not be assumed, however, that Spanish America's gold and silver were more valuable than all of its other products. This would usually be the case if only exports were considered. But most of these other commodities were consumed in the colonies. Only hides, sugar, cacao, cochineal, dyewoods, cabinet woods, and a few other commodities were sent to Spain. Total output should not be evaluated in terms of exports. After the early decades of the Colonial period, mining tended to stimulate farming, ranching, and handicraft production, in which Indians, mestizos, and even many Spaniards were primarily interested. Agriculture and the raising of livestock and poultry were seldom neglected.

Spanish exploits and experiences in the New World tended to evoke literary expression. Prior to 1800, few periods in history were so completely revealed by the records of contemporaries and participants. The conquerors and explorers were often men of literary attainment. Cortés, Bernal Díaz del Castillo, and Quesada are conspicuous examples. Balboa, Cabeza de Vaca, and, in fact, most of the leaders either wrote formal accounts of their difficulties and achievements or sent letters to members of the Spanish government. Friars who accompanied the explorers or followed closely upon their heels presented first-hand narratives of events. The Spanish monarch employed chroniclers, geographers, and historians to write of the New World. And even some men with Indian blood in their veins, such as Garcilaso de la Vega, produced accounts of Indian life and the Spanish conquest.

The numerous writers of the period were concerned mainly with war, natural phenomena, religion, and native languages. A few, such as Juan Matienzo, dealt with government and commerce. Most of their works were in prose, but quite a few expressed themselves in poetry. In fact, some 300 poets are said to have participated in a contest held in New Spain in 1585. The most famous poems of the period are *La Araucana,* written by Alonso de Ercilla y Zúñiga (1533–95), and *Grandeza Mexicana,* the work of Bernardo de Balbuena (1568–1627). The first dealt with the author's personal adventures in the war with the Araucanian Indians of Chile. The second presented a vivid account of New Spain, especially Mexico City, its beauties, wonders, and native inhabitants. Of less note is Martín del Barco Centenera's poetic account of the conquest of the Río de la Plata region. Shortly before 1600, Juan de Castellanos of New Granada produced his *Elegies of Illustrious Men,* one of the world's longest poems.

The sixteenth century was also marked in Spanish America by considerable achievements in architecture, sculpture, and painting, much of it devoted to religious purposes. Most of the painting and sculpture has perished; a few examples of the architecture still survive.

CORSAIRS, TRADE REGULATIONS, TAXES

Actuated by motives compounded of national animosity and greed, French corsairs began to attack Spanish colonial trade at a very early date. At first they hovered along the coasts of Europe or hid in the coves of the Canaries, Azores, and Madeiras. They met Columbus on his return voyage in 1493 and forced him to change his route of return in 1496. They seized two treasure-laden caravels in 1521 and captured a part of the plunder sent home by Cortés in 1522–23. By 1537 they were busy in the Caribbean, seizing treasure ships and capturing and pillaging towns—Havana, Cartagena, and Chagres, among others. When peace interrupted their raids in 1559, Elizabethan seadogs, such as Sir Francis Drake and John Hawkins, took their place, capturing bullion trains and treasure fleets, and plundering not only the towns of the Caribbean but those of the Pacific Coast as well.

Losses from these corsair and seadog raids ran into the millions, and together with the monopolistic ideal, they were largely responsible for the confinement of trade to convoyed merchant fleets sailing at stipulated dates from the Spanish port of Seville (and its subsidiary, Cádiz) to the American ports of Havana, Cartagena, Veracruz, and Porto Bello.[13] This system, in turn, led to the concentration of Spanish American trade in the hands of a few merchants at Seville, who also tried to control the import business of the colonies by stationing their agents at Veracruz, Mexico City, Panama, and Lima. Such a system proved cumbersome and expensive, raised the price of colonial imports by limiting their quantity, and predisposed the colonists to welcome smugglers. Even granting a much broader participation of Spanish merchants, its successful operation depended upon thriving manufacturing industries in the metropolis and superior sea power, neither of which Spain possessed during the closing years of the century.[14]

After the conquest of the Philippines (1565–72), trade sprang up between those islands and the Pacific coast of Spanish America. But this, too, was rigidly controlled. It was soon restricted to two vessels with a stipulated capacity of 500 to 600 tons and to the port of Acapulco in New Spain. No other jurisdiction bordering upon the Pacific was permitted to enjoy a direct trade with these islands, nor could Peru, which was allowed to carry on a limited traffic with Mexico and Guatemala, bring home goods from the Far East.

Spain's lack of ability to operate this trading system efficiently did not become clearly evident for many years. Until near the close of the century, large mercantile fleets left Seville for the Indies almost every year, bringing out a supply of goods which would appear to have been fairly adequate to meet colonial needs. For illustration, forty-two vessels sailed with the fleet in 1537, eighty-nine in 1548, seventy-one in 1585, seventy-two in 1592, but only thirty-two in 1601. Owing to the raids of corsairs and seadogs, the number of vessels returning to

Spain was likely to be less than the number going out; but the pirates were never able during the sixteenth century to capture the whole fleet or even a major part of it.

Taxes levied by Spain upon the colonies and colonial trade seem not to have been burdensome during the period under review. They certainly were not heavy during the first forty years of it. Prior to 1543, no tax was collected in Spain from the trade to the Indies, although a duty of 7.5 per cent was charged from the outset on goods as they entered the American ports. The wealth of precious metals and stones brought from the Indies would appear to have made burdensome taxes unnecessary. The crown usually took a fifth of these—a share less than had been customary in case of the mines of Spain. Remissions of gold and silver to the crown from its American colonies began to exceed 1,000,000 pesos annually by 1550. During the five-year period of 1551–55 the yearly average was 4,000,000, and it reached an average of 10,000,000 annually during the last decade of the century. Customs duties were gradually increased after 1543 until all goods going to the colonies paid 15 per cent ad valorem and all commodities coming from the colonies to Spain paid 17.5 per cent. In addition, this commerce was charged with a convoy tax that rose from 1 to 7 per cent during the century. The *alcabala,* or sales tax, amounting to about 2 per cent ad valorem, was introduced into the colonies toward the end of the century; the crown also shared a portion of the tithes and other ecclesiastical revenues, profited from a monopoly on such commodities as salt, explosives, and quicksilver, and collected a small tribute (head tax) from all male adult Indians not under the control of private encomenderos.[15]

PROMINENT VICEROYS OF THE CENTURY

A discussion of the character, policies, and activities of the multitude of Spanish colonial officials would involve tiresome detail. The colonies seem to have been overloaded with bureaucrats long before 1600. The Spanish monarchs rewarded their favorites with posts in America and sold numerous offices, high and low, to increase their revenue. Only a few of the outstanding viceroys of the century will be considered here. The total for the period was fifteen individuals, but three of them served in both New Spain and Peru, so that there were eighteen viceregal administrations, nine in the former (1535–1603) and nine in the latter (1544–1604).

Antonio de Mendoza, the first viceroy of New Spain, was an able administrator. In a day when executive clemency was rare, he usually managed to refrain from acts of brutality. He quelled rebellions; calmed bickering strife; brought the petulant conquerors under control; promoted the building of churches, schools, and hospitals; expanded the frontiers of the viceroyalty; began the codification of colonial laws; and collected revenues with a fair degree of honesty and efficiency. He was unable, however, to enforce the humanitarian laws of 1542 and thus improve the pitiable condition of the Indians. Royal recognition of his talents was expressed by transferring him to Peru, where death ended his career (1552) within a few months after he arrived in Lima.

Another skilful administrator was Martín Enríquez, the fourth viceroy of New Spain (1568–80). He repelled an attack by John Hawkins on Veracruz; strengthened the coast defenses; shielded the northern frontier against Indian raids; modified the system of local government; and supported the educational and spiritual efforts of the church. Since he found many of his subordinates unreliable, he was compelled to attend to most of the duties of his office in person. His tasks were so exacting and complaints against his decisions so numerous that he came to consider public office in Mexico a great misfortune for an honest man. One of his unusual policies was that of employing creoles in positions of governmental responsibility. Convinced of its wisdom, he recommended that the policy be continued, but his advice was seldom followed. Like Mendoza, he was transferred to Peru and died in Lima (1582) without having accomplished much of significance in his new post.

The Velascos, father and son, were among the greatest colonial administrators of the century. Luís de Velasco served as viceroy of New Spain for fourteen years (1551–64) and died a poor man at the end of his term. A relative of the royal family, he was patient, industrious, affable, and efficient. His Indian policy won him the title of "Emancipator." He urged the founding of the royal and pontifical University of Mexico and served and safeguarded it during its early years. He also promoted the expansion of the frontiers of New Spain and initiated a project to protect its capital from floods. His son, also named Luís de Velasco, was the eighth viceroy of New Spain (1590–95). Since he had already lived in Mexico for a good many years, he knew his kingdom thoroughly. Intelligent, industrious, capable, and honest, he added luster to a name already famous by promoting the textile industry (woolen and cotton); stimulating mining and agriculture; erecting new public buildings in the capital and adorning its streets and plazas; strengthening the defenses of Veracruz; and making the northern outposts more secure. Rewarded by promotion to Peru, he became one of the noted viceroys of that kingdom (1596–1604), protecting its coasts against foreign attacks, ameliorating the condition of the Indians and Negroes, quieting rebellions of natives on the frontiers, repairing the damages done by the earthquake of 1600, reducing corruption in administrative circles, and giving some attention to education. Moreover, he lived to serve another term (1607–11) as viceroy of New Spain, a term distinguished, among other achievements, by draining the lake district around Mexico City, by the suppression of a Negro revolt near Orizaba, by explorations in the Pacific Ocean, and by the sending of an embassy to Japan.

Somewhat less famous than the Velascos were Andrés Hurtado de Mendoza and García Hurtado de Mendoza. The former ruled Peru from 1556 to 1561 and was noted for his reasonably honest, though rather severe, rule. He completed the suppression of the lawlessness that had afflicted the kingdom since the days of the conquest and set up an efficient and economical government. He failed, however, to win merited appreciation from King Philip II and died in grief shortly before the end of his six-year term. His son García was more fortunate. After governing Peru for some time (1590–96), he was permitted honorably to return to Spain for his health. His administration was noted for financial reforms, the promotion of higher education and public works, and attempts to protect the natives from exploitation.

Perhaps the most outstanding of all the Peruvian viceroys of the period was Francisco de Toledo (1569–81), sometimes called the "Solon of Peru." Son of a distinguished father and a kinsman of the royal family, he served his monarch with loyalty and zeal. He began his rule with a long and arduous inspection of the most densely inhabited parts of his kingdom, its mines, its stock farms, its plantations, its vineyards, and its growing manufacturing establishments. With the view of more thoroughly indoctrinating, civilizing, and protecting the Indians, he compelled more of them to live in towns. He also promulgated numerous humane laws and regulations, but his efforts in this sphere were largely frustrated and he confronted one rather formidable native revolt. He set up local governments; tried to improve the administration of justice; encouraged the use of mercury in the silver mines; sent out exploration parties; hastened the opening of the University of San Marcos, which had been delayed for nearly a quarter of a century after its foundation had been authorized; and, in short, did what he could to bring peace and prosperity to Peru. Although he executed the Inca who led the uprising of the natives, he was not excessively cruel according to the standards of his time. He punished some of the members of the Tribunal of the Inquisition who abused their powers and took drastic measures against any clergymen found to be guilty of misdemeanor or crime.

Such were the most notable viceroys of the century. Of the eight others who have not been considered, some were corrupt and all were more or less inefficient. Taking the group as a whole, and giving due attention to the many difficulties they encountered—earthquake, pestilence, flood, foreign enemies, bewildered and often stupid Indians; ambitious and greedy conquerors and sons of the same character; the backward state of communications; exacting monarchs demanding more and more income from the colonies; untrustworthy subordinates in purchased posts; obstreperous judges, inquisitorial visitors, querulous ecclesiastics; a strange environment and problems without precedent— these Spanish dons probably deserve a rank not inferior to that of the most capable colonial administrators of modern times. The Spanish colonies would not see their like again until the middle of the eighteenth century.

CHAPTER V

The Founding of Brazil

ᾧ PORTUGAL'S GREATEST OVERSEAS ACHIEVEMENT

A third of the people of Hispanic America are Portuguese in language and culture and this third controls 40 per cent of the region's living space. The occupation and development of Brazil, well under way by the end of the sixteenth century, turned out to be the most significant achievement of the Portuguese nation overseas, more important than anything the Portuguese ever accomplished in Africa, India, and the Far East, the main centers of their colonial activities for centuries.

By virtue of agreements between Spain and Portugal, made soon after Columbus returned from his first voyage across the Atlantic, the eastern part of South America was assigned to Portugal before that continent was discovered. Although the Spaniards and not the Portuguese were probably the first to see the region, Cabral's brief examination of a section of the east coast in 1500, and other voyages to South America following soon thereafter under the Portuguese flag, confirmed Portugal's title. Some of the early expeditions carried back to Europe a dyewood similar to a dyewood of the Orient called "brazil," and that name was finally applied to Portugal's American colony, which for a time had been called Santa Cruz. Some expeditions merely stopped there briefly, as Cabral did, while on their way around Africa to the Orient. Others came to cut and ship brazilwood or to drive away French intruders.

ᾧ EARLY INDIFFERENCE

The country was not rapidly occupied because the Portuguese were more interested in India and the "Spice Islands" of the East. In fact, the settlement of Brazil might have been longer postponed if news had not arrived in Lisbon of immense riches found by Spaniards in America, of Spanish activities in the Río de la Plata Basin, and of increased

French encroachments—and if the flood of spices and silks from the Orient had not glutted the European market until trade in these commodities was no more profitable than the traffic in brazilwood.

Most of the early Portuguese settlers of Brazil were unwilling occupants, victims of shipwreck or criminals dumped ashore to shift for themselves. Their number and activities are largely cloaked in mystery; but it is known that they were scattered along the central section of the long southeast coast, that they organized simple governments at various points for the purpose of defense against the nomadic and cannibalistic native tribes, and that some of them became "squaw men," taking to themselves a number of Indian wives who bore them numerous half-breed sons and daughters. Two of the castaways—João Ramalho in the south and Diogo Alvares in the north—not only furnished wives for later Portuguese settlers but, by virtue of their influence with the Indians, befriended them in other ways.

Late in 1530, thirty years after Cabral's accidental discovery of Brazil, the Portuguese king finally sent out Martím Affonso de Souza to expel interlopers, establish a formal settlement, and organize a central government. Arriving early the next year, he captured some French vessels loaded with brazilwood, thoroughly investigated conditions in the areas of occupation, and, in 1532, founded the town of São Vicente on the coast in a province that later became São Paulo. His report to his monarch indicated, however, that the organization of the scattered Portuguese communities and the firm establishment of Portuguese control against possible European rivals would be an extremely difficult task; and the Portuguese king, lacking resources and still rather indifferent, decided to shift the heavy responsibility to private enterprise. He accordingly divided the colony into fifteen vast feudal strips and distributed them among twelve or thirteen prominent Portuguese, mostly members of the nobility, in accordance with the plan he had followed in effecting the domination of the Madeira and Azores Islands. Each feudal domain extended along the coast for an average distance of about 150 miles and into the interior to the line of demarcation stipulated in the agreements of 1493–94.

These feudal estates call to mind the "proprietary" colonies later authorized by the English government in North America. The recipients of the grants were called captains and their dominions were designated as captaincies. Granted broad powers, these feudal lords not only had the right to found towns and other settlements within their huge estates; they also had the right to distribute land, to exercise nearly all types of jurisdiction over their fiefs, to organize armies and navies, and to enslave Indians. Only the coinage of money and the imposition of the death penalty upon Portuguese inhabitants were forbidden. But the Portuguese crown did not deprive itself of all opportunity for profit. It reserved the right to levy export duties, to monopolize the trade in brazilwood, and to share a fifth of all the gold, silver, and precious stones that might be uncovered.

Thus, long before the thirteen English colonies were established in North America there was at least a chance that twelve or more Portuguese colonies would be established in a much larger area of South America. But the captaincies did not prosper. Tropical jungle, depressing heat, mountains rising abruptly from the seacoasts, and indifference or failure to co-operate proved fatal in most cases. Some of the grantees did not take possession of their fiefs, and only two of those occupied by the others revealed definite signs of prosperity at the end of fifteen years from the time their grants were made. These two were São Vicente, with the town of São Vicente and adjacent communities, and Pernambuco, with the town of Olinda and a few scattered settlements in its vicinity. The chief importance of the experiment lies in the fact that it gave the first impulse to a federal system of government and furnished the geographical background for half of the states that eventually composed the Brazilian Federation of the late nineteenth century.[1]

ଶ୍ଚ THE PORTUGUESE CROWN TAKES CHARGE
OF THE COLONY

Having failed to evade responsibility for the control and defense of Brazil, the king of Portugal decided to bring the colony under more direct royal authority. In 1549, he appointed Thomé de Souza, an illegitimate nobleman who had achieved distinction in India, as governor-general, with full administrative and judicial power over the entire colony and with instructions to establish a royal captaincy in Bahía, recently purchased from its proprietor, and hold the other captaincies together in a semblance of unity. Accompanied by more than 1,000 soldiers and settlers, some criminals among them, and by six Jesuits under the leadership of Father Manoel Nóbrega, Souza founded the town of São Salvador de Bahía the same year.

Brazil's first governor-general is remembered as a capable ruler. The captaincy of Bahía soon became a thriving center from which other parts of Brazil were occupied. Souza dispatched agents to the scattered settlements, organized municipal governments, enrolled companies of militia, imported livestock, and encouraged the cultivation of manioc, tobacco, and various other crops, giving special attention to sugar cane. In fact, the almost moribund colony was restored to life during his four-year term.

He was ably assisted by the Jesuits, who promptly began their missionary work among the natives, inducing them to settle in villages, to live in peace with the Portuguese, to cultivate a diversity of crops, to build houses and churches, and to make furniture and other useful articles. Some of the Jesuit fathers diligently learned the Indians dialects in order better to accomplish their religious and civilizing mission. In 1553 more members of the order arrived, landing at São Vicente under the direction of Father José Anchieta, and in the same year Brazil was made a province of the Society of Jesus. Like their earlier brothers, Anchieta and his associates sought out the natives at once. Climbing up the steep mountains to the plateau, Anchieta opened a school around which the town of São Paulo, later to develop into one of the most important cities of Brazil, soon sprang up. Meantime, the number of secular priests had increased and Brazil's first bishop had been installed at Bahía.

Duarte da Costa, the colony's second governor-general, was an inefficient and imprudent man who quarreled with the bishop and other authorities at Bahía, permitted the Portuguese in this and other settlements to provoke hostilities with the natives with the view of capturing slaves, and then found the security of Brazil inopportunely threatened by a French attempt to establish a settlement in the hitherto unoccupied Bay of Rio de Janeiro. Twenty years of sporadic war, which seriously retarded Brazil's progress, began soon after the new executive took charge of the government.

FOREIGN AGGRESSIONS AND INDIAN WARS

It was in 1555 that the French menace suddenly appeared. Admiral Gaspar de Coligny, a French colonial genius eager to extend the domination of France to Brazil, had sent Nicholas Durand de Villegagnon with a large expedition to carry out his purpose. Planting crops, cutting dyewood, bartering with the Indians and winning their friendship, the French colony might have prospered if harmony had not been destroyed by religious feuds between Calvinists and Catholics. The Calvinists were shortly drowned in an attempt to return to Europe and the rest of the Frenchmen were driven into the interior by Mem de Sá, the third governor-general, in 1560. There, however, they found refuge among the Indians, reorganized, and returned to the site of their original settlement with the aid of native allies. It was not until 1567 that the able and vigorous Mem de Sá, effectively supported by Nóbrega and Anchieta, finally deprived the Frenchmen of the assistance of their Indian friends and drove them from Brazil. The same year witnessed the founding of the Portuguese town of Rio de Janeiro, destined soon to grow into a flourishing community and eventually to become the capital of the colony (1763).

But Indian raids and rebellions continued to trouble most of Brazil in spite of the efforts of Mem de Sá to suppress them and restrain the oppressions of the Portuguese, and despite the noble attempts of the Jesuits to restore harmony. Although the area of Portuguese occupation expanded during the fifteen-year incumbency of Mem de Sá, he failed to complete the pacification of the colony and left the problem to his successors.

The most vigorous of the slave hunters and slave traders of Brazil were the "Paulistas," as the energetic inhabitants of São Paulo were called. Themselves part Indian, they formed alliances with the neighboring tribes and swept over hundreds of miles of territory in search of victims to sell to the planters up the coast. Neither the civil authorities, many of whom were indifferent because of the dire need for labor on plantation and ranch, nor the Jesuit fathers were able to prevent the outrageous traffic, which persisted even after Negro slaves began to be imported in fairly large numbers during the last quarter of the century.

The annexation of Portugal and its empire by Spain in 1580 soon led to further foreign attacks on Brazil. Such English seadogs as Edward Fenton, Robert Witherington, Thomas Cavendish, and James Lancaster raided and plundered most of the settlements. But the Englishmen were mainly interested in trade and booty; they seem to have had no desire to conquer the colony and subject it to their permanent rule. Frenchmen, on the contrary, revived their earlier notion of empire in the Brazilian tropics, now dreaming of an "Equinoctial France" just as they had talked of an "Antarctic France" in years gone by. Shortly after the end of the sixteenth century, Daniel de la Touche built a fort and planted a French colony on the north coast in the old captaincy of Maranhão, probably with the intention of seizing a region extending all the way to the Amazon. But the Brazilians, with some assistance from Spain and Portugal, succeeded in expelling the hated Protestant intruders—they were Huguenots—by 1615. France was able to retain only a swampy and forested region far to the north, which became the French Guiana of a later day.

This foreign menace was largely responsible for efforts by the Brazilians and the Portuguese to expand northward from Bahía and Pernambuco to the northern limits of Portugal's American domain. Between 1583 and 1623, Parahyba, Natal, São Luís de Maranhão, Pará (Belém), and other towns were founded in rapid succession, so that before the end of the first quarter of the seventeenth century Brazil had a string of settlements, some prosperous and others quite primitive, stretching along the Atlantic from Santos and São Paulo to the delta of the Amazon.

🐚 BRAZIL AT THE END OF THE SIXTEENTH CENTURY

Population increased and prosperity slowly developed in Brazil in spite of Indian uprisings and foreign assaults. Approximately 17,000 Portuguese were living in some seventeen villages and towns by 1574. Ten years later, the number had risen to 25,000, and it probably exceeded 40,000 by 1600. The civilized Indian population was smaller, since some of the natives had fled into the woods and reverted to their primitive way of life. But there were 14,000 Negro slaves in 1585 and several thousands more by 1600; and there was, of course, an ever-increasing number of mixbloods of Portuguese-Indian and Portuguese-African descent, many of whom were probably accepted as whites.

The Portuguese had not only brought into the colony specimens of all domestic animals raised in the home country—cattle, swine, goats, horses, a few sheep, and every kind of poultry—but had also introduced sugar cane, wheat, barley, grapes, and such other useful plants and fruits as were found to be adapted to Brazilian soil and climate. Although some cereals were grown, native manioc (*cassava*) was more widely used for bread. No great variety of vegetables was cultivated, but potatoes, yams, and melons were fairly plentiful. The orchards were producing grapes, olives, peaches, and other fruits and orange trees were scattered over the coastal plains. The forests were supplying nuts, lumber, and balsam as well as dyewood and tanning materials. The chief commercial crops were tobacco, cotton, and sugar cane, the last grown in abundance. Livestock, especially cattle, were multiplying rapidly in the highlands and river valleys back of the coast. The most prosperous captaincies were Bahía and Pernambuco, where some of the sugar planters enjoyed large incomes and lived in luxury. The rest were rather poor; even São Vicente, with highlands suitable for Temperate Zone crops and the raising of cattle, horses, hogs, and sheep, seemed to be unaware of its agricultural advantages, for many of its inhabitants still engaged in the Indian slave trade rather than in the cultivation of the soil and the production of livestock.

The government of Brazil was somewhat influenced by the Spanish colonial system after Spain's annexation of mother country and colony in 1580, although both were allowed to retain administrative and judicial autonomy. A Council of Finance was set up to inspect colonial revenues, a less powerful Council of the Indies was organized on the Spanish model, and the system of merchant fleets under convoy was utilized more and more in an attempt to bring colonial trade under firmer control. The title of viceroy did not begin to displace that of governor-general until 1640, however.

The Portuguese monarchs, who had deprived the captains of their political authority in 1549, slowly took over, by purchase or otherwise, the undistributed lands and economic privileges of these feudal lords and their descendants and assignees. But the government of the captaincies remained as before in the hands of royal officials entitled governors, captains, or even captains general, who were supposed, as a rule, to be subordinate to the colonial chief executive at Bahía but often were not, and nearly always claimed and exercised the right to correspond directly with the Portuguese king and his ministers. The administration of justice was largely in the hands of judges appointed by the heads of the captaincies, although the more important cases were handled by judges sent out to the colony from Lisbon. Trial by jury was unknown both in colonial Spanish America and in Brazil; and, as in the Spanish colonies, legislative bodies were lacking in Brazil and no officials were subject to election by the people save in the towns.

The Brazilian towns and adjacent suburban districts were governed by councils which corresponded roughly to the *cabildos* of Spanish America. There was, however, one important difference. The Portuguese monarchs rarely sold municipal offices and the town councils soon fell under the control of local landholders, especially the owners of large estates, instead of being dominated by royal officials as they were in the Spanish empire.

Such, in brief, were Portuguese achievements in the New World during the sixteenth century. They were far less remarkable than the achievements of the Spaniards, but they were sufficient to stake out little Portugal's claim to a huge empire.

CHAPTER VI

Spanish America Under the Later Hapsburgs (1598-1700)

The seventeenth century, unlike the sixteenth, was not a period of vigorous Spanish activity in America. Comparatively few towns were founded; the output of the mines diminished; trade between Spain and her colonies dropped to a lower level. But conditions were not entirely stagnant. Although the civilized Indian population remained stationary or even declined, emigrants from Spain arrived at the rate of 1,500 to 2,000 a year and Negro slaves were imported in greater numbers than in earlier times. Moreover, thousands of roving Indians were induced to settle in villages in charge of Catholic missionaries; some new regions were occupied by Spanish settlers, especially on the frontiers of New Spain; and educational institutions, including several new universities, multiplied. The slow tempo of material progress may be explained largely by the severe handicaps that the colonies encountered.

COLONIAL HANDICAPS

Some of these impediments may be traced to the mother country. The seventeenth century, it will be recalled, was an epoch of decline and poverty in Spain. Impotent and corrupt monarchs wasted state revenues on court favorites or spent them in European wars. Heavy taxes, imposed upon a people already lacking a strong urge toward commerce and industry, prevented the expansion of Spanish manufactures and even ruined some of those already in existence. Rising prices caused by the influx of gold and silver from America were not sufficient to induce industrial development in Spain, and application of the mercantile theory, along with indifference, hampered the growth of factories in the colonies. Economic juntas and the Cortes demanded a reduction in the exportation of manufactured goods to the Indies, but said little about the encouragement of increased production at home. To the colonists was left the choice of paying extortionate prices for the limited supply, purchasing from smugglers, setting up industries of their own, or going almost naked.

Enamored by the large inflow of the precious metals from America, the Spanish government not only failed to realize the importance of stimulating production but also failed to formulate a constructive colonial policy. The government devoted little attention to the promotion of economic activities and neglected sea power while emphasizing land armies and attempting to play a dominant role in Europe in accordance with the belief that Spain's mission was both to defend and to expand Roman Catholicism there. The frightful damage done the Spanish Armada in 1588 was never fully repaired, partly because Spaniards were slow to adopt new techniques in the construction of war vessels. Control of the seas passed to England, France, and the Dutch Netherlands, and these rival powers established settlements and naval bases not only in the Caribbean and North America but in South America as well, thus placing themselves in more convenient positions to harass and prey upon the Spanish colonies, which soon felt the effects of this new menace and Spain's loss of its maritime dominance: their scanty supply of much-needed goods from the home country was rendered uncertain,[1] their coasts were laid bare to the enemy, and the increased influx of smuggled goods that alleviated their misery could hardly compensate for the corruption and lawlessness which smuggling produced.

The colonists were also heavily loaded with taxes to meet the demands of European wars, coastal and commercial defense, and royal extravagance. The comparatively light tax burden of the previous century soon became a nostalgic memory. Old rates were increased, new contributions were levied, and a growing number of revenue officials swarmed into the colonies. Indian tributes were doubled or tripled before 1650. The *alcabala* (sales tax) was raised to 4 per cent in 1632 and to 6 per cent in 1635. The convoy tax rose to 12 per cent or more. The royal monopoly spread its tentacles. Nearly all colonial offices were sold to the highest bidder and every successful bidder demanded his pound of flesh. Stamped paper for legal transactions was forced into general use by 1640; half-annates (a contribution of half of the first year's salary) began to be collected from almost all colonial officials in 1632; and a royal license was required for nearly every business enterprise. In addition to exacting all these contributions, profligate kings confiscated gold and silver and demanded gifts. The American colonies had given Philip III 432,342 pesos in 1624 and New Spain had finished paying another donation of 1,100,000 in 1629; but 2,000,000 pesos were demanded in 1634 as the viceroyalty's share of three times as much which was needed for the erection of a new palace, and Peru made another contribution of 97,000 in 1661, despite the fact that the country had just been afflicted by a dreadful earthquake. Such were some of the handicaps thrust upon the colonies by the mother country.

There were others of a geographical nature or arising from a combination of trade restrictions and physical environment. In this connection, the salient facts set forth in the first chapter of this book should be recalled. Fully a fourth of the vast area claimed by Spain consisted of tropical lowlands covered with jungle and infested by disease and insect pests. Two large regions—one in northern Mexico and one on the borderland of Peru and Chile—had most of the characteristics of a desert. In addition, there were vast Andean mountain stretches too high and cold for comfortable human habitation. The bulk of the native population had long resided on the lofty plateaus and upland plains of the interior; and the sixteenth-century Spaniards, attracted by the semicivilized Indians and the climate, had settled down in these areas and established their rule. Few of them had remained in the Antilles or along the mainland coasts. In New Spain and Central America as well as in New Granada, Venezuela,[2] the *audiencia* of Quito, and Peru, the Spaniards had spread out over the inland plateaus and valleys, many of them far removed from the ocean; since there were few adjacent navigable rivers [3] that furnished a continuous means of communication to the sea, they confronted transportation problems far more difficult than any known to later English and French colonists in North America. They also suffered from the ravages of earthquakes and volcanic eruptions,[4] which destroyed life and property and ruined fertile upland valleys. But bad as these handicaps were, there were not many pleasant new areas for the Spaniards and their mestizo kinsmen to occupy, for swarms of pirates who followed the breakdown of Spanish sea power now rendered the tropical coasts still more uninviting, and rigid limitation of lawful ports of entry made both Chile and the great Plata Basin rather unattractive. Owing to the restriction of immigration to orthodox Spaniards, the number of immigrants who arrived annually was small, but one may well doubt that a larger influx would have brought greater prosperity, since available land was restricted not only by geographical decree and hostile Indians on the frontiers—another handicap to be reckoned with—but also by an

Political Divisions of South America during the Seventeenth Century

MAP 6

agrarian policy which permitted the accumulation of immense estates in the hands of the clergy and the descendants of the early settlers.

Smugglers and buccaneers, as already suggested, were a severe menace. Spain had been vexed by pirates and traffickers in contraband goods almost from the beginning of her colonial activities, but they became a far greater pest, from the Spanish viewpoint, during the seventeenth century. The pirates shifted their base to the islands of the Caribbean, and acquired the name of buccaneers; the smugglers plied their trade both in the Peninsula and in the colonial ports.

The seventeenth century was a time of almost universal contraband traffic with the Spanish colonies in America. It has already been noted that Spain held to the monopolistic ideal in respect to colonial trade. In order to traffic with South America, a merchant had to be a native of Spain or the son of a Catholic foreigner who had maintained his domicile in that country for twenty years. All others were forbidden to trade with the colonies through Spain or directly, on their own account or through the agency of a Spaniard or a Spanish company; and there were heavy penalties for the infraction of the rule. Yet it was often violated at both ends of the line. Foreigners loaded goods from their vessels into the flotas (fleets) at Cádiz or San Lúcar without registration at the Casa and received their value in gold and silver at the same points upon the return of the fleets. They also eluded the law by trading under the name of Seville merchants who were hardly more than factors of foreign commercial houses. As the difficulty of enforcing the law became more patent, the Spanish government sought compensation by the imposition of fines upon the interlopers. These sometimes amounted to as much as 200,000 pesos in a single year. "Under the later Hapsburgs, with the increasing demands of the colonies on the one hand, and the utter ruin of Spanish industry on the other, the dependence of the Seville export commerce upon foreign manufactures was complete. They supplied five-sixths of the cargos of the outbound fleet." [5]

The most serious and widespread development of contraband trade, however, was in merchandise introduced into the colonies directly from foreign markets. Portuguese, French, Dutch, and other interlopers smuggled their cargoes into the West Indies through the closed port of Buenos Aires, or even to the Pacific shores of Spanish America. The illicit trader was eagerly welcomed by the colonists, for he supplied their needs at reasonable prices, gave them an opportunity of enriching themselves and of adding to the comforts and luxuries of living. Two circumstances combined to make this commerce easy. One was the great length of sparsely settled coast on both the Atlantic and the Pacific side of the continent, effective surveillance over which was beyond the resources of any nation in that era. The other was the venality of the Spanish governors in the ports themselves. Apparently they often tolerated or encouraged the traffic, on the plea that the necessities of the colonists demanded it. They not only accepted bribes, but engaged in the buying and selling of contraband articles.

Direct smuggling had begun early. Sixteenth-century corsairs and sea-dogs had engaged in it as well as in piracy. In the seventeenth century, however, smuggling greatly increased. The Portuguese, taking advantage of their annexation to the Spanish empire, established their residence in the Spanish colonies and became receivers of smuggled goods. Near the beginning of the seventeenth century, they are said to have sent out from Portugal about 200 vessels annually, laden with cargoes intended largely for the Pacific provinces of Spanish America. The commodities were introduced by way of the Río de la Plata or turned over to Spanish or Portuguese agents in Brazil. By 1636 Portuguese Jews dominated the retail trade of Lima. From the English, the French, and the Dutch colonies in the Lesser Antilles [6] goods were sent out to most of the ports of the Caribbean. The feeble Spanish government tried to suppress the traffic by expelling the British, French, and Dutch settlers and removing conniving Spanish colonial officials, but the trade continued. The captain of the interloping vessel, standing off near a port, sent the Spanish governor a polite note and an attractive gift, and informed him that he had sprung a leak or lost a mast. The ship was allowed to come in with its most conspicuous portals sealed. Others were found unsealed, however, and the goods were taken out at night, products of the country being substituted for them. In a day or two the ship sailed away with its new cargo. Smaller vessels pushed up the jungle rivers and creeks and notified the inhabitants of their location by firing a cannon. At nightfall, the Spanish Americans swarmed down to the vessel in canoes laden with native commodities. A few days later, colonial families were enjoying some of the luxuries of northern Europe. The galleons which came out in the fleet in 1662, after an interruption of two years, found the American markets so glutted with contraband wares that they could dispose of only a part of their cargoes.

A multitude of restrictions, a jealous monopoly, a flood of contraband goods—such is the history of Spanish colonial commerce in the seventeenth century. The crown lost most of its treasures, the Seville merchants lost their monopoly, and the precious metals and trade of Spanish America passed largely into the hands of the subjects of rival powers.

The colonies profited economically, though not morally, from the trend of the times in commerce. But they were gravely injured by another development of the period. Some of these smugglers became buccaneers when occasion presented, and many other adventurers of the Caribbean, sometimes even supported by the fleets of their home countries, specialized in buccaneering. Three times during the century, the Spanish mercantile flota on its way from the Indies was seized and destroyed; many detached vessels were taken on other occasions, and the galleons were compelled to sail at irregular intervals. But this is not the worst of the story. So far as the colonies were concerned, indeed, it was comparatively of minor importance. The economic and naval decline of Spain had a more injurious repercussion. The colonies were left in a state "of military and naval defenselessness, forts without artillery, nominal companies of infantry without soldiers, and the inhabitants more ready to take to the hills and woods than to oppose any resistance to the invader." [7] It was around 1650 when the raids of the pirates became most destructive. Hardly a town in the Caribbean and the Gulf regions escaped unharmed, and both before and after this date, piratical or semipiratical expeditions harried the coasts of the Pacific. Between 1655 and 1671 they plundered eighteen cities, four towns, and some thirty-five villages in the Caribbean and along the Gulf. Between 1665 and 1685 Spaniards and Spanish Americans suffered losses estimated at 60,000,000 crowns, not counting damages from the destruction of ships. Near the end of the century, however, the pirates made the fatal mistake of failing to distinguish between Spanish towns and treasure and the towns and treasure of other nations, and the navies of all the European powers soon joined in their suppression.

COLONIAL EXPANSION; CONQUISTADORES OF THE CROSS

The seventeenth century can hardly be called an era of expansion in Spanish America. The bulk of the Spanish population, about 250,000 at the beginning of the century and probably still less than 1,500,000 at its close, preferred to remain in the old centers, as did also the mestizos, the only other element capable of constructive enterprise. The mother country, too feeble and bankrupt to support any vigorous advances, could not be aroused to effective effort even by the threat of European encroachments. Only the mendicant and Jesuit missionaries, who busied themselves on every frontier and bore the brunt of nearly every colonization enterprise, revealed something of the old energy. The tribes encountered everywhere after the semicivilized Indians of New Spain, Guatemala, Peru, and New Granada had been reduced to virtual serfdom, were "hostile, had few crops, were unused to labor, had no fixed villages, would not stand still to be exploited, and were hardly worth the candle. Colonists were no longer so eager for encomiendas, and were willing to escape the obligation to protect and civilize the wild tribes, which were as uncomfortable burdens, sometimes, as cub tigers in a sack. Moreover, the sovereigns, with increasing emphasis, forbade the old-time abuses of exploitation, but as strongly as before adhered to the ideal of conversion and civilization. Here, then, was a larger opening for the missionary, and to him was entrusted, or upon him was thrust, consciously or unconsciously, not only the old work of conversion, but a larger and larger element of responsibility and control." [8] In fact, before 1600, the mission was rapidly becoming Spain's most important frontier institution.

Writing of this frontier movement, Alexander von Humboldt made the following penetrating remarks shortly after 1800: [9]

> The whites advance slowly. The religious orders have founded their establishments between the domain of the colonists and the territory of the free Indians. The Missions may be considered as intermediary states. . . . As the missionaries advance toward the forests, and gain on the natives, the white colonists in their turn seek to invade . . . the territory of the Missions. In this protracted struggle, the secular arm continually tends to withdraw the reduced Indian from the monastic hierarchy, and the missionaries are gradually superseded by vicars [secular priests]. The whites, and the castes of mixed blood . . . establish themselves among the Indians. The Missions become Spanish villages, and the natives lose even the remembrance of their natural language. Such is the progress of civilization . . . ; a slow progress, retarded by the passions of man, but nevertheless sure and steady.

The Spanish monarch consciously employed the missionary as an agent of expansion and frontier defense. He usually not only bore the expense of the padre's initial equipment and transportation to his field of service, but also paid him a meager annual stipend, shared the cost of erecting mission buildings, and furnished a small squad of soldiers for protection against hostile uprisings. Hundreds of missionaries were on the royal payroll during the century, and they rendered valiant service in more than a dozen important areas, besides continuing work already begun in New Mexico and Florida. According to the letter of the law, they were the front column of two advancing lines of Spanish civilization, each of which was supposed to move forward every ten years. But the plan did not work out. A decade proved insufficient to prepare the way for the second line; the new environment often did not allure the Spaniards and mestizos, and the missionaries were loath to part with their wards. Comparatively few Spanish settlements followed the padres during the century and, even today, in some sections, the civilian column has not yet reached the frontier blazed by their heroic efforts.

In New Spain the missionaries were the main agency in carrying Spanish culture forward into Sinaloa, Sonora, Chihuahua, and Coahuila; but attempts to occupy Lower California failed. In the captaincy general of Guatemala the friars descended from the pleasant uplands and la-

Principal Mission Fields of
Colonial Spanish America

1 *The Californias*
2 *Pacific Slope*
3 *New Mexico*
4 *Texas*
5 *Neuva Santander*
6 *The Floridas*
7 *Llanos de Caracas*
8 *Cumaná*
9 *Meta-Casanare*
10 *Upper Orinoco*
11 *Guiana*
12 *Maynas*
13 *Charcas*
14 *Paraguay*
15 *Southern Chile*

MAP 7

bored among the wilder tribes of the littoral, where they suffered martyrdom almost as often as they achieved success. It was, to use the
words of one of their number, as if they had entered the "gates of Hell
from within which there was no redemption." In the *audiencia* of Panama
the story was virtually the same, while on the frontiers of New Granada
their efforts were almost as futile. They advanced into the sweltering
valley of the Atrato, where they made a number of reductions (settlements); and descending eastward from Bogotá they pursued their work
among the Indians of the plains of Casanare and the jungle valleys of the
Meta and the Orinoco, only to fall back near the end of the century,
defeated by the hostile raids of the Caribs. From Peru and the presidency of Quito, the padres crossed over the Andes and entered the tropical plains and forests of the vast region of Mainas (an area lying between the fourth and fifth parallels of latitude in the basin of the upper
Amazon), or turned far toward the south and ministered to the Moxos,
the Chiquitos, and the tribes of the Gran Chaco. In the Mainas region,
they made very considerable progress; among the Moxos, Chiquitos, and
the Chaco tribes, however, their efforts were less rewarding. The Araucanians of Chile, despite the heroic labors and sacrifices of the missionaries, remained beyond the reach of their redemptive powers. From
Cumaná, Caracas, and Barcelona (all in Venezuela) the padres proceeded slowly southward toward the interior llanos or entered the steaming valley of the lower Orinoco, in order to hold Spanish Guiana against
the intrusions of Dutch, French, and English rivals. In central Venezuela
and its great plains, they made many converts, but success in the lower
Orinoco Basin awaited a later epoch. In the Plata region, near the
beginning of the century, the Jesuits entered the fertile Paraná-Uruguay
mesopotamian area, where they were destined to win undying renown.

Such was the work of the Conquistadores of the Cross. Almost everywhere, they confronted appalling obstacles—depressing heat, drought,
famine, flood; insect and reptile pests; treacherous, ignorant, or hostile
Indians; roving Spanish encomenderos looking for natives to exploit;
Portuguese raiders in search of slaves. The mission frontier advanced,
receded, advanced, and sometimes receded again. The number of reductions which the missionaries established and of neophytes they won probably no one save the recording angel will ever know; but by dint of almost superhuman patience and energy, and by a zeal which ran to meet
martyrdom, they made a good beginning. For America, they ushered in
the great missionary age.

From the viewpoint of the Spanish monarchy, however, their work,
when completed, was but half of the process. They might, and did—
for this was their duty—partially Christianize the natives, teaching them

to say prayers, repeat psalms, produce sacred music on instruments of their own contrivance, march in religious processions, enact religious dramas, keep faith with one wife, and observe the Ten Commandments. They might, and did—this was their persistent policy—partially civilize the Indians as well, instructing them in rudimentary letters, industry, art (particuarly sacred art), agriculture, stock raising, and the application of simple medicinal remedies. But this, after all, was only in preparation for the advancing civilian phalanx. The royal plan embraced the absorption of the natives into the body politic and the creation of a new race. In this respect, Spain was the most original of all colonizing powers.

The second phase of the process, as already noted, lagged behind during the seventeenth century. In many areas the Spanish and mestizo elements approached the missions, if at all, not to settle down, but to raid, plunder, and capture the neophytes for plantations, mines, and workshops back home. They established several new towns in Sinaloa, Sonora, Chihuahua, Coahuila, and New Mexico.[10] They reconstructed pueblos destroyed by the buccaneers on the coasts of the Caribbean and the Gulf. They founded a few towns in Panama and the captaincy general of Guatemala, most of which they later abandoned, and several towns in New Granada, Venezuela,[11] and eastern Peru.[12] But they lost ground in Chile. The valiant Araucanians destroyed five of their settlements in the south and sent them fleeing across the river Bíobío, on the north bank of which they were able to establish only two to take their place.[13] In the Plata area the pueblo of Catamarca (founded in 1680) appears to have been the only new Spanish settlement of any consequence. Moreover, a considerable number of the sedentary Indians seem to have escaped to the mountains and the jungle. In South America, at least, many natives fled across the Andes and descended the eastern slopes to the forests beyond in order to escape masters whom they hated and oppressive "civilizing" agencies which they could no longer bear. The second phase of the Spanish colonization process might have developed more rapidly if the functionaries of a theoretically benevolent policy had effectively curbed exploitative tendencies.

🌿 LABOR AND POLITICS

The seventeenth century, like the sixteenth, was characterized by considerable discussion of the oppression of the Indians and by legislation designed to prevent their exploitation. A celebrated cedula (decree) dealing with personal service was promulgated in 1601. Among other things, it provided that the natives should no longer be distributed for forced labor in the fields, stock ranches, and textile factories, or in the sugar mills, building trades, and pearl fisheries, or in the olive and grape orchards, or among those engaged in collecting anil and coca leaves, or in domestic service, or in the work of draining the mines, or even in the new mines themselves. The cedula also attempted to prevent the merchants from forcing the natives to carry burdens along the trade routes, to substitute voluntary or Negro slave labor for the compulsory service of the Indians in the old mines, and to force the encomenderos to accept a fixed tribute in money or commodities in lieu of the personal service which they had so long demanded of their Indians.

This cedula, like the famous New Laws of 1542, might have developed in Spanish America a system of free labor if its provisions had been humanely carried out. But, as in the former case, this proved impossible. Distance and powerful vested interests defeated the whole program. The regulations either were not put into operation or were evaded. A cedula of 1609 met a similar fate. But the interest of the monarchy in the status of the Indians continued to manifest itself in numerous benevolent laws. The heavy volumes of Juan de Solórzano Pereira's *Política indiana* give much attention to the legal position of the Indian, and more than a fourth of the famous compilation of 1680—*Recopilación de las Leyes de Indias*—is devoted to the laws which attempt to ameliorate his woes.

It is impossible to determine how much the condition of the Indians improved, if at all, during the century. It is certain that the number of encomiendas shrank, but this reform was probably largely nullified by the growing exploitations of the clergy and the royal officials (*corregidores* and *alcaldes mayores*) and by the increase in the rate of the royal tribute. The impressed labor of the natives seems to have been indispensable to the development of Spain's colonies in the New World. The lower class of Spaniards were loath to turn their hands to manual labor, and the Indians were probably not disposed to apply themselves voluntarily to the steady performance of tasks necessary to the progress and prosperity of the Spanish establishments. In most cases, the Indians who were forced to work had their wages and hours stipulated by law. Wages varied from ten to twenty cents a day, and hours usually lasted from sun to sun, with several holidays and a minimum of clothing and food. Doubtless these regulations were often violated, but competent scholars have contended that the position of the Indians of Spanish America was probably not much worse than that of the contemporary lower classes of Europe.

The political life of the century was characterized by constant friction and quarreling and occasional revolts. Not only were there conflicts of jurisdiction between the executive officials—viceroys and captains general—and the *audiencias;* conflicts also were frequent between the civil and ecclesiastical functionaries, between the secular and the regular clergy, and even among the various orders of the regulars themselves. Several Indian and Negro uprisings occurred, and were ruthlessly suppressed. Twice during the century turbulent mobs burned the royal palace of the viceroy in Mexico, and criminals often ran riot in the leading towns and cities of all the colonies.

Owing to the venality of the judges and the distance from the tribunals of last resort, the administration of justice was defective and slow. Appeals in important cases, which had to be submitted to the Council of the Indies, required months and even years for final adjudication. The jurisdictions of the *audiencias* were very extensive, and those in pursuit of justice were often required to make long and expensive journeys. For southern South America a partial remedy was provided by the establishment of an *audiencia* in Santiago in 1609 and another in Buenos Aires in 1661, although the latter was later discontinued.

There were some fourteen viceregal administrations in Peru during the century and more than twenty in New Spain. The viceroys were hardly as distinguished as their predecessors of the sixteenth century. Some were honest and reasonably efficient; many were not notoriously corrupt or incompetent; at least five, including Luis Velasco II (already mentioned), were chief executives both of New Spain and of Peru. Without oppressing their subjects, none of them, no matter how able, could have governed to the satisfaction of monarchs so clamorous for revenues; for, in addition to most of the difficulties confronted by their predecessors, the viceroys of the seventeenth century suffered the further handicap of having to serve extravagant and unworthy sovereigns. On the whole, it must be admitted that the colonies were badly governed.

INTELLECTUAL LIFE

The seventeenth century was marked in England and northern Europe by the beginning of the Age of Science; but little of the scientific spirit reached distant Spanish America. As Humboldt has remarked, contact with the magnificent natural phenomena and the strange native races of a new world might have resulted in a great advance of knowledge had not the free range of the intellect been stifled by superstition and fanaticism. During the sixteenth century, as has been noted, Spaniards who had been ruthless in the destruction of native culture nevertheless produced many unsystematic works on geography, biology, zoology, anthropology, and Indian languages, which were marred by the interjection of many gross superstitions, but were useful sources for the historian and the scientist. Since Spaniards of the seventeenth century, whether in Spain or in America, were probably less gifted in literature, equally fanatic, and perhaps more superstitious, their writings on the New World were no better and sometimes even worse than those of their predecessors. It is impossible to determine how many of the works were Spanish and how many Spanish American, for most of the writers spent about as much time in the mother country as in the colonies. Whatever their prevailing residence, however, their preoccupations continued to be war, natural phenomena, theology, language, and government, with a strong tendency, often, to express themselves in dull, tedious, and extravagantly ornate poetry. Difficulties of printing limited the number of their productions, while a strict censorship and the Inquisition tended to confine their contents to the tenets of a rigid dogma. Eleven new universities were founded during the century, but they, as well as their predecessors, continued to devote themselves largely to canon law, scholastic philosophy, theology, and letters. Little attention was given to mathematics or medicine.

Few minds of seventeenth-century Spanish America were able to rise above the dark clouds of superstition. Comets and eclipses portended calamities soon to be visited upon the people by an enraged deity. Thunderstorms, volcanoes, and earthquakes sent them fleeing in terror to the churches in order to ask forgiveness for their sins while the massive walls tumbled down upon them and their abandoned homes crumbled in upon unremoved furnishings. If they escaped with their lives, it was only through the intervention of some saint or the Virgin. Life was filled with benign miracles from Heaven and the punishments of an angry God. Yet many Spanish Americans, and not a few churchmen among the number, persisted in a course of morality low even for the age in which they lived.

But a narrow provincialism should not be permitted to lend asperity to the student's judgment. During the same century Massachusetts divines consumed much ink on theology, attributed toothache to sins of the teeth, saw in calamities the vengeance of an offended God, gave the Indian little or no place in the Divine Plan, filled their histories with almost as many miracles as facts, and hanged witches or burned them at the stake.

Moreover, the drab depressiveness of Spanish American life was relieved by magnificent homes, churches, public buildings, plazas, and patios, which displayed a highly developed artistic taste along with considerable architectural skill. It was also graced by the charming hospitality of the upper classes, the warm sympathy of some writers for the oppressed Indians, the wit and banter of poets, and the lively display of festival and drama. Occasionally, too, there appeared a scientist who discovered the medicinal properties of a new herb or bark,[14] or, with telescope and quadrant, stood observing an eclipse of the sun which had caused the superstitious populace to flee in dread and terror; and who, even while dying, willed his body to physicians in the hope that its dissection would throw new light upon the ills that afflicted his fellow-men.[15]

A restricted "literary activity . . . cultivated by an infinitesimally small and select group of intellectuals, standing like a tiny edifice upon a vast foundation composed of an ignorant and hopeless native population"[16]—such was the situation in seventeenth century New Spain. It was no better in Peru and New Granada, and probably worse elsewhere. Upon such a scene dawned the eighteenth century, which was destined to witness important reforms and give birth to new currents of dynamic thought.

CHAPTER VII

Spanish America Under the Bourbons

🐚 CHARACTER OF THE SPANISH BOURBONS

The occupation of the Spanish throne in 1701 by Philip V, a French Bourbon prince, was a very significant event. By the European states it was interpreted as a serious threat to the balance of power. For Spain, it meant new ideas, new methods of government, new stimuli for the economy and intellectual activity—in a word, new life. For Spanish America, it was the prelude to important readjustments and reforms.

At the death of Charles II (1700), the last of the Hapsburgs, Spain was only a "little less cadaverous than its defunct master." Without army, navy, or funds, with disordered administration and respect for authority gone, without prestige or power, the kingdom "lay before Europe . . . awaiting partition as another Poland of another day." Into this crisis came the Bourbons and a "new exposure to European civilization." Little wonder that pious Spanish writers, unwilling to be Gallicized though they were, saw in the event something akin to the interposition of Providence.

Yet, from a viewpoint strictly Spanish, the coming of the Bourbons was not an unmixed blessing. Their dynasty produced a Charles IV and a Ferdinand VII as well as a Charles III and a Ferdinand VI; their inevitable involvement in European wars drained away the wealth and energy of a reviving nation; and through open doors from France eventually came to metropolis and empire more than the Bourbons were willing to admit: firmer convictions in respect to the rights and dignity of common men; new notions regarding the basis of political power; and a new radicalism that dealt old systems a shocking blow. When Ferdinand VII passed from the scene in 1833, after more than a century of Bourbon rule, he left Spain bleeding and almost empireless—and decadent once more.

⚜ COMMERCIAL REFORMS

Spanish America felt the reforming spirit of the Bourbons first in the field of commerce. In 1701 French merchants were conceded the privilege of introducing annually a number of slaves and of putting in at the colonial ports in order to purchase supplies. This concession, expanded so as to include a shipload of other commodities, was transferred to Englishmen in 1713. At the same time, the growing industries of Spain were furnishing a more bountiful supply of goods for export, and the Seville merchants were soon deprived of their monopoly of colonial trade. The *Casa de Contratación* was removed from Seville to Cádiz in 1718. Commercial companies were organized in rapid succession for the purpose of engaging in Spanish American trade: the Guipúzcoa Company in 1728; the Galicia Company in 1734; the Barcelona Company in 1755. The commercial fleet system was abolished in 1748. Nine different Spanish ports (in addition to Cádiz) were allowed for the first time in 1765 to trade with the leading ports of Cuba, Española, Puerto Rico, Margarita, and Trinidad, a privilege soon extended to Campeche (Yucatán), and direct exchange of produce was permitted between several American colonies shortly afterward. In 1778 thirteen other ports of Spain and its adjacent islands were granted the privilege of trading with twenty-four additional ports in Spanish America, including Buenos Aires, Montevideo, Valparaíso, Callao, and Guayaquil. Beginning in 1797, when Spain became deeply involved in the Napoleonic wars, neutral vessels were allowed to engage in the carrying trade with the colonies. Already, in 1764, monthly and bimonthly mail packets had been established between Spain and her overseas possessions. In all these ways, the colonies were stimulated to new economic enterprise and brought into fuller contact with European thought.

If the mercantile ideas of the Bourbons had permitted the encouragement of colonial manufacturing and if their financial demands had permitted a reduction of the rate of taxes, a permanent economic revival might have resulted. As it was, the output of the mines, fomented by a reduction in the percentage demanded by the king, increased rapidly, agricultural production expanded to supply growing colonial markets, and trade grew by leaps and bounds. Shortly before 1800 the annual production of the mines appears to have been worth about 39,000,000 pesos. Carlos Calvo estimates that the value of trade between colonies and mother country increased from 171,900,000 francs in 1753 to 430,100,000 in 1784 and 638,500,000 in 1800.[1]

The chief exports sent by the colonies to the mother country may be ascertained from a statement for the year 1747. They were, in pesos:

gold, 4,000,000; silver, 30,000,000; precious stones, 600,000; cochineal, 1,200,000; hides, 340,000; wood, 60,000; vicuña wool, 50,000; quinine, 40,000; sugar, indigo, tobacco, and other products, 2,000,000; total, 38,290,000 pesos. Among the commodities imported by the colonies were: gold and silver ware, stockings and gloves, textiles and linens, thread, hats and all kinds of articles of felt; furs, drugs, paints, perfumes, candles, haberdashery, toys, and trinkets; playing cards; articles of copper, bronze, and iron; furniture, harness, and paper; bottles and other glassware; rope and twine, canvas, tar, pitch, tackle, rigging, domestic utensils, wine, and various kinds of food. Many of these articles had come through Spain from northern Europe, but Spanish industries were furnishing an increasing proportion.

ADMINISTRATIVE REFORMS; EXPULSION OF THE JESUITS

The Bourbon era was also characterized by important administrative readjustments and reforms. The most important among them were the widespread enlistment of colonial militia for colonial defense, the final abolition of the encomiendas,[2] the introduction of the intendant system, and the expulsion of the Jesuits.

The need for reform was imperative. Not only did the direct smuggling of the previous century persist, facilitated by the privileges granted to France and England, but rival powers threatened to conquer some of the mainland colonies. Not only did higher officials engage in graft and peculation; they also revealed a tendency to defeat the royal will by their formula of *obedezco pero no cumplo* ("I obey but do not execute"). At the same time, *alcaldes mayores, corregidores,* and priests cheated and oppressed the native races until several uprisings occurred; creoles and mestizos, seeking to avoid odious taxes, or gain control of the mission Indians, or secure a larger participation in the local government, defied the royal authorities; and the Jesuits of Paraguay led their Indians in revolt (1754) against a Spanish-Portuguese boundary treaty. Moreover, the problems of disobedience and dishonesty were made more acute by constant rivalry between the civil authorities and the religious leaders, between the regular and the secular clergy, and among the civil authorities themselves.

Crying injustices were perpetrated upon the native races. From numerous reports of conscientious observers came many complaints which leave no doubt of the existence of shameful abuses. They were perhaps worst in Peru, where *corregidores* and priests combined to terrorize the Indians and deprive them of lands, wages, women and children, personal freedom—everything which men are supposed to esteem. But the evil also existed in Mexico, where the *alcaldes mayores* and sometimes the priests victimized the Indians, as well as in all of the important areas where the natives still survived. It would be an error to assume that such evils were universal, for this would be analogous to generalizing too broadly upon the abuses portrayed in *Uncle Tom's Cabin*. There were many conscientious Spaniards, else we should not have had all these reports. Yet there is no doubt that the evils were widespread.

Such were the conditions which demanded reform. The Bourbons began by creating new administrative and judicial jurisdictions. The viceroyalty of New Granada was established in 1717, abolished in 1723, and re-established in 1739. The viceroyalty of Río de la Plata was created in 1776, largely for the purpose of holding the frontier against the Portuguese. In 1731 the provinces of Venezuela were erected into a captaincy general, which was later freed from dependence upon New Granada. Cuba became a captaincy general in 1777; and the captaincy general of Guatemala was made more independent of the viceroyalty of New Spain soon afterward. The *audiencia* of Panama, no longer so necessary now that the major portion of South American commerce had ceased to pass across the Isthmus, was abolished in 1751, and this area was made to depend upon the tribunal at Bogotá. The *audiencia* of Buenos Aires, which had been discontinued in 1671, was re-established in 1783. Three years later Caracas became the seat of another, and one was created at Cuzco in 1789. Thus Spanish America was now divided into four viceroyalties: New Spain, New Granada, Peru, and Río de la Plata; four captaincies general: Cuba, Guatemala, Chile, and Venezuela; and twelve *audiencias:* Santo Domingo, Mexico, Guadalajara, Guatemala, New Granada, Caracas, Cuzco, Quito, Peru, Charcas, Chile, and Buenos Aires. Already, in these major administrative units, one may observe the geographical setting of nineteenth-century republics.

But this reorganization was by no means the most important of the Bourbon administrative reforms. Charles III, the ablest of the Bourbons, sent out *visitadores* to America in order to scrutinize the whole colonial system, and their visitations proved to be the preliminary step in the establishment of a new group of officials with numerous and weighty functions. These new officials, called intendants, were the most significant of all Bourbon innovations in the colonies. One of them was introduced into Cuba in 1765, and in less than twenty-five years, they were established in all Spanish America save New Granada. There were twelve in Mexico, eight in Río de la Plata, eight in Peru, four in Guatemala, two in Chile, and one in Venezuela. Their salaries were comparatively high, varying from 6,000 to 12,000 pesos; and although they were sometimes appointed by the chief executive officials of the colonies, more often they were chosen by the king, with whom they had always the privilege of communicating directly.

The functions of the intendants varied somewhat in different areas. In general, they were classified under four heads corresponding to the four phases, or departments, of government in the Spanish colonial system, namely, justice, general administration (*policía*), finance, and war; but in considering their manifold duties, it is necessary to bear in mind the confusion of powers which characterized Spanish government. Without going into tedious detail, it may be stated that they were directed to watch over local administration, particularly in matters of justice, protecting the Indians from their oppressors and serving as judges of first instance in cases involving the assessment of taxes and the collection of revenue; to guard against graft and smuggling; to promote internal improvements of all kinds, rural and urban; to encourage agriculture and industries not competing with those in Spain; to look after the supply and equipment of the army in their jurisdictions; to exercise the right of patronage in the regions entrusted to them; and to make detailed reports upon the population and wealth of the areas under their charge. In fact, their numerous powers constituted a limitation upon all colonial authorities, from the viceroys to the town councilmen and from the bishops to the parish priests. With their installment, governors, *alcaldes mayores,* and *corregidores* were held in check or eliminated. With reference to their qualifications, an order of 1800 remarked:

> The capable fulfillment of these . . . very important duties . . . demands that they show certain elevated talents, an exquisite instruction, a consummate prudence, and inflexible probity; it demands, moreover, that, imbued with the spirit which cannot fail to inculcate love of king and country, they find nothing delightful if not sobriety and work at all hours and on all occasions; . . . it asks that they never indulge themselves in frivolous occupations nor know other hours of distraction than those of sleep; and it asks that they show a will just, firm, and constant in order not to be deterred by any difficulties, in order to resist all . . . artful tricks.[3]

It is difficult to measure the results of the Bourbon administrative reforms. The abuses and avarice of the Guipúzcoa Company provoked a revolt in Venezuela (1749). An agent of the royal treasury who attempted to control the production of alcohol in Quito caused an uprising in that city (1765), which was quelled only by the mediation of the Jesuits; and Chilean insurgents prevented the collection of certain odious taxes in that region (1776). Visitor José Antonio Areche was partially responsible for the formidable uprising of the Peruvian Indians under Tupac Amarú, descendant of the Incas, in 1780–81. The attempts of Visitor Francisco Gutiérrez Piñeres to increase the revenues from New Granada led to the widespread revolt of the *Comuneros* (townsmen) there (1781). It was the old story of important reforms hindered by the exactions made by a needy treasury drained in supporting European wars.

The inauguration of the sweeping intendant system would have proved difficult in any circumstances, for it not only demanded a variety of talents which few men possessed, but naturally aroused the opposition of many whose offices, graft, or powers it limited or eliminated. Given its persistent emphasis upon revenues, there is small wonder that it was doomed to only partial success. The operations of peculators were considerably restricted; the oppression of the Indians was temporarily ameliorated in some quarters; and the whole tone of colonial administration was energized and somewhat improved. Yet the very thoroughness of the change which the intendancies involved tended to unsettle colonial life; and just as some of its best results began to appear, Charles IV, a weak and unworthy sovereign, ascended the Spanish throne and the French Revolution transformed the mental attitude of the Western World. The intendant system was the last effort of a rigid old order that was doomed to ultimate defeat because of inability to adapt itself to the changing conditions and demands of a new age.

The Bourbons probably numbered the expulsion of the Jesuits (1767) among their reforms; but whatever the virtues of this drastic measure from other points of view, it was, so far as the colonies were concerned, perhaps an erroneous readjustment. The expulsion of hundreds of these padres from all parts of Spanish America may have pleased many of their rivals and enemies, but it could not fail to grieve thousands of Indians whom they had protected and served. It must also have aroused the resentment of their numerous creole and mestizo pupils or relatives. Many doubtless found it difficult to believe in the justice of a monarch guilty of such a ruthless act. Nor could the Jesuits conveniently be spared on the frontiers, where they had always been a potent agency of expansion and defense. In expelling the Jesuit fathers, Charles III had acted in the interest of a regalistic control which resented what appeared to be an empire within an empire, but it may be that his apprehension was exaggerated. At any rate, it was a costly act which deprived the colonies of their best teachers and missionaries and left many of them in a disloyal mood.[4]

The rule of the eighteenth-century Bourbons was further signalized by notable improvement in the character of the viceroys sent out to

America. To span the century, twenty-two viceregal administrations were required in New Spain, fourteen in Peru, thirteen in New Granada (after 1717), and six in Río de la Plata (after 1776). Although occasionally corrupt and inefficient and frequently stern, not to say cruel, the viceroys were on the whole men of considerable integrity, zeal, enlightenment, and administrative talent. Such viceroys as Antonio Bucareli (1771–79) and the second Count of Revilla Gigedo (1789–94) in New Spain, Manso de Velasco (1745–61) and Ambrosio O'Higgins (1796–1801) in Peru, Caballero y Góngora (1779–88) in New Granada, Juan de Vértiz (1778–84) in Río de la Plata, and Manuel Guirior (1773–80) and Francisco Gil y Lemos (1789–96) in both New Granada and Peru—not to mention a few less notable rulers of earlier decades—deserve to rank among great colonial administrators of any nation or age. They devoted themselves with energy and loyalty to the economic, political, and social problems of their kingdoms, and not a few of them were patrons of learning and art.

Unfortunately, Charles IV and Ferdinand VII, the last of the Spanish Bourbons, were imprudent and inefficient monarchs whose character was reflected in their colonial agents. The viceroys of the first two decades of the nineteenth century, like their royal masters, were usually impotent and undesirable administrators, unfit to cope with the new spirit and the new aspirations which were so rapidly developing in the colonies.

THE MISSIONS AND EXPANSION OF THE FRONTIERS

The first sixty-seven years of the eighteenth century witnessed the golden age of missionary enterprise in most of Spanish America; and, as in the previous century, the missions continued to serve as important agencies of frontier defense and expansion. At the time of their expulsion, the Jesuits alone are said to have had 717,000 neophytes in their establishments. All the other orders combined probably did not have as many; but at least 1,000,000 Indians must have been living in the missions of Spanish America in 1767. Comparatively few new centers were occupied during the century, but most of the old centers were expanded and worked with greater success. Increased progress was probably due largely to the more consistent backing of the first three Bourbons, who, with all the numerous demands upon their treasury, never ceased to support missionary effort in their American colonies.

On the northern frontier of Spanish America the padres made considerable advance (as shown on Map 7). In Florida, because of the hostility of the wild Indians and of English and French neighbors, the missions declined. In New Mexico, after the Indian revolt and the Spanish reconquest near the end of the seventeenth century, missionary progress was slow. The twenty-five missions of the province, scattered for the most part up and down the Río Grande, contained fewer than 12,000 neophytes in 1744, and the number was probably no larger thirty years later. Some twenty missions were founded in Texas during the three decades beginning in 1716; but several of these were rather ephemeral, for the Indians residing in them, mostly in the vicinity of San Antonio and Goliad, hardly aggregated 2,000 in 1762. Missionary enterprise began in earnest in Nuevo Santander—a region lying between the Nueces and the Pánuco rivers—in 1746 and resulted in twenty-four settlements by 1756. The Jesuits advanced into Lower California in 1697 and founded twenty-three missions before they were expelled. The number was reduced to fourteen, however, with only about 10,000 converts by 1767.

In Central America, where the work was carried on mainly by the Franciscans and Dominicans, the missionaries made more progress than during the previous century. By 1697, after almost a hundred years of effort, the Itzas of the northern frontier of Guatemala were induced to receive some of the padres, who soon gathered them into seven villages. Their neighbors on the southwest were also partially Christianized, as were the Indians of southern Honduras, eastern Nicaragua, and the Talamanca region of Costa Rica.

In South America only two important new fields were occupied: the lower Orinoco Basin (Spanish Guiana), and southern Chile. The pacification of Spanish Guiana was effected mainly by the Capuchins, who established their first successful mission in the area in 1724, and gathered more than 5,000 Indians into eighteen villages by 1766. In Chile, after the bloody combats of the previous century, the Jesuits at last succeeded in establishing themselves among the Araucanians, where they founded eight villages before their expulsion.

With the exception of Mainas (in the basin of the Upper Amazon), most of the old fields of endeavor continued to prosper. Among the Guaranís of the Paraná-Uruguay Basin the Jesuits had thirty missions in 1767, with over 100,000 converts, in spite of the disturbances of 1754–55. At the time of their expulsion, they also had charge of fifteen reductions among the Chiquitos, fifteen in the Gran Chaco, and sixteen in the plains of the Casanare, Meta, and Orinoco. Moreover, they were administering to 31,345 neophytes of the Moxos region in 1752. In the Mainas area, however, they had lost ground; for they could claim only 15,000 souls in 1767, whereas there were as many families in 1653. Disease and Brazilian slave raids explain the diminution.

The main centers of Franciscan missionary effort in South America were southern Mainas and east-central Venezuela. In Mainas, they continued to have great difficulties with the natives and the climate and frequently ended "their days by being murdered by the very savages whom they had come to humanize." One of the Peruvian viceroys called the area a "vegetable Hell which holds its own against Heaven." In Venezuela, they continued the successes of a previous era, probably having no fewer than 50,000 Indians under their care in the vast plains south of Cumaná, Caracas, and Barcelona by 1760.

In these numerous missions, scattered from Lower California and New Mexico to Chile, and from Texas to Guiana and Paraguay, were hundreds of well-cultivated farms, orchards, and gardens, and thousands of horses, cattle, sheep, and goats. Usually there were also weaving rooms, blacksmith shops, tanneries, and warehouses. In fact, the neophytes, under the direction of the padres, engaged in most of the economic activities that were carried on by the civilian communities.

Such was the state of the missions during their most flourishing period. The closing decades of the century witnessed a decided decline in most areas, probably caused by the transfer of the wards of the Jesuits to less tactful ministers and by the general cooling of missionary zeal. In 1769 the Franciscans, supported by the military and civilians, went forward into Upper California, where, by 1806, they had gathered more than 20,000 Indians into nineteen missions. In the basin of the lower Orinoco the missions progressed, in numbers at least, until there were twenty-eight establishments with only a little fewer than 16,000 Indians in 1799. Almost everywhere else, however, there appears to have been retrogression. Recent surveys of the period, based upon authentic sources, give a depressing picture: buildings dilapidated; scarcity of missionaries, and those in the field lethargic and inadequately trained; neophytes reverting to their old roving habits or falling under the corrupt and oppressive influence of the worst elements of Spanish and mestizo society. A few years more, and only abandoned architectural ruins in forests, jungles, deserts, or grasslands would be left to remind the chance visitor of a former heroic epoch.[5]

In this century, as in the previous period, missionaries were usually supported by small groups of soldiers stationed in frontier presidios (forts). Sometimes, as in Texas, Nuevo Santander, and Upper California, the missionaries were accompanied by Spanish and mestizo settlers who founded towns at the very outset. Sometimes, moreover, military conquest preceded the successful introduction of missionaries;

and occasionally the Indians were driven farther out upon the frontiers in order to give place to ranchmen and miners, who brought with them a labor supply from the old settlements. The secularization of the missions also went on, although the large number of Indians under the missionaries at the middle of the century shows that the process did not occur with the rapidity contemplated by the law.

The epoch was, in fact, characterized by considerable expansion on the part of the civilian and military phalanx. In the founding of towns and the discovery of new mines, the eighteenth century was surpassed only by the sixteenth. Among the scores of new towns occupied, the following may be mentioned as illustrative of increased vigor: San Francisco, Los Angeles, Albuquerque, San Antonio, Montevideo, Bucaramanga and Cúcuta (New Granada), Copiapó and Rancagua (Chile). In addition to these new establishments, several old ones had to be rebuilt or refounded on account of the devastation of earthquakes or the destructive raids of European enemies. It was necessary also to spend millions of pesos on walls, coast defenses, war vessels, and armies, for on several occasions Spain's rivals tried to seize some of the mainland colonies.

Spain and the loyal elements within the colonies were able, however, to hold their own against all enemies. Cartagena and Santiago warded off formidable attacks in 1741; Río de la Plata drove out the British invaders in 1807; and other assailants were sometimes severely punished. An English expedition succeeded in seizing Cuba in 1762, only to exchange it a year later for the Floridas; and the Floridas themselves were finally returned to Spain in 1783. Trinidad was definitely lost (1797), along with a good part of Española, but these losses were more than compensated by the acquisition of Louisiana (1763). At the end of the century, Spanish America reached its maximum extent. There were then in the New World more than 3,000,000 people of Spanish descent, and a fraction of Spanish blood ran through the veins of still another 5,000,000. At the same time, the population of the mother country was well over 10,000,000. The record was, indeed, a tribute to the virility and prowess of the Spanish race.

COLONIAL SOCIETY AND CULTURE AT THE END OF THE CENTURY

Although Bourbon officials gave some attention to population statistics, apparently no accurate tables covering the whole of the Spanish colonies were ever compiled. According to the best estimates the population was as follows:

Colony	1788	1810	1823
New Spain	5,900,000	7,000,000	6,800,000
Guatemala	1,200,000	*	1,600,000
Cuba	600,000	†	800,000
Venezuela	900,000	950,000	785,000
New Granada	1,800,000	2,000,000	2,000,000
Peru	1,700,000	2,050,000	1,400,000
Chile	‡	‡	1,100,000
Río de la Plata	1,100,000	2,350,000	2,300,000

* Included in New Spain.   † Not given.   ‡ Included in Peru.

Perhaps it will do no harm to accept these figures as reasonably accurate and assume that the total population of Spanish America was 13,200,000 in 1788, some 15,000,000 in 1810, and 16,785,000 in 1823. The racial components of this population—as given by Alexander Humboldt, from whom the estimates for 1823 are taken—were as follows:

Colony	Indians	Whites	Negroes	Mestizos
New Spain	3,700,000	1,230,000		1,860,000
Guatemala	880,000	280,000		420,000
Colombia and Venezuela	720,000	642,000		1,256,000
Peru and Chile	1,030,000	465,000		853,000
Río de la Plata	1,200,000	320,000	387,000 *	742,000
Cuba and Puerto Rico	†	339,000	389,000	197,000
Total	7,530,000	3,276,000	776,000	5,328,000 ‡

* Total for all colonies except Cuba and Puerto Rico.
† Few, if any, Indians.
‡ The total population resulting from the addition of these figures differs slightly from that given by Humboldt in the preceding table.

These racial groups, whatever the number in each, furnished the basis for sharply drawn class distinctions. In addition, there was a definite cleavage between the Peninsular Spaniards and the creoles, as those born of Spanish blood in the colonies were called; and it appears that Spain actually fostered all these distinctions on the theory of divide and rule.

At the apex of the social hierarchy were the Peninsula-born Spaniards, numbering under 300,000 in 1800 but regarded as the bulwark of Spanish rule in America. They monopolized, and had always monopolized, the highest offices in Church and State. They controlled the army and the universities; they were the viceroys, the captains general, the governors, the intendants, the judges in the *audiencias;* they were the archbishops and bishops and the important officials of the cathedrals. They were also the leading merchants of the colonies. Not all of them were wealthy. Some, in fact, were poor and little better than vagabonds. But rich and poor alike looked with a certain amount of contempt upon the colonial-born Spaniards. "The most miserable European, without education or intellectual cultivation, thinks himself superior to all other white men in the new continent." Such was the view of Humboldt; and his testimony is corroborated by others.

Below the Spaniards in the social scale were the creoles, numbering nearly 3,000,000 in 1800. They owned most of the haciendas and mines, as well as much urban property. They were among the best physicians, lawyers, and notaries. They rushed eagerly into all the minor positions open to them in Church and State. They served as members of the town councils and frequently became judges or attorneys in the *audiencias;* but they were seldom permitted to become viceroys, captains general, intendants, or bishops. The wealthy among them often purchased titles of nobility and made a great display of their riches. Yet the vast majority were not wealthy. All were equally disdainful of manual labor; and since there were comparatively few honorable and lucrative positions for them in the universities, the church hierarchy, the regular orders, the army, and the civil service, they spent much time in litigation, dances, and festivals, as well as in drinking, gambling, and other forms of dissipation and vice.

The creoles came more and more to resent the discriminations set up against them by the mother country. Soon after the opening of the century, Don Melchor Macanaz, an able minister of Philip V, called attention to this resentment and advised a change of policy. "As the natives of those . . . dominions are equally deserving of filling the principal offices of their own country," he remarked, "it appears reasonable that they should not be divested of all management in their own homes. I am fully persuaded, that in those countries there are many discontented persons, not because they are under the control of Spain; but because they are cast down, and tyrannized by the very persons who are sent over to exercise the duties of judicature. Let your Majesty give these offices to subjects of that country, and by this means disturbances will be avoided." [6] The advice was not heeded, and the creoles were soon regarding "as an injustice every employment bestowed on any others than themselves."

Beneath the creoles were the mestizos, 5,000,000 of them at the end of the century. Set off from the whites above and the Indians and Negroes below, some mestizos filled the humbler positions in the parishes, convents, and missions or became small proprietors, but the vast majority were to be found among the artisans and vagabonds of the towns and cities. Still others were employed as *mayordomos* (overseers) in the mines and on the vast estates. The Spanish crown had indirectly fostered the production of this hybrid race; yet there are indications that the monarchs feared the growing class which they had helped to produce. They were careful to deprive them of their natural leaders. Social and civil position was made to depend largely upon one's complexion, and the conviction that "every white man was a cavalier" (*todo blanco es caballero*) was almost universal. The crown had therefore only to give to enterprising and aggressive mestizos patents declaring them white in order to cause them to cast their lot with the classes above them.

Next in order were the 7,500,000 Indians, still almost as numerous as all other classes combined. A few of them continued to reside in the missions; some dwelt detached in mountain fastnesses or roamed the forests and jungles, and hence could hardly be considered a part of colonial society; others were personal servants, common laborers, or humble artisans in the cities and towns; a considerable number spent their lives trudging behind mule trains through tropical jungle and along mountain trails, or "poling" rafts up and down the rivers, or as servants in the country inns; but many more were still under their chiefs in villages located near the rural mining areas or scattered over the vast estates of the creoles and Peninsula-born Spaniards. The encomiendas had been abolished, as well as most of the *mitas* (allotments of Indians for forced labor), but the vast majority were still driven to work by masters who evaded the law or to whom they were indebted; nor can it be said that the mission Indians were free, always, from forced labor and oppression. The wages of the natives were low; sometimes they were paid hardly anything at all. Many of them had some spare time for work on their little community farms and gardens or in household industries carried on mainly by the women. Poor, ignorant, exploited by a more sagacious race, superstitious, much given to strong drink, they lived in their floorless, vermin-infested huts with their pigs, chickens, and dogs. Almost unanimous testimony declares that they had failed to grasp the significant truths and lessons of the religion forced upon them and from the Catholic and native cults had compounded a religion of their own (the Cross and the Sun). Rankling hatred and a spirit of insurgency sometimes appeared. Now and then leaders arose among them and reminded them of far-off happy days before the white men came; but such leaders were ostentatiously and ruthlessly slain or bought off by patents of whiteness or titles of nobility. Truly the position of the Indians was not enviable, but that of the lower classes of Europe was not much better—and the Indians of Spanish America were still alive. Their exploitation was the huge sacrifice exacted in the interest of the ruling classes of the Old World for the development of the New.

The burden of hard labor continued to oppress the Indians because Negro slavery never took deep root in the Spanish colonies. Introduced at the opening of the sixteenth century in order to relieve the natives from heavy work in the mines and elsewhere, Negroes were brought in steadily under private license and *asiento* (concessionary) contract. Yet there were probably fewer than 800,000 in the colonies at the close of the eighteenth century and more than half of these were in Cuba and Puerto Rico. Mexico, Chile, and Río de la Plata had only a small number. Most of those not in the West Indies were the personal servants or slaves of the wealthy families of Lima, Guayaquil, Quito, Popayán, Cali, Medellín, Santa Marta, Cartagena, Caracas, and Panama. Of the remainder, more were working on the plantations than in the mines.

The Spanish slave code was comparatively humane, and there was a strong tendency toward emancipation. More than half the Negroes of Spanish America were free at the close of the Colonial period, their freedom having been obtained mainly by purchase money earned during holidays and at other spare times. If their suffering ever was great, it was probably more from neglect than severity.

Such were the social classes in Spanish America in 1800. Among the most important social institutions was, as always, the church. At the end of the century, it was organized into six archbishoprics (Santo Domingo, Mexico, Guatemala, Lima, Bogotá, and Charcas) and some thirty-four bishoprics. To the mendicant orders were added, during the course of the seventeenth and eighteenth centuries, several other orders. The clergy were never so numerous, however, as in Spain. It appears, indeed, that their number declined after 1750 to a degree not accounted for by the expulsion of more than 2,000 Jesuits. According to Humboldt, there were only 14,000 regulars and seculars in New Spain in 1803; and Rafael Altamira thinks there were no more than 35,000 or 40,000 in all Spanish America at that time. Spain, with a smaller population than its American colonies, had almost four times as many.

Nevertheless, the Spanish American church was very wealthy. It received annually large sums from gifts, tithes, and other ecclesiastical revenues and is said to have owned between one-third and one-half of all the private property in the colonies. Besides many monasteries and numerous large temples of worship elegantly and sometimes gaudily furnished and decorated, it had vast urban and rural properties and an extensive moneylending business. Moreover, the Tribunals of the Inquisition in Lima and Mexico City enjoyed large incomes and toward the last decade of the century had 2,000,000 to 3,000,000 pesos in their coffers.

Much of the income of the church was expended on charity, religious festivals, and schools. In fact, nearly every educational institution in the colonies owed its initiation and support largely to the church, which also controlled curricula and educational policy and furnished almost all the teachers. Yet many ecclesiastics of every order and degree are said to have spent their lives in luxury and dissipation little becoming the followers of the lowly Nazarene. Moreover, tithes and other dues, as already noted, were often oppressive to the lower classes, while ecclesiastical administration of real estate was not such as to bring forth the best returns. On the economic affairs of Spanish America, as on those of Spain, the church cast the blight of its dead hand.

The influence of the church in the field of learning was not an unmixed good. If it must be admitted that at least a dozen universities, scores of seminaries, and hundreds of elementary and secondary [7] schools owed their existence to the clergy, it must also be pointed out that ecclesiastical teaching was somewhat inefficient and much of the content of ecclesiastical education of doubtful value. The children were taught to memorize but not to think. Formalities and indoctrination were emphasized rather than the training of the character and the mind. Sometimes the clergy stood with flaming swords at the gates of knowledge. (This was true in particular of the officials of the Inquisition, who undertook a rigid censorship of all reading matter and placed thousands of books upon the list of forbidden literature.)

Yet, in spite of all these limitations, learning made some progress in the colonies during the eighteenth century. The Bourbons themselves, and their viceroys, were its patrons until the extravagances of the French Revolution drove them to a reversal of their policy. A new university was founded in Caracas in 1722, a second in Havana in 1728, and another in Santiago de Chile in 1738. Several printing presses were added to the few previously set up. Presses were introduced during the century into Veracruz, Guadalajara, Quito, Ambato, Bogotá, and Buenos Aires. Newspapers appeared in Havana, Mexico City, Guatemala City, Bogotá, Lima, and Santiago. While the old types of colonial literature—poetry, chronicles, treatises on Indian languages, and books on dogma, speculative philosophy, and theology—continued to appear, gradually more emphasis was placed upon medicine and other sciences, as well as upon politics and social criticism. The stream of new thought now flowing so strongly in Western Europe, and even to a considerable extent in Spain itself, could not be entirely shut out. Spanish American students returning from their European studies broke the dikes; traders from France, England, and the United States lent a hand; some of the universities felt its influence and became centers of new learning (namely, medicine, jurisprudence, and mathematics); and not a few of the churchmen themselves were swept into the current. Although it cannot be said that education was very widespread even among the whites and mestizos at the end of the century, the group of intelligentsia had greatly expanded, and the long intellectual isolation of the colonies had broken down. Baron Humboldt, who visited the region only a few years later, was often surprised at the scientific progress that had been made.

Among the scientists of the century, several deserve to be mentioned. Besides writing numerous poems, Pedro de Peralta Barnuevo of Peru produced many works on navigation, astronomy, metallurgy, engineering, and history. Antonio Alzate of New Spain published a number of articles on a wide range of philosophical and scientific subjects and gave his name to a scientific society of modern Mexico. Francisco José de Caldas, a pupil of the able Spanish scientist José Celestino Mutis, won fame by a botanical survey of New Granada and by astronomical observations in Santa Fé de Bogotá. Hipólito Unánue of Peru attained distinction in medicine and climatology and Santiago de Cárdenas even wrote a book on a "new system of navigating by air," which gained for him the title of "El Volador" ("The Flyer").

At least a score of valuable historical and descriptive works appeared during this century. The writers of greatest merit in this class were: Alonso de Zamora, Francisco de Medrano, Juan Rivero, and José Gumillo of New Granada; José de Oviedo y Baños and José Luís Cisneros of Venezuela; Dionisio and Antonio de Alcedo (father and son) of Peru; Miguel de Olivares, Pedro C. Figueroa, and Juan Ignacio Molina of Chile; Pedro Lozano, José Guevara, and Juan P. Fernández of the Río de la Plata area; and Francisco J. Alegre, Eusebio Francisco Kino (late seventeenth and early eighteenth century), Francisco Clavijero, Andrés Cavo, and Francisco Palóu of New Spain.

The period was also noted for the production of pure literature of some merit. Among the literati of the century, Antonio Valdés (author of the drama *Ollantá*), Manuel de Navarette, and Manuel José Labardén (writer of the ode *Al Paraná* and the play *Siripio*) deserve mention.

Lastly, in art, music, and architecture considerable progress was made. Most of the leading cities of the colonies contained troupes of artists, and a School of Fine Arts was established in Mexico City near the end of the century.

ᵉᴹ THE WORK OF SPAIN IN AMERICA: AN APPRAISAL

The close of the eighteenth century virtually brought to an end the constructive effort of Spain in America. The next twenty-five years were almost entirely occupied by the struggle which terminated in independence. A critical estimate of Spain's work will go far toward removing the black legend created by her colonial rivals and enemies and by partisan agitators of Spain and Spanish America. Yet the record is not as lily-white as some Hispanophiles would have it appear.

Millions of natives had been preserved, but they owed their preservation in part to their usefulness at the bottom of the economic order. The language of the mother country had been introduced and given a permanently predominant place. Yet numerous Indians could not write or even speak Spanish, and many others who knew the language preferred to employ their native tongues.

The establishment of mail systems had brought colonial minds into closer association; but communications were still very slow and uncertain, and private correspondence was difficult and unsafe. Roads adapted to carriages, wagons, or even oxcarts were few, and the ports and rivers were very little improved. Unlike Rome, Spain was not a noted builder of highways.

The land system had encouraged or permitted the concentration of large agrarian holdings in the hands of the church and the nobility, who cultivated them in very indifferent fashion. Many Indian villages continued to retain the community lands which Spanish authorities had carefully assigned them; but others had lost their *ejidos* (lands held in common by Indian villages), and the great mass of the people were landless. An aristocracy of wealth and privilege had been firmly established.

The some twenty [8] universities in existence in 1800 were probably sufficient in number to accommodate such of the sons of the upper classes as were able to attend them, even if the course of study was limited and defective. But comparatively little had been done to educate the masses.

Legal, judicial, and administrative systems had been set up, but political and geographical boundaries had been carelessly defined—a carelessness replete with difficulties for the future. Moreover, a multiplicity of officials, the widespread sale of offices, and traditions of bureaucratic dishonesty were an unfortunate inheritance for the new nations soon to appear.

Roman Catholic Christianity had been instilled, often to the point of fanaticism, into all the white and mestizo groups as well as into great masses of the natives; but numerous Indians had been very imperfectly Christianized, if at all. Moreover, both Church and State had combined to restrict thought and retard scientific development, and the church, because of its wealth, its control over intellectual life, and its habit of participating in politics, was destined to an important, inflammatory, and somewhat reactionary role in the future.

On the whole, it was a rather depressing heritage, but it contained certain elements, either in theory or in practice, which pointed the way to a new regime. "In spite of the difference in inspiration and the apparent contradiction in attendant circumstances, there is a certain connection between the highest human ideals of the revolution [namely, the Wars of Independence, 1810–25] and the deep and silent moral forces of colonial society," writes a very capable Peruvian historian. "To political and civil equality corresponds, evidently, the moral equality of all the races which was proclaimed by various intellectual leaders in Spain since the time of the conquest and was the underlying principle of the best legislation of the Indies. To the idea of popular sovereignty . . . corresponds, in essence, the idea of kingdoms, practically national groups, that existed not only in the mind but also in the vocabulary during the colonial period." [9]

Nor should the Spanish emphasis upon the artistic be forgotten. Impressive public buildings of both Church and State as well as beautiful parks and patios filled with flowers, shrubs, and trees adorned the leading towns; and some of the countryside, too, was given a romantic glamour by the stately homes of the planters, approached by avenues of palms, poplars, ceibas, or other trees. This pattern of values would continue into the National period, until many parts of Spanish America became as attractive and inspirational as any to be found elsewhere in the world. Even the poorest classes frequently exhibited good taste as well as good manners; the most miserable dwellings were likely to be surrounded by flowers and shrubbery. The major defect in the Spanish culture transmitted to America was not an absence of appreciation for the sentimental and the beautiful; it was a lack of emphasis on science, technology, and civil liberty.

CHAPTER VIII

Brazil Under the Braganzas

⁂ CHARACTER OF THE BRAGANZAS

The seventeenth and eighteenth centuries were not a happy epoch for Portugal. Restive and resentful under Hapsburg rule, and harried by foreign attacks upon their overseas possessions by the enemies of the Spanish government, the Portuguese people, especially the aristocracy, began in 1640 a long struggle for freedom from their "Babylonian captivity." In spite of intermittent assistance from England, France, and the Dutch Netherlands, the war dragged on for twenty-eight years. The head of the house of Braganza, whose claim to the Portuguese throne had been ignored by Philip II of Spain in 1580, led the revolt and took charge of the insurgent government as King John (João) IV, with the approval of the nobility and the Cortes. The Braganzas were to rule Portugal for over two centuries, and three of them were destined to reign in Brazil.

Most of the Braganzas who governed Portugal were inefficient, imprudent, unbalanced, extravagant, or corrupt; a few were enlightened and capable. Portugal was deeply indebted to the first two of them for the recovery of its independence. The third, Pedro II (1683–1706), was efficient, but despotic; it was during his reign that the national parliament (Cortes) was discontinued (1697), not to be reinstated until after 1800, and that Portugal became involved in the long War of the Spanish Succession. John V (1706–50), who continued the war, was a bigot, a spendthrift, and a crusader against the Turks, but also a patron of history, literature, and all the arts. Joseph II (1750–77) was one of Europe's enlightened despots, whose able chief minister, the Marquis of Pombal, effected an economic and a cultural revival even in face of Portugal's participation in the Seven Years' War on the side of England and the reduction of the little ally almost to the status of a vassal. María I (1777–1815), married to a silly and vicious uncle, dismissed Pombal, succumbed to court favorites, suffered from religious mania, and became insane. Her son John took charge of the government as prince regent; and it was during his vacillating rule that Portugal confronted the perils of the French Revolutionary and Napoleonic period and that the Portuguese royal family fled to Brazil (1807) in order to escape the clutches of Bonaparte.

The character of the Portuguese monarchs and Portugal's involvement in Europe's dynastic and imperialistic wars inevitably influenced the development of Brazil. The raids of British seamen and the attacks of Frenchmen at the turn of the sixteenth century already have been mentioned. These were followed by more serious Dutch aggressions and by further French attacks. Moreover, Brazil not only had to assume the main responsibility for its own defense but was compelled to share the cost of Portugal's wars and support the extravagance of its rulers. These burdens and handicaps were only partially compensated by ameliorating trade concessions wrung from Portugal by England and other European powers, by the "salutary neglect" of feeble kings, and by the reforms of Pombal.

Brazil had become a fairly prosperous agricultural colony by 1668, but the discovery of gold toward the end of the seventeenth century and of diamonds a few decades later caused a tremendous rush to the mines and the partial abandonment of the plantations and ranches, accompanied by scarcity of provisions and a rapid rise in prices. For almost 100 years, mining and the production and sale of supplies to the miners were among the major occupations of the people of Brazil. It was not until shortly before 1800 that the boom subsided and Brazilians, now greatly increased in numbers partly because of the gold seekers from Portugal, returned to the plantations and ranches near the coast or established new agricultural settlements in the west—and they returned only to discover that they could not compete with the sugar planters of the West Indies and the cotton planters of the United States. In the long run, it was the southern region of Brazil, with its corn, wheat, rice, coffee, fruits, livestock, and timber, that profited most from the mining cycle. Rio de Janeiro became the leading trading and transport center of the colony and eventually its permanent capital.

THE FOREIGN MENACE

During the first half of the seventeenth century, it appeared that Portugal might lose its American colony as well as its possessions in the Orient. Shortly after the French effort of 1612–15 to establish settlements in Brazil, the Dutch Protestants, then fighting for their independence from Spain, became a serious menace. They not only attacked the Spanish empire, which still included Portugal and its overseas colonies; they also attempted to acquire a vast commercial empire of their own. They dispatched an expedition and seized Bahía in 1624; but the Portuguese recovered this town the next year with the aid of the Spanish fleet. But with a much larger expeditionary force the Dutchmen captured Olinda and Recife in 1630, and within a few years they extended their rule over all northern Brazil, almost half of the colony.

The conquest was made under the auspices of the Dutch West India Company, which was occupying the Hudson River Valley of New York at the same time. The administration of Prince Maurice of Nassau, who was sent out in 1637 to govern the new Brazilian colony, was so mild and so considerate of the interests of the colonial inhabitants that many of them were disposed to accept Dutch rule. But Maurice's method of government failed to satisfy profit-seeking stockholders, and he finally resigned in 1644. The government then became more exacting and oppressive, and the Brazilians, already stirred by news of the successes of the Portuguese in their war for liberation from Spain, took up arms against the invaders. In fact, a small uprising occurred in Maranhão shortly before Prince Maurice left for Europe, but a general revolt might not have broken out if his successors had continued his policies. Before the end of 1645, a good part of northern Brazil—Portuguese, mixed breeds, Indians, Negroes, and not a few clergymen—was under arms.

The revolution continued for nine years and ended in the expulsion of the Dutch intruders. The people of Brazil took great pride in their prowess. The Portuguese, busy with their war for independence from Spain and reluctant to fight Dutchmen in Brazil when they were receiving Dutch aid in Europe, had extended little assistance to the American colony, and exulting colonial leaders described their prolonged struggle as the "Brazilian Iliad." But as a matter of fact, they owed their triumph in part to England. Making war against the Hollanders in Europe, the Orient, and New York, Englishmen could not look with favor upon Dutch occupation of their Portuguese ally's American domain; and it was the English government that helped to extort from the Dutch Netherlands an agreement, finally signed in 1661, to abandon their attempts to seize Brazil.

French attacks were resumed during the course of Europe's War of the Spanish Succession. Fighting on the side of England, as usual, Portugal provoked the ambitious Louis XIV of France into the authorization of raids on Brazil, and Rio de Janeiro became the victim. The first assault, in 1710, was repulsed; but Frenchmen seized and sacked the town the next year and collected a large ransom. This turned out, however, to be Europe's last attack on colonial Brazil.

Portugal thus managed to retain its big South American colony. But efforts to maintain its trade monopoly were less successful. Committed to the mercantile theory like other colonizing powers of the age, Portuguese rulers attempted to confine the trade of Brazil to the mother country, making use of convoyed fleets of merchant vessels and chartered mercantile companies to enforce their pretensions; yet Brazil's commerce fell largely under the control of English, French, and Dutch merchants. According to an estimate of the early eighteenth century, "half of the Brazil trade" was in "English hands" and the rest was "carried on by France and Holland." This estimate, which must have included the traffic of smugglers as well as the commerce of foreigners that went through Portugal on its way to Portuguese America, probably exaggerated the magnitude of both; but there is little room to doubt that most of the exports to Brazil were being supplied by these three trading nations and paid for by the gold and other commodities produced by the Brazilians. Although there were certain variations caused by occasional political and economic changes, foreign commercial encroachments, especially those of British merchants, increased during the years that followed. Despite attempts to destroy this predominance by means of Portuguese monopolistic companies and other devices, neither Portugal nor its American possession could be extricated from British economic domination. As in the case of Spain, the trade and treasure of a vast empire flowed out to alien merchants and into the coffers of foreign nations.

This breakdown of the Portuguese commercial monopoly was probably a distinct advantage for Brazil. In comparison with the narrow and rigid Spanish system, which tended to concentrate the commerce of Spanish America in the hands of Seville merchants until the reforms of Charles III, the Portuguese commercial system was always fairly liberal. Colonial ports of entry were more numerous, and far more Portuguese merchants and shipowners were allowed to share the trade. Nevertheless, the system would have injured Brazil if it had been completely enforced. High freight rates and a more limited supply would have raised the price of commodities imported into Brazil; high freight rates and a restricted market would have depressed prices for Brazilian produce.

BRAZIL'S "WESTWARD MOVEMENT"

"The story of Xenophon's Ten Thousand is but a child's tale compared with the fearless adventure of our colonial brothers," declares a Brazilian historian.[1] The "westward movement" in Brazil during the two centuries under review recalls the great migration that took place in the United States between 1763 and 1860. It involved the same search for virgin soil adapted to slave labor and the plantation economy, the same rush to the mines, the same eagerness for pasture lands, and a similar ruthless treatment of the natives. In many respects, however, the Brazilian movement differed from that of the United States. It confronted greater climatic and topographic obstacles. It was motivated in part by a desire to capture and enslave the Indians. It involved fewer emigrants and resulted in far less compact frontier settlements. Missionaries of the great religious orders, particularly the Jesuits, often went in advance, serving as buffers between frontiersmen and Indians and thus preserving some of the natives, at least for a time. The migration to the interior began before the littoral was fully occupied, and the movement was toward the north, the northwest, and the southwest as well as toward the west.

In southern areas it was the Paulistas who played the leading role. With the object of ensnaring Indians for the slave market, or finding richer lands, or discovering mines, they organized expeditions known as *entradas* or *bandeiras*—bands sometimes consisting of entire families with all their worldly possessions—which trekked hundreds of miles westward to the Spanish missions of Paraguay, to the Gran Chaco, and even to southern Mainas, or turning to the north, eventually discovered gold and diamonds in a region soon given the name of Minas Geraes (General Mines). The *entradas* resulted in the death or captivity of thousands of Indians; and the discovery of gold and diamonds caused wild excitement, followed by a general rush of miners and pitched battles between the Paulistas and immigrants from both Portugal and other parts of Brazil. From the General Mines the pioneers advanced into Goyaz, Cuyabá, and faraway Matto Grosso, where more gold was uncovered. In 1742, Manoel Felix de Lima made a long voyage of more than 2,000 miles by way of the Guaporé, the Mamoré, and the Madeira to the Amazon and down the great river to the town of Pará. A settlement called Villa Bella and Matto Grosso was established on the upper reaches of the Guaporé ten years later; soon thereafter the fort of Beira was erected at the junction of the Guaporé and the San Miguel rivers, fully 1,800 miles northwest of São Paulo. Meanwhile, other frontiersmen were moving southwest into Santa Catarina and Rio Grande do Sul, where they met kinsmen on their way northeastward from Colonia, founded in 1680, and from other settlements in Banda Oriental (lower eastern basin of the Río de la Plata).

The missionaries had almost nothing to do with this vigorous advance, for the whites and mixbloods of southern Brazil would permit little humanitarian interference in behalf of the natives. The padres were lucky if they were allowed to remain in the region at all.

In the north, however, their contribution to the expansion was large. During the early part of the seventeenth century the frontier of settlement moved rapidly along the north coast from Ceará to Pará and to the island of Marajó in the Amazon delta, covering a distance of over 1,200 miles. It then advanced up the Amazon to Gurupá (1623), to Barro do Rio Negro (Manáos, 1674), and to the junction of the Amazon with the Javary (Tabatinga, 1780), almost 2,000 miles from Pará. In the meantime, Pedro de Teixeira had led an expedition up the Amazon to the head of navigation and then over the Andes to Quito (1637–38).

From the coastal and fluvial centers of civilian occupation the Jesuits, under such leaders as Antonio Vieira, set out into the wilderness in search of souls. In the island of Marajó, in the basins of the Amazon and its southern tributaries, wherever the "black robes" appeared, the Indians by the thousands exchanged their liberty for the sway of the Jesuits and settled themselves in villages devoted to agriculture, the care of domestic animals, and the manufacture of clothing and house-hold equipment. The Jesuits had plenty of trouble with the Portuguese Brazilians, who raided their missions near and far in search of labor; but, assisted by the Capuchins, the Mercedarians, and the Carmelites, who joined in the civilizing effort shortly before 1700, they carried on with courage and tenacity. A contemporary map of the Spanish-Por-tuguese frontier represents the Jesuits as having, around the year 1749, numerous establishments on the upper right bank of the Madeira and all along the southern bank of the Amazon from the mouth of the Purus to that of the Javary. And by 1755 the Jesuit fathers were in charge of twenty-eight missions, the Capuchins controlled fifteen, and the Carmelites claimed twelve, nearly all of them in the steaming jungle and grasslands of northern Brazil.

West of the captaincies of Rio Grande do Norte, Parahyba, Pernam-buco, and Bahía, where the country is mostly arid except in the long valley of the São Francisco, the missionaries were less important than the cattlemen. Many ranchers and some planters moved into the basin of the São Francisco during the last century and a half of the Colonial era and a few of both trekked into the dry *sertão* (back country) to the north and west, where they were so cut off from the world and so im-pressed by the drought, heat, and other hardships of their environment that, like the inhabitants of the mountains and hills of Kentucky and Tennessee, they developed peculiar traits which set them apart from the inhabitants of other regions. The *sertanejo* (backwoodsman) of Central Brazil, notes Carvalho, "is somber, thin, mistrustful, and super-stitious, rarely aggressive, rash in his impulses, as silent as the vast plains that surround him, calm in gesture, laconic in speech, and, above all, sunk in an inexpressive melancholy." [2]

Brazilian frontiersmen and missionaries were thus pushing the boundaries of the colony far beyond the imaginary line of the Treaty

of Tordesillas. In many places, however, particularly in the lower eastern basin of the Plata and along the upper reaches of the Amazon, they
encountered the somewhat more feeble forward thrust of the Spaniards
and their religious cohorts. The time had come, therefore, for the
negotiation of boundary agreements with Spain, and such agreements
were signed in 1750, 1777, and 1801. They represented a triumph of
Brazilian pioneering and Portuguese diplomacy. In the main, actual
occupation was taken as the basis of possession, and Portugal, profiting by the superior vigor of its expansive forces, obtained three times
the area assigned to her by the old Tordesillas pact. Moreover, thanks
mainly to English pressure, France gave up her pretensions to the
northern basin of the lower Amazon and the right to navigate that huge
river and agreed to the river Oyapock as the dividing line between French
Guiana and Brazil.

ADMINISTRATIVE ORGANIZATION AND POLICIES

It has been noted that Brazil's development was not greatly hampered
by Portugal's commercial policy because the policy could not be consistently enforced. The economic progress of the colony may have been
more seriously retarded, however, by a somewhat burdensome fiscal
system and by restrictions upon colonial industry. Portuguese taxes
were similar to those of Spain, but hardly so numerous or heavy. Important among them were the royal fifth levied upon mines worked
by private enterprise, sales taxes, tithes, duties on imports and exports,
and a head tax upon Negro slaves. The Portuguese crown monopolized
such commodities as salt, certain liquors and beverages, brazilwood,
timber for shipbuilding, and the whale fisheries, and made vigorous
efforts to effect a monopoly of the gold and diamond mines, but without much success in the case of the gold deposits. In accordance with
the mercantile theory, colonial industries were forbidden to compete
with those of the mother country. Although the prohibitions—which
were seldom thoroughly enforced—varied from time to time, tending
to grow more numerous near the end of the Colonial period, it may be
said in general that the law did not permit Brazilians to make wine or
refine sugar, or to manufacture articles from such raw materials as
gold, silver, iron, flax, cotton, and silk. A considerable portion of the
tobacco of the colony was likewise reserved for the factories of Portugal. Restrictions relative to tobacco, gold, silver, diamonds, cotton,
and salt were most keenly felt. The high price of salt resulting from
the royal monopoly was a heavy burden for stock raisers, who required
this important article for their animals and the preservation of their
meat.

Yet, despite all these taxes and restrictions, Brazil was a moderately prosperous colony during the two centuries following 1600. The value of the gold extracted from its mines between 1694 and the end of the Colonial epoch was probably not less than $1,000,000,000 and the value of its diamonds some $20,000,000 to $30,000,000. The value of its foreign trade exceeded $16,000,000 annually during the decade following 1790. By that time the output of the mines had greatly diminished and the commodities of Brazil were once more mainly the products of farms, plantations, ranches, and forests: cotton, tobacco, sugar, cacao, rice, coffee, pepper, ginger, citrus and other fruits; some olives and grapes and a little cinnamon; indigo, corn and wheat in some sections, but more widely, manioc; meat, hides, leather, timber, dyewoods, balsam, ipecac, and other drugs and perfumes. Many of these commodities were among Brazil's exports during the last decades of the Colonial period; and Brazil received, in return, not only manufactured products of all kinds but various foods, wines, beverages, and liquors, some of which the colony itself should have produced.

An outstanding feature of the political organization of Brazil was a lack of centralization. Divided at first into twelve or thirteen captaincies, the colony numbered seventeen by the close of the eighteenth century. The unified control set up by Governor-General Thomé de Souza at Bahía in 1549 was rent in twain in 1572 by the establishment of two chief executives, one in Bahía and the other in Rio de Janeiro. This dual control was continued intermittently until 1616, when the former administrative integrity was theoretically restored by eliminating the Rio administrator. Then, in 1624, Maranhão, greatly expanded so as to include the vast region stretching from Ceará to Pará and extending westward to the Spanish frontier, was erected into a separate jurisdiction directly responsible to the government at Lisbon. During the latter part of the seventeenth and the early years of the eighteenth century, however, Maranhão was gradually reincorporated into the rest of Brazil, and eventually split up into four captaincies: Pará, Maranhão, Piauhy, and Ceará. Meantime, for nearly two centuries following 1572, it appears that the authority of the governors-general residing at Bahía often did not extend far beyond the limits of the captaincy bearing the same name. Although Brazil had become technically a viceroyalty in 1640, the title of viceroy was not consistently employed until after 1763 (there were eight viceroys before 1763 and seven afterward). In that year, as previously noted, the capital was permanently transferred from Bahía to Rio, but this change still failed to bring about a firm central administration. Theoretically, the viceroy residing in the new capital exercised supervisory authority over the chief executives of the other captaincies or provinces; in reality, however, his power outside his own captaincy was often largely nominal, except, perhaps, in the southern captaincies. Colonial administrative practice tended to create provincialism and sectionalism and forecast the ultimate adoption of a federal system of government.

Because of these numerous administrative units and the absence of a strong central authority in the colony, generalization regarding the character of the colonial regime is almost impossible. Its quality differed from time to time and from province to province. That Brazil, on the whole, was not well governed, however, seems to be a safe conclusion. The governors-general and viceroys were mostly reactionary, sometimes merely conservative, hardly ever liberal, always likely to confuse authority with despotism. Mediocre statesmen, almost all of them, some were distinguished by considerable courage and military talent. Subordinate officials usually made themselves "odious by the venality and corruption of the processes by which they governed the people." [3] Brazilian historians contend—and even the viceroys admitted—that the administration of justice was often corrupt and unfair. In all except the most important cases, which were in charge of judges sent out by the crown, justice depended upon the decisions of judges appointed by the executives of the captaincies. Only two important changes in the system had been made since early colonial days. A higher tribunal was set up in Bahía in 1608 and another in Rio in 1751.

During the ascendency of the able Marquis of Pombal in Portugal (1750–77), something of the spirit and practice of enlightened despotism was infused into the colonial administration. Pombal corrected long-standing abuses and corruption, extinguished feudal rights and privileges in the last of the ancient captaincies, removed the capital to Rio de Janeiro, injected greater unity into the administrative system of the colony, employed native Brazilians in civil and military posts, expelled the Jesuits (1759), sought to liberate the civilized Indians from tutelage, and stimulated both agriculture and such industries as did not compete with those of the mother country. Although the wisdom of banishing the Jesuit fathers may be questioned, most of his reforms were probably beneficial. But they signified an interruption of relative neglect, for everywhere the reins of government were tightened.

The temper and practices of the period are illustrated by the counsel given by one of the viceroys, Marquis de Lavradio, to his successor. Lavradio retired in 1779, after having held his post for some eleven years, and his report to the chief executive who followed him reveals a high army officer abusing his authority, acting with "asperity towards the troops and his officers" and despising the colonial militia; a system of universal military service so organized as to keep the colonials in proper "subordination"; attorneys serving as judges in cases in which they had already acquired an interest as advocates; judges thinking mainly of accumulating riches, accepting bribes, and refusing to promote harmony by discouraging litigation. These and other evils the viceroy claimed that he had tried to remedy, but in his own haughty manner, while pretending that popular "murmurs" were beneath his notice. He also claimed that he had attempted to promote the cultivation of rice, indigo, hemp, mulberry trees, and fiber for rope, and had devoted much attention to timbers, oils, balsams, gums, and useful shrubs—probably again in a highhanded fashion.

Lavradio appears to have been eager to promote the best interests of the colonists by methods which statesmen of his school approved. "As the good of the people has ever been my chief object," he avowed, "I endeavoured by all means possible to avoid all prejudice to them, and at the same time to benefit their . . . reputation. My self-love," he went on to declare, "does not bind me to the point of inducing me to defend all of my resolutions as judicious; I did what I could and what my limited talents permitted me, and I never omitted any labours which appeared likely to prevent my falling into error. Your Excellency will act with more discretion," he concluded with flattering humility, "and by correcting my imperfections and mistakes, will bring about that felicity of the people which I have ever desired, and still desire." [4] Perhaps it was neither high purpose nor capacity that was lacking in this bureaucrat of the old regime. It was rather the haughty spirit and the method that were at fault. Government might be for the people, but not of and by the people, who were not expected or permitted to do much by and for themselves.

BRAZIL AT THE END OF THE COLONIAL PERIOD

Population statistics for colonial Portuguese America are no more accurate than those for colonial Spanish America. Only rough estimates are available. According to these, the civilized population of Brazil numbered around 750,000 in 1700, well above 3,000,000 in 1800, and approximately 4,000,000 by 1823. An estimate for the year 1818 divides the races as follows:

| Whites | 843,000 | Negroes | 1,887,500 |
| Mixed | 628,000 | Indians | 259,400 |

The figure for the Indian population, unless it refers to civilized natives only, seems considerably too small; but it appears to be too large for the civilized group, even when the adjective is loosely applied. The total number of Indians in Brazil at this time probably exceeded 500,000, and it is likely that more than two-thirds of them were still uncivilized nomads.

Distinctions of class and race were not so pronounced in Brazil as in Spanish America. Nevertheless, a sort of caste system was apparent in both law and custom.

Forming the top layer of the social order were the whites, who ruled the colony and owned most of its wealth. Those born in Portugal held the majority of the offices in Church and State, although discrimination against the creoles, who, in any case, dominated the town governments, was less marked since the reforms of Pombal. Ownership of lands and of mines not in possession of the crown was largely in the hands of the creoles but fairly widely distributed among both creoles and Portuguese. Yet the colony was so immense and the whites so few that there were a great many very large estates. The whites were fond of displaying their riches in urban and rural mansions, numerous servants, and expensive apparel; but they really lacked many conveniences and luxuries then enjoyed by the upper classes of Western Europe.

Next to the whites were the *mestiços* (mamelucos), the mixed descendants of Portuguese and Indians, or at least the vast majority of them who were unable to pass into the ranks of the whites. Many of this group possessed some property, particularly those living in the southern provinces. They were small farmers and ranchmen, or skilled mechanics, or overseers on the big ranches and plantations owned by the whites, or labor foremen in the mines, or the operators of pack animals and other means of transportation. In theory, they possessed full civil rights, including the right to hold office in Church and State; in practice, they were apt to be excluded from public service unless they possessed more than average wealth and influence.

Ranking only a little below the mixbloods were the ex-slaves, both Negroes and mulattoes, who probably numbered no more than 300,000. Whether black, brown, or light, members of this group were legally barred from the priesthood and all civil employment and forbidden to hold a commission in the militia save in their own battalions. But the law was not always enforced, and they were supposed to enjoy the rights of citizenship in other respects.

At the bottom of the social order were the Indians and the Negro and mulatto slaves. It hardly seems worth while to try to determine which group ranked above the other. There was not much difference between enslavement and subjection to compulsory labor at a trifling wage.

Brazil had nearly 2,000,000 slaves in 1818, some 200,000 to 300,000 of them mulattoes and the rest Negroes. Except for the inhumanities of the slave traffic, which were less Brazilian than foreign, the slave system of Brazil was fairly mild. Its victims probably suffered more from neglect than from abuse. Custom ceded the slaves one or two days each week for work of their own, and often also a plot of ground. Since 1700 the law had recognized their right to possess private property, to exchange a cruel master for one more humane, and even to purchase their liberty. Yet the comparatively small number of free Negroes and free mulattoes clearly indicates that emancipation was proceeding very slowly.

Portugal showed less concern for the Indians than Spain did; but Portugal was not dealing with semicivilized Indians; nor can it be truthfully asserted that the Portuguese were entirely indifferent to the fate of the primitive types of aborigines who inhabited Brazil. Most of the missionaries worked among them with great devotion and usually opposed their enslavement. The Portuguese monarchs, in a series of decrees beginning in 1570 and extending throughout the Colonial epoch, endeavored to prohibit or limit their exploitation and oppression. But, as in Spanish America, the benevolent decrees were seldom enforced. In 1755 the energetic Pombal government, as already stated, declared all the Indians of Brazil free subjects of the colony, with all the rights and privileges that such a status implied. This probably meant that they were soon emancipated from slavery, but in other respects it was scarcely more than an empty gesture, since few of the natives were prepared for incorporation in the body politic on the basis of equality with their former masters. Followed four years later by the expulsion of the Jesuits, the declaration heralded the rapid dissolution of the frontier and other missions without providing any institution that adequately filled the vacuum. Most of the frontier Indians returned to the forests and their primitive life. Some of those in the more populated areas, having made peace with their civilized neighbors, continued to live in their tribal state; the majority resided in towns and villages more or less separated from the *mestiços* and the whites, a few being permitted to govern themselves and the rest placed in charge of European "directors."

Contemporary observers assert that these superior officials made no effort to improve the status of their wards. The bishop of Pernambuco declared that the directors lacked proper qualifications for their posts, and that instead of educating the Indians and promoting their interests, they sought to enrich themselves and "treated" the natives "as slaves," forcing them to "toil like beast of burthen." [5] An English writer adds a few details. He says that the new official was "invested with the power of directing all their concerns, and of punishing or re-warding them according to [his view of] their deserts. He superintends the sale of all commodities in behalf of the community, delivers to the government agents a tenth of the . . . products, and appoints the labour to be performed by those who have fallen into a state of vas-salage; and these agents act under the direction of a chief to whom is delegated still more extensive authority." [6] Apparently the English-man's last sentence refers to royal bureaucrats who participated in the oppression perpetrated by the directors and shared the spoils. The Portuguese government had never created a group of encomenderos; but it had now established a set of exploiters corresponding roughly to the Spanish *corregidores*. In all the more populated areas of Brazil, the Indians were a vanishing race.

As in Spanish America, the Roman Catholic Church was an im-portant institution in Brazil. Although the clergy were neither as numer-ous nor as wealthy as in New Spain and Peru, they owed considerable rural and urban property in addition to several imposing temples of worship—some of them elaborately furnished and decorated—in the leading towns and cities and numerous monasteries and convents. At the end of the eighteenth century, the secular organization was com-posed of an archbishop and nine bishops, the bishops of Pará and Maranhão being subject to the archbishop of Lisbon. Although Tri-bunals of the Inquisition were never set up in Brazil, the higher clergy had inquisitorial powers. Colonials accused of heresy were sent to Portugal for trial.

The church provided nearly all of the educational advantages avail-able in Brazil. The secular and regular clergy, especially the latter, founded almost all of the primary and secondary schools as well as the seminaries, and continued to support and control them. Two military academies came into existence during the eighteenth century, but at-tempts to found a university at Rio failed. Nor were efforts to set up printing presses in the colony successful until 1808. Although there were some elementary schools on the big plantations, educational facilities were meager outside of the missions and the leading towns.

The inhabitants of eighteenth-century Brazil, even the whites and *mestiços,* were for the most part ignorant and superstitious, thinking mainly of miracles, calamities, disease, and the ecstasies or horrors of Divine approval and punishment, and consuming much of their time in funerals, love-making, and religious parades. Viceroy Lavradio re-marked that his subjects were "devoid of education, licentious in char-acter," and British travelers were shocked at the lack of scientific ap-preciation.

Nevertheless, Brazilians had already produced history and literature worthy of notice as well as architecture, sculpture, and painting of some merit, and there were signs of awakening shortly before 1800. Some of the colonials had graduated from the Portuguese university at Coimbra and had even made contributions to the cultural life of the mother country. Others had written letters or chronicles describing conditions in the colony, and still others had produced fairly good poetry inspired by Brazilian life, landscapes, and history.[7] An outstanding characteristic of this literature was the love of the colonials for their native land. For example, a work published by the historian Rocha Pitta in 1730 contained this affectionate tribute: "In no other region is the sky more serene, nor does dawn glow more beautifully; in no other hemisphere does the sun flaunt such golden rays . . . ; the stars are more benign and ever joyful . . . ; Brazil, in short, is the Terrestrial Paradise discovered at last, wherein the vastest rivers arise and take their course." [8]

Moreover, toward the end of the century, Brazil began to be aroused by the new political ideas that were stirring Europe. Foreign travelers of the period took note of the fact that the "more opulent" inhabitants of Rio and Bahía were decorating homes with French engravings illustrating the exploits of French generals and acquiring the writings of French philosophes and scientists for their libraries. They might also have observed that some of the inhabitants of the colony were reading the state papers of the United States and drawing inspiration from the example of the famous Thirteen Colonies. At least one Brazilian was engaged in correspondence with Thomas Jefferson; and as early as 1789, José Joaquím da Silva Xavier (better known as *"Tiradentes,"* or "The Toothpuller"), with others of like mind, had vainly planned to set up a republic in which there should be no slaves, no monopolies, and no restrictions upon thought and industry. The plan failed because it was premature. The "conspirators" were captured and severely punished. But Brazil, like Spanish America, was now at the dawn of a new epoch.

CHAPTER IX

Beginning of the Struggle
for Self-Government

With the opening of the nineteenth century Spanish America entered the second epic period of its history. After the almost two centuries of comparative repose which followed the epoch of conquest, the heroic energy of the race exerted itself anew in a long but successful struggle for self-government and independence. Portuguese America effected its separation from the mother country through the aid of a happy accident which made possible an almost bloodless transition; but the inhabitants of the French part of Española, actually the first of the Latin Americans to break away from Europe, achieved a twofold emancipation only by means of a terrible war that passed through three phases: an armed protest of mulattoes against racial discrimination; a murderous insurrection of Negro slaves; and a combined revolt of mulattoes and Negroes against French rule.

The emancipation of the vast region extending from California, New Mexico, Texas, and the Floridas to Chile, the Río de la Plata countries, and Brazil, was an event of major importance in modern history. It was a great triumph of nationalism and republicanism, accompanied and followed by halting and hesitant advances toward individual liberty and equality of rights. It opened up an immense area to greater freedom of trade and more vigorous enterprise. It gave England, France, the United States, and all the non-Hispanic world fuller access to Latin-American resources.

CAUSES AND CHARACTER OF THE CONFLICT

New and dynamic ideas were a major cause of the demand for colonial autonomy that soon widened into a demand for complete independence. It was a phase of mankind's eternal struggle against despotism, which, in modern times, began in seventeenth-century England, found expression in the revolt of the thirteen English colonies, enacted the bloody tragedy of the French Revolution, and horrified the ruling classes of Western Europe. In the course of these bitter conflicts between peoples and governments, potent political ideals were born or reborn and given irresistible literary expression. Popular sovereignty; equality before the law; freedom of the individual to express his views, to worship as he pleases, and to choose his profession—all these and more were summed up in the articles of a new faith briefly entitled "Natural Rights" or the "Rights of Man." First adopted, though not in full measure, in the United States, these ideals seeped into the intolerant and decadent Iberian countries and infiltrated the jealously isolated Latin colonies in America, where they became a powerful spiritual force in their struggle for emancipation.

Before they appropriated these new ideals, and even before the ideals were fully formulated, the inhabitants of the colonies had keenly felt and deeply resented the heavy burdens and galling restrictions imposed upon them. Now that they had envisaged an unfettered and more just political and social order, such burdens and irritations as taxes, tithes, royal fifths, tributes, monopolies, confiscations, prohibitions, discriminations, censorship, and slavery appeared to be enormous grievances no longer sufferable. The sustaining force that drove the liberation movement to its successful termination was this vision of a new regime which had already begun to change the face of the modern world. Without it, the insurgents might not have initiated their rebellion at the very time when, with the exception of French Saint-Domingue, they were actually somewhat less oppressed than in earlier years.

Moreover, Europe's strife and the sympathetic attitude of the United States tended to convince them that the opportune occasion for drastic action had arrived. Spain's rivals were promising assistance. Aid from the United States did not appear impossible. The commercial policies of London and Washington seemed favorable. Napoleon's conquering legions had prostrated Spain and Portugal. If the colonials had not vacillated and fumbled, they might have won their independence at once. Defeated by 1816 almost everywhere save in Española and La Plata, they soon renewed their struggle in more favorable circumstances; and with the assistance of foreign merchants, privateers, seamen, and soldiers of fortune, they confronted an enemy debilitated by war and domestic discord and finally achieved their objective. "From 1808 to 1825," as Francisco García Calderón has so aptly written of the Spanish colonies, "all things conspired to help the cause of American liberty; the revolutions in Europe, ministers in England, the independence of the United States, the excesses of Spanish absolutism, the constitutional doctrines of Cádiz, the romantic faith of the Liberators, the political ambitions of the oligarchies, the ideas of Rousseau and the Encyclopedists, the decadence of Spain, and the hatred which all classes and castes in America entertained for the inquisitors and the viceroys." [1]

The war for Spanish American emancipation was similar in many respects to the Spanish Conquest. The conquest was the result of individual initiative and individual efforts rather than of the organized plans and endeavors of the state. Inspired by a mystical faith and a desire to seize a new world for Spain, the Roman Catholic Church, and themselves, the Conquerors displayed unflagging optimism, heroic will, and tenacious ambition in face of tremendous obstacles.

The same traits characterized the great leaders of the movement for autonomy and independence. Corresponding to Cortés, Pizarro, Quesada, Balboa, Alvarado, Benalcázar, and Valdivia, were Bolívar, San Martín, Sucre, Páez, Hidalgo, Morelos, and Guerrero, whose vigorous actions announced that the Spanish race had not exhausted its vital force. They exhibited a full measure of individual initiative. San Martín conceived a plan of his own; raised an army largely by his own efforts; sometimes disobeyed the orders of the Buenos Aires government; and not only liberated Chile but invaded Peru and proclaimed its independence. Bolívar defied civil authorities, devised his own military plans, violated accepted rules of military strategy, and pressed forward victoriously toward his goal. The leaders of the early nineteenth century were inspired by nationalism and a vision of the destiny of America even as the Conquerors had been inspired by patriotism, the Catholic faith, and the desire for glory and gold. Convinced of his providential mission, Bolívar fought under the auspices of the god of Great Colombia and made prophetic pronouncements regarding America's future. San Martín explained his disobedience by declaring that his destiny called him to Lima. Nor were the Liberators inferior to the Conquerors in heroic will. "They had the same audacity, the same courage, the same constancy. When all seemed lost, they retained the same faith, and started to work again. They fought against primitive forces, against nature, against primitive men." [2]

Compared with the revolution of the thirteen English colonies, the Spanish American Wars of Independence reveal more points of contrast than of similarity. Both were propelled by similar ideals and both owed their success largely to a group of remarkable leaders who seized advantage of Europe's distresses. Both were likewise civil wars; for if a third of the people of the English colonies were loyalists, fully as many in Spanish America supported the cause of the mother country, and in both instances the loyal elements were composed largely of official and mercantile classes and their satellites, although in Spanish America not a few Indians and mestizos remained for a time faithful to their monarch in Madrid and his political and ecclesiastical agents in the Indies. Here, however, the contrast begins. The insurgent colonials of Spanish America found few sympathizers in Spain, but the thirteen English colonies had many in England. Military operations in Spanish America extended over a much wider area, confronted far greater hazards of disease and topography, lasted three times as long, and cost far more both in money and lives. Finally, the Spanish Americans received no official financial or military aid from Spain's rivals, effected no more than an ephemeral unity in the course of the conflict, and failed to wrest immediate recognition of their independence from the defeated metropolis.

❦ THE "PRECURSORS"

Although several of the leaders of the successful movement for independence were undoubtedly influenced by the example of the United States, it would be an error to deny originality of conception to the colonials of the South, for some of them dreamed of independence long before the idea occurred to their Anglo-Saxon neighbors of the North. Revolts against oppression, or against policies that were resented, occurred from time to time throughout the Colonial period in both Spanish and Portuguese America. Most of them were led by creole whites; a few were headed by Indians, Negroes, or mulattoes. Several expressed a vague desire for independence; others merely demanded reforms. All were suppressed, most of them with brutal severity.

The uprisings became more frequent during the last century of the Colonial period. José Antequera, the rebellious governor of Paraguay, and his *Comuneros* talked of the "sovereignty of the people" as early as 1725. For a period of ten years, 1740–50, the residents of various Peruvian towns entertained the idea of proclaiming the Inca Felipe "King of the Seas of the North and South," by which they seemed to mean monarch of all Spanish South America, since they were in communication with centers of conspiracy in New Granada, Venezuela, Chile, and La Plata. During the same decade, dissatisfied subjects of New Spain were dreaming of founding an independent kingdom under a prince of the House of Austria. In 1765, insurgents in Quito talked of expelling the Spaniards and placing a crown upon the head of Count Vega Florida. In 1780, three emancipatory movements were under way in Spanish America: one in Chile, centering around a mysterious Spaniard named Don Juan, which hoped to receive assistance from

England and planned a constitutional monarchy to govern a region extending from the equator to Patagonia; another with centers in Caracas and Bogotá; and a third in Peru, under the leadership of none other than the Inca Tupac Amarú. The year 1781 witnessed the revolt of the *Comuneros* of New Granada and uncovered a conspiracy, headed by Antonio Rojas and two Frenchmen, to liberate Chile. Three years later, representatives of aspiring emancipators in both New Spain and New Granada arrived in London to solicit arms and munitions in exchange for advantageous treaties of commerce.

No wonder that members of the Madrid government became alarmed! As early as 1783, Count Aranda advised Charles III to establish Spanish princes upon thrones in Mexico, Peru, and Costa Firme (northern South America),[3] reserving for himself Cuba, Puerto Rico, and certain trading stations, and urged him to assume the title of Emperor. Aranda proposed to bind the three kingdoms together and to Spain by means of family compacts and treaties of alliance and commerce. If such a project had been adopted, and if the American monarchs had been willing to promulgate constitutions and set up parliaments, as Manuel Godoy is said to have suggested later (1804), the history of Spanish America might have been far different. But the stubborn Bourbons were committed to the dogma of popular repression, and propaganda and conspiracies continued.

In 1794, Antonio Nariño published a Spanish translation of the French Declaration of the Rights of Man and began to make his home in Bogotá a meeting place for intellectuals who liked to discuss the new political and social ideas. He was soon imprisoned and sent into exile, but he lived to see his country freed from the Spanish yoke before he died there in 1823. And while Nariño and his companions were reading French literature of reform, José María España and his associates were hatching a revolt in Venezuela, which ended in his capture and execution in 1797.

By 1806, Francisco de Miranda, who had been dreaming of independence for all Spanish America since the early 1780's and organizing secret societies and soliciting foreign aid since 1790, had decided that Venezuela was ripe for emancipation. But the "Immortals" who sailed with him from New York soon made the tragic discovery that their effort was premature, and several of them paid dearly for their rashness in the pestilential dungeons of Caracas and La Guaira. The majority of the Venezuelans were still loyal.

This seems also to have been true of the inhabitants of Río de la Plata in 1806–7. At any rate, they resisted British conquest. Yet the very act and manner of expelling the English troops aroused a sentiment of nationalism, while the cheap goods introduced during the English occupation created a longing for a freer commercial regime.

Meanwhile Brazil was having its insurrections and conspiracies and the first successful revolt in Latin America had occurred in French Saint-Domingue (Española). From time to time, Negro slaves escaped into the wild country back of the Brazilian coast and set up independent communities of their own. The most famous of these was Palmares, in the captaincy of Alagoas, which contained some 20,000 Negroes, defended itself for more than a quarter of a century, and was not finally destroyed until 1697. A few years earlier, in the 1680's, Manoel Beckman had led an insurrection against a monopolistic commercial company in Maranhão. José da Silva Xavier's conspiracy in Minas Geraes, exposed in 1789, has already been mentioned. Both of these Brazilian leaders were executed by the colonial authorities.

The mulattoes and Negroes of western Española, inspired by the radical ideas of the French Revolution and exasperated by racial discrimination and slavery, began their revolt in 1790. Taking advantage of tumult and war in France and Europe, the colored leaders—Toussaint L'Ouverture, Jean Jacques Dessalines, Henri Christophe, and Alexandre Pétion—succeeded in driving the French rulers from the whole island (Spain had ceded the rest of it, the larger eastern portion, to France in 1795) by the end of 1803, and on January 1, 1804, they proclaimed the independence of a new state called Haiti. (The people of the eastern region, which was later to become the Dominican Republic, were restive, however, under Negro domination.) L'Ouverture died in a French prison. The other three warriors, under the title of king, emperor, or president, became the rulers of the people they had emancipated. Dessalines was eventually chosen as the paramount hero of Haiti.

POLITICAL CONDITIONS IN SPAIN

Political disturbances in Spain, disorders which began in 1808 and continued for fifteen years, profoundly influenced the fate of her American colonies. The Franco-Spanish Treaty of Basel (1795), which had ceded to France the eastern two-thirds of Española, indicated that Spain's destiny was still to be linked with France, despite the overthrow of the French Bourbons. The Franco-Spanish alliance of 1796 and subsequent agreements led to the destruction of the Spanish Navy and the loss of Trinidad to England in 1797 and of Louisiana to France in 1800. Eight years later, Napoleon invaded the Spanish peninsula, captured the

Bourbons, forced them to abdicate, thrust his brother Joseph Bonaparte upon the Spanish throne, and dispatched agents to the Spanish colonies.

These aggressive measures provoked an outburst of Spanish nationalism. Provincial juntas (committees) sprang up in all of Spain's leading towns, and in September, 1808, a Supreme Central Junta was organized in Madrid. Soon afterward, however, it fled to Seville and then to the isle of León, where it called into existence a Council of the Regency and dissolved. The Regency, in turn, called together a Cortes, which first assembled in León and then in Cádiz. Meanwhile the British government, which had resolved that the "Little Corsican" should not be allowed to seize Spanish America in addition to Spain, now decided that he should not be permitted to control either, and sent to the Peninsula the troops that had been mobilized for operation in the Spanish colonies.

Miranda, who had returned to London after his Venezuelan fiasco of 1806, was deeply disappointed; but the cause to which he was devoted was not so desperate as it seemed. The stirring events of the period were arousing some of his compatriots to full political consciousness and a sense of their growing importance in world affairs. Thrilled by the rebellion of the Spaniards against the Corsican tyrant, they prepared to defend themselves against French conquest, and hoped to increase their political influence in the process. The doctrine of residuary sovereignty upon which the provisional governments of Spain based their action could be used by colonial leaders to justify colonial autonomy during this critical period. In the absence of the Spanish king, sovereignty resided in the Spanish people, but it did not extend to the colonies because the colonies belonged to the crown and not to the Spanish nation. Sovereignty in Spanish America should therefore be exercised by the colonies themselves until the king returned to his throne. Such was the argument of the Colonial leaders.

For a time, the Spanish insurgent governments seemed to acquiesce. The Central Junta declared in 1809 that the Americans had the same rights as Spaniards, including the right to send deputies to the Central Junta and the Cortes. The Regency, in convoking a meeting of the Cortes at Cádiz in 1810, went even further, and sent out these stirring words: "You are elevated to the dignity of free men. You are no longer in the same condition as you were before: bent under the yoke of tyranny more oppressive because you are farther from the center of power; looked upon with indifference, harassed by greed, and ruined by ignorance. . . . Your destinies now no longer depend either upon ministers, or viceroys and governors. They are in your own hands." Nobody in the colonies had uttered more revolutionary language. But the

Regency, although then in desperate straits for funds, may not have been entirely hypocritical. It was not long, however, until it changed its mind.

Twenty-six colonial deputies participated in the sessions of the Cortes of Cádiz, which was a notably liberal assembly. It proclaimed freedom of the press, abolished sales taxes and Indian tributes, removed the fetters from colonial industry, and resolved that the colonials should be admitted to public employment on terms of equality with the Spaniards. Moreover, the constitution which the Cortes promulgated for Spain and her empire early in 1812 incorporated all of these liberal principles, and the Spanish Inquisition was abolished the next year. The ideals of the political philosophers had invaded Spain.

But the colonies had not been given adequate representation in the Cortes, the obstinate Council of the Regency finally insisted upon the absolute authority of Spain in America, and as the European allies rolled back Napoleon's armies, the forces of Spanish conservatism took control again. When Ferdinand VII returned to his throne in 1814, after Napoleon had been sent into exile, he fell into the hands of the reactionaries and declared null and void both the Constitution of 1812 and the legislation of the Cortes. It was not until 1820 that the Spanish Liberals regained power and compelled Ferdinand to accept their favorite fundamental law; and, even then, their control was only temporary, for France invaded the Peninsula in 1823 in support of the Spanish king and the old regime. The reaction that followed the triumph of the absolutists was even more violent than in 1814; and political conditions were soon further complicated by intrigues for the succession, which eventually led to the Carlist wars. Such, in brief, was the turbulent history of Spain during the period when her overseas colonies were fighting for autonomy, independence, and recognition as sovereign nations.

FAILURE OF THE EARLY STRIVINGS FOR SELF-GOVERNMENT

The struggle for emancipation in Spanish America falls into two periods separated by the year 1816. The first was characterized by failure almost everywhere save in Río de la Plata and the second by slowly increasing success until complete separation from the mother country was finally achieved (1825).

Although Napoleon's invasion of Spain in 1808 caused a general ferment in the colonies, the colonial leaders, mostly creoles, were at first hesitant regarding the course they should take. At the outset, the creoles and sometimes a few Spaniards met in the town councils and in provisional juntas, protested against the imposition of Joseph Bonaparte as king of Spain, refused to receive his agents, and while preparing to set up more responsible governments, declared their loyalty to Ferdinand and sent funds to the Spanish nationalists. In view of the activities of the "Precursors," it is difficult to believe that all of their protestations of loyalty were sincere. Yet their very avowals reveal the presumed strength of royalist sentiment, and Pan-Hispanic nationalism was undoubtedly fomented by events in the Peninsula. A little later, when it appeared that Napoleon had completely subjugated Spain, some of the colonies proceeded to declare independence, alleging that the step was necessary in order to avoid French domination. Others deferred action until the restored Ferdinand left them no hope of securing larger liberties under Spain. Little could be done in Peru because of the strength of the viceroy, José Fernando Abascal, and the presence of Spanish troops cowed Cuba and Puerto Rico.

A rapid survey of disturbances in the major colonial centers seems advisable for purposes of review and clarification.

The *audiencia* of Charcas, since 1776 part of the viceroyalty of Río de la Plata, was among the first to reveal insurgent tendencies during this period. On May 25, 1809, some of the inhabitants of Chuquisaca deposed the *audiencia's* president and set up a governmental junta composed of creoles. In the following July, an insurrection in La Paz overthrew the intendant, created a "Protective Junta," and proclaimed loyalty to Ferdinand, although it is likely that the objective of the rebels was independence. Under their leader, Pedro Murillo, they waged a brief but unsuccessful war against troops sent from Lima and Buenos Aires. At the time of his execution, Murillo is said to have exclaimed: "I die; but no one will be able to extinguish the torch I have lighted."

The president of the *audiencia* of Quito was deposed and imprisoned in August, 1809, by a group of colonials who then set up a "supreme junta" with the Marquis of Selva Alegre as presiding officer. The titles assumed by the new government further revealed its aristocratic tendencies: Selva Alegre was called "Most Serene Highness" and the title of "Excellency" was claimed by the members of the junta. A senate displaced the *audiencia,* and secretaries of foreign relations, war, and justice were created; but the government proposed to exercise its authority in the name of Ferdinand. Selva Alegre and his accomplices were deposed a year later by royal forces from the viceroyalty of New Granada and the ringleaders were pitilessly executed. The colony then remained quiet until the arrival of General José Antonio de Sucre in 1821.

In the center of the Plata Viceroyalty, the new era dimly forecast by the expulsion of the British troops in 1807 had its dawn in 1810. The viceroy had revealed craven inefficiency during the British invasion, and the colonists had accordingly chosen in his stead Jacques Liniers, an experienced French military officer who had led them to victory over the intruders. In 1809, however, a royalist uprising gained the upper hand and demanded his resignation, and Liniers was soon replaced by a new viceroy appointed by the Spanish Central Junta. In May, 1810, when news arrived in Buenos Aires to the effect that Spanish resistance to Napoleon had almost collapsed, this viceroy was in turn deposed and a "Provisional Junta of the Provinces of the Plata River" organized. The entire region, excepting Charcas (eventually called Bolivia), was soon freed from Spain's control.

The new government at Buenos Aires, weakened by divided counsels, was not able, however, to extend its authority over the provinces. Expeditions sent to Paraguay failed to win over that section; its inhabitants set up their own "governmental junta" in Asunción, declared their independence from Spain in 1811, and made a similar declaration with reference to Buenos Aires in 1813. The inhabitants of Banda Oriental (later Uruguay), under the redoubtable José Gervasio Artigas, at first remained loyal to the Buenos Aires junta, but later broke away, only to fall under the temporary domination of Brazil; Artigas himself was forced to seek refuge in Paraguay (1820). Few delegates from Charcas, and none from Banda Oriental or Paraguay, were among those who assembled at Tucumán in 1816 and declared the independence of the "United Provinces." Moreover, the region continued to be menaced by invasions from Charcas and Peru. In fact, it could have no security until the royalists were driven from the Peruvian Viceroyalty.

This was fortunately realized by José de San Martín, a native of the Plata Viceroyalty who had returned in 1812, after fighting for a time in the Peninsular War, to cast his lot with the insurgents, as well as by Martín de Pueyrredón, the "Supreme Director" at Buenos Aires, who appointed San Martín governor-intendant of the interior province of Cuyo in 1814 with authority to train an army for the invasion of Peru through Chile. San Martín's busy operations in Cuyo and the Tucumán commitment were the most hopeful aspects of patriotic effort in southeastern South America as the year 1816 drew to a close.

In the captaincy general of Venezuela, the colonials began to stir within two years after Miranda's unsuccessful expedition of 1806. Excited by news from Spain, the *cabildo* of Caracas in July, 1808, declared that Ferdinand was the legal king of Spain and the Indies, but suggested that a provisional administrative junta should be established in the capital. Almost another two years passed, however, before any radical steps were taken. Then, on April 19, 1810, an open *cabildo* in

VICEROYALTY OF NEW SPAIN

Calderon× ⊙Mexico

Havana Captaincy General of Cuba

Captaincy General of Guatemala

Guatemala

VICEROYALTY OF NEW GRANADA

Carabobo× ⊙Caracas

Captaincy General of Caracas

GUIANA

Audiencia of Santa Fé
Bogota⊙ ×Boyacá

Quito⊙ Presidency of Quito
×Pichincha

BRAZIL
(Portuguese)

VICEROYALTY

Junin×

Lima⊙ ×Ayacucho

Presidency of Charcas

OF

Chuquisaca ⊙×

VICEROYALTY OF BUENOS AIRES OR LA PLATA

PERU

Rio de Janeiro⊙

Chacabuco×
Santiago⊙
×Maipú

San Lorenzo×

Buenos Aires⊙

Captaincy General and Presidency of Chile

Audiencia of Buenos Aires

Spanish America
during the Wars
for Independence
1810~25
⊙ Capitals × Battlefields

Showing Approximately the Political Divisions in 1808

MAP 8

Caracas, in which a number of leading creoles participated, deposed the captain general; created a junta while still professing loyalty to Ferdinand, and shortly afterward deported the captain general; established administrative bureaus; disavowed the Spanish Regency; directed a proclamation to other Spanish Americans asserting Venezuela's claim to a place in the rank of free nations; and issued an address to the municipal governments of the colonial capitals of South America urging them to join the movement for self-government.

Encouraged by the activities of his compatriots, Miranda returned to his native land in December, 1810, and Simón Bolívar, who had been sent by the Caracas junta to London as a member of a diplomatic mission, appeared in the capital a few days later. The champions of a vigorous policy had arrived. A general congress installed early in 1811 proclaimed the independence of the "United Provinces" of Venezuela on July 5. The next step was the drafting of a constitution, which was modeled after the Constitution of the United States but also influenced by the French Declaration of the Rights of Man. Threatened immediately by loyalist troops under the command of Domingo de Monteverde, the insurgents endowed Miranda with dictatorial power and placed him in charge of the revolutionary forces, with young Bolívar as one of his lieutenants. A desperate conflict ensued, in which the patriots managed to avoid defeat until an ill-timed earthquake destroyed their morale. The settlements in control of the rebels were almost annihilated, while those remaining faithful to the king escaped unharmed. The clergy declared that the earthquake was an unmistakable intervention of Providence; the superstitious elements withdrew from the insurgents; and Miranda was forced to sign a humiliating capitulation on July 25, 1812. Disgruntled patriots, Bolívar among them, later arrested their supreme chief and allowed him to fall into the hands of the Spaniards, who sent him as prisoner to Cádiz, where he died in 1816.

Bolívar escaped to New Granada but returned with a small army in August, 1813, regained Caracas, and won the title of "Liberator," which was conferred upon him by an extraordinary *cabildo* in that city. The "war to the death," proclaimed by that skilful and energetic commander in the previous June, was by no means over, however. Creoles, mestizos, emancipated Negroes, and Indians under Bolívar fought Spaniards, *llanero* Indians, and not a few creoles and mestizos under royalist commanders, among them a fierce Spaniard named José Tomás Boves, and neither side gave quarter or showed any mercy. By the end of the year 1814, however, the Venezuelan rebellion had once more been suppressed everywhere save in the island of Margarita. Bolívar fled to Cartagena and then to Jamaica, and remained in exile for two years.

At Bogotá, capital of the viceroyalty of New Granada, the town council avowed loyalty to Ferdinand VII in the summer of 1808; but when the viceroy called together an advisory junta in 1809 for the purpose of planning the suppression of the insurgents in Quito, the junta evinced dissatisfaction with Spanish rule and delegated Camilo Torres to frame a memorial of grievances to be transmitted to the Central Junta in Spain. The document drafted by Torres complained of discrimination against the creoles and included a threat of separation from the mother country. On July 20, 1810, an enlarged *cabildo* created a junta for the entire viceroyalty, named the viceroy as president of the new government, and reiterated its devotion to Ferdinand, an avowal which the junta repeated a few weeks later when it banished this high official and broke with the Spanish Regency.

Most of the leading towns of New Granada followed a similar course. The *cabildos,* professing loyalty to the captive king, deposed the Spanish authorities and created provincial juntas. Some of the provinces—Cartagena in November, 1811, and Cundinamarca in July, 1813—went so far as to declare independence, and nearly all framed constitutions. Unfortunately, however, they revealed no decided disposition to submit to the rule of any central government. With the hope of effecting a larger measure of unification, an "Act of Federation" had been drawn up and ratified by several of the provinces, but the government established in accordance with its terms was unable to assert its authority, and sectionalism ran riot. Instead of preparing for defense against the Spaniards and loyalists, the various regional governments quarreled and fought among themselves. Bolívar, who had marched under the banner of Cartagena in 1812–13, was later employed by the Congress of the Federation to help subdue the provinces of Cundinamarca, Cartagena, and Santa Marta. He soon conquered the first and thus enabled the general government to return from Tunja to Bogotá; but while he was besieging Cartagena and hoping to secure arms for the campaign against Santa Marta, General Pablo Murillo landed in Venezuela with a Spanish army of 10,000 men. Realizing that the chaos was beyond remedy, Bolívar abandoned this *Patria Boba* ("Foolish Fatherland") and sailed for Jamaica. Murillo, leaving half of his troops in Venezuela, captured Cartagena after a long siege and then sent his detachments into various parts of the interior, where they crushed the insurgents with terrible severity. Bogotá was occupied in May, 1816, and subjected to a reign of terror.

Meanwhile the Chileans had failed in their first effort to achieve a larger participation in the colonial government. Proclaiming their fidelity to the captive Ferdinand, they deposed the captain general in September, 1810. Calling together a general congress in Santiago the next year, they repeated their pledge of loyalty and further bound themselves to support a constitutional regime.

But the delegates soon discovered that they were hopelessly divided. Some favored independence under a republic; others opposed drastic reforms that would mean a definite rupture with the metropolis; a few urged a return to the old form of government. The more radical members soon withdrew from the congress, and the remaining deputies then set themselves up as the "Executive Power," but were overthrown a few weeks later by José Miguel Carrera, a Chilean army officer recently returned from the Spanish war against Napoleon, who ambiguously sanctioned a republican constitution and at the same time announced his fidelity to Ferdinand. Since most of his followers were radicals, there is little doubt that his goal was independence. The constitution vested authority in a junta of three members controlled by Carrera, and he and his two brothers proceeded to rule the country with stern decrees. Their action provoked Bernardo O'Higgins—himself a radical and the talented son of an Irishman with a distinguished record in the Spanish colonial service—into open opposition, and subsequent dissensions furnished the able Peruvian viceroy a favorable opportunity to smother the revolt. Although the forces of O'Higgins and Carrera eventually united, the revolutionary army was severely defeated. Santiago was captured in October, 1814, and the colonial government reinstated. Frightful reprisals were visited upon some of the insurgents; others managed to escape over the Andes to Argentina.

The captaincy general of Guatemala remained tranquil until November, 1811, when an uprising in San Salvador deposed an intendant. Among the insurgents were the priest José Matías Delgado, the friar Nicolás Aguilar, and Manuel José Arce. The movement was promptly suppressed, but with less cruelty than usual. Arce lived to become a prominent Central American politician and Delgado was finally selected as El Salvador's number-one hero. A more vigorous insurrection broke out in León, Nicaragua, in the following December, when the rebels overthrew another intendant, seized the town of Granada, and enlisted an army of 1,000 men. After an encounter with troops sent from Guatemala City by the captain general, they were induced to surrender by the promise of a general pardon, but the promise was broken and a number of them served long terms in prison. Two years later, an alleged conspiracy was discovered in a convent of Guatemala City, and its ringleaders were also compelled to pay the penalty of lingering imprisonment. A second uprising, led by Arce and Juan Manuel Rodríguez, took place in San Salvador in 1814; but it was no more successful than the first, and there were no further disturbances of consequence until 1821.

Although the Negroes and mulattoes of Haiti managed to preserve their independence, the creole and African inhabitants of the eastern section of Española were conquered by Spanish soldiers between 1806 and 1814. Incited by Anglo-Saxon immigrants, an uprising occurred in West Florida, then a part of the captaincy general of Cuba, in 1810, and a segment of the province was soon occupied by troops and revenue officials from the United States. Cuba and Puerto Rico, the main centers of the captaincy general, remained quiescent. Strong divisions from Spain compelled them to await a more favorable occasion.

Peru, as already suggested, was firmly controlled during this period by Viceroy Abascal, who ferreted out conspiracies, quickly repressed all attempts at revolt, and even sent military detachments into Charcas and Chile. The inhabitants of the Peruvian Viceroyalty had no prospect of liberation until the arrival of San Martín and Bolívar in the early 1820's.

New Spain, like Venezuela, New Granada, and Chile, was the scene of bloody combat. As elsewhere, news from Spain caused the creoles of the viceroyalty to aspire to a larger participation in the government. The incumbent viceroy, hoping to profit by catering to the creoles, and perhaps even dreaming of becoming Mexico's first king if Napoleon completely subjugated Spain, favored the creation of a general junta elected by the municipal *cabildos* of his entire kingdom. The *audiencia,* filled with Spaniards, feared and distrusted the native elements; and although unable to forestall the formation of a general junta in August, 1808, it succeeded in having the viceroy expelled from the country a month later. Four viceroys then came and went in rapid succession (1808–13). Amid the confusion, revolutionary propaganda spread by secret societies increased the longing for self-government, Valladolid became the center of an abortive revolt, and a few bold leaders determined to inaugurate a new regime.

One of them, Miguel Hidalgo y Costilla, a learned priest with a decided fondness for French political philosophy and a deep interest in the Indian masses, seems to have been uncertain about his ultimate objectives. Perhaps his goal was independence and his avowals of fidelity to Ferdinand were no more sincere than the protestations of many others. Unlike most of them, however, he was thoroughly devoted to those at the bottom of the social order. His standard, emblazoned with a portrait of the Virgin of Guadalupe, much venerated by those whose welfare he had at heart, attracted not only a multitude of Indians and mestizos but a considerable number of creoles as well. They were unconcerned with distant goals; what they desired was immediate freedom from oppression and better economic conditions. Starting from the village of Dolores in the intendancy of Guanajuato on September 16, 1810, with 4,000 untrained followers, Hidalgo began a zigzag advance toward the viceregal capital. Town after town—San Miguel, Celaya, Guanajuato, Guadalajara, Valladolid—fell at the onslaught of his ever-increasing hordes, who slew and pillaged almost without restraint. Near the end of October, he encamped with an undisciplined multitude within eighteen miles of Mexico City. So far, he had had only one serious encounter with the viceregal troops, and in that encounter his forces had held the field. He might have taken the capital if he had pressed on. But he hesitated and then withdrew to Guadalajara, perhaps distrusting the prowess of his army or recoiling from the prospect of murder and destruction which his followers might have inflicted upon the city.

Whatever its cause, the delay proved fatal. It gave the commander of the viceregal forces time to assemble his troops and take the offensive. On January 17, 1811, the insurgents, numbering around 80,000 and the royalists, only 6,000 strong—although some were soldiers seasoned by the Peninsular War—confronted each other on the banks of the Lerma River, forty miles from Guadalajara; and the royalists were all but defeated when an explosion set fire to a grass field occupied by the main body of Hidalgo's army. Stampeded by the smoke and flames, the rebels broke ranks and fled, pursued by the enemy, who perpetrated a horrible butchery. Hidalgo and his lieutenants were soon captured and executed. The heads of four of them were hung in cages at the four corners of the granary which they had recently taken by assault in Guanajuato.

The mantle of Hidalgo fell upon José María Morelos, a humble priest of mixed Spanish and Indian or Negro blood whose political ideas and purposes were fairly definite. He wished to abolish slavery, torture of prisoners, monopolies, and sales taxes. He believed in the sovereignty of the people and therefore that only Mexicans should govern New Spain.

For more than four years after Hidalgo's death, Morelos carried on the war against the Spanish colonial authorities and the Mexican loyalists. At one time, he had control of a large part of southern New Spain, including a section on both coasts. A congress which he installed at Chilpancingo issued a declaration of independence on November 6, 1813, and in later sessions at Apatzingán, promulgated Mexico's first constitution (October 22, 1814). But Morelos' star was already on the decline. Compelled to migrate from place to place with his government, he was finally captured in November, 1815, and shot to death soon afterward. The flame lighted by Hidalgo was now burning very low. Only a few guerrillas, Vicente Guerrero among them, were guided by it as they continued the struggle in the mountains to the south of Mexico City.

Such were the tragic failures of the early movement for self-government in Spanish America. They have been recounted, perhaps in tedious detail, in order to show the procedures, vacillations, confused ideas, and problems of inexperienced peoples striving to emancipate themselves from tyranny and exploitation. Spanish and loyalist arms had triumphed almost everywhere. But looking through history's perspective, one might discover lights as well as shadows. Napoleon in St. Helena, absolutism enthroned in Europe, trained Spanish soldiers free to fight in America; but the treasury of devastated Spain empty, British warriors seeking employment in colonial armies and navies, English and United States merchants and privateers looking for markets and spoils, nationalism and republicanism ready to become rampant, Bolívar in Margarita, San Martín in Cuyo, Guerrero in the Mexican *Sierra del Sur,* and Agustín de Iturbide, formerly an implacable foe of Mexican insurgents, now "sulking like Achilles in his tent"—all these elements were in Fate's balances at the end of the year 1816. Time would soon tip the beam in favor of the Spanish colonies; and Portuguese Brazil, now the refuge of the Braganzas who had fled from Europe's strife, would shortly make use of one of the royal princes to gain its independence.

CHAPTER X

The Winning of Independence

🎼 FROM FAILURE TO SUCCESS

Why did the Spanish colonies fail in their struggle for self-government during the eight years preceding 1817 and succeed during the eight years immediately following? The answer is simple.

In the earlier period both the leaders and the people were confused and divided. Some desired one thing and some desired another. Many had different objectives at different times, or never knew exactly what they wanted. The revolutionary armies were untrained, inexperienced, poorly equipped, and sometimes betrayed by colonial loyalists. Almost no assistance was received from the outside before Spain sent to America a part of the seasoned army which had been fighting the French invaders of the Peninsula.

In the later period most of the colonial leaders knew precisely what they wanted. Their firm purpose was to win independence. The insurgent forces were much better trained and equipped during the later years, partly as the result of increasing revenues and assistance from abroad: tariffs on expanding foreign trade brought in larger funds; foreign credits and loans; weapons from overseas surpluses; foreign officers and soldiers; foreign sailors and privateers who helped to give the colonials control of the adjacent seas. The Napoleonic Wars were over and the war between the United States and England had terminated. Military equipment could be purchased for cash at bargain prices, or on credit eagerly granted by speculators. The people of Europe and the United States, especially the military and merchant adventurers and the evangels of liberty, could give more attention to Spanish America. Finally, the movement for independence was now championed by more capable commanders. Most of them had suffered defeat, exile, and loss of fortune; but those who survived had profited from their failures and developed their military talents to full maturity.

✸ SAN MARTÍN AND THE EMANCIPATION OF CHILE

It will be recalled that José de San Martín had been appointed (1814) governor of Cuyo, a Río de la Plata province nestling against the Andes, with authority to recruit and train an army for the invasion of Chile. Establishing his headquarters at Mendoza, he soon displayed his genius as an organizer. Born in 1778 in the mission territory of northeastern La Plata, he was only thirty-six when he began his task, but he had been in military service for two decades and he had inherited a military tradition. His father had served in the militia of the viceroyalty and his mother was the daughter of a distinguished soldier who had fought the Indians of the northern wilderness called the Gran Chaco. Taken to Spain by his parents, José had enlisted in the Spanish army at an early age and had fought against the Moors in North Africa, in wars against England and Portugal, and in the Peninsular War. In short, San Martín was already an experienced soldier and a careful student of military affairs when he returned to the land of his birth in 1812 and began the two years of warfare against the royalists that convinced him of the futility of the overland approach to Peru.

In spite of rheumatism and other maladies, he set to work patiently and systematically. Tall, erect, with earnest brown eyes, a Roman nose, and heavy locks of wavy dark hair, he was an extraordinarily handsome man, and his impeccable morality and granite-like character soon won the confidence, if not the affection, of the people of Cuyo, who supported him loyally, contributing horses, supplies, and labor, and joining the ranks under his command. His funds were inadequate, but local taxes and contributions supplemented the appropriations voted by the rapidly shifting governments at Buenos Aires; and the women of Cuyo, San Martín's bride taking the lead, cheerfully gave their jewelry to the cause. Guns and ammunition were manufactured, a priest forging cannon from church bells, but most of the military supplies had to be imported. Chilean exiles eagerly offered their services; young men from other La Plata provinces came to Mendoza to enlist; and a few soldiers of fortune trickled in from Europe.

Prominent among the Chileans who hurried to Mendoza was Bernardo O'Higgins, destined to become the George Washington of his country. A few months older than his commander, he was the son of an Irishman with distinguished service in the Spanish bureaucracy and of a rather humble Chilean mother. After attending a primary school in Lima and an academy near London, where he sometimes conversed with Miranda and other pioneers of revolution, he returned to his native country to take charge of properties inherited from his deceased father.

His participation in the early struggle for self-government in Chile and his disastrous defeat have already been described. An unerring judge of character, San Martín welcomed O'Higgins with restrained enthusiasm.

Final preparations for the great adventure were well under way by the closing months of 1816. Carriages had been built to transport the artillery. Slings for swinging the guns on the backs of mules had been made. Portable bridges had been constructed for crossing the deep ravines. Special food and clothing had been prepared for the soldiers. And now scouts were sent out to explore the mountain trails and mislead the Spaniards. Within the limits of his resources, the methodical commander had left nothing undone. Long and often he had gazed with anxiety upon the colossal Andean range that towered high above his home in Mendoza. "What spoils my sleep," he said, "is not the strength of the enemy, but that immense mountain barrier." He knew that Napoleon, and Hannibal long before Napoleon, had led an army across the Alps. But he also knew that his task was likely to be more difficult, for the Andean passes were from 12,000 to 14,000 feet above the sea.

The advance began early in 1817 (see Map 8). On January 12, a small detachment started out in the far north and eventually arrived in the districts of Coquimbo and Copiapó, where it joined some Chilean insurgents. On January 14, another contingent began its march toward Talca and the Maule River. A few days later, the main army set out by way of the Uspallata and Los Patos passes, San Martín and O'Higgins taking the latter route. All proceeded according to schedule. Deceived by false rumors and not knowing where the invaders intended to strike, the Spanish commander had scattered his troops along a front of 1,300 miles. At the end of three weeks, the two principal divisions of San Martín's expedition united in the Chilean valley of Aconcagua, more than 300 miles from Mendoza; and although many horses and mules had perished on the way, few men were lost.

The revolutionary forces halted only four days before advancing to meet the enemy. On February 12, 1817, they attacked and put to flight some 2,000 Spanish and loyalist soldiers at Chacabuco, thirty-five miles northeast of Santiago, O'Higgins having led the two brilliant cavalry charges that decided the day. The Spanish captain general fled from the capital, which the patriots entered in triumph on February 14. An open meeting of the town council offered San Martín the office of Supreme Director of Chile, and when he declined the honor, conferred it upon O'Higgins.

All northern Chile was soon brought firmly under the control of the revolutionary government, and on February 12, 1818, independence was proclaimed. But the enemy, supported by the Peruvian viceroy, retained his hold in the south, and on March 19, made a sudden attack on the patriot troops at Cancha Rayada, near Talca, and defeated them. Then the royalists advanced rapidly toward Santiago; but San Martín rallied his forces as the enemy approached the capital and won the decisive engagement of Maipú on April 5, 1818. Suffering from a wound inflicted at Cancha Rayada and under doctor's orders to remain in the government palace, O'Higgins was not present while the battle raged. Nevertheless, he drove out near the scene of conflict in the middle of the afternoon to take part, only to find that the fighting had ceased before he arrived.

Chile's independence was now secure. The few strongholds in the far south still occupied by scattered Spanish forces were of no consequence. Already preparations for the invasion of Peru were under way. San Martín kept in touch with the faltering governments in Buenos Aires, making long journeys back and forth across the Andes and obtaining promises of continued support, while Don Bernardo gave him such aid as he could in Chile.

THE EXPEDITION TO PERU

In order to liberate Peru, it was necessary to assemble a fleet. San Martín and O'Higgins purchased some vessels from the United States and England; others they captured and held as prizes. All of them were put under the command of Thomas Cochrane, a bold though bad-tempered Scot with a distinguished record in the British Navy until he was dismissed for alleged dishonesty and insubordination. Taking charge of the Chilean flotilla late in 1818, Cochrane soon became the master of the south Pacific; and on August 20, 1820—Don Bernardo's birthday—the expedition bound for Peru left Valparaíso. It included eight war vessels, sixteen transports, 1,600 seamen and marines, and over 4,000 soldiers. Among the seamen were several British subjects, a few other Europeans, and some citizens of the United States; the soldiers included a number of Europeans, but the majority were from Chile and La Plata.

The army began to land in southern Peru early in September. But San Martín was in no hurry; he was engaged in a "war of opinion" and not a "war of conquest," he said. He set two printing presses to work, circulated propaganda, and began negotiations with the Spanish authorities while Cochrane continued to blockade the coasts, capture Spanish vessels of war, and harass the enemy's commerce. Negotiations, at first hopeful because of the Liberal revolution in Spain, failed; propaganda succeeded. The Spanish government and military forces, feeling unsafe in Lima, withdrew to the mountains early in July, 1821.

The *cabildo* of the city then invited San Martín to come in and take charge. A few days later, he was received with joyful acclaim and given the title of "Protector" by an open meeting of the council attended by prominent residents. The independence of the viceroyalty was announced to the world on July 28.

But independence was still to be won. San Martín, who soon assumed dictatorial power, controlled only the coastal area; the Spaniards and the loyalists, with an army nearly 20,000 strong, held possession of the much larger Andean region. Still hoping to achieve independence with a minimum of armed conflict, and aware that his forces were inadequate to subdue the royalists, he continued to negotiate and spread his propaganda. His subordinate officers and soldiers became impatient. Cochrane, in a fit of anger, left with the fleet for Chile, and some of the expeditionary army returned home. But San Martín refused to change his Fabian policy and attack the foe at the risk of annihilation. Finally, in the late spring of 1822, he decided to appeal to Bolívar for assistance.

BOLÍVAR AND THE LIBERATION OF NORTHERN SOUTH AMERICA

While San Martín was emancipating Chile and occupying Peru, Bolívar was engaged in campaigns so brilliant that they eventually made him one of the heroes of the whole Spanish race. Only thirty-five when he began his triumphant career, he was not a professional soldier, but he had fought intermittently for independence for a decade. Born rich (1783), he died poor (1830), having spent his fortune for the liberation of Spanish America. At the age of seven he was left an orphan in care of his uncle. His early teachers were Simón Rodríguez, an errant philosopher who was continuously "spouting Rousseau," and Andrés Bello, who eventually achieved fame as a great educator and poet. Sent abroad to complete his education, like other wealthy creoles, Bolívar visited Cuba, Mexico, and France, but spent most of his time in Spain, where he associated with the nobility and witnessed the corruption of the court of Charles IV. Falling in love with the daughter of the Marquís del Toro, he returned home late in 1802 to enjoy his bride and look after one of his estates. In less than a year, an epidemic deprived him of his wife, and he went back to Europe to assuage his grief. He witnessed the coronation of the mighty Napoleon in Paris in 1804. He talked, banqueted, danced, caroused, and still could not shake off his melancholy, which brought him to the point of suicide before he accidentally discovered his old tutor Rodríguez, who was now living in exile because of his radical notions. Tramping over the Continent together, they talked of South America's future and their patriotic yearnings. On the

Sacred Mountain in Rome, Bolívar took an oath to redeem his oppressed countrymen. Returning to Venezuela in 1807, he visited the Revolutionary battlefields of the United States while on his way. His activities during the early futile struggles for self-government have been recounted.

Prospects of success grew brighter by the end of 1817. Devotees of liberty, soldiers of fortune, and speculators from Europe and the United States began to evince an interest in Spanish America. Bolívar soon had a small navy and the support of a band of privateers sufficient to keep communications open with the outside world. Occupying the lower Orinoco, he established his headquarters at Angostura, where he collected recruits and supplies. Arms and ammunition flowed in along with several hundred professional soldiers from Europe, most of them from the British Isles. Among the foreigners were a number of officers ready to serve as drillmasters and company commanders.

From time to time, Bolívar tried to gain a foothold in northern Venezuela, but without success. Then, like San Martín, he began to think of a more daring plan. He would lead an army during the rainy season across the vast interior plains of Venezuela, ascend the lofty eastern range of the Andes, and make a surprise attack on Bogotá. This would be an extremely difficult feat; but nothing could daunt a warrior like Bolívar, hardened by years of exile and suffering into indifference to the loss of life. And he would have the enthusiastic co-operation of two men thoroughly familiar with the llanos of the region, José Antonio Páez and Francisco de Paula Santander.

Already Páez and Santander had induced or compelled the *llaneros* to enlist in the insurgent armies. In earlier years, many of them had succumbed to the influence of the clergy and loyalists and fought under the command of the terrible Boves and other loyalist chiefs.

Born in a small town on the northern edge of the Venezuelan plains in 1790 Páez had scarcely learned to read and write before he left home and sought his fortune among the cattlemen and cowboys. He soon learned to ride like a centaur, and he achieved fame as a cavalry officer by the time he reached his early twenties. Stocky and strong, with full chest and bull neck, he was ready for the boldest of exploits. Aware of his prowess, Bolívar informed him of his adroit plan and kept him busy drilling his horsemen.

Santander, two years younger than Páez, was a cultured gentleman with a college degree and a training in law. Native of a mountain village of eastern New Granada, and later a resident of Bogotá, he had been the victim of the Spanish terror of 1816 and had escaped to the wild tropical plains watered by the Casanare and Meta tributaries of the

Orinoco, where he had been living on the primitive ranches of the law-less frontier and drilling a private army. He had heard of Bolívar since 1813 and probably had known him personally. At any rate, he was aware of the Liberator's prestige; and when he learned that Bolívar was in Angostura, he immediately solicited his aid.

By the beginning of 1819, plans for the great campaign were com-pleted. Santander would return to his troops in the Meta-Casanare region; Bolívar would soon follow with the main army; Páez would re-main with the major contingents of his cowboy cavalry and harass the royalists in northern and western Venezuela.

Bolívar began his long and perilous march on May 26, just as the rainy season started. When joined a few weeks later by Santander's plainsmen, the expeditionary force numbered around 3,400, including a few hundred Europeans, mostly from England and Ireland, some of them officers. Hundreds of miles of soggy plains, swamps, and swollen rivers had been crossed or were still to be traversed, and after these, the hard climb up the slippery, rugged, and cold Andes. The rain fell in torrents, rotting the shoes from the feet of the officers and of such soldiers as wore them, rotting the clothes from their backs. Provisions spoiled. The humid midday heat was terrific. Scores died of hunger, disease, exhaustion; the rest marched on. At the end of June, they began to climb the treacherous trails of the steep mountains and soon en-countered a few royalist enemies. These they managed to put to flight; but the lower of the passes were strongly guarded, and Bolívar and his wasting army had to cross the ice-swept paramo of Pisba, 13,000 feet above sea level. Not a single horse lived to reach the edge of the Cundinamarca Plateau, and more than 1,000 officers and men perished before they arrived there. But Bolívar and the remnant of his staff soon collected fresh mounts and recruits.

Resuming the advance, they met and defeated a detachment of royalists at Pántano de Vargas (Vargas Swamp) on July 25, 1819; a few days later, August 7, they encountered and routed the enemy's main forces at Boyacá, some sixty miles from the viceregal capital. The royalists numbered about 3,000, the patriots considerably less. San-tander and the British troops were conspicuous for their bravery in both battles; and Bolívar, who directed their movements, did not hesitate to expose himself at points of danger as he moved swiftly to give orders and rally his men. Physically small and slim, with prominent nose and chin, a long face, and deep-set, flashing dark eyes, he was as agile and ferocious as an enraged tiger.

Boyacá was a decisive battle. The Spaniards and loyalists fled from Bogotá, which the Liberator occupied on August 10, 1819, with tremendous applause; the ceremonies and shouting lasted for more than a week. Then Bolívar set to work on a magnificent enterprise which kept him busy the rest of his life. Expanded according to his ambition and fancy, it included the emancipation of northern South America, and Peru and Charcas if necessary, the creation of *La Gran Colombia,* embracing Venezuela, New Granada, and the Quito *Audiencia,* and the federation of all the former Spanish colonies. He would have Páez serve as his collaborator in Venezuela, Santander in New Granada, and Sucre in Quito and elsewhere.

Although one of the youngest of Bolívar's military officers, José Antonio de Sucre eventually proved to be the most able and trustworthy of them all. Born in Cumaná, Venezuela, in 1795, he could trace his ancestry back on his father's side to the feudal lords of Flanders and on his mother's, to one of the Spanish conquerors. An industrious student of mathematics and engineering, he had been a member of Miranda's staff. Fleeing to the West Indies after the failure of Miranda's revolution, he soon returned and fought under Bolívar. Forced into exile a second time, he went to New Granada, where he helped to defend Cartagena against the Spanish besieging forces and effected an almost miraculous escape as the city was taken by the enemy. Already he had lost three brothers and a sister in the war; but their loss only increased his determination to drive out the Spaniards, and he hurried to eastern Venezuela to continue the fight. Separated from Bolívar for a time, he met him again on the Orinoco and soon became his most trusted adviser. Until early 1821, when Bolívar sent him with an expedition to liberate the presidency of Quito, he served his chief mainly in administrative and diplomatic posts. He was, for example, one of the Liberator's representatives in Venezuela during the negotiations with the Spanish General Pablo Murillo for an armistice which followed the revolt of 1820 in Spain.

It was nearly two years after the victory at Boyacá before another decisive engagement was fought. Meantime Bolívar was establishing an independent government and either pursuing the loyalists in New Granada or awaiting the result of efforts to gain independence by diplomacy. Leaving Vice-President Santander in charge of the government at Bogotá and setting up his headquarters in Cúcuta, Santander's home town, early in 1821, the Liberator soon began to advance into Venezuela, where he joined forces with Páez. On June 24, 1821, the united revolutionary army, numbering over 6,000, encountered and roundly defeated a slightly smaller number of royalists under the command of Miguel de Latorre on the plains of Carabobo, near Lake Valencia. The battle was decided by a magnificent cavalry charge led by

Páez and by the bold precision of the British battallion. The troops of the enemy were now confined to Puerto Cabello and the region of Maracaibo, from which they were expelled by the end of 1823.

After the victory of Carabobo, Bolívar rode hurriedly across the mountains of New Granada toward Quito, raising a small army as he went and encountering stubborn resistance during the latter part of his long campaign. Sucre, however, going by sea from the port of Buenaventura, had taken Guayaquil, marched up the mountains, and won the decisive battle of Pichincha (May 24, 1822) before the Liberator arrived. In this largest engagement of the war in South America, fought on the slopes of an extinct volcano some 14,000 feet above the sea, this military genius of twenty-seven had routed a Spanish army of 11,000. He was ably assisted, however, by a number of Englishmen and by a division of Peruvian troops under the command of the mestizo Andrés Santa Cruz. Sucre occupied the city of Quito the day after his victory. Bolívar joined him there three weeks later, and then rode on to Guayaquil to be lauded by its inhabitants and government—and to make preparations for the reception of San Martín.

The conference of the two great warriors on July 26–27, 1822, proved unsatisfactory. San Martín favored a royal government headed by a Bourbon or some other European prince, with its powers limited by a constitution. Bolívar preferred a conservative republic dominated by an aristocracy until the masses could be educated. Bolívar was aggressive and ambitious. San Martín was without political aspirations and capable of self-effacement, and he left Guayaquil with the conviction that harmonious co-operation with the Liberator of the North would be impossible. Back in Lima, he issued a fatherly farewell address, and then departed for Santiago, Mendoza, and Buenos Aires, where he took charge of his infant daughter, prepared an inscription for his dead wife's mausoleum,[1] and set sail for Europe, where he spent the rest of his life in voluntary exile with his only child. He died in France in 1850.

THE EMANCIPATION OF PERU AND CHARCAS

Bolívar and Sucre, mounting toward the peak of their military glory, now faced the problem of subduing the Spaniards and their colonial allies in the mountain strongholds of Peru without the assistance of the Liberator of the South. Delayed by loyalist uprisings in southern New Granada, Bolívar did not arrive until the fall of 1823; Sucre made his appearance a few months earlier. Their first task in Peru was to stabilize the politics of the coastal region. While the Peruvian leaders were quarreling among themselves and on the verge of civil war, the royalists had recovered the port of Callao and even reoccupied Lima itself for a brief period.

Nearly all of the soldiers from Chile and La Plata had gone home. Arms and supplies had to be imported. Soldiers had to be brought in from Great Colombia; recruits had to be raised in Peru. Bolívar and Sucre were not ready to advance into the Andean plateau from their headquarters in Trujillo until the middle of the year 1824. After marching for weeks along the mountain trails, they finally encountered the royalists at Junín, on the borders of Lake Reyes in the vicinity of lofty Cerro de Pasco, on August 6, 1824. It was a peculiar battle, a cavalry engagement fought with saber and lance while the rest of the troops looked on. Hardly a shot was fired, and the battle lasted only forty-five minutes. The insurgent cavalry, numbering approximately 1,100, put to flight a superior number of royalists. The enemy's losses were large, but the Spanish commander, General José Canterac, managed to save most of his army by a speedy retreat.

Bolívar hurried back to the coast, where he was having trouble with the Peruvians, and where other duties, including urgent appeals to Bogotá for soldiers and supplies, kept him busy. The patriot army at Lake Reyes hardly exceeded 8,000. The opposing loyalists numbered slightly more, and nearly as many were under arms farther south.

Major responsibility for field operations was now shifted to Sucre. Resolute, systematic, cautious, but capable of quick decisions in a crisis, Sucre was equal to the task thrust upon him. He continued his advance toward the south and finally drove Canterac's superior forces into a disadvantageous position at Ayacucho. On December 8, 1824, he opened the attack with a tremendous cavalry charge led by José María Córdova, a gallant Colombian, and the battle was soon over. With an army of less than 6,000, Sucre had almost annihilated one of well over 9,000; and by the terms of surrender, he exacted from Canterac and Viceroy José de la Cerna an agreement to withdraw all the Spanish forces from both Peru and Charcas. One of the Spanish generals refused to accept the agreement, but was forced to surrender by a revolt of his troops.

Sucre marched on into Charcas and transformed the region into a republic named Bolivia in honor of Bolívar. The last of the Spanish soldiers departed from Callao in January, 1826. Bolívar left for Bogotá in September; Sucre became the first president of Bolivia. Spanish South America was independent!

THE SEPARATION OF MEXICO AND CENTRAL AMERICA

The final act in the drama of independence in New Spain and Guatemala was short. Spain's revolution of 1820 was rather hostile toward the Roman Catholic Church and other privileged groups; the conservatives of Mexico, formerly opposed to independence, feared that the hostility might spread from the metropolis to the colonies and decided that their properties and positions could best be preserved by separation. They chose independence in order to prevent social and political reform.

The commander of the royalist forces which were hunting down the guerrilla bands in southern Mexico had failed to capture them, and the viceroy, impatient to ferret them out before events in Spain had their full impact, began to look about for a more effective general. He finally decided to confer the command upon Agustín de Iturbide, an appointment which may have reflected the influence of the conservatives whose real objectives were not disclosed to the viceroy. At any rate, Iturbide soon revealed that he knew what they were.

His record was not unspotted. Thirty-seven years old and a native of Valladolid, New Spain, he had joined the creole militia at the age of fifteen. Taking up arms against the insurgents under Hidalgo, Morelos, and more obscure leaders, he had won a number of minor engagements, treated his victims with shocking cruelty, and received the reward of rapid promotion until he had become the chief of a military district embracing the rich provinces of Guanajuato and Michoacán, where numerous complaints were soon raised against him. Accused of brutality, exploitation, and theft of public funds, he was ordered to Mexico City in April, 1816, to face the charges. Neither convicted nor exonerated and restored to his command, he was now living in rankling retirement in Mexico City upon the income of his properties. Such was the man appointed as colonel by New Spain's viceroy and ordered to eradicate the revolution in the southern sierras.

Pretending to attack the insurgents, Iturbide secretly cultivated their friendship, and on February 24, 1821, he entered into an agreement with Vicente Guerrero, who was still their chief. Named for the village in which it was signed and published, it was called the Plan of Iguala, and it contained three pledges: unity among Mexicans of all classes; independence under a Bourbon prince with his powers limited by a constitution; and protection of the Roman Catholic Church, its privileges, its functions, and its wealth. The combined forces of Iturbide and Guerrero forthwith became the "Army of the Three Guaranties."

The Plan of Iguala was generally accepted, willingly or unwillingly. Town after town fell into the hands of the new military combination, by the pronouncements of royal garrisons or by other means. A mutiny in Mexico City on July 6, 1821, compelled New Spain's last viceroy to abdicate. On August 21, Captain General Juan O'Donojú, Spain's last high official in the colony, signed the Treaty of Córdoba with Iturbide. According to its terms, Mexico was to have its independence on the basis of the Plan of Iguala. On September 27, Iturbide and his army made a triumphal entry into the old viceregal capital.

But the government in Madrid refused to provide a Bourbon prince and rejected the Córdoba agreement; whereupon a national congress assembled and "elected" Iturbide Emperor of Mexico. On May 21, 1822, he took the oath of office and the pledge to abide by a constitution to be framed and adopted later.

Meantime a wave of insurrection, aided and abetted by troops from the "Army of the Three Guaranties," had swept through Central America. Almost without loss of blood, save in El Salvador, the captaincy general of Guatemala was detached from Spanish control and annexed to the new Mexican Empire.

PRINCE PEDRO AND THE SEPARATION OF BRAZIL

Brazil broke away from Portugal shortly after New Spain severed its political ties with Old Spain. Napoleon's occupation and subsequent disorders and policies in the mother country furnished the opportune occasion.

Napoleon had intended to capture the Braganzas as well as the Bourbons, but the Portuguese royal family had eluded him. Embarking on November 29, 1807, with a retinue of some 15,000 officials and courtiers on a flotilla of thirty-six vessels under the convoy of British warships, the Braganzas departed for Brazil. On March 8, 1808, they landed in Rio de Janeiro, where they were welcomed with fervent adulation by the colonists, whose respect for the royal family fell little short of veneration.

Dom João (John), the dominant member of the family at the time, had been the acting head of the House of Braganza since 1792 because of the insanity of the queen mother, and had borne the title of Regent since 1798. Although corpulent, cowardly, and not very intelligent, he was a kindly ruler with good intentions. As his Portuguese kingdom was "caught like a shellfish in a tempest" between the "waves of England's sea-power and the rock of Napoleon's armies," John had tried to appease both antagonists. Under immense pressure from England and France, he sometimes scampered to a monastery in search of repose. When news arrived in 1807 that the French invasion was impending, his subjects were eager to defend their country to the bitter end; but John lacked the courage to undertake a desperate resistance. He wept over Portugal's plight, but fled to Brazil with a swarm of court favorites and the contents of the Treasury.

Having established his government in Brazil, he inaugurated a number of reforms—which seemed necessary now that he had lost his European dominions. He removed restrictions from commerce and industry, encouraged immigration and transportation, improved the law courts, founded a bank, set up a printing press, opened medical schools, and inaugurated both a military and a naval college and a public library. No longer a lowly colony, Brazil was declared a co-ordinate member of the Portuguese empire in 1815, with the same status as the other components. At the death of his demented mother in 1816, the Regent became John VI of the "United Kingdom of Portugal, Brazil, and Algarve." A republican uprising in Pernambuco disturbed his tranquillity in 1817, but for a time thereafter the colony was quiet. French Guiana, occupied shortly before the final defeat of Napoleon, had been turned back to France in 1815. Banda Oriental was subdued by King John's army (1820) and annexed as the Cisplatine Province.

In the end, John's rule became unpopular. He supported his horde of Portuguese courtiers at Brazil's expense, allowed them and later immigrants from Portugal to monopolize the best government posts, permitted England to coerce him into granting commercial concessions that seemed injurious to Brazilians, and clung to his notions of absolutism at a time when more liberal ideas were seeping into Brazil. His haughty and disreputable wife, Carlota Joaquina, caused further resentment; and events in Spain and Portugal increased his troubles. The tyranny of a regency in Portugal supported by William Carr Beresford, a British army officer, and the Spanish revolt of early 1820 led to an uprising of the Portuguese. The insurgents demanded that John return to Lisbon to rule as a limited monarch under a constitution modeled after the Spanish Constitution of 1812 while the Portuguese Cortes, which had not met since 1697, was being elected and installed to draft a permanent fundamental charter.

Once more John found himself unable to reach a decision. He dreaded an encounter with the Portuguese reformers, but he also observed the trend of events in Brazil with grave apprehension. Should he go back to Lisbon or stay in Brazil?

Soon after learning of the Portuguese rebellion, the Brazilians armed themselves and demanded a curtailment of royal power. Claiming the right to send deputies to Lisbon, they insisted that Brazil should be governed according to the terms of the Spanish Constitution of 1812 until the representatives of the Portuguese empire could meet, draft, and adopt one of their own. As the colonials deposed one after another of the royal governors of Brazil's eighteen provinces, John became thoroughly alarmed. In February, 1821, he issued a proclamation in which he announced his intention to send his eldest son, Dom Pedro (Peter), to Lisbon to treat with the Cortes and promised to adopt such portions of the organic law shortly to be framed as might be found convenient for Brazil.

But this announcement failed to satisfy the Brazilian insurgents. They thought that the king was maneuvering for time in the hope that their demands would be forgotten. The royal proclamation was followed by an uprising in Rio, where the popular leaders gained control of some of the royal troops and attempted to extort from John a pledge to accept any fundamental law that the Portuguese parliament, in which Brazil was to be represented, should promulgate.

Once again the king displayed his unheroic character, and now the prince who was to be the first ruler of independent Brazil took the center of the stage. While John "skulked in his palace," Pedro made his appearance, addressed the milling crowd, and swore in his own name and that of his father that the constitution soon to be drawn up in Portugal would be promptly ratified in Brazil. Wild with joyful excitement, the people rushed to the king's palace to express their gratitude. They invited John to get into his royal carriage and join the parade back to the center of the city. The frightened monarch complied; and a few minutes later, when some of the paraders unhitched the animals and began to pull the vehicle themselves, he fainted. Perhaps he recalled the specter of Louis XVI's head rolling on the ground! With returning consciousness, he wept, and between sobs he promised to grant anything that the Brazilians requested.

A call for a convention to meet in the capital in order to consider pending grievances and elect deputies for the Lisbon Cortes was sent out at once. The members of the assembly became aggressive and turbulent soon after its sessions began, however, and compelled the frightened monarch to agree at once not only to comply with the terms of the Spanish charter of 1812 but to give in advance another pledge to accept the work of the Lisbon Cortes.

But even these concessions were not enough; and when John, in a spurt of unusual courage, dissolved the Rio convention, an angry mob collected in the great square of the capital. At this juncture, however, Dom Pedro arrived with loyal troops and dispersed the crowd, while John rushed aboard a war vessel anchored in the harbor. At last, the king had made up his mind. On April 26, 1821, he left Brazil forever. On twelve ships, he departed with all the royal family except Pedro and his wife and children, with 4,000 members of the court, and with most of the funds of the bank and the Treasury. Pedro remained in the country as regent.

Soon after reaching Portugal, John took an oath to obey the Portuguese constitution. But the new parliament soon got out of hand and followed a policy that hastened the separation of Portugal's huge American colony. Practically all of the generous legislation of the period of exile was nullified; the Portuguese garrisons in Brazil were reinforced; and Pedro was ordered home to "complete his education." The Brazilians were on the point of being reduced to their former inferior status. Deeply offended, some of them set to work on a plan to gain independence through the co-operation of their regent.

The leader of the group was José Bonifácio de Andrada e Silva, whose bust was later chosen by the Brazilian government to represent his country in the Gallery of Patriots in the Pan American Union at Washington, D.C. The oldest of three famous brothers, José Bonifácio was born in Santos in 1765, the son of a Portuguese nobleman and of a mother who belonged to a pioneer family of the colony. After attending school in Rio, he went to Portugal, studied for six years in the University of Coimbra, and later received a commission from the king to collect scientific information. During his travels over Europe, he associated with some of the great scientists of the day, including Alexander von Humboldt, Joseph Priestley, and a number of specialists in chemistry. Afterwards, he taught metallurgy in Coimbra and chemistry in Lisbon. In 1819, after an absence of more than thirty years, he returned to the land of his birth. He knew that critical times were ahead both for Brazil and for Portugal.

What José Bonifácio and his associates desired was peaceful separation of the two countries and a constitutional monarchy for Brazil, and they took advantage of the disorders of 1820–22 to attain their goal. When Dom Pedro was ordered home, they urged him to remain with them. Petitions containing thousands of names and messages of support poured in to the Regent from all the important colonial towns. In January, 1822, he announced that he would stay, and José Bonifácio became his leading minister and counsellor. On September 7, Pedro declared the independence of Brazil,[2] and on October 12, a Brazilian convention proclaimed him as Emperor. The coronation ceremony took place on December the first. Meantime, preparations were made to expel the Portuguese garrisons. The insurgents had the assistance of Thomas Cochrane, the grumpy old Scot who had participated in San Martín's invasion of Peru. Cochrane took command of the small Brazilian fleet and transported the armed forces to the towns along the coast, and by the end of 1823 the Portuguese troops had been driven from the country.[3] Brazil had won its independence!

CHAPTER XI

Foreign Relations
During the Wars for Independence

🐚 COLONIAL BACKGROUND

Both Spain and Portugal were dissatisfied with the portions of the New World allotted to them by the papal bulls of 1493 and the Treaty of Tordesillas (1494). The line of demarcation was never run. The two countries failed to effect a permanent combination to enforce their claims against rival countries, and their nationals soon began a competition in South America that continued for nearly three centuries. Along most of the tributaries of the Amazon and all the eastern tributaries of the Plata, in the very heart of the South American grasslands and jungle, Spanish soldiers, missionaries, and converted Indians engaged in perpetual rivalry and combat with Portuguese explorers, prospectors, and slave hunters; and the independent nations of the continent inherited the dispute.

While the Iberian nations were thus haggling and fighting over their respective claims, they attempted to exclude all other powers from the New World. The monopoly to which they aspired was threefold: territory, trade, and navigation. That their pretensions could be enforced indefinitely was hardly to be expected; that they were fairly effectively upheld for a considerable time may be explained by the terrors of unfamiliar seas, the lingering political influence of the papacy, lack of harmony among the contesting powers, and the prestige of the Iberian kingdoms, especially Spain. The monopoly was eventually broken by the assaults of France, England, and the Dutch Netherlands. Sometimes the blows were delivered by private enterprise, acting independently or in secret connivance with state officials; sometimes the attacks were launched directly by the governments themselves. To complete the breakdown in all of its phases two centuries were required. The struggle for commerce and empire was most bitter between the years 1689 and 1763.

At the end of the period, the New World was mainly in the hands of England, Spain, and Portugal. Except for fishing rights on the banks of Newfoundland, two islets off the adjacent coast, the western third of Española, a part of the Guianas in South America, and two small Caribbean islands, France was expelled from the Americas. The Dutch Netherlands held only Aruba, Curaçao, and a share of the Guianas. England, now triumphant, confronted Spain along the Mississippi River from mouth to source (excepting the Isle of Orleans), reigned supreme beyond the Great Lakes, occupied a part of Guiana and several of the West Indies, and held an enviable position in American commerce.

Deeply aggrieved, France and Spain soon sought revenge. The successful issue of the revolt of the thirteen English colonies, as is well known, was determined largely by the assistance of these two European powers, granted mainly because of grudges growing out of the past and fears for the future. France gained no territory in the course of the conflict; Spain recovered the Floridas, which she had been compelled to cede to England in 1763. Subsequent European rivalries led France to sell Louisiana, acquired from Spain in 1800, to the United States, and so preoccupied the European nations that they were unable to prevent this young American republic from acquiring the Floridas and other territories which rounded out its domain and lifted it toward the status of a first-rate power.

POLICY SUMMARY AND FORECAST

The United States shortly became an effective rival of the European nations in Hispanic America. Participating in the competition for its trade and eventually for its investment opportunities, this country finally dominated the foreign relations of the region to such an extent that the story of Latin America's foreign relations centers largely around the American and world policies of its energetic northern neighbor.

The European nations rarely attempted to acquire territory or protectorates in Latin America after its struggle for independence got well under way. They interested themselves mainly in outlets for trade, capital, and surplus population; in the protection of their economic interests and their nationals; and in checkmating the political influence and the expansionist tendencies, commercial and territorial, of the United States. That they did not pursue more aggressive policies may be explained by the Monroe Doctrine, rivalries among themselves, and preoccupations in the Orient and Africa.

The United States not only followed the policy of territorial and commercial expansion while endeavoring to shield Latin America from non-American aggression, but tried to enlist Latin Americans in its struggle to enlarge the "rights" of neutrals and effect the freedom of the seas, and attempted, like the other stronger powers, to protect the lives and property of its nationals in Latin America. Its policy was most vigorous in the Gulf-Caribbean region, where a strategic motive mainly accounted for efforts to dominate the area to the extent deemed necessary to prevent its domination by any other strong power.

As for the Latin Americans, their main concern during their struggle for independence and as independent nations was to avoid becoming the victims and instead to make themselves the beneficiaries of the rivalries of the great capitalistic and industrial nations. They sought to profit from the contest: to sell their products in foreign markets, to obtain what they needed from abroad—capital, immigrants, the new technology—and to prevent their sovereignty from being jeopardized or curtailed in the process.

EARLY REVOLUTIONARY SCHEMES OF ENGLAND AND FRANCE

Several years before France and Spain sought to humble England by supporting a revolt in her American colonies, the idea of inciting Spanish America to revolt was considered in London and Paris. And the insurgent movement that began south of the United States in 1808 was fomented in some measure by the intrigues of England and France, Spain's chief rivals after the decline of the Netherlands.

As early as 1741 Stephen Deveros, a British subject with years of experience in the West Indies, deprecated any effort to conquer the Spanish colonies and urged his country to form an alliance with the Spanish Americans "as with a free people" and help them to gain their independence. A certain Captain Kaye, a British naval officer, presented another revolutionary plan late in 1776, and still others were proposed during the years 1779–83 while Spain was engaged in the war with England that indirectly aided the revolting English colonies in North America. Such schemes soon attracted the attention of the Hispanic colonial leaders, and they began to look to London for support.

Francisco de Miranda appealed for British aid as early as 1790, when he presented to William Pitt, the English prime minister, a plan to form a vast independent constitutional empire out of Spain's American possessions. Evidently impressed by Miranda's project, Pitt promised to give it careful consideration in case the current dispute with Spain over Nootka Sound should lead to a general war. In fact, plans were actually made to send three British expeditions to America, two to the

Atlantic and Gulf coasts and one (from India) to the Pacific coast, and the co-operation of the United States was even contemplated. But war was averted by opportune concessions on the part of the Spanish government, which not only found that revolutionary France was indisposed to fulfill the terms of the Bourbon family compact, but discovered that France dreaded the consequences of hostilities with England.

Indeed, the French leaders were so far from accepting this Bourbon alliance that they were themselves thinking of attacking the Spanish colonies. As early as 1792 the French foreign minister began to talk of expelling Spain from America and gaining access to the commerce of the Spanish colonies by means of a coalition with the United States and England, and a French admiral actually drew up a plan of operations. Presumably all Spanish America was to be permitted to enjoy independence except such portions as were considered appropriate spoils for the invading powers. The grandiose project was even suggested to London; but England was too alarmed by the extravagance of the French revolutionary leaders and the overthrow of the French monarchy to participate in such a scheme, and no further progress was made on this particular plan or others discussed a little later with Miranda, who was then in France.

The detachment of Spain from the anti-French coalition in 1795 exerted a profound influence upon British policy toward the Spanish colonies for the next thirteen years. While Spain remained under the influence of Revolutionary and Napoleonic France, instigation of revolt in Spanish America became a topic of frequent meditation among British statesmen. Miranda was pensioned and kept within reach, and preparations were made for launching liberating expeditions to America. But those in control of British policy usually took the position that armed forces should not be sent across the Atlantic unless such action became necessary in order to prevent the colonies from falling into the hands of France; and as affairs never came to this pass, England abstained from intervention until the Spanish revolt of 1808 against Napoleon's domination diverted attention from Spanish America to Spain.

Meantime, however, British agents, under instructions and sometimes contravening instructions, were engaged in activities which tended to hasten the revolt in the colonies. Thomas Picton, military governor of the island of Trinidad (which had been seized by the British fleet in 1797), was authorized to encourage revolt in northern South America, and did all he could during the next few years to foster the revolutionary spirit. Sir Home Popham, without explicit instructions, led an expedition from the African Cape of Good Hope against the Río de la Plata

Viceroyalty (1806–7); and although the colonists soon expelled the British invaders, the result was an increased desire in the region, stimulated by the flood of cheap British goods introduced during the occupation, for the benefits of a more liberal commercial policy.

INFLUENCE OF FRENCH RADICAL IDEAS AND THE EXAMPLE OF THE UNITED STATES

While these inflammatory activities were in progress, the colonial leaders were gaining inspiration from the new political ideas that were disturbing France and from the success of the thirteen English colonies. The mulattoes who started the revolt in French Española in 1790 were incited by French radical propaganda. The creole aristocracy of Spanish and Portuguese America soon became familiar with the writings of Rousseau, Voltaire, Montesquieu, and most of the French philosophes. The French Declaration of the Rights of Man, *The Social Contract,* and *The Spirit of the Laws* became their gospel and their weapons of attack. These and other similar works were in the hands of the revolutionary leaders from New Spain to Río de la Plata and Brazil.

Unlike the political authorities of England and France, those of the United States gave little encouragement to revolt in Latin America. Although there was some propaganda, authorized or unauthorized, the government seldom deviated from the norm of neutrality. Nevertheless, the influence of the United States was great. Profoundly impressed by the political ideas and character of the Founding Fathers, the Spanish American creoles, without substantial grounds for such a hope, fully anticipated aid from their brothers in North America.

Miranda declared that he conceived the idea of freeing his fatherland while fighting England during the American Revolution. He visited the United States in 1783–84 and met such prominent leaders as Alexander Hamilton, George Washington, Benjamin Franklin, Henry Knox, and Samuel Adams, and expected eventually to secure North American support for his ambitious enterprise.

Ten years later, when Antonio Nariño of New Granada was tried for sedition, one of the charges preferred against him was that he was enamored with the Philadelphia Constitution. And he not only revealed a familiarity with the revolutionary documents of the United States during his trial, but expressed admiration for Benjamin Franklin, George Washington, and other patriots.

Shortly afterward one of the conspirators in Venezuela was accused of printing the Constitution of the United States for circulation among the colonists; and at about the same time (1798) an exiled Jesuit father, dying in London, left with the United States minister a memorial in which he declared that "the recent acquisition of independence by their neighbors in North America" had made the "deepest impression" on the Spanish colonies.

Miranda, it will be recalled, came to the United States to prepare his ill-fated expedition of 1806; and the fact that it numbered some 200 Anglo-Americans must have given encouragement to the Spanish colonials despite its failure. Nor should Bolívar's sojourn of 1806 in the United States be forgotten. His itinerary included Boston, Lexington, Concord, New York, and Washington. Such an experience, at the receptive age of twenty-three, must have exerted an influence upon his later career.

Meanwhile merchants from the United States, whose trade with the Spanish colonies was rapidly increasing, were introducing liberal ideas along with their wares. Melchor Martínez, a loyal friar of Chile, described their propaganda as follows: "They magnify the riches and extent of these provinces; proclaim the injustice and tyranny with which the wealth is carried off to enrich Europe; describe the state of obscurity, abandonment, and civil nullity in which the colonists live; and offer with impudence all the aid of their great power to the peoples who may wish to shake off the yoke of legitimate and just government." [1] From these merchants the Spanish American leaders may have obtained the liberty documents which they used to win adherents in most of the revolutionary centers; and further evidence of influence coming from the North is furnished by the fact that the agents sent by Napoleon to Spanish America from 1808 on were instructed to point to the United States as a model and promise the colonials freedom and independence.

It was Napoleon's invasion of Spain that finally lighted the flame of insurgency in Spanish America, and his invasion of Portugal that eventually prepared the way for the independence of Brazil. But it was also his aggressions in the Iberian Peninsula that caused a sudden change of policy in England.

TREADING THE WINE PRESS ALONE

In the end, the Spanish Americans searched in vain for official assistance in their struggle for emancipation. The British government, after years of encouragement, turned its efforts toward the preservation of Spanish dominions in both hemispheres, even going so far as to urge the colonial leaders to reconcile their compatriots to Spanish rule. British individuals finally joined the ranks of the insurgents in hundreds and even thousands; but official aid was lacking until 1823, when the London government exerted itself to prevent Spain from receiving the assistance of other European countries in her effort to subdue her colonies.

There was never any prospect of aid to the colonies from continental Europe. French liberalism, to which the revolutionists might have looked for support, was smothered under the despotism first of Napoleon and then of the Metternich system. On one or two occasions the insurgents solicited help from the Corsican, but in vain. Nor could any who aspired to independence under native governments expect assistance from the reactionary Holy Alliance.

The Spanish Americans turned with pathetic confidence to the United States, whose political ideas and example had created an enthusiastic hope; but considerations of security and other interests prevented assistance from that quarter. In 1808, while harassed by England and France and fearing that they might seize some of the adjacent Spanish colonies, President Jefferson's cabinet resolved to communicate to the colonials the unwillingness of the United States to see them fall into the hands of England and France and its sympathy for them in case they should decide to declare their independence; but the agents sent with this message to Cuba, the Floridas, and the Mexican frontier were not authorized to promise any support. They were merely told to say, "We consider their interests and ours as the same, and that the object of both must be to exclude all European [political] influence from this hemisphere." Some of the emissaries may have used stronger language in conversing with the leaders of these colonies. But the proceedings of 1808–9, the sending of commercial agents to South America a little later, and the schemes of 1811–13 in respect to the detachment of the Floridas from Spain mark the nearest approaches to any official action that might be interpreted as inciting revolution.

Spanish American agents who hurried to the United States upon the outbreak of their struggle for self-government were unofficially heard and occasionally supplied with funds for transportation and temporary entertainment. But, aside from these polite considerations, which tended to become more rare after the Florida negotiations with Spain got under way, there was no departure from the narrow path of formal impartiality. The Spanish Americans had to tread the wine press alone.

※ BRITISH POLICY

Lord Liverpool, secretary of war and the colonies, instructed his agents in the West Indies (June 29, 1810) to discourage all suggestions of revolt. The primary objective of His Majesty's government was to preserve both Spain and its empire against the overweening ambitions of the French usurper. At the same time, the British foreign secretary refused to receive the agents of the Venezuelan insurgents until they had avowed loyalty to Ferdinand VII, and then he urged them to forget their grievances, accept a reconciliation with Spain, and support the mother country in her magnificent struggle against Napoleon. He rejected their argument that Venezuela could give Spain more efficient aid under an autonomous government, but eventually promised to use his good offices to promote an amicable adjustment between the Venezuelans and the metropolis and to shield them from France so long as they refrained from a rupture with Spain.

British policy with reference to the revolting colonies was thus clearly formulated by the summer of 1810: moral opposition, a hint of mediation, and protection from French aggression. During the next decade it was modified in only one significant respect. Gradually the London authorities advanced to a position of neutrality and a willingness to mediate upon a liberal basis. They insisted that mediation should apply to all the colonies, that no special commercial advantages be asked for Spain, and that force should not be used. But Spain declined to accept mediation on these terms and England refused to undertake it on any other.

While Spain continued to importune the London government to relent, Spanish diplomats sought mediation elsewhere on a more favorable basis; and when it appeared that Russia and possibly France might undertake the task and even go so far as to employ armed force in support of Spain, Lord Castlereagh boldly announced that England was firmly opposed to intervention of "an armed character" and insisted that mediation should be confined "within the bounds of good offices, and the employment of that just influence which must belong to any great power when laboring only to promote the welfare of an allied sovereign and his people." This announcement, made on August 28, 1817, was followed the next year by the acceptance at the Congress of Aix-la-Chapelle of Castlereagh's basic principle.

Soon afterward, however, the British cabinet was alarmed by the intrigues of France and the attitude that was developing in the United States. First came disquieting rumors of a plot to seat Bourbon princes under French auspices on American thrones. Next occurred the liberal revolution of 1820 in Spain, followed by the prospect of European intervention in that country, with France as a possible agent. And while these vexatious disturbances were taking place in Europe, it appeared that the United States was gradually moving toward recognition of the new states in Spanish America in response to commercial pressure, public opinion, and the factional support given them by Henry Clay. In 1817, seven years after the first commercial agents were sent to the colonies, preparations were begun in Washington for the dispatching of a committee of investigation, and the envoys of the United States in

Europe were instructed to drop hints to the effect that the time for recognition of the insurgent governments was drawing near. The Washington government was now held in restraint only by the uncompleted Florida negotiations and by uncertainty regarding the intentions of Europe. Learning of rifts in European diplomacy, the United States ventured to invite an understanding with the British government on the subject of recognition early in 1819. Refusing to co-operate, Castlereagh soon had cause for further alarm and worry. Clay pushed through the House of Representatives (May, 1820, and February, 1821) resolutions in favor of sending diplomatic representatives to the Spanish American states. Followed by Monroe's message of March, 1822, announcing that recognition would soon be granted, Clay's action caused the British commercial world to urge that Castlereagh take some step to prevent the United States from driving British trade from Spanish American markets.

Although convinced that the issues between Spain and her colonies could not be settled short of independence, Castlereagh still pursued a delaying action in the hope that monarchies might be set up in America. He announced his intention (May, 1822) to modify English navigation laws and establish commercial relations with the insurgent governments, and prepared to attend the Congress of Verona to fight to the finish any project for combined intervention by the European powers in the affairs of Spanish America. Then he suddenly committed suicide and left the problem to George Canning, his successor in the Foreign Office.

While somewhat less conservative than Castlereagh, Canning was not eager to change the Spanish American policy of his predecessor. Commercial recognition already had been granted in June, 1822, and Canning felt that political recognition could await further developments. While he did not object to a few American republics to counterbalance European despotism, he hoped to see a number of independent monarchies established in the New World.

But impending recognition of the insurgent governments by the United States, the pressure of British merchants, and the procedure of France rendered delay somewhat hazardous. English merchants were determined not to allow their trade to be reduced either by Spanish restrictions or by "Yankee" competition. France's resolution to suppress the liberal uprising in Spain could not be shaken by Canning's diplomatic representative at the Congress of Verona. The summer of 1823 witnessed the triumphal march of the French army across Spain. Were Frenchmen returning to the Iberian ambitions of Napoleon?

Already, during the closing weeks of 1822, French diplomats were talking ominously of placing the French fleet at the disposition of the Spanish government for the purpose of conveying Spanish troops and a Spanish prince to America, and a French newspaper was announcing the likelihood of French naval support of plans to establish Bourbon monarchs in Mexico and Peru. Discussion of these projects continued during the following spring and summer until Canning became convinced that France had "all along meditated direct interference in Spanish America." The time for diplomatic action had arrived.

Aware of the alarm in the United States regarding the designs of Russia and the Holy Alliance, Canning turned first to Richard Rush, minister of the United States in London, and proposed a joint remonstrance. "For ourselves we have no disguise," [2] Canning wrote Rush on August 20, 1823:

1. We conceive the recovery of the Colonies by Spain to be hopeless.
2. We conceive the question of the Recognition of them to be one of time and circumstances.
3. We are, however, by no means disposed to throw any impediment in the way of an arrangement between them and the mother country by amicable negotiation.
4. We aim not at the possession of any portion of them ourselves.
5. We could not see any portion of them transferred to any other Power with indifference.

If these feelings and opinions are, as I firmly believe them to be, common to your Government and ours, why should we hesitate mutually to confide them to each other; and to declare them in the face of the world?

While Rush sought advice from Washington, Canning sent consuls and commissioners to Spanish America and summoned Prince de Polignac, French ambassador to London, to conferences in which he was asked to explain French intentions. During the course of the long discussions (October 9 and 12, 1823), Canning made three important statements. In substance, they were as follows: [3] (1) England would recognize the independence of the Spanish colonies if any attempts were made to restrict her trade with them. (2) England would consider any foreign interference in the contest between Spain and her colonies as sufficient motive for prompt recognition. (3) Owing to the importance of her Spanish American interests, England was not inclined to enter upon a joint deliberation on an equal footing with other European powers, and would not do so unless the United States were invited to participate.

THE MONROE DOCTRINE

With a fairly definite idea of British attitude but without knowledge of the Polignac conferences, President James Monroe and his cabinet proceeded to discuss and formulate the policy of the United States with respect to possible joint European intervention in America. The result of their deliberations was a series of pronouncements in Monroe's annual message of December, 1823, which later became known as the Monroe Doctrine. The pronouncements differed from Canning's proposals to Rush in several important respects: They were not a joint declaration; they included no self-denying pledge against future expansion by the United States at the expense of Spanish America; and announcing a concept of two separate political spheres, they contained a warning against further European colonization in America as well as against any sort of European political interference in the Western Hemisphere.

A number of motives led the statesmen of the United States to prefer independent action. They feared that a joint statement with England might tend to make the United States, in appearance if not in reality, a mere tail to the British kite. They desired to issue a warning to Russia regarding her pretensions on the Pacific coast. And some of them were reluctant to bind the United States never to acquire Spanish American territory. Even if they had decided to accept Canning's proposal, they might have discovered that he had changed his mind in view of reassurances from Europe.

This independent course did not involve great risk to the United States, for the Holy Alliance (Russia, France, Prussia, and Austria) probably did not seriously contemplate the use of force in Spanish America. Even if the European powers had been more determined to employ force, they would have had difficulty in agreeing among themselves with respect to objectives and the contributions of each ally, and England would have offered vigorous opposition to any drastic measures they might have undertaken. Russia had no serious designs on the American Pacific coast. The Russian government had evinced a willingness to come to terms with the United States on the Alaskan boundary issue as early as December, 1822, and a boundary treaty was signed two years later in which Russia ceded all claims south of the parallel of fifty-four degrees and forty minutes.

In fact, Secretary of State John Quincy Adams felt at the time that the United States was assuming no serious risk. Unlike Calhoun, Monroe, Madison, and others, he did not believe that war was likely. Aside from the noncolonization pronouncement, and although Adams was fond of baiting England, he was interested mainly in a bold statement to Tsarist Russia, whose minister had just sent him a lecture on the sacredness of absolutist principles. If Russia and the alliance should decide upon war, they would have to encounter the British Navy; and, after all, Monroe's message was so framed that it did not commit the United States irrevocably to hostilities. The Englishman Harold Temperley has remarked that the United States could "safely blow a blast on the republican trumpet while sheltered behind the shield of England." But if that turned out to be the truth, it was also true that England was fully aware of the hostile attitude of the United States with reference to the intervention of the European reactionaries in the New World. On that point the policies of the two Anglo-Saxon governments coincided even if no joint remonstrance was made. The two nations, each following a parallel course in support of its own security interests, were destined to become the chief bulwark of Latin America's independence after that independence had been won by the Latin Americans themselves.

The United States completed the process of extending recognition to Great Colombia, Mexico, Central America, Peru, Chile, and the United Provinces of Río de la Plata between 1822 and 1825, and British recognition followed soon after. Recognition of Uruguay, Paraguay, Bolivia, and the rest came later. Some had not yet won their independence from Spain or were still a part of larger Latin American entities. The last to be recognized as independent nations by the United States—before the emancipation of Cuba and the secession of Panama —were the Dominican Republic in 1856 and Haiti in 1862.

THE EARLY NATIONAL PERIOD

CHAPTER XII

The New Nations and Their Problems

ANGLO-SAXON AND LATIN AMERICA: A CONTRAST

Thirteen English colonies in eastern North America, together with a huge back country extending all the way to the Pacific, were finally consolidated, after a long period of political strife and a four-year civil war, into a single powerful nation. A smaller number of Spanish colonies, stretching from Mexico to Chile and the Río de la Plata, eventually broke up into eighteen nations, most of them small and all comparatively weak. This is probably the most striking contrast in the history of the Americas.

There were only eight or ten Spanish colonies in the New World at the end of the Colonial epoch: the viceroyalties of New Spain (Mexico), New Granada, Peru, and Río de la Plata; the captaincies general of Guatemala (Central America), Cuba, Venezuela, and Chile; and possibly the presidencies of Quito (Ecuador) and Charcas (Bolivia), which were somewhat dependent upon New Granada and Río de la Plata, respectively. Although these colonies embraced an area of 6,000,000 to 7,000,000 square miles, their population hardly exceeded 16,000,000. The viceroyalty of New Spain, extending from southern Mexico far northward into the present states of California, New Mexico, and Texas, had more than twice as many inhabitants as any other administrative unit, but its population numbered less than 7,000,000.

Men of ambition and foresight felt that these old colonial jurisdictions provided the sinews for only a few strong nations and acted on this conviction. Agustín de Iturbide included New Spain and Central America in his Mexican empire. Simón Bolívar merged Venezuela, New Granada, and the Quito presidency into a large state called *La Gran Colombia*. Andrés Santa Cruz combined the former viceroyalty of Peru and the old presidency of Charcas in a Peru-Bolivian confederation. Political leaders in Buenos Aires tried to hold together the vast region embraced in the viceroyalty of Río de la Plata. Cuba, if some of the political leaders of the formative period could have had their way, probably would have become a part of Mexico or Colombia. If all these efforts at consolidation had succeeded, Spanish America would have been reduced to five states, with Chile forming the fifth. Portuguese Brazil and Franco-Hispano-African Haiti would have raised the total to seven; and there are indications that Bolívar was eager to include Peru and Bolivia in his vast state, thus reducing the Latin-American nations to six, all of which (possibly excepting Brazil) he aspired to unite in a confederate league designed to resist any future aggression from the outside.

But efforts at consolidation failed everywhere except in Portuguese Brazil, where the Braganza monarchs managed to hold together the eighteen captaincies of the late Colonial period and weld them into a single nation with a huge area and a population which, although no more than 4,000,000 at the outset, soon outnumbered that of any other Latin-American state. Spanish America whirled into careening chaos after expelling the colonial authorities. Iturbide's Mexican empire split into two turbulent parts, and one of these, the Confederation of Central America, broke up into five within twenty years after its separation from Mexico. Bolívar's *La Gran Colombia* dissolved in 1830 into Venezuela, Ecuador, and New Granada. Santa Cruz's Peru-Bolivian confederation lasted less than four years (1835–39). The incipient new nation of the Plata region, Argentina of the modern epoch, lost Paraguay, Bolivia, and Banda Oriental (Uruguay), and for two decades threatened to disrupt into a dozen petty states. And the inhabitants of eastern Española won their independence after twenty years of Haitian rule, and established the tiny Dominican Republic (1844).

Spanish America thus split up into sixteen sovereign nations in less than a quarter of a century after its emancipation from Spain. Including Brazil and Haiti, the total was eighteen, and the aggregate rose to twenty with the liberation of Cuba in 1898 and the secession of Panama in late 1903—though the sovereignty of these two was slightly curtailed by the United States for over three decades. In striking contrast with the trend in Anglo-Saxon America, ten or twelve colonies had become twenty nations, the largest of them (Brazil) having a population of less than 8,000,000 in 1850 and hardly more than 17,000,000 half a century later.

The founding of these new nations and the fixing of their boundaries required not merely a long and bloody struggle to break the bonds of European control; the process was accompanied by a whole series of wars among the Latin-American countries themselves, as well as by a war between Mexico and the United States and another between the

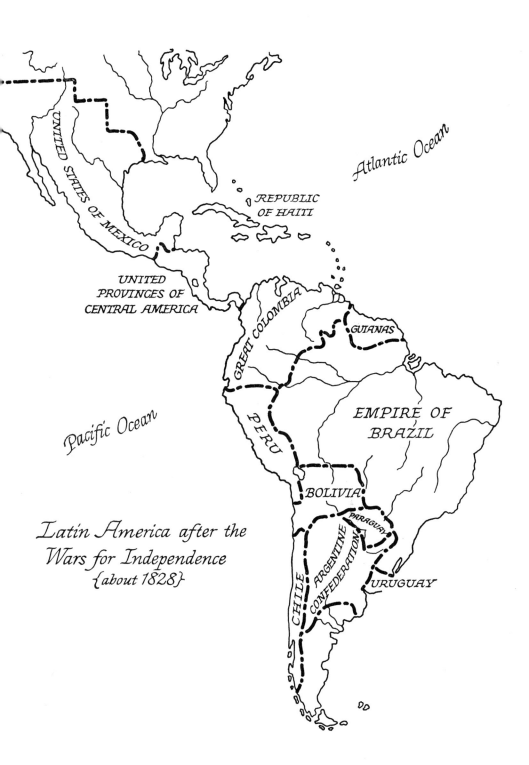

United States of Mexico

Atlantic Ocean

Republic of Haiti

United Provinces of Central America

Great Colombia

Guianas

Peru

Empire of Brazil

Pacific Ocean

Bolivia

Paraguay

Chile

Argentine Confederation

Uruguay

Latin America after the Wars for Independence {about 1828}

MAP 9

United States and Spain. The second phase of the struggle dragged on intermittently for a hundred years and—since nothing relating to nationalities and boundaries seems ever to be settled permanently—may even yet be resumed. The ten centuries of turbulence and travail that attended the birth of the modern nations in Europe were crowded into a single century in Latin America. Where secession did not lead to armed conflict, boundary disputes often did. While less bitter than the international relations of Europe, relations among the Latin-American nations were far from harmonious during the first hundred years of their independence, and the most important cause of strife among them was the problem of determining the number of nationalities into which the region should be divided and delimiting their respective boundaries. This longer series of conflicts following the protracted struggle for independence from Europe—a struggle which had already fostered the military spirit—was an important factor in the development of militarism.

🐚 MAJOR POLITICAL ISSUES IN DOMESTIC POLITICS

In addition to this grave international problem, this twofold task of determining the number of nations into which Latin America should be divided and delimiting the boundaries of each, the leaders of the young nations confronted serious domestic problems. Important among these were such issues as monarchy *versus* republic, the place of the Roman Catholic Church in the new order, centralism *versus* local autonomy (usually described as federalism), liberty *versus* tyranny, the proper distribution of the land, and the rights of labor in the growing economy.

From the very outset, of course, political leaders faced the problem of selecting the form of government deemed most appropriate for the people of their various countries. And, here again, the contrast with Anglo-Saxon America was striking.

Almost without hesitation, the founders of the United States adopted the republican form of government and advanced gradually toward the democratic republic. Although it is said that some of General Washington's officers urged him to become a king and that several of the members of the Philadelphia Convention favored a constitutional monarchy, monarchy was certainly never very seriously considered. The inhabitants of the thirteen colonies had gained political experience through long participation in local government and membership in colonial legislative bodies. In considerable measure they had governed themselves for many years, and it was not difficult to admit that they were qualified for self-government.

The liberated peoples of Latin America had a totally different background, and their leaders acted with far less confidence than did the

Founding Fathers in the United States. The Latin Americans and their ancestors had known only monarchical government, and this in its most absolute form. They had taken almost no part in political affairs during the long Colonial period except in the municipalities. They had no colonial legislatures. They had almost no experience in public administration. They hardly knew what an election was. They lacked homogeneity in race, culture, and ideals. The vast majority belonged to the primitive and mixed races which had been bound for centuries in slavery or serfdom: Indians, Negroes, mulattoes, and mestizos, ragged, barefoot, and ignorant. In nearly all the new states only a small percentage of the inhabitants were Caucasians, and not a few of these were illiterate or fanatically intolerant. Local loyalties, racial and cultural diversities, and class distinctions tended to produce animosities and social conflict. The various castes and racial groups, the scattered settlements, were conscious of almost no common interests or ideals.

Moreover, the trend in Europe at this time was not toward popular government. A conservative reaction was sweeping away the institutions set up a few years before by men inspired by the English liberal thinkers of the seventeenth century and the French philosophes of the eighteenth. The existence of the only government in continental Europe that resembled a democracy, the Swiss Confederation, was threatened by France and the Holy Alliance. Absolute monarchs sat upon thrones almost everywhere save in England, where the king's power was limited by a parliament far from democratic. In the whole Western World there was only one republic, the United States of America, and its future was clouded by internal dissension. The founders of the Latin-American nations could find little to recommend government of the people, by the people, and for the people either in the broad panorama or in the narrower domestic setting.

It is not surprising, therefore, that many of the leaders of the new nations hesitated to adopt the republican form of government. Although few, if any, preferred an absolute monarchy—the memory of Bourbon oppressions was too vivid—there were advocates of a constitutional monarchy in all the main centers of population from Mexico to Argentina. Many men of wealth and social position, white men of Spanish or Portuguese descent as a rule, dreaded the consequences of placing political power in the hands of the primitive, racially mixed, and unlettered masses, and consequently favored a limited monarchy or an aristocratic republic. This was especially true of the outstanding military leaders. Although Bolívar refused all offers of a crown, he was not opposed to an oligarchic republic, and both Antonio de Sucre and Bernardo O'Higgins agreed with him. José F. de San Martín, Bernardo Rivadavia, and Agustín de Iturbide were monarchists, and top-flight army officers toyed for decades with the idea of a lifetime presidency.

Only three nations of Latin America, however, ever ventured to experiment with the monarchical system. All the rest chose some type of the republic. Independent Brazil had two monarchs in succession; Mexico had an equal number, with forty years of so-called republican government between them; and Haiti had three, with twenty-nine years of "republican" administration between the second and the third. Monarchy was not finally discarded in Haiti until 1859, nor in Mexico until 1867, nor in Brazil until 1889. Kings might have been set up in some of the other countries if qualified princes willing to come to America could have been found and agreed upon by all the parties concerned. But the royal families of Europe and the monarchists of America had difficulty in reaching agreement; and the United States, although rather friendly toward the royal government of Brazil, was opposed to the establishment of monarchy elsewhere in the New World. In the end, the monarchs of Latin America encountered a tragic fate. Brazil's were deposed and sent into exile. Mexico's were overthrown and executed. Haiti's were disposed of in various ways: one was assassinated; another committed suicide in order to avoid capture by an enraged populace; and the third was deposed and banished.

Independent Latin America has been a land of constitutions. All of its royal governments were supposed to be limited by constitutions, and constitutions are of course a necessary part of the republican system. The republics of this region had a plethora of constitutions over the years because few fundamental charters survived for more than a decade. No other part of the world had more constitutions or observed them less. For political practice seldom harmonized with political theory; the actual system of government was usually very different from the nominal system. Haiti's theoretically constitutional monarchs were tyrants without exception. Mexico's first monarch was also a tyrant, and so was Brazil's. Mexico's Maximilian was far more respectable than Iturbide, but Maximilian had no opportunity to display his political talents. Only Brazil's Pedro II was outstanding for his moderation and statesmanship. Elsewhere in Latin America the constitutional presidents were mainly dictators in spite of the fundamental law that was supposed to hedge their power.

The republican constitutions [1] defined with great care the functions and powers of government and usually contained liberal personal guaranties, such as freedom of speech and of the press, freedom of occupation and movement, and equality before the law. Only religious toleration was lacking in most of the early constitutions, and even that was provided in the later ones. But the democratic republics, like the constitutional monarchies, were nearly always confined to the paper on which the constitutions were written. In practice, they were governed more or less as had been the colonies, according to the absolutist tradition. Men called presidents, or by some other title, frequently governed as tyrannically as if they had been viceroys or captains general. Elections were seldom either free or fair—for many years suffrage was usually limited to adult males having property or the ability to read and write. Bills of rights were no more respected than other provisions of the constitutions. Nor, as a rule, was the general welfare conceived to be the primary purpose of government. Clever and ruthless army officers or civilians, with a trophy concept of public office, seized the government in order to use it for themselves and their small cliques. And this was especially unfortunate in Latin America, where the people lacked capital, technical skill, and talent for the management of large-scale enterprises, which consequently had to be launched and managed by the government, either directly or through contracts with foreign capitalists.

ᚠᚣ THE FRUSTRATION OF HUMANITARIAN IDEALS

Yet it should not be assumed that there was no idealism in Latin America during the early National period. Some have argued that there was too much of it pouring in from France and the United States, too much perfectionism and too little willingness to adapt and compromise. Fundamentally, politics everywhere is a struggle for power, a continual contest between parties and groups for the control of government. The democratic ideal requires that the struggle shall proceed without violence and according to honorable rules and that the winners shall be compelled to serve the national interest—a high standard rarely attained in any country and too seldom approached by those of Latin America. Because of the handicaps of colonial heritage, racial and cultural diversity, and mountain and jungle topography, the mere task of maintaining order often left little energy or resources for other public services. Still, in spite of these handicaps, and despite the strong militaristic tendencies developed by the wars for independence and the petty international conflicts that followed, a little humanitarianism was sometimes compounded with the prevailing brutality and selfishness.

With the view of enlisting the blacks in the armies, but also because slavery was considered a great evil, there began with the outbreak of the wars for independence a halting movement to emancipate the Negro slaves in Spanish America—there were at this time probably not more than 300,000 of them, outside of Española, Puerto Rico, and Cuba. Later, children of slaves were declared free at birth, although retained by the masters in a sort of apprenticeship until they were grown. Complete emancipation was proclaimed in Chile in 1823, in Central America in 1824, in Bolivia in 1826, in Mexico (excluding Texas) in 1829, in Uruguay in 1846, and in all the independent countries of Spanish America except Paraguay by the end of 1854. While Negro slaves were neither numerous nor urgently needed because of the bountiful supply of Indian and mestizo serfs, their emancipation in some parts of Peru, Ecuador, Colombia, and Venezuela was no doubt considered a real sacrifice to humanitarian ideals. In Brazil, where black slaves formed a much larger segment of the total labor force, emancipation made little progress until 1871 and was not completed until 1888, after it became evident that European immigrants, particularly Italians, could be depended upon for a labor supply.[2]

Humanitarianism was less evident in the case of the Indians and mestizos. By enlisting in the armies during the struggle for liberation from Spain some of the Indians obtained exemption from the tributes that had oppressed them since the early days of the Conquest, but this discriminatory levy was not generally abandoned until around the middle of the century or later. Service in the army was a means utilized also by other members of the lower class to improve their lot; but, in general, the oligarchy of landowners, mining operators, clergymen, army officers, merchants, and the learned professions who took charge of the new nations after the expulsion of the Europeans disclosed little interest in the welfare of the masses. Here and there some zealot, like Alexandre Pétion in Haiti following 1810, or Bernardo Rivadavia in Argentina in the 1820's, or Braulio Carillo in Costa Rica in the 1830's, or Benito Juárez in Mexico in the 1850's, or Tomás Guardia in Costa Rica in the 1870's might give serious consideration to a wider distribution of the land; but significant agrarian and labor reforms were long postponed in most countries, and in many of them they were not even attempted. Debt peonage or some other system differing little from serfdom was prevalent in the majority of the nations until well after 1900.

If a fair appraisal is to be made, however, it should always be remembered that the task of retaining power and keeping order was so all-absorbing that almost no attention could be given to the promotion of the general welfare. Ambitious and intolerant leaders of the opposition, when not attempting to seize the national government, were busy trying to rule their own provinces. Champions of local autonomy abounded in every country, and it was almost impossible to govern the nations as a whole. Local chiefs had to be suppressed or paid off again and again. The federal system of government was sanctioned by the constitutions at one time or another in all the larger nations; and even when the fundamental law provided for a "unitarian" or centralist system, the local bosses—called *caudillos*—often continued to rule their provinces and not infrequently attempted to utilize them as a means of extending their dominance over the entire republic. The majority of Mexico's republican constitutions adopted federalism, Argentina's fundamental charter of 1853 sanctioned this system, and Venezuela seems to have accepted it permanently in the 1860's. New Granada became the

Central America about 1850

Shaded areas show British control

MAP 10

Granadine Confederation in the 1850's and the United States of Colombia in 1863, but renounced federalism by the constitution of 1886. Brazil, where provincialism and sectionalism were strong from the outset, became a federal republic after the overthrow of the monarchy in 1889. The doctrine of "States' rights" in Latin America, whatever may have been true elsewhere, was not based solely on principle; it was a slogan wielded in a struggle for power which diverted the energies of the national governments from constructive policies that might have improved the public services and stimulated the economy.

⅏ CONFLICTS OF CHURCH AND STATE

Church-State relations caused distraction and disorder almost everywhere, and especially in Mexico, Central America, Colombia, and Ecuador, where no other issue aroused such profound bitterness. Europe's religious conflicts of an earlier age were re-enacted during the nineteenth century in the American tropics.[3]

The Roman Catholic Church had played a leading role during the long Colonial period, and at its end was not only influential but wealthy. It engaged in many activities, social, economic, and political as well as religious. It had charge of worship, baptism, wedding ceremonies, registration of births and deaths, funerals, graveyards, administration of oaths, religious processions and festivals, holiday celebrations, frontier missions, education, hospitals, charity, and banking. It possessed not only an immense number of buildings for public worship and for housing the religious orders, but vast tax-exempt holdings of urban and rural real estate used for strictly business purposes, many industrial enterprises, and mortgages on extensive properties owned and managed by laymen; and besides its large income from these sources, it also received considerable sums in the form of gifts, tithes, and fees. In short, it controlled a goodly portion of the wealth of Latin America and enjoyed not only tax exemption but special courts for both civil and criminal cases involving clergymen.

It had, as a rule, been dominated during the Colonial epoch by the royal authorities, who used it as a means of social control and as an agent of colonial expansion. With minor exceptions, its high officials had opposed the emancipation movement; and after independence was won, they attempted to free the church from the control of the civil power. In fact, in some instances they went even further. Participating actively in politics and frequently holding public office during the early National period, they tried to control the State and make it the servant of the Church.

It is likely that many clergymen, assuming that they alone were the servants of God and the true friends of mankind, sincerely believed that they were entitled to rule the people as well as to serve as their religious and moral guides. But the majority of the political and military leaders viewed the matter in a different light. They did not believe that the State should become the instrument of the Roman Catholic Church; they felt, on the contrary, that the State should be the supreme authority in the nation, and, in societies where the Church impinged on the life of the people at every point and enjoyed an immense income, they sought to make a place for the civil authority and find revenues to implement its expanding functions.

The conflict involved both ideals and interests. In part it was a struggle for revenues, power, property, and prestige and for the creation of conditions that would attract immigrants accustomed to religious toleration; in part it was a struggle for greater intellectual freedom, the curtailment of special privileges, and the creation of wider opportunities for at least some of the people. In the end, the functions, privileges, and wealth of the Church were reduced in the interest of the State, and in the interest of those it governed, provided the State was able and willing to use its power in their behalf. In most instances, however, all that the people obtained from the expensive, bloody, and prolonged conflict was a little more freedom in religion—in which they were not seriously concerned, since they were content to remain Roman Catholics —and somewhat broader opportunities for education. The Church properties taken over by the State were not widely distributed; they fell into the hands of the oligarchy and continued to be almost as immune from taxation as they had been under the Church, and almost as inalienable.

The Church-State issue was mainly responsible for the origin of the two most important political parties—factions would perhaps be a more precise description—formed during the early National period, the Liberals and the Conservatives, or Clericals. The Conservatives, as a rule, insisted on the exercise of the *patronato*—the right to participate in the selection of high officials of the church, to be consulted in the formation of new ecclesiastical jurisdictions, and to pass upon papal documents before they were circulated within the national domain—and made slight encroachments on the traditional functions of the church in education and in some other fields, but were willing to call a halt at that point provided the church revealed a disposition to contribute to the party chest in times of stress. More under the influence of French radicalism and usually from a somewhat less affluent and aristocratic stratum of society, the Liberals seem to have lost favor with the powerful members of the clergy from the beginning; and for partisan as well as other reasons were soon demanding not merely the exercise of the patronage but the abolition of nearly all the traditional functions of the church, the suppression of the religious communities, and the seizure of church properties that were not being utilized for strictly religious purposes. By the middle of the nineteenth century these two parties, divided on other issues but especially with reference to the place of the church in the national regime, were in existence in practically every country.

℁ TURBULENCE AND TYRANNY

Much of the national histories of most of the Latin-American countries have been characterized by turbulence and tyranny. While there were variations from nation to nation, these early decades were about equally apportioned between dictatorship and military anarchy. Nor can it be repeated too often that the major factors tending to produce both were colonial heritage; conflicts of religion, race, and class; geography; and the prolonged struggle for national independence and national domains.

Absolutism was traditional. The whites and mixbloods had been accustomed for centuries to the despotism of viceroys and captains general, and to the imposition of their own authority, as masters and labor bosses, upon the working class below. The Indians, the largest racial group in many countries, had long been dominated by local tyrants, priests, or native chiefs who had been allowed to survive as instruments of social control. The Negroes and mulattoes, numerically predominant in Española and a significant element in Venezuela, Colombia, and some of the other tropical regions, were slaves and serviles. Too many members of the upper class were determined after independence to occupy dominant positions in the governments; few were willing to accept subordinate roles, and while the aristocracy was not numerous, there were not enough high posts for all either in Church or State. The power-drive was overwhelming among the army officers, who could not be reconciled to the obscurity that civilian rule would have imposed upon them. Like the generals of Alexander the Great, those of Bolívar, San Martín, Iturbide, and Toussaint L'Ouverture—and their lieutenants after them—were determined to dominate until the end. In a region where a multiple series of wars had to be fought for independence and the delimitation of national boundaries, the shackles of militarism were firmly fastened upon the people. The ignorant, impoverished, and morose masses, lacking the intelligence to perceive their own best interests, could not resist the recruiting officers or the seductive appeals of men on horseback with their brilliant uniforms, provocative slogans, and promises of loot and redemption. The sword had been the arbiter for so long that it was difficult to find or even envisage any other. Government by the counting of ballots at the polls or in legislative assemblies appeared inane and absurd to men lacking the democratic tradition and experience in democratic procedures. It seemed more heroic to determine issues with saber and machete, pistol and musket. The vanquished faced the rising sun and the firing squad like martyrs or pined away in nostalgic exile. And the anarchy of passion and imperious wills was fostered and protected by geography. The centers of settlement in nearly every country were widely scattered or surrounded by mountain walls, parched deserts, or matted jungle, and lack of efficient means of transportation made them so difficult to reach from the main seat of government that disobedience and insurgency could not be suppressed in their incipient stages.

The result of all this was an almost perpetual crisis. When the crisis did not arise from domestic conditions it was produced by menace from the outside, by threats of aggression from neighboring countries or Europe. No words were employed more frequently by the leaders of these young nations than *la crisis* and *el abismo*. Yet hope was never abandoned; on the contrary, there was usually a messianic tone in political utterances: "liberator," "savior of the country," "restorer of order," "founder of peace," "deliverer of the people," "champion of the national honor." No doubt there were some sincere reformers and patriots among the rulers, but often the governments seemed to be operated by shifts of fortune hunters who abused and betrayed every noble cause. Whatever the character of these imperious personalities, however, the political history of the epoch is practically synonymous with their biographies.

They are difficult to classify. The majority were army officers, but some were civilians who managed for a time to outwit or retain the loyalty of the military. Many were ephemeral rulers, elevated and deposed by capricious fortune, men whose names hardly deserve to be recalled; but not a few were dominant for more than a decade. Some were whites and some were Indians or Negroes, but the majority were mestizos or mulattoes, except in countries where the Caucasians managed to consolidate their position because the more primitive groups were less numerous or less successful in their thrusts for power. A few were sober and abstemious; many were sensual and corrupt, some constantly under the influence of strong drink. Some were pious or pro-church, a few were atheists or freethinkers vigorously opposed to the church, more seem to have been little influenced by their religion. Some had constructive programs; others had none; a few were mere soldiers of fortune.

Perhaps their most common characteristics were their willingness to gamble with fate and their fondness for titles, pomp, and ceremony. The road to power was bloody, and hazardous even for the leaders. Failure meant imprisonment, expatriation, or facing the victor with back to adobe wall and a last look at the palms, the blue mountains, and the wheeling buzzards. And success was hardly less perilous than failure. Power must be maintained by censorship, propaganda, and the sword, and the system was expensive. Funds had to be secured from excise taxes, tariffs, tributes, forced loans, confiscations, shares in the profits of concessions and monopolies, debasement of the currency, and bond issues sold to foreign investors or local speculators. Enemies, traitors, and assassins lurked everywhere; catastrophe always hovered near. Sooner or later a filthy prison, death, or ostracism was almost certain to be encountered. Ex-dictators were seldom tolerated; only the most fortunate were able to escape to foreign lands with a sufficient sum, taken from enemies or the treasury or obtained from partisans, to ensure a comfortable old age. As for pomp and ceremony, it appears that medals, ribbons, uniforms, and parades were in part a pose for political effect and in part an expression of innate fondness for display. The ruler was rare who did not cover his entire chest with decorations or accumulate sonorous titles a quarter of a page long.

Dictators with a constructive bent usually tackled such problems as communications, transport, education, and whatever barriers impeded their progress, or tried to stimulate agriculture and industry in other ways. As a rule, however, they expended the major part of their resources in suppressing insurgents and constructing commemorative monuments and public buildings in the national capitals and their home towns. They usually proclaimed eternal devotion to democracy, liberty, and country and eternal hostility to special privilege. Sometimes they meant what they said, but often such avowals merely embroidered a demand for the opposition to clear out and make room for a new shift of the crew.

The histories of the young nations, as already suggested, were not all the same. There were, in fact, marked differences among them. A few had nothing but despots as their rulers; a good many had along with their tyrants a leaven of autocrats who revealed a large measure of respect for the liberties of the people. Some—Mexico, Guatemala, Nicaragua, the Dominican Republic, Venezuela, Ecuador, Peru, Paraguay, Brazil—were conspicuous during this period or later for their long-term rulers. Others had a rapid succession of chief executives. Chile, Argentina, Costa Rica, and monarchal Brazil advanced fairly steadily toward order and liberty. Mexico, until 1867, the Dominican

Republic from 1844 to 1880, Honduras and El Salvador from 1839 to 1900, Paraguay from 1870 to 1900, Colombia from 1849 to 1903, and Venezuela from 1846 to 1870 were in chaos most of the time; and Uruguay, which was to become a model republic, seethed with almost continuous revolt. Ecuador began with despotic stability, sank into fifteen years of roaring turbulence, achieved order under a pious tyrant, and fell into another period of anarchy. Peru, after a chaotic beginning, attained comparative stability only to descend again into near chaos and lose its boundary war with Chile.

With reference to the history of Latin America as a whole during the period from independence to the closing decade of the nineteenth century, the following generalizations may be offered for illustration and justification in the chapters that follow: (1) Violent attacks upon the wealth and functions of the Roman Catholic Church occurred in all the nations save Haiti, the Dominican Republic, Nicaragua, Peru, Uruguay, and Brazil, and some efforts were made to curtail its power in most of these countries. (2) The forces of tradition and reaction were defeated in almost every country in which a vigorous Church-State conflict occurred, with the exception of Colombia and Ecuador, where theocratic oligarchies temporarily triumphed. (3) Turbulence, despotism, and violence retarded but did not entirely prevent economic and cultural advance; the governments of even the most primitive and turbulent countries, such as Haiti, Bolivia, and Paraguay, adopted constitutions committing themselves to compulsory and gratuitous elementary education for the masses. (4) Progress toward political democracy was not made in many of the republics, although a few—Costa Rica, Chile, Argentina, and Brazil—seemed to be moving in that direction; army officers were the chief executives of most of the republics at the end of the period, as the following list shows:

1. Haiti—General Teresias A. Simon Sam (1891–1902)
2. Dominican Republic—General Ulises Heureaux (1882–99)
3. Mexico—General Porfirio Díaz (1884–1911)
4. Guatemala—Manuel Estrada Cabrera (1898–1920)
5. El Salvador—General Tomás Regalado (1898–1903)
6. Honduras—General Policarpo Bonilla (1895–98)
7. Nicaragua—General José Santos Zelaya (1893–1909)
8. Costa Rica—Rafael Iglesias (1894–1902)
9. Colombia—Miguel Antonio Caro (1894–98)
10. Venezuela—General Cipriano Castro (1899–1908)
11. Ecuador—General Flavio Eloy Alfaro (1895–1901)
12. Peru—Nicolás Piérola (1895–99)

13. Bolivia—Severo Fernández Alonso (1896–99)
14. Chile—Federico Arrázuriz (1896–1901)
15. Argentina—General Julio Roca (1898–1904)
16. Uruguay—Juan L. Cuestas (1897–1903)
17. Paraguay—General Juan B. Egusquiza (1894–98)
18. Brazil—Manoel Campos Salles (1898–1902)

The dates in parentheses indicate the periods of uninterrupted dominance. Porfirio Díaz's dominance actually began in late 1876. Eloy Alfaro became chief executive of Ecuador again in 1906 and held the post until 1911. Generals were at the head of the national governments in ten of the eighteen countries in 1898, but General Roca of Argentina was not a dictator. It is likely that the army was the dominant political force in 1898 in all the republics except Costa Rica, Bolivia, Chile, Argentina, and Brazil. Bolivia's Conservative civilian government was deposed by revolution in 1899, and Colombia's most prolonged revolt of the National period, 1825–1900, began in 1899.

CHAPTER XIII

Haiti and the Dominican Republic

🕮 HAITI

The long story of disorder and despotism in independent Latin America begins in the island of Española—30,000 square miles of mountain, jungle, savanna, and tropical valleys—scene of the first European colony in the New World, seat of the first independent government in Latin America, and eventually the domain of two rival nations, one Franco-African and the other Hispano-African. The population of this little theater of impending conflict, around 1790, was less than 700,000 and overwhelmingly Negro and Negroid. Seventy or eighty thousand whites and a much smaller number of freedmen were exploiting 500,000 slaves. The western third of the island, where between 30,000 and 40,000 resident Frenchmen lived from the sweat and toil of some 450,-000 black and mulatto slaves, and treated with contempt more than 20,000 "free people of color," was rather densely settled; the eastern two-thirds contained hardly more than 125,000 inhabitants, 40,000 Spaniards and the rest yellows and blacks, a good many of them enslaved and the remainder theoretically free but fettered by peonage and poverty.

The weak Spanish colony of Española, its manpower drained off by the mainland settlements, had not been able to defend itself against the intrusion of French buccaneers, who gained a foothold on the northwest coast in 1630 and were soon joined by other Frenchmen. In 1697 Spain had recognized the title of France to the western borders of the island, which included only the irregular area between the outer mountain ranges and the sea—the limits of the French colony were not definitely fixed until 1777—and never reached more than twenty-five or thirty miles inland. The French portion was mostly impressive scenery; but there were some fertile alluvial plains, and French enterprise and ingenuity, utilizing the hard labor of African slaves, soon transformed buccaneer hunting grounds into plantations producing sugar cane, cotton, tobacco, cacao, and indigo. Elaborate irrigation systems, highways, and sugar mills were constructed to serve the plantations; distilleries, brick yards, lime kilns, and potteries were operated as subsidiary industries. It was not long until the sugar production of French Saint-Domingue exceeded that of all the British West Indies combined. By the 1780's France was importing most of its tropical products from this small colony.

All this prosperity was founded upon an immense concentration of imported Negroes and a caste system based upon both wealth and color. The *grands blancs,* the white masters of the plantations, together with the French royal officials, were the ruling class. The more numerous *petits blancs* served as overseers and skilled workmen or followed minor independent occupations in the towns. Rigid distinctions in wealth and social prestige caused bitter antagonism between these two classes of whites. The freedmen (*affranchis*) competed with the *petits blancs* or tried to ape the *grands blancs,* but racial discrimination doomed them to an inferior social status and denied them even the political privileges of the *petits blancs.* Whether yellow or black, however, the *affranchis,* or at least some of them, did not scruple to hold less fortunate colored men as slaves. This slave class, composing about nine-tenths of the total population, had neither civil rights nor social standing, yet the color line prevailed even here, the some 40,000 mulatto slaves holding themselves superior to their fellow bondsmen. Each layer of society in French Saint-Domingue regarded every other with extreme jealousy or profound contempt.

This discordant social structure could not withstand the shock of the French Revolution. It exploded and erupted in the black smoke and red flames of prolonged, confused, and bloody civil war. The turmoil lasted more a decade (1791–1803); exterminated or banished all the whites; brought death and destruction to thousands of mulattoes and blacks; thrust up an able group of Negro and mulatto warriors; and ended in the liberation of both the slaves and the colony.

Independence, proclaimed on January 1, 1804, had been won by intrepid Africans, aided by yellow fever and Europe's strife, but it left the reduced population face to face with grave economic, political, and social problems. French Saint-Domingue had been destroyed, but the first experiment in Negro self-government within the pale of civilization was still to be conducted and tested, under distinctly unfavorable conditions and without much hope of aid or sympathy from an unfriendly world.

The physical environment, as already suggested, was not altogether favorable. It was not so much that Haiti, as the new nation was called, was situated in tropical seas. The Negroes were used to the tropics. It was rather that it was mountainous and dispersed. Steep ranges rising abruptly to an average height of 3,000 feet, but with some peaks soaring to an altitude of 8,000, were a serious obstacle to communication. Urban centers were confined to the seaboard. Distinctions between town and country were accentuated. Sectionalism was fostered. Control of the central government over the provinces was weakened by topographical barriers.

Since there were no important mineral deposits in Haiti and since much of the valuable timber had been cut away, the chief resource of the country was the fertility of its soil. But the sloping terrain exposed it to rapid erosion; and with the exception of the well-watered Plaine du Nord, the more level parts could be fully exploited only by means of systematic irrigation. Yet the elaborate works built by the French planters had been ruined by war and neglect, and the skill and energy required to restore them were lacking. Given leaders with the knowledge of what needed to be done and the will to do it, there was still a labor problem. Apparently labor could be had only by compulsion, but the various labor codes promulgated over the years for that purpose gradually became ineffective. The more untractable cultivators drifted away to the foothills and the mountains, where the necessities of a simple life could easily be obtained and where coffee could be gathered and sold for cash with a minimum of effort. The diminishing group of planters—mostly mulattoes, but some Negroes—abandoned the land and moved to town, where they could live on their dwindling rents and the public treasury, which was sustained mainly by duties on imports and exports. A policy of land distribution was inaugurated early and continued for several decades, but such sharecroppers and small farmers as remained in the plains were left largely to their own devices, and were soon producing little more than food for themselves and the local markets. This agricultural transformation involved the substitution of coffee for sugar as the Haitian staple and signified the total abandonment of intensive agriculture upon which had rested the wealth and commercial renown of French Saint-Domingue.

Social problems were as difficult as those arising from the physical environment. More than half of the population was under the influence of early years spent in African jungles and tribal societies, and almost none of the people had any experience save that known in the Dark Continent, suffered in slavery, or gained in one of the most barbarous wars in history. The culture of Africa had more meaning, for the blacks at least, than the civilization of France, which they had observed almost exclusively in the person of the slave driver and the invading soldier. The vast majority were peasants, and half of these were residents of the foothills and mountains, fugitives from civilization as they knew it, dwelling in isolation by preference, worshipping African gods, and following the ways of their ancestors little modified by contacts with Western civilization.

Only urban Haiti, composed for the most part of the new ruling class and its servants and attendants and forming no more than 5 or 10 per cent of the total population, consciously modeled its life upon European forms and patterns. Here dwelt the elite, hardly more than 1 per cent of the inhabitants, with its nucleus the *affranchis,* who were the only group with any experience in the management of public affairs, but including such rough and rude men of action as the troubled times brought forward. Representing authority, since they filled the offices and possessed what education and wealth there were, the members of this elite class were proud of their European style, which was the badge of their social superiority and the sanction of their claim to distinction, and were ardently patriotic in the sense that most of them were fiercely determined never to surrender the control of Haiti to any outside authority. As a class, however, they lacked a vivid feeling of social responsibility, differing little in this respect from the aristocratic French planters of the colony, who seemed to be their model of what a ruling class should be. Remembering the colonial hierarchy and its social attitudes, they regarded with disdain both unskilled labor and the tasks once performed by the humbler whites and the free men of color. Caring little for the sons of the people, they provided only a literary education for their own, with a government post as the ultimate objective. The result was a few journalists and men of letters, a good many lawyers, an array of politicians and bureaucrats, and no engineers, skilled artisans, and scientific farmers to promote the material advancement of the country.

Color prejudice also prevailed. Deeply rooted in colonial experience, it had been fomented rather than allayed by the long civil wars that began in 1791. For a few months the Negroes and mulattoes had collaborated in the expulsion of the French because France had threatened both, but previous jealousies between blacks and yellows could not be forgotten by the revolutionary generation. Since the elite were predominantly mulatto, color prejudice often merged with other distinctions separating the aristocracy and the masses, but it persisted. The whites had been extirpated, constitutions and laws declared all men black and equal, but the Black Republic continued to be divided by a color line, not only socially but politically. The Negro party was called Nationalist; the mulatto party, Liberal.

And there was extreme militarism. The long war preceding independence had deprived Haiti of every inhabitant experienced in civil government; produced a number of outstanding warriors, such as Toussaint L'Ouverture, Jean Jacques Dessalines (Haiti's paramount national hero), Henri Christophe, and Alexandre Pétion; and militarized the country. After thirteen years of combat the only authority recognized was the authority derived from military rank. No civil administration existed and none was ever firmly established. Almost without exception the rulers were generals. Nor did this extreme militarism lack justification. An army seemed to be required to effect the unification of Haiti proper, a task not accomplished until 1820, as well as to liberate and govern the eastern two-thirds of the island and defend the whole against foreign menace and aggression. No foreign power deigned to recognize Haiti until after France took that step in 1825, and it was 1838 before a reasonably satisfactory settlement was reached with France, a settlement that left Haiti deeply in debt for indemnities to the descendants of the late planter class. The eastern part of Española, conquered and lost by Toussaint, was recovered in 1822 and lost again in 1844; and still the Haitians refused to reconcile themselves to its secession.

Violence and instability were the natural result of this colonial heritage, physical environment, social and political cleavage, and foreign danger. Whatever the numerous constitutions—there were fourteen of them by 1886—may have stipulated with reference to the sphere of government and the rights of the governed, political power in Haiti was seldom actually curbed by the fundamental law, and it was always attained, exercised, and defended mainly by naked force. Changes in personnel were effected by military coups or campaigns; and although really destructive civil wars were rare, military uprisings were sufficiently numerous to create an atmosphere of insecurity and make the possession of power an end in itself, a prize to be enjoyed to the utmost while enjoyment was possible.[1]

The early decades of Haitian political history were but a continuation of the internecine conflict that began in the last years of the Colonial period. The expulsion of the French authorities at the end of 1803 dissolved the alliance between the Negro Dessalines, heir of the Negro Toussaint, and the mulatto Pétion, heir of the mulatto André Rigaud, whom Toussaint had driven into exile. It was only two years before the old feud was renewed by the assassination of Emperor Dessalines (Jacques the First) by Pétion's adherents. The civil war that broke out in 1806 between Pétion and Christophe, Toussaint's surviving black lieutenant, dragged on intermittently for fourteen years. Adopting the forms of a feudal monarchy, Christophe (Henri I) ruled northern Haiti as he would an army (1806–20), dividing his subjects into workers and soldiers and rigidly enforcing L'Ouverture's compulsory labor system of an earlier day, while Pétion, his milder adversary in the south and west, seeking both to please the elite and placate the masses, tried to found an aristocratic republic, but actually exercised dictatorial powers and finally obtained a life-presidency with the right to select his successor. Embodying the only principles ever of basic significance in Haitian politics—Christophe's individual dictatorship and Pétion's dictatorship of the elite—these two leaders set the political course for the future. The black Nationalists followed the precedent set by Christophe, aspiring to a crown or a lifetime hold on the chief executiveship; the Negro and mulatto elite followed the example set by Pétion and favored an aristocratic dictatorship operated by a long-term president and a parliament in which they could display their forensic talents. Rival leaders struggled violently for political and administrative posts, and the masses, who might have been compelled to enlist in the armies in any case, sought escape through civil wars from grinding poverty.

If any other issues besides personal and class rivalry (accentuated by the color division) and the rewards of power and plunder were ever involved, they were these: rotation in office, responsibility of the military to the civil authorities, and responsibility of the executive to the legislative body. The religious issue was unimportant in Haiti; the Roman Catholic Church was not strong, and the ecclesiastical authorities in Rome were comparatively indifferent. The elite were Catholics because that religion seemed appropriate to their status; the masses were devoted to the cult of Voodooism, with its magic, charms, spells, and superstitions; and all religions were tolerated, although the Roman Catholic Church was favored officially by the terms of the Concordat of 1860.

Alternations of chief executives were less rapid in Haiti, however, than in many of the other Latin-American countries. During the first eighty-five years of the National period there were only fourteen administrations, and since three of these covered only four years between them and since Emperor Dessalines ruled for only two, the other ten averaged nearly eight years each. Pétion died in 1818; King Henri I died in 1820; and by the end of 1822 Jean Pierre Boyer, Pétion's protégé and Haiti's only really long-term autocrat during this period, was ruling the whole island. This reunion, followed soon by recognition on the part of several European powers, gave some promise of a new era; but in spite of legislative and judicial forms borrowed from France, civil government was not developed. Boyer followed the military-executive tradition, and although continuing to distribute land to the peasants, devoted little attention to education. No great economic or social development occurred. After twenty-five years in office (1818–43), and the accumulation of a small fortune, Boyer was overthrown by ardent young mulattoes who complained that he had limited the patronage to "old-timers" and demanded that Pétion's earlier liberal policies be put into practice. The "new era" promised by the reformers proved sterile, producing four years of chaos during which three black generals occupied the presidential palace in rapid succession and Spanish Santo Domingo was lost, and ending in the twelve-year monarchical dictatorship of Faustin Soulouque (1847–59), brutal and corrupt imitator of Dessalines and Christophe. The Liberals, under the leadership of Fabre Geffard, another mulatto, seized the government in 1859; but when eight years of "regeneration" failed to redeem the country, or alter the hard fact of military dictatorship, another upheaval occurred, and after still another series of dictatorships and revolutions the Liberal elite finally lost power and any chance they may have had to lift their nation to a higher level. An educated black general from the mulatto south—his name was Lysius Salomon and he was married to a beautiful French wife—took charge of the government in 1879 and held it, in spite of incendiary insurgents, until 1888.

The mulatto Boisrond Canal was the only president of Haiti (1876–79) during the century who ever tried seriously to observe the constitution. Convinced that most of his country's political ills sprang from the arbitrariness of the national executives, he seems to have respected the fundamental law. But the members of the *Corps Legislatif,* although mostly belonging to his own party, spent so much time asserting their supremacy and lecturing him on his duties that they forgot to enact the promised reforms of the latest "new era" and condemned his administration to futility. The elections to determine Canal's successor were conducted far more honestly than usual, and the Nationalist opposition won. The defeated candidate then provoked a disturbance and threatened a coup, whereupon Canal intervened and suppressed his own party—and then resigned in utter disillusionment a year before his term expired, convinced that the constitutional regime was a failure.[2]

Did any changes that might be described as progress take place during the first eight decades of Haitian independence? In the absence of satisfactory statistics, this is not easy to determine. Population slowly increased, but per capita production probably declined, certainly production for export. The masses, freed from slavery before they were released from French control, escaped from the exploitation of compulsory labor, but they did not escape from conscription into the armies, nor did they receive any appreciable benefits from education or other social services. As late as 1875 there were only a little over 19,000 pupils in Haiti's schools, and no doubt nearly all of these were the sons and daughters of the aristocracy, some of whom completed their education abroad. This small group, mostly mulattoes but including a few Negroes, made some cultural advance, as evidenced in their newspapers, books, and other literary productions. After they lost control of the government and the opportunity to develop and display their oratorical talents in the *Corps Legislatif,* they produced a number of creditable works on Haitian problems. The remedies they prescribed for their country's ills were a sounder and more practical education; honesty in public office; the abandonment of color prejudice and class discrimination; divorce of the army from politics; and more efficient exploitation of natural resources. But many decades would have to pass before their elaborate prescription could be filled.

Haiti was no more disorderly than the average Latin-American nation during the twenty years following the violent overthrow of Lysius Salomon in 1888. Three of the four black generals who ruled the country during these two decades managed to cling to the government for an average of more than six years each, only a few months less than the seven-year term prescribed by the constitution under which they were supposed to govern. But an era of ephemeral chief executives and political and fiscal chaos began in 1908 after the last of the four black generals was ousted by a revolution. Military uprising followed military uprising with accelerating speed until the Black Republic was threatened with extinction.

🐚 THE DOMINICAN REPUBLIC

Haiti's Spanish-speaking neighbors in the less crowded eastern part of Española, where the population numbered around 200,000 in the 1840's, revealed only a little more efficiency in the exploitation of their material resources and no greater capacity for orderly self-government. Here, as in Haiti, there were mountain barriers that hampered government, trade, and communication and arid sections requiring irrigation; but fertile land and timber were more abundant. Here were a good many whites—although they were outnumbered by both Negroes and mulattoes—comparatively few ex-slaves, a little less illiteracy, a somewhat higher level of culture, and almost no racial conflict, for the Haitian policy of Africanization, which had increased the darker element in the population and driven many white families into temporary or permanent exile, seems, quite surprisingly, not to have appreciably increased color prejudice among the Dominicans themselves. And yet, in spite of these apparent advantages, the inhabitants of this side of the island were unprepared for liberty and democracy when they won their independence in 1844 because they had received no training in politics or public administration under Spain and had been given no effective voice in government during the two decades of Haitian rule. They soon revealed passionate intolerance, extreme local and regional loyalties, and utter inability to resist the trend toward militarism, which seemed necessary for a time because of almost constant threats from militarized Haiti. The Dominican Republic, like its closest neighbor, was tyrannical and turbulent.

During the first forty years following its release from Haitian domination it was disturbed by revolution every twelve months or so; and although many of the uprisings were suppressed, a few succeeded in overthrowing the national government, which always depended for its support upon the armed *caudillos* who controlled the provinces. Constitutions were frequently discarded or amended—there were eight or ten of them by 1887—and seldom accorded much respect. Military ability was the paramount qualification for high office; almost every chief executive was a general, and army officers usually filled most of the cabinet posts just as they dominated the local governments.

As a rule, the various constitutions prescribed a single term of two to four years and barred immediate "re-election," but each "president" usually attempted to perpetuate his rule. Yet, until the late 1880's, no ambitious politician was able to retain power for more than six years in succession. The opposing forces, organized in two or three bitterly antagonistic groups ("Reds," "Blues," and, at one time, "Greens"), were evenly matched, and therefore frequently alternated in power; but since personalities far outweighed principles, a few outstanding chiefs managed to seize the government repeatedly, after spending the intervals in exile—defeated candidates and their partisans usually found asylum in Curação, St. Thomas, Puerto Rico, or Venezuela—and borrowing from speculators the funds required to purchase the *elementos de guerra* (sometimes gunboats as well as arms and munitions) for another campaign.

In a land free from decided race prejudice (though deeply divided in other respects), where no color line distinguished the partisan organizations, men of all colors dared aspire to the highest offices. And men of all colors succeeded in capturing them about as often as their numbers warranted. This meant, of course, that men of darker hue ruled most of the time, either in person or in the background. While the whites may have furnished most of the ideology, such as there was of it, and some of the strategy as well, the dominating political personalities, of the earlier and the later period alike, were mulattoes or Negroes.

Pedro Santana, who had charge of the government on four different occasions and for a total of eleven years, was largely Spanish but part Indian or African. A rough ranchman, farmer, and lumberman from the southeastern section of the island, he was the outstanding warrior of the independence period and the nation's first president. Buenaventura Báez, Santana's protégé and soon his bitterest rival, was a well-to-do mulatto from the southwestern part of the country who held the reigns of government on five different occasions between 1849 and 1878 for a total of fifteen years. Gregorio Luperón, who became the uncompromising opponent of Báez shortly after Santana's death in 1864 and who, without occupying the presidential post for long, was a powerful political chief for twenty years, imposing and deposing "presidents" almost at will, was a Negro from the northern coastal region. Ulises Heureaux, who put an end to Luperón's dominance, in the early 1880's, was a young Negro from the same region, whom Luperón had sponsored and treated almost as a son. Leaders of Spanish descent—such as Manuel Jiménez in the 1840's and Ignacio María González, Ulises F. Espaillat, and Padre Fernando A. Meriño (later an archbishop) in the 1870's and 1880's—were never able to govern for more than two or three years at a time. The fact that Father Meriño attained the highest political post in the country indicates that clergymen were not entirely divorced from politics; but conflicts between the civil and the ecclesiastical power were never very serious, especially after 1865.

Although there were a few notable exceptions, such as Jiménez and Espaillat, practically all these rulers, including the padre, were despotic, and most of them were tyrannical and brutal, if not corrupt. Santana turned his country over to Spain in 1861; Báez was willing to sell it in any market that seemed to offer him personal and pecuniary advantage, and almost succeeded in his negotiations with the corrupt clique that surrounded President U. S. Grant. Heureaux was the worst of the lot, even more ruthless, cruel, and depraved than Buenaventura Báez. Perhaps it is symbolic of the immense divergence between Dominican political ideals and actualities that the number-one hero of the nation, Juan Pablo Duarte, should have spent most of his life in exile. An admirable and tragic figure who organized the movement for independence, he was banished by Santana in 1844. He buried himself so completely on the remote frontier of Venezuela that he was generally believed to be dead; but when he heard that Spain had regained control of his country against the will of his compatriots, he returned home and offered his services to the leaders who were fighting the second war for independence. His offer, however, was rejected and he departed again for Venezuela, where he died in 1876. He was among the few leaders of his day who had firm confidence in the capacity of the Dominicans to rule themselves and steadfastly insisted upon their freedom from the control of Haiti or any other foreign power.

For a few years after the beginning of the fourth quarter of the century the situation in the Dominican Republic seemed promising. Under the dominance of Luperón, political conditions improved for a time. Chief executives retained control for the brief terms prescribed by the latest constitution and transmitted their authority to their successors without much commotion. Cubans and other foreigners entered the country and improved ranching and planting by introducing more efficient methods in the livestock and sugar industries. Finances improved under better management and some attention was given to the public services. The old colonial university, closed for many years, was reopened and reformed; public schools multiplied; a normal school was founded and placed under the direction of the distinguished Eugenio M. Hostos; and a veritable literary revival began. But appearances turned out to be deceptive. Under the long tyranny of the corrupt and extravagant Heureaux social and economic progress proved impossible.

A native of Puerto Plata, where he was born in 1845 or 1846, Ulises Heureaux was probably a full-blooded Negro, although some say that he was part Syrian. After attending a Methodist mission school for a time, he set to work for a French merchant but then soon joined the military uprising against the Spanish authorities who were governing the country in the early 1860's. He fought under the leadership of Gregorio Luperón, the able Negro warrior from Heureaux's home town; for almost twenty years Heureaux continued to follow this *caudillo* as he headed revolt after revolt against Buenaventura Báez and other Dominican chief executives. A good part of their time was spent in concealment or exile. Heureaux's poverty was so extreme on one occasion that he engaged in a duel for the possession of a blanket, emerging from the contest with a shattered right arm after murdering his antagonist. For twenty-four months he and Luperón had command of an armed vessel, *El Telégrafo,* which they employed to harry the Dominican coast. Though far more honorable and patriotic than his younger companion in arms, Luperón served as chief executive of his country for only a few brief periods, and Heureaux, soon after he seized the government for himself, drove his old *caudillo* into exile.

Heureaux did not act as president during the entire seventeen years of his dominance. Half a decade was required to establish full control and remove the constitutional barrier against re-election. But no one could operate the government without Heureaux's approval and support, and he ruled directly and continuously from 1887 until 1899.

Covetous of both wealth and power, Heureaux was devoid of all scruples. He robbed the treasury of millions and spent them extravagantly. He ceded Haiti a part of the national territory in return for a large bribe. He plunged his country into hopeless debt and imperiled its independence, borrowing recklessly from foreign speculators and permitting them in return to build docks, railroads, and other public utilities and even to take charge of the nation's customhouses and finances. Ruthlessly smothering all aspirations for liberty or reform, he subjected the Dominicans to pitiless tyranny. The cruelties of the last years of his rule are almost incredible. He blanketed the country with spies and assassins and fed many of his victims to the sharks. He murdered nearly everybody who opposed him or was ever suspected of the remotest hostile intent. A shrewd, bold, and skilful warrior with a magnificent physique, he could not be deposed by revolution. Assassination proved to be the only means of putting an end to his terrible rule. On July 26, 1899, while Heureaux was at the little town of Moca on one of his frequent tours of inspection, he was killed by Ramón Cáceres and a youthful companion. Emerging from a restaurant, apparently without his bodyguard, the tyrant was shot while searching his pocket with his sound arm for small coins to present to a beggar. Already practically bankrupt at the time that Heureaux was assassinated, the republic entered a period of political and fiscal disorder that soon led to the intervention of the United States government.

CHAPTER XIV

Mexico

⊛ FIFTY YEARS OF TURMOIL

Turbulent during the last decade of the Colonial period, Mexico fell into almost complete anarchy shortly after winning its independence in 1821. Order was not finally and fully restored until Porfirio Díaz consolidated his power in the 1880's.

Few of the elements of discord that perturbed other parts of Latin America were absent. The country was large, and composed of rugged mountains, arid plateaus, jungle lowlands, and 6,000,000 to 7,000,000 heterogeneous, uneducated, and politically inexperienced people. Independence itself was the result of a reactionary movement intended to evade the impact of a liberal uprising in Spain and avoid social change. Republicans were soon fighting monarchists and federalists combatting centralists. Liberals demanding a civil and secular regime rose up against Conservative landlords, army officers, and clergymen. Insurgent Indians fought against oppression and for land and plunder. Mestizos preferred the army to peonage and the miserable wages of town and industry. Local *caudillos* fought to control their feudal districts. Dramatic military heroes shuffled back and forth between the rival factions. And the shadow of foreign intervention floated in over the chaos.

Agustín de Iturbide, the first ruler of independent Mexico, had brutally opposed the separatist movement while it was led by men interested in the liberation of serfs and slaves, but he had joined it as soon as it became aristocratic and reactionary. After the expulsion of the Spanish authorities he employed his army and a shouting mob to compel the Mexican constituent congress to choose him as monarch instead of the Bourbon prince hoped for by the clergy and other Conservatives. He took the oath in May, 1821, and was crowned as Emperor Agustín I the following July. A successful mestizo with a shady past, he strutted for twenty months on the imperial stage, a tinsel monarch reigning over, but hardly ruling a vast empire of nearly 2,000,000 square miles—including both Mexico and Central America down to the northern border of Panama—and inhabited by some 8,000,000 subjects, the overwhelming majority composed of Indians and mixbloods living in dire poverty and ignorance, many of them not even able to understand the official language. In theory, the emperor was not to be an absolute monarch; his power was supposed to be limited by the national assembly and the constitution it intended to draft. But Iturbide was headstrong and despotic. He seized silver and gold from the mineowners, exacted forced loans, imprisoned assemblymen, and dissolved the assembly before the constitution was framed.

By the end of 1822 insurgents were again on the march, and within a few months the whole country was seething in revolt. Vast arid plateaus in the north, jungles in the east and south, mountains almost everywhere, immense distances, bad roads, and an unfaithful army—all these handicaps made it impossible for Iturbide to enforce his authority. On March 19, 1823, he presented his resignation to such members of the national assembly as he could persuade to appear for the purpose; early in April this "rump parliament" accepted his abdication, voting him a large pension on condition that he leave the country and set up his residence in Italy. Gambling on rumors that certain European powers were planning to assist Spain to reconquer her American colonies, he returned home a year later, posing as the great champion of Mexican nationalism. But the Mexicans were in no mood to welcome him. Already a new constitutional convention had declared for a federal republic and pronounced him an outlaw to be seized and executed if ever again he should set foot on national soil. Probably ignorant of this harsh decree, Iturbide landed near Tampico and advanced into the interior, hoping to rally an army of supporters. Captured a few days later, he was shot on July 19, 1824.[1]

The federal system adopted earlier that year turned out to be the system most favored by the Mexicans. Except for brief periods, the title of the independent nation has since been the United States of Mexico. But the rights of the states were rarely respected. They had their governors and legislatures, but these were often imposed upon them by the national authorities in Mexico City. Nor, on the other hand, were the officials of the several states disposed to obey the federal constitutions or collaborate with the officials in the national capital except under threat or compulsion.

The first president of the republic was a mestizo named Guadalupe Victoria, a minor hero of the war for independence. The only thing noteworthy about his administration was his success in completing his four-year term, a feat that few other Mexicans were able to imitate during the next three decades. Victoria's successor, Vicente Guerrero, another independence hero and a mestizo who had risen from a very humble status, seized control of the national government before it could be transferred to the aristocratic president-elect; but Guerrero was deposed and executed within a few months, and thereafter chief executives, most of them army officers, followed one another in speedy succession. The national government became a sort of flying trapeze—which, however, some of the generals and occasionally a civilian ventured to ride repeatedly. Three white aristocrats—Anastasio Bustamante, Nicolás Bravo, and José Joaquín de Herrera—tried it twice each. The ardent anticlerical reformer Valentín Gómez Farías mounted it five times, and Antonio López de Santa Anna, the shrewd militarist and deft *pronunciamiento* artist, displayed his skill on eleven different occasions and managed to hang on for as many years.

A creole, like most of the others after the downfall of Guerrero, Santa Anna was the worst of the group. Having neither principles nor a sense of direction, he fought on both sides of every issue that arose. He was a royalist before he became a patriot. He supported Iturbide and then helped to depose him. He championed both federalism and centralism. He slyly permitted Valentín Gómez Farías to make the first serious attack on the Roman Catholic Church in Mexico in 1833 and then allied himself with the clergy and posed as the savior of Catholicism. He led an army against the Texans when they rebelled against his tyranny, and after being defeated and captured, managed to obtain release by a false pledge to return to Mexico and have Texan independence recognized. Driven from power early in 1837, he recouped his fortune by a "heroic" attack on a detachment of French marines sent out in 1838 to exact indemnity for injuries to French nationals. Leaping into power again in 1841, he set up a centralized and corrupt dictatorship.

He was overthrown by a popular uprising and compelled to leave his country in 1845, but he got in touch with President James K. Polk and persuaded him to facilitate his return. Expecting Santa Anna's assistance in the settlement of difficulties (regarding claims and the annexation of Texas) that had caused the outbreak of war between the United States and Mexico, or with some other objective, Polk let the exile pass through the blockade from Cuba to Veracruz; but having safely landed, the turncoat demanded a continuation of hostilities and managed to seize the national government once more. When peace negotiations promised to terminate the war, he protested vigorously and went into exile again.

Although he established himself on a large plantation near Cartagena,

Colombia, not far from the place where the great Bolívar spent his last days, he soon became a reactionary monarchist. Called back home by the Mexican clergy and monarchists early in 1853, he took charge of the national government with the title of "Dictator" and "Most Serene Highness." After more than two years of despotism, extravagance, and plunder, during which he sent an agent to Europe to search for a prince for Mexico and sold a strip of territory—the Gadsden Purchase—to the United States, he was deposed by a popular revolt and expelled from the country a third time. Offering his sword a few years later both to the republican reformer Benito Juárez and to Emperor Maximilian, he received a double rebuff and was forced to remain abroad until 1874. He spent the last years of his life dictating his memoirs. He liked to be called the "Napoleon of the West." A millionaire in 1855 when he was finally driven from power, he came home in 1874 poor and almost blind and died in poverty in Mexico City in 1876.

Corrupt, ruthless, and cruel, Santa Anna was also eloquent, dramatic, and clever. A soldier of fortune, he did nothing for his country but exploit it and disturb its peace. When he first became president in 1833, Mexico, in spite of the secession of Central America a decade before, had an area of well over 1,500,000 square miles. When he was finally deposed twenty-two years later, the national domain had shrunk to around 760,000. More than any other Mexican, Santa Anna had been responsible for this tragic loss of territory, which might have been avoided entirely (or possibly with the exception of Texas) if it had not been for the machinations, tyranny, and demagoguery of this unprincipled charlatan and one of his imitators, Mariano Paredes, who whipped up an anti-Yankee fury for political purposes. José Joaquín Herrera,[2] one of the few honest Mexican chief executives of the period and Mexico's only real statesman before 1855, was eager to settle the difficulties with the United States without resort to war, and might have succeeded if Santa Anna and Paredes had not interfered. The depths into which Santa Anna plunged his country were so profound that it could sink no lower and survive as a republic.

There was no national unity. Military chiefs dominated the outlying states or even larger regions. Feudal lords ruled their huge haciendas. Indians raided the settlements of the northern frontier or took refuge in mountain and jungle fastnesses farther south and made frequent sorties against the more densely inhabited sections. The clergy, with an annual income many times larger than the revenues of the national government, refused to contribute to its support, making loans only to such national authorities or insurgents as were willing to pledge themselves to protect its properties and privileges. The big landlords demanded protection at the expense of somebody else; they paid almost no taxes. The army consumed more than half of the national revenues and the bureaucracy devoured the rest, leaving almost nothing for education or the other public services. The budget was never balanced. In spite of the millions received from the United States in payment for territory, the national debt, foreign and domestic (the latter held also to a large extent by alien speculators), was around 150,000,000 pesos. Robbers infested the countryside; beggars and thieves swarmed in the leading towns and cities. A deep chasm separated the poor from the rich. For 90 per cent of the people there was neither opportunity nor liberty. Equality before the law did not exist. The many were exploited by the few: the army officers, the landlords, and to a considerable extent the clergy preyed upon everybody else. Frightened by the Spanish Revolution of 1820 and the French Revolutions of 1789 and 1848 and by sporadic mass uprisings in Mexico, the upper classes had sought, and were still seeking, to protect themselves and their possessions and privileges by means of a military dictatorship or a monarchy supported by a titled nobility, an established church, and mercenary soldiers.

BENITO JUÁREZ AND THE REFORM MOVEMENT

After deposing "His Most Serene Highness" in 1855, Benito Juárez and the little group who surrounded him—a few Indians and creoles and more mestizos—began the hard task of lifting their nation from the abyss. Their ideas and inspiration came mainly from France and the United States, but their courage and resolution were tempered by the hard blows of experience. They were determined to transform Mexico into a secular and democratic commonwealth. They attacked the privileged groups because they had been hampered and abused by them, but they felt a keen sense of responsibility for their even more unfortunate countrymen. Like most liberals everywhere, they were striving for opportunity and power for themselves, but they intended to use both to open the doors of opportunity for the masses below.

Among this group of reformers many names stand out: old Valentín Gómez Farías, a physician who had envisaged the goal as early as 1833 and had been trying in vain for years to move the nation toward it; Melchor Ocampo, a great landowner with an interest in the living conditions of his peons, who had seen the light as early as 1851; Ignacio Ramírez, the caustic mestizo iconoclast; Guillermo Prieto, popular journalist, poet, and sentimentalist; Francisco Zarco, a most able and persuasive journalist; León Guzmán, a bland and convincing zealot; visionaries like Ponciano Arriaga and Isidoro Olvera; sensible champions of reform like Doctor José Antonio Gamboa; politicians like Santos Degollado, Manuel Gutiérrez Zamora, Manuel Doblado, Jesús González Ortega, and José María Iglesias, who transformed themselves into army officers for the sake of the cause; the aristocratic Lerdo de Tejada brothers, Miguel and Sebastián, enthused by ardent nationalism and humanitarianism; the ever-faithful José María Mata, neither brilliant nor able, but always willing to serve with such talents as he had at any post assigned him; Juan José Baz, the firebrand whose burning zeal for his objectives led him to advocate a dictatorship in order to attain them; Ignacio Comonfort, zealous and capable, but weakened by his Roman Catholic conscience and the influence of his devout mother; two outstanding Indian leaders, old Juan Álvarez, stoical, faithful, and self-effacing warrior from the southern sierra, and Ignacio Manuel Altamirano, ardent revolutionary who berated Juárez because he thought his actions were too deliberate. All these and many more joined in the reform movement; but Benito Juárez, a full-blooded Zapotec Indian from the state of Oaxaca, soon stood out above the rest and eventually became Mexico's paramount hero.

Born in a small Indian village in 1806, Juárez had managed to work his way through school in preparation for the priesthood, perhaps because no other profession seemed to be open to him. Later he had turned to law and politics, and by 1855, when he first became prominent on the national stage, he had held every office at the disposal of his native state. Exiled by Santa Anna, he spent several months in New Orleans, where he worked as a printer and cigar maker. Then he returned home and joined the successful revolt against the corrupt tyrant. As national minister of justice and afterwards as president (1858–72), he vigorously and unwaveringly supported the reform movement, which immediately abolished the special military and ecclesiastical courts and within the next decade deprived the church of its immense holdings in tax-exempt real estate, disbanded the religious communities, forbade the clergy to hold office, authorized civil marriage and civil registry of births and deaths, took control of the cemeteries, inaugurated religious toleration, separated Church and State, and proclaimed the responsibility of the state for the education of the youth. All these measures, along with an elaborate bill of rights and universal manhood suffrage, were embodied in the new constitution of 1857—Mexico's fifth since independence—and in amendments thereto adopted in 1873–74.

Unimpressive in personal appearance, a small, ugly, swarthy man with a low, soft voice and lacking the eloquence that characterized many of his followers, Benito Juárez possessed a combination of courage, tenacity, balance, serenity, and a sense for timing which many of them lacked.

He became the symbol of the movement for law, evenhanded justice, liberty, democracy, and nationalism because no other leader had these traits in such a full and well-rounded measure and because he managed to survive all the perils of a tragic decade which swept into eternity many of the members of his group. He was an able and honest administrator and always a civilian; men fighting to curb the army and the church which had sought to use it as a shield dared not thrust him aside lest they destroy the appeal of their ideology and lose their battle. They might criticize him for his plodding ways or his stubbornness, or for clinging to power after 1867 when his work seemed to be finished; but few of them failed to realize that he was the only living Mexican with the character and capacity required to inaugurate and stabilize the new era toward which they were striving. He was indispensable, and those who had joined his standard knew it. Whatever his faults, however lacking in brilliance and personal magnetism, he was the embodiment of the ideals and aspirations of Mexico's underprivileged. He was a Jefferson without Jefferson's mastery of literary style and political philosophy, a Lincoln without Lincoln's power to sway and convince by the written and spoken word. Unlike most Latin-American leaders, and many political leaders everywhere, he was a man of action rather than of well-turned phrases. Such letters and state papers as he left to posterity were probably written in large part by his more facile secretaries and cabinet officers. For these reasons, and because his reputation has grown with the years and his personality has become enveloped in mythology, the historian can never hope to recapture the real Juárez and determine his exact dimensions. But it will be sufficiently accurate for general purposes to describe him as a character with many admirable traits who became a symbol of the highest ideals of Mexico's most noble leaders for all time. In honoring him as the image of their number-one hero, the Mexicans reveal their own high ideals.[3]

The sober historian is compelled to admit that the reform movement led by Juárez was in many respects a failure. Little was done to increase landownership among the poorer classes or in behalf of the workers. Nor was there much improvement in public education or other public services.

The base of landownership might have been expanded by distributing among the people the immense holdings of the church, portions of the big estates owned by laymen, and such public lands as could be made available. The original intention of the reformers was to force the sale of ecclesiastical lands at prices so moderate that Indians and mestizos could afford to buy them; but civil war and foreign intervention compelled the Juárez government to adopt the policy of seizure without compensation and emergency sales for badly needed cash to aristocrats and speculators, both domestic and foreign, thus adding a few more recruits to the landed oligarchy but conferring no benefits upon the poor.

There was some interesting talk about paring down the big estates of the lay landlords and sponsoring resettlement upon these and about colonization on the public lands still in possession of the government. Two speeches made during the constitutional convention of 1856–57 advocated such a policy.

Ponciano Arriaga protested that abstract rights were being stressed and basic economic rights and guaranties ignored. The French Revolution of 1848 had raised the question of property on behalf of the French proletariat, and Mexico's poverty-stricken millions should not be forgotten. Men were discussing foreign colonization; might not Mexican colonization on the uncultivated lands of the republic be possible with the aid of the government? Arriaga recommended that owners of large and idle estates be obliged to cultivate them or turn them over to those who would. The reform should be planted in a system of small land grants.[4]

Isidoro Olvera, invoking the French Revolution of 1789 and its policy of taxing the rich for the benefit of the poor, urged the land barons to stave off a future peril by acts of Christian charity. Predicting that the landless would some day rise up in their wrath and despoil the propertied class, he exhorted the rich to "direct the drama by sacrificing a small portion of their substance to save the whole, instead of wasting it on foolish revolutions and armed resistance, capable at most of temporarily weakening the movement but never of crushing it." There might still be time to "remedy evils without serious damage to any fraction of society," but there would certainly be grave danger in procrastination. Noble heads might fall, as did Louis XVI's. Members of the constitutional assembly and the government "should reflect seriously on the dangers and the necessity of expelling them," and the rich should also reflect on their real interests and aid the public power to save the country by the betterment of the poor classes and by settling definitely a social question that was assuming dimensions both "gigantic" and "menacing." [5]

The subject was brought up again in 1869 by radicals who felt that Juárez and the Liberals had grown too cautious. The constitution proclaimed that all men were equal, but equality did not exist, they declared. So long as the people were "devoured by poverty and ignorance . . . democracy" would be "an illusion, morality a dream, legal equality a sarcasm. . . . A small number of Mexicans own the territory of the

Republic, the vast majority of the citizens possess not an inch of land; almost every village is obliged to work for the landlord in return for a meager fare." [6]

But the men who proposed a general agrarian reform at this early date only planted an outpost and towered above their fellows in lonely eminence. Nothing was done. The masses had to be content with civil liberty and universal suffrage.

One of the reform measures actually injured the Indians, for Indian villages were included among the corporations forbidden to hold lands, and the way was thus paved for the distribution of the *ejidos* (common lands owned by the villages) among individual natives, who generally lacked the astuteness to retain their portions as private property. Although the mistake was discovered and some attempt made to remedy it, the process of division was resumed in later years to the great disadvantage of the Indians.

Juárez and his reformers thus stopped far short of the goal some of them had envisaged. They did little for the Indians or the lower classes in general. They built few roads or railways or schools. Although Gabino Barreda won some renown as a promoter of primary and secondary education, there were probably no more than 200,000 pupils in the public schools in 1872. The reforms were largely political and civil, and more theoretical than practical. But it was probably impossible for the reformers to go further than they did. Too much energy and resources were required to combat the enemy during twelve long years of revolt and civil war. The armies of the Conservatives and the clergy fought desperately and fanatically from the outset, advancing into battle with the sacred emblems of the church and with shouts of "Long live religion; death to the heretics!" And for nearly five years the reactionary cohorts had the support of a French expeditionary force.[7]

In fact, Mexico never enjoyed complete tranquillity at any time during the Juárez regime. Although conditions were somewhat more stable near its end, Porfirio Díaz was profoundly dissatisfied and was striving for power. Revolting once against Juárez and twice against Juárez's successor, Sebastián Lerdo de Tejada, Díaz seized Mexico City late in 1876 and soon had himself "elected" constitutional president. In 1880 he handed the reins over to a trusted lieutenant, who faithfully handed them back in 1884. Díaz had returned to stay. Apparently he had few supporters at first other than the military, whom Juárez had failed to reform, although he had reduced the size of the army in the late 1860's. The landlords and the clergy allied themselves with Díaz later, but he never won the allegiance of the masses in spite of his efforts to use Juárez as a continuing symbol.

🐛 THE DÍAZ DESPOTISM

In the early 1880's Mexico stood at the dawn of another new era. With mortmain abolished and the nation secularized and stabilized, it was ready for a material, if not a social and cultural, transformation. Already foreign capital and immigrants were beginning to flow in in larger streams than ever before. Mexico would now be claimed as a part of the industrial and capitalistic order of the Western World.

The son of humble parents, Díaz was born in 1830 in a small village in the state of Oaxaca. A mestizo with as much Indian as Spanish blood in his veins, he never acquired more than the rudiments of creole culture until after he married his second wife and formed an alliance with Mexico's white aristocracy. Educated at first for the priesthood, he later studied law and received a law degree without mastering that subject. But this mattered little; during the turbulent years following his graduation in law there was not much opportunity to practice his profession, and he had far more talent for guerrilla warfare. Even before receiving his degree, he had spent several months in the army, fighting in the war against the United States. He joined the revolt against Santa Anna in 1854 and battled for more than a decade against the Mexican Conservatives and their French allies. At the end of the long and hazardous war he was only thirty-seven, but he had won a reputation as a capable and loyal officer. A stocky man with full chest and fine head, he appeared taller than his actual five feet eight inches because of his erect posture and his fondness for riding big horses. Possessing a superb physique, he also had an agile mind. But he was not by any means a profound thinker. Whatever political, social, or economic philosophy he acquired was not the result of any hard mental exertion of his own. He absorbed it from his more intellectual associates. His brainwork centered on the problem of managing the military and manipulating the politicians.

The French army had hardly been withdrawn from Mexico before Díaz developed an overweening ambition to rule his country. He offered himself as a candidate for the presidency in 1867 and again in 1871. Defeated both times by his old friend and law professor, Benito Juárez, he decided to adopt another method of attaining his objective, but his insurrection was quickly smashed by a loyal general of his old chief. Five years afterwards, when Sebastián Lerdo de Tejada, who took charge of the national government at the death of Juárez in 1872, revealed a strong desire for another term, Díaz made a second military thrust for power after setting forth his political platform in two *pronunciamientos* which declared among other things that the states and the municipalities had been deprived of their autonomy, that the courts had been reduced to subserviency, that elections were controlled by the incumbent chief executive, that the country was being sacrificed to foreign investors, and that dictatorship and *continuismo* must be terminated by free suffrage and faithful observation of the constitutional proscription against re-election to the presidency. Díaz was again severely battered by Lerdo's generals, but already he had made contacts with salesmen of military supplies in the United States. Escaping over the border after his defeat, he reorganized his forces, equipped them with the latest inventions in firearms, and sent them back across the frontier while he made his way by sea and land to his native Oaxaca where other troops awaited him. Two revolutionary armies soon converged upon Mexico City, one led by Díaz himself and the other by General Manuel González. The government was overthrown late in November. The learned, arrogant, and lazy Lerdo fled to New York, where he died in 1889, and José María Iglesias, another rival for the chief magistry, was brushed aside a few weeks later.

Díaz had captured the trophy at last, and would soon be ready to violate every pledge he had made, thoroughly illustrating the cynical adage that political platforms are "made to get in on and not to stand on." His working program has been well described by the phrase *pan ó palo* (bread or a club): bread for the minor bureaucrats willing to conform and collaborate; more than bread—fortune and luxury—for the influential journalists, politicians, and army officers who would agree to help perpetuate his rule; but the club and worse—imprisonment and death—for the stubborn, the overly ambitious, and the zealots who demanded political and civil liberty.

It will be recalled that the reform movement led by Juárez had three main objectives: to establish democratic government, to broaden the base of landownership, and to foster economic development, and that Juárez and his group, while failing to attain any of the three, made some progress toward them all against the violent opposition of the Conservatives and their clerical and French supporters. Díaz sacrificed the first and second objectives for the third, changing the motto "Liberty, Order, and Progress" to "Progress, Order, and Peace."

Within four years Díaz had his system running fairly smoothly. Lerdist partisans who tried to make a landing at Veracruz after seizing two Mexican warships were frustrated, and residents suspected of sympathizing with the movement were shot in cold blood. Opportune "accidents" struck down so many prominent leaders known to be hostile to Díaz that other dissidents were terrorized and peace and order assured. State governors and municipal heads were displaced by the dictator's henchmen. The national congress and the various state legislatures were gradually transformed into mock debating societies. Bandits and other bold, bad men were compelled to make a choice between almost certain extinction and a chance to join the *rurales* (rural police) and help exterminate any possible competitors. In order to make this rural police force more attractive, its members were equipped with swift horses, silver-embossed saddles, efficient rifles, and seductive uniforms. Faithful and obedient *jefes políticos* (political chiefs) were appointed to command these new guardians of peace and order and supervise all local affairs. Money, suavity, and threats were employed to win over or intimidate the press.

As the year 1880 approached, Díaz realized that it was too early to violate his pledge regarding rotation in office; but he knew how to manage the situation without exposing himself to great risk. Assuming a role which Mexicans later described as the "Great Elector," he pronounced the name of Manuel González, an able and loyal mestizo general, and easily "procured" the chief magistry for his collaborator and friend.

González was not fettered by any platform pledges whatever. He was pledged only to remain loyal to Díaz and take no steps to prevent his return to the presidency in 1884. He was free to break every promise his chief had ever made, particularly that clearly implied promise about concessions to foreigners; and his four-year term was a period of brisk negotiation with railway concessionaires, land surveyors and land speculators, mining companies, and alien capitalists of every sort. He also signed a contract with British bondholders, who had not enjoyed a dividend on their Mexican holdings for many years; but the national congress, perhaps under the influence of Díaz, who either desired the credit for himself or thought his puppet might win too many strong foreign friends, refused to ratify the agreement. Regarding the extent and magnitude of bribery and pilfering that went on under González, the historians disagree. The majority of them declare that both were as large and widespread as economic conditions would permit. Others are of the opinion that the corruption was exaggerated not only by the pro-Díaz press but by the "opposition newspapers" which he had already begun to finance in order to turn them loose on friends whose prestige was rising too high for the master's comfort. Whatever the truth of the matter, González had been so badly smeared by the end of his term that the return of Díaz to the presidency in 1884 was greeted with loud applause.

Díaz was now no longer a rough guerrilla chieftain. The cut and arrangement of his hair were different and his clothes were more becoming. In fact, he had acquired all the attributes of a Spanish gentleman —except a familiarity with history and literature and skill in spelling. His second wife, Carmelita Romero Rubio, whom he had taken on a honeymoon to New York in 1881, had polished and domesticated him without in any way curbing his "yen" for political power. She had married a promising politician and she knew it; that is why she linked her fate with a mestizo widower twice her age and far below her social status. Carmelita's father, Manuel Romero Rubio, who had grown rich by buying up cheap church property during the early days of the reform, ardently approved the match. He had been a *Lerdista* until the political trend became too obvious to be misjudged; whereupon he carefully trimmed his sails in the hope of securing a cabinet post and perhaps even the presidency in due time. He was promptly awarded a place in Díaz's cabinet, and he continued to hold it until his death; but when he finally summoned the courage to suggest his presidential aspirations to his son-in-law, Díaz is said to have squelched him by pointing out how fatal such aspirations had been in several other instances. The Rubios were mainly responsible for two important changes in the relationships of the dictator: they gradually severed his connections with his old Indian and mestizo comrades, and they promptly destroyed whatever hostility or suspicion he may have felt toward the Roman Catholic Church.

Díaz soon put aside all compunctions regarding rotation in office. Posing as the nation's reluctant indispensable man, he imposed himself upon the country repeatedly and permitted his minions to hold office as long as they remained faithful or could not be changed without serious risk. Such political parties as came into existence were organized mainly by his partisans. There were political conventions, but they accepted the despot's dictates and were assembled only to deceive the public. In order to lighten the campaigning, Díaz had the presidential term extended to six years in 1904, and at the same time added a vice-president in order to ease the apprehensions of any who might be worried about his seventy-four years. Vice-President Ramón Corral was a rich creole who had made his fortune by speculating in lands and mines and selling Yaqui Indians into slavery; he had almost no personal magnetism or political talent, suffered from a deadly disease, and therefore could never outshine his chief.

Continuing his earlier administrative policies, Díaz now also followed the economic policies inaugurated by González: more *rurales;* more local political chiefs; more municipal "presidents"; more eloquent ornaments in the legislative halls; special commissions of one kind or another to promote economic and cultural advance or satisfy the hungry politicians; more and bigger newspapers with more and bigger subsidies, even subsidies for the opposition press when it was attacking possible political rivals, and for such foreign-language journals as were willing to sing the praises of Mexico and its great ruler; more and more interviews graciously accorded foreign writers, investors, and tourists; concession after concession to alien capitalists who employed the right Mexican attorneys, concessions embracing mines, timber, immense tracts of land, the right to search for and exploit or refine petroleum, contracts granting the privilege of developing every kind of private business or installing and operating every type of public utility. Foreign investors received a cordial welcome in Mexico. They were not hampered by heavy-handed regulations, and unless they were blatantly dishonest, they had nothing to fear from the carefully dominated courts. Díaz looked mainly to foreign capitalists and technicians to carry out his program of material progress; his task was to provide security and peace for alien investors and the few Mexicans who collaborated in their enterprises. As the decades passed, petty graft gave way to profiteering and large-scale peculation by a few army officers, some overlords in the outlying states, and a small group of "insiders," known as *científicos,* in the capital. Perhaps the aging despot was not fully aware of all that went on; but he could hardly have failed to learn of some of it. The Gilded Age in the United States encompassed Mexico. But the *Yanquis* were not the only ones who handled the gold; British investors and other Europeans got their share along with the North Americans and some of the Mexicans.

Few rulers ever received such extravagant praise as was showered upon Porfirio Díaz during the long years of his reign. He was described as a Cromwell, and more than a Cromwell, "the Moses and the Joshua of his people," a composite of Washington, Jefferson, Lincoln, Solon, and the Twelve Apostles. Even Elihu Root, who certainly should have known better, uttered this glowing tribute early in 1908: "It has seemed to me that of all men now living, General Porfirio Díaz of Mexico was best worth seeing. . . . If I were a poet, I would write poetic eulogies. If I were a musician, I would write triumphal marches. If I were a Mexican, I should feel that the steadfast loyalty of a lifetime would not be too much in return for the blessings he has brought my country. . . . I look to Porfirio Díaz as one of the great men to be held up for the hero-worship of mankind." [8] And not a few, some Mexicans among them, could still be found years after the despot's downfall and demise who would sturdily defend his regime and declare that Mexico had not produced a greater statesman. The substance of their argument was that Díaz brought peace to Mexico for the first time in its national history, and not only a long era of peace but prosperity and international renown as well.

This cannot be denied. Díaz restored order and maintained it for decades, thus making possible the rapid development of the nation's material resources, which he also fomented by his concessions and his fiscal policies. He reorganized the public finances; scrupulously met the financial obligations of the country; balanced the budget in 1894 for the first time since independence; eventually funded the public debt at a low interest rate; subsidized railways, port works, and municipal public utilities; stimulated mining and, to a lesser extent, agriculture and the livestock and manufacturing industries; fostered the extraction of petroleum; made some improvements in sanitation; re-opened the National University; founded and supported professional and secondary schools; and spent enough money on normal and primary schools to reduce illiteracy by 6 per cent or more in a multiplying population. In his private life he was sober and comparatively chaste. In Díaz's case, at least, absolute power did not corrupt absolutely. If he amassed a large fortune, it was never discovered.

But his rule was unnecessarily brutal. The agents of his despotism—some of the army officers and state caciques, and particularly his *jefes politicos* and *rurales*—terrorized the people, jailing them for no adequate cause, depriving them of just trials, drafting dissidents into the army or forced labor gangs, and shooting prisoners under the pretense that they were trying to escape from the officers of the law (*ley fuga*). The Yaqui Indians of Sonora were provoked into rebellion by encroachments upon their lands and then subdued and sold into slavery. The Mayas of Yucatán suffered a similar fate. The natives crowded together on the southern end of the great plateau were gradually deprived of their village commons (*ejidos*) and forced into peonage on the plantations or compelled to work in the expanding industries. The minions of the despot also dealt very harshly with labor in the mines and factories. Labor unions were resented; protesting workers were shot, bayoneted, or jailed under the assumption that they had been incited by radicals and enemies of the regime. These horrible abuses were too widespread to be hidden from the Mexicans, but the more intelligent and articulate groups either blamed them upon the dictator's unruly henchmen or accepted them without shock. The little creole clique who surrounded the despot developed a sentiment of scornful depreciation for the Indians and the lower-class mestizos, if not for all the colored races, and it is likely that their feeling was finally shared by the transformed half-Indian who dominated the nation for a third of a century.

Nothing is more certain than the failure of Díaz to rule Mexico in the interest of the majority of its inhabitants. The upper classes, the Roman Catholic Church, and the foreigners were his main concern. They enriched themselves at the expense of the masses. The rural workers fared worst of all. Their wages remained stationary in a period of rising prices, while the wages of laborers in transportation enterprises, in mines, in factories, and in the civil service increased; and expansion of primary school facilities was confined mainly to the cities and the larger towns.

Sullen and sometimes explosive resentment against the regime began to disclose itself shortly after 1900. A strike in Monterrey in 1903 was followed by another in the Cananea copper mines of Sonora in 1906, by strikes and mob violence in the textile mills of Puebla and Orizaba in 1907, by still more strikes the following year, and by a small insurrection, quickly suppressed and largely concealed, in 1909. The financial panic of 1907; subsequent crop failures in some sections; hunger of the masses; frustration among the young intellectuals who could find no outlets for their talents; the growing self-consciousness of the industrial workers; the feeling that the aged despot was under the control of a small clique of greedy Mexicans and agents of foreign corporations; rivalries over the succession—all these caused anger and restlessness which boded ill for the future.

CHAPTER XV

Central America

🔖 JOSÉ ARCE AND FRANCISCO MORAZÁN

Although Central America north of Panama was exempted from one of the influences that tended to generate militarism elsewhere, since it had won its independence from Spain without much bloodshed, and its independence from Mexico without any, this region nevertheless sank into military anarchy shortly after the beginning of the National epoch. Its history merely continues the story of despotism and disorder that characterizes so much of the vast empire recently controlled by Spain.

A confederation composed of the five provinces into which the colonial captaincy general had been divided—Guatemala, El Salvador, Honduras, Nicaragua, and Costa Rica—was formed in 1823–24. Officially entitled the United Provinces of Central America, it continued its feeble existence for about fifteen years and was governed by two chief executives, Arce and Morazán.

The Confederation's first president, José Arce, a leader of Spanish descent, confronted a peculiarly difficult task. The new republic had no national capital, no army, practically no finances and few sources of revenue, almost no roads, and hardly any passable trails. Its five provinces, really sovereign states in spite of the name, were separated by mountain and jungle and extremely jealous of one another. Its leaders were ambitious, stubborn, sensitive, intolerant, and inexperienced in public affairs. Its inhabitants were a miscellaneous lot aware of almost no common interests or ideals. In a population of somewhat less than 1,500,000, not 100,000 were whites. Around 900,000 were pure Indians, living in villages or tribes; more than half as many were mestizos; and 15,000 to 20,000 were Negroes and mulattoes, some of them enslaved. Only in Costa Rica were the Caucasians more numerous than the mixed and primitive inhabitants. Most of the whites possessed education, culture, and property; the Indians, Negroes, and mixbloods were almost entirely illiterate and extremely poor, although many of the Indian villages still owned community lands (*ejidos*).

It is clear that it would be no easy task to forge a nation from these materials and set it on the road to progress. And a cloud on Arce's title to the presidency added to his troubles. He had not received as many votes as the Conservative candidate, but a combination of Liberals and Moderates in convention had awarded him the office. He was considered a Liberal, but he first offended the members of his party by trying to appease the Conservatives and then infuriated them by joining their rivals, who were quite reactionary, some of them monarchists who would have had no objection to the restoration of Spanish rule. Having thus aroused violent partisan passions, he further fanned the flames by intervening in the political affairs of the provinces.

The result was revolution. Uprisings began in 1826, continued through 1827, and were so widespread by the middle of 1828 that Arce was compelled to resign several months before his four-year term expired. Already in control of most of the states of the Confederation by that time, the Liberals seized Guatemala City shortly afterward and sent Arce into exile. He lived in Mexico until the confederation collapsed and then tried to come back to El Salvador, but it was not until the last years of his life that he was permitted to return. At the age of sixty, he died (September 14, 1846) in poverty in his native city, San Salvador. Such was the fate of the George Washington of Central America.

Meanwhile Francisco Morazán, the second president of the confederation, had played his brief role on the Middle-American stage and encountered an even more tragic fate. A native of Tegucigalpa, Honduras, where he was born in 1792, he managed to educate himself, make his way in local politics, develop his military talent, and marry a wife who brought him a small dowry. Some say that his paternal grandfather was a Corsican named Morazani; at any rate, Francisco Morazán seems to have inherited some of the military genius and enthusiasm for change that characterized a more noted Corsican whom many Latin Americans of this period liked to imitate. In 1827, at the age of thirty-five, Morazán joined the revolt against Arce, and soon became the outstanding military and political figure in Central America. First he served as chief executive of Honduras; then he gained supreme command of all the Liberal forces in the region; and finally, in 1830, after leading his troops over mountain trails, battering the Conservatives, and banishing a number of their leaders, he was "elected" president of the Confederation.

Already in possession of the state governments, except that of isolated

Costa Rica, when their leader took charge of the Confederate government, the Liberals had inaugurated their program of reform, in which Morazán now vigorously collaborated. Ecclesiastical courts were abolished, religious orders dissolved, protesting clergymen banished, church properties seized, and a few lay schools opened. Morazán hoped to introduce civil marriage, religious toleration, and jury trial, the last of which had already been put in operation in Guatemala; but the constitutional amendment he sponsored providing for all these reforms failed to be adopted. He also tried to stimulate economic progress by attracting immigrants and granting a concession for interoceanic communications.

In spite of revolts, Morazán managed to retain power for two terms; but at the end of his second, early in 1839, the Confederation was left without a president because extreme disorder had prevented the elections. Instead of continuing at the head of the national government, the capital of which he had shifted to San Salvador, he chose for some unknown reason to head the state of which this town was the capital. He did, however, yield to the persuasion of his partisans and try to restore the collapsing union, a task which proved to be impossible. After a number of bloody battles, he was finally crushed and banished by Rafael Carrera, a Guatemalan warrior backed by the Conservatives. "He is now fallen and in exile," wrote a distinguished traveler named John L. Stephens. "I verily believe they have driven from their shores the best man in Central America."

With a few faithful followers Morazán sailed for Peru early in 1840; but some of his companions disembarked in Costa Rica, which had remained practically untouched by the reforms or the hatreds they produced, and comparatively free from clerical domination, religious fanaticism, and revolt. Costa Rica had fallen, in 1836, under the control of an innovating dictator named Braulio Carillo, who was busy distributing land among the peasants, abolishing church holidays, and founding the coffee industry. Financed by friends in Peru and Central America, Morazán returned from his ostracism early in 1842 and attacked Costa Rica with a small squadron and a few hundred recruits. Aided by the companions he had left behind two years before and by the dissatisfaction of Costa Ricans under the iron rule of Carillo, he was able to seize the government and banish the dictator; but when he tried to use this little country as a base for the revival of the Central American union, conscripting its citizens and levying forced loans, he aroused a fury of resentment. The Costa Ricans flew to arms; Morazán was soon defeated, betrayed, and captured; and on September 15, 1842, the anniversary of Central America's declaration of independence from

Spain, this Thomas Jefferson of Middle America faced the firing squad.

But time has been far more generous to Morazán than to Arce. The policies for which he stood—freedom of speech, of press, of religion; reduction of the wealth and power of the church; lay education supported by the state—were destined finally to triumph and perpetuate his fame. Greatly admired in the Central America of later years, Morazán became the outstanding national hero of Honduras, and monuments, plazas, and public buildings were named in his honor throughout the region.

With the fall of Morazán and the disruption of the Confederation, the five sovereign republics of Central America came into existence; but the ideal of unity survived and frequently disturbed their politics. It was often invoked and cultivated by warrior-politicians actuated by motives not primarily connected with unification. Central America, or most of it, became a land of petty tyrants who battled for domination within each republic and meddled in the politics of neighboring states in the name of unity, religion, or reform. Many of the wars were thus international as well as civil. Local insurgents often expected and usually received the support of warrior-politicians beyond national boundaries. Some of the rebel recruits were likely to be exiles trying to fight their way back home; others were sympathizers from adjacent republics; and both were frequently supported by the governments of the neighboring nations.

THE EPOCH OF RAFAEL CARRERA

For several decades after the dissolution of the Confederation, the political history of each of the four northern nations was closely connected with that of the others. The chief executives of Guatemala, the most populous of the four, exercised great influence in the other three, and especially in Honduras and El Salvador. Costa Rica generally managed to avoid embroilment in the disorders of the other republics. The political history of the some forty-five years following the collapse of the Confederation falls into two well-defined periods, the first dominated by Rafael Carrera and the Conservatives and the second by Justo Rufino Barrios and the Liberals.

Rafael Carrera was a mestizo of illegitimate birth, more Indian than Spanish, who got his start as a pig driver and hog dealer. He managed to save enough money to buy a small farm and house in the village of Santa Rosa, situated in the forested hills east of Guatemala City, and became sufficiently conspicuous by 1837 to be entrusted with a company of militia delegated to enforce sanitary regulations in his district during an epidemic of cholera. This post, conferred upon a half-Indian at the age of twenty-three, turned out to be more important than might have been anticipated. For this cholera scourge and the young man it summoned from obscurity soon led to the downfall of the Liberals in the state of Guatemala and the destruction of the Confederation. Rural priests accused the Liberals of poisoning the wells in order to exterminate the Indians and make room for colonies of foreign whites. It was not cholera that was causing the death of the natives, they declared, but poisoned water; Morazán and his ruthless partisans were planning to turn Central America over to heretics and infidels and destroy the Roman Catholic religion! Alarmed and enraged by these charges (although they were false), the Indians seized such weapons as they could muster and went to war. They were joined by a horde of mestizo peons, and Rafael Carrera became their leader. With two priests in his mobile headquarters preaching a sort of medieval crusade, in less than three years he made himself master of Guatemala, destroyed the Confederation, and drove Morazán from Central America.

Having found their military leader, the Conservatives and their clerical allies set to work to nullify all the reforms the Liberals had enacted and restore the past. In order to carry out their plans it was necessary not merely to retain control in Guatemala but to seize the governments of El Salvador, Honduras, and Nicaragua as well. They did not need to worry about Costa Rica; it was in Conservative hands after the overthrow of Morazán.

In the main, the Conservatives succeeded in carrying out their program of reaction. For nearly a quarter of a century Carrera and the clique who used him dominated the four northern states. But this was no easy feat. The Liberals were always on the alert to regain their power, and Conservative lieutenants sent out to control the neighboring republics sometimes got out of hand. On one occasion indeed, in 1848, the Liberals actually recouped their position in Guatemala itself and banished Carrera to Mexico; but he soon came back and recovered his command of the Guatemalan army.

An attempt by the Liberals to regain power in Nicaragua, where they had been driven from the government with great slaughter in 1845, caused one of the most exciting episodes in Central American history and brought Costa Rica for a time into the turbulent current of Middle-American affairs. Liberal agents went to California to purchase arms and supplies and enlist recruits. Their first detachment of mercenaries and soldiers of fortune sailed from San Francisco in 1855 under the command of the notorious William Walker, and other adventurers continued to pour in until their commander had sufficient military forces to rout the Nicaraguan Conservatives and have himself "elected" president of the republic. The filibuster chief probably aspired to rule the entire region; but the Central Americans suspended their local broils and took up arms against the foreign invaders. With aid and encouragement from the outside, from Cornelius Vanderbilt and the British government, the allied armies soon subdued the filibusters, who were already weakened by tropical heat and fevers, and drove them away. When Walker renewed his efforts to carve out an empire, he was captured and shot.

Juan Rafael Mora, then president of Costa Rica, was an outstanding leader in the war against the filibusters, and his military achievements won for him undying fame. He became Costa Rica's number-one national hero, rising to eternal renown on a wave of "Yankeephobia" produced by the Mexican War and filibuster aggressions.

Rafael Carrera did not take personal command of the troops furnished by Guatemala for the filibuster war. He was busy serving his second term as president of his country, having completed his first administration of four years in 1848. Before his second term ended, a subservient congress declared him president for life, with the right to choose his successor when he felt the end was near. With the defeat of the filibuster horde and the disgrace of the Liberals who had called them in, the Conservatives seemed firmly seated in all five countries. Nevertheless, their troubles were not over. The Indians and some of the mestizos became restive in Guatemala, and the Liberals finally fought their way back to power in El Salvador and Honduras. By the time Carrera had restored order at home and finished a bloody war against the combined Liberal forces of these two countries and restored Conservatives in both, his health had begun to break. Since the death of his wife in 1857 he had been indulging in strong drink and other debaucheries even more freely than in earlier years. On April 14, 1865, at the age of fifty-one, he died from a violent attack of dysentery.

THE EPOCH OF JUSTO RUFINO BARRIOS

With Carrera gone, the Central American pendulum soon took another swing. Armed with new weapons—Winchester and Remington repeating rifles—the Liberals made a concerted attack upon the Conservative strongholds. Guatemala, the former center of reaction, now became the most vigorous center of reform. On June 20, 1871, six years after Carrera's death, Justo Rufino Barrios and Miguel García Granados entered Guatemala City in triumph after many months of planning and revolution. Violently opposed to everything that Carrera and the Conservative and clerical clique who controlled him had done, they were determined to shatter the power of the white aristocracy and the church, set up a state system of education, foster economic development, restore the old confederation, and obtain for the mestizos—often called Ladinos in Guatemala—better opportunities and a larger place in the political life of the country.

They began their efforts at once to curtail the power of the church, expelling the Jesuits, whom Carrera had brought back into the country, before the end of the year. The onslaught continued during 1872 and 1873, accompanied by civil war between Liberals and Conservatives. Before peace was finally restored at the end of 1874, all the religious orders in Guatemala had been disbanded, their properties confiscated, and most of their members, along with several dignitaries of the secular organization, banished from Central America.

García Granados, an "aristocrat of vast learning," had framed the program of revolution, probably under the influence of the Juárez group in Mexico and memories of Morazán, and had furnished a good part of the guns and equipment for the rebel army. It was natural therefore that he should have the presidency of the country. But young Barrios, a member of a prosperous mestizo family, was the dynamic force and the military genius of the rebellion, and García Granados turned the government over to him in 1873.

Liberal executives were already in control of El Salvador and Costa Rica before the Guatemalan revolutionaries seized their national capital, but they were not zealous Liberals like Barrios, and they soon lost his confidence. Although García Granados and Barrios collaborated for a time with the Liberal president of El Salvador in consolidating Liberal control in Honduras, Barrios went to war with both countries in 1876 in order to "elect" presidents whom he could trust more fully; and seven years later he intervened again in Honduras and set up another chief executive there. The management of Guatemala and these two neighbors kept him so busy that he hardly had time to promote Liberal interests in Nicaragua or to deal with the Liberal executive whom he distrusted and disliked in Costa Rica.

This Costa Rican autocrat, Tomás Guardia, was no ordinary man. Although of humble origin—his mother was from Panama, his father a frontiersman—he had managed to seize the government of this little country in 1870 and inaugurate a vigorous program of development, promoting railways, telegraphs, agriculture, and mining. Having thrust aside the little oligarchy that had dominated Costa Rica most of the time since independence, he proceeded to crush its power by expropriating a part of its lands and putting them in the hands of small farmers. He established a family rule of his own, but it lasted less than twenty years. He was succeeded by his brother-in-law, Próspero Fernández, who was followed in turn by a relative of both named Bernardo Soto. Soto, however, at the end of his term in 1889, permitted a fair election in which the opposition won, and thus terminated the reign of family oligarchies in Costa Rica and smoothed the way for democracy.

One of the things Barrios disliked about Guardia was Guardia's moderation in dealing with the Roman Catholic Church. For this autocrat merely insisted on religious toleration in the hope of attracting skilled immigrants. Shortly after Guardia's death in 1882, however, Fernández expelled the Company of Jesus, suppressed all religious communities, secularized the cemeteries, and adopted a system of state education. And even the Conservatives ruling in Nicaragua, responding to the spirit of the epoch, followed moderately liberal policies.

Early in 1885 Barrios decided that the time had come to consolidate Central America under the Liberal regime. The political situation seemed propitious. The executives of El Salvador and Honduras were supposed to be his allies; he had placed them in power. Fernández, a Liberal, was in charge of Costa Rica. A moderate Conservative was governing Nicaragua. In February, Barrios accordingly announced his determination to restore the old confederation at once.

But the reaction to this sudden announcement was decidedly unfavorable. Nationalism and vested interests were threatened. Only Luís Bográn, Liberal president of Honduras, approved unification under Barrios' leadership. The other three governments disclosed strong opposition, and the plan was frowned upon by both Mexico and the United States, since they felt that unification could be achieved only by the use of force. In spite of this opposition, however, Barrios refused to give up his scheme. He led his army through the mountains into El Salvador—and was mortally wounded in his first battle. After the death of Barrios the Guatemalan troops were called back home and the project was abandoned.

In spite of the tragic failure of this part of his program, Barrios had helped to bring about many significant changes in Central American life. Conservative oligarchies had been driven from power not only in Guatemala but in El Salvador and Honduras as well. In all three countries the temporal power of the church had been crushed, religious toleration, civil marriage, and state-supported public schools introduced, and a policy of general secularization carried out. These "reforms," and improvements in transportation, communication, agriculture, and stock raising, widened the opportunities of some of the people in these three republics; and similar developments occurred at the same time in Costa Rica under the Guardia dynasty and to some extent in Nicaragua under moderate Conservative rule. The 1870's and 1880's witnessed the arrival of the telegraph, the railway, the telephone, and electric power, a great expansion in coffee production, and the beginning of the banana industry. Central America emerged from medievalism and entered the modern age under Justo Rufino Barrios and his cohorts.

It should be observed, however, that Barrios was not a complete liberal in the modern sense. He did not permit freedom of speech and of the press or fair elections, or allow the legislative bodies or even the courts to limit his power. He was a dictator; and although he was a benevolent dictator in some respects, he failed to improve the lot of the Indians, who made up more than half of Guatemala's population, or that of the mestizo artisans and unskilled workers. He continued the system of peonage, compelled the laboring class to work for trifling wages on the roads and public buildings and allowed the Indians to be deprived of some of their *ejidos*. Barrios the mestizo, like Juárez the Indian, neglected the native race and the mestizo working man.

THE END OF THE CENTURY

Soon after the death of Barrios the three northern states of Central America succumbed to anarchy again; and Nicaragua, which had been comparatively tranquil for thirty years under moderate Conservative rule, followed them for a time in the early 1890's, but was shortly stabilized by José Santos Zelaya, who inaugurated the customary Liberal reforms before he became a ruthless despot. Of the eight republics of northern Latin America five had the appearance of stability in 1898— Haiti, the Dominican Republic, Mexico, Nicaragua, and Costa Rica— but only the last of the five had attained a measure of liberty and democracy as well. Haiti was dominated by a Negro army officer who had seized power in 1891 (Simon Sam); the Dominican Republic had been in the iron grip of a tyrant (Ulises Heureaux) since 1882; Mexico had been subjected for more than twenty years to the rule of a despot (Porfirio Díaz) who had little regard for the common people; in the very year 1898 a man (Manuel Estrada Cabrera) destined to oppress the Guatemalans for over two decades had grabbed the reins of power after a chief executive had been assassinated; and an army officer (Tomás Regalado) whose dictatorship would last until 1903 had oc- cupied the executive mansion in San Salvador; Honduras was under the military control of another army officer (Policarpo Bonilla) who was planning to dictate his successor before the end of 1898 after domi- nating the country for three turbulent years. But all of the five republics of Central America had "gone Liberal" and were well on their way to fame as producers of bananas and coffee. The population of the region, approximately 1,600,000 in 1842, was now three times that number.

CHAPTER XVI

Formation and Collapse of *La Gran Colombia*

THE FORMATION

Iturbide's empire in northern Spanish America was a tragicomedy. Its emperor was a ridiculous charlatan; the experiment did not have the slightest chance to succeed. The effort to weld the vast viceroyalty of Río de la Plata into a single independent state was a miserable failure from the outset, as we shall soon observe. Santa Cruz's Peru-Bolivian Confederation was ephemeral and insignificant. Only one of the early attempts to build a great state in Spanish America commands respect. This was the effort to create *La Gran Colombia,* an enterprise conceived by Simón Bolívar.

The iron yoke of Spanish despotism in America was not severed by the swords of a handful of intrepid leaders. Men of every color and status made their contribution to the success of the long and bloody conflict. Liberation was achieved in large measure by the daring and sacrifices of a multitude of more or less obscure warriors of different races and classes, from the Negro slave and the Indian serf to the mulatto and mestizo artisan and the aristocratic creole. Yet liberation from Spanish rule required leadership of the highest talent; and the second phase of the great enterprise, the establishment of stable governments under free institutions, demanded even greater wisdom and skill. The extreme poverty and ignorance of the masses, diversities of race and class, rugged terrain and unfavorable climate in much of the region, tropical diseases and pests, lack of efficient means of transportation, scarcity of revenues, local and regional loyalties and rivalries, intolerance to the point of fanaticism, threats (imagined or real) from abroad, the duration and character of the struggle for independence (at times more like a civil war than a war against Spain), the problem of determining the number of the new nations and their boundaries— all these handicaps need to be recalled again. Unity among the outstanding leaders was an urgent necessity if the second phase of the immense task was to be successfully completed.

Regarding the method of solving the problem of efficient self-government there were conflicting points of view. Not only were there constitutional monarchists and several kinds of republicans, as already noted; opinions also differed with reference to the type of leaders who should assume major responsibility for providing the new republican governments.

Some contended that the work of the great warriors had been finished with the completion of liberation from Spain, that the task of government should now be turned over to the civilians, and that, in fact, there could be no genuine liberty until the liberators had retired to private life or ceased to exist. Others, feeling that those who had led the fight against Spain had incurred a heavy responsibility for setting up liberal governments to take the place of the colonial despotism, argued that the great captains had the capacity to become great statesmen as well, or that, in any case, they alone were capable of defending the new nations against outside foes and maintaining order while demobilizing the revolutionary armies. Not a few military men, some of them of no more than mediocre ability, were by no means reluctant to accept the latter view, feeling that they had the right for a generation or two to make their living by ruling the nations they had created.

Although those who championed the civilian view gained the sympathy of the liberal world, it is likely that they did not fully comprehend the magnitude of the task before them. Government by lawyers, planters, businessmen, clergymen, and intellectuals would not only have to wrestle with the problems confronted by the warrior-liberators; it would also have to brave the contempt of many military men for "doctors, lawyers, theorists, and demagogues" without practice in slaying the enemy or controlling the masses. Civilian governments would have to cope with tremendously difficult geographical, economic, and social problems and at the same time win and hold the loyalty of outstanding military leaders while effecting a prompt demobilization of the armies (there were probably not less than 50,000 men under arms in Spanish South America in the early 1820's, and many private citizens also possessed arms) at a period when the boundaries of the new nations were still unsettled, when Spain and the Holy Alliance were still feared, and when treasuries were so empty that governments could not grant satisfactory bonuses and pensions or even pay off army salaries long overdue.

Of the many immediate causes for the political turbulence of the early National period in Spanish America, failure to carry out a rapid demobilization of the revolutionary troops was probably the most serious. Although caused in part by scarcity of funds, this failure resulted mainly from lack of harmony between the military and the civilian leaders. There would have been many groans and protests, but a firm and united effort on the part of these two groups might have succeeded in putting these soldiers and minor officers to work in civilian occupations.

But confusion was even worse confounded by discord within both of the rival groups themselves. In the midst of the dire poverty of the period and in an environment where no honor brought such prestige as a government post (sons of colonials who had been deprived of this privilege for 300 years were now hungry for what neither they nor their ancestors had been permitted to enjoy), every warrior-politician and every even moderately ambitious citizen was consumed with eagerness for high office, and scandalous internal squabbles disrupted both the military and the civilian groups. Worse still, the members of each group promptly decided that bullets were a better instrument for political success than ballots and began to tamper with the army instead of trying to persuade the lieutenants, captains, colonels, and brigadier generals that their duty was to stay away from political caucuses, obey the laws, and support the legally constituted governments. Although civilians and army officers were about equally at fault in this respect, perhaps the ambitious military were more ready to utilize the army for political purposes. At any rate, the army officers were better acquainted with the army's rank and file, and they always had a bow of two strings, since they might obtain military promotions in the scramble even if they failed to land somewhere near the top in the bureaucratic reorganization.

It is clear that the military men had the advantage in the 1820's; and since this was a fact, it might have been wiser for the civilians to have reconciled themselves to conditions as they were. If they had resigned themselves to the stark realities, and if the great captains had been able to work in harmony, the history of the period under review might have been less confused. Willing and able to pull together, a few outstanding members of the military group might have established fairly large and respectable states with solid governments and a moderate degree of personal liberty for everybody. The civilians, if they had been sufficiently imbued with patriotism and "passion for anonymity," possibly could have buttressed the generals with an enlightened "brain trust." Among the military leaders in South America at this time, those who might conceivably have assumed the role of statesmen with promise of success were Simón Bolívar, José de San Martín, Antonio José de Sucre, Francisco de Paula Santander, José Antonio Páez, Juan José Flores, Andrés de Santa Cruz, José de la Mar, Agustín Gamarra, and Bernardo O'Higgins.

Working in loyal collaboration and aided by a half-capable civil service, in which some of the lesser veterans of the great war could have participated after shedding their uniforms, these ten great captains might have hewn out two or three large, orderly republics as successor states to the Spanish empire in South America—Argentina, for instance, including not only present-day Argentina but Uruguay and Paraguay as well; a consolidation of what is now Chile, Peru, and Bolivia; and Greater Colombia, embracing New Granada (now called Colombia), Venezuela, and Ecuador. But of these ten great and near-great captains of the heroic age, only Bolívar and Sucre and San Martín and O'Higgins collaborated in good faith; and San Martín—who disliked both politics and public administration, favored constitutional monarchies with European princes at their head, lacked good health, and perhaps feared a dangerous clash with Bolívar—withdrew from the scene in 1822 after liberating southern South America and a part of Peru, leaving the rest of the task to others. Sucre, however, while loathing politics and administration, although he had uncommon talent for both, faithfully supported the great Liberator until struck down by the hands of assassins.

Deprived of San Martín and lacking sound advisers, O'Higgins was helpless. Soon driven from Chile, which he had governed well for the first three or four years after he became its chief executive at San Martín's suggestion in 1817, he spent the remainder of his life in ostracism in Peru.

Without San Martín, the Río de la Plata provinces across the Andes succumbed to decades of disorder. Returning to his home country early in 1829, he refused to undertake the task, which many of his fellow-citizens begged him to assume, of giving stability and liberty to his native land and went back instead to Europe, where he remained until his death in 1850. His second renunciation, like his first, has been highly praised, since nations must have their heroes; but a tremendous burst of assertiveness at this critical juncture might have been of greater service to Argentina.

With La Mar, Santa Cruz, Gamarra, and a host of army officers of lesser caliber, all jealous of Bolívar and ready to betray him while uttering honeyed words, and all working at cross purposes, there was little hope for stability and progress in Peru and Bolivia. Certainly there was no hope of the loyal collaboration of these generals with any leaders elsewhere.

Only *La Gran Colombia,* in the 1820's, seemed promising. And even in this case, as it turned out, the grandeur was only an illusion.

But here was Bolívar, the progenitor, very ambitious but also ardently patriotic, a genius who towered above them all in spite of his many faults. Here was Santander, able in both politics and administration. Here was Páez, the grand cowboy cavalry commander of Venezuela with his amazing mass appeal. Here was Flores, the youngest of this group of young men ranging in age from the middle twenties to the early forties, whose talents for government were not fully disclosed. And after his return from Bolivia, where he had given that infant nation three years of enlightened government, Sucre appeared on the scene, married a lady with a noble title, and fondly hoped to retire at last from the burden and turmoil of public life—Sucre, the finest character produced by the revolutionary epoch and ready to collaborate in spite of his reluctance. It was a promising nucleus of talent.

And *La Gran Colombia* was a large and promising nation. Formed during the years between 1819 and 1822, it sprawled from Guiana, south of the lower Orinoco River, to Guayaquil and beyond, embracing an area of more than 1,000,000 square miles and bordering two great oceans. Its climate and soils were adapted to both tropical and Temperate Zone crops. It contained immense grassy plains, some magnificent forests, and not a few metals and precious stones: gold, silver, copper, iron (but apparently no good coking coal), platinum, emeralds, and diamonds. But it also contained huge ranges of lofty mountains and some almost impenetrable swamps and jungles; its rainfall was badly distributed (in many areas far too much, and in some seasons far too little); its climate was depressingly hot except in the higher altitudes; its extreme heat, its insect pests, and its many diseases were a great affliction for both men and beasts. Its population in the middle 1820's numbered 2,500,000 to 3,000,000. (Many had lost their lives during the long war; almost every family was mourning its dead.) The inhabitants were very unevenly distributed, the main centers of occupation separated by mountain and jungle barriers or immense reaches of level plains. The whites, residing mainly in the larger settlements, made up less than a fourth of the total. There were still more than 100,000 Negro slaves, living mostly along the Caribbean and the Pacific coasts, but also in the Cauca Valley and in most of the mining regions of New Granada, and to some extent on the great plains, which now held fewer people and smaller herds because of the ravages of the revolution. But the bulk of the "people of color" was composed of

Indians (over 200,000 of them still "running wild"), mestizos, mulattoes, and "free" Africans, groups which together far outnumbered all the rest. The majority of the Colombians who were not enslaved were serfs or peons, although a good many of the lower classes were free men who served as overseers on the plantations and in the mines or worked as artisans in the various towns, from Angostura (later Cuidad Bolívar, on the Orinoco), Caracas, Valencia, and Trujillo to Santa Marta, Cartagena, Bogotá, Popayán, Quito, Cuenca, and Guayaquil. Although these and other urban centers were three centuries old, none of them really rated as cities, for none had a population of over 50,000 to 60,000.

This was Colombia in the middle 1820's. It could not be transformed or even greatly improved within any short period. But the great captains might at least have held it together and laid the foundations of progress if they had been able to utilize the advice and assistance of the more talented civilians, and if, always excepting Sucre, they had not quarreled among themselves instead of making a joint attack upon the problems of military demobilization, public finance, transportation, education, public health, and general economic development.

Serious trouble first started in Venezuela, where some clever schemers persuaded Páez early in 1826 to head a movement for greater autonomy. This brought him into conflict with Santander, who had charge of the central government while Bolívar was away in Bolivia and Peru. Soon after the Liberator left Lima, belatedly, on his way back to Bogotá and Caracas, Santa Cruz, La Mar, and Gamarra staged barracks revolts and attempted not only to take over Peru but to speed Sucre's departure from Bolivia, which he left in August, 1828, after his right arm had been shattered in putting down another presidio (garrison) uprising, ostensibly designed to hasten the payment of salaries and bonuses. The insurgent Colombian troops in Lima left for Ecuador, where, with the backing of the Peruvians, they next tried to annex part of that country to Peru. Meantime, the military and civilian leaders in *La Gran Colombia* were calling citizens and soldiers together in open meetings of the town *cabildos* and telling the central government at Bogotá what it ought to do. The chaos had begun. But the story of the formation and disruption of Greater Colombia can best be told with Bolívar in the center of the stage.[1]

POLITICAL IDEAS OF BOLÍVAR

In spite of his passions and weaknesses, Simón Bolívar may have been the wisest—he was certainly the most versatile—member of this assemblage of warrior-politicians, although Santander, a college graduate with a law degree, had a more formal education. Bolívar was an industrious reader and a rather profound thinker. Well versed in history and political theory, possessing a telescopic vision and a vivid imagination, he was a magnificent orator, a great dramatist, and a remarkable letter writer. Although he knew little about science, technology, or economics, he had a fairly clear conception of his epoch and the particular environment in which he was acting, and was able to predict the future of Spanish America so accurately that its future almost seems to have been determined by his predictions.

Long deeply concerned with political institutions, he became primarily and fundamentally interested in them as the struggle for independence terminated. His basic political ideas were set forth in four documents which have become famous in Spanish America—a long letter written from Jamaica, a lengthy discourse at Angostura, the constitution which he drafted for Bolivia, and a communication recommending this fundamental law to the constitutional convention of Bolivia.

A "Memorial to the Citizens of New Granada," sent out from Cartagena under the date of December 15, 1812, was one of the earliest formal expressions of his political ideas. In this document he attributed the recent failure of the independence movement in Venezuela to utopian liberalism, federalism, and the political incapacity of the Venezuelans. "We had philosophers for governors," he said, "philanthropy for legislation, dialectics for tactics, and sophists for soldiers." The theorists were loath to employ coercion. Every village and every province wished to govern itself, and the state would not take a man's life even for the high crime of treason. Each conspiracy was followed by a pardon, which was followed by another conspiracy and another pardon, and the result was anarchy. The Venezuelans lacked the virtues required to operate a democratic system of government, for these could not be acquired under an absolute monarchy where the rights and duties of citizens were unknown. In particular, the people of Venezuela were incapable of a prudent and orderly exercise of the right of suffrage. The "rustics of the countryside" voted mechanically; the "intriguing inhabitants of the towns and cities" were so ambitious and impetuous that they became a tumultuous faction. A free and fair election was never seen, and the government was placed in the hands of "disloyal, inept, and immoral men." This failure of the electoral system, this violently partisan spirit disorganized and disrupted the state. "Our division and not the arms of Spain returned us to slavery." Let this be a warning to New Granada.[2]

But neither New Granada nor Venezuela heeded the advice. Foolish factions paved the way for Spanish reconquest in the one, and Bolívar went down in defeat again in the other. His letter from Jamaica, dated September 6, 1815, and written to an "English gentleman," expressed the views of an involuntary exile saddened by three failures, two in Venezuela and one in New Granada. "The position of the inhabitants of the American hemisphere was purely passive for three centuries," he declared. "Their political existence was null. We were on a plane even lower than that of servitude, and for this reason it will be all the more difficult to raise ourselves up to the level where we may enjoy liberty." "America was not only deprived of its liberty," he continued, "but it was also deprived of the privilege of actively participating in the tyranny which dominated it." The Americans were in worse condition than the subjects of the despotisms of Persia, Turkey, and China, because the subjects of these countries were oppressed by their own rulers, who were the agents of the despots, while the residents of Spanish America were oppressed by satraps sent over from Spain. Reduced to the status of mere laborers and consumers, they were people abstracted, "absent from the universe in all that related to the science of government and the administration of the state." They were seldom permitted to become viceroys, governors, archbishops, or bishops; they were never allowed to become diplomats; and they took part in military affairs only as subordinates.

The Spanish Americans had therefore risen suddenly from their low status "without previous training; and, what is worse, without practice in public affairs, to represent on the world's stage the lofty dignities of legislators, magistrates, fiscal administrators, diplomats, generals, and all the other supreme and subordinate authorities which form the hierarchy of a regularly organized state." And recent events in Venezuela and New Granada, where the leaders had fought one another and fallen before the enemy, had demonstrated that "perfectly representative institutions" were not adapted to the character, customs, and enlightenment of the people. In both countries democratic societies and assemblies, popular elections, a passionate partisan spirit, and extreme federalism had frustrated the independence movements and returned the inhabitants to slavery. "Until our compatriots acquire the political talents and virtues which distinguish our brothers of the North, entirely popular systems, far from being beneficial, will, I very much fear, come to be our ruin."

Montesquieu had said that it was more difficult to deliver a people from servitude than to subjugate a free people, and the history of all times had proved the accuracy of this assertion. Yet the people of South America, moved by a blind instinct which causes all men to seek the greatest possible happiness, had manifested a desire to establish liberal and even perfect institutions. Mankind's maximum happiness would certainly be attained in societies based upon the foundations of justice, freedom, and equality; but "are we capable of maintaining in its true equilibrium the difficult burden of a republic?" "Is it possible that a people but recently freed from its chains can ascend into the sphere of liberty without melting its wings like Icarus and plunging into the abyss? Such a marvel is inconceivable; it has never been seen."

Would it be advisable, then, to set up monarchies? Such a system would neither be useful nor possible, Bolívar contended. Kings would be interested in increasing their wealth, possessions, and power, and the pursuit of these ends would lead to wars of conquest. Existing abuses would not be reformed; the regeneration of Spanish America would not even be attempted. The people preferred peace and opportunity to develop commerce, agriculture, and the sciences and arts. They desired republics rather than kingdoms. Perhaps some system might be found that would represent a compromise between the two. "The states of America need the kindly guardianship of paternal governments which will cure the wounds and sores of despotism and war." They should avoid the anarchy of demagogues on the one hand and the tyranny of monocrats on the other.

Such, in substance, were the political ideas expressed by Bolívar in 1815. Less than four years later, when a constituent assembly met at Angostura, after the great victory of Boyacá, to frame a fundamental charter for Venezuela, he announced his views in greater detail.

He began by an examination of the character of the people and their heritage from Spain. The inhabitants of his America were neither Indians nor Europeans, he declared. Indeed, it was difficult to determine the family to which they belonged. The European element had mixed with the American and with the African, and the African had mixed with the Indian and the European. Moreover, none of the groups had any knowledge of, or experience in, government. Fettered by the triple yoke of ignorance, tyranny, and vice, they had been unable to acquire wisdom or power or virtue. "Slavery is the child of darkness; an ignorant people is the blind instrument of its own destruction," he said. Intrigue and ambition would take advantage of credulity and lack of experience. The masses would mistake illusions for realities: "license for liberty, treachery for patriotism, vengeance for justice." It would be difficult to persuade the people that happiness consisted in the practice of virtue, that they must obey the law, that justice was essential to the exercise of liberty. Rousseau had said that liberty was a nourishing food, but that it was difficult to digest; and the weak citizens of Spanish

America would have to develop greater intelligence and a more robust spirit before they could digest that salutary nourishment of freedom.

Only democracy, Bolívar admitted, was capable of providing absolute liberty. But what democratic government had been able to attain at the same time not only power and prosperity, but permanence as well? Had not all republics been ephemeral, and were not all the great and enduring states of history monarchies and aristocracies?

Venezuela had already declared itself a republic, proscribed kings and all the titles, distinctions, and special privileges that accompanied the royal system, and pronounced itself in favor of the rights of man and freedom to work, think, speak, and write. He admired the noble aspirations which prompted this course; but he was compelled to point out that Venezuela's federal constitution was entirely impracticable. It was true that such a system was in operation in the United States; but the people of North America were unique in their political virtues and moral enlightenment, and the survival of even that nation under such a system was nothing less than a miracle. The Spanish Americans and the English Americans were not even remotely similar, and this model should not be followed in Venezuela. Had not Montesquieu said that all laws should be adapted to the people for whom they were made?

Bolívar urged the members of the convention to be moderate in their aspirations. Unbridled liberty and absolute democracy were the reefs upon which all republican hopes had been shattered. Social perfection and perfect systems of government were noble ideals, but the legislators were dealing with men and not angels. A steady nerve and a firm hand would be necessary to prevent this heterogeneous multitude of diverse racial origins and cultures from plunging into anarchy. The executive power should be made very strong, and the senators should serve for life. The citizens should be divided into two groups, the one active and the other passive. Qualifications for active participation in government should be carefully weighed. Mobs of turbulent, blind, and blundering people should have no part in elections. Voting should be safeguarded. The liberties of the nation would depend upon the orderly and wise performance of this important function.

Bolívar then suggested that a fourth power be added to the legislative, the executive, and the judicial. After carefully considering the methods of effectively regenerating a people debased by tyranny, he proposed a Moral Power, which he found described in the laws designed to maintain virtue among the Greeks and Romans. "Let us take from Athens its Areopagus," he exhorted; "let us take from Rome its censors and domestic tribunals; and making a holy alliance of these moral institutions, let us revive in the world the idea of a people which is not content with being free and strong, but desires to be virtuous as well. Let us take from Sparta its austere establishments, and having formed of these three streams a fountain of virtue, let us give to our republic a fourth power." The Areopagus would have dominion over the education of the children and the youth, over the hearts of the adults, over customs, public spirit, and republican morality. It would have its books of virtue and vice, in which would be registered its proceedings, its lists of moral principles, its judgments passed upon the acts of citizens and officials. This Moral Power was fully described in the draft constitution which he submitted to the Angostura assembly.

Although this phase of his plan was rejected because of unpleasant memories of repression during the Colonial period and the fear that his Moral Power might lead to moral despotism, in general the members of the convention followed Bolívar's advice. But the constitution was framed for a nation not yet free from Spanish bondage and was never put into full operation. In 1821, after further military triumphs, another fundamental law was drawn up for New Granada and Ecuador as well as Venezuela. It provided for a centralized republic, with Bogotá as the capital, divided the sprawling nation, still partially occupied by the Spaniards, into twelve departments and thirty-six provinces, and proclaimed all the freedoms except that of religious cults. On this occasion the Liberator was too busy with military operations to exert any direct influence on the deliberations of the convention. A few years later he was to complain bitterly of the defects of this constitution, which, by its terms, was not to be revised until the end of ten years; but for the moment he made no comment. Elected president under the regime it prescribed, he took the oath of office, expelled the Spaniards from Venezuela with the aid of Páez and others, and soon departed with full discretionary powers for Ecuador in order to join Sucre, leaving Santander in charge at Bogotá. These extraordinary powers were conferred upon Bolívar in accordance with a provision of the new constitution itself (Art. 128).

After he and his able lieutenants had finally driven the royalists from a region almost as large as the present-day United States, he was called upon for advice in providing a constitution for Bolivia. His response, May 25, 1826, indicates that his fundamental political conceptions had not greatly changed. He attempted to draft a model constitution for all of northern South America, perhaps even for all Spanish America. For almost three years he had been dictator of Peru and president of Colombia as well.

The constitution which he proposed was quite conservative. Designed as a compromise between a monarchy and a republic, it was virtually a monarchy in disguise. The government was vested in executive, legislative, judicial and "electoral" powers. The chief executive bore the title of president, but his term was for life and he was given the right to choose the vice-president. The legislature was composed of three houses: tribunes, senators, and censors, with the last likewise serving for life. In fact, the censors were another version of his Moral Power of 1819. They were to supervise education, the press, and the conduct of public officials; they were to promote the arts, the sciences, and public morality. Officials subject to election were few, and a literacy test was required for voting.

The message which accompanied his draft constitution revealed clearly his distrust of the masses. He remarked that tyranny and anarchy formed an immense ocean of oppression which surrounded a small island of liberty perpetually lashed by furious waves and hurricanes. He said that elections were the great scourge of republics, since they tended to produce anarchy, the most immediate and most terrible danger of popular governments. Yet the personal guaranties which he provided were fairly ample, religious liberty being included among them, and the constitution abolished slavery.

Foreseeing that his fundamental charter might arouse apprehension among the democrats, he sought to reassure them by contending that the powers of the president were greatly curtailed. In this connection he also remarked that Spanish America contained neither great wealth nor powerful ecclesiastics, nor an ambitious clergy, nor great nobles. Without these supports rulers could not become dangerous, and any who aspired to become kings or emperors would be deterred by the fate of Dessalines, Christophe, and Iturbide. No power was more difficult to maintain than the power of a new prince; the fall of Napoleon I was convincing evidence of that. Men need have no fear that monarchs would be established in America. Thrones would turn out to be royal scaffolds; crowns would be but so many swords of Damocles suspended above royal heads. It was evident that the Liberator had given considerable thought to the subject of monarchy.

His grand plan for the political future of Spanish America was now taking full shape. He wished to consolidate Bolivia, Peru, Ecuador, New Granada, and Venezuela into one vast state under his conservative constitution. This large entity would then become the dominant unit in a sort of league of Latin-American nations, and the whole area would be given stability and prestige, he hoped, under the patronage of Great Britain. The congress soon to assemble at Panama was designed to form the new league. Perhaps he himself might become the life-president of the states of northern South America and select Antonio José Sucre as his successor.

𝕊𝕄 THE DISSOLUTION

Whether the Liberator exaggerated the dangers which threatened Spanish America at that period is a question difficult to answer. There could have been only two motives for exaggeration: a desire to frighten the people into the adoption of stronger governments, and an eagerness for supreme power.

His private correspondence does not positively convict him of harboring extreme personal ambitions. It rather suggests that he was anxious at times to retire, but continued at the head of the government in the hope of giving stable institutions to the people whom he had liberated.

As he surveyed the new nations from the lofty peaks of the Andes, the scene which presented itself to his keen vision was alarming enough. Chaos was reigning in Chile and the Río de la Plata; anarchy was beginning to threaten Mexico and Central America; a tyrant was ruling in Paraguay.

During the next three or four years conditions not only became worse in most of these states, but anarchy began to sweep over the vast region which he himself had freed from Spain. Moreover, his anxiety was heightened by fear of the Spanish Bourbons and the European Holy Alliance.

Reluctantly, perhaps, he undertook to remedy the evils which he observed. He warned the political leaders and the people against the federal system and the excesses of democracy. He urged the adoption of his model constitution in Peru and Greater Colombia. He appealed to England for help. He left Lima in late 1826 for Guayaquil and Quito to calm the disorders caused in part by his own imprudent agents, and then went on to Bogotá. There he was vested with extraordinary powers to settle difficulties which were threatening a bloody civil war in Venezuela, where Páez was planning a coup d'état. While trying to calm the storm in Venezuela he continued to advocate another convention and waited impatiently for the assembly which met in Ocaña in 1828 to give *La Gran Colombia* a more conservative and vigorous constitution. When the convention of Ocaña ended in a tumult and he barely escaped assassination, he resumed his dictatorship in the hope of resisting the tide of anarchy and expelled Santander from the country for alleged complicity in the assassination plot. In 1829 he hurried south to help Sucre deal with the war between Ecuador and Peru.

But the waning strength of his declining years was not equal to the burden which he took upon his frail shoulders. The task of liberating half a continent had depleted his energies. He could not construct the great state of his dreams; much less was he able to bring into existence a Latin-American league of nations.

The very nature and scope of his enterprise defeated him. The magnitude of his undertaking and his frank warnings and confessions aroused the fears and jealousies of those who called themselves democrats and liberals, many of whom, like Santander and Páez, were men of power and determination. He promoted anarchy by his attempts to cope with it. Opponents declared that he was ambitious, that he would become a tyrant. Crowns offered by ardent friends in good faith and ambitious enemies in bad faith tended to frustrate his efforts. Men who sought refuge in a monarchy headed by a European prince involved him in grave embarrassments. In order to avoid offense to the kings of Europe, in order not to provoke intervention by reactionary governments across the sea, he must either keep silent or resort to vague and evasive language. Even in private letters he could merely point out the difficulties which would attend the establishment of a monarchy.

Moreover, he shrank from drastic use of force because this would give plausibility to the arguments of those who said he was a potential despot, and perhaps also because he was at heart a liberal. He was too lenient with the insurgency of Páez; and although he put down other revolts and conspiracies with a sterner hand, he was loath to adopt a general policy of blood and iron in order to preserve his ideal state. He preferred moral suasion.

The last five years of his life were filled with anguish. Shortly after he finished the bloody work of driving the Spaniards from their last South American strongholds, a note of extreme pessimism began to appear in his letters and interviews. All is bad and bound to become worse was almost a constant refrain. The specter of a race war in which the inhabitants of European descent would be exterminated sometimes haunted him, and he talked of an albocracy—a government by the whites. He was eager to give his people a stable regime as well as independence from Spain, but he feared his glory would be tarnished in the process. His popularity was waning among the liberals of Spanish America and the whole Western world. The great liberals of Europe, perhaps even including Lafayette, although he wrote with superb tact, disclosed anxiety regarding his ambitions. Henry Clay and Jacksonian Democrats in the United States scolded him. Newspapers in both Europe and America questioned his motives. Conspirators planned to destroy him. Ambitious captains revolted against his rule. Partisans and opponents aroused the people. Seething mobs surged along the streets of a hundred towns and villages shouting their views pro and con. Painfully wounded by the opposition and its bitter criticism, which seemed to betray base ingratitude, he was a Hamlet now, perplexed and paralyzed by doubts and fears. No help came from England whose aid he eagerly sought, no effective aid from anywhere. Bolívar and Sucre finally stood almost alone confronting the anarchy that both had predicted and feared.

As the year 1830 dawned, all Spanish America, save dictator-ridden Paraguay, seemed to be a raging sea of anarchy, and stark despair seized the Liberator's soul. "There is no faith in America," he said, "between either men or nations." "Treaties are pieces of paper; constitutions, books; elections, combats; liberty, anarchy; and life, a torment." [3]

Slowly dying with tuberculosis, aggravated by his strenuous life, Bolívar resigned and left Bogotá in April, 1830. Spanish America was ungovernable, he declared. In attempting to give freedom to these people he had merely plowed the sea. The region was rapidly falling into the hands of frenzied mobs, becoming the prey of petty tyrants of every race and color. It would be devoured by crime, extinguished by ferocity. If it were possible for any portion of the world to return to primeval chaos, this would be the final doom of Spanish America. On June 4 enemies assassinated Sucre, his dearest friend and most faithful collaborator. The two men had not seen each other since February, when Sucre left Bogotá for Venezuela in the vain hope of preventing its secession. They had exchanged their last letters in May, as Bolívar began his voyage down the Magdalena toward the coast and as Sucre mounted his horse for the long ride to Quito to join his wife and infant daughter. News of Sucre's assassination in a forest north of Pasto had reached the Liberator in Cartagena at the end of June. It was soon followed by reports of the secession of Ecuador under the leadership of Flores. Bolívar's dream was now shattered; Greater Colombia was completely disrupted. Exiled from Venezuela by the dictatorial decree of Páez (written by Antonio L. Guzmán who had but recently presented Páez's offer of a crown), unwanted in New Granada, the dying warrior spent his last days at a country place near Santa Marta. Into his feeble hands, as the end drew near, an attendant, a Spaniard, is said to have placed a book. Its title was *Don Quijote*. Glancing at the old classic again, the dying Liberator was reminded of three broken and frustrated idealists —Jesus Christ, Don Quijote, and Simón Bolívar.[4]

It is likely that Simón Bolívar never quite understood why he failed to accomplish the second phase of his great task. He did allude to some of the causes, however, as already observed. He referred frequently to mass ignorance, the danger of a race war, the insubordination of rude and ruthless army officers, the selfishness and faithlessness of some of the prominent citizens, the mania for government employment, the peculations and tyranny of local agents (military commandants, intendants of the departments, prefects of the provinces), the imprudence of emissaries who negotiated ruinous foreign loans, inability to balance the budget—expenditures were nearly always twice as large as receipts —and general resistance to the payment of taxes.

This was a formidable array of obstacles, but there were others that he failed to mention. In spite of his many long and ardent journeys from one end of his great state to the other, he seems never to have fully grasped the significance of the immense geographical handicaps. Nor did he ever attack the problem of demobilization with a vigor that disclosed a complete understanding of its importance. This mistake, serious as it was, is not difficult to explain. He was uncertain about the plans of Spain and the attitude of some of the other European powers. He adored the military machine which he had organized and which had carried him to lofty heights of fame, and there was always a tender spot in his heart for the veterans of the long war and the families of those who had lost their lives in battle. (For these victims of the war he was extravagant, with both his own private fortune and the funds of the state.) Toward the end of his life he remarked that the bitter feud between Santander and Páez caused the ruin of Greater Colombia; but his own break with Santander, which had its beginnings in late 1824, was more significant. It may also be suggested that he undertook too much when he attempted to dominate Peru and Bolivia as well as *La Gran Colombia;* that he talked and wrote too freely and frankly (not for the historian, but for the good of his cause); that he should never have attempted to induce Peru and Colombia to accept his conservative constitution of 1826, but should rather have sought to stabilize Greater Colombia under the fundamental law of 1821, which appears to have served fairly well until efforts were made to repudiate it; that he should not have unsettled and weakened his friends by so much talk of resigning; that he should never have encouraged or permitted his agents, many of them army officers, to create an uneasy and even turbulent atmosphere by convening one town council after another; that he lingered too long in Peru, enjoying the adulation of flatterers and the caresses of his mistress (Manuela Sáenz) instead of hurrying to Bogotá, Valencia, and Caracas to deal with the disturbers of the peace; and that he should have backed Santander, who had the law on his side, in Santander's clash with Páez, and subdued that Llanero chieftain. Nor should one forget that the Liberator's health had been shattered and that physical exhaustion may have befogged his mind and sapped his will.

It is not easy to arrive at firm conclusions regarding the traits and achievements of this complex and remarkable man. Of one thing, however, the historian may be certain. There was little that he did not sacrifice for his country. He could not give it more than he had.

CHAPTER XVII

Republics of the Northern Andes

SUMMARY OF SIMILARITIES

Spanish South America broke up into nine states shortly after the last of the Spanish garrisons were expelled, and Portuguese Brazil raised the total to ten. The population of the entire continent in 1830 was barely 12,000,000, perhaps no greater than it had been three centuries before. Brazil, by far the largest nation in both population and area, had no more than 4,000,000 inhabitants; Uruguay, the smallest, had less than 75,000! Colonial administrative divisions, geographical influences, diversities in racial composition, and the ambitions of local and regional chiefs all fostered the spirit of separatism. Differences in colonial background, language, and form of government set Brazil off from the rest. Intimate relationships arising from proximity, and similarities in racial composition or physical environment, make it convenient—and not inappropriate, at least during the early National epoch before time and change accentuated national divergencies—to deal with the republics of Spanish origin in groups composed of three countries each: (1) the republics located mainly in the northern Andes; (2) those of the southern Andes; and (3) those of the Plata region.[1]

The three republics of the northern Andes are quite similar from the standpoint of both geography and racial characteristics. Situated in the tropics, they all have their lofty mountains, jungle coastlands, and vast plains, although the plains of Ecuador are much less extensive than those of the other two and Colombia has a larger share of Andean ranges. The population of each is made up of Indians, Negroes, whites, and mixtures of the three races, with the whites decidedly in the minority. Nevertheless, this white minority—about a third of the population in Colombia, a fifth in Venezuela, and a still smaller fraction in Ecuador—managed during the early National period to maintain its political, social, and economic supremacy; for while there was no intense racial prejudice, few of the mixed and primitive peoples were able to rise above their colonial status of artisans and unskilled workers. The position of the Roman Catholic Church was strong in all three republics, though it was less powerful and a less disturbing factor in politics in Venezuela than in the other two.

For several decades the history of the three nations followed a similar course. All three were fairly stable under conservative regimes imposed by Bolívar's generals until perturbed by new men and new ideas. Then they plunged into extreme disorder, from which they were temporarily extricated at different periods: Ecuador in the 1860's by Gabriel García Moreno, Venezuela in the 1870's by Antonio Guzmán Blanco, and Colombia in the 1880's by Rafael Núñez.

At the end of the epoch, Venezuela was quite different from its two neighbors. Ecuador had only recently ceased to be a vast monastery and Colombia was conservative and theocratic; Venezuela, in contrast, seemed progressive and secular. None of the three, however, had achieved a stable democratic or civilian regime. Militarism still predominated; and although the Africans had been freed from slavery and the Indians exempted from the discriminatory head tax of the Colonial period, a wide gulf still separated the classes. Rural laborers were no better off than serfs and those in the towns worked for a pittance and begged on the streets to avoid starvation. Although the state had assumed a measure of responsibility for schools, education was still left mainly to the clergy and private initiative in Colombia, and was still very inadequately supported by the state in Ecuador and Venezuela in spite of the repeatedly announced enthusiasm of Eloy Alfaro and Guzmán Blanco for the enlightenment of the people. With little opportunity to better their condition, the lower classes in these countries seemed doomed, generation after generation, to work on the sugar and cacao plantations, the coffee *fincas,* or the big ranches, or as artisans, porters, muleteers, boatsmen, miners, pack animals, and household servants. Apparently there was no escape except into the armies.

VENEZUELA

It will be remembered that the large republic founded by Bolívar while the people of this region were collaborating in the war against Spain had held together less than ten years. Venezuela—with a population of around 800,000 in 1830 and fewer than thrice that number in 1900—had been the first to secede. For the first sixteen years after separation —until 1846—the country was governed by the ranchman and warrior José Antonio Páez, or by executives whom he controlled. Páez, the picturesque commander of cowboy cavalry from the Venezuelan llanos during the war for independence from Spain, was able to prevent any serious revolutions. Although the son of a poor family, and perhaps not altogether Caucasian himself, he governed in the interest of a white oligarchy of merchants, planters, clergymen, and army officers who favored a centralized republic dominated by an aristocracy of wealth and culture in alliance with the church.

The political group who overthrew Páez and his partisans called themselves Liberals and soon began to advocate a federal system. Although deeply divided by doctrinal disputes and clashing ambitions, they ruled the country for several decades and theoretically transformed it into a federal republic under the title of the United States of Venezuela. But since they usually controlled state elections, and therefore state governors and legislatures, the change, which was embodied in the centrofederalist constitution of 1858 and the purely federalist constitution of 1864, had little significance in practice. What they actually established was an unstable federation of *caudillos,* each of whom tried to occupy the position of supreme *caudillo* at Caracas. Like most of the Conservatives who surrounded Páez, the Liberals were white planters and intellectuals; but their group embraced a few members from the lower classes, and in 1854 they freed the last remnant of the Negro slaves, with compensation to the owners, and adopted universal manhood suffrage shortly afterward.

The overthrow of Páez and the Conservative oligarchy by the so-called Liberals, who were also actually an oligarchy, was facilitated by a shift in the political affiliation of José Tadeo Monagas. A Conservative ranchman supported by Páez for the succession in 1846–47, Monagas soon went over to the Liberals, suppressed the Conservative Congress, placed his brother, José G. Monagas, in the presidential palace in 1851, took charge of the government again in 1855, and tried to perpetuate his rule. This caused a split in the Liberal oligarchy and a vigorous revolt by a coalition of dissident Liberals and the displaced Conservatives, who drove the Monagas family from power in 1858.

The next twelve years were the most turbulent in Venezuelan history. Both the Liberals and the Conservatives splintered into violent factions, each following a personal leader, usually an intrepid army officer. The masses were incited and dragooned, and the nation was laid waste by almost continuous civil war. Between 1858 and 1870 Venezuela had seven chief executives, including the old Llanero warrior Páez, who returned from exile in the United States and set up a two-year dictatorship, and including two members of the Monagas clan, his bitter rivals since 1847. The most powerful factions were the "Blues," who sometimes allied themselves with the remnants of the Conservative oligarchy, and the "Yellows," who were ostensibly extreme federalists. Despite the fact that the Negro slaves were emancipated and universal suffrage proclaimed, there was actually less respect for personal liberty, the ballot, the law, and the constitution than during the Páez regime. The nation was almost destroyed and foreign intervention seriously threatened before a dominant leader finally arose and restored peace and order.

The new leader was Antonio Guzmán Blanco, the son of the popular journalist, agitator, and politician Antonio L. Guzmán. An aristocrat of pure Spanish blood who had spent a decade fighting his way to supreme power and whose devotion to the motley masses was probably far less ardent than he professed, Guzmán Blanco held the country in his iron grip for nineteen years (1870–89). The federal constitution under which he ruled prescribed a two-year term and prohibited two terms in succession, and, like many other Latin-American politicians of his day, he went through the pretense of surrendering his power while exercising rigid control behind the scenes. While his marionettes carried out his orders, he spent the intervals in Europe, selling government bonds and negotiating concessions to "develop" the nation he ruled as a vast plantation.

Although dishonest and despotic, committing many brutalities and accumulating a private fortune at public expense, he was able and sometimes patriotic. Hostile toward the Roman Catholic Church—mainly, it is said, because the clergy refused to join in the celebration of his military triumphs; certainly the temporal power of the church had already been greatly curtailed—he suppressed the religious communities and seized their property; legalized civil marriage; inaugurated a civil registry; took control of the cemeteries; issued decrees making primary education free and compulsory under state control; proclaimed religious freedom (toleration of non-Catholic faiths had been granted in 1834); and threatened to set up a state church independent of Rome. He also had the laws codified and financed the construction of roads, bridges, railways, telegraphs, schools, and many expensive public buildings. His vanity was immense and ridiculous. With public funds he erected numerous monuments to himself, inscribing his name on almost every structure built by the national government during his long rule, and like Napoleon he had the legal codes named in his honor. He spent the last decade of his life in exile in Paris, living in a fine mansion and associating with the elite. One of his daughters became the wife of the Duc de Morny.

Politics became turbulent again in Venezuela after the ousting of Guzmán Blanco in 1889. Chief executives, whether army officers or civilians selected by them, were ephemeral until 1899, when Cipriano Castro, with the aid of Juan Vicente Gómez, seized the government and consolidated his tyranny.

ECUADOR

In the meantime the southwestern section of Bolívar's *La Gran Colombia* had seceded and formed a new state under the title of Ecuador. Its leading sponsor and first chief executive was Juan José Flores, a mestizo from Venezuela who, though eventually married to an Ecuadorian wife, never saw the land he was to rule until he arrived there in the 1820's with the liberating army under Bolívar. He allied himself with the wealthy white families and imposed his authority by means of a military establishment composed mainly of foreign soldiers (Colombians and Venezuelans).

To maintain order in this turbulent little country (its population was about 500,000 in 1930 and barely 1,500,000 in 1900) with its ambitious minority of whites, its primitive and mixed races easily ensnared into the armies, its restless and violent army officers, its tremendous mountain barriers, and its lack of any genuine national spirit, required uncommon capacity. To have promoted progress in addition to keeping order would have demanded nothing short of genius. Flores was able to effect a measure of stability, but he appears not to have given serious attention to anything else except his own selfish interests. His main objectives seem to have been the retention of power and the accumulation of wealth for himself and his relatives and intimate friends. He was a soldier of fortune. A revolution organized in the coastal region, with Guayaquil as its center, might have expelled him from the country in 1834 if he had not succeeded in making a compromise with Vicente Rocafuerte, its principal leader.

According to the terms of this agreement, Rocafuerte was to become the next president of the country, but Flores was to retain command of the army. The alleged, and probably the actual, causes of the revolt were tyranny, heavy taxes, and the peculations of the Flores regime. After serving as provisional president for a time, Rocafuerte called together a convention which framed a moderately liberal constitution.

A native of Guayaquil who had lived for years in France, the United States, and Mexico, Rocafuerte was a diplomat and pamphleteer rather than a soldier. Familiar with all the liberal ideas of his day, he thought of applying some of them in Ecuador, but his alliance with Flores restrained him. He made some improvements in finances, in education, and in other public services, but undertook no drastic changes in the social order.

At the end of Rocafuerte's constitutional term in 1839, Flores, who still commanded the national army, had himself "elected" for a second period. Having lost during his first administration some of the territory of the old Quito presidency which the new nation of Ecuador claimed to inherit, he now tried to recover it by supporting a revolt in southern New Granada. The result was a brief but futile and expensive war. Ambitious to perpetuate his rule, he assembled another constitutional convention in 1843 as his second term drew to a close. Composed mainly of hand-picked delegates ready to carry out the despot's will, the convention framed a very conservative constitution and elected Flores president for a term of eight years. But this was not enough; he soon demanded and obtained from the subservient assembly a grant of "extraordinary powers," and then proceeded to fetter the press and persecute the opposition.

Smarting under a tyranny imposed by a foreigner, the Ecuadorians rose up in a tremendous revolt in 1845. Seeing the writing on the wall, Flores was shrewd enough to negotiate a good bargain with the insurgents, who agreed to respect his property and continue his salary for the rest of his term provided he would leave the country. He went to Europe, where he managed to obtain funds for another effort to recoup his political fortune, but was unable to force his way back into Ecuador. He did not return until he was called back in 1860 by another spin of the wheel and given supreme command of the army.

His fifteen years of exile were very turbulent years for Ecuador, a period during which the native colonels of the war for independence from Spain fought one another in order to determine who should rule their country. In the course of their petty combats the Negroes were freed (1851–52) from slavery and the Indians from tribute, and the religious issue was raised by the expulsion of the Company of Jesus and minor attacks on the property and functions of the church. Then a strong man appeared, a vigorous reactionary, who gave the nation an era of peace—peace without liberty. His name was Gabriel García Moreno.

Like most of the other Ecuadorian political chiefs of the early National period (a mulatto named Ramón Roca served a term as president 1845–49—and spent most of the rest of his life in jail), García Moreno was of pure Spanish blood. Studious and ambitious, and married to a wealthy wife who belonged to a family with considerable political influence, he completed his education in France, where he was shocked into extreme conservatism by the Revolution of 1848, and returned home to enter politics. After almost a decade of pamphleteering and fighting, he finally seized the national capital in 1860 and, with the aid of Flores, firmly seated himself in power. For the next fifteen years he completely dominated the country, serving as its supreme executive most of the time.

A ruthless tyrant with some constructive tendencies, he not only maintained order but promoted the economic development of his country and tried to improve the moral standards of its people, including the clergy. Managing the national revenues honestly and efficiently, he opened new schools, financed the construction of roads and public buildings, and initiated Ecuador's first railway. A rigid disciplinarian, he permitted neither freedom of speech nor freedom of the press, neither religious toleration nor freedom of elections. Apparently very pious himself, he spent long hours in prayer and meditation, placed the nation under the guidance of the Roman Catholic Church, and in impressive public ceremonies dedicated it to the Sacred Heart of Jesus. During the later years of his rule Ecuador became an immense monastery. Clericalism and Conservatism were so firmly established that the Liberals were unable to shatter their power until twenty years after his assassination in August, 1875. Although two Liberals managed to capture the government during the first decade after his death, one of them held it for only a few months and the other had to betray his party in order to complete his four-year term.

The Ecuadorian *caudillos* who finally led their Liberal cohorts to victory over the Conservatives, so firmly established in power by the theocrat García Moreno three decades earlier, were Flavio Eloy Alfaro and Leónidas Plaza Gutiérrez, who followed the customary liberal policies with reference to the church, destroying its monopoly of education and religion and drastically reducing its wealth, power, and functions. Like other Latin-American Liberals, they favored state-supported lay education, religious toleration, civil marriage, state control of graveyards, and civil registry. Between them they dominated the national government for some twenty years.

Both were natives of the hot coastal region, always more progressive than the mountain areas of the interior, although neither was a native of Guayaquil, the leading port city. Alfaro was born in 1842 in Montecristi, a small town where skilled artisans and merchants made their living by weaving and marketing "Panama" hats. Plaza Gutiérrez was born twenty-four years later in the port town of Bahía de Caraquez. Alfaro was mainly responsible for the courageous and determined leadership that finally resulted in the restoration of the Liberals and eventually became the more famous of the two.

Few men in history had a more stormy and perilous career than Eloy Alfaro. He spent a third of his life in exile, mostly in Panama, and

THE EARLY NATIONAL PERIOD
252

another third in military campaigns against the Conservatives. He then ruled Ecuador for a total of eleven years, with a five-year interval between his two terms, and after breaking with other leaders of his party, began his last revolution at the age of sixty-nine. His first administration lasted from 1895 until 1901, when he transferred the presidency to Plaza Gutiérrez whom he had favored as his successor and for whose "election" he was mainly responsible. His second administration covered the period from 1906 to 1911; and it was early the next year that he started his last revolt. Defeated and imprisoned, he was soon murdered and mutilated by a Quito mob; but a few years later a monument was erected to his memory in Guayaquil. Alfaro not only inaugurated Liberal "reforms"; he also stressed the material development of his country, and is especially noted for his successful efforts to have the railway between Guayaquil and Quito completed, the longest and most important railroad in Ecuador.

Plaza Gutiérrez followed the policies laid down by Alfaro, supporting the construction of railways, telegraph lines, and telephone exchanges, building schools, and completing the secularization of the country. But the two became enemies in 1905, falling out largely because of a dispute over the presidential succession; and it was Plaza Gutiérrez who crushed his former chief's revolution early in 1912. Plaza suffered like Alfaro from the disease of *continuismo,* but he retired in 1916 at the end of his second term, handing the reins over to another Liberal who managed to complete a four-year period and transfer them to still another Liberal.

COLOMBIA

Under the official title of New Granada, then the Granadine Confederation, the United States of Colombia, and finally the Republic of Colombia, the center of Bolívar's grand state achieved early stability, with the promise of both order and liberty. In 1849, however, the area descended into the chaos of radicalism, federalism, and militarism, from which it was finally rescued for a time in the 1880's by a converted (or turncoat) radical in close alliance with the clergy.

For more than thirty years New Granada was ruled mainly by army officers who had won fame during the long war against Spain. Although they were for the most part an able group with some appreciation for democracy and civil rights and not afflicted with the disease of *continuismo,* they finally developed such extreme partisan fervor that they split the nation asunder and almost extinguished it. A population of slightly more than 1,500,000 in 1830 had not increased to much over 3,000,000 by 1885, and was probably as miserable at the end of the epoch as at its beginning.

This nucleus of *La Gran Colombia* had not been extremely disorderly under the decade of Bolívar's rule—although as already stated, he had felt it necessary to assume dictatorial powers in 1828 after conspirators had tried to assassinate him—and had succumbed to only a temporary period of turbulence after his resignation and the loss of Venezuela and Ecuador. Francisco de Paula Santander, a hero of the war against Spain and for some time vice-president under Bolívar (although their political association was severed in 1828), put the country back on an even keel during his term as chief executive (1833–37), giving it a sound administration and promoting both economic and cultural progress.

The next president was a scholarly civilian, José Ignacio Márquez, victorious in a reasonably fair election in spite of the opposition of Santander, who felt that his successor should be another military man. Dr. Márquez took his task seriously, sought the co-operation of all groups, tried to enforce the law, provoked a revolt in southern New Granada by suppressing some monasteries which had only a few residents and therefore seemed superfluous, but managed to serve out his term.

Márquez was followed by two generals, closely related to each other by marriage and business affiliation, Pedro A. Herrán and Tomás C. Mosquera. They both acquitted themselves with distinction, preserving the peace, making serious efforts to promote economic and cultural advance, and at the same time respecting civil and personal liberties. As the end of Mosquera's term approached in early 1849, the future seemed unclouded.

Then the turmoil suddenly began. The Colombian intellectuals, as fervid, energetic, and active as any to be found in Latin America or elsewhere, were profoundly moved by the Revolution of 1848 in France and by the ideology upon which it was based. They not only dreamed of a perfect society but decided to inaugurate one at once—in New Granada. Students and teachers, young and old, crowded around the building in which the national congress was assembled to choose Mosquera's successor, since none of the candidates had won the recent election, and not only shouted for their man, General José Hilario López, but threatened the lives of the balloting congressmen, some of whom finally cast their votes for López "in order to avoid assassination." Inaugurated on April 1, 1849, the new administration launched "grand and transcendental reforms," abolishing slavery, the death penalty for crime, the government monopoly of tobacco, and all limitations on freedom of press and religion.

The reformers provoked a widespread revolution, of course, but they managed to suppress it and write their program into a new constitution, the Constitution of 1853, the first in Spanish America to separate Church and State. They banished some of the protesting clergy from the country.

Although federalism was a part of their creed, they did not apply it at once. They suffered a reversal in 1854 when their next president was deposed by a military adventurer and the government fell into the hands of the Conservatives. But the Conservatives, hoping to build dykes to shield at least some parts of the nation from the tidal wave of change, suddenly became federalists too. They began to confer the status of statehood upon the provinces in 1855, and were mainly responsible in 1858 for inaugurating the Granadine Confederation.

Now there were multiple centers of conflict instead of one. The outlying members of the confederation seceded, formed a new compact under Tomás C. Mosquera, a Conservative turned radical, seized Bogotá in July, 1861, and began forthwith a violent attack upon the church, dissolving the religious orders, confiscating ecclesiastical properties, depriving clergymen of all their traditional functions except that of conducting public worship, and sending a number of them into exile. Asserting the right of national and local political authorities to inspect the conduct of the clerics and to participate in the selection of all clergymen from parish priests to archbishops, they not only deprived the Roman Catholic Church of its wealth, functions, and power but actually subjected it to the state. All these drastic "reforms" were embodied along with extreme federalism in a new constitution framed in 1863, which changed the official title of the nation to the United States of Colombia.

The turmoil that began in 1849 lasted nearly forty years. Between 1851 and 1885 the country was ravaged by four general civil wars and fifty local revolutions. Men abandoned fortune and family, "as in the great religious periods of history," went out to defend their convictions, and fell "nobly, with the ardour of Spanish crusaders." The fundamental charter of 1863 guaranteed unrestricted freedom of discussion and opinion, complete free trade in firearms, and the sovereignty of the states. It also limited the presidential term to two brief years and prohibited two terms in succession. Elections, including those in the nine states, were almost continuous. But they were never orderly or fair. They were bloody combats in which voters risked their lives. No president ever violated the dogma of rapid rotation—or ever permitted the opposition to win! Although the Conservatives sometimes managed to get control of state governments, for a period of twenty years not a single Conservative served as chief executive of the nation.

A vigorous reaction was bound to occur sooner or later. There was not a more brilliant journalist or political philosopher among all the brilliant Colombians than Rafael Núñez; and, for many years, there had not been a more ardent champion of radicalism and local autonomy. But he had withdrawn from the national political combat in the 1860's, abandoned his wife, entered the diplomatic and consular service, and gone to Europe, where he spent more than a decade in serious study and observation of politics. Whether these investigations and the sad condition of his fatherland under the rule of his party had caused him to modify his political attitude no one can tell. Shortly after his return he ran for the presidency as one of the candidates of the Liberal party and failed to win. A native of Cartagena, where he was born fifty years before (1825), he had no intimate contacts with the ruling clique. Nor were presidents chosen from Cartagena; its ancient renown had vanished. But he did not join the Conservatives; he organized a little faction of his own, composed of dissident Liberals, and called it the Independent Liberal party.

Late in 1876 the Conservatives launched a widespread revolution and asked him to join them, but he refused, remarking that he did not care to embark on a foundering ship. The revolt was suppressed after months of bloodshed.

In 1878 he became a member of the national congress and was chosen as temporary president of that body. One of the duties of this post was to administer the oath to the incoming president of Colombia. Núñez seized the occasion to make one of his eloquent speeches and promulgate a slogan: "We have arrived at a point where we are confronted by this dilemma," he said, "fundamental administrative regeneration or catastrophe." But there were still doubts regarding his political sympathies and aims.

The next year Núñez was elected president, mainly by the votes of his new party, although a few radical Liberals and some Conservatives cast their ballots for him. His inaugural address was a plea for tolerance, peace, and intellectual and economic progress. Since the constitution restricted his term to two years and prohibited immediate re-election, he surrendered his office early in 1882, but not until he had imposed his successor and secured for himself the position of "first designate." Moreover, he soon entered into secret communications with the Conservatives, who promptly decided to make him their candidate for 1883. Since he was already the preference of the Independents, this Conservative support assured him of victory.

His second inaugural address was a final appeal to the radical Liberals to join the moderates. "One epoch of our history has passed," he said, "and we ought to consecrate our united and loyal efforts to the task of facilitating the peaceful arrival of another that must succeed it. The Hispanic-American republics . . . are entering one by one into a period of stability . . . after years of discord and war. We must undertake a similar evolution under the auspices of a policy truly liberal, incompatible with all intolerance and as free from the dogmatism of those who believe too much as from that of those who believe too little. As an irrevocable member of Colombian liberalism, I shall spare no pains . . . to bring together its scattered forces, for I consider it synonymous with morality and justice in action. . . . May Divine Providence grant us sufficient virtue and foresight . . . to . . . turn resolutely from the tortuous and dangerous path which . . . has brought us to the brink of a terrible abyss." [2]

But the radicals were too suspicious and exasperated to heed his appeal. They considered him a traitor, and they began a formidable revolt before the end of the year 1884. In maintaining his government Núñez had to depend largely on the Conservatives, for many members of his own party abandoned him; by the time the civil war ended he was completely in Conservative hands. From a balcony in Bogotá he announced to a milling crowd below that the Constitution of 1863 was dead. He was now ready for a complete reversal of the radical trend. The vague phrases he formerly employed were clarified and the meaning of "regeneration" disclosed. "Enervating particularism should be replaced by vigorous generality [centralism]. . . . Religious sentiments should be invoked as an aid . . . to culture; the system of education ought to be based primarily upon the Divine teaching of Christianity. . . . The press should be a torch and not a firebrand, a tonic and not a poison." Thus he spoke to a convention of carefully selected Conservatives called together late in 1885 to frame a new constitution.

The fundamental document duly drafted and promulgated (1886) reduced the states to departments, restored the Catholic Church to all of its ancient privileges and prerogatives, and insured it an annual subsidy in lieu of its confiscated real estate, which Núñez had helped to dispose of years before. Agreements signed with the papacy shortly afterward restored the power and prestige of Roman Catholicism in Colombia. The clergy took charge of the schools and censored the textbooks. The press was fettered. The reaction was almost as thorough as in Ecuador. The new constitution did not actually proscribe other religious faiths, but they were not really tolerated. Here was another huge monastery!

Núñez, who preferred to live on a small plantation called Cabrera on the outskirts of Cartagena, continued to rule Colombia by means of deputies in Bogotá until his death in 1894. And despite his death, the Conservative regime which he inaugurated endured until long after 1900. At the end of the nineteenth century Colombia's population was only a little more than 4,000,000 and the resources of the country were still largely undeveloped. The herds of livestock were mostly of an inferior breed; and although two or three modern sugar mills had been established and the cultivation of bananas had been started on a large scale in the Santa Marta region, agriculture was still in a backward state. Coffee culture, for which the nation would shortly become famous, was still hampered by political disorders and inefficiency in cultivation and marketing. There were hardly 400 miles of railway or good roads in the entire country. Barely a tenth of the school-age population was enrolled in the schools. A short revolution occurred in 1895 and a longer and more violent uprising began in 1899.

CHAPTER XVIII

Republics of the Southern Andes

CONFLICTS AND CONTRASTS

Although the mighty Andes are the most striking feature of their geography, Peru, Bolivia, and Chile might as appropriately be described as republics of the South Pacific as republics of the southern Andes, if recent custom had not applied the first term to an entirely different region. For the waves of the Pacific Ocean beat against the shores of Peru and Chile for nearly 4,000 miles, Bolivia once bordered the Pacific, and the Pacific is the main outlet of all three countries.

Closely connected during the long Colonial period—although separate administrative and judicial divisions, Chile and Bolivia (Charcas) were subordinated to the viceroyalty of Peru most of the time—they were also intimately associated during the achievement of national independence and the demarcation of national boundaries. The question of whether Peru and Bolivia should form two separate states was not decided until 1841, and between that date and 1883 Chile seized the whole of Bolivia's coastal provinces and three of Peru's. The formation of the southern Andean nations and the delimitation of their domains required four wars besides the war with Spain.

Chile is radically different from Peru and Bolivia, which are very much alike. Chile is mostly Caucasian, with only a small admixture of aboriginal blood; its Indian population was never dense and was soon largely absorbed. Peru and Bolivia, in sharp contrast, are mainly Indian and mestizo. Situated in the South Temperate Zone, Chile has a better climate and a less difficult topography than its tropical and subtropical neighbors, although the Andes raise much of them both above tropical heat, and the Humboldt Current cools the Peruvian coastal valleys. Chile's national domain is the smallest of the three; but, perhaps mainly because of its better climate, less baffling topography, and racial homogeneity, its political and economic advance was far more rapid. The population of Chile, around 1830, was about 1,000,000; Peru and Bolivia had approximately 1,250,000 each. Chile suffered a decade of anarchy after winning its independence and then became the most stable republic of Spanish South America. It was disturbed by only three revolutions between 1837 and 1900. Peru and Bolivia, especially the latter, enjoyed only brief periods of tranquillity during the first three quarters of a century after winning independence.

CHILE

Freed from Spain shortly before 1820, mainly through the efforts of San Martín and O'Higgins, Chile began its national career under the auspices of the latter. Contending that Chileans were not qualified for popular government, Bernardo O'Higgins tried to gather all political power into his own hands; but otherwise his rule was characterized by a moderate liberalism. A firm believer in public education, he revived the *Instituto Nacional,* which had been founded in Santiago at the end of the Colonial period; established a public library in the capital city; and opened a number of Lancasterian schools under the direction of a noted Englishman named James Thompson. Other reforms inaugurated by the dictator included abolition of coats-of-arms and titles of nobility; the suppression of brigandage by means of an efficient police force and criminal courts; the suppression of bullfights and cockfights; the abolition of Negro slavery; and prohibition of the colonial practice of selling public office.

Some of these measures antagonized the wealthy and influential Chileans, who were especially disturbed by the financial policy of O'Higgins and his proposal to abolish the entailment of estates. At the same time, many men of liberal tendencies began to denounce their ruler for his alleged tyranny, and a number of military chiefs were not slow to reveal their eagerness for power and the spoils of office. Prominent among these chiefs was General Ramón Freire, who headed a revolt early in 1823; and shortly afterward an open meeting of the Santiago *cabildo,* which had chosen O'Higgins as Supreme Director a few years before, collaborated with Freire to force the dictator's abdication and departure from the country. O'Higgins, as already stated, spent the rest of his life in restless exile in Peru.

The abdication of the Supreme Director was followed by a decade of ruinous disorder, during which there were no fewer than eleven chief executives and three different constitutions. Five revolutions occurred between 1827 and 1829 alone. Presidents were ephemeral figures placed in and thrust out of office at the will of the military and the populace. The new nation suffered severely: "Vandalism in the country, commerce paralyzed, industry at a standstill, finance in disorder, credit vanished, and politics revolutionary." Chile passed from "liberty to license, and from license to barbarism."

This decade of furious strife was not, however, a mere struggle among military leaders for dominance and the spoils of office. Ideas were involved; and by 1828 political issues were pretty clearly defined. Two parties—or factions—were formed, the Conservatives (called "Pelucones" or "Bigwigs") and the Liberals ("Pipiolos" or "Novices"). The latter stood for local autonomy, curtailment of the temporal power of the Roman Catholic Church, and minor reforms in the agrarian system. The former, composed largely of the clergy and the owners of large estates, championed the interests and privileges of these two groups.

Since the beginning of Chile's struggle for independence men of liberal or radical tendencies had been in charge of the government. Although the leaders of this group had too often allowed lust for power to outweigh other considerations (thereby contributing to the defeat of their party), their major defect was that they were dogmatists rather than statesmen and hence were unable to create a strong government and maintain peace. After overwhelmingly defeating them in 1830 at the battle of Lircai, the Conservatives took charge of the political destiny of Chile. The overthrow and virtual destruction of the Liberal party and the thorough organization of their antagonists meant the beginning of a stable, if somewhat reactionary regime; and a war against Peru and Bolivia further consolidated Conservative power.

The most conspicuous figure in the new government was Diego Portales. A shrewd businessman with a gift for practical politics, he did not aspire to the presidency. He preferred instead to play the role which Bismarck and Cavour were later to play upon different stages. Taking charge of the important portfolios in the president's cabinet, he became minister-dictator. He has been called the "Founder of the Chilean Nation," a title which rests upon the following achievements: organization of a strong civilian party; destruction of local *caudillos* and bandits; reorganization of Chilean finances; the founding of a national militia; support of primary and normal schools; the sponsoring of a civil code; and, most of all, upon the calling of a national convention which drafted the Constitution of 1833, the organic law under which Chile was governed until 1925.

This constitution was such as might have been expected from solid and prudent conservatism. It provided for a highly centralized republic under a president with absolute veto power indirectly elected for a term of five years, a bicameral legislature with a conservative senate, and a highly dignified national judiciary. It declared the Roman Catholic religion to be the religion of the nation, prohibited worship by any other cult, and guaranteed to the church the secure possession of its properties; but it reserved to the state the right to exercise ecclesiastical patronage and excluded clergymen from the higher civil offices of the country. Property qualifications were required for the presidency and for membership in the national legislative body. But excepting the failure to accord freedom of worship, which was not a severe handicap where nearly everybody was Roman Catholic, personal and property guaranties were definite and ample, and the duty of the national and municipal governments to foster education was emphatically proclaimed. Thus the constitution was conservative rather than reactionary. Liberty and security were assured, but participation in elections and the administration of government was strictly limited. This was not democracy, but neither was it extreme conservatism. Reactionary tendencies were in the dominant party rather than in the fundamental law, and Conservative presidents were soon founding normals for the training of teachers and schools for the children of the people, along with a national university and schools of law and engineering.

Although Portales was killed by mutineers in 1837, his work had been too thoroughly done for his death to affect it. Chile had emerged from the *caudillo* period. Two insurrections occurred during the ten-year term of Manuel Montt (1851–61), but they represented a fight between the reorganized Liberals and the Conservatives over such issues as the limitation of the power of the executive, extension of the franchise, freedom of the press, and relations of Church and State. They did not signify a tendency to return to the era of militarism. Nor did the revolution of 1891 represent such a tendency. To all appearances, a civilian order had come to stay.

As Montt's last term drew to a close, the Liberal elements once more became active. In fact, a reorganization of parties took place in 1857. Moderate Conservatives and moderate Liberals combined in a National party—the Montt-Varista party, as it was usually called—while the reactionary Conservatives who had been offended by restrictions placed on the church and the abolition of primogeniture, evinced a willingness to co-operate with the radical Liberals, whose policies for the most part were anathema to them. Violent opposition to Montt was the cohesive force which brought together such obviously incompatible groups as the latter two, and when the president prepared to dictate his successor, sporadic outbreaks warned him that such a policy would result in the re-enactment of the bloody scenes of 1851. He accordingly made a concession to the opposition. He turned away from Antonio

Varas, the candidate of his preference, and gave his support to José Joaquín Pérez, a statesman more acceptable to the Liberals. Pérez was elected, and his inauguration (September 18, 1861) in some ways marked the beginning of a new regime in Chile. For one thing, it indicated that the balance of power was slowly shifting from the landed aristocracy to the merchants and mine owners of the cities. The control of the government was passing into the hands of the Liberals—that is, liberals after the order of the Whigs of eighteenth-century England.

During the next three decades five able executives wielded the national scepter, each maintaining power for a five-year term, with the exception of the first of the group, who served two terms, and the last, who was overthrown by a revolution. Although their domestic programs were interrupted by a war with Spain (1866) and with Peru and Bolivia ("War of the Pacific," 1879–83) as well as by uprisings of the Araucanian Indians in southern Chile, numerous important Liberal measures were enacted.

The administration of Domingo Santa María (1881–86) was especially noted for religious and other reforms: the law of civil marriage; the law of civil registration of births and deaths; the removal of practically all restrictions upon the use of cemeteries; a constitutional amendment permitting a two-thirds majority of the chambers to pass a law over the executive's veto; removal of all property qualifications for voting.

Chile appeared to be entering an era of real democracy. Unfortunately, however, Santa María did not refrain from electoral interference. Not only did he resort to official intervention in almost every conceivable form in order to control the congressional elections of 1885; he also prepared to name his successor in 1886. His conduct provoked an unfavorable reaction even among some of the congressional groups who supported him, but Santa María had his way. His candidate, José Manuel Balmaceda, was elected.

Balmaceda was one of Chile's most picturesque presidents. In his early days—he was born in 1838—he had shown an inclination for the priesthood, but his faith had been shaken by wide reading in literature and science. In the silence of the fields, where he devoted some time to agricultural pursuits, the tendency to revolt against the religious spirit became more pronounced; and having become a liberal, a reformer, a laical and almost an atheistic thinker, he entered politics. In the Chamber of Deputies at Santiago he was an eloquent and towering figure before he entered the cabinet of Santa María as minister of interior and cult. In this latter capacity he is supposed to have been the major influence in bringing about the clerical and constitutional reforms which characterized Santa María's administration.

Balmaceda's first task upon assuming office as chief executive was to harmonize the various Liberal factions which had appeared during the last years of his predecessor's rule. After having effected a measure of solidarity, he embarked upon an ambitious program of public works and educational promotion and reform, utilizing revenues from nitrate of soda for these purposes. He also put through legislation reducing the voting age from twenty-five to twenty-one years and equalizing representation. But graft unfortunately appeared in the execution of the contracts for public works, and the clerical and oligarchical groups were tireless in their machinations against him. By 1890 the opposition secured the balance of power in Congress, and a spirited struggle ensued between the national legislature and the national executive. When Congress refused to vote the budget for 1891, Balmaceda declared that the budget for the previous year would be considered as in effect. He also refused to dismiss his cabinet, which was out of harmony with the congressional majority, threatened to nationalize the nitrate industry, and planned to dictate his successor by electoral interference. Congress thereupon attempted to depose him, and in January, 1891, a civil war broke out. It proved to be a very sanguinary struggle, but the forces of Balmaceda were finally routed in the following August, whereupon the president abdicated, leaving a high army officer, who had remained neutral during the war, in charge of the government. Balmaceda remained in hiding in the Argentine legation until September 19, 1891, when he committed suicide in order to avoid prosecution by his political enemies, who had come to power on the previous day. There was historical irony in this bitter contest. The overthrow of Balmaceda had been accomplished mainly by the Conservatives in the name of the Liberal principle of parliamentary responsibility!

Thereafter, for several years at least, the power of the Chilean presidents declined and congress played a role of increasing importance. In fact, the presidential system made way for a sort of parliamentary system. Most of the immediate successors of Balmaceda, although men of ability and distinction, failed to exert any great influence upon the march of events. By a law of 1891 executive interference in elections was forbidden and the right of electoral supervision, local as well as national, was conferred upon the municipalities. Moreover, the lower middle class and the proletariat were already beginning to make their voices heard in national affairs. An indication of the trend of the times may be seen in the occurrence of the first labor strikes during the administration of Balmaceda and the organization of the Democratic party in 1887. According to the view of Luis Galdames, a Chilean historian, the era of the Democratic Republic had dawned.

Yet it can hardly be contended that the Chilean masses wielded any very great influence. There was universal manhood suffrage with only a literary test not rigidly applied; there was also a larger measure of political liberty and of freedom from electoral domination by the employment of military force, but the democracy failed to develop its potentialities by making use of the devices placed in its hands. It was too ready to sell its votes for a week's wages; it was somewhat handicapped by the property qualifications still required of senators and deputies; and it was unable to organize a strong party based upon a program of genuine democratic reform. The Chilean people, in short, lacked the wisdom and power to push through important measures of social legislation. Aside from laws designed to prevent epidemics and improve the health of the masses—laws which would benefit all classes—aside from the beginnings of labor legislation and the establishment of certain benevolent institutions supported in part by the state, the most signal triumph was in the field of primary education. The number of primary schools was doubled between 1890 and 1910, and the revenues devoted to this purpose bulked large in the national and local budgets. And yet the primary schools were sufficient at the latter date to take care of only about one-half of the children of school age; the curriculum of these institutions did not furnish a basis for entrance into the secondary schools; and illiteracy among the masses stood at an appalling height.

Nevertheless, Chile now deserved to be classed among the progressive states of Latin America. Many changes had occurred during the century: numerous irrigation works; somewhat better sanitation; an expanding railway system; new copper mines; coal mines; and rich nitrate properties, snatched away from Bolivia and Peru, under development —the majority of all these financed by the proceeds of government bonds sold (mainly in England) at good prices, with low rates of interest. In 1800 the population numbered around 600,000—approximately 100,000 unsubdued Indians, some three times as many mestizos, and the rest whites. By 1900 it had increased fivefold to over 3,000,000, and was melted into almost a racial, if not a social unity.

✂ BOLIVIA

Bolivia and Peru alike were dominated by foreign generals for some time after their liberation from Spain. Bolivia was dominated until 1828, it will be recalled, by Antonio José de Sucre, that able and honorable Venezuelan hero of the independence period who later married an Ecuadorian wife. Peru was ruled in turn by San Martín of Argentina; by Bolívar, a native of Venezuela; and by José de la Mar, an aristocrat from Ecuador. The Bolivians began to govern themselves in 1828,

and the Peruvians started on their career of self-government the next
year. Both republics confronted tremendous social and topographical
problems.

A small minority of whites and a few mestizos—there were only about
40,000 people of Spanish descent in Bolivia and perhaps not more than
three times as many in Peru—owned practically all the wealth that
existed: the mines, the best lands, and the valuable urban properties.
The Indians, although they had managed to retain some of their *ejidos,*
were nearly all extremely poor and densely ignorant, and the same was
true of the vast majority of mestizos. The condition of the Negro and
mulatto slaves—about 40,000 to 50,000 in Peru, almost none in Bolivia
—requires no comment. The "free people of color" were no better
off than the Indo-Hispanic mixbloods. The Roman Catholic Church
was strong in Peru but not a very significant factor in the politics of
Bolivia.

Bolivia's geographical position and topography, however, were far
more baffling than Peru's. Bolivia's Pacific coast lands, although rich in
minerals, were a complete desert, and, as already stated, were soon
lost to Chile. The foothills and vast plains on the eastern side of the
country, because of immense distances to markets and lack of roads,
were difficult to develop or even to occupy. Most Bolivians were doomed
to live in the high plateaus and valleys lying between the two giant
ranges of the Andes that traversed their country from north to south.
The region they inhabited ranged from 5,500 to 16,000 feet above the
sea and averaged about 10,000. The elevation of La Paz, which soon
became their capital, was nearly 13,000 feet! Peru, while having likewise to contend with the lofty Andes and an immense tropical region
stretching beyond them to the Amazon Basin, also possessed numerous
fertile coastal valleys cooled by the Humboldt Current and watered by
rivers leaping down the steep Andean slopes, as well as good ports and
a convenient location for its capital on the Pacific.

While both were disorderly during the early National period, and so
retarded in their development that they became an easy prey for the
aggressive and more efficient Chileans, their turbulence did not syn-
chronize. Bolivia was fairly stable during the decade following 1829
under the firm rule of Santa Cruz, while Peru entered a period of military chaos for which no magician was found until Ramón Castilla
seized the government in 1845. For the next forty years Peru, although
upset by not a few barracks uprisings and electoral wars, was somewhat less disrupted than Bolivia, which tumbled into anarchy after the
downfall of Santa Cruz in 1839 and had few periods of repose during
the next four decades. While the white aristocracy in Peru either won

over the mestizos who rose above the mass or held the reins of government firmly in their own hands, the mestizos controlled Bolivia most of the time.

Andrés Santa Cruz, the only approximate facsimile of a statesman produced by Bolivia during the early National period,[1] was half Indian, the son of a minor Spanish official and an "Inca princess." He ruled despotically but set the nation on the path of modest progress by promoting mining, agriculture, household industries, and road building, codifying the laws, and giving some attention to education. He might have dominated his country much longer than a brief decade if his driving ambition to confederate Bolivia and Peru had not provoked a war with dissident Peruvians and Chile. Conquered early in 1839 by a combination of invading Chileans and insurgents in Peru, Santa Cruz was forced into exile, from which he never returned.

Two years after Santa Cruz's defeat and banishment José Ballivián was catapulted into power by a tremendous victory over a Peruvian army that had invaded his country. The presidency was awarded him in compensation for Bolivia's second emancipation. One of Bolivia's few supreme executives of pure Spanish descent, he promised to give the people an economic and political order as grand and inspiring as its mountains and scenery, but exhausted his resources and energy putting down revolutions and trying to imitate the "Little Corsican." Like Santa Anna, his contemporary in Mexico, he imagined he was another Napoleon. He was a *pronunciamiento* artist with some skill in war, but he never won the affections of the Bolivian people or held for long the loyalty of his army officers. He was deposed and permanently banished late in 1847.

Bolivia's next chief executive, Manuel Isidoro Belzu, held on perilously for nearly seven years and imposed his son-in-law as his successor. A man of the people, an illegitimate mestizo (mestizos are often called "cholos" in Peru and Bolivia), Belzu was not only a demagogue but a sort of early Trotsky. His rule was a terrible shock to the small wealthy class. He governed by means of and for the Indians and the urban proletariat, and showed no respect for the persons and property of the deposed plutocracy, who were abused and pillaged by his rioting mobs and soldiery. Winning over the masses, whom he had no time to educate, by bullfights, liberal showers of coin, and license to plunder, he reduced legislators to figureheads, suppressed freedom of the press (which meant nothing to his illiterate followers), and persecuted his enemies, who never ceased to conspire and revolt against him.

Like many another Spanish American despot, Belzu's utterances were far better than his policies. Note what he said, for instance, in one of his last messages to Congress. Lamenting empleomania, disdain for work, and indifference to the common good among the upper class, he declared that all the recent revolts in the name of liberty and country were nothing more than attempts to secure government posts and raid the national treasury. Institutions of secondary and higher learning were corrupting the youth, who were taught to interpret liberty and law as synonymous with license and revolt. The arts and sciences were neglected. The laborious Indians and the cholo artisans were the sentinels of order and the stout defenders of public security. While the wealthy were habitually conspiring, "these poor citizens were confounding the traitors and saving the nation." He claimed that he had honestly tried to serve the underprivileged masses but that his motives and purposes had been calumniated and he had been called a Socialist and accused of setting the poor against the rich. It is possible that he was more sincerely humanitarian than the Bolivian historians have been willing to admit. His fervid partisans were not the sort who write history.

Belzu's son-in-law, Jorgé Córdova, held the reins for less than three years, and the white aristocrat who ousted him was betrayed and deposed in less than four. Belzu came back in 1864 from a tour in Europe, the Holy Land, and Egypt and seized the government again, but was soon murdered by Mariano Melgarejo, a terrible cholo who terrorized and debased his country for more than half a decade.

If Melgarejo was not a monster, he was at best a lecherous and hard-drinking brute. He possessed a gorilla physique, a luxuriant beard, and a booming voice. Crassly ignorant and violently argumentative, especially when drunk, he contended that Napoleon was a greater general than Bonaparte and threatened to shoot a subordinate who maintained that Bolivia could not give military aid to the pope without a navy or a merchant marine. He taught his favorite war horse to drink beer, forced some of his army officers to lie down and roll like poodles, commanded his soldiers to march through second-story windows, and decreed that his birthday should be celebrated with the shifting cycle of Easter. He reduced his legislators to the status of nonentities; muzzled the press; jailed, murdered, or banished his political enemies; threatened to execute members of his cabinet when they talked of resigning, and compelled them to ride hundreds of miles over mountain trails with him and his army. Finally overthrown early in 1871, he escaped to Peru. He was killed in Lima near the end of that year by his son-in-law and the brother of his favorite mistress.

The next "president" was murdered in a personal quarrel, and his successor, the son of José Ballivián, lived only a few months after his inauguration. Then, after a brief interval, Hilarión Daza captured the government and began an era of corruption a little better than that of Melgarejo only because it could hardly have been worse.

This pathetic story of Bolivian politics has been given in some detail in order to explain why it was so easy for Chile to crush Bolivia during the war that broke out in 1879 and ended in the final and permanent seizure of Bolivia's Pacific coast. Already Brazil and Chile had induced Melgarejo, by titles, gifts, and flattery, to make territorial concessions to each of them. By 1868 his string of honors unrolled as follows: "Well Deserving of His Country in a Heroic and Eminent Degree, Provisional President of the Republic, Captain General of its Armies, Grand Citizen of Bolivia, Conserver of Public Order and Peace, Grand Cross of the Imperial Order of Crossbearers of Brazil, General of Division of Chile."

It may seem almost miraculous, but political conditions began to improve in Bolivia immediately after the war with Chile. A political faction which called itself the Conservative party took over the government and continued in power for almost twenty years. The most significant opposition faction described itself as the Liberal party. The army still continued to serve as the main bulwark of political control, but it ceased for a time to operate as the springboard to success in politics. The new era was symbolized by the "election" of two presidents who had made small fortunes in mining, Gregorio Pacheco and Aniceto Arce, both mestizos who demonstrated that the army was not the only avenue to political advancement in their country. Pacheco served out his four-year term (1884–88) and effected a peaceful transfer of his power to Arce. Although Bolivia still had no good roads, stage coaches had arrived in the 1860's and its first railway was under construction. Little advance had been made in agriculture or manufacturing, but a mining "boom" had started. There were few public schools and no good educational institutions of any type; and yet the children of the wealthier groups managed somehow to acquire the kind of schooling they desired either at home or abroad. Bolivia was obviously not a country that would draw immigrants from the more advanced nations of the world, but it did attract a few foreign speculators, some of whom appeared on the scene even during the barbarous rule of Melgarejo.

The Constitution of 1880, drafted and adopted by the Conservatives, required property and literacy tests for voting and holding public office, denied religious toleration while asserting the state's right of ecclesiastical patronage, and guaranteed the property and privileges of the clergy. But, like the fundamental law of 1871, it also included a meaningless declaration in favor of gratuitous and compulsory primary education, presumably to be largely financed and controlled by the state.

Taking charge of the national government in 1899, the Liberals carried out their reforms, which included an extension of the suffrage, encouragement of public schools, abolition of special courts for the army and the clergy, religious toleration (1905), state control of cemeteries (1908), civil marriage (1912), and a more vigorous development of natural resources. They also effected boundary agreements with Chile and Brazil which resulted in the construction at the expense of these two countries of railway outlets for Bolivia to the Pacific Ocean and the upper Amazon, and they transferred the capital from Sucre (old Chuquisaca) to La Paz, where it remained. Outstanding among the Liberal presidents were José Manuel Pando (1899–1904) and Ismael Montes (1904–9). Meantime Bolivia's population had slowly increased from slightly more than 1,000,000 in 1825 to barely twice that number in 1900.

PERU

Twelve "presidents" had their brief day of glory and troubles in Peru during the sixteen years that intervened between the forced departure of José de la Mar in 1829 and the triumphant arrival of Ramón Castilla in Lima in 1845. It was a period of bloody contest among the white and mestizo "generals" for the control of the government and the contents of the treasury, which became a more lucrative prize toward the end of the period because of mounting income from the sale of guano, one of the world's best fertilizers. The tenure of such civilian aristocrats as chance and the army thrust into the national palace was provisional and ephemeral.

Castilla was a mixture of Indian, Spanish, and Genoese Italian that turned out reasonably well. A native of the southern desert region of Tarapacá and a competent officer in the armies that defeated Spain, he married an aristocratic lady of pious Arequipa and formed an alliance with the aristocracy and clergy. Although actually chief executive of Peru (on two occasions) for only thirteen years, he was a dominant political figure for more than twenty. Essentially conservative as he was, he carried out certain policies, incidentally or otherwise, of a liberal and progressive character. With the view of enlisting the support of Indians and Negroes during a revolution which he led in 1854, he proclaimed the emancipation of African slaves and the abolition of the head tax exacted from the Indians since early Colonial days. With revenues obtained from heavy levies or royalties on guano and nitrates, he serviced the public debt, subsidized or stimulated in other ways the construction of railroads and telegraphs, fostered education, enlarged the Peruvian navy, and tried to encourage immigration and the settlement of vacant lands, particularly in the region east of the Andes.

According a measure of respect to civil rights and the constitutional limitations on his power, at least during his first term (1845–51), he sponsored the adoption of two fundamental charters. The last of them, the Constitution of 1860, was destined to survive, although not without many violations, for sixty years. It sanctioned a centralized system of government in which the heads of the provinces were appointed and controlled from Lima and failed to provide religious toleration, but it contained reasonably liberal and humane personal guaranties. It not only prohibited Negro slavery—Chinese coolies were taking their place —and Indian tributes, but declared forced army recruiting—one of the scourges of the time in Spanish America—a crime. Literacy and property tests for suffrage, however, largely disfranchised the masses.

Castilla's second term, which began in 1855, terminated in 1862. He imposed his successor and then died in 1867, after which Peru entered another period of disorder and rapidly rotating chief executives. General Mariano Ignacio Prado occupied the government for two periods aggregating only five years; General José Balta held on for nearly four years (1868–72) and almost bankrupted the nation by his heavy expenditures for railways and his liberal distribution of public funds among his supporters. Manuel Pardo, Peru's first civilian president of any significance, managed to serve out his full term (1872–76), but was assassinated shortly after he retired. General Prado then came back for his second period, but fled to the United States and Europe, allegedly in search of assistance and better *elementos de guerra,* shortly after the Chilean armies landed in his country in 1879.

Prado was succeeded by Nicolás Piérola, who was soon chased into the mountains by the Chilean army of occupation, and was replaced by two ephemeral chiefs: one, a scholarly civilian promptly deposed by the Chileans; the other, an army officer driven from the high post by General Andrés Cáceres and the band of guerrillas he assembled in the Andes during the course of the war with Chile. Although the war was lost, the army was not condemned or denied political power. On the contrary, militarism secured a new lease on national politics. Cáceres ruled from 1885 to 1890 and transmitted the government to another army officer of whom he approved.

The generals retained control of the Peruvian national government until Nicolás Piérola drove them from power in 1895 after a bloody civil war. Like Eloy Alfaro, his Ecuadorian contemporary, Piérola's political career was perilous and exciting. He headed four different revolutions, spent fifteen years in exile, governed his country directly or indirectly for ten, disturbed its peace for half a century, and managed to survive until he reached the ripe age of seventy-four.

Born of Spanish parents near Arequipa in 1839, he studied theology and law, but soon became more deeply interested in journalism and politics. By the time he reached twenty-five he had edited two newspapers and married the granddaughter of Iturbide, ill-starred emperor of Mexico. Expelled from Peru in 1866, he established his residence in France and made friendly contacts with French bankers. Returning home three years later, he served as minister of finance and floated huge bond issues in London and Paris for the construction of Peruvian railways under the management of Henry Meiggs. Accused of "graft" in connection with these large transactions, Piérola was never convicted; but his reputation was somewhat tarnished and he soon left for Chile. Using that country as a base, he made two unsuccessful attempts to overthrow the Lima government, but after the outbreak ·of the War of the Pacific in 1879 he went back to his native land and managed to have himself proclaimed as dictator for the purpose of confronting the crisis. He was unable, however, to stem the tide of Chilean invasion by hurling his decrees at the enemy. Forced from power before the war was over, he left for the United States and Europe.

Returning home in 1890, he entered the contest for the presidency at the head of a new organization called the Democratic party. His campaign was marked by mass appeals, marching mobs, and street fights, and before the voting took place he found himself in jail for disturbing the peace. He lost the election, of course, but he soon escaped from prison and fled to Europe. When he returned in 1894 with the idea of running for the presidency again, he found his country so thoroughly organized against him that he left at once for Chile.

More determined than ever to seize power, however, he soon landed in southern Peru and started a revolt. After months of fierce fighting he finally seized Lima in March 1895; in the "elections" that followed immediately he triumphed at last. The trophy was now his for the second time.

Piérola served out his term of four years and then helped his candidate for the succession win the election of 1899. But he lost control of Peruvian politics in 1903 and was never able to recover his power. During that year and on two subsequent occasions, one of them in

1908, he campaigned for the presidency without success. At the age of seventy he finally decided to live in quiet retirement at his Lima home, where he died in 1913.

Although not lacking in talent as a statesman, Piérola was mainly a demagogue. He promised the people much and gave them little, ruling mainly in the interest of the upper classes. Husband of an emperor's granddaughter, he posed as a democrat, but he really preferred to surround himself with men from the old and aristocratic families. Claiming to be a friend of the Peruvian workers, he carried out no effective measures in their behalf. Conversing with the Indians in their own tongues and assuming the title of "Protector of the Native Race," he levied a salt tax which imposed a great hardship on the natives, who must have salt for their food and their animals. He did practically nothing to promote the welfare of the Indian and mestizo masses; he left them where he found them—in rags and ignorance.

Peru's inhabitants, decimated by civil wars and the ravages of disease, had multiplied very slowly. Numbering around 1,250,000 in 1825, they scarcely exceeded 3,300,000 in 1900. Three minor universities had been added to the ancient San Marcos, but educational facilities for the masses were pitifully inadequate. With its guano exhausted and its nitrates taken by Chile, Peru was now poor and loaded with debts. Some advances had been made, however, in the cultivation of sugar cane and cotton in its irrigated coastal valleys, in the development of mining, and in the construction of railways and public utilities, although a good part of these public services were owned by foreigners, Englishmen in particular.

CHAPTER XIX

The Plata Nations

🐚 PHYSICAL ENVIRONMENT AND POLITICAL TRENDS

Geography and tradition might have united the inhabitants of the Río de la Plata region if stubborn political, social, and psychological influences had not interposed. The great rivers which empty into the Plata estuary—the Paraná, the Paraguay, and the Uruguay—dominate a large part of this section of South America and tend to give it unity, and its people had been fairly closely associated during the Colonial period, especially after the creation of the Río de la Plata Viceroyalty in 1776.[1] But provincial loyalties, the ambitions of local and regional chiefs, and interference from the outside stultified all efforts to hold the parts together.

The region's population when the struggle for independence from Spain started in 1810 was hardly more than 800,000: something over 200,000 in Paraguay, 50,000 or so in Banda Oriental (Uruguay), and the rest mostly in the vast provinces west of the Paraná which later became the Argentine republic. Except for the cultivated fringes around the urban centers, the major part of the region was open range where herds of cattle and horses fattened on the succulent grass.

Like Chile and southern Brazil, most of the Plata area is located in the Temperate Zone, although the northern section of Argentina and half of Paraguay are subtropical. It is a region of great plains. The mountains are confined to the western border. Except for the absence of moderating ocean breezes and the infrequency of destructive cyclones, Paraguay's climate resembles that of the Gulf coast of Texas and Mexico. Argentina and Uruguay, although not so cold in winter, are generally similar in surface and climate to the Middle West of the United States—parts of Argentina, however, resemble the arid trans-Mississippi west.

The basic occupations of the three River Plata republics, during the early National period and later, were ranching and farming. Relatively poor in minerals, all have fertile soils, and Argentina and Paraguay, particularly the latter, have some valuable forests. Rainfall is abundant and usually well distributed throughout the year in both Uruguay and Paraguay; in two-thirds of Argentina it is scanty.

The inhabitants of Argentina and Uruguay were largely Caucasian at the beginning of the National period and tended to become more completely so as the years passed. The aborigines were eventually absorbed or exterminated—most of the Indians of Argentina by the 1880's; those of Uruguay earlier—and the few thousand Negro slaves introduced during the Colonial epoch and the first decades of independence finally disappeared almost without leaving a trace. The people of Paraguay, in striking contrast, were, and have continued to be, mainly Indians and mestizos, the whites accounting for only a small fraction of the total.

Although tranquil for half a century while its neighbors were wallowing in the mire and blood of civil combat, Paraguay plunged into a raging sea of troubles in later years, and remained there while Argentina and Uruguay gradually advanced, the first more rapidly than the second, toward stability and prosperity, their economic development promoted in large measure by an influx of European immigrants which Paraguay failed to attract in any considerable numbers. In effective development of their material resources, in public health, in education and culture, Argentina and Uruguay eventually attained front rank among the Latin-American nations; Paraguay lingered among the most backward.

ARGENTINA

For more than twenty years after the beginning of the movement for independence, Argentina suffered as severely from civil strife as any part of Spanish America. The twelve leading towns—soon increased to fourteen—set up as many states, which clamored, one and all, for full autonomy in spite of the fact that they assumed the title of provinces. There was no effective national government until 1835 or later, and a viable unity sanctioned by a federal constitution was not achieved until 1880.

The largest of the fourteen provinces, the province of Buenos Aires, which included the important port and city of that name, soon became the wealthiest and most populous of the group. For many years both the government of this province and such national governments as existed had their seat in the city of Buenos Aires. The *caudillos* of the outlying provinces, while squabbling bitterly among themselves, fought desperately against the public authorities in Buenos Aires, whether provincial or national, and frequently tried to raid and plunder this rich province. Most of the fighting in these cut-throat wars was done by brutal cowboy cavalry, composed mainly of heavy-drinking, hard-riding, half-Indian, half-civilized daredevils, widely known as Gauchos, who, between campaigns, looked after the livestock and slaughtered the wild cattle roaming over the immense level pampa of Argentina and the rolling prairies of Uruguay. But the Gauchos were usually led by the shrewder men of the towns, one of whom, townsman, ranchman, and Gaucho combined, finally put an end to the worst of their bloody combats. Many local uprisings and several general revolts occurred, however, after his day. Political stability was not attained in Argentina until 1880, and by that time Uruguay and Paraguay had long since definitely and permanently seceded.

John Milton is said to have remarked that the petty wars among the early Saxons were no more "worthy of being recorded than the skirmishes of crows and kites." The civil combats of the first decades of Argentina's national history might be dismissed with a similar comment if no issue had been involved except the struggle for plunder and power. But some of these embattled politicians had ideas and ideals.

One of them, for example, Bernardo Rivadavia, acting at first as the leading cabinet member of the governor of Buenos Aires province (1821–23) and later as head of a short-lived national government (1825–26), undertook to carry out a significant program. He abolished tithes and ecclesiastical privileges, dissolved monasteries, quietly granted religious toleration, founded the University of Buenos Aires, promoted primary education (including some Lancasterian schools), federalized the city of Buenos Aires, and substituted long-term leases for the sale of public lands. If his reforms had not been frustrated by the confusion of the period, Argentina might have avoided many serious difficulties in later years.

Another outstanding leader of these turbulent decades was José G. Artigas, a ranchman and Gaucho warrior of Uruguay and a fervent admirer of the United States who early championed an intelligent federal system of government, such as Argentina was finally compelled to adopt after forty years of confusion. He also became Uruguay's paramount hero, for reasons to be explained later.

The *caudillo* who exterminated most of the other Argentine *caudillos* and gave Argentina a mighty impulse toward unity was Juan Manuel Rosas. Born in Buenos Aires in 1793, he spent most of his early years on his father's big ranch down near the southern Indian frontier, where he gained the respect and admiration of the cowboys, organized a uniformed Gaucho guard to protect the livestock from the raids of thieves and Indians, and accumulated vast properties for himself. It was as a commander of Gaucho cavalry that he rode into power (although a good many Negroes and mulattoes joined his army later), but he had the support of a number of clerics, who felt that he was the only man capable of bringing about order and peace, and the backing of not a few Buenos Aires land magnates, especially those associated with him in the profitable beef trade.

Rosas's legal office was that of governor of the province of Buenos Aires (1829–32 and 1835–52), but he managed to thrust his agents into the other provinces and make himself the representative of the nation in foreign affairs. Few Latin-American countries ever had a more able or more ruthless dictator. He suppressed at least six revolutions and exterminated nearly every prominent provincial *caudillo*. He imprisoned, assassinated, or executed thousands and compelled thousands more to flee the country, filling Uruguay and Chile with Argentine exiles. He drove the Indians back from the southern frontier settlements, divided their lands and those of his political enemies in huge estates among his supporters, and with cold ingratitude prevented the Gauchos from hunting wild cattle and horses and reduced them to peonage. A firm nationalist despite his alliances with the federalist faction, he imposed a rigid centralism, refused to recognize the independence of Uruguay or Paraguay, conquered most of Uruguay for a time, and involved himself in serious conflicts with England and France. He managed the country's finances honestly and made no raids on the properties of the church, but he forced the clergy to bow to his will. Voluntarily or involuntarily, they hung his portraits in the temples, showered him with praise, and mentioned him in their prayers. He was finally overthrown by a combined army of Argentines, Brazilians, and Uruguayans under the command of Justo José de Urquiza, a hard-riding ranchman from the northeastern province of Entre Ríos, who had supported the tyrant for two decades and made a fortune supplying his armies. Escaping to a British steamer, Rosas spent the last twenty-five years of his life in England, dying there in 1877.

After expelling Rosas, Urquiza took charge of the national government as provisional president, called together a constitutional convention which framed a constitution in 1853 and elected him constitutional president, and ruled the whole nation, with the exception of the big province of Buenos Aires, until 1860. He signed commercial treaties with foreign countries, encouraged immigration, stimulated education, especially primary schools, and earned a reputation for statesmanship. He was unable, however, to conquer the province of Buenos Aires. After two brief wars with that province, he retired to Entre Ríos, which he continued to control as governor or political "boss" until he was assassinated in 1870.

Shortly after Urquiza turned over the national government—which then had its seat in the town of Paraná—to a rather weak executive named Santiago Derquí, the province of Buenos Aires conquered the federal army and entered the federation more or less on its own terms. These were naturally not satisfactory to the rest of the federation, and the problem was not finally settled until this big province was subdued by the others in 1880. The city and port of Buenos Aires was then detached from the province of Buenos Aires and turned over to the national government as a federal district, like the District of Columbia in the United States, in accordance with the plan temporarily in operation under Rivadavia more than a half-century before.

By Urquiza and his immediate successors Argentina was effectively organized (1853–80) as a confederation, although its fourteen units continued to be called provinces instead of states. With some later modifications, the Constitution of 1853, drafted and adopted by the convention which Urquiza convoked, continued to operate as Argentina's fundamental charter for almost a century. By a broad interpretation of its provisions the federal authorities frequently interfered in the political affairs of the provinces, and when the Indian frontier to the west and south was conquered and settled by the whites, these vast border regions were not organized as new autonomous provinces, as in the United States, but were retained permanently as territories under direct national control. Thus the Argentine national government became far more centralized than the federal government of the United States upon which it was modeled. The Argentine constitution contained, however, an ample bill of rights safeguarding the liberties of the people. It even included religious toleration, mainly with the view of appealing to immigrants of all faiths; but the Roman Catholic Church was supported by contributions from the national treasury, and the national government exercised a measure of control over it.

Santiago Derquí was followed by three able chief executives, two of them civilians: Bartolomé Mitre (who conquered Derquí's government), Domingo F. Sarmiento, and Nicolás Avellaneda, each of them serving for the six-year term stipulated by the constitution. Elections were not free or fair and, besides the four brief civil wars between the province of Buenos Aires and the confederation, there were numerous local disturbances in the outlying provinces; yet conditions were more stable than in previous decades. Following the policies initiated by Urquiza, all three presidents emphasized foreign trade, immigration, and education. In fact they went a step further than Urquiza, who limited his promotion of transportation to the introduction of regular steamboat schedules on the rivers, and initiated a policy of national subsidies for railways. Dealing tactfully but firmly with the church, they also inaugurated a full secular regime.

Mitre, a native of the city of Buenos Aires and a member of an aristocratic family, achieved distinction as a general, a journalist, a historian, and a capable civil administrator. Deeply attached to his home province, he was also an ardent nationalist, and suggested on one occasion that the entire province be federalized. Nevertheless, when in 1874 he was defeated for a second term (his first term ended in 1868), he joined a revolt—which the national government promptly suppressed.

Sarmiento (1868–74), though born in poverty in the western province of San Juan, had made an outstanding record as educator and writer before he became president. In exile during the tyranny of Rosas, he had taught school in Chile and had been sent by the Chilean government to investigate systems of public education in the United States and Europe. Because most of his life was devoted to educational activities he became widely known as Argentina's "Schoolmaster President." He established during his presidency a number of normal schools, employing instructors—both men and women—from the United States, opened many other schools, and urged national appropriations for elementary education in the provinces, which were mainly responsible, under the constitution, for primary schools. Sarmiento developed a great admiration for the United States. He had read the works of Benjamin Franklin at an early age and had later become familiar with the New England writers, with the educational theories and practices of Horace Mann—he knew both Mann and his wife personally and the latter published an English translation of one of Sarmiento's books in 1868—and with the remarkable career of Lincoln. But the "Schoolmaster President" was not merely a great champion of popular education; he was also an exponent of material progress, and he helped to advance his nation toward an era of great prosperity. Attributing the rapid economic development of the United States to the education of its people, he sought the same end through the same means in Argentina.

Avellaneda (1874–80), a scholarly politician from the western province of Tucumán, was Sarmiento's minister of education and his choice for the presidency. Victorious in the manipulated national election, he not only continued the policies of his patron; he also directed his minister of war, Julio Roca, to complete the conquest of the frontier tribes, an assignment which General Roca carried out thoroughly in 1878–79. But, as in the days of Rosas, the Indian territory was turned over in huge tracts to the land barons instead of being granted as small homesteads or sold on easy terms to those who needed them and might have become better citizens by virtue of land ownership. With Roca's trained and seasoned army and with the backing of the other provinces, Avellaneda then turned on the province of Buenos Aires, subjected it to military control, and federalized its main city and port, compelling its government to establish a new capital at La Plata.

Roca now became the official candidate for the succession. Backed by Avellaneda and a league of provincial governors—known as the "Córdoba clique" because Córdoba was the center of the organization —he easily won the national election and took charge of the national government in 1880. Although his administration was a period of peace and unprecedented growth in national wealth during which the railways, financed mainly by English capital, doubled in length and caused a rapid rise in land values and an equal expansion in cultivation, his six years in office were marked by the beginning of an era of imprudent speculation and extravagance, and his collaboration with the Córdoba League in imposing his brother-in-law, Miguel Juárez Celman, as Argentina's next president prepared the way for a financial and political crisis from which the country did not fully recover until near the end of the century.

Juárez Celman (1886–90) was Argentina's worst ruler since the days of Rosas. An alliance was formed during his administration between the national government and corrupt business interests, and the growing prosperity of the country was seriously checked by reckless inflation of the paper currency and excessive borrowing, by extravagance and scandal in public finance, and by favoritism in the granting of public lands, monopolies, and concessions. The debauchery in the capital was reflected in the provinces, where the local politicians caught the infection of wasteful borrowing, speculation, and graft. This financial orgy, together with Juárez Celman's despotic tendencies and his interference in the provinces, provoked widespread indignation. The "Radical Civic Union," organized in 1890, issued a manifesto which not only denounced the economic abuses of the administration but other abuses as well: its suppression of the suffrage and its exercise of arbitrary authority in both the national government and the provinces. In short, the regime was damned as "an ominous and intrusive oligarchy," and the vehement Leandro Alem, demanding the overthrow of the president by armed force and the establishment of a provisional government by a fair and "uncontrolled" election, started a revolt in Buenos Aires. The uprising was suppressed after two days of bloody fighting, but the government was "killed." Hostile public opinion forced Juárez Celman to give way to Vice-President Carlos Pellegrini, who served out the remainder of the term.

Pellegrini (1890–92) and his three successors were occupied with financial troubles, provincial interventions, boundary disputes with Brazil and Chile, and the activities of the "Radical Civic Union." Pellegrini did much to "retrieve the disaster" which had befallen the nation. He stopped the construction of public works, dismissed superfluous officials, recovered large tracts of public land which had been improperly alienated, suspended the amortization of the public debt, and founded a national bank. But he caused considerable resentment by imprisoning and afterwards exiling Alem and his friends and forcing Luís Sáenz Peña upon the country as president in 1892. Most of Sáenz Peña's efforts were devoted to the maintenance of his position. He did not have the support of Congress and was compelled to dismiss his cabinet on several occasions. He also had to suppress a revolt led by Alem, whom the Radicals had proclaimed president in 1893. Although he took one of the leading members of the Radical party into his ministry, the death of this minister compelled other changes, and in January, 1895, Sáenz Peña resigned in favor of Vice-President José Uriburu, who adjusted a boundary dispute with Brazil (1895), resumed full service (1897) on the national foreign debt, and added to the cabinet two new ministers, those of agriculture and public works.

General Roca, who was elected chief magistrate of Argentina for a second term in 1898, signed a law during the following year providing for the redemption of the paper currency—at the rate of 44 centavos in gold for each paper peso—and reached a settlement of a boundary controversy with Chile (1902), a dispute which had threatened more than once to result in war between the two neighbors. With the beginning of the redemption of this paper, so imprudently issued a few years before, and with this boundary adjustment, Argentina may be said to have fully recovered from the crisis occasioned by the misgovernment of Juárez Celman and the economic depression of the 1890's. The nation's population, hardly more than 1,000,000 in 1825, now exceeded 6,000,000. The stream of immigrants arriving from Europe was once more expanding after a period of contraction following the year 1889, when a total of nearly 219,000 arrived. Educational institutions were now numerous: five universities, a score of normal schools, and many hundreds of primary and secondary schools. Two of the newspapers of Buenos Aires—*El Tiempo* and *La Nación*—deserved to rank with some of the greatest in the world. Argentina had attained leadership among the Latin-American countries in economic development and cultural progress.

🦅 URUGUAY

The almost incessant civil wars of the early National period in Uruguay remind one again of John Milton's remark about the bickerings and combats of the ancient Saxons. Yet the kitelike, crowlike skirmishes of the early Uruguayans deserve a few paragraphs even in this rapid narrative. They were the birth-pangs of a little nation destined eventually to command the appreciation and respect of the well-informed world. The early Uruguayan *caudillos* were fanning the flames of nationalism and making a niche for themselves as national heroes— more or less inadvertently, for some of them probably did not go beyond an aspiration for ample autonomy in a loose Río de la Plata federation.

José G. Artigas, already mentioned as a pioneer exponent in this region of a federalism similar to that adopted in the United States, expelled the Spanish colonial officials and garrisons from the eastern side of the great river basin only to be crushed shortly afterward by an invading army from Brazil which banished him to Paraguay, where he died in exile thirty years later (1850) at the ripe age of eighty-six. (The very appropriate last words attributed to the tough old warrior-ranchman were "Bring me my horse!")

Juan Lavalleja earned immortal renown by heading a daring little group of thirty-three Uruguayans who crossed over the broad estuary from Buenos Aires one dark night in 1825 and began a revolt against Brazilian domination. Nobody knows whether he was fighting for the independence of this section or for its annexation to Argentina. The intrepid Thirty-three were aided and abetted by the Argentines; and the result was a three-year war between Brazil and Argentina, terminated by the mediation of British agents, who induced the two belligerents to set up a buffer state between them and pledge themselves not to intervene in its internal affairs thereafter, a pledge repeatedly broken by both during the ensuing decades.

Two other Uruguayan *caudillos* perpetuated their fame through the permanent political factions they organized. Fructuoso Rivera, a guerrilla ranchman who always looked toward Brazil for support, founded the Liberal party, which was called "Colorado" because of the crimson color of its flag. The more aristocratic Manuel Oribe, looking westward across the Plata estuary for succor, and for employment during periods of ostracism, was the founder of the Conservative party, called "Blanco" because its flag was white. Thereafter most Uruguayans became members of one faction or the other at birth and rarely changed their allegiance.

Quite unlike most Spanish-American *caudillos* in this respect, those of Uruguay did not assume that every triumph in civil war demanded a brand new constitution. The Uruguayan constitution adopted in 1830 was preserved almost unchanged for nearly a century, although actually it was frequently violated for at least half that period. It contained the usual bill of rights and, even at this early date, permitted the exercise of dissident faiths by omitting the customary prohibitory clause. This preference for toleration indicated a desire to attract immigrants and presaged a program of secularization, which progressed slowly until in the 1880's the Roman Catholic Church was left in a preferred position, with a small subsidy from the national government in return for state patronage, but with its functions and temporal power greatly reduced.

Already the national government had assumed major responsibility for the education of the Uruguayan youth. The Horace Mann and Domingo F. Sarmiento of Uruguay was Pedro José Varela, who set up a private organization for the founding of schools and the promotion of better methods of instruction as early as 1868, after returning from a study tour in Europe and the United States. He was both the moving force and the guiding spirit behind the decree of 1877, promulgated by Dictator Lorenzo Latorre, which provided for compulsory education and established a national school board, and for several years Varela was the leading member of the board and superintendent ("inspector") of public instruction. Owing largely to his efforts and enthusiasm, the national government was supporting well over 300 schools by the middle 1880's and at least two normal schools, one for men and one for women. Forty years earlier (1849), in harmony with the customary Latin-American stress on higher education, a national university had been founded in Montevideo.

Uruguay was becoming prosperous and progressive in spite of frequent revolts, some of them by factions of the Colorado party and more representing attempts of the Blancos to gain political recognition. It was not until 1894 that a chief executive was able to complete his term without suppressing a rebellion, and not until around 1900 that the more numerous and powerful Colorados began to conciliate their rivals and permit, except in some of the provinces, their participation in public affairs. In fact, party rivalries resulted in two civil wars after the beginning of the new century, one in 1904 and another in 1910. But most of these conflicts, especially after 1868, were electoral revolts which seldom involved the whole nation or even spread beyond the capital and a few of the smaller towns. W. H. Hudson, the distinguished British naturalist, may have been too enthusiastic when he wrote as early as 1885 that Uruguay was the "perfect republic," but he had spent several years riding over its gorgeous, undulating plains; and he declared further that the people had by no means been reduced to misery by the "knot of ambitious rulers all striving to pluck each other down." "The unwritten constitution, mightier than the written one, is in the heart of every man," declared Hudson, "to make him still a republican and free with a freedom it would be hard to match anywhere else on the globe." [2]

The major port of the nation was usually filled with ships, and British-financed railways were fanning out across the republic from its capital. Immigrants had begun to enter Uruguay even during its most turbulent days. Montevideo alone contained around 100,000 aliens in 1900. The population of the country, less than 75,000 in 1830, had increased more than tenfold during the seven decades that followed. Lush fields of corn and wheat were encroaching upon broad pastures teeming with sheep, cattle, and horses. Foreign trade was growing rapidly. The national capital had good port facilities, fine public buildings, tramways, a large gas plant, telephones, and electric lights.

PARAGUAY

Paraguay, the first country in Spanish America to win its independence, was ruled continuously by tyrants until 1870. Three of them spanned a period of fifty-nine years, and the third might have held power much longer if he had not been crushed by a war with Argentina, Brazil, and Uruguay in combination.

Far removed from the sea, and having comparatively little trade with their neighbors during the Colonial period, the Paraguayans were rather isolated for nearly three centuries, and their isolation continued into the National period. Lacking precious metals, Paraguay did not arouse much enthusiasm among the Spaniards, and its white population was therefore quite small. Its white settlers were sufficient, however, with the aid of missionaries, to reduce the natives of a good part of the eastern half of the region to a sedentary mode of life. The western half, across the Paraguay River, continued to be the haunt of roving savages. The southeastern section, once the center of flourishing missions long since disrupted by the expulsion of the Jesuits (1767) and the raids both of Brazilian slave hunters and of Spanish ranchers and planters, now languished in the shadows of its vineclad ruins. In the rest of the region east of the Paraguay River the majority of the Indians were reduced to serfdom, later changed to debt peonage. And there were a few hundred Negro slaves.

Considerable miscegenation occurred during the Colonial epoch in spite of the sparsity of Caucasians, and hybridization continued, of course, during the National period. This constant mixing of races and the reduction of the white population by war and other fatalities eventually resulted in the decided predominance of the mixbloods.

The major products of Paraguay were maize, manioc, tobacco, sugar cane, cotton, various fruits and vegetables, and an abundance of Paraguayan tea (yerba maté) made from the leaves of shrubbery that required almost no cultivation. In addition, of course, there were poultry and some livestock. An inspection of land titles as late as 1826 revealed that half of the land in eastern Paraguay still belonged to the state, which had added to its holdings by confiscations. But the despots adopted no agrarian policy designed to create a citizenery of independent farmers. The state lands seem to have been cultivated by compulsory labor or share croppers.

José Gaspar Rodríguez de Francia, Paraguay's first dictator, dominated the nation for almost twenty-nine years. Mainly responsible for the expulsion of the Spanish authorities and for secession from Argentina, he frankly assumed the title of Dictator in 1814, after serving for over two years as member of a national executive committee and as "First Consul." Fearing an invasion of soldiers, conspirators, or ideas from Brazil or from the lower Plata region, he "hermitized" the nation. Although himself a white man, half Spanish and half Portuguese, he dealt sternly and brutally with other members of his race because he realized that they were the most likely to oppose his tyranny; but he also struck down practically every Paraguayan who raised his head above the anonymous toiling crowd. Viewing the clergy with disdain, he dissolved the monasteries and appointed his own vicars and curates, depriving the papacy of all authority in Paraguay.

While vigorously repressing the upper class, he utilized the rabble. The Indians and mestizos spent a good part of their time in the employment of their tyrant. They constructed roads, bridges, barracks, and forts, worked on the state farms and ranches, or served in the army and the spy corps. If they had any time left, they cultivated such small plots as were available, cared for such animals and fowls as they possessed, and engaged in household industries and local trade.

Dividing the country into military districts, Francia governed the some 200,000 to 300,000 Paraguayans by means of spies, state police, and a loyal army. He was not himself a military man. A student of history, law, and theology, he bore the title of Doctor as well as Dictator. But he diligently drilled his troops and personally selected their equipment.

In fact, he assumed all the burdens of administration. He had only four attendants and secretaries and a trusty military guard; and while there were a few judges, they made no decisions until they had consulted him. Honest, frugal, and abstemious, he demanded only a small salary, lived in the rambling colonial palace on a few pesos a day, rode daily for a few hours about Asunción or out into the country to look after his duties or for fresh air, and left properties valued at only 35,000 pesos at his death in 1840.[3]

About his private and inner life, his ideals and his motives, little is known for certain. Contemptuous of the opinions of his contemporaries, untouched by their praise or calumny, he was also unconcerned about what posterity might think of him. Shortly before his death he destroyed all of his papers. Perhaps he coveted only power and a country to rule. Perhaps he loved the Indians and mixbreeds en masse (though he seems to have despised them individually), and wished to shield them from the oppression of the whites of Paraguay or any other section of South America. It is true that he subjected them to rigorous discipline, but probably he thought this was what they needed. Although he possessed a striking physique and a keen mind, he suffered from attacks of epilepsy and melancholy. Deadly serious and stern at all times, his most brutal acts were confined to the period between 1818 and 1823, when one of of the fleeting national governments of Argentina set in motion a conspiracy to extinguish him. Hundreds were jailed, tortured, executed, or banished before he felt secure. Between 600 and 700, perhaps the majority of them political prisoners, were still in jail when death finally ended his reign.

Carlos Antonio López got control of the government shortly after Francia died. A native of Asunción, López was a huge rotund mestizo who practiced law for a time in the capital but later retired to his wife's large farm in order to avoid arousing Francia's suspicion or jealousy. Like Francia, he began his rule as First Consul, reducing his associate to a figurehead. But López refused to assume the title of Dictator. He preferred to govern as president under a constitution drafted by himself with the aid of a cleric. As might have been expected, it merely legalized his power and cloaked his despotism. A unicameral congress was given the right to choose the national chief executive, but this must be done by open acclamation! A ten-year term was stipulated for the president, but no barrier was set up against re-election. The subservient assembly which ratified the constitution in 1844 selected López, of course, for Paraguay's first president. Ten years later a puppet congress "elected" him for a second term, and in 1856 it voted him a life tenure with the authority to choose his successor in his last will and testament. Constitutional limitations were thus a mere pretense; López was a despot.

But he was in some ways an enlightened despot in the seventeenth-century European manner. He opened the ports of Paraguay to foreign commerce, stimulated the development of its resources, began the emancipation of its African slaves, and made efforts to educate its youth. He also encouraged immigration for a time, but trouble with aliens and their home governments caused him to abandon this policy. As in the days of Francia, the government continued to own and manage numerous farms and ranches; indeed, under López, it went much further and monopolized the trade in tobacco, lumber, and Paraguayan tea. Fearing that Paraguay might be attacked by its neighbors, the dictator constructed a number of forts, expanded his army and improved its equipment, purchased gunboats and merchant vessels in Europe, and imported foreign experts in military affairs and the manufacture of munitions. Toward the end of his rule he had a short railway built, mainly for strategic purposes, for he appears to have given little attention to the improvement of land transportation.

His rule was considerably milder than Francia's. (Rigor was less needed; most of the conspirators and potential rivals were dead.) It was also somewhat less personal: a bureaucracy was set up to handle the details of administration. But the government was far too extravagant. López coveted wealth as well as power and managed the nation as if it were his own vast estate. The despot and his family lived off the fat of the land. His wife and two daughters ordered their clothes from Paris. His three sons enriched themselves by preying upon the country. Francisco Solano, the eldest, although a mere youth when his father seized the government, was on the official payroll from the outset. A sort of crown prince, he held a high rank in the army, occupied a cabinet post, and served as a roving diplomat. The fat despot who so easily dominated the servile nation failed to control his family. Perhaps contrary to his best judgment, shortly before his death in 1862, he designated Francisco Solano as his successor.

The second López was a tyrant with few redeeming qualities. Born in 1826 on his father's estate 100 miles or so from Asunción, he had almost no formal schooling. Petted and pampered by indulgent parents and by those who later sought his favor, he became vain, arrogant, and corrupt. He not only drew a salary from his father's government but terrorized the people in business transactions to his own great advantage. He was sent to Europe in 1853 as general representative and purchasing agent for his father's government. Visiting England, Spain,

Italy, and France, he bought arms, ammunition, and steamers, hired experts to supervise the building of fortifications and arsenals and the erection of an iron foundry, and made some hasty observations on politics, diplomacy, and military strategy. After nearly two years abroad, he returned home with uniforms for Paraguayan officers, an Irish mistress with a dark reputation, and some explosive ideas.

It was these dangerous ideas, which may have been suggested or diligently cultivated by his mistress, Madame Lynch, that finally involved him in war with Argentina, Brazil, and Uruguay. He came back from Europe with a Napoleonic concept of his military and political talents, the conviction that his country should maintain the balance of power in the Río de la Plata region, and perhaps the desire to become monarch of an enlarged domain. Both Brazil and Argentina looked with covetous eyes upon Paraguay as well as Uruguay, but Paraguay's preceding dictators had managed to preserve the national territories by a mixture of caution and firmness, avoiding entangling alliances while taking advantage of the rivalries of their two big neighbors. Instead of profiting from the lessons they should have taught him, the younger López rushed headlong into the international power-struggle and demanded a voice in every arrangement. With tactless arrogance and the worst sort of timing, he provoked a combination of his enemies and found himself confronted by a triple alliance when he might easily have dealt with them one at a time.

His political career may be summed up in a single sentence. He was a bellicose tyrant and blundering diplomat who oppressed and plundered his nation and left it in ruins. The war against the triple alliance, waged almost entirely on Paraguayan soil, began late in 1864 and lasted until early 1870. Whether from love of country or in mortal fear of their tyrant, the Paraguayans put up a bold and stubborn defense and died fighting until the last. Two-thirds of the nation's inhabitants, numbering approximately 800,000 when hostilities began, were exterminated. Francisco Solano López was not among the survivors. He either committed suicide or was killed by the Brazilians. Eliza Lynch stayed with him until the end and buried his corpse in the sand. She then managed to escape to Europe with all the treasures she could assemble or entrust to gallant accomplices. After a visit to Jerusalem and long years in Paris, she died in utter poverty.

The two great victors kept troops in Paraguay for six years after the war ended and nibbled at its territory, but their rivalries reduced the portion of each. The country survived but fell into military anarchy as soon as its enemies departed. There were elections as well as revolts, but elections were a farce. It was a political axiom that no government ever permitted itself to be defeated at the polls. The opposition could win only by winning a decisive battle or effecting a sudden military coup. Five "presidents" ruled the country between 1870 and 1880—with the consent of the army. The most tenacious of the military chiefs was Bernardino Caballero, who managed to cling to the government from September, 1880, until November, 1886, and to govern for several years afterward through puppets, some of them hard to manage. Yet, in spite of turbulent and wretched conditions, some foreign capital was invested in Paraguay and a few immigrants entered the country. British speculators bought Paraguayan government bonds even while the nation lay prostrate; and after a decade of defaults, they negotiated a new arrangement in 1885 that included an immense allotment of public lands, which they tried to dispose of at a profit by promoting a Paraguayan "boom."

Prospects for the development of the country seemed favorable for a time, but proved to be rather illusory. Paraguay at the end of the century was still desperately poor. Only a single short railway had been built and no good roads. The majority of its inhabitants—around 500,000 in 1900, not including some 65,000 to 70,000 Indians who roamed over the wild region in the north and in the Chaco to the east—were engaged in primitive farming. Most of the larger enterprises—ranches, tea plantations, lumber companies, firms exploiting quebracho forests, the lone railroad—were owned either by foreigners or by a small group of immigrants. Less than 30,000 pupils were enrolled in the primary schools and only a few hundred were attending the small university which had been established in Asunción in 1892 and the School of Law opened a decade earlier in the same city. Although Paraguayans talked of the cultural progress that they had made since 1870, their poets, journalists, historians, and other writers were far from numerous and the cultural advance of the nation was confined to the small upper class, composed mainly of officials and their kinsmen and a few hundred European immigrants.

CHAPTER XX

From Empire to Republic in Brazil

🦅 EMPEROR PEDRO I

Brazil, under a constitutional monarchy until 1889, was somewhat more tranquil during the first eight decades of its independent existence, especially during the forty years following 1849, than even the most orderly nations of Spanish America. Portuguese America had no prolonged and bloody struggle for independence, a less powerful clergy to oppose the rising tide of secularization, no sudden shift from monarchal absolutism to the republican system. The major political issues of the period were nativism in opposition to the Portuguese inhabitants residing in the country; absolutism *versus* a limited monarchy; slavery and abolition; centralism *versus* local autonomy; and jealousies among the several states. During the early days of the republican period, and probably previously, personalities often counted for more than issues. In fact, only a small minority of the people interested themselves in politics. The monarchy gave way to a republic dominated by big landlords and high-ranking members of the army and navy; poverty and ignorance still excluded the masses from holding office or voting. Population, which numbered around 4,000,000 in 1823, crowded 18,000,000 by the end of the century. Meantime, Brazil's declining sugar economy of the late Colonial period had largely been replaced by one of coffee and rubber, with livestock, corn, manioc, and some wheat, vegetables, and fruits produced for local consumption. Between 1822 and 1902 Brazil was governed by two emperors, four regencies, and four presidents. Both of the emperors and one of the presidents were overthrown by the menace of armed force.

The first ruler of independent Brazil was Emperor Pedro I, who was so proclaimed on October 12, 1822, with the understanding that Brazil should have a written constitution. Dom Pedro was not well qualified for his exalted and difficult position. He was only twenty-four years old.

Born in 1798, he was still a small boy when he fled with his parents to the American colony, and he had grown up amid the quarrels and confusion of the royal household. Neglected by his parents, he spent more time in the stables than in the palace, and roamed the streets of the capital at will. Such education as he received was acquired in a haphazard manner. He developed a fondness for mechanics, music, horses, and rowdy living. Quite unlike his father, he was handsome and courageous, and a superb horseman. Generous and rather democratic, he was at the same time impulsive and stubborn, and not incapable of cruelty. Sentimental, romantic, and fond of French philosophy, he liked to think of himself as a liberal; but his notions of liberalism were vague and his despotic tendencies often cropped out. His wife, Leopoldina, the Austrian princess whom he had married in 1817, was a distinct asset. Cultured, intelligent, athletic, and almost beautiful in spite of her Hapsburg chin, she soon won the hearts of the Brazilians, who developed a deep attachment for her after she supported the independence movement.

But Brazil was a sprawling, backward colony, with disconnected settlements scattered along the coast for 4,000 miles, its people sharply divided into races and classes and inexperienced in the practice of government. Nearly half of its 4,000,000 inhabitants were Negro and mulatto slaves and less than a fourth were whites. The remainder were Indians, the majority of them still in the tribal state, and blends of the three races. It is likely that not over 5 or 6 per cent of the people could read and write. This meant that the majority of the whites and nearly all of the primitive and mixed groups were illiterate. The wealth of the country was concentrated in the hands of a few hundred thousand native land magnates and Portuguese-born merchants and officeholders. At least four-fifths of the population belonged to the impoverished and servile classes. Deep animosities divided the Brazilian coffee and sugar planters and ranchmen, on the one hand, and the Portuguese merchants and bureaucratic nobility, on the other. And these were the only two groups that would be associated with the young emperor in the management of his government. Unlike the multitude of slaves, the 300,000 to 400,000 freedmen, the 500,000 Indians, the numerous mix-breeds, and even the poorer whites, this affluent and official class could not be ignored by any ruler committed to a constitutional government. He could not govern without them. It remained to be determined whether he could govern with their collaboration.

For two or three years after the departure of his father, Pedro's political career was a success. His important contribution to the independence of Brazil made him immensely popular. Later, however, his popularity rapidly waned among the Brazilians, and they finally became profoundly dissatisfied with the youthful monarch whom they had proclaimed so joyously on his twenty-fourth birthday.

Pedro first offended his subjects in connection with the framing and adoption of a constitution. The representatives of the new nation called together in the constitutional convention which assembled in Rio de Janeiro in 1823 included, of course, both native-born and Portuguese-born subjects, and bitter quarrels between the two groups soon began. Provoked by the violent debates, which dragged on for weeks, the emperor drove out the assembly at the point of the sword before it finished its work; he then set up a constitutional commission of his own, and promulgated the document which it framed without submitting it to any representative body for ratification.

The fundamental law of 1824 did not differ greatly from the draft the national convention had almost completed before it was dismissed. It contained an ample bill of civil rights and personal guaranties, including religious toleration under an established church. At the same time, it gave the monarch broad powers, including the right to dissolve the assembly and call for new elections, to appoint the governors of the provinces, and to select the senators from triple lists presented by the provincial authorities; but the Brazilians apparently had not expected their country to advance from absolutism to representative democracy in one sudden leap. While there was considerable demand for local self-government, which the constitution obviously did not grant, the main cause of offense was the despotic procedure of the emperor, which was a contradiction of his professed liberalism.

Dom Pedro's highhanded dissolution of the national convention and the failure of the constitution to satisfy the aspirations of the autonomists in the provinces incited a rebellion in the North, where republican sentiment suddenly waxed stronger. Four of the provinces in this region attempted to secede and form a republican confederation, and for a time it appeared that two or three others might join them. Since these were among the largest administrative units in Brazil, the emperor was threatened with the loss of half of his dominions. But Pedro, in striking contrast with the pusillanimity of his father, acted boldly and vigorously. With an army trained in part by foreign experts and with a small navy under the command of the British Lord Thomas Cochrane, he speedily suppressed the revolt and imprisoned or executed its ringleaders.

The emperor and his advisers then devoted their attention to foreign relations. A settlement with the Portuguese government headed by King John and recognition of the new nation by the leading European powers —recognition had been accorded by the United States in 1822—were considered to be of utmost importance; but there was also an urgent frontier problem. It will be recalled that a revolt backed up by the government at Buenos Aires began in 1825 in Banda Oriental, which had been annexed to Brazil several years before as the Cisplatine Province, and that the uprising soon led to war between Argentina and Brazil. The solutions finally reached in these foreign problems resulted in further loss of prestige and popular favor.

Satisfactory relations with Portugal and the leading European powers depended largely upon the co-operation of England. But England's support could not be obtained gratuitously. In order to secure British assistance in inducing King John to recognize Brazil's independence, the emperor agreed to abolish the slave trade, to grant special tariff concessions to British merchants, and to pay Portugal, always in debt to English capitalists, the sum of £2,000,000 as compensation for surrendering its claims to its former colony. The terms of these British-Portuguese agreements provoked hostility among the Brazilians, especially the slaveholding planters, who felt all the more aggrieved because the treaties were signed and put into force without consulting the national assembly. And to make matters worse, Dom Pedro, shortly after the death of King John in 1826, began to spend large sums in an effort to obtain the Portuguese crown for his eldest daughter, Maria da Gloria.

In the meantime the imperial troops were failing to win the war against Argentina and the Banda insurgents down in the Cisplatine province. The loss of life and national reputation in this prolonged struggle naturally irritated the Brazilians; and irritation turned into deep resentment against Dom Pedro when he finally agreed, under British pressure, to give up the province and recognize its independence as a buffer state between Argentina and Brazil.

While suffering defeats or paying dearly for victories in foreign relations, the emperor continued to exasperate the Brazilians by his domestic policies. He not only ignored the national parliament in connection with the negotiation and ratification of treaties; he waited until 1826 to open its first session and probably would have postponed its opening longer if he had not urgently needed funds. During this and subsequent sessions his foreign policy was criticized, and he had difficulties in securing appropriations. Finally, in 1829, the headstrong monarch, whose agents had already begun to suppress newspapers and subject the provinces to tyrannical treatment, dissolved the national assembly.

A further cause of resentment was Pedro's brazen relations with his mistresses—particularly the Marchioness of Santos, whom he kept in the royal palace—and the cruelties he inflicted upon the popular young empress. When she died in 1826, it was generally believed that her death was caused in part by the abuses of her husband; it was even reported that he had beaten his wife. But Pedro's morals were not much improved either by this tragic event or by his marriage to another European princess in 1829.

It was becoming more and more evident that independent Brazil's first monarch was no better than many of the dictators of the early National period in Spanish America. By the end of 1830 all the devotion and respect of former years had practically disappeared. He was now supported only by a few subservient Brazilian office-seekers and by his Portuguese-born subjects, whose numbers had been considerably enlarged by eager newcomers who had migrated to Brazil with the view of securing government posts or making their fortunes as merchants under the special favor of the monarch. More and more Dom Pedro surrounded himself with the hated Portuguese clique; and early in 1831, after the arrival of news of the overthrow of Charles X in France, the Brazilian leaders decided to rid themselves of their monarch too. During the first week of April they mustered their forces, won over his army, and compelled him to abdicate.

Leaving his only son and two of his daughters in Brazil, Dom Pedro and his second wife and his eldest daughter set sail for France. They could not land in Portugal because Pedro's brother, Dom Miguel, had usurped the throne and refused to allow the Brazilian Braganzas to enter the country. But the exiled monarch, who still imagined he was a liberal, determined to assert his daughter's rights and free Portugal from the tyranny of his brother. Borrowing funds in England, he assembled a small army and navy, captured the Madeira Islands, launched from this base an expedition against the usurper, and succeeded in deposing Miguel early in 1834 and replacing him by Maria da Gloria. Still young —less than thirty-six—Pedro probably looked forward to years of comparative repose. But a complication of diseases already had set in, and death terminated his stormy career on September 24, 1834.

In some respects Pedro I had served Brazilian interests, although he had conferred no appreciable benefits upon the masses of the people. He had collaborated with the native leaders in achieving emancipation from Portugal, granted Brazil a constitution (which he rarely respected), obtained recognition of the new nation from the major powers, preserved its unity by holding its eighteen original provinces together (Brazil was not really entitled to the Banda, since its population was mainly Spanish), and imposed domestic peace after a fashion. But he plunged the nation into debt; he was despotic (which may have been unavoidable in the circumstances) and personally immoral; and during the last years of his reign he seemed to care more for Portugal and the Portuguese than for Brazil and the Brazilians. He therefore not only lost his throne but tarnished his fame and thus failed to attain the exalted position which he might have occupied in the national esteem as Brazil's paramount national hero—an honor later conferred upon José Bonifácio de Andrada, who had advised Dom Pedro for a time and who became the tutor of Prince Regent Pedro after the first Pedro was dethroned.

🎵 PEDRO II, AMERICA'S LAST MONARCH

This infant prince—only six years old in 1831—was probably the most valuable contribution Pedro I made to the nation he helped to found, for this son was fated to become the only great monarch ever to wear a crown in America. But José Bonifácio did not live to witness the enlightened and benevolent rule of his distinguished pupil. The enemies of the "Patriarch of Independence" soon had him dismissed from his royal tutorship, and he died in 1838 when the second Pedro was still too young to assume the burdens of government. A regency, composed of three aristocrats and later of one, ruled in his name for almost a decade.

It was a turbulent period, during which revolts in the provinces remote from the center of government retarded national development. Conditions were almost as chaotic as in most other nations of the epoch in Latin America. Ambitious provincial leaders were clamoring for a larger measure of self-government and imposing their imperious wills by military force. It appeared at times that Brazil would break up into several small nations. The Liberal faction which controlled the regency during most of the decade departed from its doctrine and became centralistic and rigidly authoritarian. There were uprisings at one time or another in fifteen of the provinces. In the hope of calming the discontent, it was decided in 1840 to make the youthful Pedro emperor. Although only fifteen, he was so serious, intelligent, handsome, and ingratiating that he was already admired and loved by all who knew him. In July, 1840, he was proclaimed Pedro II, apparently with great rejoicing and general approval. Although his advisers probably dominated him for some time, he was destined to rule Brazil for nearly half a century and to become noted throughout the Western World as a wise and magnanimous sovereign.

Disorders continued in a few of the provinces for another decade, but thereafter Brazil enjoyed nearly forty years of uninterrupted domestic peace. Unfortunately, however, the nation confronted two serious international conflicts. The first was a war lasting several months against the Argentine dictator, Manuel Rosas, who seemed to be determined to conquer Uruguay with the aid of the Blanco party. As observed elsewhere, Rosas was defeated and banished early in 1852 by a combined army of Brazilians, Uruguayans, and Argentinians. The second war, likewise mentioned in another connection, was the long war with Paraguay which broke out late in 1864 and continued until early 1870. In both instances, traditional interest in Uruguay was largely responsible for Brazil's involvement. The first struggle was comparatively inexpensive; the second, in which Brazil took the lead, cost the nation more than 50,000 lives and many millions of dollars. Thus domestic revolts or foreign wars distracted the second Brazilian monarch for a total of over fifteen years. Yet hardly a year passed without definite contributions on his part to the national welfare.

An autocrat at times, but never a despot, Pedro II endeavored to safeguard the rights and liberties of his subjects. He used with moderation the broad powers granted him by the constitution of 1824. He was careful in his selection of provincial governors, senators, and ministers, although he rarely found men capable of filling these posts to his complete satisfaction. He pretended to govern in accordance with the will of the nation as expressed in the elections; but he knew that the elections were never fair. Well aware of the disposition of the faction in power to browbeat and defraud the opposition, he tried to effect a just rotation in office and give each faction its turn by utilizing his appointive power and his right to dissolve the national assembly. He also tried repeatedly to improve the election laws, but his efforts were largely futile. (Suffrage was hedged by property qualifications, but for some unknown reason literacy tests were not required.) A firm believer in religious toleration, he offended less tolerant members of the clergy by his intellectual independence and his religious policies. Opposed to Negro slavery, he was eager to effect its abolition with fairness to the slaveholders and without arousing their hostility; and although he failed to attain this objective despite his great moderation, the slaves were nevertheless freed by 1888; and they owed their emancipation mainly to the emperor, his daughter Princess Isabel, and a handful of Brazilian collaborators like the eloquent Joaquím Nabuco. Knowing full well that large armies and navies were a heavy burden on the people and always a potential threat to order and liberty, he endeavored to pare the military establishment down to the minimum required by Brazil's position in South America and to prevent its officers from meddling in politics. He was careful not to interfere with freedom of speech and of the press, even when journalists and politicians attacked him unjustly or advocated a republic. He was also much interested in criminology and prison reform, opposed to capital punishment, and generous in his use of the pardoning power.

His efforts to promote the education and moral progress of Brazil were unceasing. He spent a considerable part of his time visiting schools, contributed his personal funds to their support, and educated a number of Brazilians at his own expense. His messages to the national parliament repeatedly urged larger appropriations for schools of all types. His long rule witnessed great cultural advance among the upper classes. Among the masses, however, progress was far from rapid. It would have been greater among all classes if the monarch had received more hearty co-operation from the Brazilian political leaders. Primary education was under the provincial governments, which failed to give it the support it deserved. At the beginning of his reign it is likely that no more than 5 per cent of the people could read and write; at its end the percentage of literacy was probably twice as large and the nation could boast a distinguished array of writers and scholars, including some scientists, particularly in the field of medicine and metallurgy.

Much concerned with public health, Pedro II urged the adoption of many practical measures to improve it and constantly advocated sanitation and the control of epidemics. Yet sanitary measures were inadequate and preventable diseases continued to ravage the people because sanitation and prevention were expensive and the politicians could not be fully aroused to the importance of appropriations to safeguard the national health.

The great monarch was eager to develop the material resources of his empire. He stimulated agriculture by encouraging immigration and the importation of modern machinery; promoted transportation and communications by subsidizing steamboat lines, railways, and telegraphs; and gave manufacturers his approval and support. At the end of his reign Brazil had a respectable merchant marine, 6,000 miles of railway, 12,000 miles of telegraph lines, cable connections with foreign nations, the beginnings of a telephone network, the largest coffee production in the world, herds of livestock second only to Argentina's among the Latin-American countries, and numerous small manufacturing plants. Well over 500,000 immigrants had entered the country since 1840, and its foreign trade, although now slightly smaller than Argentina's, had increased in value from $61,000,000 in 1840 to $242,000,000 in 1888. Its population, in spite of tropical climate and the heavy toll of disease, had more than doubled during the period.

It would be absurd, of course, to attribute all this progress, which might easily have been greater, given a less primitive mass of people and a better physical environment, to the character and policies of the emperor. It was the result of the efforts of millions of Brazilians, many thousands of skilled immigrants, the growing demand abroad for food and raw materials, and the impact of foreign capital and technology.

Yet there is no doubt that Pedro II was a great man and a great states-man. Rojas Paúl of Venezuela thought that Brazil under the second Pedro came nearer being a republic than any other Latin-American country of his epoch, and Mitre of Argentina described his rule as a "crowned democracy." Victor Hugo, who knew the Brazilian emperor well, called him the modern Marcus Aurelius and declared that if all monarchs were like Dom Pedro there would be no republicans in the world. They were according him unstinted tribute, and, indeed, it would be difficult to praise him too highly.[1]

A distinguished Brazilian historian, Manoel de Oliveira Lima, has intimated that conditions could have been improved more rapidly in Brazil if its sovereign had been more resolute and vigorous. But this is doubtful. Nobody ever denied that he was most active and industrious. He had to govern the nation as it was with the collaboration of such men as were available. If he had acted with greater determination and vigor he might have provoked a dangerous reaction that would have compelled him either to set up a military despotism or to abdicate. He was fully aware of the dilemma which he confronted. As early as January 10, 1862, he wrote in his diary: "I am very sad, though it is necessary to show a cheerful face. Many things trouble me; but it is not possible to remedy them immediately. . . . There is much lack of zeal, and love of country is mostly mere talk! To see what is desirable to do but not to be able to contribute towards it except slowly . . . is a torment of Tantalus." [2]

Pedro II is a phenomenon not easily explained. With Braganza, Bourbon, and Hapsburg blood and brains, he received no heritage that forecast a model monarch. Unless he was one of history's accidents or a gift of Providence, his character and wisdom must be attributed in large measure to the training he received from his tutors, who seem to have been diligent and conscientious in the development of his will, emotions, and ideals as well as his intellect and physique. A frail and delicate child, he grew up with a strong body—he was six feet, three inches tall—a sound and inquiring mind, excellent personal habits, perfect balance and poise, and a keen sense of responsibility for the welfare of the nation he was to govern.

Above everything, Pedro II was devoted to his country and his people. He viewed himself as both the teacher and the physician of Brazil, with the mission of educating Brazilians by example as well as by precept and of administering, to the best of his ability, to their physi-cal, social, and moral ailments. He traveled over nearly all the provinces to discover their needs and over a good part of Europe and the United

States in quest of ideas and methods. Yet this great monarch, who certainly held a high rank among the statesmen of the nineteenth century, was finally overthrown and expelled from his country. Why?

Some of the causes have already been suggested. The pillars of his empire were the landowning aristocracy, the clergy, the intellectuals, and, in the last resort, the army. The slaveholding planters were alienated by the abolition of slavery (1871 and 1888). The leaders of the Roman Catholic Church did not like his rationalistic tendencies and his broad tolerance of Protestants and Masons. The intellectuals, particularly the lawyers, gradually developed, under a regime which granted them the utmost freedom, a strong republican sentiment, based not so much on the feeling that Dom Pedro was not a capable and magnanimous monarch as upon the conviction that the monarchical system was incongruous in America and upon the desire to have Brazil take its place among the republics of the New World. There was also a longing among the professional politicians, many of whom were lawyers or planters, for fuller self-government in the provinces, a craving which the emperor refused to satisfy because he felt that the common people were not yet sufficiently educated and that the local leaders still lacked the requisite devotion to the national welfare. Some of the officers of the army and navy, the recipients of both merited and unmerited popular esteem because of their service in the wars against the tyrant Rosas and against Paraguay, especially the latter, were dissatisfied because Dom Pedro did not approve of their active participation in politics or grant them more honors and higher pay. There was also some resentment toward Princess Isabel, the heiress to the crown, and her French husband, who, though deaf, diffident, and aloof, was expected to influence the policies of his consort.

For all of these reasons, late in 1889, the army and navy with a few republicans and landowners—the rest of the nation was too ignorant or indifferent to exert its influence on either side—deposed and banished Dom Pedro, who was then old and ill and too kindly to assert his rights at the cost of fratricidal strife. With the Empress Tereza, a Neapolitan princess whom he had married forty-six years before, and with his daughter Isabel and her husband and three children, he departed for Europe. Then sixty-four years old, his patriarchal beard and hair were white. Although his energies had been depleted by worry and work, his tall figure was still erect and he bore his troubles with dignity. After visiting Portugal and the tombs of his Braganza ancestors, he established his residence in France, where he was welcomed with great courtesy and respect. Still mentally alert and eager, he read widely, attended the lectures of learned societies, and composed sonnets until a few weeks before his death in December, 1891. He was buried by the side of the ex-empress (who died shortly after their banishment) in the old Portuguese Church of São Vicente, but in 1920 his remains and hers were brought back to Brazil and deposited in a small chapel at Petropolis, a town long ago named in his honor, almost concealed in the tall hills not far from Rio de Janeiro.

❦ EARLY YEARS OF THE REPUBLIC

The republican constitution, promulgated on February 24, 1891, was in many respects similar to that of the United States. It provided for the three customary departments of government, each of them separate and distinct from the others, and for a national congress to be composed of two houses, the senators representing the twenty states and the federal district and the deputies representing the people. The senators, sixty-three in number, were to be elected by direct vote for nine years, one-third going out of office every three years. Members of the Chamber of Deputies were to be chosen for terms of three years by popular vote on the basis of population, but each state was to have at least four representatives. In general, the powers conferred upon congress were the same as those of the national legislative body in the United States, and national suffrage was granted to all male citizens twenty-one years of age who were able to read and write—with the exception of beggars, common soldiers on pay, members of religious orders, and organizations whose rules or vows implied the surrender of liberty. The functions of the president were likewise very similar to those of the chief executive of the United States, but his power with respect to legislation was some-what broader: he could issue decrees, instructions, and regulations for the faithful execution of the laws and ordinances of congress. Both the president and the vice-president were to be elected for a term of four years, and the former was not to be eligible for immediate re-election. The judicial power was conferred upon the supreme court and such inferior courts as Congress might create. All federal judges were to be appointed by the president and to hold office for life unless removed by judicial procedure. The jurisdiction of the federal courts was in most respects similar to the jurisdiction of analogous courts in the United States, including the power to pass upon the relative spheres of the state and national governments.

The constitution of 1891 also contained a somewhat elaborate bill of rights. Among its provisions were: freedom of worship, speech, and the press; trial by jury; and abolition of the death penalty. Church and State were separated, marriage was declared to be a civil institution, and cemeteries and public instruction were secularized.

The constitution permitted the federal government to intervene in the various states (1) to repel foreign invasion or the invasion of another state; (2) to maintain a republican form of government; (3) to re-establish order at the request of any state government; and (4) to secure the execution of federal laws and judgments. And this power of federal intervention was destined to be used too frequently and to give rise to the most delicate problems.

The first four years of the republic were far from tranquil. In February, 1891, the constituent assembly chose General Deodora da Fonseca, who had been chief executive of the provisional government, as president and Floriano Peixoto, a high officer of the navy, as vice-president. Fonseca proved to be selfish, tactless, and dictatorial, dissolving Congress, urging a revision of the constitution, interfering in the affairs of the states, and making himself generally obnoxious. He had been in office only a short time when a group of prominent Brazilians protested against his corrupt and arbitrary rule. Although opposition to him was widespread, it was strongest in São Paulo and Rio Grande do Sul. Before many months, the army and a portion of the navy, Admiral José de Mello being among the naval insurgents, abandoned him. Finally, on November 23, 1891, the warships stationed in the harbor of Rio de Janeiro threatened to bombard the city and forced Fonseca to resign in favor of Vice-President Peixoto.

Peixoto was even more unsatisfactory than his predecessor, however. Not only did he depose several state executives and place the capital under martial law, he permitted his administration to indulge in extravagance, bribery, and corruption and forced Ruy Barbosa, the distinguished editor of *Jornal do Brazil,* to flee the country in order to avoid arrest. A famous Gaucho chieftain named Gumercindo Saraiva began an uprising in Rio Grande do Sul in 1892, and Admiral de Mello resigned as minister of marine early the following year in order to begin another naval revolt. After eight months of fighting and the loss of thousands of lives, the insurgents were finally suppressed. The presidential campaign of the spring of 1894 took place while the conflict was going on, and Prudente de Moraes Barros, a distinguished lawyer of São Paulo, was elected. It was freely predicted that Peixoto would refuse to surrender his authority at the expiration of his legal term (November 15, 1894), but the prediction was not fulfilled. Brazil had narrowly escaped an era of militarism, however, and the military element continued to be a menacing problem.

The restoration of order and the elimination of militarism from the government were the most substantial achievements of the Moraes Barros administration (1894–98). He granted amnesty to the participants in the recent rebellion, but expelled numerous army officers from civilian posts to which they had been appointed by his predecessor. He gradually discarded praetorian methods of government, and put down uprisings in several of the states, the most formidable of them being the revolt of the Brazilian mystic Antonio Maciel [3] on the frontier of Bahía. Moraes' administration was also noted for an attack upon political corruption and the settlement of a boundary dispute with Argentina (1895). He found himself unable, however, to solve the financial problems which confronted the nation.

Partly by the aid of Moraes, Manoel de Campos Salles (1898–1902), another Paulista, won the presidency against the candidate of the militarists in 1898. The campaign took place in the midst of a financial crisis, and the president-elect immediately visited Europe, where he negotiated with the Rothchilds a loan of £10,000,000. The terms were somewhat onerous, but the loan aided the country in surmounting its most urgent financial difficulties. Returning to assume his duties, Campos Salles began at once a policy of retrenchment and a search for new revenues, securing the latter in the main by levying a stamp tax and increasing import duties. He strongly opposed federal interference in state affairs; and boundary disputes were settled during his administration with Bolivia (1901–3, the Acre territory) and with France (1900, French Guiana).

CHAPTER XXI

Intellectual Life

🕮 LATIN AMERICA'S INTELLECTUAL REVOLUTION

Latin America not only had its wars for independence; it had a revolution for independence. The wars were fought mainly against a political and economic system. The revolution was directed at a system of thought, against scholasticism, spiritual repression, and intellectual fetters, and its ultimate objective was to baptize the new generations, or a part of them, in the exhilarating stream of modern and contemporary ideas. It not only confronted the divine right of kings and the old commercial notions with Rousseau's *Social Contract* and the economic theories of Adam Smith, John Stuart Mill, and Jeremy Bentham; it undertook to revise all the traditional concepts and place Latin-American thinking abreast with the age. Its aspirations went far beyond the expulsion of the minions of European despotism and the severance of economic fetters; it envisaged an intellectual and spiritual emancipation, a Revival of Learning.

The Wars of Independence, prolonged as they were, nowhere lasted more than two decades, and triumph had to be achieved mainly by the sword. The intellectual revolution started before the wars began, continued long after the wars terminated, and was carried on by men who, while not averse to employing the customary arbiter, the sword, if it seemed expedient, utilized mainly their pens and their vocal cords. The duration of this intellectual revolution is not difficult to explain. Latin America had fallen far behind much of the Western world, and the progress of enlightenment was retarded in the region by poverty, by the dead weight of ignorance, superstition, and intolerance, by political ineptitude and military ferment. But the intellectual leaders, steeping themselves in positive and natural law, political theory, and what was then called "political economy," and gaining an acquaintance with modern history, social philosophy, geography, botany, medicine, and some of the other sciences, persisted in their struggle.

New ideas regarding man, the social order, and the universe began to seep in during the latter half of the eighteenth century. The flow increased with the beginning of the Wars of Independence and helped to undermine the foundations of this anachronous medievalism. Later the ideas pouring in from the outside took on the semblance of a flood. Four or five hundred years after the Humanists began to appear in Europe, Latin America produced Humanists of its own, who gradually replaced the dying scholastics in the old colonial academies and in the royal and pontifical colleges and universities, opened new seats of higher learning (in Buenos Aires, Santiago, Montevideo, and elsewhere), and vigorously disputed with clerics and peripatetics in the forum and the press. Frequently they paid the penalty of imprisonment or exile for their bold ideas and innovations; but they managed to find ink and paper in the jails, or to expound their views in more tolerant neighboring states, or, if their ostracism sent them as far afield as the United States, England, or France, they gained access to still more books and other novel ideas. For, unlike the Humanists of an earlier epoch, these belated Humanists of Latin America did not seek the new learning so much in dusty tomes and manuscripts, in ancient lore, as in the new treatises of the eighteenth and nineteenth centuries.

They did not become proficient in many of the applied sciences— in technology, in invention. Living in countries without much good coking coal and with such coal as they had seldom conveniently located in respect to their iron ore, they were hampered by lack of the basic material resources for the development of the major technical skills. They were also handicapped by a traditional aversion to the manual arts, by their late start, and by the perpetual heat of their vast tropical regions. Although they did a good many things surprisingly well, they rarely became experts in anything, with the possible exception of poetry and law—not even efficient in politics and the brutal military art in spite of all the time they devoted to these occupations. As a rule, they were more interested in the understanding of ideas than in their practical utilization. They seldom felt the urge to become specialists; their models were the European encyclopedists, whose writings were the first to stimulate their minds and emotions.

As late as 1913 James Bryce, the distinguished British historian and diplomat, declared that Latin America had not produced "any thinker or poet or artist even of the second rank." [1] His conclusion was doubtless reached without sufficient investigation and he was probably mistaken; but his assertion, to the extent that it was true, refers to a failure that can in large measure be explained by the sudden exposure of Latin Americans to this immense accumulation of new learning, to this flood of new books, to which they had not previously gained full access because of the obscure mantle of colonialism that had enshrouded them. They were far behind in their reading; they liked to read because reading was a delightful new experience, and a long time was required for them to catch up. It also seemed necessary to summarize this new knowledge, and to translate it for such of their associates as had learned to read and think after the long years during which such occupations were not encouraged.

Their achievements in architecture, landscaping, sculpture, painting, and music cannot be dwelt upon here. Both space and competence prevent it. Suffice it to say that they seem to have lacked neither taste nor the germ of capacity in these fine arts.

It is true that they produced no great books in the fields of science and philosophy; but they wrote good poetry, revealed a genius for languages, exhibited talent for treatises on all branches of law, made some contributions to botany, geography, and medicine, produced not a few histories of literature and literary histories, published some novels and short stories, revealed talent as journalists and polemists, became apt *pronunciamiento* artists, displayed uncommon oratorical gifts, and sometimes rose to the rank of *pensadores* (thinkers), at least in the opinion of their compatriots. Writing about the same time that Bryce expressed his adverse conclusion, Francisco García Calderón, a Peruvian critic, declared: "He who knows Latin America only by its imperfect social framework, its civil wars, and its persistent barbarism sees only the outward tumult; there is a strange divorce between its turbulent politics and its refined art." [2]

Whatever one may conclude about the merit of their literary product, its quantity cannot be disputed. They blanketed their towns and cities with the output of their printing presses. They were thrilled after a long twilight of repression to see their literary compositions in print. Few oligarchies were ever more vocal, more prolific with the pen, than this Latin-American literary group of the early National epoch, whose members shuffled back and forth between the government buildings and their writing desks, between printing establishments and jails, between republic and republic, between the home countries and lands overseas. Their collected works, depending mainly upon circumstances and longevity, filled from three or four to more than fifty volumes. Their contemporaries in the United States and Europe were absorbed in commerce and industry, busy with devices and inventions to speed production and distribution. The Latin-American intellectuals were mainly concerned with ideas and literary style, although most of them played a part in politics, and politics always involved them in polemics and sometimes in civil wars.

They liked to express lofty ideals and glowing sentiments in torrents of words. The framing of long constitutions—the longer the better; the perfection of the national laws; the writing of national anthems; the compilation of legal codes; the delivery of orations on anniversaries of independence or at the tombs of dead heroes whose mutilated bodies had been reclaimed from the battlefield or whose remains had just been shipped home from exile; the denunciation of a tyrant or some other evil thing; a wail about the mundane fate of man; an intimate description of how it feels to fall in love and of the lady involved; an ode to a newborn child; verses on the condor's freedom or the "last" Inca's fierce determination to resist enslavement; an epic on the noble Indian or the vanishing cowboy; a portrayal of the ecstasy produced by a distant peak or a nearby waterfall; an allocution to poetry itself; a discourse on liberty, justice, or duty, on the relics of an ancient civilization, or on the latest events and trends in Europe; a polished summary of the most recent discoveries in astronomy or medicine; a flowing exposition of the latest theories in philosophy, metaphysics, literature, or social organization—nothing made them happier or contributed more to their self-esteem.

García Calderón insists that Latin-American thought was "not divorced from action." "It reflected the political unrest," he says; "it prepared or justified political transformations." [3] But the word was often the end as well as the beginning. Action was comparatively unimportant except in political and military maneuvers or in escaping from the clutches of an angry antagonist. In other spheres it was left largely to the unsophisticated and the underprivileged, who bore the burden of manual toil and even the brunt of military combat. Although there were some notable exceptions, this little aristocracy of letters, in spite of the fine sentiments embodied in its flowing sentences, was not deeply concerned with the welfare of the masses. The task of uplifting these dumb and degraded multitudes must have seemed almost hopeless anyway. It was much easier to dismiss them from the mind or salve the individual conscience and the national pride by erecting a façade of noble laws, while making no serious attempt to enforce them. In general, the best efforts of the members of the literary groups were devoted to self-expression and self-improvement. On this point, at least, their attitude suggests a cold realism. The task of keeping up with the thoughts and moods of the world overseas was heavy enough without assuming any additional burdens. By concentrating on the problem of self-instruction and self-development at least a few men in each republic could scale the tall ladder of learning. Perhaps God and gravity would cause this top layer of culture to trickle down as fast as those below could absorb it. Without improved means of production or the skill to use them, many humble hands were required to produce the bread of life for the lowly multitudes and the wealth needed by the aristocracy to purchase their material comforts and cultural amenities.

The effort to absorb all the learning and art of the nations that had got a long head start and were still rapidly advancing, if all this culture was to be absorbed, was sufficient to keep the men of letters occupied. The effort not only required vigorous intellectual activity at home; it demanded frequent journeys and long sojourns abroad. In fact, it soon led to a division of labor. Not a few of the elite established permanent residences in Europe—especially in France, which became their Mecca—where they basked in the sunshine of wisdom and watering places, crowded the restaurants and viewed the boulevards, and frequently did a stint in diplomacy, negotiating loans or commercial treaties, placating creditors and claimants, attempting to soothe the papacy, and searching for outlets for the minerals, metals, animal products, and tropical commodities produced by their peons, often under the direction of foreign technicians. Although the home governments were usually willing to subsidize the education and the publications of the literary aristocracy, provided its members made the proper contributions to the newspapers, wrote an occasional tribute to a dead hero, or aided a favorite general to draft his recollections of battles fought in behalf of the right cause, still this intellectual life, because of empty treasuries or the frequency of political upsets, required considerable personal funds or friendly private subsidies.

This relative neglect of the masses, this reluctance to undertake vigorously the task of enlightening the minds of the common people and raising their level of life, restricted the scope of the literary appeal. But primary education was not entirely neglected. Mutual instruction and a few night schools were early thought of; the Lancasterians were busy in some of the towns even before emancipation had been completed. In later years a growing disposition was revealed to admit that general education was the duty and the function of the state, so that by 1900 the majority of the governments in the region had accepted the principle of state responsibility for the educational task and issued decrees or passed laws declaring primary education both free and compulsory. But revenues were scarce, the people and the governments alike usually lacked sustained enthusiasm for mass education, competent teachers willing to undertake the mission were few, and the laws were rarely implemented and enforced. Yet, with the multiplication of the descendants of the oligarchy, the spread of wealth, the arrival of European immigrants, and the gradual reduction of inertia, the number of literates slowly increased. While it is likely that no more than 25 or 30 per cent of Latin America's population of around 43,000,000 in 1885 and some 62,000,000 in 1900 were able to read, and that nearly half of these were too poor or indifferent to exercise their talent, the number who could and did read was nevertheless several times larger than it had been in the 1820's when the population was only some 20,000,000 and the percentage of literacy considerably lower. One of the most severe limitations on the literary appeal was the multiplicity of national boundaries and the lack of intercommunication among many of the national units. Although there were not a few exceptions, the reading public was roughly divided into eighteen separate and distinct compartments. It was therefore quite restricted even in the largest or the most progressive nations, and it included only a tiny group in the others.

Yet, unless it be assumed that the members of this intelligentsia were writing for the sheer enjoyment of self-expression or for a foreign market (which some of them were in considerable degree, and most of them to some extent), they must have felt that their reading public compensated for its limited numbers by its enthusiasm and its readiness to respond to literary appeals and inspirations. And there is strong evidence that they were not mistaken. Nations ruled by small oligarchies were easily swayed by men of letters and oratorical talent because a little well-directed persuasion was often sufficient to change the delicate balance of power and turn the tide of politics. The best evidence that literary men had prestige and influence is the attention they received even from the crudest politico-militarists. They were either showered with subsidies or subjected to persecution. They were never ignored. While no large number of lives may have been saved by shouting "Don't shoot me; I'm a poet," it is a fact that most high officials who were not generals paraded the title "Doctor" and that the generals themselves did not disdain to seek and demand honorary degrees. The scale of values included at least two kinds of prowess: literary and military.

The Latin-American humanists of the early National period do not yield themselves readily to the refinements of classification. They were too versatile to fit into neat categories. In addition to being planters, ranchmen, mine-owners, politicians, and generals, or most of these, they were likely at the same time to be lawyers, poets, journalists, orators, short-story writers, novelists, linguists, amateur historians, naturalists, geographers, and social philosophers, or three or four of these rolled into one. Their grasp of the theoretical and practical sciences, perhaps excepting medicine, was by no means firm; but they might roughly be divided into encyclopedists and near-encyclopedists if this weakness could be overlooked and if several of them had not devoted most of their time to belles lettres and the history and criticism of literature. A classification consisting of only two categories with a vague line separating them would not be very helpful, however; and consideration of each type of production in its turn would not only expand this narrative beyond all reasonable limits but would require a monotonous reappearance of most members of the cast. Perhaps as illuminating a procedure as any would be to select a few outstanding members of the literati, largely on the basis of their "progressive outlook" but without ignoring the claims of the various countries, and comment briefly on their works, leaving the rest to the specialists in literary history and criticism. This is the procedure which has been adopted in the sections that follow.[4]

WRITERS OF THE CARIBBEAN COUNTRIES AND MEXICO

That even the smallest countries were not incapable of producing literary lights and able exponents of culture is illustrated by Eugenio María de Hostos (1839–1903), whose name is usually associated with the Dominican Republic, where some of his best works were published, although he was born in Puerto Rico, lived for a decade in Chile, and spent some time in the other republics. Novelist, moralist, social philosopher, jurisconsult, and educator, he founded the first normal school in that little republic (1880) and ardently championed the education of women. Much appreciated in his day, his writings continued to be popular wherever Spanish was read. If further exhibits are needed to support the thesis of the literary fecundity of the small nations, the writings of other Dominicans may be offered: those of Félix María del Monte (1819–99), for instance, composer of the Dominican national anthem, renowned poet, and long the intellectual leader of the republic; or Doña Salomé Ureña de Henríquez (1850–97), poetess who extolled the virtues of home life and the "good" Indian, gave birth to sons and inspired them to achieve literary fame, and founded a school for "young ladies"; or Manuel de Jesús Galván (1835–1911), whose novel *Little Henry,* published in 1882, dealt deftly with the clashes between the Spaniards and Indians in the days of Columbus and his immediate successors and is considered one of the best pieces of fiction written by a Spanish American during this early National period.

Literary figures of some prestige appeared even in turbulent Central America. Guatemala lays claim to Antonio José de Irisarri (1786–

1868), pioneer journalist, author of poetic satires and burlesques, philologist, and diplomat, who spent a good part of his life in Chile and in the United States; José Batres y Montúfar (1809–44), who produced finished models of "jocose" narrative abounding in local color and interrupted by skeptical digressions; José Milla (1827–82), who wrote both local history and historical novels containing realistic portrayals of Guatemalan life; and Lorenzo Montúfar (1823–98), who published a seven-volume "survey" of Central American history. The literati were less numerous in the other Mid-American countries, but they all had their journalists, versifiers, essayists, and historians. One of them, Juan José Cañas (1826–1900), wrote autobiographical poetic narratives of his adventures in the gold mines of California, in the filibuster war against William Walker, and in the diplomatic service, and published popular verses dealing with steamship captains and articulating the tender sentiments attending the departure of steamers from the ports.

Mexico's claim to cultural renown during the early National period is based upon her romantic poets and dramatists, who dwelt upon the ways in which the tyrants brought tragedy to lovers, death and destruction to the ancient Indian chiefs, and the wrath of God upon themselves; upon an array of journalists, some writers of short stories and novels, and a few historians; and upon at least two *pensadores,* one of them assuming the name himself and the other earning it, at least in the esteem of later generations of Mexicans, by his thoughtful works. Among the dramatists and poets were Ignacio Rodríguez Galván (1816–42), whose "Vision of Moctezuma" and "Prophecy of Guatémoc" are typical of his best productions, and Fernando Calderón y Beltrán, whose talent is well displayed in "The Withered Rose," "The Soldier of Liberty," "The Nightmare of a Tyrant" and "The Return of the Exile." Among the most prolific Mexican historians were Carlos María de Bustamante (1774–1848), who wrote an account of Mexico's War of Independence in six tomes; the reactionary Lucas Alamán (1792–1853), who published three volumes of "dissertations" on Mexican history and then five volumes on the history itself; and the even more prolix writers Francisco Arrangóiz (1830–89) and Niceto Zamacois (1825–86). The journalists are too numerous to mention; the list would have to include almost every Mexican with a college degree and some who by-passed this approach to literary prestige. Three of the Mexican journalists must be given passing mention, however, because they were much more than journalists. Ignacio Ramírez (1818–79) was journalist, poet, orator, amateur historian and political economist, educator, reformer, and philosophical skeptic who liked to shock an ardently Roman Catholic country by the declaration that God does not exist. Ignacio Manuel Altamirano (1834–93), a full-blooded Indian, achieved distinction as journalist, poet, orator, novelist, and short-story writer and for his talent in recounting legends and traditions and describing customs and folkways. Guillermo Prieto (1818–97) was not only a very able journalist but a poet, an orator, a reformer, a writer of memoirs and travelogues, a compiler of textbooks on history and political economy, and a public official fairly familiar with Mexico's problems of public finance. The two *pensadores* deserve special attention because they envisaged nearly everything of significance that happened in Mexico during the century that followed their deaths, with the possible exception of the long Díaz dictatorship and the tremendous impact of foreign capital and technology.

The first of the Mexican "thinkers" and the one who boldly assumed the name—or rather published a literary journal entitled *El Pensador Mexicano,* from which his pseudonym was derived—was José Joaquín Fernández de Lizardi (1776–1827), poet, pamphleteer, humanitarian, and Mexico's first novelist. Living in poverty, peddling his poems and pamphlets on the streets, serving several terms in jail but seldom permitting himself to be silenced, he ridiculed and reproved all the errors, abuses, follies, and vices of his day, took his stand for religious toleration, emancipation of the Negro slaves, free and compulsory education, reading societies where books could be rented cheaply, abolition of large landed estates, and distribution of lands among the poor. Although he attended college for a time, Lizardi could not afford the tuition and the fees required for a degree. He achieved literary fame without much aid or direction and was struck down at an early age by tuberculosis.

The other Mexican *pensador* of the early National period was José María Luís Mora (1794–1850), who held several degrees, including the degree of Doctor of Theology, but early became a critic of the wealth, privileges, temporal power, and educational functions of the Roman Catholic Church, and advocated the seizure of its properties, mass education under the direction of laymen and at the expense of the federal government and the various state governments, the expansion of ownership of rural and urban property, and the curtailment of the size and privileges of the army. He thus laid the foundations for the abortive reform movement of 1833–34 (led by Gómez Farías, whom he advised and supported), for the incomplete reforms of the Juárez period, and for some of the drastic changes of the twentieth century. Perhaps this is the reason his fame has increased with the years; but there was a good deal of the aristocrat in Mora despite his meager earthly possessions, for his concept of the sacredness of property, other than that of the church, did not differ from the views of the laissez-faire school of the mid-nineteenth century, and he even advocated fairly large property qualifications for voting and office holding. Journalist, national historian more interested in interpretation than in facts, political theorist and philosopher, economist after a fashion, and educator of some distinction, Mora wrote discourses which are more like those in the *Federalist* than is any other publication of the epoch in Latin America (though he never cited those famous papers and may never have read them).

SOME LITERARY LIGHTS OF THE BOLIVARIAN COUNTRIES

Occupying close to first place in point of time as well as in rank among Latin America's nineteenth-century Humanists was Andrés Bello (1781–1865), a native of Venezuela who spent nineteen years of his life in Europe, mostly in England, and nearly three decades of it in Chile, where he edited newspapers, occupied several government posts, and became the first rector of Chile's National University (inaugurated in 1843). Among his writings were translations of essays on physiology, medicine, physics, and the other sciences; a book on cosmography, "or a description of the universe in accordance with the latest discoveries"; newspaper articles on the free importation of books and freedom and responsibility of journalists, on the chaos of laws in Latin America and the importance of legal codes, on Spanish orthography, and on the annual message of the president of the United States and the comparative influence of public opinion in the two Americas; a poem in praise of poetry; an ode to agriculture in the Torrid Zone, in which he lovingly described the tropical plants and the lush tropical landscapes; a poetic prayer for all mankind; a treatise on international law, the first to appear in the Latin world overseas; a Castillian grammar for use in America, one of the very best ever published; and an address at the opening of the University of Chile so well rounded and forward-looking that it deserves to be copied by the most progressive university presidents of the twentieth century, for he urged equal attention to the sciences and the humanities and advised American scholars to utilize source materials available in the New World and make their own first-hand investigations.

If it seems to be an inadequate tribute to recall that Venezuela produced a Bolívar, a Sucre, and a Bello during this early National period, then three other names may be selected at random and added for good measure: Juan Vicente González (1808–66), editor, educator, historian, pamphleteer, and "Hercules" of polemics; Cecilio Acosta (1818–81), lawyer, journalist, poet, philosopher, and moving orator; and Antonio Leocadio Guzmán (1801–84), linguist, polemist, somewhat prejudiced historian, demagogue who knew how to stir the masses by his spell-binding harangues, and father of Antonio Guzmán Blanco, who dominated Venezuela for two decades. But Bello, to whom Chile may have as just claim as Venezuela, was at once the most versatile, the most scholarly, and the best balanced of this literary group, although more aristocratic than any of them, and, if the others are to be judged by their utterances alone, less vehemently concerned with the improvement of the lower classes.

Colombia produced an array of journalists and jurisconsults, novelists and dramatists, literary critics and historians, essayists, political theorists, and social philosophers. Among them was José Eusebio Caro (1817–53), who pioneered in Colombian journalism, both political and literary, held several government posts, sang of family life, freedom, and love of country, and put a poem [5] in the mouth of the "last Inca":

> To-day arriving on Pichincha's slope,
> The deadly cannon of the whites I flee,
> Like the sun a wanderer, like the sun aflame,
> Like the sun free.

> Upon my tomb the condor will descend,
> From heaven the condor, bird of liberty,
> And building there its nest, will hatch its young,
> Unknown and free.

Among the Colombian literary group were also Jorge Isaacs (1837–95), son of a Spanish mother and an English Jew converted to the Roman Catholic faith, poet of slight distinction, historian of a radical revolution, and author of *María,* a novel that went rapidly through dozens of editions because it was replete with realistic detail and delicate romantic melancholy that captured the attention and expressed the sentiments of an entire epoch and a whole people; José Manuel Restrepo (1781–1863), author of a four-volume history of the struggle for independence in northern South America that has never been surpassed; and José María Samper (1828–88), the most versatile of a highly polished and versatile group: poet, playwright, and historian; journalist and editor at one time or another of a dozen newspapers and two or three literary magazines; lawyer, diplomat, politician, and writer of books of travel; author, in short, of a score of works and a successful businessman besides!

One of Samper's most illuminating works is a little volume published in Paris in 1861, an *Essay on the Political Revolutions . . . of the Hispanic-American Republics* in which he tried to uncover the causes of these frequent civil wars and describe in broad strokes the barriers to social and economic progress in these countries. He dwelt upon the character of the Spanish Conquest, which he described as an "armed speculation"; upon the repressions of three centuries of Spanish rule, during which the despotic monarchy and the church condemned the Spanish Americans to the bleak "obscurity of an immense colonial prison"; upon the militarism engendered by the long struggle for independence; upon the primitive and mixed races that nobody had taken the trouble to enlighten and rescue from disease, hunger, and ignorance; upon the pride and vanity of the whites, which he considered a heritage from Spain and its colonial system; upon the disposition, also handed down from the Colonial epoch, to consider government as an end in itself instead of a means of stimulating social and economic advance; and upon the immense handicaps of topography and climate. Centering attention for a moment upon the intellectual and spiritual phase of the struggle, he described it as a contest between the liberty and enlightenment of the nineteenth century and the obscurantism and intolerance bequeathed by sixteenth-century Spain.

But Samper, at this time at least, was not a pessimist. He was a member of a Romantic school that believed in the unlimited potentialities of human progress. He advocated mass education by every available means; separation of Church and State; promotion of transportation, communication, and immigration; scientific surveys of natural resources; a wholesome balance between laissez-faire and state promotion of enterprises that private capital was reluctant to undertake; consolidation of the smaller republics so as to provide more adequate public revenues and greater international prestige and influence; fuller local autonomy to permit the people to gain experience in the management of public affairs as the national units were cemented by better means of transportation and communication; and reduction of the size of armies while improving their equipment and efficiency, excluding the regular military forces from politics, and training a military reserve of citizens with Switzerland as a model. Later Samper abandoned his role as a radical and freethinker, re-entered the Roman Catholic Church, described his doubts and anguish and their resolution in a little volume entitled the *History of a Soul,* tried to reconcile the radical and the moderate Liberals, became engulfed in the torrent of reaction, and ended his days in deep spiritual depression.

Ecuador's literary fame would not be insignificant if it had to be based for the early National period upon the works of a single man; for Ecuador's Juan Montalvo (1832–89) was a giant among polemists, a remarkable essayist, and one of the Spanish world's great masters of prose. Although he spent most of his life in hurling literary explosives at Ecuador's dictators (Gabriel García Moreno and Ignacio Veintemilla), he found time to write *Seven Treatises* and *Chapters that Cervantes Forgot,* works which, because of their refined elegance, noble sentiment, and rebellious spirit, won for him eternal renown. But while Montalvo stood out above the other Ecuadorian writers he did not stand alone. Ecuador's early literary group, to name only a few, included José Joaquin Olmedo (1790–1847), politician, diplomat, journalist, and poet, who, at Bolívar's suggestion, wrote an immortal ode to the victory at Junín; Juan León Mera (1832–94), poet, novelist after the manner of James Fenimore Cooper, literary critic, historian of Ecuadorian literature, antiquarian, and amateur scientist; voluminous writers on Ecuadorian history, such as Pedro Fermín Ceballos (1812–93) and Federico González Suárez (1844–1917); and Ecuador's Liberal pioneer, Vicente Rocafuerte (1783–1847), who translated some of the works of Thomas Paine, Thomas Jefferson, and John Quincy Adams, wrote essays on the last phase of the independence movement in Mexico, on a new system of jails, and on the advantages of religious toleration, and published a text on moral philosophy, based mainly upon extracts from the Bible, for use in Lancasterian schools—whose writings, in short, fill sixteen small volumes recently published by the Ecuadorian government.

Peru of the early National epoch had almost a plethora of poets, some reactionary or cynical with the cynicism of frustration, but more of the Romantic type, who imitated their European masters with servility, each trying to excel the rest in disappointment and to utter louder lamentations than his colleagues. But Peru also produced Francisco de Paula González Vijil (1792–1875), a liberal padre with a political urge, who wrote long treatises defending the state against "the pretensions of the Roman Curia" and the American bishops against the encroachments of the papacy, and published numerous pamphlets advocating religious toleration, mass education, and the suppression of tithes and ecclesiastical privileges, or opposing dictatorship and the death penalty for crime. Peru produced Clorinda Matto de Turner (1854–1909), wife of an Englishman, who published in 1889 a novel, *Birds Without Nest,* which depicted the wretchedness of the Peruvian Indians and the depravity of their oppressors, a work destined to be followed later by many others dwelling on the same theme. Still more important, Peru furnished the environment and historical background for an imposing literary personality named Ricardo Palma (1833–1919), who not only composed verses during his early years but began to publish in 1872 an almost endless series of *Traditions,* nine volumes of historical anecdotes filled with wit, humor, satire, merriment, and a little scandal and prevarication which put him in a class by himself. And the Peruvian literary group included some scholars who delved into the history of their country, such as Sebastián Lorente (1813–84) and Mariano Felipe Paz Soldán (1821–86).

Even turbulent Bolivia could offer a few journalists, *raconteurs* of exploring expeditions, and short-story writers, who fawned upon or denounced its despots, issued their verses under the title *Tears* or *Melancholies,* or published tales woven about the history and traditions of a sufficiently distant past. One of its literary lights was the Argentine wife of the rabble-rouser Belzu, who spent most of her time in Peru after the assassination of her husband in 1865; and the terrible Melgarejo was lauded and advised by a lawyer-journalist named Mariano Muñoz. What has been said of army-ridden Bolivia can also be said of dictator-ridden Paraguay; but space does not allow for elaboration.

A SAMPLE OF THE LITERATI OF URUGUAY, CHILE, AND ARGENTINA

Many of Argentina's literary figures of the early National period began their careers in exile in Uruguay or Chile during the long years of the Rosas tyranny and stimulated the literary movement in the two countries in which they found refuge. But there is no doubt that Uruguay and Chile would have produced their literati without these refugees.

The verses of Uruguay's patriarch of letters, Francisco Acuña de Figueroa (1790–1862) were assembled and published as early as 1846, in a collection which filled twelve volumes! Among his poems were the Uruguayan national hymn and heart-stirring stanzas on an African mother, intended to put an end to the slave trade under the Uruguayan flag. Of greater merit were the works of Alejandro Magariños Cervantes (1825–93), poet, playwright, and novelist who sang of palms, Plata breezes, and ombú trees and portrayed Uruguayan pastoral life in all of its romantic and rowdy phases. His most popular work was *Caramurú,* a thrilling novel dealing with Indians, Gauchos, dangerous love, and daring escapades. Toward the middle of the period Juan Zorilla de San Martín (1855–1931) began his notable literary work, publishing his first volume of poems in 1877, reading his patriotic ode "La Leyenda Patria" in 1879 at the unveiling of an independence monument, and publishing his masterpiece in 1888, a long epic poem, or novel in verse, entitled *Tabaré,* which dealt with warfare between the Indians and whites and the tragic love of a Charrua half-breed for a Spanish maid, and ended after the death of the hero with these moving words: "The Indian is silent forever, like his race, like a desert, a tongueless mouth, a heavenless eternity." (Cooper or Longfellow would certainly have sent the noble half-breed to the "Happy Hunting Ground" in spite of his heavy taint of Caucasian blood.) *Tabaré* made its author famous throughout the Spanish-speaking world. Among Uruguayans dealing with the national history of their country were Francisco Bauzá (1851–99), who never got beyond the short colonial background except on the literary theme, and Isidoro De-Marie (1815–1906), who also published three volumes of biographical sketches.

Chile's early literary movement got its start under the leadership of the Venezuelan Andrés Bello and a Spaniard named José Joaquín Mora, and under the provocation of the Argentine exiles. The Chilean elite of the early National epoch, like that of the other major countries, included able journalists, polemists, novelists, dramatists, historians, and *pensadores;* but comparatively few poets were among them, perhaps because of the somber and practical Basque origin of most of the whites. Perhaps the Chilean historians, probably the ablest of the period in Latin America, may be considered as an almost satisfactory compensation for the lack of versifiers. Among the most prolific of the writers who concerned themselves with Chile's past were Benjamín Vicuña Mackenna (1831–86), part Scot, Miguel Luís Amunátegui (1828–88), and Diego Barros Arana (1830–1907). José Toribio Medina (1852–1930), an amazingly industrious historian and bibliographer, began his long and very productive career in the middle 1880's.

In the field of fiction the Chilean elite of the epoch may stake their reputation without much risk on a single towering figure, Alberto Blest Gana (1830–1920), whose literary career falls into two distinct periods, separated by a long hiatus during which he paid the pleasant penalties of fame by being thrust into the diplomatic service as minister to France and England. He began with short stories on Chilean themes; won the prize in the national literary contest of 1860 with a novel entitled *The Arithmetic of Love;* published his masterpiece, *Martín Rivas,* in 1862; and closed the first period of his activity the next year with *The Ideal of a Madcap.* Blest Gana attacked some aspects of Chilean society without mercy; but he was a deft portrayer of social customs and a close observer of the national life, and the Chileans liked his works. In fact, they rated him as Spanish America's greatest novelist. But at least one other Chilean who wrote fiction, a member of the Blest Gana school named Martín Palma (1821–84), who affiliated himself with a radical group, deserves passing attention for his frank confession of social and political purposes. Among the Chileans who went to California in 1849 in search of gold, Palma came back a freethinking reformer full of zeal for the Chilean underdogs. Beginning his agitation as a pamphleteer, he published his first novel, *The Secrets of the People* in 1869, and it was greeted with general applause in spite of, or perhaps partly because of, aristocratic hostility. He then expanded the work into four volumes with an introduction in which he said: "We have in mind the improvement of the people. Our customs are examined attempting to improve them, our vices to correct them, our virtues to enhance them . . . for the sake of exalting the dignity and independence of man." [6] Palma was didactic, but he inculcated his lessons cleverly with striking portrayals of poverty and vice. In a later novel, *The Mysteries of the Confessional,* published in 1874, and afterwards in a three-volume English translation under the title of *Julia Ingrand: A Tale of the Confessional,* he gave his anticlerical propensities full play.

The Chilean poets might be omitted entirely if one of them had not fitted himself so neatly into the plans of the more renowned reformers of his day. Eusebio Lillo (1826–1910), journalist as well as poet, was among the founders of an influential literary journal and the editor of a little magazine with a title that embodied its purpose, *The Friend of the People.* In his younger days, as one might expect, he wrote two cantos entitled *Crazy with Love;* then he composed the Chilean national hymn; but when he published a "Hymn to Equality" and helped to stir up a revolt by his polemics he was banished from the country (late in 1851). Taking refuge in Peru, he published a long poem, *Fragments of the Memoirs of a Proscript,* in which he recounted his experiences in exile and described the ancient and noble city of Lima in verses disclosing a delicate feeling for nature in its kindlier moods. Next he applied his imaginative and speculative gifts to mining in Bolivia, and finally came home a wealthy man, to join Santa María, Balmaceda, and the anticlerical reformers, hold important government posts, and become the executor of Balmaceda's will after the reformer-president committed suicide.

Chile's *pensadores* were also *luchadores,* fighters for social, political, and intellectual regeneration. The two who bear the title without much contradiction are Francisco Bilbao (1823–65) and José Victorino Lastarria (1817–88).

Bilbao was a reformer and social philosopher who thought he had discovered the causes for the misery of the Chilean common people in the Spanish heritage, the exploitations of the oligarchy, and the repressions of the Roman Catholic Church. "Our past is Spain," he wrote. "Spain is the Middle Ages. The Middle Ages were Catholicism and feudalism." Both feudalism and Roman Catholicism, declared Bilbao, continued to impose their fetters on Latin America, whose progress was further hampered by a multiplicity of bellicose states too poor and weak to push the engines of progress. The two Americas presented a striking contrast, the English United States, free and progressive, and the Spanish

"Disunited States," impoverished and suffocated by their past. "In the United States we see all the elements of their history united in a movement toward greater and greater liberty. In the Disunited States we see the impotent efforts of liberty falling and rising again, always threatened, never secure, living through all the vicissitudes of a terrible alternation between despotism and attempts at freedom." [7] In Europe during the 1840's, Bilbao witnessed the failure of popular uprisings there but returned home in the hope of applying the ideas of the French insurgents in Chile. Organizing the Equality Society shortly after he arrived and arousing the people from one end of the country to the other, he became a ringleader in the frustrated revolt of 1851. Banished the same year, he went to Peru and attempted to spread his ideas there. He wrote a pamphlet to explain how the people might be governed without destroying their liberty, and a biography of one of the Peruvian saints in order to contrast earlier saintly virtues with the vices of the day and show how love, charity, and sacrifice were needed to improve the sad condition of the Indians and other colored races in that country. And, as if this were not enough, he attacked most of the dogmas of the church. Compelled to seek another place of refuge before the end of the decade, he managed somehow to assemble the funds for a second sojourn in Europe, but soon returned to America and established his residence in Argentina. Here, among other works, he wrote his *Law of History,* which, after the rejection of many previous philosophies on that subject, turned out to be the law of human progress through Divine inspiration, freedom, and brotherly love; and, more important still, he published his *American Gospel,* the gospel he had been trying to persuade his fellow-Americans to accept ever since his return from France in 1850—the gospel of "un-Spanishing" themselves, of emancipating themselves from the habits, customs, and attitudes inherited from Spain—in short, the gospel of Liberty, Equality, and Fraternity. He descended to his grave in Argentina in 1865, after two decades of shouting in the wilderness. He had demanded too much too soon; but he had planted some seed in soil not altogether barren and the harvest would eventually come.

Lastarria was less impetuous than Bilbao and more influential in his time. His intellectual interests were broad and diverse. He wrote on history, geography, law, politics, literature, education, and social philosophy; taught some of these subjects in the colleges and the university; and became a patron of young men of letters and a fairly successful politician, holding high government posts for many years. His ideas about the baneful influence of the colonial heritage were similar to those of Bilbao; and although less hostile toward the church, he also agreed with Bilbao in advocating the complete separation of Church and State.

But he did not approve of the radical ideas of the Revolutionists of 1848, either in Europe or in Latin America, and he not only lamented the miscegenation that had occurred in Latin America but seemed pessimistic regarding the potentialities of the mixed and primitive elements in its population. Compared with Bilbao he was aristocratic and moderately conservative. While advocating government support of education and government promotion of transportation and immigration, he recoiled from any drastic expansion of the functions of the state, especially its interposition in production and distribution, because he feared that the end would be "stateism" and the destruction of liberty. He felt that individual freedom, an abundance of well-selected immigrants, and practical education for the masses were the safest and surest means of economic progress.

Argentina of the early National epoch could safely rest its case on the literary works of two tall figures, Domingo F. Sarmiento (1811–88) and Juan Bautista Alberdi (1810–84); but this would require the neglect of the poets—not to mention the novelists, dramatists, and historians—and Argentina swarmed with poets. Neither Sarmiento nor Alberdi made much effort to write verses, and Alberdi even thought that Spanish America had far too many poets. Able and many-sided as these two personalities were, especially Sarmiento, they could not fully incarnate the intellectual and emotional life, the vigorous vitality, of this immense and turbulent land. They failed, for example, to foresee the growing affections of their people for the Gauchos, whom Alberdi hardly mentions at all and whom Sarmiento, who has been called the "Gaucho in literature," openly condemns as barbarians even though secretly he may have felt the magnetic attraction of affinity.

These rough mounted men of the great plains pulled at the heart-strings of most sophisticated Argentines and attained mundane immortality as they left the pampas forever and rode their fleet ponies out into the great beyond. Crude, cruel, and pugnacious as they were, they had their minstrels, their *payadores,* who improvised their mournful songs as they strummed their worn Spanish guitars and produced their poetry, their folksongs, of the open range:

> The palm-tree is over the grass,
>   The sky is over the tree;
> I am over my horse,
>   My sombrero is over me!
>
> I wish that I had been born
>   Wild grass out on the plain;
> And never had seen you passing,
>   And never had suffered this pain.[8]

The pain he suffered was some kind of love pain. But it would disappear and so would he, and then Argentina would feel the pangs of regret and nearly every Argentino would want to be a Gaucho or else have the cowboys return from their last long ride. From this nostalgia sprang the Gaucho epic which had its vogue decade after decade. The great masters in this form of literature were Hilario Ascasubi (1807–75), whose most popular work was *Santos Vega, El Payador,* and José Hernández (1834–86), whose masterpiece was *Martín Fierro:*

> And this is my pride: to live as free
> As the bird that cleaves the sky;
> I build no nest in the careworn earth,
> Where sorrow is long and short is mirth;
> And when I am gone none will grieve for me
> And none care where I lie.[9]

But old Martín was mistaken. Almost every literate Argentino grieved for him and set up such a loud wail that Hernández had to bring him back. In 1879, seven years after he wrote of the disappearance of Martín Fierro, Hernández published *The Return of Martín Fierro.* Cowboys and Indians improve when they become rare and when pent-up urbanites begin to seek compensating adventure in books about the faraway and the long-ago.

It is a pity to neglect the numerous Argentine poets who dealt with other themes, but the misdemeanor must be committed if any space is to be conserved for the historians and for Alberdi and Sarmiento. Worse still, the novelists and dramatists must also be omitted. The most outstanding writers on Argentine history during the early National epoch were Vicente Fidel López (1815–1903), Mariano Pelliza (1837–1902), Bartolomé Mitre (1821–1906), and Adolfo Saldías (1859–1914). Their works are usually characterized by a fluent style and a somewhat exaggerated nationalism. López also wrote historical novels and made contributions to literary magazines. Mitre, still more versatile, was not only historian, general, and politician; in his younger days he was a poet who dreamed of the laurels of Homer, and in later years he became the founder of *La Nación,* one of Argentina's great daily newspapers.

But no other Argentine writers of the early National period have risen so high as Alberdi and Sarmiento in the admiration of the critics, whether of Argentina or other American countries. These two have been elevated to that sparsely populated Seventh Heaven, perhaps higher than Mount Olympus itself, to which only *pensadores* are ever admitted. They were not only literary masters when they half tried; they were social philosophers, at times almost profound. Alberdi had no love for ornate and grandiloquent phrases; he preferred pungent "punch lines" whose meaning could not be mistaken. Sarmiento could make words do anything, but he rarely attempted to make them rhyme. Both wrote with a purpose and seldom without effect. Sarmiento produced fifty-two volumes—far too many; only about one in ten represented him at his best. Alberdi turned out less than half that number, the majority not published until after his death, but a larger fraction of them approached the top range of his capacities. If Alberdi is examined first, Sarmiento will seem to be overshadowed, and the effect is likely to be reversed if Sarmiento is given priority, for they were contemporaries with more or less the same ideas, emotions, and objectives, Sarmiento more prolific and passionate and Alberdi calmer and rather more profound.

Sarmiento leaped into fame in the 1840's by the publication of four books: his fictionalized biography of Facundo, adding the subtitle *Civilization and Barbarism* to emphasize the heavy downward drag of the thinly settled pampas on the national culture, and in order to flay the cowboy cut-throats and their ruthless leaders; his recollections of his native province of San Juan (*Recuerdos de [una] Provincia*), in which he recorded his hardships and his efforts to educate himself and others, described his family and his teachers, and told of his encounters with the tyrants of hill and plain; his *Travels in Europe, Africa, and America,* one of the world's great travelogues; and *Popular Education,* which contained the educational philosophy that he distilled from his experiences in Argentina and Chile and from his observations during his tour of investigation abroad. These four, all published before his fortieth year, the last of them, the *Recuerdos,* appearing in 1850, were his best works.[10] They contained in substance the message of his life. Nearly all that he sent through the presses later was repetition, deemed necessary to clarify, elaborate, defend, and make effective his gospel.

"To govern is to educate." This was his main theme. Without educating the sovereign, without educating all the people, there could be no genuine republic and little national progress. Public education is the duty and function of the state and should be supported by taxation. Teachers in the public schools should be trained laymen with the zeal of the early Christian missionaries. The model and the tremendous results could be observed in the United States, where the vast majority participated in politics, obeyed the law, acquired skills in agriculture, industry, and commerce, made the nation rich, and laid the foundations for literature, art, architecture, and all phases of higher culture. It was the business of government to provide the conditions for progress by equalizing opportunities, setting free the genius of the individual, and attracting immigrants from the most advanced countries to stimulate economic development and furnish the natives good examples of industry, thrift, and intelligence in economic activity.

Regarding the handicaps of colonial heritage, Sarmiento had less to say than many other Spanish American writers of his time, although he felt that contemporary Spain had little or nothing to contribute to these new nations overseas, save possibly the manual labor of her poor sons. Until late in life Sarmiento looked upon scanty, widely scattered, and disassociated population as the major handicap retarding Argentine development. He found it difficult to wax enthusiastic about the virtues of frontiersmen, although those of the Anglo-American West almost aroused his admiration and he later remarked that his *Facundo* was designed in part as propaganda. Toward the end of his life he began to feel that neither education nor immigration was effecting the transformation he expected and tried to bring all Spanish America under the focus of his powerful mind in order to discover some other cause than the "barbarizing" influence of the frontier for the prevailing turbulence and backwardness. In one of his last books, *Conflicto y Armonías de las Razas,* he seemed to find it in the difficult problem of amalgamating the conflicting races and cultures, and perhaps in a fatal inferiority of the Indians, Africans, and mixbloods. But his mind was already impaired by age and ill health and the volume was never finished, so that the reader cannot be sure whether these were the tentative musings of an ailing and disillusioned old man or the final revision of a philosophy of history.

Alberdi devoted his intellectual and literary talents to journalism, jurisprudence (especially constitutional law), and economics. Although a year older than Sarmiento and possessing a college and university education which his great contemporary could not afford, Alberdi's rise to fame was slower. His first important book, and by far his most famous, did not come off the press until 1852. Entitled *Bases and Points of Departure for the Political Organization of the Argentine Republic* and intended to bring about the establishment of a constitutional federalism permitting full civil rights, including religious toleration, in the hope of promoting liberty and order and a rapid influx of immigrants, the volume promptly went through several editions and exerted a profound influence. Succeeding works, which flowed freely from his pen, were mainly elaborations of his *Bases* and treatises on the constitution of 1853, itself largely embodying his principles and suggestions. In 1876 he published a life of William Wheelwright, a Massachusetts promoter who built railroads and established some other public services in Argentina and Chile, in which this Yankee pioneer was praised for his able attacks on two of Latin America's enemies, the wilderness and lack of transportation. Perhaps Alberdi's most significant and interesting work, aside from his *Bases,* is his *Economic Studies,* published after his death, in which he attempts to analyze the economic problems of Latin America and the causes that retarded its advance.

Alberdi matched Sarmiento's "To govern is to educate" with his maxim of "To govern in America is to populate," to settle the vast stretches of vacant land with inhabitants able and willing to work. It was not that Alberdi did not favor education just as Sarmiento favored immigration; there was only a difference in emphasis. In fact, Alberdi considered well-selected immigrants as the best agents of practical instruction. "Every European who comes to our shores," he declared, "brings us more civilization in the habits he spreads among our people than many books of philosophy. The perfection that is not seen, touched, and felt is not well understood. A hard-working man is the most edifying catechism." The education of the masses should have practical utility. Teaching the common people to read without teaching them the skills to earn a better living and instilling a desire to improve their level of life would do them little good; the courses of study in the academies, institutes, and universities should include more than Latin, literature, law, and theology. What have these educational centers been but "factories of charlatanism, idleness, demagoguery, and titled arrogance?" "These countries need more engineers, geologists, and naturalists than lawyers and theologians. . . . Literature has fulfilled its mission . . . in South America." It should no longer be permitted to strangle science. Economic pursuits are the best means of teaching the youth good behavior. "Industry is the supreme tranquilizer. It leads to happiness and wealth and through these to order and liberty; examples of this are England and the United States." [11]

The habits, customs, attitudes, and value-patterns inherited from Spain should be cast aside; Latin America needs more scientists, technicians, and skilled laborers not afraid of hard work and fewer poets, politicians, journalists, clergymen, and army officers. It needs greater individual initiative and stronger ambition for material improvements, citizens more ready to collaborate in private enterprises for the common good and less inclined to look to political authorities for salvation. "The peoples of the North have not owed their prosperity and greatness to the power of their governments but to the power of their individuals. These are the products of egotism rather than patriotism. By making his own private fortune each individual contributes to that of his country." The Latin Americans will never be saved if they wait for some patriot to save them. "Societies which expect their happiness from the hands of their governments are hoping for something which is contrary to nature." Nations become rich, powerful, and highly civilized by virtue of the work of free individuals who are masters of their persons, properties, lives, and homes. To proceed on any other principle is to erect an omnipotent state, which is the negation of liberty and will become a fatal barrier to material and spiritual progress. So wrote Alberdi at the age of seventy, citing at one point Adam Smith's *Wealth of Nations*.[12] He and Sarmiento came nearer viewing their world through Anglo-Saxon eyes than did any other Latin-American writers; but it is likely that neither ever established a model workshop or farm, or ever soiled his hands with physical labor if he could avoid it.

℥⍟ SOME BRAZILIAN LITERARY FIGURES

Brazil's population, outnumbered in the 1820's only by one other Latin-American country (Mexico), had outgrown Mexico's by some 3,000,000 to 4,000,000 by the 1880's and was several times larger than that of any other nation of the region. But Brazil's progress in education was slow, less rapid than Argentina's or even Chile's, Uruguay's, or Costa Rica's. The constitution of 1824 consigned primary and secondary education to the provinces, which disclosed little zeal for the enlightenment of the people. The central government was responsible only for higher education and elementary education in the capital. At the end of the imperial period the total enrollment in the primary schools was no more than 225,000, hardly a tenth of the school-age inhabitants, and secondary schools were far from adequate. Opportunities for professional education, to which few besides the sons of the oligarchy had access, were much better, especially in law, engineering, art, and literature; but it is likely that the number of literate Brazilians, even in the late 1880's, did not exceed 1,500,000 out of a total population of some 13,000,000 and that a considerable number of these had little interest in books. Yet, in spite of this widespread inability or indisposition to read, the reading public in Brazil probably had been larger since the middle of the century than in any other Latin-American nation.

Whatever its comparative size, it was assiduously cultivated by the Brazilian elite, who were no less articulate, if somewhat less versatile, than the little aristocracies of letters in the Spanish American countries. It is true that the Brazilians had less serious political problems to worry them, especially after 1850 and before 1890; but they could agitate the slavery issue, air other social enormities, express their republican longings, portray their gorgeous landscapes, or find inspiration in the vanishing Indian and frontier life or the age-old themes of love, loneliness, and human tragedy.

Although one of Brazil's early patriots and intellectuals, José Bonifácio de Andrada e Silva (1763–1838), was an able scientist as well as a poet and a politician, the Brazilian intelligentsia of the early National period were not much interested in any of the sciences except medicine, mathematics, and botany. They devoted most of their time to poetry, fiction, political oratory, journalism, and history. There were almost no social philosophers and very few dramatists.

Among the writers dealing with Brazilian history were José Ignacio de Abreu e Lima (1796–1869), Francisco Adolpho Varnhagen (1816–78), and João M. Pereira da Silva (1819–98). Among the political orators and publicists were Joaquím Nabuco (1849–1910), who was also a poet, a diplomat, and a reformer noted for his antislavery campaigns and his interest in public education, and Ruy Barbosa (1849–1923), a very able lawyer and a gifted linguist as well as a talented journalist and a moving orator. One of Brazil's outstanding international lawyers of this period was Antonio Pereira Pinto.

In the field of poetry only a few stand out above the multitude of mediocrities. Brazil's pre-eminent verse writer was Olavo Bilac (1865–1918), one of the most gifted poets in the Portuguese world. António Gonçalves Dias (1823–64) won the hearts of his countrymen by his "Song of Exile" and his skillful utilization of Indian themes. Casimiro de Abreu (1837–60) was a very moving singer of *saudades,* reeking with homesickness and nostalgia. Antonio de Castro Alves (1847–71) was a humanitarian in verse, the flaming firebrand of the abolition movement, which he did not live to see completed. His most famous poems are his "Voices from Africa" and "The Slave Ship." Some critics have called him a "condor bard" because of his soaring grandiloquence: "Christ! In vain you died upon a mountain. . . . Your blood did not erase from my forehead the original stain. . . . My children are the cattle of the universe, and I a universal pasture. Today America feeds on my blood. . . . Enough, O Lord. . . . For two thousand years I have been wailing a cry. . . . Hear my call yonder in the infinite." [13] The slave ship floated the Brazilian flag:

My God! My God! but what flag is this that impudently flutters at the masthead. Silence, Muse . . . weep, and weep so much that the banner will be bathed in your tears. . . . Green-gold banner of my country, kissed and blown by Brazilian breezes, standard that enfolds in the light of the sun the divine promises of hope. . . . Horrible fatality that overwhelms the mind! Let the waves through which Columbus opened a path . . . shatter this hour the polluted ship! The infamy is too much! . . . Rise up from your ethereal realm ye heroes of the New World! Andrada! tear that banner down! Columbus! shut the gates of your sea! [14]

One of the earliest of the Brazilian novelists was Joaquím Manoel de Macedo (1820–82), who wrote love stories in which he portrayed the frivolous society of Rio or Brazilian rustic life and made an irresistible appeal to the women. His *Little Brown Girl,* which appeared in 1849, was so well received that he soon followed it up with *The Blond Young Man.* José M. de Alencar (1829–77) not only wrote tales of Indian life filled with descriptions of nature that rivaled Cooper and with noble savages that fell in love with aristocratic Portuguese, his most popular works of this type being *O Guarany* and *Iracema;* he also dealt with the mining regions, with the men of the arid backlands, and with the cowboys on the distant frontiers. Alfredo d'Escragnolle Taunay (1843–99) published among other works of merit a tragic love story of the Matto Grosso jungle entitled *Inocencia,* which the literary critics associate with Isaacs' *María,* sometimes awarding the prize to the Brazilian. Brazil's greatest literary personality, Joaquím Machado de Assís (1839–1908), poet, playwright, and novelist, did not reach the zenith of his productive powers until after the beginning of the republican epoch.

CHAPTER XXII

A Summary View of Foreign Impacts

🦅 EXPANSION OF FOREIGN RELATIONSHIPS

The severance of the political ties that had bound the Latin Americans for three centuries to overseas powers marked the beginning of a new and broader exposure to the great formative forces of the nineteenth century. Independence itself had been largely the result of external factors: new ideas regarding the rights of man, which increased the dissatisfaction of Latin Americans with their colonial status; rivalries of power politics and mercantile interests, which provided them with funds obtained from levies on foreign trade and shielded them from outside interference in behalf of the imperial nations struggling to retain them; loans from foreign speculators expecting large returns on their capital; assistance from foreign seamen and soldiers motivated by eagerness for gain and adventure, as well as by devotion to liberty. The people of Latin America continued to feel the weight of traditional institutions and habits, but now they were open to the penetration of ideas and interests from every quarter. British political institutions and creeds, especially the landed aristocracy, the parliamentary system, and the doctrine of free enterprise; such political concepts from the United States as federalism, the separation and balance of powers, bills of rights, and state responsibility for education; the political and social philosophy, revolutions, and towering political figures of France; Europe's literary forms and moods, such as Classicism and Romanticism; a continuous stream of merchants and emigrants; thrusts of political and economic power from the United States and the major European countries—these were some of the significant foreign impacts after 1825.

But there were still others. Ill-defined boundaries between the Latin-American countries and the United States or the remnants of European empires gave rise to territorial disputes. Latin America's geographical position between the Occident and the Orient involved the region in international rivalries for naval bases, coaling stations, and commercial routes across the American isthmus. Perhaps most important of all, Latin-American military conflicts tended to provoke foreign interposition in the form of mediation or coercion. This was fundamental and inevitable; the Latin-American nations could not indulge in prolonged civil wars and delay the development of their resources without involving themselves in trouble with the more dynamic foreign countries. With a population of only some 20,000,000 at the beginning of the National epoch and hardly more than 62,000,000 in 1900, the Latin-American nations occupied a seventh of the land surface of the earth; and the great powers were not losing any of their vigor by becoming more highly industrialized and capitalistic. The glories of empire, in the old territorial sense, might be fading somewhat, or a combination of circumstances might limit imperial opportunities in the Americas; but the demands for food and raw materials and for outlets for manufactured goods, capital, technical skills, and surplus population were growing stronger.

Disorderly as the Latin-American countries were during this early National period, they did not by any means repel all traders, emigrants, or investors. Their foreign commerce increased in value from $50,000,-000 or $60,000,000 in 1825 to $700,000,000 in 1870, around $800,-000,000 in 1885 (including Cuba and Puerto Rico), and more than $1,000,000,000 in 1900. Foreign nationals residing in the region probably numbered close to 1,000,000 in 1885 and three times as many in 1900, the majority of them in Argentina, Brazil, Uruguay, Chile, and Mexico, but from a few hundred to several thousand in the other countries. Foreign investments, including those of alien residents loath to become citizens, perhaps aggregated not less than $5,000,000,000 by the century's end. Traders, especially salesmen, pursued mankind everywhere. Great open spaces and unexploited resources in Latin America served as a challenge to emigrants and venture capital, and even revolutions furnished golden opportunities for traffic in firearms and munitions.

These expanding interests of the foreign nations meant that Latin-American domestic disorders and violence produced ever-increasing reverberations in the major capitals of the Western World. By pressing forward to claim these countries for capitalistic culture, the great powers embroiled them in disputes over injuries to alien persons and property and determined in considerable degree their role in the broad economy of the West. The functions assigned to the Latin Americans until somehow they could manage to exert greater influence in determining their destiny, were twofold: the production of food and raw materials for export, and the reception of finished goods, capital, technology, business management, and emigrants from the more crowded and more intensively developed nations. With the orientation and dynamics of their economies thus largely directed from the outside, their most efficient industries tended to be those producing for the foreign market, some of them owned and operated, along with most of the more efficient means of transportation, by foreign capitalists. Production for the home market was primitive, haphazard, or incidental. Manufacturing, in particular, lingered largely in the handicraft stage, its output intended mainly for the masses who lacked means to purchase imported goods.

BOUNDARY DISPUTES AND RIVALRIES FOR NAVAL BASES, COALING STATIONS, AND INTEROCEANIC ROUTES

Boundary disputes with foreign powers involved only France, England, and the United States.[1] The boundary between French Guiana and Brazil was not determined until the late 1890's. Fifty years earlier, when the French government disclosed a disposition to enlarge its South American holdings, it was held in check by Great Britain; the final settlement by arbitration may have been influenced in part by the well-known attitude of the United States with respect to European territorial expansion in the New World. The boundaries of both British Guiana and British Honduras were long uncertain, but again the policy of the United States tended to restrain European aggression. British rights of residence, trade, and forest exploitation in Belize were transformed into dominion when the region became a crown colony in the 1860's, but the territorial limits of the colony were not significantly enlarged. The English government revealed some tendencies to expand British Guiana at the expense of Venezuela during the half-century preceding the 1890's; but the interposition of the United States shielded the weaker country from territorial infraction.

It was the United States that extracted the greatest benefits from its boundary dispute with a Latin-American country. The limits between the United States and Mexico had not been fixed when Mexico won its independence. Texas was acquired, it will be recalled, by pacific penetration, revolt, and annexation at the behest of the newly formed Texas Republic. But this did not settle the boundary issue. Mexico's strenuous objection to the annexation, together with the unpaid claims of American citizens against Mexico and expansionist tendencies in the United States, led to the Mexican War of 1846–48 and the annexation of our vast Southwest. And still the boundary was not definitely fixed. The final settlement involved the acquisition of even more territory from Mexico

—the Gadsden Purchase of 1853–54. The efforts of England and France to prevent the expansion of a nation which they considered at the moment a dangerous rival proved futile. Effective restraint required close co-operation among four powers—not only France and England but Mexico and Texas as well—and the risk of war with the United States. The necessary collaboration could not be effected. Mexico lost half of its national domain and might have lost more if domestic discord in the United States had not checkmated the expansionists. The slavery issue was mainly responsible for saving Mexico from further mutilation, just as the problems of Reconstruction and the abatement of greed for territory frustrated the later efforts (1869–73) of a clique of speculators to annex the Dominican Republic.

In the contest for naval bases, coaling stations, and isthmian trade routes at the expense of Latin America, only the United States and Great Britain profited during this period, and their gains were modest.[2] Great Britain permanently annexed the Falkland Islands, to which Argentina had a good claim, in 1833 and the United States made no protest. Citizens of the United States secured all the profitable concessions for the utilization of the isthmian commercial routes; but the Washington government, eager to forestall English expansion from the Belize center, agreed to a treaty in 1850, the Clayton-Bulwer Treaty, which bound each of the contracting powers to refrain from the acquisition of domain or exclusive control of interoceanic routes in the region. Few treaties ever caused greater dissatisfaction in the United States; and yet, despite frequent protests and threats, the agreement was never seriously violated by either party. The rivalry of the Anglo-Saxon powers sometimes set one Central American country against another, but on the whole it tended to shield them from aggression. The United States might have secured a naval base (Samaná Bay) in the Dominican Republic in the late 1850's if England, France, and Spain had not interfered. (Searching for cheaper fertilizer, the United States also considered the acquisition of some guano islands claimed by the Latin-American governments but desisted when no guano was found [Galápagos Islands] or when Latin-American titles proved too strong [Lobos and Aves Islands]. Navassa Island, however, was seized by the Washington government in spite of Haitian protests.)

Only France and Spain, among the European powers, revealed significant imperial aspirations in America during the period under consideration. The French attempt to dominate Mexico will be summarized shortly in another connection. Proffers of a French protectorate made by some of the leaders of the Dominican Republic in the 1840's were rejected by the Paris government, partly because opposition was anticipated from the United States and England. The seizure of this little country by Spain in the early 1860's, while the United States was busy with the Civil War, was at the invitation of the Dominican dictator, Pedro Santana, after he had conducted a fake plebiscite. The ravages of disease and revolution in the colony caused a change in attitude in Madrid and led to Spain's withdrawal early in 1865.

Attempts of the great powers to settle disputes within or among the Latin-American countries rarely succeeded. The most outstanding achievement was the British mediation in the war of 1825–28 between Brazil and Argentina, which resulted in the creation of Uruguay as a buffer between the two contestants. British good offices in the war between Chile and Santa Cruz's Peru-Bolivian Confederation in the late 1830's proved futile, and so did the efforts of United States and European diplomats to terminate the War of the Pacific between the same countries over the nitrate territory in 1879–83. Occasionally, however, the arbitration of boundary disputes by agents of the major powers before such disputes had culminated in war was more successful.

TROUBLES ARISING FROM FOREIGN COMMERCE, IMMIGRANTS, AND INVESTMENTS

Commercial interchange and the migration of capital, technology, and surplus population were perhaps the most important phases of the foreign relations of Latin America even during the early National period. Sometimes constructive and sometimes exploitative, these economic, technical, and immigrant impacts often produced complications and provoked or served as a cloak for aggression.

Most of Latin America's immigrants [3] were supplied by Italy, Spain, and Portugal; but France, the Germanies, Great Britain, and other countries provided enough to cause difficulties in periods of extreme disorder. The major part of the foreign capital during the decades under consideration, excluding the holdings accumulated by immigrants who retained their alien status, was British, and Britishers likewise captured the lion's share of Latin-American foreign trade. French capital and commerce were fairly important from the outset, however, and the United States, various German states, Spain, and other European countries were competitors in trade and to some extent in investment. Citizens of the United States played a surprisingly significant part in the supplying of the new technology, introducing steam engines, cotton gins, some textile machinery, and telephones; constructing a good many railroads, tramways, and gas plants; and operating several steamboat lines.[4]

Nearly all of the Latin-American government bonds sold abroad during the early National period were marketed in England and France, especially England, but a few were disposed of in the United States and probably some elsewhere. The young nations which inherited the old Spanish empire were considerably indebted to British merchants, army and navy officers, and shipowners by the time their struggle for independence terminated; and since Great Britain was the only country in the world at that time with a large accumulation of capital, it was but natural that these new nations should have floated their first issues of government securities in the London market. It was a period of frantic speculation in England, destined, of course, to end in a tremendous financial panic. The face value of Spanish American bond flotations during the years 1822–25 aggregated £17,929,000 and Brazilian sales raised the total to £21,129,000! Every Latin-American nation in existence at the time marketed one or more loans in London, with the exception of Argentina, Francia's hermit Paraguay, Boyer's island republic of Haiti (which floated a 30,000,000-franc issue in Paris), and Bolivia, which had just been born. No doubt some of these four would have been included in the speculation, which also embraced canals, pearl fishing, mining, and real estate, if the panic had not come too swiftly. Even the fictitious "kingdom of Poyais," a mythological realm reputed to be located somewhere in Central America, sold an issue of £200,000! The Mexican national government and one of the Mexican cities borrowed a nominal total of £7,000,000. Bolívar's *La Gran Colombia* borrowed £6,750,000; Brazil, £3,200,000; Peru £1,816,000; Chile, £1,000,000; and the Central American Confederation, £163,000—before the market collapsed. A loan of £1,000,000 went to the province of Buenos Aires, but none to the weak and fleeting Argentine national governments, perhaps because nobody thought of it in time.

Unscrupulous merchant bankers put out false propaganda, rigged the market, fleeced the Latin-American governments and British investors, and made enormous profits for themselves. The disorderly Latin-American countries might have failed to meet their obligations in any case, but the just conviction that they had been cheated made defaults a mathematical certainty. By the end of 1827 every one of them had ceased to service its bonds. Payments were resumed by Brazil in 1829; other governments continued in default for decades. There is no way to measure the extent to which these imprudent issues injured their credit, since it was also affected by their civil and international wars, but it is a fact that most of them had to postpone further flotations for thirty or forty years. Parts of these early debts were inherited by Ecuador, Venezuela, and the sovereign states of Central America which came into existence with the collapse of *La Gran Colombia* and the Central American Confederation.[5]

But unpleasant memories finally faded away in England. British investors of the 1860's and 1870's, acting as if they had forgotten or never heard of the misfortunes of their forebears in the 1820's, took another plunge. Between 1860 and 1875 they bought huge issues of Latin-American government bonds, a total of over £108,000,000 figured at par. On February 1, 1877, the nominal value of their Latin-American government bond investment stood at approximately £127,-000,000, and over £85,000,000 of the total were in default! Only four of the fifteen countries involved—Argentina, Brazil, Chile, and Colombia —were paying dividends, and Colombia began another long period of default in 1879.

Political disorders and ineptitude in the management of public finances account only in part for this general failure to service their obligations. More important causes were repeated scandals in the process of flotation and extreme eagerness for the development of public services. Peru's huge foreign debt of nearly £33,000,000 was mainly the result of immoderate enthusiasm for railroads, inculcated in considerable measure by Henry Meiggs, a dynamic Yankee promoter. Mexico's almost £28,-000,000 were the heritage of reckless borrowing in the 1820's and 1860's. Bolivia's £1,654,000 were floated for the purpose of building a railway in an Amazonian jungle. Venezuela's £6,616,800 and Ecuador's £1,824,000 were, for the most part, accumulations from the early borrowing of *La Gran Colombia.* Uruguay's £3,164,800 represented prudent flotations for laudable purposes; the securities were in temporary default because of a depression and a revolution. A part of Guatemala's £542,800 stemmed from 1825, but most of the debt dated from 1869. Costa Rica's £3,304,000, the Dominican Republic's £714,300, Honduras's £5,398,570, and Paraguay's £1,505,400 represented flotations as scandalous as any recorded in international finance. Paraguay had just been laid waste by five years of war; the other three were dominated by dictators with a trophy concept of government. In each case Latin-American public authorities connived with clever European manipulators to defraud both foreign investors and their own people. Although the announced purpose of each loan was to build or lengthen a railway, most of the proceeds filled the coffers of the negotiators. Within two or three years every issue of these four governments went into default. French investors, who financed Haiti, participated in the Mexican and Honduran flotations, and bought some bonds issued by Peru and the Argentine national government and provinces, also suffered severe losses.

Beginning with the late 1880's, however, the debt record of many of the Latin-American countries decidedly improved. By the end of the year 1890 the face value of British investments in Latin America exceeded £425,700,000: government securities £194,400,000 and economic enterprises £231,300,000. Ten years later the total, in spite of the economic depression of the early 1890's, was slightly above £537,800,000, with nearly £308,700,000 in economic enterprises and the rest in government bonds,[6] while the par value of French investments in Latin America aggregated over $600,000,000, German investments in the region were only slightly smaller, and investments of citizens of the United States, concentrated mainly in northern Latin America, were in excess of $320,000,000. Foreigners owned by 1900 all the oceanic shipping lines communicating with Latin America; nearly all of Latin America's railways and most of the shipping companies operating on its great rivers; all the submarine cables; the majority of the gas plants and tramways in the region; not a few of its port facilities; most of the enterprises exploiting the nitrate deposits and many large companies engaged in the mining of metals; numerous ranches, plantations, and farms; several firms taking out forest products; a multitude of mercantile firms and many commercial banks; and the most efficient manufacturing and processing plants. In short, while the Latin-American upper classes were absorbed in political wrangling, civil war, and literary and diplomatic activities, or indulging in absentee farming and ranching—many of them spending a good part of their time overseas—foreign capitalists and alien residents were developing and extracting Latin-American resources and building and operating Latin-American public services.

It was a situation fraught with trouble. Foreign consuls and diplomats spent most of their time for decades reminding the Latin-American governments of their unpaid debts or scolding them about their maltreatment of foreign nationals and foreign interests. The settlement of claims for injuries to the persons and property of aliens and the payment of interest and sinking funds on government bonds were issues eternally debated. Naturally objecting to coercion, the Latin Americans insisted that the use of force to collect debts and support reclamations for personal and property damages was unjust and illegal. One did not any longer imprison or chastise one's debtor, they argued. Aliens should find their remedies in the local courts. Foreign diplomats should intervene only when national judiciaries manifestly failed to administer justice; otherwise the alien resident who refused to become naturalized and the foreign trader and investor would be accorded a privileged position.[7] But the governments of the stronger powers, by and large, took a different view, rejecting in practice the legal theory of the equality of states on the ground that those of Latin America fell far below the standard the more advanced nations had a right to expect in the maintenance of order and the independence and honor of their courts. The stronger powers never quite demanded of Latin America the privilege of extraterritoriality which they were then imposing upon the Orient, but they did not stop far short of it.

The wages of despotism, disorder, and deficient technology were not death, but they were painfully high. Foreign merchants and shipowners complained to their home governments of irregularities in tariff collection, port charges, and port administration and of injurious and arbitrary acts affecting merchant vessels and their crews and cargoes. Foreign investors and alien immigrants complained of violence suffered during revolutions, of the abuses of military and civil officials, of unjust taxes, forced loans, seizures, confiscations, breached contracts, and defaults on public debts. Foreign governments responded to the appeals of their nationals, demanded redress, and not infrequently employed force or threat of force to exact indemnity or compliance with contracts.

COERCION BY FOREIGN POWERS

An account of all the instances of armed coercion in behalf of foreign persons and property during this long disorderly period would require more than a volume. War vessels of all the major powers moved menacingly along the coasts and often blockaded ports or bombarded coastal towns and cities. France sent a naval detachment to Haiti in 1825 and compelled the Boyer government to sign an agreement to pay a heavy indemnity to the descendants of the French planters of the later Colonial period; bombarded Veracruz in 1838 and collected 3,000,000 francs for French claimants; blockaded Argentina from 1838 to 1840 and again from 1845 to 1850; forcefully reminded Venezuela in 1864 and repeatedly thereafter of unsettled pecuniary claims of Frenchmen; invaded Mexico in 1862; and kept its gunboats always within reach of its diplomats and consuls. Spain landed a military force at Tampico, Mexico, in 1829; menaced Venezuela more than once a few decades later; and in the 1860's not only temporarily occupied Peru's Chincha Islands (rich in guano) but bombarded both Callao and Valparaiso. The United States landed its Marines in Uruguay; sent a part of its navy up to Asunción to redress the grievances of its citizens; debarked military forces in Panama to protect a railway owned by American investors; fought a war with Mexico in part to collect pecuniary claims; and threatened (in the late 1850's) to occupy the northern section of that country in order to maintain peace and stability. England joined France in the blockade of Argentina in 1845–50; bombarded or blockaded the port settlements, at one time or another, of nearly every Latin-American country that bordered the seas; and kept its American squadrons ready for instant action. Germany entered the fray in the 1870's; and even little Holland sent its war vessels to the coast of Venezuela.

Summaries of four episodes may serve to illustrate the troubles growing out of this economic and personal phase of the foreign relations of turbulent Latin America. Ulterior motives were involved in one of the four and suspected in two others.

Anglo-French naval operations in the Río de la Plata region were intended in part to compel Manuel Rosas, the Argentine tyrant, to respect British and French nationals, to release those whom he had imprisoned or forced into his armies, to make amends for their maltreatment, and to open the great rivers of the area to foreign trade. They were also designed in part to deflect attention from domestic and European problems and to force Rosas to keep Argentina's pledge to refrain from violating the independence of Uruguay. After Louis Napoleon gained control of the French government (1848), the British feared that he might be tempted to add the Plata Basin to the French empire. The two European powers not only blockaded Argentina; they also engaged in hostilities with Rosas, captured his small navy, and supported the Uruguayans in their struggle to maintain their independence. The French government actually subsidized the Montevideo government and encouraged the organization of a foreign legion composed mostly of French immigrants but including some Italians, the noted Garibaldi among them, and a few other aliens. Years of intermittent hostilities and large expenditures of money neither obtained redress from the stubborn Rosas nor opened the great arteries of commerce; and, while it is true that the European governments helped the Uruguayans in their capital to resist the tyrant's siege until his South American enemies were almost ready to assemble their forces and drive him from power, it is still a question whether European intervention prolonged the dictator's rule or shortened it. British suspicions of Louis Napoleon's motives were probably unfounded, but if he had attempted to conquer any part of the Plata region he would most likely have encountered British resistance. The United States, then absorbed in the problems of Texas, the Mexican War, and the Oregon boundary, probably would have taken no immediate action.[8]

Having acquired in 1846–48 a vast segment of territory bordering on the Pacific coast, and considering the construction of transcontinental railways impossible in the immediate future, the Washington government centered its attention on the isthmian routes with the view of finding rapid means of transportation between its two coasts. The most convenient of these turned out to be the railroad across Panama, begun in 1849, completed early in 1855, and largely utilized by citizens of the United States on their way to and from California. On April 16, 1856, almost 1,000 passengers landed at Colón and proceeded across the isthmus on four trains. Late in the afternoon a drunken adventurer named Jack Oliver, who probably hailed from the deep South, ate a slice of watermelon belonging to a black fruit vender of Panama City and refused to pay for it. When the Jamaican Negro made a dignified protest in his broad English, Oliver whipped out his revolver. The Negro either dodged or outran the bullet and soon returned with a roaring rabble. The Panama Railway station and the rambling wooden structure advertised as a hotel, both filled with citizens of the United States, were besieged. Eighteen of the passengers were killed, sixteen wounded, and many more robbed. Asserting that the municipal police force called out to protect the immigrants joined in the assault and that the governor of the Colombian state of Panama was remiss in his duty, the Washington government demanded full indemnity and guaranties of security for the future as well. Aware of the chronic emptiness of the Colombian treasury and eager to get control of the Isthmus of Panama, Secretary of State William Marcy proposed to make a cash payment to Colombia and assume the claims in return for naval bases and an agreement to set up two joint autonomous governments along the railroad right-of-way. The national authorities in Bogotá stoutly refused to acknowledge responsibility and appealed to England and France for support; but both European governments declined to interfere, and the British minister in Washington advised his Colombian colleague to admit responsibility for mob violence and settle the claims promptly, since the United States might be in a mood to heal its domestic discords by a foreign war. The naval bases in the Bay of Panama were not ceded, nor was the proposal to establish joint local governments accepted. But the riot claims were soon adjusted by means of a joint commission which awarded a total of $160,000 to 126 claimants.[9]

It is difficult to give specific details regarding the reclamations which led to the collaborative effort of France, Spain, and England to coerce Mexico in the 1860's and served as an excuse for drastic French intervention.[10] The nationals of all three countries had grievances, well founded or not, for which they advanced heavy claims. The grand total for unserviced government debts and injuries to persons and property amounted to many millions. Ostensibly, though not actually—for some of them were fraudulent—the French grievances were the most serious of the group. Disagreements among the powers engaged in the coercive action soon caused the withdrawal of England and Spain, leaving Louis Napoleon free, so far as they were concerned, to carry out his scheme of empire.

In his letter of July 3, 1862, to Marshal Elie F. Forey, Napoleon clearly revealed his real motives. Presenting his justification for spending "men and money to place an Austrian prince upon a throne," he wrote:

> In the present state of the world's civilization, the prosperity of America is not a matter of indifference to Europe, because it nourishes our industries and gives life to our commerce. We have an interest in seeing the Republic of the United States become powerful and prosperous; but it is not at all in our interest that she shall grasp the whole of the Gulf of Mexico, dominate from there the Antilles and South America, and become the sole dispenser of the products of the New World. If the United States should become master of Mexico, and consequently of Central America and the passage between the two oceans, there would indeed be no other power in America.
>
> If, on the contrary, Mexico shall preserve her independence and maintain the integrity of her territory, if stable government be established there by means of French arms, we shall have opposed an impenetrable dike to the flood waters of the United States; we shall have safeguarded the security of our colonies in the Antilles and those of ungrateful Spain; we shall have established our benign influence in the center of America, and this influence will radiate to the north and the south, create immense markets for our commerce, and procure raw materials indispensable to our industry. . . .
>
> Thus . . . are involved our military honor, the demands of our policy, the interest of our industry and our commerce, all of which oblige us to advance upon Mexico, boldly plant our flag there, and establish a monarchy —if not incompatible with the national sentiment of the country—or at least a government that will promise something of stability.[11]

Commerce and empire and "containment" of the United States, then, were Napoleon's actual objectives. There was not a word here about the claims of Frenchmen, although these would be vigorously pressed upon the Maximilian government later. And while Napoleon may have supposed that the majority of the Mexicans, at least the majority of those possessing wealth and culture, had despaired of the republic and were ready to try another experiment in monarchy, it is likely that his reference to national sentiment was mainly pretense. More than five years were required to convince him that his Austrian prince was unwelcome, and more than the intrepid and tenacious resistance of Benito Juárez and his Liberals was necessary to compel the withdrawal of his armies. The termination of the Civil War in the United States and mounting resentment there; the coolness of the British government toward the French Mexican venture after the death of Lord Palmerston;

opposition in France, and a growing menace across the Rhine—perhaps all these factors were involved in Napoleon's final decision to abandon his dream of empire in America.

Whatever the reasons, he recalled his troops in 1866–67 and left his Hapsburg puppet to confront Mexican national sentiment without further outside assistance. The Mexicans soon captured Maximilian and shot him at sunrise (July, 1867), just as if he had been an upstart Mexican general and not a scion of one of Europe's most distinguished royal families. The episode was expensive and tragic for all concerned. If some Frenchmen collected their claims, others lost millions of francs which they invested in Maximilian bonds (subsequent Mexican governments repudiated the loans), and many thousands lost their lives on Mexican battlefields. Latin Americans, keenly aware of the cost of such coercive enterprises to themselves, hoped that the lessons taught by Juárez' Mexico and Rosas' Argentina might not be ignored forever.

The fourth episode in this rapid series concerned Venezuela, where serious troubles began early in 1849, with the passage of a moratorium law which inflicted injury upon foreign as well as local creditors. The British chargé d'affaires summoned war vessels and presented the Caracas government with the choice of a British naval bombardment or an agreement to assume the debts owed to British creditors on which a moratorium had been granted. Venezuela agreed to assume the debts —and, of course, was compelled to accord the same treatment to other foreign creditors. The total amounted to almost 2,000,000 pesos (about $1,600,000).

The next twenty-five years, as noted in an earlier chapter, were an unusually turbulent period even for Venezuela, and foreign traders and investors as well as aliens settled in the country were frequently abused. Moreover, there were not a few of a speculative and inventive turn of mind who managed to frame up grievances. Nationals of eight or ten countries were involved, but especially those of France, England, Germany, Spain, Italy, and the United States. First and last, the reclamations advanced amounted to more millions than passed through the Venezuelan treasury in a decade. Spain broke diplomatic relations and called in war vessels on two or three occasions; but France usually took the lead, and, as a result, exacted preferential treatment for French nationals a good part of the time. The most vigorous measures were taken while the United States was in the midst of the Civil War. The Venezuelan government was compelled to pledge 40 per cent of its customs receipts to meet the monthly payments; and since most of the national revenues came from duties on foreign commerce, this was almost the equivalent of an equal percentage of the national receipts.

France alone collected around 6,000,000 francs. It was not until near the end of the Guzmán-Blanco regime (1870–88) that the pressure was temporarily relaxed.[12]

BULWARKS OF LATIN-AMERICAN SECURITY

Were there no remedies for such assaults? One obvious remedy, although it was largely theoretical during this early National period, lay with the Latin-American countries themselves. Where no concealed objectives were involved in these European grievances, trouble could have been avoided by putting a stop to civil wars, administrative excesses, and faulty judicial procedures. But this threefold remedy was not generally applied, and in the circumstances probably was not actually available.

Bad as it was, Latin America's international situation might conceivably have been worse. During a rather perilous epoch for the weaker nations of the world, when the Orient, the Pacific Islands, and Africa were being subjected to European imperialism, the Latin-American countries managed to maintain a considerable measure of independence.

This suggests what was actually the case: that the nations of the region did not lack certain bulwarks of defense. And these were not merely the two customarily mentioned: the policy of Great Britain backed by the strongest navy in the world and the parallel policy of the United States promulgated by James Monroe in 1823 and elaborated by his successors. These were important; but there were other bulwarks also, some less significant and some resting on foundations which penetrated deep into the fundamentals of power politics. Latin America was a long way from Europe, and the European nations may have been more vitally interested in other undeveloped regions. Latin Americans, for the most part, were ardently nationalistic and ready to fight and die for their independence. The moral code of the epoch required a degree of respect for the sovereignty of nations ruled by Caucasians, even if such nations had no more than a respectable veneer of European culture. Finally, Europe's suspicions, distrust, strife, and unsteady power-balance tended to shield the Western Hemisphere from drastic aggression. The European situation was generally too tense for any single power or any possible combination of powers to attempt large-scale imperialistic operations in America. There was constant danger of attack on the rear as well as the likelihood of vigorous resistance from the Anglo-Saxon countries, which would feel that their security was being threatened, England being disposed to act to maintain the European power-balance, which could be upset by annexations in America as well as in Europe, and the United States likely to follow the course prompted by the sentiments embodied in the Monroe Doctrine.

That this United States-British combination, each party acting in its own interest but each following the parallel course dictated by those interests, was a significant bulwark was demonstrated by what occurred during the American Civil War. For that brief epoch one member of the combination was not able to implement its American policy, and the other, mainly for that reason, it seems safe to assume, did not offer resistance to Spain's occupation of the Dominican Republic or France's occupation of Mexico. It required simultaneous action by the Anglo-Saxon team to make this bulwark effective. But even if France and Spain had planted themselves more firmly in the New World at this time, they probably would have been expelled as soon as the next European crisis arose, driven out by one or both of the Anglo-Saxon powers, perhaps with some aid from the Latin Americans.

But what protection was there for the Latin Americans against the Anglo-Saxon countries? The British government during this epoch was not ambitious to expand its holdings in America; but if its aspirations had pointed in that direction it would probably have been held in check by the United States and the requirements of the British power-balance policy in Europe. For the United States there was generally no effective outside restraint, as demonstrated by Texas, the Mexican War, and the unhindered pressure on Colombia in connection with the Panama Riot, to mention only three cases. There were, however, certain internal restraints: domestic discord, public sentiment, national conscience.

So much for Latin America's bulwarks of security against conquest. Most of them did not serve during this period as barriers to the employment of coercion in the collection of contract debts or indemnities for injuries to persons and property. Engaging to some extent in such coercive procedures itself, the United States usually stood aside during these years so critical for Latin America and permitted the European powers to impose their will. But the Washington government or some of its diplomats always disclosed interest and never failed to express uneasiness when ulterior motives were suspected. There were only two available retorts, either bold defiance of the European powers or defiance moderated by a measure of appeasement, which involved acceptance by the United States of a degree of responsibility for the conduct of Latin-American nations in their relationships with the outside world. Although the second policy, an appeasement policy, was not finally adopted until shortly after 1900, when Theodore Roosevelt added his famous "corollary" to the Monroe Doctrine, certain antecedents pointing to the new policy can be found in the period now under review. They related to Mexico and Venezuela.

As early as February 10, 1857, the minister of the United States in Mexico concluded the negotiation of a treaty by the terms of which the United States government agreed to lend Mexico $15,000,000 and to set aside $4,000,000 of the total for the payment of the Mexican debt to European bondholders. British bondholders were so enthusiastically in favor of the pact that they sent an agent to Washington to lobby it through Congress. Neither President Pierce nor President Buchanan was willing to submit it for approval, but for some time thereafter the English diplomats in Mexico City had standing instructions to insist that Mexico reserve for the satisfaction of British creditors and claimants a portion of any sums received from the United States.

The subject was brought up again in 1859 by Senator Sam Houston, and in 1861 Secretary Seward authorized Thomas Corwin, then United States minister to Mexico, to enter into negotiations with the view of appeasing European creditors and averting intervention. The Seward-Corwin plan provided a loan sufficient to pay interest at the rate of 3 per cent per annum for five years on Mexico's funded foreign debt, estimated at $62,000,000. The plan was accepted by President Juárez, but it failed to obtain the approval of either the United States Congress or the European governments.

Further suggestions of the same nature were made in 1867 and 1869, both by the agent of the British bondholders and by the chargé of the United States in Mexico, but Seward was not disposed to deal with the problem, since "no portion of the [Mexican] consolidated debt . . . was contracted to this government or citizens of the United States." Mexico was left to its own devices in the solution of its European financial problems.

For more than a decade the United States government was on the point of taking a hand in the settlement of Venezuela's financial difficulties with foreigners. Two of the four secretaries of state who served during the twenty years following the American Civil War favored the appointment of official agents to collect Venezuelan customs and distribute a part of the income among American and European claimants. First made by Hamilton Fish in 1869, the proposal was later opposed by William B. Evarts, taken up by James G. Blaine, and finally rejected by Frederick T. Frelinghuysen. It might have matured if the governments at Washington and Caracas had been of the same mind at the same time for a sufficient period to work out the details, and if the European powers—especially France, which had secured a preferential status in 1864—had been less impatient and aggressive. In a slightly different concatenation of circumstances, Venezuela in the 1870's or 1880's, and not the Dominican Republic in 1905, would have been the first Latin-American nation to have its customs collected and its debts paid off by representatives of the United States! [13]

CHAPTER XXIII

Relations with Great Britain and the United States

Until shortly after the middle of the nineteenth century the United States and Great Britain were rather bitter rivals in respect to Hispanic America. In order to frustrate the projects of the Holy Alliance, Canning had invited the co-operation of the United States in 1823; but this did not mean that the two branches of the Anglo-Saxon family were in complete accord. Canning was more provoked than pleased by the Monroe manifesto. Its protest against armed intervention by the Continental powers in Spanish America tended to support Canning's policy, but it contained two other ideas that aroused his apprehension. It forbade future colonization in America by European nations and it suggested that America and Europe were separate worlds. These pronouncements had political and commercial implications unacceptable to the British foreign secretary, and his vigorous efforts to counteract them during the remainder of his life (1823–27) increased distrust of England in the United States. The rivalries of the two Anglo-Saxon countries sometimes benefited the new Latin-American nations and sometimes injured them.

EARLY EVIDENCE OF MUTUAL JEALOUSIES

Latin America had long been considered an important potential market for British goods, and profound economic changes of the early nineteenth century made this market even more desirable for Englishmen. British industries had undergone a remarkable development during the previous century. Total exports had mounted from an annual value of £1,505,285 in 1701 to £41,717,000 in 1801, and British manufacturing industries had reached a very efficient stage compared with those of other countries. But while the opening decades of the new century saw no decline in efficiency, they witnessed a decided shrinkage in the total of British exports. Their value in 1822, for instance, was less than £37,000,000. The decrease was caused largely by the impoverishment of Europe and the efforts of Europe and the United States to encourage home industries by erecting tariff walls. These circumstances enhanced the importance of Latin-American markets, and British trade with the new republics expanded rapidly, reaching an aggregate value of over £5,500,000 in 1822 and more than £7,500,000 in 1823. The United States, with a Hispanic-American trade amounting to more than $26,000,000 in 1822 and almost $31,000,000 in the following year, was becoming Britain's most formidable commercial rival.

English capitalists, likewise interested in the region, encountered few competitors until after the middle of the century, except for occasional investors from France or from the United States, the latter mainly in Cuba, Mexico, and Central America. Most of the new governments of Latin America immediately negotiated loans with British merchant bankers, and English investors became deeply involved in mining and other enterprises. British capital in Latin America amounted to around £25,000,000 by 1827, with most of the government bonds of the new states already in default.

Because of heavy losses from early ventures and lack of competition, British investors watched Latin America both less hopefully and less anxiously than British mercantile interests did. When the Colombian agent in Europe suggested in 1823 that the Spanish American states might give preferential commercial treatment to foreign countries which accorded them prompt recognition, the London *Times* accused the United States of grabbing the bait and attempting to "forestall the merchants of Great Britain." Coming to the support of the *Times,* the London *Examiner* scolded British ministers for allowing the North Americans to take the lead "in establishing profitable connection with the immense, fertile, and improving States" of Latin America. Already, in 1819, a member of the House of Commons had remarked that the cession of the Floridas to the United States was a mere "sop to Cerberus" that stimulated his appetite for more in the form of commercial advantages; and in September, 1822, a group of London merchants urged government support on the ground that citizens of the United States were crowding them out of Spanish American markets.

Still more convincing evidence of British jealousy is disclosed in the arguments used by Canning to convince the British ministry of the advisability of prompt recognition of the revolting colonies. He declared that it was the purpose of the United States to organize a "Transatlantic League, of which it would have the sole direction." "I need only say," he continued, "how inconvenient such an ascendancy may be in time of peace, and how formidable in case of war." After he had forced his recognition policy through the cabinet, he wrote in high exultation: "The deed is done, the nail is driven. Spanish America is free; and if we do not mismanage our affairs sadly, *she is English.*" [1]

A similar attitude of jealousy was revealed in the United States. Henry Clay, when advocating the recognition of the Spanish American states, heaped scorn upon Secretary Adams for truckling to England: "If Lord Castlereagh says we may recognize, we do; if not, we do not." Attempting to arouse the mercantile interests, the New York *Commercial Advertiser* pointed to the "vast markets about to be opened to the enterprise of the world in the late American colonies of Spain," and expressed the fear that the "vigilant and indefatigable John Bull" would capture them. Distrust of England was one of the motives for reluctance to accept Canning's proposal for a joint remonstrance against European intervention in 1823. In his observations on Mexico, published in 1824, Joel Roberts Poinsett called attention to the alarming magnitude of British economic activities; and on the eve of his departure as minister to Mexico, received a letter reflecting his mood: "Make a good commercial treaty for us and take care that John Bull gets no advantage of you—if anything get the weather gauge of him." [2]

Such were the mutual jealousies of the Anglo-Saxon nations as they initiated their intercourse with the new nations of Latin America. Britain held almost every advantage during the early years of the contest: the prestige of a great and victorious power; better trained diplomats; the good will of Spanish Americans won by the aid of hundreds of British subjects during the Wars of Independence and by Canning's opposition to European intervention in the struggle; capacious markets; and an abundance of capital to lend to the needy republics. The United States, on the other hand, had only the advantage of a manifesto whose vagueness was not clarified, of prior recognition of the insurgent governments, and of being a republic—and the last was hardly an advantage in certain quarters where monarchal sympathies and admiration for the British system of government were strong. The rivalry was disclosed at many points and in numerous ways. It was most vigorous in the countries nearest to the United States. Although not indifferent, the Washington authorities were less concerned with European activities in southern Latin America.

THE PANAMA CONGRESS OF 1826

The rivalry of the Anglo-Saxon nations was clearly revealed in connection with the Panama Congress. Exaggerating the importance of Latin America and the designs of the United States, British officials

feared that their rival would commit the Latin Americans to its views in respect to maritime rules and regulations and threaten British commercial and maritime predominance. Edward J. Dawkins, sent as observer by the English government at the invitation of Colombia, was instructed to detach the United States from a position of leadership and induce the young states to lean upon the experienced arm of Britain. Any project for "putting" the United States "at the head of an American Confederacy would be highly displeasing" to England. The delegates of the Washington government were directed at the same time to advocate the rights of neutrals, restriction of blockades, and maximum freedom of commerce. They were instructed to urge that "whatever may be imported from any foreign country into any one American nation or exported from it in its own vessels may, in like manner, be imported into or exported from the same nation" in vessels of other nations. Secretary Clay, who wrote the instructions, had not forgotten the War of 1812 and the arrogant treatment of neutrals throughout the Napoleonic period. "At all times," he remarked, "there has existed more inequality in the distribution among nations of maritime than of territorial power. . . . But when a single nation finds itself in possession of a power anywhere which no one, nor all other nations, can successfully check or countervail, the consequences are too sadly unfolded in the pages of history." [3]

The British press did not fail to note the significance of these instructions. On May 18, 1829, shortly after they were published, the London *Times* remarked: "There is an obvious anxiety throughout these long documents to assume . . . that all 'American' states are to constitute a system and a community of their own, recognizing interests and establishing maxims for their regulation as affects each other, and for their separate, exclusive, nay repulsive use, as regards the other nations of the world. The first obvious consequence of such a scheme, if adopted by Mexico and the states of South America, would be to place the United States at the *head* of the new federation, in virtue of superior strength, maturity, . . . commercial and political resources." A pamphlet published in England the same year declared that the United States had urged infant republics, "without the possibility of becoming maritime states for many generations, if at all," to adopt in their relations with Europe the "highest pretensions, which, in the maturity of her naval strength, the United States herself ever ventured to urge— and even then without the remotest hope of success." Instead of advising these budding states to cultivate the most friendly relations with Europe and to avoid meddling where their interests were not concerned, the United States had urged them to take the "highest ground" in their negotiations, to insist that "free ships shall make free goods," to demand a "definition of blockade," and to make an "inroad into our navigation act." [4]

But Englishmen were unduly excited. The United States accomplished nothing at Panama. Its delegates did not attend the assembly. One of them died on the way; the other had not left for Panama when news arrived that the congress had adjourned to meet again at Tacubaya, Mexico. The British agent, while not attending the formal sessions, held frequent informal conferences with the Latin Americans, upheld English prestige, and reduced the influence of the United States, whose views regarding maritime rules and regulations were not fully accepted by its American neighbors.[5]

RECIPROCAL SUSPICIONS REGARDING CUBA

Canning and American statesmen suspected each other's intentions in regard to Cuba from the moment he became foreign secretary until death ended his career. On October 11, 1822, Canning informed the British minister in Washington of indications that the United States intended to seize the island, but cautioned him against imputing such a design to the administration lest the charge suggest the very evil which it deprecated. "The Yankees may be just the rogues that we have always taken them to be, but which I was willing to hope that they might have resolved to be no longer," he remarked in 1825. Still uneasy with respect to the ambitions of the United States, he instructed Dawkins in 1826 to warn the Spanish Americans that a concerted effort on their part to drive the Spanish authorities out of Cuba might result in the occupation of the island by their North American neighbor.

American officials were equally uneasy with reference to the designs of Great Britain. The prospect of England's seizure of Cuba alarmed Monroe's cabinet in the autumn of 1822, and the American minister in Madrid was directed to investigate the rumor that England was trying to induce Spain to cede the island to her. In June, 1823, Jefferson remarked in a letter to Monroe that the acquisition of Cuba by England "would be a calamity." With respect to Canning's proposal of a joint remonstrance against European intervention in Spanish America in 1823, Madison inquired suspiciously as to whether Cuba and other Spanish possessions were not involved in the projected pronouncement. Shortly before Canning's death the minister of the United States in Madrid sent to the State Department alarming reports of British designs on both Cuba and the Canary Islands, and there is evidence that Canning was thinking of attacking Cuba in case of hostilities with Spain.

The mysterious procedure of France in the West Indies and the more or less open schemes of Colombia and Mexico to deliver Cuba from the Spanish yoke added to the anxiety of the Anglo-Saxon powers, each of which tried to restrain the other by disavowing any aggressive intentions, by expressing the desire that Cuba should remain in possession of the mother country, and by declaring that the island should not be permitted to fall into the hands of another. England sought to commit the United States and France to a triple guaranty of Cuba to Spain; the United States, unwilling to sign such a covenant, attempted to enlist the European governments in a concerted effort to relieve the tension by inducing Spain to recognize the independence of her former colonies, thus circumventing the plans of Mexico and Colombia. The European states manifested a real interest in the American suggestion but found Spain as indisposed as ever to recognize accomplished facts. Nevertheless, these very rivalries may have prolonged Spain's possession of her valuable colony, for, as the London *Courier* remarked, Cuba had become the "Turkey of trans-Atlantic politics," tottering to her fall, and kept from falling by those who contended "for the right of catching her in her descent." Colombia and Mexico were first dissuaded by England and the United States from invading the "pearl of the Antilles" and then reduced to impotence by domestic discords. But England attempted to gain an advantage at the Panama Congress by representing herself as far less meddlesome and selfish than the United States in her Cuban policy.

And so the rivalries and jealousies continued. British interest in Cuba centered mainly on questions of commerce, investment, strategy, and slavery. A prosperous Cuba might supply revenues to enable Spain to meet her obligations on large outstanding British government loans. A badly administered and insurgent Cuba would mar this prospect and possibly lead to the annexation of the island by the United States, a step which would strengthen America's position in the Gulf-Caribbean region and bolster the Southern slave power. For all these reasons, Great Britain set her face firmly against the acquisition of Cuba by the United States.

The British government insisted on the suppression of the slave trade with the island, but appears not to have meddled with the status of slavery itself. There was, however, sufficient meddling by enthusiastic British abolitionists to arouse uneasiness on the part of Southern politicians in the United States. Nor was the London government willing alone to offer Spain a guaranty of territorial integrity, although it attempted repeatedly to persuade the United States to sign with England and France a tripartite agreement insuring Spain's perpetual control of

Cuba, and employed its navy to interrupt the contraband slave trade and the raids of filibusters who organized their expeditions in the United States. Moreover, England probably tried to prevent Spain from selling the island to the United States in 1848–54, when the Washington government attempted to purchase it, and certainly to moderate Spain's Mexican policy with the view of preventing the United States from taking advantage of a Hispano-Mexican war to occupy this Spanish colony.

It must be admitted, however, that British efforts were largely superfluous. Cuba was indeed retained by Spain until 1898, but for this British policy deserves little credit. Public opinion in the United States was divided on the Cuban issue, and Spain's resolution against sale of the island to the United States needed no tonic. England employed every resource and device of diplomacy, but a more profound understanding of the situation might have spared her the anxiety and the trouble.

MEXICO THE BUFFER

Canning considered cordial relations with Mexico the key to his "later American policy." In one of his memoranda urging recognition of the Spanish American states, he remarked: "I believe we now have the opportunity . . . of opposing a powerful barrier to the influence of the U.S. by an amicable connection with Mexico, which from its position must be either subservient to or jealous of the U.S. In point of population and resources it is at least equal to all the rest of the Spanish colonies, and may naturally expect to take the lead in its connections with the powers of Europe." After converting the cabinet to his viewpoint, he boasted: [6] "The Yankees will shout in triumph; but it is they who lose most by our decision. The great danger of the time . . . was a division of the World into European and American, Republican and Monarchical; a league of worn-out Govts., on the one hand, and of youthful and stirring Nations, with the United States at their head, on the other. *We* slip in between; and plant ourselves in Mexico. The United States have gotten the start of us in vain; and we link once more America and Europe."

Englishmen soon planted themselves in Mexico, won the friendship of its conservative groups, and gave the representatives of the United States plenty of trouble, delaying their efforts to obtain commercial and boundary agreements with Mexico and nagging the United States minister, Joel R. Poinsett, into imprudent involvement in local politics which eventually resulted in his recall from his post. But the British government was unable to shield Mexico from the consequences of the distrust and bitterness which Englishmen helped to arouse. After inviting citizens of the United States to settle in Texas, the Mexican government eventually became alarmed, subjected them to oppression, and caused them to revolt, secede, and set up an independent republic.

British officials then transferred their attention from Mexico to Texas and attempted to use that republic as a buffer. But again their efforts proved futile. Success hinged upon the attitudes of France, Mexico, and Texas, and they all failed to co-operate. France refused to lend aid to the extent of armed resistance; Mexico refused to recognize Texan independence and threatened to reconquer Texas; the Texans voted to accept the destiny that Great Britain was so eager to have them escape. In spite of British opposition, despite Mexico's vehement protests, Texas was annexed to the United States in 1845, nine years after its separation from the Aztec republic.

Naturally infuriated by the loss of a large segment of their national domain and still not convinced of the futility of expecting European assistance in their effort to redress their grievances, the Mexicans appealed to France and England for sympathy and aid and prepared for war. Feeling that no wrong had been done in annexing Texas, irritated by the maltreatment of its citizens, and not averse to further expansion of its boundaries, the United States was equally belligerent. Almost bankrupt, poorly armed, rent by factional strife, Mexico received no support from England or France in her war with the United States and finally accepted defeat and the loss of an immense slice of territory, for which she obtained several million dollars in partial compensation.

A few years later, Dictator Santa Anna sold to the United States another small strip known as the "Gadsden Purchase" (1853) in order to terminate a boundary dispute and compose other difficulties. Further appeals to England for support, at this time and later, were fruitless. British efforts to prevent the alienation of Mexican territory to the United States, limited to warnings and diplomatic overtures, had little weight. The indirect British pledge given to Mexico in 1825 to shield her from aggression proved a broken reed. Convinced that remonstrance unaccompanied by the use of military force tended to incite rather than check the expansionists of the United States, the British government finally decided to change its policy.

RIVALRY IN CENTRAL AMERICA

Meantime the two Anglo-Saxon powers were waging a vigorous contest in Central America, where England had developed interests long before the United States won its independence. Belize and the Mosquito Territory on the mainland and the islands in Honduras Bay were the main centers of British activity. English subjects had resided in Belize for the purpose of cutting logwood and collecting other forest products since 1662; had alternately occupied and abandoned certain of the Bay Islands since 1642; and maintaining fitful settlements along the Mosquito Coast, had associated more or less intimately with the natives of the area since the closing decades of the seventeenth century. By a series of treaties extending from 1786 to 1814, however, the English government had acknowledged that it had no sovereign rights in the region.

British agents in Central America, as elsewhere, expressed alarm regarding the intentions of the United States, but American statesmen evinced little interest there until the acquisition of California from Mexico became a certainty. Englishmen therefore had only to deal with the Central American governments, which they easily managed by setting state against state and faction against faction. Central Americans

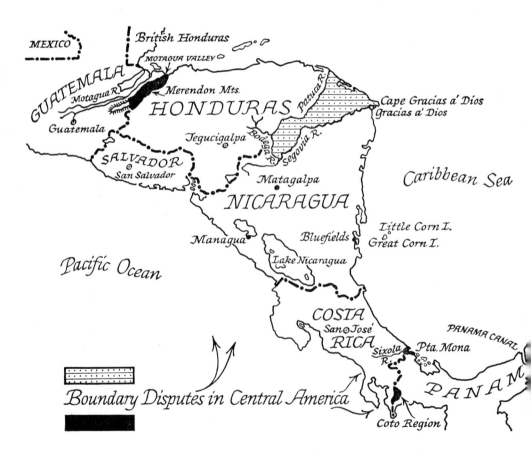

Boundary Disputes in Central America

MAP 11

appealed to Washington for assistance in vain during this early period; the United States seemed unconcerned. British settlers expanded their operations in Belize without obtaining immediately the status of a crown colony. The British government supported its subjects, however, in the occupation of the largest of the Bay Islands, and British agents also induced the primitive Mosquito "king" to extend his dominions to the mouth of the San Juan River and the town of San Juan; and when Nicaragua contested his claim, the British government came to the assistance of the native monarch with armed force and renamed the village Greytown. Clearly, it was England's intention either to control the isthmian commercial routes or prevent the United States from dominating them.

The interest of the United States was finally aroused by these and other English activities, by persistent Central American requests for succor, and by the prospect of new possessions on the Pacific coast. Loath to enter the fray in the Nicaraguan region before finishing the Mexican War, the United States first authorized its ministers in Bogotá to negotiate a treaty relating to Panama (1846). But hostilities had scarcely ended before action was begun on a larger front. Diplomats were sent to Honduras and Nicaragua to secure agreements regarding the utilization of the interoceanic routes; and when these were signed in terms which the United States was not willing to ratify, negotiations were opened with England by the Whig administration, which had won the elections of 1848.

The result was the Clayton-Bulwer Treaty, signed in Washington on April 15, 1850, after a vigorous diplomatic encounter, a pact which, as shortly became evident, was interpreted in contradictory fashions by the opposing governments. Secretary Clayton's original objective had been to clear the way for the construction of a canal by an American company which already had secured a concession, but public opinion in the United States had forced him to undertake the task of obtaining from Britain an agreement to withdraw altogether from Central America. Minister Bulwer's prime concern was to extract from the United States a pledge not to dominate the region or its commercial routes and to do this without committing England to immediate withdrawal. Both diplomats thought, or pretended to think, that they had accomplished their purpose, but it shortly became obvious that neither had attained his goal. The United States adopted the view of Clayton and demanded that Britain clear out of Central America immediately. The British government accepted Bulwer's view and made no move to get out at all.

Moreover, the nationals and agents of the two governments in the contested area committed acts which increased the tension. English settlers and officials in Greytown interfered with American trade and transit; citizens of the United States on their way to California, where gold had been discovered, often involved themselves in altercations with British residents and their native allies. Britain's seizure of the Bay Islands in 1852 with the view of making them an English colony intensified the situation. Matters developed from bad to worse until in July, 1854, an American man-of-war bombarded Greytown and burned it to the ground, an act plainly in defiance of the British protectorate over the Mosquito Kingdom which claimed jurisdiction in Greytown; and the London government might have retaliated with armed force if it had not been engaged in the Crimean War. The state of bitterness between the two countries was not improved by the dismissal in 1855 of John Crampton, who had been soliciting recruits for the Crimea while acting as British minister to the United States.

The climax was reached in 1856, when the United States obtained evidence of active British opposition to William Walker and his filibusters, who were engaged in the conquest of Central America with fair prospects of success because the United States permitted defiance of its laws forbidding such operations. While President Pierce was winning the plaudits of press and politicians by breaking diplomatic relations with Britain and recognizing the Walker government, the conflict in the Crimea suddenly ended and the situation became extremely critical.

༄ THE BRITISH RECESSION

Both sides talked of war, but the crisis soon passed without armed conflict. It passed because England decided to relax her opposition to the southward expansion of the United States and then gradually abandoned, one by one, the many points of resistance which she had formerly held. Unmistakable indication of a change in attitude first appeared in June. On June 14, the London *Economist* remarked:

> We could not hinder the ultimate absorption by the Anglo-Saxon republicans of the whole of Central America if we would. . . . We can have no interest in upholding the present wretched and feeble governments of Spanish America. Our interest lies all the other way. We wish ourselves for no extension of territory on that continent. . . . Desiring no territory, we desire only prosperous, industrious, civilized, and wealthy customers. . . .
>
> Central America peopled and *exploited* by Anglo-Saxons will be worth to us tenfold its present value. We have no fear that our countrymen will be excluded from the commerce of those provinces. We have no fear that our ships will be prohibited from crossing that isthmus when the two seas shall be joined by a canal.

Other journalists soon uttered similar sentiments. *Blackwood's Magazine* declared: "The paths of Britain and America do not cross. The Isthmus of the New World is the goal of Transatlantic ambition. . . . The Isthmus of the Old World is the cynosure of British policy." The London *Times* saw no reason to resist the expansion of overseas kinsmen, unless "some real interest" could be "shown to be at stake." "North America under strong, civilized, uniform, and prosperous government" should meet with British approval. "It does not become us to play the dog in the manger with our fast-growing progeny across the Atlantic. They have too many good reasons, as well as too many bad ones, against allowing us to stand in their way for the sake of mischief or pride." [7]

British statesmen and diplomats soon fell in line. On June 16, 1856, Benjamin Disraeli rose in the House of Commons to give the ministry his advice. England would be wise, he said, to abandon her opposition to the "so-called 'aggressive spirit' of the United States." Such opposition would not prevent Yankee expansion; it would only involve England in struggles that might prove disastrous. Britain had suffered no harm from American annexations; on the contrary, they had added to the prosperity and power of his country. He therefore advocated a sort of reciprocity whereby Britain, by recognizing this expansion as it occurred, might persuade the United States to abandon the two-spheres conception embodied in the Monroe Doctrine as obsolete in an age of steam and expanding international trade and investment.

Economic interests were carefully weighed. The southward expansion of the United States was likely to bring stability and higher levels of living in the regions acquired, thereby enlarging the market for British goods. A war with the United States would unleash a swarm of privateers and produce economic consequences which could not lightly be dismissed. British trade with the United States, now that American tariffs had been reduced, was larger than British commerce with all northern Latin America. The cotton trade of the United States alone was more important than the British stake in Mexico and Central America combined. Thoughtful appraisal of the situation dictated a change of policy.

British holders of Mexican bonds set to work on a scheme designed to divert into their coffers any cash which the United States might pay Mexico for territorial or commercial concessions, presented their plan to the Mexican government and the minister of the United States in Mexico City, and sent the Mexican attorney of the bondholders to Washington for the purpose of sounding some of the political leaders. Partly as a result of these machinations, perhaps, Minister John Forsyth negotiated a treaty early in 1857 providing for a loan of $15,000,000 to the Mexican government, $4,000,000 of which was to be applied to the British convention debt, in return for a favorable commercial arrangement. Forsyth's action was unauthorized, and the loan agreement was not accepted either by President Pierce or President Buchanan; but the idea impressed British diplomatic circles, and English ministers in Mexico were forthwith given standing instructions to the effect that the Mexican government would be expected to pay a portion of any sums received from the United States to British creditors and claimants.

W. G. Lettsom, then in charge of the British legation in Mexico, made some very significant remarks [8] on July 22, 1857, regarding American negotiations for control of territory in northern Mexico; "I conceive that the absorption of *half* . . . of Mexico by the United States would inflict greater injury on British Interests than if the whole . . . were annexed to that Country," he declared. Explaining the meaning of his statement, he continued:

If half the territory of Mexico is so absorbed, Mexico, as before, will be burthened with all her present liabilities, while the resources remaining at her disposal to cover them will be diminished by one half, and in this case I need hardly remark that it will be useless to expect she will fulfill her engagements. The manner in which the revenue of Mexico is always frittered away prevents the development of the resources of the Country, while the tariff is constantly such that consumption is impeded as much as possible.

Were the whole of . . . this Republic annexed to the United States the latter Country would have to assume the liabilities of Mexico; the position of the numerous British claimants . . . would be at once ameliorated, while with the general activity then pervading this Country, with the development of its resources, and with the increase of its population, new wants would arise, and these British commerce would be called upon to provide for.

In July, 1858, Lord Malmesbury, British foreign secretary, told George M. Dallas, minister of the United States, that he and other British statesmen believed that "all the southern part of North America must ultimately come under the government of the United States," and that, far from objecting to what seemed to be the "inevitable course of things," he felt that American control would benefit the region, the United States, and "the rest of the world." [9] Late in 1860, as Great Britain, France, and Spain laid plans for a coercive expedition to Mexico, England invited the United States to join in the enterprise; and when the Washington authorities not only rejected the invitation but protested against European intervention, the British minister in Mexico commented: "If the position of the United States . . . is authorized and maintained, I cannot but view it as binding that country to assume the moral obligation toward other nations of restoring peace and order in Mexico, and of preventing the recurrence of scenes which disgrace humanity and neutralize . . . the international rights and natural commercial relations of civilized nations." [10]

But the United States was by then in no condition to assume such a "moral obligation"; that would be postponed until after 1900. The Civil War, upon which its energies would have to be concentrated, was rapidly approaching. British participation in the joint coercive action against Mexico seems not to have been motivated, however, by a desire to circumscribe the influence of the United States. England's purpose was rather to divert Louis Napoleon from his European aggressions and to obtain satisfaction from Mexico for debts and claims.

The same softening of British attitude likewise became evident in Central American affairs. Lord Malmesbury's statement to Dallas in July, 1858, applied to that region as well as to Mexico; and as early as March 13, 1857, he had written to President Buchanan: "Pray bear in mind that beyond the point of honor respecting the Mosquito Indians we possess no interest in Central America, and that, so far from wishing to create one, we would not accept such a 'damnosa possessio' . . . if it could be offered to England as a gift." [11]

On November 28, 1859, the British government signed a treaty with Honduras acknowledging that the Bay Islands belonged to that republic and recognizing also the sovereign rights of Honduras over the portion of the Mosquito territory which lay within its frontiers. Negotiations with Nicaragua resulted two months later in an agreement to recognize the sovereignty of that little state over the part of Mosquitia that fell within its boundaries, the natives of the region to be granted a sort of home rule until they should agree to incorporate themselves into the Nicaraguan republic. Copies of these treaties were transmitted to the United States as soon as they were ratified, and the hope was expressed that they might "finally set at rest the questions respecting the interpretation of the Clayton-Bulwer Treaty." It was a clever stroke, and notwithstanding the fact that England still retained Belize with boundaries extending south to the Sarstoon River, Buchanan expressed his entire satisfaction in his annual message of 1860, which contained one of the few cordial references to England that had appeared in an American presidential message up to that time.

Although England withdrew from Mexico after disagreements with Napoleon and persuaded Spain to take the same action, it appeared for a time that the Civil War might furnish the occasion for a reversal of policy. The British government organized the Belize settlements into a full-fledged crown colony in 1862, continued to watch over its Mosquito wards in Nicaragua, and verged on intervention in the struggle between

North and South. For reasons which need not be related here, however, England did not intervene in the Civil War in the United States. The Union forces triumphed, but the American merchant marine was almost destroyed; and shortly afterward Great Britain began a rapid transformation from aristocracy to democracy. The clash of views regarding political institutions gradually ceased, and for a considerable time maritime rivalry disappeared as a disturbing factor. Purely economic rivalries continued and Irish and other anti-British groups in the United States occasionally tried to stir up trouble; but conditions in Europe, Asia, and Africa were so critical, and Great Britain confronted such formidable antagonists in those regions, that the friendship of the United States was urgently needed, and the two Anglo-Saxon nations continued to move toward an era of harmony.

So far as Latin America was concerned, few causes of friction arose during the rest of the nineteenth century. British merchants continued to enjoy a major share of Latin-American trade, larger on the whole and in most countries than was the commerce of the United States. British investors ventured large sums in Latin America, particularly after 1880, much more capital than was invested by citizens of the United States or by the nationals of continental Europe.[12] Except in Cuba and Mexico, and to a lesser extent in Central America, Peru, Chile, and a few other countries, the merchants and capitalists of the two nations were not sharp rivals. Nor did the governments themselves appear to have been seriously concerned, although James G. Blaine expressed uneasiness regarding British activities in Chile and Peru.[13] Only with reference to the control of projected communications between the Atlantic and the Pacific and in respect to interpretation of the Monroe Doctrine did any official clash seem possible.

✺✺ EFFORTS TO REVOKE THE CLAYTON-BULWER PACT

Efforts to modify or abrogate the Clayton-Bulwer Treaty of 1850 were resumed by the United States in 1881. Alarm at the prospect that a canal across Panama would be constructed by a French company headed by Ferdinand de Lesseps led to a public demand for an American canal under the control of the United States, and the United States government asked for release from the pact which bound it not to seek exclusive domination of the isthmian routes. The British government refused to grant the request and buttressed its position by arguments difficult to refute. Probably with the view of making it harder for the French company to raise funds, the United States turned to Nicaragua and negotiated a canal treaty with that republic on terms which ignored the earlier treaty with Great Britain; but Grover Cleveland, who became president before the Nicaraguan pact was ratified, withdrew it from the Senate, and thus relieved the tension with England. It was soon discovered, however, that Britain was still maintaining intimate relations with the natives of Mosquitia in close proximity to the Nicaraguan route, and systematic opposition, which finally led to their incorporation into the state of Nicaragua in 1894, was promptly begun by the United States. At least that issue was settled.

Meantime American journalists and politicians continued to demand the revocation of the Clayton-Bulwer Treaty and the construction and control of a canal by the United States government, and British authorities began to temper firmness with moderation. When sharply questioned on the issue in the House of Commons, Sir Edward Grey, undersecretary of state for foreign affairs, replied that there was no reason to suppose that the United States did not intend to respect its treaty obligations. And Secretary Richard Olney soon revealed that Grey's confidence was justified so far as the second Cleveland administration was concerned, for Olney condemned arguments designed to prove that the agreement was obsolete and declared his decided preference for "a direct and straightforward application to Great Britain for a reconsideration of the whole matter." However, before the initiation of direct negotiations which finally resulted (1901) in a new treaty satisfactory to the United States, a crisis arose over a boundary dispute between England and Venezuela and severely tested the friendly relations of the two governments.

⚜ THE VENEZUELAN CRISIS

The limits between British Guiana and Venezuela had never been clearly defined. Intermittent negotiations extending over a period of nearly fifty years had ended in the severance of diplomatic relations between England and Venezuela in 1887 and in appeals by the Caracas government to the United States for support. The time seemed opportune to force a settlement. Ambassador Thomas F. Bayard wrote from London in 1893: "Great Britain just now has her hands full in other quarters of the globe. The United States is the last nation on earth with whom the British people or their rulers desire to quarrel. . . . The . . . European nations are watching each other like pugilists in a ring." [14] Invocation of the Monroe Doctrine and plain talk to England would win approval in the United States, where a flamboyant jingoism was developing and political orators and journalists were shouting for the enforcement of the Monroe Doctrine and a new era of territorial and commercial expansion.

On July 20, 1895, Secretary Olney sent off his now famous instructions to London. They contended that the Monroe Doctrine was applicable to the Venezuelan boundary dispute with England and contained a good many emotional irrelevancies. Insinuating that the British government intended to reduce Venezuela to the status of a crown colony, Olney declared that the people of the United States believed that popular self-government was for "the healing of all nations, and that civilization must advance or retrograde accordingly as its supremacy is extended or curtailed." Intimating that the European nations should withdraw from their possessions in the New World, he asserted that "distance, and 3,000 miles of intervening ocean" made "any permanent political union between any European and any American state unnatural and inexpedient." Boasting of the wealth and prowess of his country, he declared: "Today the United States is practically sovereign on this continent and its fiat is law." [15] A short communication emphasizing the contention that the Monroe Doctrine would be violated if Great Britain expanded the boundary of Guiana beyond the limits which it had in 1823 might have been more astute.

Olney's "spread-eagleism" naturally ruffled the disposition of Lord Salisbury, head of the British Foreign Office. He denied applicability of the Monroe Doctrine to the dispute, pointedly rejected the manifesto, refused to submit the question to arbitration except in reference to certain specified areas, and taking exception to Olney's statement regarding the absurdity of European possessions in America, maintained that the "union between Great Britain and her territories in the Western Hemisphere" was "both natural and expedient."

After conferring at length on the matter, Cleveland and Olney decided to request Congress to authorize and finance a commission to determine the boundary with the view of compelling England to accept its findings. In his message of December 17, 1895, Cleveland declared: "When such a report is made . . . it will be the duty of the United States to resist by every means in its power . . . the appropriation by Great Britain of any lands . . . which after investigation we have determined of right belong to Venezuela."

The message and the diplomatic correspondence were handed to the press at once and were greeted by tremendous applause. The House of Representatives, without a dissenting voice, adopted a resolution incorporating the president's suggestions; and after debating the measure for three days the Senate unanimously concurred in the action of the House.

The British nation was equally firm during the closing weeks of 1895 in supporting the stand taken by Salisbury. Parliament was not in session, but the press, with little knowledge of the issue or the soundness of the official position, contended that it was preposterous for an American commission alone to determine a British boundary and for the president of the United States to presume to support its findings by resort to force. The newspapers of both parties were indignant. The London *Chronicle,* the mouthpiece of the Liberals, though firm, was a bit more moderate than the rest. "There is one answer to President Cleveland and America," it declared. "If an enlarged application of a neglected doctrine is to be enforced with all the might of the United States, at least let us be assured that the United States will make itself responsible for the foreign policy of all the petty, impetuous little states on the two continents. There is no international right without a corresponding duty. . . . Unless the United States formally proclaims a protectorate over all of the South American Republics, we are bound to protect our citizens." At least one other writer made a similar suggestion during the course of the controversy, and George W. Mathew's statement of late 1860 regarding Mexico had contained essentially the same idea of a "corresponding duty."

Several Englishmen and a few Americans who tried to calm the excitement were indirectly assisted by an important episode in Africa. On December 29, 1895, Leander Starr Jameson raided the Dutch Transvaal with a small armed party of Rhodesians. The hostile expedition proved a fiasco, and the invaders were promptly captured and imprisoned by Paul Kruger, the Transvaal's Boer president; but German animosity toward Britain then suddenly revealed itself in German public opinion and in the Kaiser's congratulatory telegram to Kruger. Japan's defeat of China in 1895 had already disturbed conditions in the Far East and Turkish massacres in Armenia were unsettling the Near East. Clearly it was no time to risk a war with the United States, and British statesmen began to search for a pacific settlement of the Venezuelan affair.

On January 12, 1896, the Foreign Office sent Lord Playfair on a confidential mission to the residence of the American ambassador in London to propose that England accept the Monroe Doctrine and try to induce other powers to accept it, and, further, to state that the British government was willing with minor reservations to submit the Venezuelan boundary controversy to arbitration. These proposals, followed by conciliatory utterances by publicists and politicians in both the United States and England, eased the tension, and the crisis entirely passed by the end of July. Within the next few months all arrangements for arbitration were completed. The entire boundary was submitted to the arbitral tribunal, but with the understanding that "adverse holding or prescription during a period of fifty years" would constitute a good title to territory. On October 3, 1899, the arbiters announced their decision. Since England was awarded all areas occupied for half a century, she probably received more territory than she would have been entitled to according to the boundary as it stood at the time of Monroe's manifesto of 1823, but less than she might have taken if the United States had not shielded Venezuela. But British suggestions regarding the responsibility of the United States for the conduct of Latin Americans in their relations with foreign countries were ominous. They forecast Theodore Roosevelt's "corollary" and American interventions in the countries of the Caribbean.

The significance of these various rivalries for the Latin Americans cannot be accurately determined. The economic competition of the Anglo-Saxon powers probably was beneficial. Their political rivalries probably did more harm than good. It is likely that British opposition hastened the territorial expansion of the United States at Mexico's expense. It certainly did not prevent it. It may be that the United States impeded British territorial encroachments in Central America and limited them in Venezuela, but the United States certainly did not prevent British annexation of the Falkland Islands (1833) or make any protest against continued British occupation of that strategic bit of territory claimed by Argentina. Nor did the United States shield the Latin Americans during the nineteenth century from any forceful action that the British government desired to take in order to redress the grievances of British subjects. Finally, the rivalries of the Anglo-Saxon nations may have delayed the emancipation of the Cubans, but opposition of the antislavery groups in the United States rather than any European remonstrances was the main factor in preventing American annexation of their island.

CHAPTER XXIV

Latin America and Latin Europe

The most significant phase of the relations of Spain and Italy with Latin America during the last three quarters of the nineteenth century was the impact of immigrants with their fertility, brawn, and skills. In other respects, their relations were comparatively unimportant. France, in contrast, supplied only a few hundred thousand immigrants but exerted a powerful influence in political and cultural fields and became a fairly strong competitor in trade and investment.[1]

SPAIN UNRECONCILED

Many of the Peninsula-born Spaniards were either killed or expelled from Latin America during the two decades following 1810, but Spanish emigrants began to enter the region shortly thereafter; and between 1850 and 1900 they arrived in as large numbers as had migrated to the Spanish American colonies during the whole of the Colonial period. The total exceeded 2,000,000 by the end of the century, the major recipients being Argentina, Brazil, Chile, Mexico, and Cuba. Capital ventured in Latin America by Spaniards living in Spain—invested mainly in urban and rural real estate and in mercantile firms—probably amounted to $50,000,000 or more by 1900.

In the 1850's, when the remnants of the Spanish empire in the New World as well as the newly-formed Latin nations were thought to be threatened by the aggressions of the United States, especially by filibuster raids against northern Mexico, Central America, and Cuba, Spanish propaganda sounded the racial alarum in an effort to induce the Spanish Americans to unite among themselves and with Spain for the purpose of stemming the tide of invasion. Newspapers were founded, books were published, and diplomats exerted themselves with this end in view.

Early in 1856, for instance, the Spanish minister in Washington held conferences with the diplomatic representatives of the Hispanic countries resident there for the purpose of discussing plans of union, and a project was drafted which proposed to bind the Latin nations in a pact pledging themselves not to permit the abridgement of their independence or the infringement of their territorial integrity, but to treat the invader or offender of any member of the prospective alliance as a common enemy. Although no provision was inserted at the time that would include Spain in the union, the Spanish government approved the action of its minister and considered it of sufficient importance to communicate an account of it to the Cuban captain general.

But while some Spaniards urged *rapprochement* between mother country and colonies, the government in Madrid was slow to put aside the resentments of the past and quick in attempts to redress the grievances of its nationals. It bombarded Tampico in 1829, took vigorous action against Mexico again in 1856–62, tried to coerce Venezuela in the 1860's, and not only seized Peru's Chincha Islands but bombarded Valparaíso in 1865–66. And as if all this were not enough, the Spanish queen, dreaming of finding kingdoms for her sons, supported the adventurer Juan J. Flores in efforts to conquer a part of northwestern South America in the late 1840's, and the Spanish army occupied eastern Española (the Dominican Republic) in 1861–65.

These aggressive actions, together with bitter memories of the past and sympathy in Latin America for Cuba and Puerto Rico, which were still Spanish colonies, tended to stultify efforts to achieve harmony until near the end of the century. Yet some progress toward reconciliation was made. Beginning with the recognition of Mexico's independence in 1836, Spain slowly extended this favor to other Spanish nations of the New World, finally completing the process in the early 1890's. At the same time numerous treaties relating to extradition, postal and telegraphic communications, literary, scientific, and artistic property, and commercial affairs gave evidence of the abandonment of the policy of aloofness. And near the end of the century Spaniards evinced their growing interest in their kinsmen across the Atlantic by founding the Ibero-American Union, while the Spanish government laid aside old grievances and invited them to join the mother country in the celebration of the fourth centenary of the discovery of America.

THE SWARMING OF THE ITALIANS

Almost 4,000,000 Italians arrived in Latin America between 1825 and 1900. Argentina, Brazil, and Uruguay were the major recipients, but many thousands went to Chile, Paraguay, Venezuela, and Mexico, and most of the other nations received several thousands each. More than a third of the total eventually returned home or moved elsewhere, but population of Italian or part-Italian descent in Latin America probably exceeded 6,000,000 by 1900. It made up about a third of the inhabitants of Argentina and Uruguay and formed almost as large a portion of the population of southern Brazil.

The contribution of these immigrants to the economic development of Latin America cannot be accurately measured, but there can be no doubt of its significance in such countries as Argentina, Uruguay, Brazil, Paraguay, Chile, and Peru. They gave a strong impetus to the wine industries of Argentina, Chile, and Peru, to the Brazilian coffee industry, to the cultivation of cereals in Argentina, Uruguay, and Brazil. They were also active in mercantile enterprises, in the cultivation of fruits and vegetables, in the dairy industry, in banking and manufacturing, in the building trades, in barbering and bootblacking, and in various public works, supplying much of the labor for the construction of railways and port facilities.

Italian steamship companies began to make regular voyages to Latin America in the late 1870's, and within a few decades four companies were engaged in the traffic. This steamship capital, a part of which might be allocated to Latin America, was one of the earliest investments in the region made by Italians of the home country. Another early investment was in banking enterprises, the first of them established in 1872 and four others founded by 1890.

Emigration was generally viewed by Italian leaders as an inevitable misfortune. One of them remarked in 1896: "It alone can provide a safety valve against class hatreds. It is . . . the great and sole avenue to salvation for a country wanting in material resources but fruitful of men." Gradually an emigration policy was evolved. The emigrant was to be protected and utilized for the benefit of Italy. A law of 1901 gave the minister of foreign affairs the power to suspend emigration to any place in the public interest or whenever "the life, liberty, and property of the emigrant" was "at stake." Emigration must be protected, it was said, in order that it may not be "miserably lost to our country, our nationality, and our economic and political future." [2]

Beginning with the 1880's, the Italian government was prompt to protect the lives and property of Italians in foreign lands. At times, emigrants were warned not to sign contracts or prevented from going to Argentina, Brazil, Uruguay, or some other Latin-American country. At times, the Italian navy was employed to speed negotiations for the settlement of claims. The Ernesto Cerruti case against Colombia illustrates early coercive action. A retired Italian army officer, Cerruti, had migrated to that country in 1868, married a Colombian wife, and established his home in Cali, in the fertile Cauca Valley. His property was seized during the revolution of 1885 and confiscated on the charge that he had aided and abetted the insurrection. Unable to obtain redress, the Italian minister asked for his passports and an Italian warship was sent to enforce the Italian government's demand for indemnity. Claiming a special relationship with Colombia because of its guaranty under the treaty of 1846 of a part of Colombia's territory (Panama), the United States requested Italy to desist, and urged that the Spanish king be chosen as mediator. The case was submitted to the Spanish monarch, but his decision proved unsatisfactory to the Bogotá government and it refused to accept it; whereupon Italy continued to press the claim, and the United States again intervened, expressing deep concern and declaring that it was bound to Colombia "by strong ties of tradition and common interest." The case was finally submitted to President Cleveland, who handed down a decision in favor of Cerruti in 1897. Italian policy might have been more drastic if the United States had not interposed.

FRENCH AGGRESSIVENESS

As already observed, Napoleon Bonaparte once dreamed of making Spanish America a part of the French empire, and the restored French Bourbons (1815–30) disclosed eagerness to establish princes on Spanish American thrones. The French navy compelled Haiti in 1825 to sign an agreement to pay for the damages suffered by French planters during the thirteen-year bloody insurrection of 1790–1803, bombarded Veracruz in 1838, blockaded Argentina in 1838–40, and joined the British navy in coercive action against the River Plata republic in 1845–50; and although the French government refused to commit itself to England either on the Texas issue or on the question of interference in the war of 1846–48 between the United States and Mexico, it collaborated with Great Britain in efforts to prevent filibustering expeditions organized in the United States from invading Cuba, in the proposal of a tripartite pledge to preserve this island in Spanish possession, in negotiations for the use of South American rivers, and in machinations to defeat attempts of the United States to acquire commercial and naval-base concessions from the Dominican Republic (1856–57). In similar manner in 1855, the French chargé in Ecuador tried to dissuade the Quito government from ceding some of the Galápagos Islands to the United States and made the threat that Emperor Louis Napoleon would turn his attention to the New World as soon as the Crimean War was concluded.

French intervention in Mexico in the 1860's was but the culmination of this aggressive policy. Suspicion of French intentions was aroused in Washington as early as 1852, and French diplomats in Mexico were soon causing deep uneasiness by plans for blocking the expansionists of the North. These plans forecast the true intent of the French project that was initiated in 1861. The reason announced by France, England, and Spain for the joint expedition against Mexico was the desire to avenge outrages suffered by their nationals and to force Mexico to honor her financial obligations; but the ulterior designs of Louis Napoleon soon became evident. They were revealed in his now famous letter of July 3, 1862, to General Forey, already quoted in Chapter XXII. His purposes were to prevent the territorial expansion of the United States at the expense of Latin America, to protect French trade with the region, to encourage French investments in the various Latin countries of America, and to expand French dominion and influence in the Western Hemisphere.

But Napoleon's Mexican venture failed miserably. His puppet, Ferdinand Maximilian, never ruled the whole of Mexico or enjoyed a day of tranquillity. Because of the hostility of the United States, whose aid against France was eagerly solicited by Liberal Mexicans and other Latin Americans, and owing to the menacing attitude of Prussia, opposition in France, and the dogged determination of Benito Juárez and his Mexican soldiers surreptitiously supplied with American arms, Napoleon finally withdrew French troops in 1867, abandoning the unhappy Hapsburg monarch to the tragic fate which shortly overtook him. Louis Napoleon thus suffered a blow to his prestige, and resentment toward the United States for its part in the affair and for other reasons was long felt in France.

However, in spite of French aggressiveness (which gradually abated after the downfall of Louis Napoleon), no other foreign country had more influence in Latin America than France wielded until well after 1900. The role of French political ideas in the Wars of Independence already has been described. French thought, French literary moods, themes, and forms, political events in France, and French propaganda continued to sway the intellectuals, artists, and politicians of the region.

THE PERSISTENCE OF GALLIC INFLUENCE

Napoleonic imitators sprang up in Mexico, Central America, Bolivia, Paraguay, and Peru. In deposing their emperor in 1831, the Brazilians were thinking of the French overthrow of the last of their Bourbons the previous year. The Revolution of 1848 in France had its reverberations from Mexico to Chile and Argentina. After causing a Conservative reaction in Mexico, it became one of the inspirations of the reforms of the Juárez epoch. It encouraged reform efforts in Ecuador and then provoked the clerical reaction led by García Moreno, who had been shocked by revolutionary excesses while sojourning in Europe. It incited a radical movement in Colombia (then called New Granada) which led to the adoption of Latin America's first constitution separating Church and State (1853). Partly responsible for the revolt of the radicals in Chile in 1851, its political and humanitarian doctrines sustained the victims of the Rosas tyranny in Argentina in their plans for liberation. French legal codes served as models all over Latin America. French Romanticism echoed in Latin-American literary circles, and Paris became the Paradise of Latin America's aristocracy.

Of no less importance in Latin America were French criticisms of the American policies of the United States. Motivated by jealousy, racial and cultural affinities, fears regarding the security of French possessions in the New World, and economic rivalry, these criticisms became most vehement during the decade following the Spanish-American War and continued until long after 1900.

The potentially rich Mississippi Valley, which soon became a great source of wealth, once belonged to France, and the products of this enormously fertile region competed with French commodities in the world markets. French attitude regarding this subject is illustrated by Comte D'Haussonville, a descendant of Rochambeau and an honored guest of the United States in 1881 at a festival commemorating the centenary of the surrender of Cornwallis at Yorktown, who made a rapid journey across the continent from New York to San Francisco and was reminded of the melancholy past. The French count wrote later: [3]

> I recall that with the happy feelings of satisfied curiosity there was mingled a certain degree of sadness when I read on the railway time schedules and heard pronounced by foreign lips the names of cities and stations, large and small, which called to mind their French origin: La Nouvelle Orléans, Saint Louis, Vincennes, Saint Geneviève, Versailles; for I said to myself: It was Frenchmen who christened these places, but where is France now? . . . I experienced other feelings also. While traveling across immense plains where the steam plow was at work . . . with a view to the approaching seedtime; . . . when crossing large rivers by which I knew wheat, cattle, and fruit were carried to the sea for export to Europe; or when I saw the glare of mighty furnaces and the accumulation at the depots of great containers of petroleum, I became aware that a powerful rival was preparing himself to deal terrible blows to our agriculture and our manufacturing industries, and that it would be necessary to defend ourselves against the invasion of his products.

Such was the jealousy aroused by the fact that the United States had profited from French misfortunes. Racial and cultural sentiments were also a potent motive for this carping criticism. They were in part responsible for Napoleon's quixotic Mexican expedition; and M. Reclus, writing shortly afterward in *Revue des Deux Mondes* (1868), sought to console Frenchmen with respect to the fiasco by reminding them that, "fortunately for France, the affinity of languages" assured "for her literary and scientific works a decisive influence" among the Hispanic Americans, and that the "grand memories of the Revolution" would "render them only too indulgent toward our contemporary history. . . . They recognize with a sort of filial piety that they owe their emancipation to the ideas proclaimed by the men of '89; in spite of all our political blunders, we inherit a part of the spiritual gratitude dedicated to our ancestors." Another contributor to this journal (1893) pointed out that French political, administrative, scientific, and cultural ideas were in the ascendant in Mexico; that the Mexican civil code was almost a literal reproduction of the Code Napoleon; that cultured Mexicans were reading more French than Spanish books and sending their children to Paris to finish their education. Such Mexican admiration filled the writer with pride; but the growing power of the United States aroused strong misgivings, and he ended his article with a warning to the Latin Americans, particularly the numerous Indian groups, that too close association with the Anglo-Saxon republic would mean extermination, and with a fervent hope that France would assist the Latins of America in defending themselves from this grave danger. Other French journalists were in agreement; one of them thought that an alliance with Latin America might be inconvenient in view of the sensitiveness of the United States but urged the need for a cordial understanding and a growing intimacy between the Latin peoples of Europe and America.

Fully expecting the United States to resume its expansionist policies sooner or later, Frenchmen feared that a sudden outburst of American imperialism might deprive them of French Guiana and the French West Indies, remnants of an empire which reminded them of a glorious past. Napoleon alluded to this uneasiness in 1862, and it appeared again in 1890 in the discussions provoked by James G. Blaine's Pan-American activities, when Frenchmen asserted that the United States was planning to expel the Europeans from all of their American possessions.

The Venezuelan boundary controversy of the 1890's aroused further apprehension, and French journalists generally agreed that the United States was taking another step in its policy of excluding Europe from the Western Hemisphere. One writer warned that an attempt to assert "the pretensions of Mr. Cleveland" universally would bring the United States into "conflict with all Europe." Nor would England's submission obligate other powers or induce them to tolerate "such odious interference." [4] Another journalist charged that the United States intended at the opportune moment to seize all of Europe's American colonies—perhaps the European governments, adopting Russia's policy in respect to Alaska, should sell them to the United States in anticipation—but declared that he did not believe the United States was foolish enough to consider the year 1896 a fit occasion for this robbery. On the contrary, he felt confident that if France should be "forced to make a naval demonstration in the waters of Rio de Janeiro for the purpose of establishing" her "rights in the contested territories of French Guiana, the admiral commanding the American fleet would do us the honor of coming aboard the French admiral's vessel to dance." Surely the American officer would consider it more comfortable to dance on a French man-of-war than over a volcano! [5] French anxiety regarding the security of her American possessions became so evident that the German emperor thought France might be persuaded early in 1898 to join a concerted action against the United States mainly on the basis of preserving them.

French desire to share the trade and investment opportunities of Latin America was strong and persistent. Commercial motives were largely responsible for French recognition of the new states long before the mother country was willing to do so, and trade furnished one of the justifications for Napoleon's intervention in Mexico. France's commercial aspirations had not been thwarted before 1860. The value of her trade with Latin America had risen from less than $3,000,000 in 1825 to $30,000,000 in 1848, to $80,000,000 in 1855, and to more than $123,000,000 in 1860. But already a marvelous industrial transformation was taking place in the United States, the effects of which France was destined to feel in the markets and industrial enterprises of Latin America. French trade with the region was valued at only a little over $144,000,000 in 1896, at somewhat less in 1900, and at only $158,000,000 in 1905. French investments in Latin America, however, exceeded $600,000,000 at the end of the century, as already observed, and were rapidly expanding. The United States was, of course, not France's sole competitor in the field—England was more important and Germany was beginning to build up its trade and invest its capital—but owing to the reputation of the "Yankees" for shrewdness, they seemed most formidable, both in prospect and in reality. Frenchmen accordingly decried the new Pan-American movement as a scheme to build a Chinese wall between Europe and the Americas and denounced the Monroe Doctrine as an instrument of economic aggression.

But the policy of the French government after the downfall of the third Napoleon was far milder than the utterances of the French press. Asked by the United States whether the French canal company was sponsored by the national government in Paris, French officials replied politely and honestly that there was no connection between the two, and the sympathies of France seemed to be with the United States in its efforts to terminate the South American war of 1879–83 in which Chile conquered the nitrate fields formerly belonging to Peru and Bolivia. Although somewhat disturbed by French activities in respect to Venezuela in the 1880's and in respect to the Dominican Republic and Haiti before the end of the century, the United States suffered no great anxiety because of France's official Latin-American policy. French criticisms of the policies of the United States require emphasis mainly because of their undoubted influence in Latin America, where French books and periodicals were widely read and where French views were often adopted and supported by Latin-American writers.

CHAPTER XXV

Latin-American Interrelations; the First Pan-American Conference

DISCORDS PREVENTING EFFECTIVE COLLABORATION

In a sense, the Spanish American colonies were united under the Spanish monarchy; but their unity was based on the dependence of each major administrative division upon the royal government in Madrid rather than on intimate relations among themselves. Although the struggle for independence brought them closer together, political and geographical factors and lack of economic interdependence kept the new republics apart during the nineteenth century. The main causes of friction among them were (1) indefinite boundaries; (2) disputes over navigation of international rivers; (3) the military operations of political refugees across international frontiers; and (4) the ambition of certain nations or political leaders to seize territory or natural resources in possession of their neighbors, to promote political affiliations beyond their borders, or to create larger unities by coercive methods.

A number of influences tended, however, to promote harmony. Important among them were the persistence of the desire for unity that developed during the early National period, population too sparse to cause serious disturbances along international frontiers, preoccupation with perplexing national problems, and threats from stronger foreign nations. The United States and (less frequently) the European countries attempted to settle Latin-American disputes; but they also engaged in rivalries that sometimes set the small states against one another and pursued aggressive policies that caused the Spanish Americans to seek protection in alliances or multilateral diplomacy. Although the desire for unity occasionally embraced Brazil, the latter rarely revealed any strong sentiment for Hispanic-American solidarity. Having no special reason to fear the strong powers after achieving domestic harmony in

Line of Demarcation

Expansion of Brazil

1 The original Brazil
2 Added before 1850
3 From Venezuela, 1859, 1905
4 From Colombia, 1907
5 From Ecuador, 1904
6 From Bolivia, 1867, 1903
7 From Paraguay, 1872
8 From Argentina, 1895
9 From Uruguay, 1891

The Question of the Pacific

A Yielded by Bolivia to Chile
B Yielded by Peru to Chile
C Disputed by Peru and Chile

Other Disputed Areas

a The Gran Chaco
b Ecuador, Colombia and Peru
c Venezuela and England disputed till 1899

d ⎫
e ⎬ Boundary disputes between Colombia and Venezuela
f ⎭

Area of Friction in South America in 19th and 20th Centuries

MAP 12

the 1840's, and winning one boundary dispute after another in subsequent years, the Portuguese inhabitants of America tended to hold
themselves aloof from the projects for regional concert proposed by
their more disorderly neighbors, and no effective concert was attained
during the century.

NINETEENTH-CENTURY WARS

Latin-American disputes led to frequent frontier skirmishes but seldom
to more serious hostilities. Central America, having dissolved into five
small states soon after gaining independence, was often upset by international boundary quarrels, by petty armed collisions arising from rival
political affiliations, or by feeble attempts to restore political unification
by military force. Mexico and Guatemala had a boundary dispute that
was not settled until shortly after 1900. Haiti was reluctant to recognize
the independence of the Spanish-speaking inhabitants of the eastern
two-thirds of Española and invaded their domain on two occasions.
Colombia engaged in minor border conflicts with Venezuela and Ecuador; the latter had more disturbing conflicts with Peru; and Argentina
and Chile had quarrels about common frontiers. But Brazil, with more
uncertain boundaries than any other Latin-American country, adjusted
most of them without armed conflict. The Hispanic-American countries
had five real wars among themselves during the nineteenth century,
but only two or three of these were of serious magnitude.

The first of them, the war between the United Provinces of Río de la
Plata and Brazil, was caused by a bitter dispute over the small region
that later became Uruguay. The dispute had been inherited from the
Colonial era, and the Portuguese in Brazil and their more or less independent Spanish neighbors had engaged in intermittent hostilities
since 1814. In 1825, however, the Buenos Aires government supported
a revolution in the region, which Brazil had recently annexed as the
Cisplatine Province, and the war began in earnest. It continued for
three years until, with the mediation of Great Britain, a peace treaty
was signed (September, 1828) erecting Uruguay into an independent
buffer state.

The second war resulted from the opposition of Chile and Argentina
to the formation of the Peru-Bolivian Confederation by Andrés Santa
Cruz, the Bolivian dictator. Announced in 1835, this new consolidation
immediately aroused the hostility of Bolivia's southern neighbors. With
the aid of irreconcilable Peruvian exiles, Chile invaded southern Peru
and occupied the town of Arequipa in October, 1837, but the invaders
were compelled to accept a peace agreement within a few weeks. Rosas,
the Argentine dictator, sent an army into the Bolivian province of

Tarija in June, 1838, but his troops were promptly forced to withdraw. The Chileans, however, soon resumed the struggle with greater success. Under the command of General Manuel Bulnes, the Chilean army routed the forces of Santa Cruz at the battle of Yungai in January, 1839, and the confederation was forthwith dissolved. Its ambitious champion escaped to Ecuador and soon departed for Europe, where he died a quarter of a century later.

The third war was caused by factional strife in Uruguay and the aggressive tyranny of an Argentine dictator. Having gained control of most of the Plata provinces by 1835, Manuel Rosas was ambitious to expand his dominions and refused to recognize the independence of either Paraguay or Uruguay. The latter, torn by the bitter conflicts between the Blancos led by Manuel Oribe and the Colorados headed by Fructuoso Rivera, seemed to be an easy victim. When Rivera raised the red standard of revolt in 1836, Oribe appealed to Rosas for aid, and the Argentine despot soon sent an army across the Río de la Plata. But Rivera, supported by some of the neighboring provinces of Argentina and by the French government—which was having trouble with Rosas over commercial matters and the maltreatment of French immigrants—managed to drive the forces of the Argentine dictator out of Uruguay toward the end of 1839.

The next year, however, the French government effected an understanding with Rosas and withdrew its war vessels, leaving the tyrant free to renew his operations against his small neighbor, and Rosas sent his army back across the Río de la Plata in 1842. Commanded by Oribe and with many Uruguayan Blancos in their ranks, the invaders swept rapidly across Uruguay and laid siege to Montevideo. But the city was held so firmly by Rivera and his Colorados, supported by three Argentine provinces, by a legion of foreigners including the brilliant Giuseppe Garibaldi, and eventually by the harassing operations of French and English war vessels (1845–50), that the forces of Oribe and Rosas were unable to take it. The bloodiest phase of the war began in 1851 with the formation of an alliance composed of the Rivera government, Brazil, and the Plata provinces of Corrientes and Entre Ríos. After forcing Oribe to abandon the siege in October, the allied army crossed the Río de la Plata, routed the troops of the Argentine dictator, and forced him to flee the country. Uruguayans proudly described the long struggle as *la guerra grande* (the great war) and called Montevideo the "New Troy."

A little more than a decade later, at the end of 1864, a shorter but far more calamitous conflict began. It grew out of old enmities between Brazil, Argentina, and Paraguay, disputes over boundaries and trade, and reciprocal suspicions of imperialistic designs. With the defeat and exile of Rosas, Brazilian influence became dominant in Uruguay, and Brazil took advantage of the situation to force a boundary settlement and dictate the terms of a loan guaranteed by Uruguayan revenues. Shortly afterward, in 1854, Dom Pedro II, at the request of Venancio Flores, the Colorado president of Uruguay, sent an army of 4,000 into the country and kept it there for two years. Its withdrawal furnished the signal for the opposing party to seize the government and for rough treatment of Brazilians residing in Uruguay. Failing to obtain satisfaction, Dom Pedro intervened again in 1864 in behalf of Flores and his Colorados, who were now in revolt.

The Blancos appealed at once to Francisco Solano López of Paraguay, whose ambition and distrust of Argentina and Brazil had caused him to organize and maintain a large army and build some forts and an arms factory. López called upon the two governments to explain their attitudes toward the Blanco government in Montevideo and protested against the presence of Brazilian troops in Uruguay on the ground that they tended to disturb the balance of power in the Plata region; and when his remonstrances were ignored, he opened hostilities against Brazil and occupied a part of the province of Matto Grosso. Moreover, with the view of invading southern Brazil, López asked Argentina's permission to send his troops across Corrientes; and when General Mitre, the Argentine chief executive, refused the request, the Paraguayan dictator declared war on Argentina (March, 1865). By this time, Venancio Flores had gained control of the Uruguayan government with the aid of Brazil and formed a secret alliance with both Brazil and Argentina, so that López found himself confronted by a triple enemy. The war lasted for five years and ended only with the death of the Paraguayan tyrant. The cost in blood and revenue was enormous. Opposing armies numbered 20,000 and even 30,000. Paraguay was finally invaded, with heavy losses on both sides, and laid waste. The frightfulness of the war may be judged by the fact that Paraguay's population was reduced by combat and starvation from around 800,000—some writers say more than 1,000,000—to only a little more than 221,000, with less than 29,000 men among the survivors.

The last of the nineteenth-century wars was the war between Chile on the one hand and Peru and Bolivia on the other. Known as the "War of the Pacific," or the "Nitrate War," it had its background in an ill-defined boundary, but its immediate occasion was a dispute over the exploitation of the nitrate deposits (fertilizer, explosives, iodine) of the Pacific coast region between the nineteenth and twenty-fifth parallels of south latitude. Also involved before the hostilities ended was Bolivia's outlet to the Pacific Ocean.

Chile, whose territory did not extend farther north than the twenty-fifth parallel at the beginning of the National period, soon began to appreciate the economic importance of nitrates and to lay claim to the region as far north as the twenty-third parallel, a claim which, of course, Bolivia contested. The two countries agreed in 1866 to recognize the twenty-fourth parallel as their common boundary, to divide the revenue equally between themselves in the area extending from the twenty-third to the twenty-fifth, and to permit the nationals of each to work the nitrate beds; but the agreement proved unsatisfactory. Bolivians felt that their government, headed by a corrupt and extravagant dictator named Mariano Melgarejo, had conceded too much. Disputes soon arose over the division of the nitrate revenues and special taxes levied by Bolivia against Chileans engaged in excavating the product, and at length, in 1874, another treaty was negotiated. By the terms of this agreement Bolivia recognized the twenty-fourth parallel as the permanent boundary and bound itself for twenty-five years not to increase the taxes collected from Chileans operating in Bolivian territory and Chile consented to give up all claims to revenues collected north of the boundary.

Meanwhile Peru had become involved in the problem. Chile had secretly offered, during the negotiations which culminated in the treaty of 1866, to aid Bolivia in conquering the Peruvian provinces of Tarapacá, Arica, and Tacna, provided Bolivia would cede to her all of the Bolivian littoral to the south of these. Bolivia had rejected the proposal, but the secret soon got abroad. At the same time, the Peruvian government, under the influence of foreign speculators in Peru's public debt, adopted the scheme of purchasing the private nitrate enterprises operating in Tarapacá, monopolizing the nitrate beds in that province, and effecting an agreement with the *caudillos* of Bolivia to control the supply and price of guano and saltpeter. Alarmed by the aggressive attitude of Chile, the Bolivians listened attentively to Peruvian proposals, signed a secret treaty of alliance with Peru in 1873, and undertook, evidently at Peru's behest, to increase export taxes in 1875, but desisted under the strongest pressure from Chile until 1878, when Chile became involved in difficulties with Argentina; whereupon the Bolivians levied a tax against all nitrates exported by the Nitrate Company of Antofagasta, the most important nitrate enterprise of the Chileans operating in Bolivian territory. Protesting vigorously, the company refused to pay the impost and the Bolivians seized its property with the view of selling it for taxes. The Chilean government not only protested but sent troops to seize Antofagasta. The Peruvian government came speedily to the support of its ally, and in February, 1879, the War of the Pacific began.

Hostilities continued for four years in spite of efforts by the United States to mediate, and ended disastrously for Peru and Bolivia. With greater domestic harmony and superior forces, and with the encouragement and support of disgruntled nitrate exploiters and resentful holders of old issues of Peruvian bonds which they expected a victorious Chile to service,[1] Chile not only occupied the entire nitrate area but Arica, Tacna, and Lima as well. Thus victorious, the Chilean government forced Peru to agree to the Treaty of Ancón (signed in 1883 and ratified early in 1884) and obliged Bolivia to accept a truce (April, 1884). By the terms of these pacts, Chile retained all of the territories of Bolivia bordering on the Pacific, the Peruvian province of Tarapacá, and the right to occupy Arica and Tacna for ten years, after which the destiny of these two provinces was to be decided by a plebiscite and the winner would pay the loser 10,000,000 silver pesos. But the plebiscite was never held and the problem of Arica and Tacna embittered the relations between Peru and Chile until it was finally settled in 1929. Meantime Bolivia continued to lament the loss of its nitrates and its outlet to the Pacific.

⚜ PACIFIC SETTLEMENT OF DISPUTES

That the small nations of Latin America should favor the pacific settlement of disputes with stronger powers is not surprising, for they had little hope of victory in contests with them. That they frequently adjusted disputes among themselves by peaceful means is both a tribute to their sentiments of solidarity and the result of pressure from the outside. Good offices were urgently proffered by foreign nations in almost every instance. The United States and England were the most active.

Such interposition in quarrels among the Latin Americans probably exerted some influence upon the policies of the stronger powers, for if they were to urge pacific settlement in good grace, they must themselves be willing to accept their gospel in disputes with Latin America. The Monroe Doctrine, while not interpreted as prohibiting the redress of just grievances by overseas powers, was probably another restraining influence. Although the United States sometimes employed force or menace to effect settlements of its own claims, as in the cases of the Mexican War, the Panama Riot of 1856, and the naval expedition against Paraguay in 1859, it was usually willing to submit its complaints to tribunals of arbitration and reclamation commissions; and the European governments composed at least fifty differences with the Latin-American countries in the same manner between 1823 and 1900.

The number of Latin-American controversies adjusted by pacific means is more impressive than their international wars. Practically all of them, as already suggested, inherited boundary disputes from the Colonial period, but settled most of them by 1900 without the use of force. Some sixteen were compromised by arbitration and half as many others in whole or in part by direct negotiation. Moreover, Latin-American disputes over the navigation of international rivers had ceased by that time and the pecuniary claims pressed by the great powers had been adjusted repeatedly by pacific processes. The day would eventually come when all of the Latin-American nations would sign solemn covenants binding themselves to settle all inter-American difficulties in a peaceful manner and to refrain from using war as an instrument of American policy.

THE MOVEMENT FOR LATIN-AMERICAN SOLIDARITY

In an epoch characterized by intense rivalry among the great powers and too frequently by the use of force, the policy of the weak and turbulent states of Latin America with reference to these powers was naturally a defensive policy. Although the Latin Americans did not adhere formally to the Monroe Doctrine or promulgate a similar doctrine of their own, they were greatly concerned with its application, which they approved or solicited on several occasions. The Calvo Doctrine, announced by the Argentine international lawyer Carlos Calvo shortly before 1870, they accepted with hearty appreciation and with the hope that it might moderate the employment of armed force in the collection of contract debts and pecuniary claims for injuries to alien persons and properties.

But they did not view either the Monrovian manifesto or the Calvo effort to abate the employment of force as a sufficient guaranty of their territorial integrity and political independence. And they had reason for their doubts, especially in respect to the Monroe Doctrine, which offered no firm and specific pledge to shield them against all non-American aggression, contained no guaranty of security against the United States, and tended to place them under the tutelage of the government which sometimes insisted on regulating their conduct with reference to foreign countries and thus limited their freedom of action. They felt compelled therefore to seek security against the United States as well as against other foreign countries, and a series of Latin-American conferences and congresses was one means they tried to utilize in their quest.

The first of the series was the Panama Congress of 1826, already mentioned. The powers feared at that time were Spain and the Holy Alliance. Apparently against the wishes of Bolívar, at whose instance the assembly was convoked, the United States was asked to send delegates by the vice-president of Colombia and the government of Mexico (which soon appeared to regret its action). The United States was not thought of as a member of the proposed league of nations, which was rather envisaged as a Spanish American federation under the patronage of England. The congress was a complete fiasco. Delegates of the four governments represented—Great Colombia, Peru, the Federation of Central, America, Mexico—signed treaties which were never ratified.

The second congress, which met in Lima in 1847–48, was convoked mainly for the purpose of adopting defensive measures against Juan José Flores, the Venezuelan soldier of fortune who was reported to be acting in behalf of the queen of Spain in an attempt to reconquer some of the states of South America's Pacific coast. Delegates were present from Chile, Bolivia, Peru, Ecuador, and Colombia (then called New Granada). Having recently (1846) obtained from the United States a guaranty of the permanent possession of the Isthmus of Panama, the Colombian government was in a friendly mood and advocated that the Latin-American states sign a pledge that they would always maintain diplomatic agents in Washington. But the United States–Mexican war was then in progress and the Colombian representative at Lima found the sentiment toward the United States so hostile that he decided not to present the proposal until he had received further instructions from Bogotá. He informed his government that "all the American republics" were very suspicious of their Anglo-Saxon neighbor and that their delegates at Lima were beginning to feel that the United States was more to be feared than Europe. Nevertheless, he was told to present his project; and when he did, it was rejected. Like its predecessor at Panama, the Lima Congress accomplished practically nothing of enduring value. Three treaties were signed; but the Flores threat soon vanished and they were not ratified.

Two Spanish American diplomatic conferences, one in Santiago and the other in Washington, were held in 1856, largely because of growing uneasiness regarding the United States aroused by its recent territorial acquisitions from Mexico, by the raids of "Yankee" filibusters into northern Mexico, Cuba, and Central America, by vigorous demands of the United States for indemnity for its citizens who had been killed or injured by a riot in Panama earlier in the year, and by awareness that England was becoming less disposed to oppose American expansion toward the south. It was a period of widespread alarm in Spanish America. Predicting a race war, Manuel Carrasco Albano of Chile urged Latin-American solidarity. Francisco Bilbao, another prominent

Chilean, saw in the United States an imperialistic Russia unrestrained by the balance of power and called frantically for a congress to effect unity. Juan N. de Pereda, the Mexican minister in Guatemala, wrote a long memorandum on the subject, in which he contended that the Latins of America were in grave danger, that a conference of plenipotentiaries should be assembled for the purpose of forming an offensive and defensive alliance, and that it might be advisable to extend the alliance to other Latin countries, particularly Spain. Such were the apprehensions that drove the diplomats of Colombia, Mexico, Guatemala, Costa Rica, Venezuela, and Peru to assemble in Washington, and those of Peru, Chile, and Ecuador to hold a conference in Santiago. Both groups drafted and signed treaties of alliance; but the "Yankee" danger subsided with the approach of the Civil War, and these pacts also remained unratified.

Civil conflict in the United States soon revealed to the Latin-American countries a serious dilemma. If a powerful United States was a potential danger, a weakened United States was also to be dreaded, for it could no longer ward off European aggression. France, England, and Spain invaded Mexico, and Spain reannexed the Dominican Republic and made attacks on both Peru and Chile. The Mexican minister in Washington, who had at first rejoiced at the prospect of a dissolved union north of the Rio Grande, thinking that Mexico would have less to fear, was not long in discovering the dilemma and changing his mind. His reason for doing so he stated as follows on April 4, 1862: [2]

Before the civil war commenced in the United States, it appeared that they were the only enemies that Mexico had, because their . . . usurping policy had deprived us of half of our territory and they were a constant menace against the integrity of what we had left. Nothing therefore was more natural than to see with pleasure . . . a division which . . . [promised to] make almost impotent against us each of the parts that remained. But unfortunately the sedition from which we expected such favorable results had hardly begun when we discovered another danger from which the power of this country had freed us and against which its present unity would be the surest guaranty. . . . We therefore find ourselves in the presence of the hard alternative of sacrificing our territory and our nationality at the hands of this country or our liberty and our independence before the despotic thrones of Europe. The second danger is immediate and more imminent; in evading the first, we may count upon the future and the lessons of experience.

Once more the Spanish Americans began to advocate a congress and to discuss the advisability as well of inviting the United States to participate. Most of the Latin diplomats seemed to think it would be a good thing to have the United States represented, provided Washington could be persuaded to send delegates, but they soon learned that the Lincoln government was too deeply absorbed in domestic problems to deal with any others. The Costa Rican diplomat, whose country had taken a leading part in the military conflict with William Walker and his armed adventurers, could not forget the past nor feel secure in respect to the United States for the future. He remarked that moderate, just, and upright men like those who formed the Lincoln administration might not always rule the destinies of this great republic, and therefore urged that an effort be made to persuade the United States to contract the solemn obligation to respect, and compel others to respect, the independence, sovereignty, and territorial integrity of its sister republics and pledge itself specifically not to acquire any part of their territory, or permit filibuster expeditions, or infringe upon the rights of these republics in any manner whatsoever.

The Hispanic Americans finally decided not to invite the United States to the contemplated congress, which met at Lima in 1864–65, with delegates present from eight Spanish American states: Colombia, Venezuela, Ecuador, Peru, Chile, Argentine, Bolivia, and Guatemala. Another treaty of alliance was signed, only to meet the fate of agreements made at previous assemblies.

The Colombian government planned a congress at Panama in 1881, for the purpose of dealing with arbitration in America, but it failed to convene on account of the War of the Pacific. Five years later the Colombian president, uneasy regarding the policy of the United States in respect to the Isthmus of Panama and the projected canal, and resentful of the procedures of the stronger powers with regard to the complaints and claims of their nationals against Latin America, instructed his minister in Paris to sound out his colleagues on the advisability of a Spanish American meeting to consider these subjects. The Colombian minister accordingly urged his associates from Argentina, Uruguay, Bolivia, and Guatemala—the Chilean minister was not present at the conference because of illness—to prevail upon their governments to take part in a conference for the purpose of bringing about a general union that would enable them to resist the aggressive tendencies of the United States and the "unjust claims" of the nationals of the great powers of Europe. But the assembly failed to materialize.

Another attempt, sponsored by the government of Ecuador during the critical stage of the Anglo-Venezuelan boundary dispute, fared only a little better. Convoked for the purpose of considering the implications of the Monroe Doctrine and effecting the organization of a "cohesive force" capable of preventing the European nations from flouting and abusing the "weak states" of America, the conference did not begin to assemble in Mexico City before the Venezuelan crisis had passed. Delegates who finally arrived in August, 1896—those from Ecuador and Central America—decided not to inaugurate a formal congress but merely to organize themselves into a sort of junta and draft a report. One of the results was a document (1) declaring that the enforcement of the Monroe Doctrine ought not to depend upon the "unilateral" policy of the United States but should require the consent and co-operation of "all and each of the other republics," (2) calling for abolition of intervention and territorial annexation on the American continent, and (3) approving obligatory arbitration in glowing terms.

Without dealing with assemblies of a regional nature or those concerned with law, sanitation, and other subjects, it is safe to conclude that the nineteenth-century Latin-American international movement was, in most respects, a failure. It probably made some contributions to peace and harmony, but it led to no effective solidarity and no common policy in confronting the outside world.

THE FIRST PAN-AMERICAN CONFERENCE

Meantime the United States, at first largely actuated by economic motives, had become interested in the American international movement. The first invitations to a Pan-American conference to be held in the United States were sent out as early as 1881; but for partisan reasons in the United States and because of the war then raging between Chile and Peru and Bolivia, the invitations were cancelled.

The conference finally met in Washington late in 1889; but its only achievements worthy of note were the actual presence of delegates from all the independent nations of America except the Dominican Republic, the organization of a committee to study the feasibility of a Pan-American railway, and the creation of a "Commercial Bureau of the American Republics" under the direction of a governing board headed by the United States secretary of state. The conference revealed that the Latin Americans did not trust the United States and that some of them were suspicious of one another. Secretary James G. Blaine's proposed customs union reminded them of the German *Zollverein* and Otto von Bismarck's policy of "blood and iron." The delegates could not even reach an agreement on the question of commercial reciprocity.

The discussions and proposals of the Hispanic Americans clearly indicated that they were seeking security not only against non-American nations but against American countries as well. For instance, the delegations of Argentina and Brazil submitted this recommendation: "In cases of war a victory of arms shall not convey any rights to the territory of the conquered. Acts of conquest, whether the object or the consequence of the war, shall be considered to be in violation of the public law of America."[3] They probably had the United States and Chile in mind, but the seizure of Paraguayan territory by their own countries during the recent war could have been recalled. Agreement could not be reached on the recommendation; but after the delegates of eleven countries had signed a resolution favoring a Pan-American treaty of arbitration, Blaine introduced a similar proposal on arbitration and conquest and it was accepted. Its effectiveness depended, however, upon the negotiation of a general arbitration treaty, and no such treaty was signed and ratified during the century.

The Latin Americans, as might have been expected, also disclosed anxiety regarding the prospect that the strong powers would continue to press vigorously the claims of their nationals. A juristic committee of the conference recommended the adoption of a declaration to the effect that "a nation has not, nor recognizes, in favor of foreigners any other obligations or responsibilities than those which are established in favor of the natives, in like cases, by the constitution and the laws."[4] The Latin-American delegates were thus trying to prevent the strong powers from elevating to a privileged position such of their nationals as were residing in or having economic relations with Latin America and thereby reducing Latin-American citizens to a subordinate status. All the delegates voted in favor of the recommendation except those of the United States, who opposed it, and the delegates from Haiti, who abstained from voting.

One of the Argentine representatives, Vicente G. Quesada, was disturbed, or pretended to be disturbed, by the potential aggressiveness of the United States. Quesada visited Mexico on a diplomatic mission soon after the congress adjourned, his main purpose being to ascertain the views and plans of the Mexican government with reference to its powerful neighbor, to give the Mexican leaders assurance of Argentina's moral support in withstanding pressure exerted from Washington, and to point out the singular mission which geography imposed upon Mexico to serve "as a dyke against the invading torrent" of political and economic power from the north.

No other Pan-American conference was held before the end of the century. But at least two events occurred to keep alive Latin-American fears of and irritation with the United States. One was the Spanish-American War, to be discussed later, which aroused uneasiness throughout Latin America in spite of strong sympathies for the Cubans. The other was the drastic procedure of the United States in its relations with Chile.

The trouble with Chile arose from the *Itata* affair and culminated in the *Baltimore* incident. The United States had exhibited offensive zeal in the capture of the *Itata,* a vessel which left California with arms and munitions for the Chilean insurgents in revolt against President Balmaceda; later it showed imprudence in permitting some sailors from the *Baltimore* to go ashore in Valparaiso shortly after Balmaceda was overthrown by the aggrieved revolutionaries. As might have been expected, the seamen soon got into a fight with the Chileans, in which several Americans were killed or injured; whereupon the United States proceeded to exact a heavy indemnity (1891–92) by resorting to a threat of war.

THE RECENT PERIOD

CHAPTER XXVI

Dynamics of Latin-American Economic Development

☙ LATIN AMERICA'S DECIDED DEPENDENCE UPON FOREIGN TRADE AND FOREIGN CAPITAL

To a greater extent than in many countries the economic development of the Latin-American nations has been the result of impacts
from the outside. The nature and significance of these impacts during
the nineteenth century have been described in previous chapters. They
were more significant perhaps after the 1890's than before. Production
in the Temperate Zone republics of Latin America was vigorously
stimulated by the large influx of immigrants, and this influence was
important also in other republics where their numbers were much
smaller. Even more significant were two other factors: (1) the vigorous
search of the highly industrialized nations for outlets for manufactured
goods, capital, and technical skills; (2) ever-increasing demands by
such nations for foods and raw materials. The most efficient producers
in Latin America, whether immigrants, alien capitalists, or natives, had
their eyes on foreign markets for their output. National economies
were developed with this objective in mind and it determined the contours of national transport systems and the commodities upon which
economic effort was centered. It was not until well after 1900 that
much thought was given to production for home markets. If production for domestic consumption became efficient in some lines it was
largely because most of the output, or at least a good part of it, was
intended for export. Methods of producing foods or cheap consumer
goods for the masses at home were rarely given much attention by
either the economic leaders or the governments. The oligarchies depended on imports for their finished products and considered foreign
commerce more important than domestic. Latin America became a

weak outlying segment of the great industrial economies of the West.[1]

These foreign impacts and the rapid growth of population caused a vast expansion in foreign trade. From less than $1,000,000,000 in 1885 the value of the foreign commerce of Latin America increased to nearly $3,000,000,000 in 1913, and after a brief recession at the outbreak of World War I the total skyrocketed to a peak of more than $6,000,000,000 in 1920. A slight contraction then set in, but the aggregate climbed back to well above $5,000,000,000 in both 1928 and 1929. Thereafter, of course, a decided decline occurred because of the severe world depression; but the second global conflict, like the first, vigorously stimulated exports until the peak of 1920 was approached again in the middle 1940's and far surpassed in 1947. Total Latin-American foreign trade was valued at $14,600,000,000 in 1951. Mainly because the Latin-American nations were debtor nations and because imports were difficult to obtain during the two global wars, the exports of the region and of each of the republics that comprised it were usually much larger than their imports.

On the basis of their exports, the Latin countries of America divided themselves into three groups: (1) states such as Mexico, Bolivia, Venezuela, and Chile whose exports were confined almost entirely to minerals and metals; (2) countries whose exports were composed mainly of farm, ranch, and forest products: Argentina, Brazil, Uruguay, Paraguay, the six countries of Central America (although some of these exported small quantities of gold), and the three island republics; (3) nations such as Colombia, Peru, and Ecuador, which exported both groups of commodities in approximately equal percentages. Many commodities exported from the region were produced in large measure by foreign corporations. Capitalists from the big industrialized nations organized business enterprises and sent them into the Latin-American countries to produce sugar, bananas, nitrates, industrial metals, petroleum, and other foods and raw materials and ship them out to the more highly developed regions.

It is hardly necessary to point out that the principal imports of the Latin-American republics, as in the early National period, were manufactured products, but it should be noted that many of them also imported such agricultural commodities as cereals, flour, canned foods, and dairy and pork products. Bulking large among the manufactured goods brought in were, of course, clothing and various textiles; iron, steel, and numerous metal products; railway rolling stock; electrical equipment and many kinds of machinery; vehicles of almost every type, from bicycles to airplanes; typewriters and other office equipment;

sundry chemicals and pharmaceuticals; and newsprint, as well as many other paper products.

Until the early 1930's, and later in some countries, the national governments of the region obtained their revenues mainly from tariff levies on both exports and imports. It required a world depression and urgent suggestions from foreign financial advisers to turn their attention to other important sources of revenue such as income and inheritance taxes.

Whether for export of surpluses or for imports needed by the oligarchies and the upper middle class, few nations of the world were more dependent upon foreign markets. Practically the only commodities that they did not produce primarily for export until well after 1900 were corn, manioc, beans, peppers, certain native fruits, and yerba maté (Paraguayan tea); *pulque, chicha,* and a few other alcoholic or soft drinks; some machine-made consumer goods of cheaper grades; a number of handicraft articles for the poorer classes; and revolutions. Anywhere from a third to more than four-fifths of the leading commodities produced in the region were sent abroad, and most of the countries specialized in one, two, or three export commodities. Tin accounted for more than 70 per cent of Bolivia's exports; copper and nitrates made up 60 to 75 per cent of Chile's; bananas over 70 per cent of Panama's and well above 80 per cent of Honduras'; petroleum nearly 90 per cent of Venezuela's; sugar and tobacco 80 per cent of Cuba's; coffee and bananas 80 to 90 per cent of Nicaragua's; copper, petroleum, and cotton about 75 per cent of Peru's; and coffee from 50 to 90 per cent of the exports of the leading coffee countries, such as Brazil, Colombia, Guatemala, El Salvador, and Haiti. (Map 13 gives further details on this point.)

This extreme dependence upon world markets, and particularly upon such a limited number of export commodities, was very hazardous. Both the national revenues and the general prosperity of most of the countries were determined by conditions over which they had practically no control. A sudden drop in the price of one or two export products, outbreak of war among the powers, a tariff rise, or failure of a crop was often tantamount to financial calamity. Beginning with the period of World War I, and a little earlier in some cases, several of the republics initiated efforts to widen the base of their economies by diversifying agriculture and stressing manufacturing industries; but such economic changes required both time and heavy outlays of capital.

The pace and magnitude of the flow of capital into the region varied, of course, with both local and world economic and political conditions; but the stream expanded and speeded its tempo after 1880. Foreign investors were not greatly interested, however, either in the diversification of Latin America's agriculture or in fostering its manufactures. A large fraction of the funds they made available was invested in government bonds, the proceeds of which were used to pay off budgetary deficits or to build railroads, port works, highways, and other public services. The rest of the foreign capital consisted mainly of direct investments in these public services or in mining, agricultural, forest-product, banking, mercantile, and petroleum enterprises. Only a small percentage of the total was invested in establishments designed to turn out finished goods, although considerable sums were placed in packing houses, sugar mills, and other types of processing plants. It is true that certain factors were tending to increase this percentage; growing pressure in the highly industrialized countries for the export of manufacturing equipment, a definite trend toward alliances between the capital-goods industries and investment bankers and shipping firms, and Latin-American manipulation of tariffs and currencies were gradually forcing foreign capital into enterprises calculated to reduce the region's dependence upon the outside world. This applied, however, mainly to larger countries such as Argentina, Brazil, Chile, Colombia, and Mexico, where diversification was most feasible.

The amount of foreign capital operating in the region at any particular date cannot be precisely determined; but there is no doubt that the total increased fairly steadily up until the 1930's in all the countries except Mexico, where a contraction occurred after the overthrow of Porfirio Díaz in 1911. The aggregate (excluding the properties of alien immigrants) was around $9,000,000,000 in 1914, $12,000,000,000 in 1929, and $11,000,000,000 in 1940. The British investment, including the Canadian, was larger than any other until shrinkage set in following 1928. Next in importance was the French investment, until it was exceeded by the investment from the United States shortly after 1900 and by that from Germany a decade or so later. The capital stream flowing in from the other European countries was much smaller, but the nationals of practically all of them made investments in Latin America—especially those of Italy, Spain, Belgium, the Netherlands, and Switzerland—and some capital likewise flowed in from Japan. Of the $12,000,000,000 of alien funds active in the region in 1929 nearly three-fourths were from the Anglo-Saxon countries. World War II and its aftermath sharply reduced both the Japanese and the European investment, which probably aggregated no more than $2,250,000,000 in 1950. Private investments of citizens of the United States at that time were more than twice as large; but the aggregate of foreign capital operating in the region was less than two-thirds of the aggregate in

Export Products
of Latin America

Mainly agricultural, forest and pastoral
Mainly mineral
Agricultural, forest, pastoral and mineral

Countries Dangerously
Dependent on one or two
Export Commodities

Country	Commodities	Percentage of Total Exports
Bolivia	Tin	71.4
El Salvador	Coffee	89.2
Honduras	Bananas	82.3
Panama	Bananas	73.6
Venezuela	Petroleum	89.0
Brazil	Coffee, Cotton	64.6
Costa Rica	Coffee, Bananas	81.0
Chile	Copper, Nitrates	66.2
Cuba	Sugar, Tobacco	78.6
Dom. Rep.	Sugar, Cocoa	73.1
Guatemala	Coffee, Bananas	95.2
Haiti	Coffee, Cotton	77.4
Nicaragua	Coffee, Bananas	83.5

MAP 13

1929 and even less than the total in 1914, and some of the Latin-American republics were clamoring for gifts and loans from abroad.

Naturally this foreign investment was not evenly distributed among the various countries. The major recipients were Argentina, Brazil, Chile, Mexico, Peru, Uruguay, Cuba, Venezuela, and Colombia. The first six of these, in fact, were the chief centers of investment until Mexico had its twentieth-century revolution and until capital was attracted by Cuba's sugar, Venezuela's petroleum, and Colombia's oil and government bonds. In proportion to their size, however, Guatemala, Costa Rica, Honduras, Panama, and the Dominican Republic did not lag far behind their larger neighbors as fields for the investment of foreign capital.

AN APPRAISAL OF THE ADVANTAGES AND RISKS OF FOREIGN DYNAMIC FORCES

This flow of money from the highly developed nations and the technology that accompanied it were important stimulants to Latin America's economic advance, but there were certain limitations that will be pointed out shortly. The most fundamental factors were the pressure of the industrialized nations for markets for manufactured products and their constantly increasing demand for the foods and raw materials that the region could produce. Next in significance was probably the immigrant impact. Around 11,000,000 immigrants entered Latin America between 1885 and 1956 and close to 7,000,000 of them stayed there to make their contribution to its economic development. They came from almost every nation in the world but principally from Italy, Spain, Portugal, Germany, France, and the Slavic countries. There were no more than 300,000 to 400,000 from China and Japan, and the number from Turkey, Syria, and other parts of the Orient was perhaps somewhat smaller. The major recipient countries in Latin America were, of course, Argentina, Brazil, Mexico, and Uruguay, but tens of thousands entered the other larger countries and Cuba, and many hundreds settled in the smaller republics. The newcomers were for the most part poor and unlettered, but they were industrious, ambitious, and not without native intelligence, and they furnished good examples for the older population just as men like Sarmiento and Alberdi had expected. The Latins among them—and the Latins composed the overwhelming majority—were also fairly easy to absorb. In the introduction of more efficient farming and superior breeds of livestock and in the establishment of manufacturing and processing plants the immigrants were usually the pioneers.[2]

The heavy impact of foreign capital, trade, and immigrants caused less difficulty than during the early National period in such countries as Argentina, Uruguay, Chile, Peru, Colombia, and Mexico under Díaz, but considerably more trouble in Venezuela and several of the smaller countries of the Caribbean area; and attempts to use immigrants as propaganda media sometimes caused disturbance or uneasiness almost everywhere. Germany, Spain, and Italy were the principal offenders in this effort to draw their nationals in Latin America into the cultural and power conflicts of the time.

The large inflow of capital undoubtedly increased the tempo of economic development, caused a slow rise in wages, and helped to liberate some of the serfs; but few who are fully informed regarding the details would be bold enough to argue that foreign money was always utilized to the advantage of the region in which it was invested. Some of the scandals that accompanied British investments during the early National period have already been discussed. It is likely that others occurred during the recent epoch but were not exposed by official investigation. The record of the investment bankers of the United States during the 1920's, as disclosed by two Senate hearings shortly after the beginning of the world depression, was marred by bribery, greed, and bad judgment, and it is likely that the record of other foreign investors was no better. Governments dominated by foreign capitalists or revolutions financed by them were not unknown in the smaller countries of the region. The truth of the matter is that there was not a little dishonesty, chicanery, and faulty judgment on the part of both the lenders and the borrowers; and, worse still from the standpoint of Latin America, there was almost no planning. The foreign investors were in pursuit of profits they hoped to make by supplying the world's industrialized regions with food for factory workers and minerals, metals, and other raw materials; they were not primarily concerned with the development of the nations in which their money was invested. The Latin-American leaders wanted to pay off old government debts or current budgetary deficits, to create new government revenues, and to reap personal profits by sale of materials to new enterprises, or from commissions or "handouts" of one sort or another; they rarely had any blueprints for balanced national development. This haphazard and selfish procedure, along with bad judgment, profiteering, and a good deal of speculation in lands and other natural resources, often greatly reduced the benefits of foreign investment.

The international difficulties that arose from foreign economic activities and the presence of aliens must also be taken into account in estimating these benefits. They were similar to the difficulties that arose during the early National period; but there was at least one important difference: the attempt of some of the European governments to use immigrants and the sons of immigrants in the struggle for influence and power.

Foreign merchants and shipowners engaged in commerce with the various Latin-American nations continued to complain to their home governments regarding tariffs, port charges, port regulations, and arbitrary acts affecting merchant vessels and their crews and cargoes. Their complaints, some arising from genuine grievances and others with little foundation, often led foreign governments to support them in efforts to secure redress.

Foreign investments and immigrants who clung to their original nationality caused similar political difficulties. The immigrants not only suffered from administrative abuses and political disorders in the more turbulent countries, but sometimes aided and abetted them or presented trumped-up claims to their home governments. Foreign investors and their enterprises permeated Latin-American life. Foreigners, whether living in Latin America or residing abroad, financed and constructed numerous railways, telephone systems, electric plants, port facilities, and other public services and frequently controlled and operated them for years after they were completed; bought or leased lands and engaged in agricultural enterprises both large and small; controlled shipping companies and trunk airlines; acquired and exploited many mines and most of the nitrate, asphalt, and oil deposits; financed, built, and managed meat-packing plants, textile mills, and other industrial establishments; and purchased huge quantities of Latin-American government bonds. Revolutions and arbitrary acts of Latin-American administrative and military officers injured alien persons and properties, and disputes occurred with respect to taxes, contracts, defaults on loans, utility rates, labor and sanitary regulations, and distribution of profits. Foreigners not only raised loud complaints but made appeals to foreign offices, and sometimes the final result was coercion of the Latin-American governments by the more powerful countries and consequently the impairment of Latin-American sovereignty. Often the aliens had valid grievances and the final adjustments of their complaints were reasonably fair; but when a keen sense of justice was lacking abroad, the foreigners were likely to be favored because they had the backing of powerful governments. To such procedures, if not to the general policy of protecting and promoting foreign commerce and investments, especially in its more vigorous phases, the term "economic imperialism" may be applied without much hesitation.

The penalties connected with political disorder, despotism, and deficient technology must therefore be placed in the balance along with dishonesty, chicanery, speculation, profiteering, and lack of planning, before an accurate appraisal of the beneficial effects of these economic and immigrant impacts can be arrived at. The highly developed nations, or rather some of their producers, shippers, investment bankers, and business managers, certainly profited, and the Latin-American countries, as already suggested, reaped advantages from accelerated development, taxes, rising wages, wider opportunities for employment, and liberation of the workers from debt peonage; but in some cases the penalties—for which the Latin Americans were largely, though not entirely, to blame—were heavy indeed. It is not possible to determine the exact weight of such penalties because power politics and possibly other factors were involved; but the intervention policy inaugurated by the United States following the Spanish-American War was certainly adopted in part because of the problems arising from foreign trade, foreign investments, and the presence of alien residents in the Caribbean countries; and loss or curtailment of sovereignty is not generally regarded as a light punishment.

The United States reduced five of the Latin-American nations to the status of quasi protectorates within less than two decades. The Washington authorities were activated by a mixture of economic interest, benevolence, and defense strategy; but the last was probably the basic motivation. The United States was determined to dominate the Caribbean area to the extent deemed necessary to prevent its domination by outside powers, and the European nations suspected of ambition to intervene in the region or control it were expected to act under the pretense of protecting the persons and properties of their nationals.

The Cuban protectorate was set up in 1902 with a naval base and the security of foreign investments as the main goals. The Panama protectorate, established late in 1903, was closely connected with the determination to control, build, and operate the isthmian canal. The security of foreign investments, the urgency of pecuniary claims, a naval base, and the desire to promote economic progress and democracy figured among the motives two years later for the domination of the Dominican Republic, some of whose political leaders were asking for intervention. A potential rival canal, the supposed ambitions of foreign powers, and the brutal tyranny of a dictator seem to have been the major causes for intervention in Nicaragua in 1909. Extreme disorders and resultant injuries to the persons and property of foreigners and danger of intervention by European governments were probably the main reasons for extending American control to Haiti in 1915. In the three island republics and Panama, if not also in Nicaragua, some efforts were made to promote democracy and economic advance and to improve the life of the people by education and sanitation.

In respect to the entire Caribbean region, the fear of European intervention was increased by the joint coercion of Venezuela in 1902–3 by Great Britain, Germany, and Italy and by a decision of the Hague Tribunal early in 1904 to the effect that these three powers should have priority in the payment of the contracted debts and claims of their nationals. It seemed to be a reasonable conclusion that this strange decision handed down by a group of lawyers presumably devoted to international peace would tend to incite coercive action against other disorderly and remiss countries. In fact, some efforts were made by the United States during the Theodore Roosevelt and Taft administrations to extend the protectorate policy to at least three more Caribbean republics—Honduras, Guatemala, and Costa Rica; but while there was almost as good a case in respect to the first two as there had been for intervention in Haiti, the Dominican Republic, and Nicaragua, suggestions for a protectorate over Costa Rica seemed to betray too crass a "dollar diplomacy"; members of Congress revealed a growing reluctance to consent to further extension of the system; and all three efforts failed. The abuses of Cipriano Castro, even after the settlement of 1903–4, were very irritating both to foreign investors and to Theodore Roosevelt, but the problem was finally solved by preventing Castro's return to Venezuela after he had gone to Europe for medical attention.

It is very interesting to observe that the empire of the United States reached its maximum dimensions under Woodrow Wilson, the avowed anti-imperialist, who disliked "dollar diplomacy" but was zealous for the promotion of democracy in Latin America. Wilson did not recall the American Marines or proconsuls from a single protectorate and even added Haiti to the four established by his predecessors. He did refuse, however, to intervene in Mexico or other Latin-American countries for the primary purpose of promoting or defending economic interests. His armed interventions of 1914 (Veracruz) and 1916 (the Pershing Expedition) had other objectives.

Harding and Hughes and Coolidge and Kellogg tended to follow the old policies laid down by Roosevelt and Root and Taft and Knox until a vigorous reaction in both the United States and Latin America finally forced a change. Then a recession began, slowly at first under Herbert Hoover and Henry Stimson, but more rapidly under Franklin D. Roosevelt, Cordell Hull, and Sumner Welles. All the protectorates were finally abandoned by the early 1940's.[3]

Mexico's case was unique among the Latin-American countries. Aliens lost many of their Mexican properties, especially their lands, railways, and oil wells, some of which were expropriated without the "full, prompt, and adequate compensation" required by the rules of international law; but Mexico largely escaped the customary punishment for such raids upon foreigners and their possessions. The New Freedom, the New Deal, and two global wars were mainly responsible for Mexico's impunity, for they increased democratic fervor in the United States and aroused deep sympathy for little nations and humble men. The Washington government sometimes hovered on the verge of vigorous intervention but was restrained either by humanitarian sentiment or by global distractions, and the European powers were held in check both by the United States and by Europe's strife.

It does not seem necessary to dwell upon the policies pursued by the European nations with respect to their economic interests and their nationals in Latin America. The scope of their official operations was narrowed but intensified during part of the period under consideration. Most of the South American countries, excepting Venezuela, were not harassed by force or menace; but European navies were industriously employed elsewhere in Latin America, especially those of Germany and Great Britain, and if France and Spain were more moderate than during the early National period, Italy almost made up for the difference. The significant point to be noted is that European aggressiveness was sufficient to furnish an important motive for the vigorous Caribbean policy of the United States.[4]

The main concern of Latin-American leaders in all such relationships was to obtain what they needed from the outside world without jeopardizing or seriously impairing their sovereignty in the process. To this fundamental problem they devoted no little diplomatic effort. They often tried to induce the wealthier and stronger powers to sign agreements to refrain from using force or menace in connection with the persons and properties of their nationals in Latin America. Insisting that all disputes arising with respect to the subject should be adjusted by Latin-American administrative officials and courts, they pleaded their case repeatedly in Pan-American and world assemblies; but the only satisfactory pledges they ever obtained were from the United States. In view of critical world conditions after 1914, however, this concession from the leading American power, together with the policy laid down in the Monroe Doctrine, served as a mighty bulwark. The United States was not willing to permit other great powers to indulge in policies which it renounced and which might become a threat to the hemisphere's security. The Mexican case was a striking example.

With their eyes upon Mexico's assertion of economic nationalism, other Latin-American countries—particularly Argentina, Guatemala, and Bolivia—revealed some disposition to follow Mexico's lead. But few ever followed it fully, and at the middle of the twentieth century practically all of them seemed eager for foreign funds. They were being reminded, however, by the big neighbor which was supposed to have most of the world's available capital that the best way to attract foreign investment was to create the "proper climate." President Harry Truman declared early in 1949 that he had no intention of reviving the "old imperialism," but his "bold new plan," otherwise known as "Point IV," included no license to confiscate or seriously hamper American enterprises abroad. It seemed to envisage both a more thoughtful and generous attitude on the part of capitalists and pledges of "good treatment" on the part of retarded countries as a prerequisite for large investment in such countries.

The conclusion suggested by this brief summary of a very important subject can be stated in a few sentences. It should not be assumed that either immigrants or alien capital investments in underdeveloped countries are always and everywhere an unmixed blessing. The result will depend upon individuals and governments on both sides. Perhaps of greater significance than either private capital or immigrants in Latin America are the foreign markets eager for its products and high-pressure salesmanship of foreign goods. After the second or third decade of the twentieth century more and more attention was devoted in the region to production for home markets, and this emphasis seemed likely to continue. By diversifying production and expanding domestic consumption, perhaps Latin America would soon generate within itself the major dynamics of its economic development.

In any case, the Latin-American revolt against "colonialism" had become a factor that could not longer be ignored. A strong sentiment described as "economic nationalism," accompanied by more careful economic planning, greater control over foreign enterprises, and more stress on saving and investment by natives, was becoming increasingly evident in almost every country.[5] Whether this sentiment—and generous loans and grants by foreign public agencies—would restrict the flow of private capital into the region had not yet been fully revealed, although such a result appeared probable as Latin America entered the sixth decade of the new century.

CHAPTER XXVII

Northern Latin America: The Island Republics

The general economic depression of the 1890's revealed that the economies of the Latin-American countries were firmly linked to those of the great capitalistic and industrial powers. Latin Americans not only shared the economic vicissitudes of the rest of the world from that time onward; they also felt the shocks of global war and the drafts of power politics.

ECONOMIC, POLITICAL, AND SOCIAL TRENDS

With the exception of a few of the republics, which experienced a period of severe political turmoil or confronted peculiar economic problems, Hispanic America enjoyed a period of material prosperity from the end of the nineteenth century until 1920 and from 1922 through 1928 or 1929. Immigrants and foreign capital flowed in as never before; [1] railways and highways were constructed and airlines inaugurated; production of old commodities expanded—silver, gold, copper, zinc, lead, tin, meat, wheat, coffee, sugar, and most of the rest; such new commodities as petroleum, vanadium, nickel, iron ore, and manganese were exploited; sanitary works were installed in most of the leading cities; magnificent public edifices were erected; municipal parks were laid out and ornamented; streets were paved and avenues widened.

The region descended with the rest of the world into the painful economic slump that began in 1929. The dollar value of Latin-America's exports, which had risen from some $600,000,000 in 1900 to over $3,000,000,000 in 1928, dropped to little more than $1,000,000,000 in 1932 and stood at considerably less than $2,000,000,000 in 1939.[2] Every nation in the region interrupted payments on a part or the whole of its foreign-owned government bonds, and nearly all of them adopted rigid exchange regulations which curtailed their imports and hampered the outflow of such profits as alien business enterprises yielded. Many firms, native and foreign, went into bankruptcy. Public services deteriorated.

With the approach of the second global war, however, a new era of prosperity began. European governments spent billions for Latin-American products; the United States expended even more on lend-lease to the various countries and for their critical materials. The value of Latin America's exports, converting inflated currencies into inflated dollar equivalents, ranged from $5,000,000,000 to $6,000,000,000 in the 1940's and was boosted to over $7,300,000,000 in 1951 by the "cold war" and Korean operations, both volume and value in terms of gold dollars exceeding volume and value in the same terms of the aggregate exports in 1928. But population, approximately 62,000,000 in 1900, increased from less than 104,000,000 in 1928 to well above 155,000,000 in 1950, and Latin Americans not only keenly felt that they were comparatively poor but attributed their relative poverty to the disadvantages of specializing in the production of food and raw materials and of alien ownership of large segments of their public services and material resources.

The decades following 1930 therefore witnessed vigorous efforts in many of the countries to establish manufacturing industries, diversify agricultural production, and "nationalize" foreign enterprises by purchase or otherwise. It was too early for accurate appraisal of their ultimate success. Some new crops appeared everywhere, light manufacturing industries greatly expanded in the majority of the countries, and Argentina, Brazil, Chile, Peru, Colombia, Venezuela, and Mexico either developed considerable heavy industry or were on the point of doing so. Yet all eventually discovered that they were handicapped by scarcity of venture capital and raised a clamor for foreign funds, hoping to obtain government grants, cheap government loans, or minority private investments in enterprises controlled by themselves. Lamenting their alleged state of economic subjection to the great powers in the past, they worked up an intense devotion to "economic nationalism."

The first thirty years of the century, with some exceptions, seemed to disclose a slow trend toward civilian government, growing political stability, and a larger measure of democracy. But a series of revolutions in 1930 and 1931, followed by several long-term dictatorships and reverberations of European totalitarianism, signalized a reversal, so that from the viewpoint of political democracy conditions were little better in 1956 than in 1900, though somewhat better by 1958.

Aside from a rapid increase of population, which was the result not only of a large influx of immigrants, particularly during the first decade or so, but also of a declining death rate attributable mainly to better sanitation, several striking social developments occurred during the period. Among them were: rapid urban growth; expansion of the middle class; the rise of labor movements; land reforms (actual or merely vaguely projected); reduction of illiteracy; achievements in poetry, music, painting, and architecture; and the appearance of a group of novelists who attained world fame.

In international affairs, the Latin Americans advanced from the passive-defensive to the active-defensive, participating in world conferences and world organizations as well as in those confined to the Americas. Irritated and alarmed during the early years of the century by the defensive expansionism of the United States, they passed through a period of deep distrust and hostility toward this country into an era of mildly suspicious harmony after their big Anglo-Saxon neighbor developed a more conciliatory policy. Sharply divided in sentiment during the first global war, they were almost unanimous in supporting the United States and its allies during the second. They were also firm collaborators, for the most part, in the struggle against Communist expansion, although they often disclosed dissatisfaction because of a feeling, justified or not, that the United States was relegating them to a secondary position in its esteem and was not sufficiently aware of their problems.

Northern Latin America, on the whole and until the 1940's, was less prosperous than southern Latin America. Mexico entered a long revolutionary period shortly after the financial panic of 1907. The island republics and those of Central America were retarded by insurrection, corrupt or oppressive governments, or falling prices for their sugar, coffee, cacao, tobacco, and bananas. Agriculture and the mineral industries, fairly prosperous until the end of World War I, never fully recovered from the recession that followed until World War II lifted them out of the deep depression of the 1930's.

CUBA LIBRE

Shortly after 1900 two new Latin-American nations, Cuba and Panama, joined the eighteen of the nineteenth century. Both owed their independence in part to the United States.

Restless under Spanish rule, the Cubans had expressed their discontent in 1848–51 in the Narciso López conspiracies, which seemed to be motivated in part by a desire for annexation to the United States. Tranquil for a time after these were suppressed, the island had fought a Ten Years' War for independence in 1868–78, and had been subdued only at the cost of 200,000 lives and hundreds of millions of dollars' worth of property.

Spanish taxes, though sufficiently burdensome to cause vexation, and subject to favoritism and bribery in the process of collection, were not heavy enough to justify the loud complaints that were made. The "fundamental dissatisfaction of the Cubans" in respect to the internal revenue system arose from the fact that they "objected to paying any taxes at all that were imposed by the Spaniards and not by themselves." [3]

Discrimination against creoles, which had long caused complaint in the Spanish colonies, continued in Cuba. Cubans especially resented the fact that Spanish immigrants, who arrived in rather large numbers, received special favors from the colony's officials. Natives of the island were rarely permitted to hold public posts except in a very subordinate capacity. The captains general and (later) the governors general sent out from Spain completely dominated Cuban political life and caused still further bitterness by enriching themselves at Cuba's expense.

Although the Spanish government had permitted Cuba to engage in trade with foreign countries after 1818, it had subjected this commerce to high duties and to certain discriminations in favor of the mother country; and Cubans had become more and more insistent upon trading with the United States without the inconvenience of heavy tariffs and harsh regulations. Spain had finally ratified a reciprocity treaty with this country in 1891, but the United States had revoked the agreement three years later.

This revocation, at the depth of the economic depression of the 1890's, provoked the tremendous economic discontent and fostered the overwhelming desire for independence which culminated in another revolution early in 1895. Spain found it most difficult to quell the rebellion or reconcile the Cubans to any measures short of home rule or even independence. After the war had dragged on for three years, the United States, because of commercial and strategic objectives and humanitarian sentiments, intervened in spite of the displeasure of the leading European powers and helped the Cubans to break the Spanish yoke. Spain's domination in the Americas [4] officially ended in the spring of 1899, and Cuba was granted limited self-government on May 20, 1902. During the last phase of the struggle, Cuba produced able propagandists and generals: José Martí and Tomás Estrada Palma, Antonio Maceo and Máximo Gómez. Martí, an outstanding poet and journalist and the victim of a fatal Spanish ambuscade, was later selected as Cuba's supreme hero. Estrada Palma became the new nation's first president.

The first Cuban elections were held in 1901 while General Leonard Wood was still head of the military government of the island. A national convention framed a constitution, which separated Church and State, guaranteed ample personal and property rights, made provision for free and compulsory primary schools, and contained an amendment which authorized the United States to occupy a naval base in Cuba and intervene in the political affairs of the country for the purpose of promoting sanitary measures, supervising foreign government loans, and maintaining a government capable of protecting life and property. The partisans of one of the candidates for the presidency refused to go to the polls because they objected to the personnel of the national electoral board, and Estrada Palma won the election for a four-year term beginning in 1902.

Sixty-seven years old at the time of his inauguration, Estrada Palma was noted for his sincere patriotism and high sense of honor. His administration was characterized both by respect for the constitution and the liberties of the people and by honest employment of public revenues to foster the construction of roads, railways, and public schools and promote the cultural and material development of the new nation. He accepted the nomination of the Moderate party for a second term; but the Liberal faction soon discovered that the Moderates had registered scores of fraudulent names, and not only abstained from voting but hinted at revolt. In fact, they staged an uprising a few months after the election, and by the end of the first week in September, 1906, they were threatening the capital. Estrada Palma, himself innocent and probably unaware of the fraud until after his electoral victory, appealed to the United States for advice and assistance. President Theodore Roosevelt sent William Howard Taft and Robert L. Bacon to Havana in the hope of solving the problem without full-scale intervention; but their efforts failed, and Taft assumed the role of governor late in September, to be replaced soon afterward by Charles E. Magoon.

Magoon's main tasks were to keep the Cubans quiet by the promotion of public works and to prepare effective laws to govern electoral procedure. The legal work was assigned to an Advisory Law Commission composed of nine Cubans and three citizens of the United States, with Colonel Enoch H. Crowder as chairman. General Mario García Menocal was the presidential candidate of the Conservative party (the successor of the Moderates) in the fall of 1908, and José Miguel Gómez was the standard-bearer of the Liberals. In an honest, well-managed election, Gómez won the prize. On January 28, 1909, Magoon turned the government over to him and thus terminated the first intervention of the United States in Cuban national politics.

Gómez made himself popular by his oratory, his smiling intimacy with the people, and a wide distribution of political favors. Depriving the municipal officials of their proper and legitimate functions, he handed out urban concessions and other contracts to political henchmen, restored cockfighting, sponsored a notorious amnesty bill, put into operation an even more notorious lottery system, and built up a strong military establishment in order to win more friends and insure himself against the fate which had overtaken his predecessor in 1906.

In spite of his single-term pre-election promise, Gómez attempted to obtain the Liberal nomination for the presidency in 1912; and when Alfredo Zayas got the nomination, Gómez used his influence to favor Mario García Menocal, the Conservative candidate, who won the election. Cuban chief executives were thus forming the habit of imposing their successors.

García Menocal was the first Cuban president to serve for two terms (1913–21). Veterans of the recent war for independence threatened to revolt during his administration, but were bought off by an increase in pensions or held in check by fear of intervention by the United States, and a Negro insurrection collapsed because of the landing of American Marines. Menocal, whose father was an American and an officer in the United States Army Engineering Corps, welcomed capital from the United States; and his eight-year government was an epoch of wild speculation and upper-class prosperity based upon wartime prices for Cuban products, especially sugar, and rising land values. It was also noted for considerable progress in public works, sanitation, and education.

Cuban politicians expressed their preference for more rapid rotation in office by adding an amendment to the national constitution in the early 1920's forbidding two presidential terms in succession, so that Cuba's next president, Alfredo Zayas, the Liberal leader who had lost the election in 1912 mainly through the opposition of Gómez, served only four years. It was a period of extremely hard times. The price of sugar suddenly plummeted after the end of the global war, and bankruptcy not only overwhelmed many of the speculators but threatened the Cuban Treasury. Two bond issues floated in the United States and the rigid supervision of Colonel Crowder prevented a fiscal collapse, but conditions were still very bad when Gerardo Machado, another member of the Liberal party, took charge of the government in 1925.

A businessman and the candidate of business interests, both foreign and domestic, Machado became independent Cuba's first tyrant, perhaps because he was eager to lift the nation out of its slump. He had been in office less than two years when he obtained from a pliant congress an extension of his administration; and as if this were not enough, he pushed through a puppet constitutional convention an amendment repealing the bar against immediate re-election and providing for a presidential term of six years. Elected in November, 1928, for a six-year period, he commenced his new administration on May 20, 1929. With the onslaught of the world depression he sharply reduced the salaries of civil employees, but enlarged the army and engaged in nepotism and peculation.

This highhanded procedure and official dishonesty made the opposition furious. Several members of the Radical party, accused of plotting against the government, were arrested and deported in August, 1930. A few weeks later, the students of the University of Havana, angered by an attack on a student parade, rioted and demanded that Machado be deposed. But an obedient congress thereupon gave the president the right to suspend freedom of expression and assembly, and the despot not only dismissed a number of professors and padlocked the university, but closed numerous other schools. The situation became even more tense when the Supreme Court declared all laws and decrees issued since 1928 null and void. A revolution, under the leadership of former president García Menocal, broke out early in August, 1931, and gravely threatened Machado's government; but he managed to suppress it. A reign of terror then began, with both Machado police and the underground opposition involved in a series of murders. Finally, in August, 1933, the opposition leaders, having ascertained that the Franklin D. Roosevelt administration was not in sympathy with Machado, forced the tyrant to abdicate and leave the country. He died in Miami, Florida, six years later.

Prominent among the leaders who rid Cuba of Machado was a young sergeant named Fulgencio Batista, who soon became the country's strongest political figure. Controlling the situation from behind the scenes, he left the presidency to others until 1940, after which he took charge of the government in person for a term of four years and then transmitted it to Ramón Grau San Martín, who apparently won the office in a free and fair election. Grau San Martín was followed in 1948 by Carlos Prío Socarrás. Both executives, though apparently liberal and democratic, were accused of large-scale graft and corruption, and Batista, who seems not to have been very active in politics for some time, deposed Prío early in 1952. An autocrat of a rather mild and benevolent type, Batista, while not averse to a little illegal enrichment, governed the country in the 1940's if not in the 1950's mainly in the interest of the common people, promoting primary education, improving public health by sanitary measures, fomenting economic development, and at the same time befriending labor and permitting a large measure of personal liberty.

Meantime, economic conditions slowly improved. The value of exports, which had dropped from a peak of approximately $794,000,000 in 1920 to considerably less than $64,000,000 in 1934, exceeded $766,-000,000 in 1951. Since this last figure is in terms of depreciated dollars, Cuba's exports were still far below their value in 1920; but 1920 was a "boom" year, and Cuba had diversified her production until her people were less dependent on the export industries—sugar, tobacco, fruits, winter vegetables—for employment and livelihood. Wages and working conditions had improved since the 1930's and labor's purchasing power had tended to benefit the smaller merchant class and the lower ranks of lawyers and physicians. Cuba's population, approximately 2,000,000 in 1907 and nearly 4,000,000 in 1931, was rapidly approaching 5,500,-000 in 1950. The population of Havana and its suburbs was close to 1,000,000 and the inhabitants of seven other cities averaged well above 130,000 each.

THE DOMINICAN REPUBLIC AND HAITI

The United States intervened in the Dominican Republic (1905) and Haiti (1915) during the early years of the twentieth century as in Cuba, Panama, and Nicaragua—and for the same strategic, humanitarian, and economic reasons. The assassination of Ulises Heureaux in 1899 had left the Dominican Republic in a bankrupt condition, which the Dominicans themselves seemed unable to remedy because of the turmoil of civil strife. Haiti's incessant revolutions culminated in 1915 in the overthrow of an ephemeral chief executive and his butchery by a mob which violated the French legation in seizing him.

The national economies of the two small countries shared the vicissitudes of the period: first an era of prosperity, especially during World War I, then a brief recession and a slow recovery, followed by a severe depression in the 1930's, eventually cured by the war economies of the second global conflict and subsequent years. The dollar value of Haiti's exports increased from an annual average of slightly more than $14,-500,000 for the years 1910 through 1913 to over $22,500,000 in 1928, shrank to $4,100,000 in 1938, and exceeded $49,500,000 in the inflated dollars of 1951. The dollar value of the exports of the Dominican Republic expanded from less than $7,000,000 in 1905 to nearly $59,-000,000 in 1920; dropped to less than $15,300,000 in 1922; rose to well above $28,500,000 in 1928; dived to considerably less than $8,000,-000 in 1934; and soared to almost $119,000,000 in 1951, in terms of the depreciated dollars of that year.

The population of the two republics increased at a rather rapid rate: Haiti's expanded by nearly 250 per cent between 1900 and 1950, reaching a total of some 3,112,000 in the latter year, and the Dominican Republic's increased by at least 300 per cent during the same period, numbering approximately 2,121,000 in 1950. Because of improved sanitation and migration from the rural areas, the population of the Dominican urban centers grew rapidly. The inhabitants of Ciudad Trujillo, only 30,957 in 1921, numbered 181,533 in 1950. The growth of Haiti's towns was slower; Port au Prince, with a population of approximately 110,000 in 1921, had only 142,840 in 1950. The capitals were by far the largest towns in both countries, which were still mainly rural.

Since control of the Dominican customs did not prevent revolutions, the United States felt compelled to inaugurate full-fledged intervention in 1916 and establish a government under the direction of the secretary of the navy. Six years later, however, a Dominican named Juan Bautista Vicini Burgos was set up as president; and in 1924, after the electorate had chosen General Horacio Vásquez as chief executive, the United States withdrew its Marines.

Supported by an American-trained National Guard, presumably guided by the maxim that the military should back the legal government and refrain from meddling in political affairs, Vásquez enjoyed a period of tranquillity. But the rather popular president finally became ambitious to prolong his rule. Calling together a convention mainly for that purpose, he had a constitution framed and adopted which extended his term from four to six years. Discontent aroused by this change and his other dictatorial tendencies finally led to a revolution headed by Rafael E. Ureña, which succeeded in deposing Vásquez early in 1930 mainly because General Rafael Leónidas Trujillo, commander of the National Guard, refused to come to his assistance. Ureña then became provisional president, but Trujillo controlled the elections which followed within a few months, and thus seized the trophy for himself.

The Dominicans soon discovered that they would be subjected to another long-term dictator, fully as cruel as the terrible Heureaux but far more capable. Trujillo, a shrewd and ruthless mulatto, enriched himself and his kinsmen and favorites by every means he could contrive. But the heavy demands for Dominican products by the big nations involved in war and postwar defense—sugar, coffee, cacao, tobacco, molasses, and more recently some corn, bananas, and beef were the main exports —eventually brought incomes to his countrymen far larger than in earlier years. The national revenues expanded enormously, and what the despot and his relatives and favorites did not take for themselves, they spent for the improvement of ports, the adornment of towns, the building of public works, and the multiplication of schools. Economic, social, and cultural advance was not as rapid as might have been achieved under a less voracious and severe management, but progress was made in nearly every aspect of the national life except the political and the moral.

An important result of Haiti's twenty-year military occupation (1915–34) by the United States was the transfer of power from the Negroes to the mulattoes. A succession of mulattoes headed the national government, under American supervision or on their own responsibility: Sudré Dartiguenave (1915–22); Louis Borno (1922–30); Eugene Roy (1930–31); Sténio Vincent (1931–41); and Elie Lescot (1941–46). Most of them were as capable rulers as Haiti could provide; but they belonged to the racial minority, and the Negro masses were restive under their dominance. Long restrained by the National Guard, which had been drilled and instructed by army officers of the United States, they finally won over the contingent whose duty was to defend the presidential palace and ousted Lescot in 1946. A Negro named Dumarsais Estimé then took control, but was in turn deposed in 1950 by Colonel Paul Magloire, the strong man of the new Haitian army, who was likewise deposed in December, 1956.

With its badly-eroded hills and a crowded population lacking education and skills, Haiti was probably the poorest country in Latin America. Most of its inhabitants were undernourished and disease-ridden; but a sunny disposition and a keen appreciation for music and festival seemed to make them happy in spite of poverty and ill health; and they had registered progress in recent years in sanitation and agricultural diversification. Among their exports in the early 1950's were not only sugar, coffee, and cacao but bananas, sisal fiber, castor beans, and vegetable oils. Foods grown for domestic consumption were manioc, corn, rice, yams and a few other vegetables, and fruits. Favorite animals were donkeys, goats, pigs, and barnyard fowls, but a few cattle, horses, and mules also were raised.

CHAPTER XXVIII

Northern Latin America: Mexico and Central America

✠ REVOLUTIONARY MEXICO: FROM MADERO TO CALLES

The years following the fall of Porfirio Díaz in May, 1911, were a period of radical transformation, an epoch of changes more momentous than any that had occurred in Mexico since the sixteenth century. Revolution followed close on the heels of revolution for an entire decade. The destruction of life and property was terrific. Population in 1921 barely exceeded that of 1900 and was almost 1,000,000 less than in 1910. Although exports were expanded in order to purchase military supplies and other requirements, production fell off. Government and government-guaranteed securities held abroad went into default.

Uprisings gradually ceased after May, 1920, however, and though a former president (also a president-elect) was murdered, no national government was overturned during the following decades. After reaching a peak dollar value of nearly $424,000,000 in 1920, Mexico's exports began to contract, slowly at first but more rapidly after 1930, reaching a low of less than $83,000,000 in 1933; and although they then began to expand, markedly after 1940, reaching a total of more than $629,500,000 in 1951 (in terms of depreciated dollars), their actual value was still less than in 1920. But exports were no longer an accurate gauge of Mexico's economic progress, for manufacturing industries had expanded, farms and plantations were producing more and a greater variety of commodities, and comparatively fewer people were directly concerned with production for export. In short, as in Cuba's case, the home market had expanded at the expense of the foreign market because the workers and the lower middle class were able to purchase and consume larger quantities of goods produced in Mexico. Income had not only been somewhat more evenly distributed, but population had rapidly increased since 1921, having grown from 14,-300,000 in that year to 26,000,000 in 1950.

The fundamental causes of the revolt against Díaz were: (1) The rapid growth of capitalism, largely under foreign control, which resulted in increased concentration of land, monopolistic developments in trade, and rising food prices; (2) the gradual development of a middle class—composed mostly of mestizos but including a few whites and Indians; and (3) a dictatorship which encouraged foreign investment and foreign enterprise, favored the church and the remnants of the creole aristocracy, restricted the economic opportunities of the new middle class and deprived it of political expression, and not only oppressed the great majority of the people but permitted and connived in the shameful exploitation of the Indian masses. The immediate causes of the uprising were: (1) The economic recession of 1907; (2) the scanty crops of 1907 and 1908; (3) the bloody suppression of strikes in the Cananea copper mines of Sonora (1906) and the cotton mills of Orizaba (1907); (4) increasing fear of "Yankee imperialism"; (5) widespread political agitation; and (6) possibly the influence of competing foreigners for Mexico's oil lands and other properties.

It was a long revolution because the middle and lower classes had difficulty in formulating a program and finding sympathetic leaders with requisite administrative capacity, because of the revival of old military propensities, and because the forces, foreign as well as domestic, opposing the movement were very tenacious and very powerful. After the overthrow of Díaz, the leaders of the revolution faced a situation not unlike that confronted by the new Latin-American nations immediately after their separation from Spain. Although a middle class had begun to develop and the masses were more assertive, there were the same lack of political experience on the part of the leaders, the same paucity of resources, the same tendency toward riotous militarism, and the same privileged groups—the army high command, the creole landed aristocracy, and the conservative church—to be dealt with. If the growing intelligence of the Mexican people enabled them better to appreciate their interests and, as a consequence, brought them to the support of the revolution, their waxing assertiveness made them more difficult to manage, and the potent influence of foreign investors was usually (and quite naturally) exerted in behalf of the old regime.

Political, labor, and agrarian agitation had begun in Morelos, Puebla, Yucatán, and other states as early as 1906 and 1907, and excitement increased in 1908 when James Creelman published in *Pearson's Magazine* (March) the substance of his startling interview with Díaz, in which the dictator stated that since his country was then ready for democracy, he would allow free political opposition and retire in favor of any opponent legally elected. Political "hopefuls" began to appear at once. Prominent among them were General Rodolfo Reyes, José Limantour, and Francisco Madero. But Díaz soon revealed that he did not mean what he was supposed to have said. He adroitly sent Limantour and Reyes to Europe on financial and diplomatic missions and imprisoned Madero during the heat of the electoral campaign of 1910, in which the dictator was inevitably chosen for another term.

Poorly advised by his octogenarian counsellors and contemptuous of the talents of his prisoner, the dictator misjudged the situation and released Madero shortly after the election. Madero fled to Texas, sent out a call for revolution, and issued a program which demanded "effective suffrage and no re-election," the abolition of the *jefes políticos* (local bosses and agents of the central government), and, rather vaguely, the redistribution of lands. Within a few months, all dissatisfied factions had rallied to Madero's support, from the conservative followers of Reyes to the radical labor and agrarian reformers. Capturing Ciudad Juárez early in May, 1911, Madero soon began his triumphal march toward the capital. Díaz abdicated on May 25 and departed for Europe, and Madero became chief executive of the nation before the end of the year. All attempts to divert him from his goal had proved futile; but he had risen to power not so much because of the appeal of his reform program as because of his daring in taking the leadership in an assault upon a dictatorship hitherto supposed to be impregnable.

Small and unimpressive except for his sincerity, weak-willed, impractical, handicapped by a large following of greedy relatives belonging to the landholding aristocracy, Madero was clearly not the leader that the revolution demanded. And this was soon revealed. The reactionaries, backed by vested interests, foreign and national, revolted in the Center and the North. Agrarians, led by Emiliano Zapata, began a formidable uprising in the South. Henry Lane Wilson, the American ambassador, assumed an antagonistic posture from the outset. Victoriano Huerta, commander of Madero's army, proved a traitor. Late in February; 1913, Madero was deposed and shot, and Huerta took charge of the government.

Temporarily, at least, the revolution had been stymied. But President Woodrow Wilson opposed Huerta from Washington, and not only Zapata and the reformers but many ambitious military leaders fought him in Mexico. In July, 1914, Huerta was forced to resign and seek refuge abroad. Revolution then ran riot for more than a year; but thanks largely to the assistance of Woodrow Wilson, Venustiano Carranza finally emerged as the dominant figure in October, 1915. Like Madero, however, Carranza turned out not to be the leader for whom the middle class and the masses were looking. A member of the landed aristocracy of the North, he had taken up arms against Huerta less on account of interest in the common people than because of a burning desire for power. He issued one reluctant decree ordering lands to be granted or restored to Indian villages, but many of the provisions of the radical constitution of 1917 were placed in that document in defiance of his wishes, and he made no attempt to put any of them in force save those which required the nationalization of subsoil minerals. It soon became evident that he was stubborn, tyrannical, inefficient, perhaps corrupt, and certainly indifferent to the demands of the people for agrarian and labor reforms. He was finally driven from power (May, 1920) by a group of military and civilian leaders—Álvaro Obregón, Plutarco Elías Calles, and José Vasconcelos among them—who took the reform movement more seriously.

The most noteworthy achievement of the Carranza period was the framing of the constitution of May 1, 1917. It was a document filled with concepts friendly to labor: protection of women and children, eight-hour day, a minimum wage, workmen's compensation, housing, social insurance, profit sharing, the right to strike, boards of arbitration and conciliation. It contained detailed provisions with reference to agrarian reforms; the nationalization of petroleum and other subsoil treasures; ownership of property, particularly agricultural lands, by foreigners; and educational and religious matters. In brief, it was the most elaborate social welfare program ever issued in Mexico.

Obregón, Calles, and their associates carried out this program with great zeal for more than a decade, until Obregón was assassinated (1928) and the enthusiasm of Calles began to wane. Mexico became the scene of a mighty crusade of social uplift and transformation that extended from the capital to the remotest village of Indians and mestizos. A veritable war was waged on poverty, disease, and ignorance. An eyewitness and a careful observer wrote in 1927: [1]

Probably there is not in the world so elaborate a system of social welfare under state control. . . . The tremendous campaign of the Federal Sanitary Department against smallpox and other infectious diseases, vaccination of hundreds of thousands of individuals monthly, the inspection of foods and beverages, go hand in hand with an educational program that adds a thousand schools annually, develops teachers, provides material equipment and mental pabulum for added thousands of the lower classes. Agricultural credits, banks, loans of seeds and tools and animals seek to fill the gap in the agricultural situation. Colonization laws seek to introduce new farmers. Macadam roads for the automobile thread the desert reaches. Irrigation reservoirs prepare for their irrigation. Most of the work is being done effectively and economically, and under expert advice where necessary.

Millions of acres of land were placed in the hands of hundreds of Indian villages and thousands of heads of families. Hundreds of mestizos were granted small farms. A vigorous effort was made to recover for the nation the water, timber, lands, and minerals with which it was endowed. The Roman Catholic Church, because its leaders were considered as enemies of the reform movement, was subjected to rigid supervision and even persecution. Foreign investors suffered serious losses which were never fully indemnified. Neither the remonstrances of foreign governments nor the opposition of landlords and clergy could stay the march of social revolution. The republic was in the hands of its Indians and mestizos. It was a new era for old Mexico.

REVOLUTIONARY MEXICO: CÁRDENAS AND HIS SUCCESSORS

Obregón and Calles, both from the virile and progressive North (Sonora), took turns in the presidency until Obregón was murdered by a religious fanatic in 1928. Calles, once a poor and almost shoeless schoolteacher, was the most outstanding personality in Mexico for some time thereafter. He continued the program of reform and development for a few years, but gradually accumulated a fortune and began to reveal conservative tendencies. Pretending to respect the constitutional proscription against continuing in power, he let others occupy the presidency under his dominance, living in ostensible retirement on his large rural estate or in a luxurious home in Mexico City surrounded by guards in brilliant uniforms. Mexican politics became mildly reactionary until Lázaro Cárdenas shattered his power and banished him from the country in 1936.

Cárdenas was a mestizo more Indian than Spanish, a native of a small village in the state of Michoacán, where he was born in 1895. Although the son of a poor family, he managed to obtain a primary education, to learn the printer's trade, and to hold some minor public offices before he enlisted in one of the revolutionary armies. Stocky, strong, and intelligent, he won rapid promotion and advanced to the rank of general in his early twenties. In 1928, at the age of thirty-three, he became governor of his native state and proceeded to distribute lands among the land-hungry Indians. Late in 1930, while Calles was busy manipulating his puppets, Cárdenas was elected president of Mexico's National Revolutionary party, the most influential political organization in the country, and with the support of Calles, he received that party's nomination for the presidency of Mexico in 1934. He might have won the election without exertion, but he was determined to renew the reform movement and felt that he needed to meet the people and discover their specific needs. He campaigned in every city, town, and village in the nation and made himself so popular with the common people—the peons, the Indians, the little mestizo farmers and ranchmen, the workers—that within twelve months of his inauguration for a six-year term (under the amended constitution) in 1934, he was able with their backing and that of friendly army officers to defy Calles and his army and bureaucratic clique.

The tempo of reform was accelerated during his administration. He distributed more acres among landless families, constructed more irrigation works and highways, installed more sewers and sanitary water systems, and built more schools than all his revolutionary predecessors combined. He expanded state-ownership of railroads, seized foreign-owned factories and oil wells, thrust the state into the national economy in other ways, and championed the cause of labor. Mexico was in some respects a socialist nation at the end of his presidential term; but alien capitalists still controlled the mines, most of the public utilities, and many of the larger factories. Although government enterprise was competing with private enterprise, private property had by no means been abolished. There was even some talk of dividing the community-held lands of the Indian villages among family heads in private fee-simple ownership. But this appeared to be an imprudent and unlikely step, since most of the family plots would be too small for efficient separate operation.

With the inauguration of Manuel Ávila Camacho on December 1, 1940, the zeal of the reformers abated again. As a matter of fact, arable soil was not plentiful in Mexico. No more than 10 or 12 per cent of its land could ever be profitably cultivated, even after all available water had been conserved and utilized. Most of the national domain was mountainous, swampy, or arid. After all of the agrarian reforms of Cárdenas and his predecessors, half of the people engaged in agriculture were still hired hands who possessed no lands of their own either as members of villages with community property or as private individuals. Not unaware of the situation, Ávila Camacho stressed manufacturing industries and a highway system designed to bind the local markets together into a national market and to accommodate national and foreign tourists. But he was actually more conservative than Cárdenas and less concerned about petty dishonesty in government. He treated private property with greater respect, adjusted the claims of foreigners and began to pay them, took no effective measures against speculation and rising prices, permitted bureaucratic larceny to spread. He continued, however, to distribute some land, refrained from interference with freedom of the press, and, in general, governed the country in the interest of the majority of the people.

Ávila Camacho was succeeded in 1946 by Miguel Alemán, another moderate Liberal and Mexico's first civilian president since Francisco Madero was murdered in 1913. The agrarian movement almost came to a halt. Foreign capitalists began to be courted. No effective measures were taken to hamper speculation. Prices continued to soar. The Mexican peso was devalued. Bribery and petty graft became more prevalent. But efforts to foster sanitation, education, manufacturing, and the exploitation of natural resources were not relaxed, and the press was left largely free to denounce the evils of the time.

Daniel Cosío Villegas pointed to the achievements of the years since the departure of Díaz, but complained of the lack of integrity in administrative circles. The "Revolution"—to use a term applied by the Mexicans to the entire epoch following 1910—had created "new institutions, an extensive network of highways, impressive irrigation projects, thousands of schools, a goodly number of public services, solid industries and agricultural developments"; it had achieved the three important objectives of "political freedom, agrarian reform, and labor organization." But the record of too many of its leaders had been marred by dishonesty. "Widespread administrative corruption, unabashed and insulting, behind a cloak of immunity," had "undone the program of the Revolution." [2] Silva Herzog, another Mexican, declared that the creative and progressive tendencies of the new regime were being stultified by "new-rich officials and ex-officials, traffickers of governmental influence, and dealers who profited from public-works contracts or the sale of inferior materials." [3]

With a program no different from his two immediate predecessors except that it demanded greater morality in government, Adolfo Ruiz Cortines, an engineer, became president late in 1952. But he seems not to have applied any drastic remedies. A multiparty system was probably the fundamental political requirement if the nation was to achieve cleaner and more efficient government. Mexico's only party with any chance of winning elections was an official party. While there were considerable mobility and flexibility in its organization, changes of personnel and policies could be effected only by joining the party and working within its ranks.

Nevertheless, the Mexico of the 1950's was very different from the Mexico of the first decade of the twentieth century. From 1916 through 1951, more than 102,000,000 acres of land had been distributed among villages inhabited by some 2,300,000 Indians, and tens of thousands of mestizos had been added to the private landholding class. More than 42,000 miles of highways, nearly a third of them paved and half of the rest graveled, accommodated over 350,000 automobiles in a land which had hardly any roads for wheeled vehicles forty years before. Power plants, irrigation works, factories, and schools had multiplied, along with artists, labor unions, and literary societies. Towns had grown into cities. Almost half of the people were living in urban centers of 2,500 inhabitants and more. With a population of only 615,376 in 1921, Mexico City numbered 2,234,795 inhabitants in 1951. Guadalajara's population had grown from 143,376 to 388,149 during the same period; Puebla's from 95,535 to 217,576 and Monterrey's from 88,458 to 348,270. The mestizos and many of the Indians had become integrated with the creoles and were sharing the national culture. The mestizos, with the support of the Indians, now held the balance of power. The faces of the masses were smiling with hope. But Mexico's expanding population was actually pressing hard upon its resources, and it would not be easy for these masses to emancipate themselves from poverty. Reformers who failed to realize this fundamental fact doubtless would continue to complain of "subtle reactionary" maneuvers and contend that the Revolution would "be over when there" were "no proletarian hungry, no illiterates, no greedy landlords," and no alien ownership of material resources and means of production, and when "a real democratic order under law and human rights" had been established.[4]

PANAMA, COMPARATIVELY STABLE AND DEMOCRATIC

Encouraged and shielded by the United States, Panama seceded from Colombia late in 1903 and established an independent republic under a constitution which separated Church and State, proclaimed religious liberty and other individual freedoms, provided for a centralized form of government, and set a four-year limit on the presidential term of office, without, however, prohibiting more than one term (in succession or otherwise). The Theodore Roosevelt administration, interested in acquiring control over the Canal Zone on terms which Colombia had refused to concede, obtained from Panama not only the right to construct, fortify, control, and operate the canal but also the right (until it was revoked in 1939) to intervene in the domestic affairs of the republic for the purpose of preventing political disorders and promoting works of sanitation.

With a population of around 300,000 in 1904 and some 800,000 in 1950, Panama was a liberal and comparatively tranquil republic during the first half-century of its national existence. Its political conduct was influenced by the United States, which, at the invitation of the government of the little country, helped to disband its army in 1904 and supervised its national elections in 1908, 1912, and 1918. Panama was governed by a small group of white or largely white families, but individuals of other races—a few Indians and many more Negroes whose grandfathers and fathers had come from the British West Indies —held some minor government posts. The first president, Manuel Amador Guerrero, was a leader in the secession conspiracy and a fairly satisfactory chief executive; but the number-one hero of the republic was Tomás Herrera, who had proclaimed Panama's independence in 1840 and maintained it for more than a year.

Only one president, a popular leader named Belisario Porras who organized a strong personal faction of his own, served for more than a single term before 1949, and one of his two terms was short (1912–16 and 1919–20). Florencio Arosemena, head of a Liberal faction, was the first chief executive driven from office before his term expired. He was deposed early in 1931 by a coalition of Independents and Conservatives, under the leadership of Harmodio Arias, who were restless because of the hard times occasioned by the world economic depression and exasperated by electoral frauds and financial dishonesty. Another president who served for two terms (1940–41 and 1949–50) was Arnulfo Arias, Harmodio's younger brother, who revealed decided despotic tendencies and was overthrown twice. In the absence of an army, the police force became the instrument of power. Colonel José Remón, chief of the police, seized the government in 1950, but was assassinated early in 1955. Ricardo Arias Espinosa, a civilian who then took charge of the national executive power, permitted an election the next year. The new president, Ernesto de la Guardia, was inaugurated on October 1, 1956.

Panama's resources were still largely undeveloped. Its principal crops were bananas, coffee, and sugar; but cotton, rice, corn, tobacco, and a variety of vegetables and fruits were also grown as well as herds of livestock. Its forests produced not only lumber, cabinet woods, and medicinal plants but coconuts and tagua nuts; salt, sponges, pearls, and tortoise shells were taken from the sea. Of the several minerals known to exist, only gold was exploited in significant quantity. Small manufacturing plants turned out processed foods, beer, rum, whisky, toiletry, furniture, matches, tile, wearing apparel, and various tobacco products.

The Panama Canal was an important source of income both for laborers and local merchants. The annuities paid by the United States to Panama, in addition to the original $10,000,000 for control and utilization of the canal, were raised from $250,000 at the outset to nearly

$2,000,000 in 1955. Panama's exports rose from an annual value of less than $2,000,000 in earlier years to over $15,000,000 in 1951— more than a threefold increase after making allowance for the depreciated dollar. The population of Panama City at mid-century was nearly 200,000. The combined population of Colón and David, the other two leading towns, was close to 100,000.

𑁉 OTHER MIDDLE AMERICAN COUNTRIES

Costa Rica's orderly government of the people, by the people, and for the people was interrupted only twice during the period under review (1917–19 and 1948–49). The other four older republics of Central America continued as before to be harried by militarism or oppressed by tyranny. The population of the five countries almost doubled between 1900 and 1950, expanding from around 4,100,000 to slightly less than 8,000,000. Exports—mainly coffee, bananas, hides, forest products, and gold—rose from an annual average value of approximately $25,-500,000 during 1901–5 to over $107,000,000 in 1928 and then dropped to less than $25,500,000 in 1935, but rose above $290,000,000 in the inflated dollar equivalent in 1951. Urban population increased more rapidly than the population of the nations as a whole. The population of the capital cities in 1950 ranged from slightly less than 100,000 in San José and Tegucigalpa to almost 300,000 in Guatemala City.

One of Costa Rica's deposed presidents, Alfredo González Flores, was a radical who proposed tax and agrarian reforms; the other, Rafael Calderón Guardia, was accused of Communist affiliations. The first was overthrown by Federico Tinoco, an army officer, who served as dictator for two years (1917–19) before he was compelled to give way to a democratic regime. The second was deposed by an insurgent organization called the National Opposition, led by Otilio Ulate and José Figueres. Ulate became president in 1949 and was succeeded four years later by Figueres, a left-wing coffee planter and the son of a Spanish immigrant, who appears to have been the free choice of the voters. Costa Rica's rate of illiteracy was one of the lowest in Latin America: around 20 per cent. One of the most pressing problems of the republic in the early 1950's was the construction of good roads to and in its outlying provinces.

Following a period of revolutions and ephemeral presidents terminated by the assassination of President Manuel E. Araujo, El Salvador in 1913 fell under the control of the despotic Meléndez dynasty. Two brothers, Carlos and Jorge Meléndez, and Alfonso Quiñones Molino, a brother-in-law, oppressed the people for fourteen years. The republic then became more tranquil and free until it was again upset by a revolution late in 1931. The leader of the revolt, Maximiliano Hernández Martínez, set up a dictatorship which continued until 1944, when he was compelled to surrender the government to a less tyrannical chief executive. But the country was unable to shake off the domination of the army and the police. Major Oscar Osorio seized the government in 1950 and dominated the nation until 1956, when he imposed Colonel José María Lemus as his successor by means of a tightly-controlled election.

Guatemala writhed under the iron despotism of Manuel Estrada Cabrera, a mestizo lawyer, for a period of twenty-two years (1898–1920). A scholarly eyewitness in 1918 described his tyranny as follows: [5]

The administration firmly maintains its authority by means of a large standing army and police force, and promptly and mercilessly checks the slightest manifestation of popular dissatisfaction. An elaborate secret service attempts, with a large measure of success, to inform itself fully of everything which occurs in the Republic. Supposed enemies of the party in power are closely watched, through their neighbors, their servants, and even through the members of their own families. . . . It is dangerous to express an opinion on political matters even in private conversation. . . . The formation of social clubs is discouraged because of possible political results, and it is impossible for a man prominent in official circles to have many friends without arousing distrust. Persons who fall under suspicion are imprisoned or restricted in their liberty, or even mysteriously disappear.

Several efforts to assassinate the tyrant were frustrated, and avenged by the ruthless execution of large numbers of citizens, many of whom were probably innocent. Earlier attempts at revolution had also failed, with tragic consequences for their promoters. It was not until April, 1920, that the despot was finally deposed by armed revolt. He died in prison four years later, at the age of sixty-seven, after having been deprived of his ill-gotten millions.

The fall of Estrada Cabrera was followed by a decade of intermittent civil war and then by another despot somewhat less cruel and more constructive, an army officer named Jorge Ubico, who took pride in his resemblance to Napoleon Bonaparte. Ubico's rule was terminated in 1944 by a military coup, but a group of civilian reformers soon got control of the government, with Juan José Arévalo and then Jacobo Arbenz Guzmán serving as president. Organized labor enjoyed a period of power and progress; but the Arbenz administration succumbed to Communist domination before agrarian reforms were completed, and General Carlos Castillo Armas, with encouragement and assistance from the United States, seized control of the country early in 1955 and drove Arbenz and his associates into exile, and with financial aid from the generous big neighbor attempted moderate agrarian reforms, but was murdered in July 1957.

Honduras was the most turbulent nation of Central America during the first third of the twentieth century. Practically all of its little despots held the reins of power as long as they had the support of the army; but only one, Francisco Bertrand, held them for as long as six years, until a huge mestizo named Tiburcio Carías Andino seized them early in February, 1933. Discouraging his opponents by a small air force and a few armored tanks, Carías continued his Conservative rule until 1948 and imposed his successor. Whether he was to some extent responsible for the dictatorship inaugurated late in 1954 by Julio Lozano Díaz was a question that awaits clarification. Lozano Díaz was compelled to give way to Juan Manuel Gálvez, a former president of Honduras, in September, 1956.

In Nicaragua, after José Santos Zelaya's overthrow in 1909 by a coalition of dissident Liberals and Conservatives with the ardent approval of the William Howard Taft administration, there ensued a period of disorder. The Conservatives, supported by United States Marines, were unable, however, completely to pacify the country. Representatives from the United States supervised the national elections in 1928 and 1932, and the deposed Liberals triumphed both times. Six months after Juan B. Sacasa took charge of the government in 1932 the United States withdrew its military forces from Nicaragua. With Sacasa's nephew, General Anastasio Somoza, in command of the National Guard, prospects for political stability seemed promising. The bandit-like insurgents under César Augusto Sandino soon dissolved and their leader was assassinated shortly afterward. But Somoza promptly developed an ambition to rule the country, deposed his uncle a few weeks before the end of his term, and after setting up and pulling down two puppet chief executives, had himself "elected" president late in 1936.

Establishing a dictatorship which lasted for twenty years, Somoza achieved notoriety both for the length of his dominance and for the wealth he accumulated at the expense of his country. At the outbreak of World War II he visited the United States and persuaded President Franklin D. Roosevelt to agree to finance a highway—the Rama Road —from a point twenty miles north of Managua to a point on the Escondido River from which it is navigable to the Caribbean Sea. The road, which eventually cost the United States more than $12,000,000, was constructed in order to appease the dictator, who complained that Nicaragua was being gravely injured by the failure of the big neighbor to build a canal across the country under a long-term option acquired in 1916 actually for the purpose of preventing the digging of another canal in competition with the one across Panama—an option for which the United States had paid $3,000,000. And Somoza used this leverage at a time of world crisis when the United States was already planning to grant the major part of the funds required to build an Inter-American Highway through Central America from the northern boundary of Guatemala to Panama City. Assassinated in September, 1956, the tyrant was succeeded by his son Luís Somoza.

CHAPTER XXIX

Northern South America, Peru, and Bolivia

🐚 ECONOMIC AND SOCIAL TRENDS

Of the five republics included in this chapter, Venezuela and Colombia experienced the most rapid economic development during the period under consideration. Peru registered greater economic advance than did Ecuador and Bolivia, and Bolivia developed at a slower pace than Ecuador. Petroleum was the main basis of Venezuela's growing prosperity. Colombia's was grounded on coffee, petroleum, bananas, sugar, livestock, and expanding light industries; Peru's, mainly on long-staple cotton, sugar, petroleum and other minerals, and metals: tungsten, antimony, zinc, lead, vanadium, and copper; Ecuador's on cacao, bananas, coffee, castor beans, "Panama" hats, balsa wood, petroleum, rice, textiles, rugs, and a shrinking trade in tagua nuts; Bolivia's, unsteadily on tin, copper, lead, wolfram, silver, some petroleum, and animal products. Foreign capital and enterprise, especially money and management from the United States and Great Britain, were active in all of them, though on a larger scale in Venezuela, Colombia, and Peru than in the other two.

Venezuela's exports rose in the 1940's to an annual average value of well above $1,000,000,000 measured in the depreciated dollars of the period, and exceeded $1,300,000,000 by 1951. The gold-dollar value of her exports had been slightly less than $15,000,000 in 1898 and $1,000,000 less than that in 1905. Rising to more than $52,500,000 in 1919 and over $150,000,000 in 1929, they had dropped no lower than $90,300,000 during the economic depression that followed (1933).

Having a gold-dollar value of $19,000,000 in 1898 and only a little over $9,000,000 in 1906, Colombia's exports exceeded $87,000,000 in 1919 and $130,500,000 in 1928. They shrank to $47,500,000 in

1933, but slowly expanded thereafter until they exceeded $453,000,000 in the depreciated dollars of 1951.

In similar manner, Peru's sales abroad, amounting to almost $22,-000,000 in 1900, soared to $162,000,000 in 1920, dived to less than $60,000,000 in 1921, and climbed to $134,000,000 in 1929. But the economic depression drove their gold-dollar value down to $38,000,000 in 1932, after which Peru's foreign sales began to expand again, finally reaching a total of over $252,500,000 in 1951, a sum hardly equivalent to the figure for 1920 in terms of the same gold currency.

Ecuador's exports rose in value from an annual average of around $9,000,000 during the early years of the century to over $22,000,000 in 1920, then fell off and never reached that figure again until the period of the second global war. In the depreciated dollars of 1951, they were valued at somewhat more than $52,000,000, or about $4,000,000 above the gold-dollar figure for 1920.

Bolivia's exports showed approximately the same trend as Ecuador's. Evaluated at around $10,000,000 in 1903, they averaged over $53,-500,000 annually during the years 1916–20, declined to approximately the level of 1903 in 1933, and then moved up to an average of approximately $100,000,000 yearly in 1946–50, the equivalent of about $50,000,000 in gold dollars.

Population multiplied rapidly in all these countries except Bolivia. Colombia's inhabitants increased nearly threefold between 1900 and 1950; Ecuador's more than doubled, Peru's doubled, and Venezuela's almost doubled; Bolivia's expanded by some 80 per cent. The population of Colombia was crowding 11,500,000 at the middle of the century. Peru's was approaching 7,000,000 and Venezuela's 5,000,000. The inhabitants of Ecuador and Bolivia numbered slightly more than 3,000,-000 each.

There was a noticeable drift to the cities, particularly to the capitals, after the second quarter of the century. Lima's inhabitants increased from 250,000 in 1926 to 835,468 in 1950; Bogotá's rose from 201,593 to 547,440 during the same period; the residents of Caracas multiplied from 135,000 to 488,000; those of Quito from 80,700 to 212,873; and the population of La Paz from 109,750 to 321,063. Maracaibo's inhabitants increased from fewer than 75,000 in 1926 to 232,000 in 1950, while Barranquilla's expanded from 90,000 to nearly 257,000 and Guayaquil's grew from approximately 100,000 to almost 263,000. As elsewhere, the people migrated to the cities in the hope of finding more profitable employment or superior cultural advantages.

⚙ REFORM AND REACTION IN COLOMBIA

The new century opened with a civil war raging in Colombia, the most destructive the country had suffered since the war for emancipation from Spain. "The three-year struggle caused incalculable losses. On the battlefields 100,000 men or more perished; thousands were maimed for life; commerce was ruined . . . production almost negligible; and paper money, issued in increasing quantities to meet the needs of the government, depreciated so much that a paper peso was worth less than one centavo in gold." [1] The middle of the century witnessed a reign of terror. "The police were reorganized into a shock force, and the national army into a party militia with a belligerent general staff. . . . Many villages were destroyed, some completely wiped out. The prisons became the scene of tortures. . . . The death toll from 1949 to 1951 has been estimated at 50,000. . . . The exact figure will never be known, for during this time the Colombian newspapers carried only such information as the government . . . saw fit to print." [2]

Between these two tragedies Colombians led a fairly peaceful existence. There were a few riots, a very destructive one in Bogotá in April, 1948, and more than a few strikes, especially in the oil fields and in the Santa Marta banana zone. A strike in the banana region late in 1928 resulted in the death of scores of workers and the wounding of many more when the military forces of the country were employed to suppress it. But there were no civil wars. Nor were there any dictators, with one exception, among the chief executives. Freedom of speech and of the press prevailed. The constitution and the law provided for religious toleration, although Roman Catholic zealots gave the Protestant missionaries trouble and the church officials were often able to dominate the state schools. The political opposition was free to do almost anything within the law—except elect a president or the majority of the members of the national congress, or control the assemblies in the administrative departments! The Conservative party, dominant until 1930, made certain that the Liberals kept within bounds. A coalition government effected an arrangement in 1910, however, making possible a Liberal representation in Congress, and for a good part of the next two decades Liberals also held a few cabinet posts.

Soon after Colombia's long revolution which began in 1899 had been suppressed, General Rafael Reyes was "elected" president. Reyes, like Núñez, was a "self-made man," but Reyes was more tolerant than his Conservative predecessor and more eager to develop Colombia's material resources. Born in a mountain province of Boyacá in 1850, he had little formal schooling. The death of his father and the poverty of his family compelled him to begin work at the age of twelve. A few years later the Reyes tribe moved to Popayán, where he and his three brothers engaged in commerce, shipping quinine and other forest products to foreign markets. At the age of twenty-four Rafael joined his brothers Enrique and Nestor in an adventure as daring as any ever attempted by the Conquistadores. It was nothing less than the exploration and occupation of the vast forested region stretching southeastward from the slopes of the Andes toward the great Amazon Basin. The area turned out to be rich in quinine, rubber, sarsaparilla, wild cacao, vegetable ivory, and precious woods. Rafael Reyes spent almost ten years there and suffered severely from the hardships inflicted by the hot and humid climate, insect pests, tropical diseases, and hostile savages. His brother Enrique died of malignant fever, and his brother Nestor was eaten by cannibals; but Rafael brought out the body of the one and the bones of the other and returned to resume his business enterprise. In spite of all his efforts, however, the firm of Reyes Brothers collapsed as the result of a financial panic, a fall in the price of quinine, and the high cost of operations in the jungle. Rafael Reyes arrived in Cali late in 1884 a very discouraged man with financial ruin staring him in the face.

But another door of adventure swung open before him. The revolution against Núñez had begun, and Reyes joined the Conservative military forces at once. With his small army, he swept like a whirlwind across Colombia, and by the time the insurgents were suppressed he had become a general. He then went as a delegate from the State of Cauca to the constitutional convention of 1886, and during the next ten years he held several important political posts, including a seat in congress. At the outbreak of the Liberal revolt of 1895, he took to the battlefield again. A whirlwind ten years before, he was now a tornado. In less than three months the revolt was crushed. Without question the outstanding commander of the Conservative troops, Reyes offered himself as a candidate for the presidency in 1897, but was persuaded to withdraw before the election was held. Shortly afterward he entered the diplomatic service, went to Europe, and later headed the Colombian delegation to the Pan-American conference in Mexico City (1901), where he attracted attention by a paper on his jungle explorations and by his pro-Spanish pronouncements. He came away from Mexico full of admiration for Porfirio Díaz.

Reyes took charge of the national government on August 7, 1904, for a term of six years. Then in his early fifties, he was growing bald and stout. With his tall figure, massive frame, and heavy mustache trained in Teutonic fashion, he resembled a Prussian field marshal. Arrogant and impatient, he collided with the Congress soon after his inauguration, imprisoned some of its members, drove others away from the capital, and closed the legislative sessions. He then set up a national assembly of his own to carry out his will. The components of this hand-picked group of twenty-seven, three from each of Colombia's nine administrative departments, faithfully discharged the duties assigned them. They stamped with their approval nearly every measure the dictator recommended: government contracts for public works; mining and oil concessions; appropriations for night and technical schools; multiplication of local administrative units to furnish more jobs for the dictator's partisans or to provide more efficient management; and even an extension of the dictator's term from six to ten years. His purpose was clearly to attract capital as Díaz had attracted it by relieving it of the burden of multiple negotiations. It would be easier and simpler, he assumed, for prospective investors to come to terms with a one-man government and an assembly of puppets.

In order to increase the flow of capital from the United States, Reyes decided to close the breach that had occurred in 1903–4 with the "taking of the Canal Zone" by the Theodore Roosevelt administration. His diplomats negotiated a treaty with Secretary Elihu Root agreeing to recognize the independence of Panama in return for $2,500,000 of badly needed cash and important privileges of transit through the projected canal. But when Reyes proposed to submit this agreement to his puppet assembly for approval, the gathering storm broke loose. The Liberal opposition now had a patriotic issue to add to their other grievances; the national domain was on the verge of permanent mutilation. The dissident Conservative politicians, who longed for the legislative posts which the dictator had rudely snatched from them, now felt the impulse of nationalism that permeated the people. Aware of the developing crisis, Reyes withdrew the pact and promised to call together the Congress which his malleable assembly had displaced. But these concessions failed to dissolve the lowering clouds, and a quick investigation disclosed that the dictator could not count upon the support of his wavering generals and police. Fearing that he might not be able to weather the tempest, he quietly left the capital in June, 1909, and on July 13, at Santa Marta, signed his resignation. He sailed from the country on a world tour a few days later and did not return for a period of ten years. Arriving back home in 1919, he settled down on his small estate in the Cauca Valley, where he died in 1921 at the age of seventy-one. An aggressive hulk of a man with tremendous energy and great skill in military operations, he lacked the culture of the aristocratic poets, lawyers, and journalists who were accustomed to rule the nation in collaboration with the higher clergy.

Longing for a more harmonious and a more democratic regime, the politicians who deposed Reyes called together a constitutional convention which passed an amendment providing for minority representation of the Liberals and set up a coalition government under a moderately conservative scholar from Medellín named Carlos Restrepo. But the old-line Conservatives soon recovered fuller political control and retained it until 1930, when a sharp division in their party and the vacillation of the bishops and archbishops resulted in the election to the presidency of Enrique Olaya Herrera, a wealthy six-foot, bald-headed, moderate Liberal and ex-ambassador to the United States, who formed another coalition government.

An indemnity of $25,000,000 paid by the United States in installments during the years 1922–26 had fostered an era of development, which was further stimulated by the proceeds of government bonds sold in the American market and by other streams of capital which trickled in from the same source. An enlightened Conservative, a law professor named Miguel Abadía Méndez, had been so eager to prevent political disturbance that he refused to dominate the elections that had conferred the chief executive office upon Olaya Herrera. The Liberals, easily outvoting the Conservatives in 1934, chose Alfonso López as president and sent a party majority to congress.

In a reforming mood after being out of power for half a century, the Liberals promptly amended the constitution of 1886. They reduced the temporal power of the church and deprived it of its educational control, made larger appropriations for primary and secondary schools, gave more attention to sanitation and public health, passed friendly labor laws, and initiated some agrarian reforms which they never completed. All these measures provoked bitter complaints in which the Conservative politicians mingled their voices with those of the clergy, and not only protested but refused to take part in national elections on the ground that their ballots would not be fairly counted. But there was no revolt. López was succeeded in 1938 by Eduardo Santos, a scholarly journalist and a mild-mannered Liberal, whose motto was *"conviviencia"* ("live together in harmony") and who slowed down the tempo of change in the hope of preserving political tranquillity. Santos was followed by López, who was elected for a second term and seemed radical enough. Nevertheless, he was too moderate to please the extremist followers of Jorge E. Gaitán, who split the party in 1946 and thus helped to restore the Conservatives to power.

The presidency went to Mariano Ospina Pérez, a wealthy, intelligent, and supposedly moderate Conservative with relatives in both political camps, who assumed office with the intention of utilizing the services of the moderate Liberals as well as the Conservatives. But efforts at conciliation failed. Hounded on the one side by the reactionaries led by Laureano Gómez, an engineer and a newspaperman whose ideas of government resembled those of Benito Mussolini and Francisco Franco, and on the other, by the volcanic and utopian Gaitán, whose explosive eloquence stirred up trouble, Ospina Pérez finally declared a state of siege in the disaffected areas. The situation developed into a reign of terror after the assassination of Gaitán in Bogotá in April of 1948 during a Pan-American conference presided over by Gómez. The capital was looted and set on fire by a mob said to have been egged on by Communists. The conference continued its deliberations, but Gómez went into hiding and soon fled to Spain. The government bombarded towns and villages in half of the country and fettered the press. The police hunted down the Liberals and shot them in cold blood or locked them up in unsanitary prisons. Many of the Liberal leaders went into exile, while the rural followers of the late Gaitán fled in droves to neighboring countries or sought to conceal themselves in the Colombian cities.

Martial law continued its reign. Returning home in 1949, the reactionary Gómez won the presidency in a one-sided election. The Liberals, still deeply divided and certain that their partisans would be coerced at the polls, refused to put up a candidate. Gómez took charge of the government, filled the newspaper offices with censors, denied the few Protestants in the country liberty of worship, issued pronouncements warning against the menace of Anglo-Saxon anti-religious materialism, ruled by decree, and intensified the terror. But since Franco claimed to be the first to discover the calamitous Communist peril, his Colombian disciple sent a detachment of troops to Korea, and, incidentally, acquired guns and planes to suppress insurgent Colombians and removed from the scene certain potentially dangerous Liberal army officers.

Stricken with a heart attack, Gómez began to relax the rigor of his dictatorship in 1952, and was finally driven from power in June, 1953, by General Gustavo Rojas Pinilla, who installed a military government and tried to restore order and security under Conservative domination. Notwithstanding a decade of turbulence and tyranny, inflated prices for coffee and other Colombian products brought prosperity, at least to the managers of the economy. But rising salaries and wages hardly kept pace with increasing costs of living. Colombia's political, if not her economic, future was still clouded as she entered the second half of the century. Rojas Pinilla was deposed in May, 1957.

🎏 VENEZUELA'S INCREASING WEALTH
AND PERSISTENT DESPOTISM

Venezuela's mineral wealth is fantastic. Huge deposits of recently discovered iron ore have been added to unlimited quantities of petroleum. But the great majority of Venezuelans remained poor tenant farmers or day laborers working for the big planters and ranchmen. Too little of the national revenues from oil and iron had been spent to fertilize the land, improve farming methods, enlighten the people, and develop their skills. Too meager attention had been given to production for home consumption.

Arciniegas has described the country as an "oil heaven" for the military group, and characterized the despotism of the mestizo General Juan Vicente Gómez, who held the country in his iron grasp for twenty-seven years (1908–35), in the following pertinent phrases: [3]

> A former cattle-rustler, swift and heavy-handed, given to few but trenchant words, he had the air of a barbarian patriarch. . . . Like Manuel Rosas of Argentina, Juan Vicente looked upon his country as his ranch. On his ranch he was boss. Those who thought of opposing him were thrown into underground dungeons where they suffered terrible tortures and rotted away in tropical dampness. The phrase "thought of" is used advisedly, for Juan Vicente could read what was going on in people's minds. Besides being a dictator, he was something of a wizard.

The immediate predecessor of Gómez was Cipriano Castro, a cruel and rapacious mestizo mountaineer born in the energetic Andean section of western Venezuela in 1858. With scant opportunity for formal education, Castro began work on a cattle ranch at an early age, entered politics in 1884, and became governor of his native state of Táchira four years later. He took part in an unsuccessful revolt in 1892 and was expelled from his country. For seven years he lived on the eastern frontier of Colombia, rustled cattle, and bided his time. When he finally crossed back over the border with an intrepid guerrilla band, he was promptly joined by several of the professional warriors. Advancing rapidly toward the capital, he chased the government out and installed himself in Caracas in October, 1899. The ablest of the guerrilla officers who supported Castro in his thrust for power was Juan Vicente Gómez.

Castro's political career was extremely hazardous. No mountaineer had ever ruled the nation before. Venezuela had been dominated by its plainsmen or the intellectuals and generals of Caracas and the seaboard. It was perhaps the realization that he was engaged in a desperate enterprise that made him so cruel and so eager to accumulate a fortune. He was determined to hold on to the government as long as he could and to lay up a large treasure for possible years of exile in case he lost control. He obtained considerable sums by means of government contracts, concessions, and monopolies, and within a few years he sent heavy bank deposits to Curaçao and New York. He had almost no moral scruples. He not only plundered the nation; he jailed and executed his opponents or compelled them to flee the country in order to escape death or imprisonment. He governed Venezuela as if he owned the country and was constantly in conflict with foreign governments because of his abuse of their citizens and subjects. He was one of the most irresponsible tyrants that Latin America ever spawned.

Late in 1908 he became seriously ill—or so it was said—and went to Europe for an operation. He was succeeded by Juan Vicente Gómez, who had been the strong right arm of the Castro government from the outset. But now Gómez decided to dominate the country in his own right and not in the interest of his former chief, who was forced to wander for years in exile, a "man without a country." Sometime in 1916 Castro established his residence in San Juan, Puerto Rico, where death overtook him late in 1924.

His successor broke all records in Venezuela for length of despotic domination. Gómez held the nation in his iron grip for twenty-seven years, until death ended his tyranny in December, 1935. Like Castro, he was a mountaineer and ranchman from the state of Táchira, and, like his immediate predecessor, he was a mestizo, although probably with more Indian traits than Castro had. Born in 1857, Gómez spent almost no time in school and set to work as a small farmer and then as a ranchman, just as Castro did. Like Castro again, he took part in the civil war of 1892 and was forced to flee the country; and, like Castro once more, he took refuge in Colombia, where he prospered as a livestock man, and as a cattle thief, it is said. Under Castro he served not only as an army officer but as vice-president and as acting president for brief intervals.

Gómez was a shrewd and efficient warrior; and after he took charge of the national government at the end of 1908 he gathered around himself a number of able administrators and journalists who tried to polish and gild his reputation at home and abroad. His rule differed little from Castro's except in one important respect: he carefully cultivated the friendship of foreigners and foreign governments. He promptly settled all the claims of aliens and welcomed investments from abroad. Venezuela possessed rich petroleum deposits, but had no money, technicians, or equipment to extract, refine, and market the oil. Gómez and his supporters formed a partnership with foreign capitalists which proved profitable for both sides. Workers in the oil fields also appear to have received reasonably good pay. The main trouble was that Gómez and his little coterie did not use the Venezuelan share to promote the welfare of the nation; they kept a large part of the profits for their own private purses. Gómez accumulated millions before he died. He invested most of his fortune at home, however, in fine horses and cattle, in lands, houses, and hotels; the property remained in Venezuela and the national government recovered the major part of it after the dictator's death. Moreover, he redeemed the foreign debt of the country and refused to float foreign loans when he could easily have borrowed millions in New York or London. Debts were either repugnant to him, or else there was a limit to his greed, enormous as it was. He must be given credit for paying off these foreign obligations and for his harmonious relations with other nations. The fact remains, however, that Gómez was a despot and not even a benevolent despot. He was among the world's most cruel tyrants. Many hundreds were imprisoned, tortured, killed, or driven into exile during his long rule. Under him Venezuela had peace and made considerable material progress, but enjoyed neither liberty nor democracy, and almost nothing was done to redeem the mass of the people from poverty and ignorance.

Gómez was succeeded by his long-time war minister, General Eleázar López Contreras, likewise a native of Táchira; but the new chief executive was not a tyrant. He seems to have been a mild devotee of democracy, and during his administration he granted the Venezuelans a considerable measure of freedom. He also gave some attention to education, public health, and the welfare of the common people. Retiring from the presidency in 1941, he transferred the government to Isaías Medina Angarita, no doubt his choice for the presidency, and, moreover, another son of Táchira. The men from the mountains were crowding out the *Llaneros* and the *Costeños*.

This dominance of the mountain men could not last forever. Medina Angarita was a less satisfactory ruler than López Contreras, whose conscience may have been quickened by the threat of death from tuberculosis. Both of these army officers, however, were men largely of Spanish blood and more civilized than Castro and Gómez as well as fully aware of the mood of the Venezuelan people, who had rocked Caracas and other towns at the time of Gómez' death with demonstrations of hatred toward dictatorship which nobody in Venezuela could soon forget. The problem that may have puzzled them both was this: how to open the floodgates of democracy without inviting ruinous turmoil. López Contreras unbarred a tiny portal in 1941 when he permitted Congress to collaborate with him in the choice of his successor, but he left Medina Angarita to wrestle with the problem in 1945. Forbidden to serve another term immediately after the end of his five-year administration, General Medina could not decide whether to select the next president with the advice of the national legislature or leave the choice to the will of the people as expressed at the polls. The Democratic Action party, along with some Communists and more radicals, grew impatient; and army officers, actuated by fear that the stream of "black gold" might be diverted or dried up, joined them. On October 19, 1945, the legal president was hauled off to prison.

A junta of army officers and leaders of the Democratic Action set themselves up as the national government, with Franco-Spanish Rómulo Betancourt as presiding officer. Some of the officials of the defunct regime were hustled off to Miami, Florida, by plane; others went to jail. A good deal of private property, acquired unjustly or not, was seized by the provisional government. Then revenge and persecution ceased. Labor organizations were not only permitted but encouraged, and larger and still larger sums of oil revenues were spent on sanitation, schools, the adornment of the towns and cities, the building of roads, and the purchase of shares in a joint merchant marine formed in collaboration with Venezuela and Ecuador.

"But," in the words of Arciniegas,[4] "the essential problem still remained unsolved," the problem "of finding a stable, democratic formula of government. Betancourt, wily and quick-witted, quashed the plots the military were already scheming to halt the march toward democratic solutions."

And finally, to the surprise of Latin America, Venezuela arranged for free, general, unrigged elections. Testimony of the most varied sort bears witness that it was an absolutely democratic election. It took place in December 1947. . . . On that day in city and village the people were up at dawn to take their place in the lines at the voting booths. There was enthusiasm, liberty, and respect. The ballots were of different colors [white, black, green, and red], the only way voting could be handled in a country where a large proportion of the people is illiterate. . . . The majority voted for Acción Democrática.

The man chosen for president was Venezuela's famous novelist, Rómulo Gallegos, a gray-headed man of sixty-three who had tasted the bitterness of exile after serving as director of several academies and a college for teachers. Inaugurated in February, 1948, he was overthrown before the end of the year.

His benevolent attitude toward labor had alarmed the business interests and the generals, who were not only alarmed but infuriated by his efforts to reduce their plunder and his suggestion that oil royalties be increased. They feared that he might slaughter the fowl that was laying the golden eggs. When he finally made mild proposals for redistribution of arable lands, the army officers decided to tolerate him no longer. He was replaced by a three-man military junta, which was soon dominated by its strongest member, Colonel Marcos Pérez Jiménez, who outlawed the Democratic Action party and made himself president, first by a fraudulent election (1952) and then by a pliant constitutional assembly. The oil wells continued to respond to the pumps. The iron ore began to move to United States markets. The flood-gates were still closed against the dangerous populace. But Pérez Jiménez was deposed early in 1958.

LIBERALISM AND MILITARISM IN ECUADOR

After some insurgency at the beginning of the century, Ecuadorians settled down and seemed to be moving toward a fairly prosperous and more democratic era. Liberal president followed Liberal president every four years. Probably each supreme chief manipulated the elections in favor of a party successor; but, after all, the Liberals were in the majority. Liberty of the press usually prevailed, martial law was rarely proclaimed, and the people were left free to cultivate their orchards and their wheat, barley, and corn fields for the home market and weave their fine straw hats, grow their cacao, and collect their tagua nuts for export. Only one government was turned out by a military coup (1925), after which the politicians seemed determined not to let it happen again. They illustrated their resolution by placing the reins of government in the hands of Isidro Ayora, a distinguished physician, and keeping him in power, more or less against his will, until the late summer of 1931.

Meantime, the recession of 1921–22, the decimation of the cacao trees by a leaf disease, and the arrival of the great economic depression had created discontent and radicalism on one side, and the rise of totalitarianism in Europe had caused reactionary reverberations on the other. As in some other countries of Latin America, militarism forged to the front. But conditions in Ecuador became more chaotic than elsewhere. Not less than twenty chiefs of state, set up and pushed out by the jarring military coterie, came and went during the next sixteen years, four of them within a week or two after being thrust into the president's office. Only José M. Velasco Ibarra (1934–35, 1944–47), an oldtime *caudillo* with a Fascist *mystique* to mesmerize the multitude, and Carlos Arroyo del Río (1940–44), an able lawyer and businessman from Guayaquil, were able to cling to power for any length of time.

With the inauguration of Galo Plaza, son of Leónidas Plaza Gutiérrez (associate of Eloy Alfaro and twice chief executive of the nation), politics entered a calmer stage. A stalwart giant, born and educated in the United States, where he later served for a period as ambassador, Don Galo was voted into the presidency by one of the freest and fairest elections ever held in Ecuador. Ruling with the consent and backing of the people, he cowed the restive army chiefs. Calling in specialists from the outside, he made a mighty effort to push his country along the path of prosperity and enlightenment, using his office to promote productivity and expansion in manufacturing and diversity in agriculture, stressing rice and bananas as well as the customary crops. Committed to liberty and democratic procedures, he refused to impose his presidential successor, and the astute and eloquent José María Velasco Ibarra won the election for that office in 1952. Velasco Ibarra's association with Dictator Juan D. Perón while an exile in Argentina caused some uneasiness among Ecuadorians, which was not relieved by the new president's attempts to muffle the newspapers and his apparent drift toward despotic reaction. But Velasco Ibarra neither gave free reign to his messianic complex nor lost the support of the army, and was therefore able to complete his four-year term. His successor, Camilo Ponce Enríquez, a member of the Conservative party, won the election of July 1956 by a narrow margin and was inaugurated at the end of the following August, but confronted a period of political restiveness and disorder.

Lecturing in the United States in the spring of 1954, Plaza praised his compatriots and predicted a democratic future for his country: [5]

> The people are good and hard-working to a degree of intensity that in some cases borders on desperation when the barest necessities of life have to be hoed out of a steep slope of the Andes ten thousand feet above the sea. They possess ancient virtues that have not been lost . . . ; they are hospitable, patient, and have an extraordinary ability for handicraft.
>
> The people have a long-standing tradition of love of freedom, ever present throughout the history of the nation, from revolt against taxation by the Spanish king in the seventeenth century, through the heroic Wars of Independence, to the permanent struggle for liberty throughout the convulsive history of the republic. The people of Ecuador have never tolerated despotism for long, nor have they ever exchanged freedom for bread.

When Ecuador tames her army officers, when her political leaders become less intolerant, when her citizens become more enlightened and escape from their poverty, democratic hopes may be fulfilled.

CIVILIAN DICTATORSHIP AND MILITARY DESPOTISM IN PERU

There were still two Perus at the beginning of the twentieth century as before: two nations, two peoples. One was the Peru of the ruling class, mainly white. The other was the Peru of the back-country masses, mainly Indian, and of the workers on the coastal plantations, in the oilfields and manufacturing plants, in the coastal towns, mostly part-Indian but with a sprinkling of Negroes, mulattoes, and poor whites. The members of the oligarchy, the majority of them residents of Lima but some dwellers in other urban centers bordering the Pacific, felt no urge to change the political, economic, and social order under which they had lived so comfortably—except in times of civil wars, which usually sprang from rivalries among themselves. Adoption of the procedures of democratic, representative government would set in motion the stagnant multitudes and create difficult and dangerous problems. If incited by demagogues, the masses might not only deprive the oligarchy of their power and wealth; they might snuff out their lives or banish them from the country. The oligarchy therefore preferred dictatorships in order to avoid the risk. There was no more conservative group in all Latin America. Religious toleration was not permitted until well after 1900. No constitution required compulsory and gratuitous primary education for the people until 1919, and this requirement was not consistently enforced.

The most outstanding political figure of the period was Augusto B. Leguía, a clever and forceful little man hardly more than five feet tall and weighing less than 140 pounds. Born in 1863 in the town of Lambayeque, a few score miles up the coast from Lima, he belonged to a family of small means. But he managed to acquire a business education and work his way into the outer fringe of the aristocracy by virtue of his success in banking. President of Peru during 1908–12, he was forced into exile a few years later. He spent the World War I period in London as commission merchant distributing Peruvian and Latin-American war products, and making tidy sums gambling on the races. Going back to Peru in 1919, probably richer than when he left, he ran for the presidency again and won; but fearing that political rivals intended to bar him from his office, he drove the legal president out of the capital, seized the government before the time arrived for his inauguration and maintained himself in power for eleven years.

By means of widespread propaganda and the servicing of the foreign debt, he restored Peruvian credit. Then he floated large issues of bonds in the United States and smaller issues in London. Adding to the proceeds of bond sales such revenues as he could collect in Peru, including an income tax levied for the first time, he spent large sums on ports, railroads, highways, city sewers and streets, and smaller sums on education. With a loyal army, a mounted constabulary, and an efficient police force, he ferreted out conspiracies, killed some of his opponents and critics, sent others to jail or out of the country, and subdued or destroyed opposition parties and newspapers. Members of congress either supported his policies or lost the next election. Although he sponsored some labor laws, apparently they were largely for display in progressive circles abroad. So likewise was some of his Indian legislation. His attitude toward all workers, whether white-collar or manual, was rather stern. His sympathies were with the merchants, mine-owners, and bankers; but he treated the landed aristocracy with great deference.

If the world depression had not struck Peru, he might have ruled the country as long as he lived. There was some political dissatisfaction on account of his suppression of certain political factions and his tight control of the rest. There was intellectual bitterness because he closed the University of San Marcos in retaliation for student demonstrations. Bitterness also developed among the workers because he not only dealt sternly with strikes but abolished their schools and forced their founder, Víctor Raul Haya de la Torre, to flee for his life. But economic grievances were probably a stronger motive for the uprising which forced him to resign in August, 1930. Business was bad. Unemployment mounted. The tax burden was becoming very irksome. The dictator was accused of extravagance and misappropriation of funds—and both charges were true. It was felt that accomplishments were not in proportion to expenditures, and the feeling was probably justified. But all the economic ills of the country were attributed to his government; and this, of course, was not just. A military revolt in Arequipa was followed by student and labor riots in Lima. The officers of the dictator's military staff began to waver. His police force, resentful because he had organized a mounted constabulary trained by Spanish officers, was in a disloyal mood. Leguía packed his baggage, filled his portfolios with Peruvian paper *soles,* sent other funds to foreign banks, and embarked with his family for England. But the Peruvian navy forced him to return before he had gotten far out to sea! Most of the family's property was seized and Augusto B. Leguía died in prison early in 1932.

Colonel Luís M. Sánchez Cerro, leader of the Arequipa military uprising, took control of the government late in 1930, suppressed a revolt of workers and radicals in Trujillo with brutal thoroughness, and maintained himself in power until he was assassinated in 1933; whereupon General Oscar R. Benavides became dictator for six years and then imposed a civilian aristocrat named Manuel Prado as chief executive. José L. Bustamante, a wealthy lawyer and diplomat, became president in 1945. He was given almost unanimous support at the polls by Haya de la Torre's APRA (American Popular Revolutionary Alliance) party. This group, called the "Apristas," was a radical underground organization composed of mestizos, mulattoes, Indians, and young intellectuals who had bound all of them together and formulated a program which included labor and social security legislation, parcelization of the big

estates, and a demand for a larger share of the profits of foreign enterprises: mining, petroleum, agricultural, and manufacturing. For the two
decades since their party was founded in 1923, their leaders had been
killed, jailed, and persecuted in every conceivable manner. Haya de la
Torre had spent most of the time in exile or in prison. The Apristas
were accused of every imaginable crime—falsely for the most part, since
Haya held firmly to the doctrine of peaceful change—and deprived of
the right to participate in elections; but Bustamante had powerful rivals
among the ruling groups and needed APRA votes. They elected a large
representation to Congress and were given three cabinet posts in return
for their support.

But Bustamante hated the Apristas, who had now changed their name
to the People's party, and searched diligently for an excuse to resume
the persecution. He found it in the assassination of a newspaper editor
and a revolt in Callao, for which the members of the party were probably
not responsible. Its cabinet members were dismissed, its congressmen
were forced to flee for their lives, and Haya de la Torre was eventually
(late 1948) compelled to seek asylum in the Colombian embassy, where
he was protected even by Conservative Colombian diplomats until he
finally went into exile again in 1954. The People's party was now practically destroyed; the oligarchy's dreadful uneasiness had vanished.

The oligarchy naturally applauded Bustamante, but a powerful army
officer named Manuel Odría had quarrelled with the president and had
been ousted from his cabinet position. Sulking for a time in Arequipa,
Odría finally led an army revolt in October, 1948, deposed Bustamante,
jailed hundreds of Apristas, attacked San Marcos University with
armored tanks, dismissed its Aprista rector and a number of its faculty,
and set up a military despotism. At the very beginning of his revolt, he
had threatened to hang the radicals from the lampposts of Lima. He
sought to justify his conduct later by a statement which recalls the days
of the Bourbon tyranny: [6]

> The fundamental reason for the existence of the revolutionary govern-
> ment I head is to eliminate the sectarian danger that for more than twenty
> years, and under four political regimes, has done nothing but commit crimes
> of every order against all individuals and institutions. *Aprismo* has sys-
> tematically threatened the individual, the family and the home, the school
> and the church, the military and civil institutions, and the nation itself.

The truth of the matter seems to be that this organization had merely
demanded a new deal for the Indian, the mestizo, and the mulatto workers and all the underprivileged with a moderation that could not always
be expected from the leaders of such people. But the Aprista program
was a threat to the wealth and privileges of the oligarchy, and the

politicians who had governed Peru as far as possible in the aristocratic interest had crucified the organizers of the movement from the start. With the election of Manuel Prado, however, and his inauguration late in July 1956, the customary Peruvian despotism became less severe. Prado was a civilian who had ruled the country with a stern but rather benevolent hand during the World War II period and would probably not resort to tyranny.

Social conditions in Peru were not quite the same in the 1950's as they had been a century earlier. Some of the rich were richer, but many of the poor were not quite so poor. Wages and salaries were considerably higher and probably represented greater purchasing power in spite of the rising costs of living. Sanitary conditions were less wretched, schools were far more numerous, the rate of literacy was considerably higher, and religious intolerance was less pronounced. Transportation—railroads, highways, even airways—and communications were far more efficient. Petroleum was being exploited at a rapid rate and many other minerals and metals were in process of vigorous extraction. But there had been little progress toward democracy since the winning of independence.

LIBERALISM, MILITARISM, AND RADICALISM IN BOLIVIA

Two decades of Liberal domination ceased in Bolivia in 1920 with the violent overthrow of José Gutiérrez Guerra. The Liberals had split into two factions, and one of them, after taking a few Conservatives into its camp, had organized a new faction called the Republican party. The Liberals had revealed their progressiveness not only by changes in the relationship of Church and State; they had promoted the economic development of Bolivia by building wagon roads, encouraging the construction of railways, and fostering mining, farming, and ranching. Bolivia had lost the rubber territory of Acre to Brazil in 1903 just as she had lost her Pacific coast territory to Chile at an earlier period. But both Brazil and Chile had made retribution by financing railway outlets, one from La Paz to the Pacific and another running around the rapids of the Mamoré and Madeira rivers so as to furnish access to the Amazon. These reductions of the national domain could not be avoided, and the Liberals had made the best of a bad bargain.

The Liberals—and the Conservatives before them—had succeeded in curbing militarism, and had permitted the press to have a measure of freedom uncommon in the country. The Republicans, taking advantage of the eagerness of American bankers to manage the flotation of foreign bonds, sold large issues of government securities in the United States and continued to foster the exploitation of the nation's resources. But they were rather extravagant, they showed scant respect for the liberties of the people, and they neglected public education and failed to prevent the army officers from meddling in politics.

Bautista Saavedra, the first of the Republican presidents (1921–25), tried to induce the army to help him prolong his rule. Hernando Siles, the second (1926–30), set up a dictatorship and subjected the country to martial law, using the world depression and labor agitation as an excuse. Both sold government bonds in the United States at large discounts, with high interest rates, and on terms which, if enforced, would have given the bankers excessive control over the national economy; and Siles spent the money thus obtained rather lavishly in preparation for a war with Paraguay over the Chaco boundary.

As economic conditions grew more critical, Siles called the Nazi Hans Kundt to La Paz, made him chief of staff, and announced that the presidential election, scheduled for May of 1930, would be postponed "for reasons of national welfare." These maneuvers aroused the resentment of army officers, rival politicians, and a Defense League which had been organized during the Chaco war scare of 1928 for the purpose of fostering patriotic sentiment and obtaining subscriptions for the purchase of armament. Students and workmen rioted in La Paz, General Carlos Blanco Galindo started an uprising in the railroad and mining center of Oruro, and soon the inhabitants of nearly every town in the country declared themselves in favor of revolution. Blanco Galindo and his insurgents seized the capital on June 28, 1930; Siles and Kundt took refuge in foreign legations; and a military junta with the victorious general at its head was set up to govern the nation pending elections.

Blanco Galindo promised that the election for president would be held promptly; and, surprising as it may seem, he kept his promise. The old habit of military domination had not yet been fully revived. The victory at the polls in January 1931 of honest, capable, and democratic Daniel Salamanca, prominent among the founders and leaders of the new party until he was shunted aside by Saavedra and Siles, seemed to be a good omen. But the war with Paraguay (1932–35) soon brought the army officers to the fore and blasted all democratic hopes. The war into which Salamanca was driven reluctantly went against Bolivia; but when the president made an inspection tour to the front lines and attempted to shuffle his commanders, he was arrested and deposed. The vice-president, José L. Tejada Sórzano, then took charge of the government (1934–36) and the war ended in victory for Paraguay. The Bolivian generals had not covered themselves with glory, but they had convinced themselves that they knew what was wrong with their country and that only they could apply the remedy.

The remedy ranged from socialism to fascism, with a heavy dose of xenophobia added. Army officer followed army officer in the presidential palace during the next decade (1936–46). Colonel David Toro occupied it long enough to outline a socialist program and expropriate the properties of the Standard Oil Company. Hermán Busch, half German, stayed longer, but died either from suicide or assassination in 1939. General Carlos Quintinilla's occupancy endured for two years, and General Enrique Peñaranda and General Gualberto Villarroel dwelt in the mansion for three years each. On July 17, 1946, a mob aroused by political gangsters invaded the government palace, seized Villarroel, and hanged him on the arm of a lamppost.

Civilian despots ruled Bolivia during the next four years, but the government then passed into the hands of another general, Hugo Ballivián, descendant of José Ballivián, one of the nation's "Little Napoleons" of a century earlier. Hugo Ballivián was driven from power in less than a year, however, by the ardent followers of Víctor Paz Estenssoro, formerly professor in the University of San Andrés in La Paz. The new president and his party—MNR, which stands for National Revolutionary Movement—were more than a little radical. They not only championed the interests of the workers; they took over the properties of the big mining magnates—Patiño, Aramayo, and Hochschild—in 1952 and launched a sweeping agrarian program late the next year: homesteads in tropical eastern Bolivia and the big haciendas elsewhere were divided among the landless, leaving owners with a modest acreage and the promise of payment for the rest of their lands with twenty-year government bonds. Hoping to discourage communism and foster the development of a higher level of living for the impoverished masses, the United States began to make large grants to the Bolivian government in 1953.

Practical education for the Indian and mestizo masses, more productive agriculture, farm-to-market roads, and the multiplication of light industries were Bolivia's most desperate needs at mid-century. Inaugurated in August, 1956, after an election largely dominated by Paz Estenssero, Hernán Siles Zuazo, son of former president Hernando Siles, took charge of the executive mansion amid financial and political conditions that barely fell short of chaos: conspiracies, strikes, declining production of minerals, confusion in agriculture, and a runaway inflation. Probably influenced by the example of Lázaro Cárdenas of

Mexico, the leaders of the National Revolutionary Movement had armed the workers in the mines and other industries and the Indian peasants in order to defy and intimidate the Bolivian army. But they were having great difficulty in controlling their armed supporters.

CHAPTER XXX

Southern South America and Brazil

𝄞 ECONOMIC AND SOCIAL TRENDS

Chile, Brazil, and the three republics of the Plata region felt the impact of world economic conditions during the new century: twenty years of comparative prosperity before and during World War I; a brief recession; partial or complete recovery followed by a tremendous depression; and then another prosperous period troubled by price inflation. Argentina, with a somewhat more diversified production, weathered the storms of recession and depression more successfully than the rest. The value of her exports climbed from slightly above $149,000,000 in 1900 to more than $1,000,000,000 in 1919, dropped to less than $500,000,000 in 1921, climbed back to approximately the 1919 figure in 1928, and fell precipitously after 1929; but the value of her sales abroad at the lowest point of the great depression was approximately $84,000,000 above the aggregate for 1900, and the annual average for 1948–51 exceeded $1,300,000,000, measured in the depreciated dollars of those years.

In contrast with Argentina, the value of the exports of the other countries at the depth of the great depression fell well below their value at the opening of the century. Brazil's exports during the period under consideration averaged somewhat less than Argentina's, but exceeded Argentina's in dollar value during the years 1948–51. Expanding from slightly less than $182,500,000 in 1900 to over $582,500,000 in 1919, Brazil's foreign sales did not reach the 1919 level again until after 1940. The low for the depression period was over $22,500,000 short of the figure for 1900! But the figure for 1951 exceeded $1,750,000,000— considerably larger than the aggregate for 1919 even in terms of the gold dollars by which they were measured in 1919.

Chile's exports, which sold for not quite $61,000,000 in 1900, expanded to somewhat more than $272,000,000 in 1918 but failed to rise much higher before the world depression. Valued at $276,500,000 in 1929, they plummeted to hardly more than \$35,000,000 in 1932, rose falteringly during the next decade, and finally approached \$377,-000,000 in 1951, an aggregate actually smaller in terms of gold dollars than the total for 1929.

The exports of Uruguay, which sold for less than \$30,500,000 in 1900, rose to nearly \$162,000,000 in 1919 and not only failed to rise higher during the next two decades but actually dived to a low of hardly more than \$18,500,000 in 1934. Then they gradually expanded, reaching an average of more than \$215,000,000 annually for the years 1948–51, but still fell short of the figure for 1919 in terms of gold dollars.

Paraguay's exports, which averaged around \$5,000,000 annually during the early years of the century, exceeded \$15,000,000 in 1928, but shrank to less than \$4,000,000 in 1936. Expanding slowly thereafter, they averaged some \$31,000,000 annually during the quadrennium of 1948–51, which meant that they barely recovered the value they had in 1928 in terms of the gold dollars by which they were measured in that year.

All five of the countries had their epochs of reform, apparent or actual, and their periods of reaction. Only Uruguay, and perhaps Chile, made indisputable progress toward democracy, but none save Paraguay failed to register considerable social and cultural advance.

Population increased rather rapidly in all the republics, but most rapidly in Argentina, Brazil, and Uruguay, mainly because these three received a much larger stream of immigrants. Paraguay's population expanded from 600,000 in 1900 to 1,405,600 in 1950; Chile's, from some 3,100,000 to 5,885,000; Uruguay's, from approximately 936,000 to over 2,365,000; Brazil's, from some 17,319,000 to over 52,645,000; Argentina's, from 4,500,000 to 16,200,000.

The growth of cities was still more remarkable, except in Paraguay. Fully half of the inhabitants of Chile, Uruguay, and Brazil and nearly two-thirds of Argentina's were living in urban centers of 3,000 and above in 1950. Santiago had a population of 1,500,000; Rio de Janeiro and São Paulo had in excess of 2,000,000 each; Montevideo's population was approaching 900,000 and that of Buenos Aires was over 3,000,000. More people were now living in Buenos Aires than in Paris, and Rio's inhabitants outnumbered Rome's. Too many people were crowding into the cities in southern Latin America, as in Mexico, Colombia, Peru, and Venezuela.

The migration, as already pointed out in another connection, was due to the presumed economic and cultural advantages of the urban communities. Educational facilities and sanitary conditions were less satisfactory in most of the rural regions, but the main attraction of the cities was the prospect of employment in factories, commercial houses, and government. Paraguay, having few manufacturing plants and insufficient public revenues to afford a well-to-do bureaucracy, was still 70 per cent rural. The population of Asunción numbered only 200,000 at the middle of the century; population of other Paraguayan towns ranged from 11,000 to 41,000.

🐚 REFORM IN URUGUAY

Taking the lead in the reform movement, Uruguayan statesmen soon transformed their little country into a democracy in fact as well as in name. Revolutions ceased. Elections, formerly a farce, now became orderly and reasonably fair. Presidents quietly surrendered their offices at the end of their constitutional terms. The people, under liberal and progressive government, advanced in education and culture while increasing in numbers and prosperity. Foreign capital, mainly from England and the United States, flowed in rapidly, in spite of social legislation which some considered too radical. Transportation and communication facilities expanded. Power plants and factories multiplied along with sheep, cattle, horses, and acres planted in corn and wheat.

Outstanding among Uruguayan political leaders of the period was José Batlle y Ordóñez, twice president of the republic (1903–7 and 1911–15), twice head of the National Council of Administration, and for forty years the guiding spirit of the Colorado party. The son of General Lorenzo Batlle, a former president of Uruguay (1868–72), he was born in 1856 and educated in his home country and in Europe. Although he had studied law, he devoted himself mainly to journalism and politics. After writing for various newspapers for several years, he founded one of his own, *El Día* (1886), and made it his mouthpiece for the rest of his life. His first task in politics was the renovation of the Colorado party, which had lost prestige under unworthy leadership and had never formed any close connection with the common people. He set out to make it more democratic, to give it a program and endow it with the cohesion and strength necessary to carry out its purposes. A large, intelligent, earnest, and magnetic man with unlimited reserves of energy, he so far succeeded by 1903 that he was the victorious candidate for the presidency.

As chief executive, he confronted an intolerable situation in the government of the departments. The Blanco party, which had not been able to capture the presidency a single time since 1865, had revolted in 1897 and extorted the privilege of appointing the political chiefs of six of the eighteen departments into which the republic was then divided for administrative purposes; and these six units had become the "fief" of a political boss named Aparicio Saravia, a wealthy ranchman of scant culture and less political integrity. A civil war of nearly two years' duration was required to break the hold of the *caudillo* over these departments, and the remaining two years of Batlle's administration had to be devoted mainly to repairing the damages.

Followed in the presidency by Claudio Williman, an enlightened and progressive Colorado who inaugurated a number of educational, judicial, administrative, and financial reforms and left a surplus in the Treasury, Batlle became president a second time on March 1, 1911. Having spent a good part of the preceding four years in Europe observing its most democratic governments, he had now formulated a reform program which he was determined to put into practice. Four years were too short to get all of his innovations started, but he laid the foundations for social legislation that shortly placed Uruguay in the vanguard of the progressive nations of the Western world. He and his loyal successors during the twenty years following 1911 wrote on the statute books laws providing for an eight-hour day, factory inspection, indemnity for accidents, a minimum wage, the right to strike, and abolition of the death penalty. Projecting the government into the economy, they nationalized telephones, electric plants, and fuels, created a state mortgage bank and a state insurance bank, erected a national refrigeration plant, and began a state railway system. Inaugurating national income and inheritance taxes, they utilized the increased revenues for the improvement of sanitation and schools and the construction of highways and public buildings. Among purely political reforms worthy of note were an electoral law which virtually eliminated fraud and a new constitution (adopted in 1917, effective on March 1, 1919).

The constitution separated Church and State, provided ample personal guaranties, and abolished property qualifications for voting and holding public office; but its most singular provisions created a National Council of Administration, to be composed of nine members chosen by direct popular vote at the time of the presidential elections and to represent all parties in proportion to the number of ballots cast by each. The main objective of the new organization was to limit the power and functions of the presidents and avoid the evil of dictatorship. It was to have jurisdiction over public instruction, public works, labor, manufacturing industries, agriculture, sanitation, charities, and finance, and to have charge of elections and the administration of electoral laws. The main functions retained by the president were the power to appoint and remove cabinet members, diplomatic and consular representatives, and civil, police, and military officers; the duty of calling together the national legislature and proposing legislation and the right to approve or disapprove acts passed by this body; and authority to serve as commander-in-chief of the military forces and to represent the nation on ceremonial occasions. Although the administrative departments were provided with elected administrative boards and representative assemblies, each of them had to have an administrative head appointed by the national chief executive.

During the next decade Batlle either served as member of the National Council or advocated his reform program in public addresses and the press until most of it was adopted. When he died in 1929 almost the entire nation mourned his loss. The new Legislative Palace completed a few years before included a Hall of the Lost Footsteps—*Salón de los Pasos Perdidos*—a spacious room dedicated to the nameless citizens of the republic who had contributed in their humble way to its progress and then passed on; and it was there that Batlle's body rested in state while the whole nation marched by in worshipful homage. Uruguayans would hear his heavy footsteps no more; would never again see his big frame slouching on the town rostrums and the improvised village platforms. His clarion voice was forever silenced. But he would not soon be forgotten in Uruguay. Public squares, streets, schools, and hotels would be named in his honor; monuments to his memory would be erected in the town plazas; and his close relatives would occupy high posts in the national government. José Artigas, who lived and died before Batlle was born, continued officially to occupy his niche as Uruguay's paramount hero; but this well-balanced though zealous reformer of a later day seemed destined to occupy a larger place in the hearts of his countrymen. José Batlle had won immortality by transforming his little nation into a model republic.

It will be observed that Uruguay's new constitution still left to the president the two main instruments of power often utilized by dictators: the police force and the army; and Gabriel Terra, who took charge of the government in the midst of an economic crisis in 1931, employed both two years later to dissolve the National Congress and the National Council of Administration and set up a dictatorship in Uruguay. He offered a triple justification for these drastic steps: the severity of the depression, the dangerous agitation of Communists and other radicals, and the administrative paralysis caused by the organic reforms of Batlle and his associates. Promulgating another constitution in 1934, which nullified the Batlle system, Terra continued his despotic rule until June 19, 1938, when he turned the government over to General Alfredo Baldomir. Although Baldomir was Terra's brother-in-law and probably owed his election to the manipulation of his kinsman, he immediately announced his intention to adopt more democratic procedures and kept his promise. But the Terra experience was not forgotten by Batlle's disciples.[1] They not only returned to the plural administrative council in 1952 but abolished the presidency.

Uruguay was now the freest, most justly governed, and close to the best educated country in Latin America. Lacking coal, petroleum, iron ore, and most of the industrial metals, its prosperity depended largely upon processing and light industries, agriculture, and the livestock business. But its soil was still fertile, it had no vexatious agrarian problems, and no serious provocation for class conflict, since no deep chasm separated rich and poor. There were some dissatisfied citizens, of course. No country is without them. But they belonged mainly to the opposition parties—the Blancos, lately called the Nationalists, and the Socialists—and to rural groups who complained, not without justification, that too large a share of the public revenues were spent in the capital to the neglect of the country towns and villages.[2]

✑ TURMOIL AND TRANQUILLITY IN PARAGUAY

Turbulence persisted in Paraguay for more than a decade after the opening of the new century, but politics became far more stable following August of 1912. For a period of twenty-four years thereafter, the Liberal faction, which had ousted the Conservatives in 1904, kept the army and the police force quiet or held them in check and succeeded in frustrating nearly all attempts to shorten administrations by means of armed revolt. A group of fairly progressive civilian presidents, two of them the sons of immigrants, governed the country in a mildly autocratic fashion: Eduardo Schaerer (1912–16); Manuel Franco (1916–19) and José Montero, who completed this four-year term after Franco's death; Eligio and Eusebio Ayala (1921–28); José P. Guggiari (1928–32); and Eusebio Ayala again (1932–36). They stimulated agriculture, adopted a land policy designed to increase the number of small family-owned farms, encouraged immigration, promoted public education, and fostered handicraft and light mechanized industries. They also allowed the Paraguayans to enjoy a large measure of freedom for the first time in their lives.

But this orderly progress was interrupted by the Gran Chaco War with Bolivia. The military heroes of the war, provided with ideas by some intellectuals with authoritarian or totalitarian propensities, denounced the "outmoded liberal democracies" of the nineteenth century and promised a "new era" in Paraguay. The epoch of the progressive Liberals came to an end in February, 1936, with the overthrow of Eusebio Ayala by Colonel Rafael Franco and the new "authoritarians." On September 7, 1940, after a succession of three short-term dictators,

General Higinio Morínigo, a stocky mestizo more Indian (Guaraní) than Spanish in appearance, seized the government. A professional soldier forty-three years of age, without education but with native shrewdness and strong despotic tendencies, Morínigo subjected the country to nearly a decade of tyranny that resembled the epochs of Francia and Francisco Solano López.

Although a revolution forced Morínigo out in August, 1948, the government went into the hands of the Colorado Conservatives. An old civilian *caudillo* named Federico Chávez leaped into power two years later and maintained his position until he was deposed in May, 1954; General Alfredo Stroesser, a Paraguayan of part German descent like Eduardo Schaerer, took control of the government by military force a few months later.

Paraguay was still primitive and 80 per cent illiterate, much of its resources in the hands of foreigners, mainly capitalists from Argentina, who owned three-fourths of a foreign investment that totaled $60,000,-000. The quebracho forests (tanning materials), the lumber mills, the tea plantations (yerba-maté), several immense ranches, and the few mechanized factories were all owned by aliens or by the naturalized sons of European immigrants. The common people—mostly Indians or mixbloods—worked either for the foreigners or in the handicraft industries, or cultivated their small eroded farms with obsolete tools. A few highways and a railway had been built, but the roads from farm to market were either dusty trails or muddy ruts. Oxcarts and pack animals were still the customary mode of transportation. But perhaps a note of optimism is not out of place. Harris G. Warren, who has recently observed the country at close range, concludes his survey with this statement: [3]

"Paraguay has known glory and despair but never disgrace. There is an inherent vitality in her people that has led the country slowly forward, that has overcome tremendous handicaps and healed terrible wounds. So long as that vitality endures, Paraguayans can hope that their land may yet become the Paradise of Guaraní legend."

Paraguay cries out for political education, manual skills, intensive development of its resources, and personal freedom.

"RADICALISM," CONSERVATIVE REACTION, AND "PERONISM" IN ARGENTINA

Ruled since the 1850's by an oligarchy of lawyers, literati, and big landlords, Argentina's masses became more restless and assertive in the late 1880's and early 1890's, expressing their new mood by strikes on the docks and enlistment in the Radical Civic Union organized by

Leandro Alem and Hipólito Irigoyen. After Alem committed suicide in 1896 and Irigoyen began to teach in a school for girls, things seemed to quiet down, but discontent actually continued to spread. The trouble arose mainly from the fact that the oligarchy was educating the lower classes without providing an outlet for their sharpened minds and heightened ambitions, and that some of the people were appropriating European democratic and radical ideas. Nearly all of the best farming and grazing areas were owned in huge tracts by the descendants of the old Spanish settlers or by foreign companies, mostly British. None of the presidents—not even Sarmiento, who had sojourned in the United States twice and must have acquired some familiarity with its public-land policy—ever adopted an agrarian system calculated to create a group of small independent farmers. Immigrants who came to Argentina in the hope of becoming landed proprietors soon found that little land was available except in the hot and humid North or in the arid Northwest and Southwest. Condemned to day labor on the big haciendas and *estancias* (grain and flax plantations and sheep and cattle ranches) or to the apparently perpetual role of tenant farmers living in rural huts or in drab, neglected country villages with few cultural advantages, more and more of them migrated to the cities, where they helped to found small industries or set up small commercial enterprises of their own.

Still unreconciled, they were ready to listen to agitators who promised them better opportunities, whether the agitators were the sons of immigrants or the politically ambitious younger sons of the aristocracy. They joined not only the Civic Union but also the Socialist and the Democratic Progressive parties. A bloody, though futile uprising in 1905, followed by smoldering discontent and increased labor agitation, frightened the oligarchy into the acceptance of electoral reforms proposed in 1912 by one of their more sensitive and humanitarian presidents, Roque Sáenz Peña, who had vainly tried to placate Irigoyen by a cabinet post.

In 1916, for the first time in the history of the nation, its adult males, without the customary barriers of literacy and property qualifications, freely cast their secret ballots in every province for electors who were to choose the president. Hipólito Irigoyen, candidate of the Radicals and recipient of some other leftist votes, was elected by a narrow margin. Son of an immigrant family of humble Basque origin, he had managed to obtain a college degree, study some law, acquire a small ranch, and perfect a loyal political organization. A kindly mystic like his uncle, Leandro Alem, who had contributed to his education and given him his early training in politics, Irigoyen was tall, self-possessed, and enigmatic. He addressed political gatherings in vague and mysterious language which men felt rather than understood. They readily assumed that there was profound wisdom in his verbose pronouncements and went away convinced that he was a friend of poor people like themselves.

Taking charge of the presidency late in 1916, he faced a difficult task. Committed to radical reforms by his electoral promises and party connections, he confronted the crisis of World War I, the impatience of the crowd, and a critical opposition—with a party composed of men untried in public life and lacking a tradition of devoted public service. Probably in defiance of the sentiment of the more intelligent citizens, he refused to break relations with Germany. He contributed very little to enlightened legislation because he was handicapped by parliamentary opposition and the postwar economic slump and spent too much of his time and energy in securing control, often by dubious methods, of the various provincial governments. Capricious in his official conduct, he justified only in part his reputation as friend of the workingman. He successfully sponsored legislation controlling hours of labor, stipulating minimum wages, providing for sanitary working conditions, protecting women and children, and authorizing arbitration of industrial disputes. But the law also penalized strikes, and he sternly suppressed strikers in Buenos Aires.

Since the Argentine constitution prohibited two successive terms, Irigoyen was not a candidate in 1922; but he supported the campaign of Marcelo T. Alvear, a moderate Radical of aristocratic lineage and possessor of more than moderate wealth, and Alvear won the election. The affluent aristocrat did not betray his party, yet the Radicals, according to the Latin custom, split into two factions near the beginning of his term, the supporters of the president and the followers of Don Hipólito. The result was virtual legislative paralysis. A workmen's pension act was passed, but it proved so unsatisfactory to labor that it was soon repealed. Farm legislation enacted during Alvear's term was potentially of greater consequence. Farm tenants and a few small farmers were granted a measure of government aid and the British railways were brought to an agreement to colonize the lands adjacent to their lines with farmers on small holdings, with fixed tenure and the prospect of ultimate ownership.

Irigoyen was elected for another term in 1928 in spite of the split in his party. It was a tragic mistake. Now approaching seventy-eight, he was too old to carry the heavy burdens of his office. As in his first administration, he tried to look after every detail in person; but his growing senility not only resulted in postponement of important measures demanded by the onslaught of the world economic depression; it permitted a group of sycophants to surround the old man, charge fees for expediting the interests of groups seeking favors, and steal the public revenues. Debts mounted; public bills and salaries of government employees remained unpaid. Official communications went unanswered and legislative enactments piled up unread and unsigned in larger heaps than in former years. The Conservatives fretted and boiled. University students in the capital paraded in protest. Many of Irigoyen's followers fell away in disgust and disillusionment. The time had come for the oligarchy to return to power.

General José F. Uriburu, son of a former Conservative president and an influential figure in the army, led the revolt which began early in September, 1930, in Buenos Aires. "Troops from the suburban barracks started toward the center; cadets from the military academy were . . . joined by students of the university; with the rector and professors at its head, the gigantic demonstration moved through the principal avenues down to the central Plaza, and the government unfurled the white flag of surrender. . . . It was . . . a spontaneous movement by the people at large" [4]—at least by the people of the capital, which contained almost one-fifth of the nation's inhabitants. Uriburu placed himself at the head of a government "composed almost exclusively of men whose names" carried "aristocratic connotations." Imprisoned for a time, Irigoyen, ineffective champion of the Argentine common people, died in 1933, "as poor as when he was born."

Uriburu persecuted Don Hipólito's party, postponed elections, intervened in twelve of the fourteen provinces, where he set up local governments attuned to his purposes, and made himself so unpopular that he was finally compelled to permit the pretense of an electoral campaign. The Irigoyen faction of the Radical party was not allowed to vote, however, and the Conservative candidate, General Agustín P. Justo, with adequate official assistance, won an easy victory over the candidate of a coalition of the Democratic Progressive and the Socialist parties.

Taking charge of his office on February 20, 1932, Justo made conciliatory appeals for harmony and tried to lift the nation out of the depression, but without notable success. Graft was not eliminated from the government. Exports continued their downward plunge, unemployment increased, swelling the relief rolls, and dissatisfaction intensified; but there was no revolution because the masses had no leaders. In a shamelessly fraudulent election, Justo imposed as his successor Roberto Ortiz—once a Radical but now a moderately conservative lawyer grown rich by inheritance and from corporation fees—and threw in the reactionary Ramón S. Castillo as vice-president in order to placate the old guard.

Inaugurated early in 1938, Ortiz followed a rather progressive policy which might have cured some of the evils of the time if he had not sickened and died in the middle of his term. He removed the trammels from the press, insisted on fair congressional, provincial, and local elections, treated the commoners and even labor with respect, and made attempts to assist the tenant farmers and effect a wider distribution of land. Although economic conditions had begun to improve when he handed over the government to Castillo, that reactionary martinet from conservative Córdoba reverted to the old pattern of corrupt elections, political repression, and bureaucratic dishonesty, and the country slowly drifted from dictatorship toward totalitarianism of the Spanish and Italian brand. Among the group of young army officers who deposed Castillo in June, 1943, was Colonel Juan D. Perón, who was not unfamiliar with the Nazi and the Fascist systems of Adolf Hitler, Benito Mussolini, and Francisco Franco.

Other army officers occupied the presidency while Perón held a cabinet post (the ministry of labor) which enabled him to organize the workers and the underprivileged into a powerful political machine. Actually in control of the government after a few months, he befriended labor, created numerous government positions for the lower class, collected funds for charity and hospitals, won the support of many of the clergy by pious pronouncements and the introduction of religious instruction into the public schools, raised large revenues from heavier taxes, from contributions exacted from public employees and labor unions, and from profits made by purchasing farm products at controlled prices and selling them in hungry world markets. He also filled the schools, colleges, and universities with his propagandists, subjected the press to close supervision, and harangued the multitudes in affectionate and nationalistic terms describing the glorious destiny he envisaged for them and their country. Neither Hitler nor Mussolini ever roused the people to greater exaltation and loyalty. With plenty of money from mysterious sources to spend on the poor and the afflicted, and assisted by his second wife, Eva Duarte Perón, herself an actress and a "rabble rouser," and also by other "spellbinders," Perón muffled the campaign of his opponents and easily won the presidency in 1946. Moreover, he triumphed again in 1952 by the use of similar tactics. Although he rarely executed any of his opponents, no Argentine dictator ever sent more men to prison or into exile or more completely dominated the life of the nation.

Born of Spanish immigrant parents in 1895 in a dull and lonely village on the frontier of Buenos Aires Province, he was taken to bleak, windswept Patagonia a few years later. There the father, who had been working as a field hand, rented some land from a Polish immigrant and sent his children to a country school. The family moved to Buenos Aires in 1905, where Juan finished his preparatory studies and entered the Military Academy (1911). In 1928, at the age of thirty-three, he married a schoolteacher, the daughter of a Spanish immigrant, who died ten years later, leaving him a widower without children. By that time he had moved up toward the top in military and government circles. Among the troops who deposed Irigoyen, he attracted attention by his discipline and enthusiasm on that occasion and rose rapidly thereafter, becoming a professor of military history in the War College, military attaché to the Argentine embassy in Chile, and military observer in Italy, where he came into direct contact with Mussolini and the Fascist military organization. He also visited Hitler's Germany and Franco's Spain, and returned to Argentina at the end of 1940 convinced that totalitarianism would soon sweep over the world and eager to adapt it to Argentine conditions. He even talked of making Argentina a world power—without iron or coking coal, with a rather limited supply of petroleum, and with a population then numbering hardly 16,000,000! But his vision included an alliance of South American totalitarian dictators leading delirious masses all dominated by his tall, handsome presence, his eloquence, and his prestige. Eva Duarte Perón, whom he married shortly after he came back to Buenos Aires, blindly shared his dreams and imagined herself a princess benevolent riding the "wave of the future" to a glorious apotheosis.

His grandiose schemes, domestic and international, were tremendously expensive. Taxes were piled upon taxes. Contributions made by his followers, willingly or unwillingly, grew larger and larger. The paper currency depreciated. Living costs rose more rapidly than salaries and wages. Farm production, fettered by price controls, fell off. A nation which had ranked among the world's largest exporters of mutton and beef was compelled to have its meatless days each week. Sobered by these hardships and calamities and by the death of Eva in 1952, Perón curtailed his ambitions and trimmed down his great economic plans, but continued his dictatorial arrogance. Having denounced foreign investors repeatedly and having bought out the alien-owned railways and municipal utilities, he found himself in need of more capital than he could extort from his people and was compelled to borrow from the United States Export-Import Bank in order to surmount his fiscal difficulties. Trouble with the Roman Catholic Church, which he injudiciously nagged into opposition, further weakened his hold on the country, until he felt it necessary in the summer of 1955 to announce that he would retire after the completion of his term, which the constitution he had sponsored in 1949 had fixed at six years. But the officers of the army and navy were unwilling to accept his promise. They drove him from power and into exile in September, 1955, and Major General Eduardo Lonardi seized the government, but was replaced shortly afterward by General Pedro Aramburu.

It is still too early to pass judgment on the dictatorship of Juan Domingo Perón, but from all appearances the Argentine people had been duped again, perhaps less from accident and unconquerable circumstances than in Irigoyen's case; for Irigoyen, while capable of duplicity in dealing with political rivals, never attempted to deceive the common man [5] or succumbed to an overweening craving for wealth and power. With less credulity on the part of its people and more moderation and efficiency in management on the part of its leaders, Argentina might forge far ahead of most of the Latin nations of the New World.

CHILE'S TROUBLESOME ECONOMY AND RESTLESS DEMOCRACY

Chile moved along smoothly under her moderately liberal autocrats after the revolution of 1891 until her economy was upset by world forces shortly before 1920. The opening of the Panama Canal destroyed her bunkering business and caused unemployment in her coal mines. The invention of synthetic nitrates broke down her natural nitrate monopoly. The swift drop in copper prices struck a third blow. The value of Chile's exports in 1919 was less than 40 per cent of what they brought in 1918.

The people looked in vain to the government for a remedy. The president was impotent under the modified parliamentary system adopted after the fall of President José M. Balmaceda in 1891. Parliament did little or nothing either because its members placed factional and personal interests above the national welfare or because leadership to impose cohesion was lacking. Some Chileans began to sigh for the days of strong presidents.

The time was ripe for a reformer, and the reformer promptly made his appearance. Arturo Alessandri, an eloquent lawyer with a strain of Italian blood, offered himself as candidate for the presidency in 1920. His party, called the Liberal Alliance, was composed largely of labor and middle-class groups, but it also included scores of Liberals of the lesser landed aristocracy who joined his organization either because of their habitual opposition to the Conservatives or because they favored the policies of the new leader as more promising than any others in the crisis. Alessandri proposed an elaborate program of social and political reform: abolition of the quasi-parliamentary system; greater autonomy for the provinces; election of the president by direct popular vote; separation of Church and State; improvement of the legal status of women; modernized labor legislation; extension of the free public school system; either an income tax or a heavier tax on real estate; and national control of banks and insurance companies.

The campaign was close and bitter. All the more conservative factions combined in a Union party and supported Luís Barros Bargoño, a wealthy banker and son of the famous historian Diego Barros Arana. Returns to the election officials indicated that Alessandri had won by five electoral votes, but the constitution required that both houses of Congress should make the final decision, and the Conservative party still hoped that some device could be found to defeat Alessandri. The situation was so tense, however, that Congress refused to employ questionable means and submitted the problem to a special board described as the "court of honor." The board finally decided that Alessandri had received a majority of one electoral ballot, and the "first president of the Chilean people" was inaugurated on that slim margin in December, 1920.

Known admiringly as the "Lion of Tarapacá" because of his birthplace, his roaring voice, and his shaggy mane, Alessandri had promised the people nearly everything. But he soon discovered that miracles were hard to perform. He had a strong and massive physique and an abundance of energy and intelligence, but his earlier conservative record tended to raise doubts regarding his sincerity whenever he faltered. The economic depression continued. An earthquake in 1922 caused tremendous losses. The cost of government increased, while revenues declined until they were insufficient to pay the multiplying public officials and support the military establishment. Don Arturo's conciliatory policy in reference to the Tacna-Arica dispute with Peru became another cause of dissatisfaction. Worst of all, the parliament was obstreperous. Conservative groups dominated the Senate, and the members of the Liberal Alliance who controlled the lower house soon had disagreements, so that Alessandri, like most of his predecessors since 1891, found himself powerless.

The outcome was a series of almost bloodless "palace revolutions" which deposed him and his two brief successors, recalled him from exile only to have him resign a second time, coerced and overreached the national legislature, and finally put the country in the hands of

Colonel Carlos Ibáñez, who controlled the government from 1925 until 1931. Although Ibáñez ruled as dictator during most of the period, he was careful to fill the public offices with civilians and bow to the popular demand for national elections; and he was probably the actual as well as the ostensible choice of the voters for the presidency in May, 1927.

Virtually all the reforms advocated by Alessandri had been achieved by July, 1929. The reformer had been ousted but his program was enacted with the backing of the army, and seems not to have been unpopular because of the instrument employed. Chile was given a new constitution in 1925, which restored the presidential system, granted larger autonomy to the provinces (at least in theory), and segregated Church and State. Progressive labor legislation was passed, along with other measures intended to provide for the welfare of the masses. An income tax was adopted and sweeping educational reforms emphasized primary schools in order to eliminate illiteracy.

The costs of the program were met in part by the new tax and increased revenues provided by rising prosperity, but more largely by the proceeds of government and government-guaranteed bonds floated abroad, mainly in the United States. These were only the material costs. There were others. The reforms were made at the expense of personal liberty and political persecution. Freedom of the press was violated and numerous political leaders were imprisoned or banished. Ibáñez was not less a despot because he was progressive.

He made some serious mistakes. He suppressed those who dared to oppose him with too much vigor, borrowed too much "easy money" abroad during the expansive years preceding the autumn of 1929, and failed to comprehend the magnitude of the terrific world depression when it struck. Nothing, however, and nobody, not even an enlightened despot, could cope with the crisis. Ibáñez could not prevent a sharp break in the prices of nitrate and copper with all the consequences that such a break entailed. He formed a cabinet of civilian experts early in July, 1931, but stubbornly refused to assent to their demands for drastic economies and the restoration of constitutional guaranties.

As the nation sank deeper and deeper into the depression, its misery and resentment became explosive. Students in the two universities of the capital declared a four-day strike and took possession of the buildings; and although they were soon ejected by force, it was evident that they had aroused widespread sympathy. Schoolteachers, engineers, clerks, and other workers began a policy of passive resistance to the government and planned a general strike. Rapidly a national demand developed for the elimination of the dictatorship and the restoration of constitutional government. After three days of street demonstrations and clashes between the populace and the police, Ibáñez resigned and fled to Argentina in order to avoid further spilling of blood (July 25, 1931).

Acting chief executive then followed acting chief executive with accelerating speed until Arturo Alessandri, victorious in the presidential election of late 1932, took charge of his office in December of that year. Sixty-four years old and less optimistic than in 1920, he was no longer an innovator. He merely returned to the people their constitutional liberties, did what he could for the unemployed, and preserved the reforms of the previous decade.

Alessandri was followed in 1938 by a Popular Front government—Radicals, Liberals, Socialists, Communists—headed by Pedro Aguirre Cerda, a wealthy lawyer, businessman, and vineyard-owner, who was succeeded in turn by Juan Antonio Ríos, a member of the Radical party who despised the Popular Front and rejoiced in its collapse. But the next president was Gabriel González Videla, a lifelong Radical who revived the *Frente Popular* and soon regretted his action. These leftish administrations all stressed manufacturing industries, financed many new industrial plants, and injected state funds into the economy in several other ways, but they also applied a liberal share of the annual budgets to education, sanitation, and social relief and adopted a vast program of social insurance. Growing expenditures for the public services and the creation of new economic enterprises greatly enlarged the tax burden, and uncontrolled inflation outran the ascending curve of salaries and wages. Chileans were still restive and resentful after thirty years of reform, some of them ready to listen to Communist appeals and even to join the party. One of the most serious problems that confronted the nation was the agrarian problem, for which no adequate solution had been adopted. Ownership of land remained highly concentrated. Workers and tenants on the big haciendas led a miserable existence.

The old war horse decided early in 1952 that the Chileans might be induced to give him another chance. Taking advantage of their smoldering discontent, Carlos Ibáñez, in spite of his seventy-four years, spent most of his time in a vigorous campaign against the Radical-dominated regime and its domestic and foreign policies. He promised to push up the prices of copper and nitrates and still expand exports, to prevent strikes by bringing capital and labor together in a common patriotic effort to increase production, to shorten government payroll lists, to substitute honesty and efficiency for alleged corruption and mismanagement, and not only to put an end to inflation but to bring domestic prices down. In a rather turbulent but reasonably free and fair election held early in September, he won an overwhelming victory, in which Communists and followers of the "party line" were said to have collaborated with the reactionaries. But he certainly could not have been elected without a large supplement of old-time Liberal ballots.

His despotic record and his association with Perón caused uneasiness in some quarters; but he neither proposed any extreme measures after his inauguration, nor set up a dictatorship, nor catered to Argentina's strong man. He probably had learned his lesson along with other Chileans, most of whom still preferred democracy to any other system and continued to have faith in it in spite of economic hardships and political frustration.

🐚 ECONOMIC INSTABILITY AND MACHINE POLITICS IN BRAZIL

Brazil's economy suffered peculiar setbacks during the first thirty years of the century when otherwise her people might have prospered. In 1912, just as Oriental plantation rubber began to drive Amazonian wild rubber from the market, coffee prices started to tumble because of overproduction. World War I, expanding the demand for Brazilian sugar, vegetable oils, and strategic materials, provided only temporary and partial relief. The years 1919–22 witnessed a serious recession. Recovery began in 1923, however, in spite of political turbulence, and the next few years were a rather flourishing era. The value of exports rose in 1929 to the highest point in the nation's history up to that time.

The state of São Paulo furnished Brazil's first three civilian presidents: Prudente de Moraes Barros and Manoel de Campos Salles, both already mentioned in a previous chapter, and Francisco de Paula Rodrigues Alves (1902–6), whose term was signalized by the settlement of two boundary disputes and the modernization of Rio de Janeiro. The boundaries between Brazil and two of the Guianas—British and Dutch—were adjusted by agreements with the respective colonial powers. With the able assistance of the prefect of the city and Dr. Oswaldo Cruz, Rio de Janeiro was transformed from a backward colonial town into one of the most beautiful and sanitary capitals of the world.

The next chief executive was Affonso Moreira Penna from Minas Geraes, who owed his election to a combination of state organizations determined to break the São Paulo monopoly. Large issues of paper currency during the previous decade had greatly depressed the value of the *milreis,* and the new president had run on a platform of financial reform. Establishing a bank of conversion, he redeemed a good part of the currency and made plans to place the country on a gold basis, but these were interrupted by his death and the disturbing effects of the global war of 1914–18.

The presidential campaign of 1910 was very exciting. The Conservatives, joined by the military group, presented as their candidate Marshal Hermes da Fonseca, nephew of General Deodora da Fonseca and resident of Rio. The Liberals and all those who distrusted military politicians supported the distinguished Ruy Barbosa, a Bahía lawyer and journalist. Although the eloquent Liberal candidate campaigned vigorously, pleading for a more strict adherence to the constitution which he had helped to draft in 1890 and for the elimination of the military from civilian affairs, Nilo Pecanha, president since the death of Moreira Penna in 1909, exerted his influence in support of Hermes, and Hermes won the election. Charging fraud and intimidation, the Brazilian navy, which had opposed both President Deodora and President Peixoto in the 1890's, revolted again; but Marshal Hermes sternly suppressed the rebellion, shot some of its leaders, and bombarded Barbosa's home city. Further trouble might have ensued if Barbosa, who had planned to make another whirlwind campaign against the militarists in 1914, had not been influenced by the rubber and coffee depression and the outbreak of war in Europe to withdraw his candidacy in the interest of Wenceslau Braz of Minas Geraes, who won the election and served as chief executive during the war period.

Rodrigues Alves of São Paulo was chosen for a second term in 1918, but was too ill to take charge; whereupon Epitacio da Silva Pessôa of the state of Parahyba managed somehow to triumph in a special election. It was during his term (1919–22) that Brazil was troubled by the postwar recession; but the president supplemented falling revenues by new issues of paper currency which he used to favor his own and neighboring arid states with large storage dams built at government expense and to celebrate the centennial of Brazil's independence by a grand and expensive exhibition. It was also during his term that the decree of banishment issued against the Braganza family in 1889 was repealed—a gesture which signified that Brazilians no longer feared the possibility of re-establishing the monarchy.

The administration of Arturo Bernardes of Minas Geraes (1922–26) was a period of turmoil. Uprisings, mostly barracks revolts, occurred in the capital and in eight different states. Army officers, who considered the president a bitter enemy of the militarists, first tried to defeat him in the electoral campaign and then attempted to prevent him from taking charge of the government. The son of Hermes da Fonseca, with the intention of making his father dictator, raised the flag of revolt and shelled the capital shortly before Bernardes was inaugurated; but President Pessôa quickly put down the rebellion. Bernardes confronted sedition and revolt in the states of São Paulo, Santa Catarina, Rio Grande do Sul, Matto Grosso, Amazonas, Pará, Sergipe, Bahía, and Rio de Janeiro in 1924 and 1925. Rebels in the state of São Paulo seized its capital in July, 1924, and held it for three weeks before federal troops forced them to withdraw. The revolt which Bernardes suppressed in Rio Grande do Sul earlier the same year was probably one which he should have supported. Its objective was to depose a corrupt dictator named Borges de Madeiros who had dominated the state for a quarter of a century. Bernardes maintained a state of siege in a good part of the republic during most of his administration and occupied himself largely with the problem of restoring peace. Nevertheless, he effected some financial adjustments, reduced the deficit, created a National Council of Labor, launched a housing program, regulated work in the bakeries of the Federal District, and signed a law providing for annual vacations for laborers in banks, manufacturing industries, and mercantile establishments.

Bernardes was succeeded in 1926 by Washington Luis Pereira de Sousa, a former governor of the state of São Paulo, who had a reputation for efficient administration. The new president was compelled to deal with some uprisings at the beginning of his term, but he performed the task with marked success and brought the reign of martial law to an end early in 1927. He then set to work on the coffee market and financial problems and started an extensive road-building program, but highway construction was interrupted by the world depression.

Brazil was clearly not a tranquil country during the 1920's! Effective and progressive functioning of the government was rendered most difficult by lack of communications, the high rate of illiteracy, political intolerance, state and sectional rivalry, the absence of thoroughly organized national parties, and a strong tendency toward militarism.

Although much larger than the United States, excluding Alaska, Brazil had less than 20,000 miles of railway as late as 1930 and comparatively few motor roads, and its airways had hardly been initiated. The military strategy of the country was based mainly on the principle of keeping the waterways open: the sea, the Amazon, and other rivers.

Immense distances and divergences in climate, racial elements, and economic pursuits combined with political decentralization to foster state and sectional loyalties. The northern part of the country was a region of tropical forests, arid brushlands, scrubby livestock, primitive farms, and big plantations; the vast area from Minas Geraes southward was a land of minerals, coffee, wheat, cattle, and pine forests. The

North and the Center were inhabited by mixed races, largely unlettered, with the Negro and the mulatto predominating; the South was almost entirely white, the recipient of hundreds of thousands of Italian, Portuguese, and German immigrants, and much better educated.

The local administrative divisions had been jealous of their autonomy since colonial times; and, as must have been observed already, the ambitious states of São Paulo, Minas, and Rio de Janeiro, especially the first two, had sought to rule the country since 1890 and succeeded in doing so. National parties hardly existed. Rival state organizations, controlled by wealthy aristocrats and political oligarchies, took their place. Presidential candidates were chosen in caucuses or conventions composed largely of members of the national congress, who were in turn the supporters and creatures of the various state administrations. Nominations were thus determined by the controlling political forces of the more wealthy and populous states.

Equally disturbing were official domination of elections and the strong tendency of army officers to meddle in politics. Officials of both the national and the state governments nearly always interfered with electoral freedom, the prevailing open ballot making such interference easy. The first two chief executives of the republic, it will be remembered, were army officers, and so likewise was Marshal Hermes da Fonseca, who served as president from 1910 to 1914. Moreover, high officers of the army and navy were largely responsible for the revolutionary disturbances of the 1920's.

THE GETÚLIO VARGAS EPOCH

In the presidential campaign of March, 1930, Julio Prestes of São Paulo, member of the Conservative party, was the official candidate. He was opposed by the Liberal politician Getúlio Vargas from the southern cattle state of Rio Grande do Sul, with João Pessôa, governor of the state of Parahyba, as his running mate. In the natural order of things, the successor of Washington Luis should have been from Minas Geraes or the state of Rio de Janeiro; but the president and the other leading Paulista politicians allowed themselves to be swept away by state ambition. The election was bitterly contested, but the official candidate won as usual. The opposition charged that Washington Luis had employed military forces in Minas Geraes and Parahyba to secure the election of his candidate and had fraudently deprived these states of their legally elected representatives to the national congress. A dramatic turn was given to these and other political events by the assassination of João Pessôa in July. Threats of revolution filled the air.

Finally, in the following October, Vargas began a revolt for the purpose of eliminating the president-elect and dissolving Congress. Minas Geraes, Pernambuco, and a few other states rallied immediately to his support, while the main backing of the outgoing government came from the state of São Paulo and the state and Federal District of Rio de Janeiro. The struggle threatened to become widespread and destructive. Nearly 300,000 men were under arms and both opponents had a small air force. After a few skirmishes, however, in which the casualties were rather numerous, the president's army deserted him and he was forced to abdicate (October 23, 1930).

A military junta took charge of the government pending the arrival of Vargas, who reached the capital early in November and assumed the office of national executive "as chief of the victorious revolution." He was to become the republic's first long-term dictator. He ruled for fifteen successive years, then served a second, less-dictatorial term; in short, he practically dominated the nation until his death in 1954.

Born in 1883 in a frontier village near the Argentine border of Rio Grande do Sul, Vargas was the son of a ranchman and farmer of moderate wealth. He attended a military academy, served in the army for a short time, then studied law and became interested in politics. After some years in the state legislature, he went as one of Rio Grande do Sul's representatives to the national congress. Making political friends in the capital, he soon advanced to a cabinet post. Big loan contracts were negotiated with New York bankers while he was national minister of finance. Observing that prospects were good for obtaining millions in foreign money for Rio Grande do Sul, he resigned from the cabinet in order to assume the presidency of his home state (the chief executives of several of the Brazilian states bore the title of president) and sell some bonds in the United States. The office was his by the grace of "boss" Borges de Madeiros, who knew that no rough ranch-man like himself could manage such transactions as deftly as this in-gratiating, midget-like ex-minister of finance. Although the New York bankers probably had not foreseen what was soon to happen, Vargas, in effect, had their assistance in his thrust for power.

In accordance with the program of his "Liberal Alliance" and the promises he made during his insurrection and ensuing months, Vargas treated labor with benevolence (though despotic), stimulated mining, helped to promote diversity in agriculture by stressing rice, wheat, cacao, sisal hemp, jute, and citrus fruits, aided sugar and coffee planters, supported cattlemen, subsidized manufacturers and protected their market, and at the same time devoted a good portion of the national revenues to education and sanitation. Government revenues were rather scanty until the demands of World War II extricated the country from the depression. But Vargas defaulted on the foreign-owned public debt in 1931 and gradually gained control of the receipts of the state and local governments. Refusing to resume payments with the coming of the war, he imposed his own conditions on foreign creditors in 1943–44, paring down principals and drastically reducing interest rates with impunity because the United States and Great Britain were too eager for his collaboration to champion the cause of private interests. On the contrary, the United States spent hundreds of millions in Brazil on lend-lease, airfields, and such war materials as rubber, manganese, quartz, and iron ore, and the Export-Import Bank lent many millions more for the Volta Redonda steel mill and other purposes. The last years of the Vargas dictatorship were a flourishing period, though marred somewhat by continuous inflation caused by scarcity of manufactured civilian goods and the great stress on exports. His nationalistic pronouncements and decrees probably did not retard development, since foreign capital would have been absorbed by taxes and war production at home in any case.

Brazil was harassed by political troubles as well as by economic hard times during the first years of Vargas' rule. The year 1931 was marked by riots in various states and rebellions in Pernambuco and São Paulo. In the summer of 1932, before order had been restored, the Paulistas began large-scale hostilities with the aim of assaulting the capital; but the federal troops moved swiftly, prevented the insurgents from receiving aid from other dissatisfied states, and suppressed them before the end of the year. Compelled to accede to the demand for a new fundamental law, Vargas permitted the election of delegates to a convention late in 1933; but he never allowed the new constitution (adopted on July 16, 1934) to hamper his authority, even though the convention paid him the compliment of electing him president for his "first regular term." The new organic law did not suit him. It accorded too much respect to state autonomy, contained too many personal guaranties, and erected the same barrier to two successive presidential terms that had been written into the constitution of 1891. Vargas confronted a small Communist uprising led by Carlos Prestes late in 1935 and uncovered an alleged widespread Communist conspiracy. Speculation was rife regarding his successor as his "first regular term" approached its end. Vargas, however, did not offer himself as candidate; he merely executed a *coup d'état* a few weeks before the time scheduled for the elections, issued another fundamental law by executive decree, dissolved Plinio Salgado's green-shirted *Integralistas* (a flag-waving fascist organization), and established a more thorough dictatorial regime.

The new constitution outlined a highly centralized government, which abolished the federation and gave the president almost unlimited powers. The puppet legislative body was to have two "chambers," a Chamber of Deputies selected by "indirect suffrage" and a Federal Council of some thirty members, ten of whom were to be appointed by the president and the rest selected by the state governors and legislative bodies. In addition, a Council of National Economy was to be created, made up of "representatives of the various branches of the national economy . . . designated by professional groups or unions recognized by law," in such manner as to give "equal representation to labor and management"—clearly a suggestion of Mussolini's "corporative state." But, aside from revealing the state of mind of the amiable little despot or some of the advisers who surrounded him, the document was of little consequence. Vargas never got around to submitting it to a plebiscite as he had promised. In fact, he practically ignored the constitution and continued to rule by decree.

What he did was sufficiently drastic. He not only abolished the machine-ridden federal system; he also abolished all local autonomy, put his henchmen in charge of both state and municipal governments after dissolving the legislative assemblies and town councils, assumed full control over the press, and set up a busy propaganda bureau.

In May, 1938, he barely escaped assassination, not by an enraged Brutus striking a blow for liberty, but by Plinio Salgado's green-clad troopers, who attacked his official residence (Guanabara Palace) and actually broke into his study, where he and his daughter were still at work late in the afternoon. But the intrepid little man and the equally intrepid little lady seized revolvers and held the assailants at bay— assisted by the dictator's brother (Benjamin Vargas) with his machine gun and a few palace guards—until the slow-moving government troops finally arrived. Some of the attackers were shot down as they tried to escape; others were hunted down in a nearby forest to which they had fled. Hundreds who had occupied strategic points in the capital were routed out and killed or captured; thousands from various parts of the country were rounded up and sent to prison camps.

Vargas had no more trouble with armed insurgents and conspirators until World War II drew to a close. Then Brazil resumed her restiveness. Upper-class Brazilians began to chafe under the political and economic rigidities of the regime. The lower classes, who had looked upon the dictator as a benefactor, were exasperated by rising prices and scarcities in consumer goods. Aware of the explosive situation, Vargas unmuffled the press in the hope that the escaping steam would lower the pressure. It was hotter than he expected and inflicted some burns. Consulting his closest advisers, he tried to cool the boiler by another device. He announced his intention to hold national elections before the end of the year and to permit universal suffrage without any literacy test except for women.

But who would be the candidates? Two promptly showed up: General Eurico Dutra, thought to be the dictator's favorite, and Brigadier Eduardo Gomes of the airforce. The military men were again revealing their ambition. Although Vargas did not volunteer to run for the presidency, his shifting of police chiefs, his release of Communist prisoners, his genuflections in the direction of other left-wing groups and labor organizations, suggested that he would not be hard to draft. A political organization called *Queremistas* ("We Wanters") suddenly filled the air with its pleas for the continuation in power of the courageous little man with smiling black eyes and neatly-chiseled profile from the bold cattle country. The army and the opposition, anticipating another coup like the one of 1937, went into action. Troops marched and tanks rolled on Rio's streets. Vargas was deposed (October 29, 1945) without the firing of a shot.

The president of the Supreme Court took charge of the government and made sweeping changes in personnel before election day. Vargas did not offer himself for the presidency, but he made a successful campaign for senator in his native state. General Dutra, backed by his Social Democratic party (which was neither very social nor very democratic), won the election and took control at the beginning of the new year. His administration sponsored a new constitution (1946) which proclaimed all the liberties and exuded deep attachment to the people. It also outlawed the Communists and continued Vargas' program of industrialization, agricultural diversification, education, and sanitation. But production did not keep pace with growing domestic and foreign demands and prices continued to soar.

The demoted dictator used his office as senator to organize his political friends and the labor and leftist groups and to needle the administration. Campaigning for the presidency in 1950, he easily triumphed over his divided and confused opponents. Chief executive of Brazil for a second time, Vargas fought shy of dictatorship. Perhaps he feared the army; perhaps he felt too old. Facing fiscal problems which he could not solve, refusing to give up his "economic nationalism" and let foreign investors try their hand, threatened by a downward plunge in coffee prices, which had risen to unprecedented heights, maddened by withering press attacks and efforts at impeachment, informed of the hostility of the dominant military group, the tired old man put a bullet through his heart (August 24, 1954) after dictating a farewell letter in which he complained bitterly of ingratitude and spoke of persecution by a conspiracy of international scope.

Vice-President João Café Filho, said to be an honest and moderately able politician noted for his deep devotion to democratic procedures, was left in control of the government while the nation confronted economic, political, and social problems difficult enough to baffle a superman: vast farming areas too inefficiently cultivated to feed the rapidly-growing population, pitifully inadequate railroads and highways, price inflation and poverty, mass ignorance and widespread lack of skills, revenues inadequate to master the vast tropical stretches and their diseases, the best arable lands and other wealth so unevenly distributed that class bitterness could not be avoided. But if more Brazilians were miserable than ever before because of the sharp upward curve in population, more Brazilians were also better off than they used to be. Their greatest needs were political harmony, hard work, less greed on the part of the well-to-do, and more patience and prudence on the part of the people.

After a hotly contested election and the displacement of Café Filho by a military coterie, the successful candidate, Juscelino Kubitschek, was inaugurated as president at the end of January, 1956. The grandson of a Czech immigrant, the new chief executive owed his electoral triumph mainly to the followers of the deceased Vargas. Announcing the melodramatic motto "Fifty years of progress in five," he proposed vigorous efforts to stimulate agricultural and industrial production and thus not only prevent further inflation but reduce the cost of living. He was undoubtedly too optimistic, but he has the assistance of both foreign technicians and foreign capital in his efforts to solve the nation's problems and provide a more abundant life for its impoverished masses.

CHAPTER XXXI

Some Literary Masters

⁂ LATIN AMERICA'S LITERARY AND ARTISTIC ATTAINMENTS

No countries attach more importance to their artists and intellectuals than do the republics of Latin America. They are proud of the great figures in whom they think their culture has flowered. The place of the artist and the intellectual in the esteem of the Latin Americans corresponds to the place occupied by the great inventor and successful businessman in the value patterns of the United States. The fact that each nation's supreme hero, like the paramount heroes of most other countries, is usually a warrior or a politician cannot be taken to indicate any lack of appreciation for the artist and the thinker. These heroes have been selected by the warrior-politicians, and mainly because of their contributions to the independence movement or some political reform of the early National epoch.[1]

The artists and intellectuals of the recent period cannot, of course, be dealt with fully in this volume; but they must be given sufficient attention to illustrate their significance in Latin-American civilization. The painters, sculptors, and musicians must be consigned to more competent hands; it would be presumptuous to attempt to evaluate them here. It may be noted in passing, however, that some won renown not only in their home countries and in most of Latin America but in other parts of the world as well, and that the first half of the twentieth century was marked—particularly in Mexico and Brazil but likewise in some of the other republics—by both high achievement and increasing interest in the fine arts. The historians—far more numerous than during the early National epoch, and some of them rather more thorough and reliable than their predecessors—will also be omitted.[2] The purpose of this chapter and the one that follows is to convey a general idea of the talents of the literary men, the thinkers, and the critics of the Latin-American social order.

With the exception of Martí and Rodó, the writers considered in this chapter are renowned primarily as poets. Other masters of prose or poetry could easily be added, and some of them will be considered in other connections in Chapter XXXII. The rest must be left to the historians and critics of literature.[3]

☙ CUBA'S MARTÍ

José Martí (1853–95), Cuba's outstanding agitator for national independence and the nation's paramount hero mainly because he gave his life for this cause, was poet, journalist, literary critic, and essayist. Although his poetry ranks high for a sincere simplicity unparalleled save in folk ballads, he is more famous for his mastery of prose and his moving oratory. His newspaper articles, on almost every conceivable subject but dealing with Cuban aspirations for independence more often than with any other, were characterized by originality and an intimate personal touch. Few better descriptions of life in the United States in the 1880's and 1890's, particularly in New York City and its metropolitan area, can be found in any language. His eloquence thrilled his audiences or caused them to weep. His letters, whether bearing on Cuba's suffering and longing for freedom or on any other subject, form a unique category in the Spanish tongue because of their simple intimacy, deep insight, and sparkling imagination. His prose has been described as a "Wagnerian orchestra . . . a symphony of a fantastic forest where invisible gnomes enchant our ears with a flock of harmonies and our eyes with a tempest of colors." It was certainly outstanding for its trumpet-like sonority and its incendiary quality. "There are cries," said Martí, "that sum up an entire epoch. . . . I am not a man speaking, but a people protesting." And again, wittingly or unwittingly describing himself: "Genius is simply anticipation; it foresees in detail what others do not behold even in outline, and as others do not see what the genius sees, they regard him in amazement, weary of his splendor and persistency, and leave him to feed upon himself, to suffer."

Many who knew Martí intimately, or even met him only once, left a record of his personal charm and power of attraction. Rubén Darío declared: "Never have I met . . . so admirable a conversationalist. He was harmonious, intimate, and gifted with a prodigious memory—swift and ready with quotation, reminiscence, fact, image. I spent several unforgettable moments with him." [4] Another admirer said: "He who has never heard Martí in a moment of confidential intimacy does not realize the full power of the fascination of which human speech is capable." [5]

Martí's writings were—and still are—lauded in both Latin America and Spain. They have been collected by his admirers with loving enthusiasm and industry and published in several editions. The latest, which started through one of the Havana presses in 1939, will consist of some sixty small volumes.[6]

GUTIÉRREZ NÁJERA AND NERVO OF MEXICO

Mexico's two great literary figures were Manuel Gutiérrez Nájera (1859–95) and Amado Nervo (1870–1919). The first was beset by unresolved religious conflict and often oppressed by profound pessimism. The second, now Buddhistic, now pantheistic, was mystically serene and deeply religious, with almost an Indian humility and resignation, in spite of occasional skepticism.

Journalist, editor, writer of whimsical sketches and short stories, frequently signed with the pen name "El Duque Job," Gutiérrez Nájera excelled in the field of poetry, and many consider him the greatest Mexican poet. The son of pious middleclass parents, he was early harassed by religious doubt; and his life was cut short by long hours in newspaper offices and heavy drinking. He was by no means handsome: of medium height, he had a large head and slightly oblique eyes, his face was unsymmetrical, his nose "cyranesque," his mustache sparse and bristly, and his mouth turned to one side, perhaps from inveterate cigar-smoking. But despite his ugliness and his humble origin there was at times a proud aloofness in his attitude. His *nom de plume* suggests an aristocratic agony. "A seeking soul, torn by doubt, a prey to a dominating vice, distilling his query into melodious beauty—a vagrant spirit caught between a vanishing world and a nascent era—a nature shedding his inner grace upon everything touched by his pen—such was the suffering poet who died midway upon the journey of his life, mourned by the continent to which he had given the gifts of his . . . song and the impulse of fresh artistic conquests." [7] He put new melody into Spanish verse and greater imagery and agility into Spanish prose. He was a man of many moods, but he was rarely happy because he could never control his appetite for alcohol or resolve his religious doubt either by affirmation or resignation. He could be whimsical, elegiac, and tenderly melancholy, but seldom really cheerful and optimistic.

Sometimes his black despair skirted the edge of blasphemy. In his *Monologue of the Unbeliever* he suggests that life is an unmerited penalty given without our consent, asks whether living is worth the pain, and tells why he does not commit suicide. It was not because he feared to meet the God who gave him what he did not ask, but because he knew his suicide would either kill his mother or bow her with grief for the rest of her days, since she would believe that his soul was burning in the eternal flames. "To recall, to pardon, to have loved, to have been for a moment happy, and then . . . to recline wearily upon the snowy shoulder of oblivion" [8]—there was nothing else in life. He finds no beacon and no God in the big churches and cathedrals: "The colossal temple, the immense nave, is dank and dreary, the altar without flowers; all is dark, very dark. The candles are extinguished! Lord, where art Thou? I seek Thee in vain! Where art Thou, O Christ? I call Thee in fear, because I am alone. . . . And there is nobody at the altar! Nobody in the nave! All is submerged in sepulchral gloom! Speak! Let the organ sound! Let me see the candles burn . . . ! I am drowning in the darkness. . . . I am drowning!" [9]

One of Gutiérrez Nájera's most famous poems bears the title *Dead Waves:*

> The noble rivers to the ocean flow
> Past field and forest, meadow-bank and lawn,
> Reflecting in their silvery changeful glass
> The stars of heaven, the pale tints of dawn. . . .
>
> In the white marble fountain, lo! the stream
> Is mischievous and playful, sporting there
> Like a young girl that in palace hall
> Scatters the pearls that form her necklace fair. . . .
>
> The waves that in the mighty ocean swell
> Assail the craggy rocks, upsurging high;
> Their raging fury shakes the solid earth,
> And rises up in tumult to the sky. . . .
>
> How different is the current dark and still,
> Doomed to imprisonment which knows no end,
> Living beneath the earth in gloomy depths,
> Down deeper than even the dead descend! . . .
>
> Like such a stream, to all the world unknown—
> Like such a stream, whose prisoned waters roll
> Surrounded by thick darkness—such are you,
> O dark and silent currents of my soul! . . .[10]

Does the theme not remind one of Thomas Gray's *Elegy*, except that Gray was thinking of the dead Englishmen who never had a chance to develop their talents, while the Mexican poet, like many of the literary masters of the time in Latin America, was thinking of himself? Recall, for instance, these two stanzas:

Full many a gem of purest ray serene
The dark, unfathomed caves of ocean bear;
Full many a flower is born to blush unseen,
And waste its sweetness on the desert air.

Some village Hampden, that with dauntless breast
The little tyrant of his fields withstood,
Some mute inglorious Milton here may rest—
Some Cromwell, guiltless of his country's blood.

"I was born in Tepic," wrote Amado Nervo toward the end of his life.[11] "My real name should have been Ruiz de Nervo, but my father shortened it. His first name was Amado, and he gave it to me. Whereupon I became Amado Nervo, and what appeared to be a pseudonym . . . and what was in any event a rare combination, was of no little worth to my literary fortune. . . . I began to write when I was a mere child. . . . I have never had, nor have I, any particular tendency. I write as I please. . . . I support only one school, that of my deep and eternal sincerity. I have written innumerable bad things in prose and verse, and some good ones; but I know which is which. If I had been wealthy, I would have written only the good ones, and in that case there would be today only a little volume of my writings—a book of conscientious art. . . . It was not to be! I was compelled to make a living in a country where almost nobody reads books and where the only form of diffusion was the periodical. Of all things that grieve me, this is the greatest: the small, precious . . . book that my life did not permit me to write—the free and only book."

Here was a little posing and more than a little exaggeration; but it is a fact that Nervo had to work for a living. He studied for the priesthood but soon left the seminary to take up newspaper work in Mazatlán and Mexico City, at a period when the press was not free to discuss the issues of the day. By the time he had reached thirty (1889) he had managed somehow to lay his hands on enough money for a sojourn in Paris and Italy, and five years later he became secretary of the Mexican legation in Madrid, a post which he held until 1918 when he was appointed minister to Uruguay and Argentina. He died in Montevideo the next year. His *Complete Works,* published in Madrid in the 1920's, fill too many (twenty-nine) volumes; but the autumn of his life was a bed of roses. His writings included essays, short stories, literary criticism, poetic prose, and poetry. His poetry was noted for amazing variety in both theme and meter. He liked to pretend that he was writing in the person of a druid, a Merovingian king, a plant, or a butterfly. In his verse forms he was as anarchic as Walt Whitman, whom many Latin-American poets admired. If he was often sad, he was usually also serene. "He was one of those rare souls who manage to escape from the torments of the outer world to the peace of the world within." [12]

One of Nervo's longest poems bears the title *Sister Water,* a theme suggested to him by St. Francis of Assisi. Here he writes in pantheistic mood of water underground, above ground, and spouting from fountains, of water in all the shapes it assumes—snow, ice, hail, vapor, sea mist, or conforming with the contours of every kind of receptacle—and not only makes the water speak but draws lessons from its pliability and resignation. Another poem, *Miraculous Bird,* written in 1910 after his first flight in an airplane, illustrates the manner in which invocations of the past rise like incense from his pages: [13] "Miraculous bird, colossal white bird that brings to realization the dream of the ages, you have reconquered for the fallen angel the wings which he lost fighting with the gods. . . . Fathers who sought this anxiously and died without beholding it, poets who for centuries dreamed of such gifts—lamentable Icaruses who provoked laughter—today, over your tombs, there flies, buzzing, the miraculous bird of the snowy wings that crystallizes the dream. . . . Let a divine exultation flood our spirits, and a *Te Deum Laudamus* burst from our lips, and let old melancholies perish." But the poet did not fail to feel apprehension about the baneful uses to which the new invention might be summoned. "Stain not the celestial bird with missions of war. . . . It was born for the message of friendship and to sow kisses of peace among men!" In an essay written shortly after the first world conflict, in which aviation played only a very minor part, he predicted transoceanic flights and beheld visions of the nocturnal skies illumined by signs upon huge wings bearing the legends: "Paris to New York," "London to Mexico," "Madrid to Buenos Aires." "The airplane will give back to us," he said, "the majesty of the forgotten stars . . . and . . . the stars are pale and ardent instructors that teach us many things. . . . They civilized the Chaldeans, the Egyptians, and the Greeks, the Nahuas and the Mayas."

NICARAGUA'S DARÍO

Those who know Nicaragua only by its political reputation or for its bananas and gold mines will be surprised to learn that this turbulent little country produced in Rubén Darío (1867–1916) a supremely gifted writer judged by many to have been the greatest poet who ever sang in the Castilian tongue. "He crystallized an epoch," says Goldberg; "he transformed a language; he infused new life into the Castilian muse; . . . he became . . . a legendary figure even during his . . . life. He belongs not only with the greatest poets that have written in the Spanish tongue, but with the masters of universal poesy." [14] A cosmopolitan crucible, he fused all bloods, all inspirations, all feelings, and became the poet of Spanish America par excellence.

Perhaps the less said about Darío's personal life the better. He was conspicuous for his romantic long hair, his broad, dark-skinned face, and his slender aristocratic hands, and notorious for his amorous escapades. Of Spanish, Indian, and Negro extraction, he scarcely knew either his mother or his father, and was brought up by relatives and family friends. A born poet, he wrote this little elegy before he was thirteen: "Your father died, it is true; you weep for him, and are right; but resign yourself, for there exists an eternity where there is no suffering . . . and where the just dwell in song amid white lilies. . . ." [15] Darío soon became known as the "boy poet," and admirers began to give him money or find work for him on newspaper staffs, in grammar schools, or in public libraries. He spent some time in El Salvador and Guatemala and then set out for Chile (1886), where he remained for four years, published a collection of verse and prose sketches, wrote for the Chilean journals, and established through the influence of a friend a permanent connection with *La Nación,* the great Argentine daily owned by Bartolomé Mitre. Back in Central America, it was not long until he was sent to Spain on a double mission, to represent both Nicaragua and *La Nación* at the quadricentennial of the discovery of America. Returning to America by way of Cuba and Colombia, he met Rafael Núñez, who appointed him forthwith Colombian consul at Buenos Aires, with permission to visit Paris before he took up his official duties. He remained in Argentina until 1898, when *La Nación* sent him back to Spain to write a series of articles on European subjects. He spent several years in the former mother country and published one of his finest works there in 1905— *Songs of Life and Hope.* He greeted the Pan-American Conference in Rio de Janeiro in 1906 with a *Salutation to the Eagle.* He became Nicaraguan minister to Spain in 1908 and, according to some reports, was named as a delegate to the Mexican centennial celebration two years later but failed to appear in Mexico City because of the objection of the Díaz government under pressure from the United States. Tours and sojourns in various parts of Latin America and Europe followed. For almost a decade the poet had been in wretched health because of too much drinking and other dissipations. He arrived in the United States late in 1915 for a lecture tour, and not only failed miserably but contracted double pneumonia. Subsidized during his illness by the tyrant Manuel Estrada Cabrera, he rallied enough to return to his native Nicaragua, but died in León shortly after he arrived.

Throughout his life—or most of it at least—Darío oscillated between paganism and Christianity, Epicureanism and religion, eroticism and contemplation. He liked brilliant uniforms, fine lace, shining jewels, sweet aromas, flaming flowers, and the refinements of classic Greece and eighteenth-century France. He sought in his verses to escape from the mud and murk of his sordid life into an imaginary world of ideal beauty. "Art for art's sake" was usually his motto. His symbol was the swan, a beautiful bird that served no utilitarian purpose. During the last years of his life, however, he began to dwell upon more mundane and practical themes. Abandoning his ivory tower and entering the hurly-burly of life, he sought to arouse the Spanish race from its apathy and sloth, denounced Theodore Roosevelt, condemned the Russo-Japanese War, published an ode to Mitre, and wrote a long laudatory hymn to Argentina.

His ringing call to the Spanish people on both sides of the Atlantic seems to have been the expression of a twofold uneasiness. He not only feared aggression from the United States, but seems to have foreseen the cataclysm of 1914–18: [16]

Glorious, numerous races, blood of our fertile Hispania,
Valiant fraternal spirits, luminous souls, all hail!
Come is the moment long yearned for, when voices aquiver with gladness
New hymns will chant. All about us the air is alive with vast portents. . . .
And here in the box of Pandora, whence issued so many misfortunes,
Suddenly we have discovered, smilingly pure, talismanic . . .
The heavenly queen of light—Hope that descends from the skies!

Darío's portrait of the mighty Theodore is unforgettable: "It is with the voice of the Bible, or the verse of Walt Whitman, that one should approach you, hunter! Primitive and modern, simple yet complex, with somewhat of Washington and more of Nimrod! You are the United States; you are the future invader of that ingenuous America in whom glows indigenous blood, and which still prays to Jesus Christ and speaks Spanish. You are a proud and powerful exemplar of your race; you are cultured, skilful; you oppose Tolstoi. And dominating horses, or assassinating tigers, you are an Alexander-Nebuchadnezzar. (You are a professor of energy as today's madmen declare.) You believe that life is a conflagration, that progress is an eruption; that wherever you send the bullet, you implant the future. . . . To the cult of Hercules you join the cult of Mammon; and lighting the way of facile conquest, Liberty raises its torch before New York." The poem ends with a warning and a defiance:

> Take care!
> The daughter of the Sun, the Spanish land doth live!
> And from the Spanish lion a thousand whelps have sprung!
> 'Tis need, O Roosevelt, that you be God himself . . .
> Before you hold us fast in your grasping iron claws.
> And though you count on all, one thing is lacking—God! [17]

Among Darío's earlier poems, there are a few of peculiar charm for their vividness and rhythm. Here is a description of a tropical sea scene. The old sailor referred to is probably an Englishman: [18]

> The sea as in a silvered glass
> Reflects a sky as gray as zinc;
> Afar some birds in bands, like stains,
> Into the polished surface sink.
>
> The sun, a disk opaque and round,
> Slow climbs the zenith, old and sick,
> The seawind rests within the shade,
> Its pillow a cloud-bank gray and thick.
>
> The waves heaving with leaden heat
> Beneath the wharf their moan begin;
> A sailor sitting on a coil of rope,
> Puffing his pipe, is rapt in thought
> Of fog-clad home and distant kin.
>
> A wandering wolf, the old seadog;
> Brazilian suns have tanned his skin;
> Typhoons in China, fierce and wild
> Have seen him drink his flask of gin. . . .
>
> In tropic siesta he falls asleep. . . .
> The tropic siesta: the locust old
> Essays her guitar hoarse and thin;
> The cricket plays in monotone
> On the single string of her violin.

PERU'S CHOCANO

José Santos Chocano (1875–1934), Peruvian journalist, propagandist, and poet, was exuberant, grandiloquent, and bombastic, a blasting trumpet with more power than grace, and yet capable at times of producing simple, spontaneous, and beautiful verse. He frequently wrote of himself, but more often he wrote of Spanish America, its plants, flowers, trees, rivers, mountains, and history. "I am sure," he declared near the end of his life, "that . . . I have been most characteristically Hispano-American, with all the qualities of the race and its corresponding defects, or better still, inevitable excesses." [19] He was certainly

Spanish American and sometimes Pan-American and Pan-Hispanic; but he had considerably more than his share of defects, and his excesses must have been sufficient to raise the general average.

His father was a Peruvian army officer and his mother was the daughter of a Spanish immigrant who had made and lost a fortune in the Peruvian mines. Poetry and the intrigues of love and politics were the main interests of his life, but he loved Peru and his America as well as the women of every country he visited. He achieved fame as a poet and a Don Juan before he reached his middle thirties. Without wealth, he had to earn his living. He began writing for the newspapers while in his teens. A partisan of Nicolás Piérola, he assaulted the Cáceres government with his youthful and vehement pen and toward the end of 1894 was thrown into an underground cell at Callao, where he remained until Piérola seized control at Lima six months later. Then he was released, made editor of *Diario Oficial,* and given a chance to publish his poems at government expense. He was sent as a roving diplomat to Central America in 1901; and after remaining there for two years and winning the friendship of the two leading tyrants of the region, Zelaya and Estrada Cabrera, he was transferred to the Peruvian legation in Colombia and then to Spain.

His tour of duty in Spain lasted nearly five years, during which he published two of his most noted works: *Soul of America* (Madrid, 1906) and *Let There be Light!* (Paris, 1908). He lost his secretaryship of the Peruvian legation in Madrid by his scandalous conduct and had barely enough money at the time of his dismissal to pay his fare to New York and Guatemala City, where he sold his pen to Estrada Cabrera and founded a newspaper called *La Prensa.* Shortly after the overthrow of the Díaz regime he set out for Mexico and won the friendship of Madero, after whose downfall he was expelled from that country. It was not long, however, before he became the special secret agent in New York of both Pancho Villa and Venustiano Carranza! A few years later he returned to Guatemala and championed the cause of Estrada Cabrera again; in fact, his championship was so ardent that he barely escaped with his life after the tyrant was deposed early in 1920. A residence of several months in Costa Rica followed, and then, after an absence of over sixteen years, he returned to Peru in order to see what bargain he could make with Augusto B. Leguía. Apparently he remained in the good graces of this handsome midget dictator for only a short time, for Chocano soon involved himself in his customary amorous escapades, assassinated a distinguished literary rival, and escaped to Chile, where he was shot to death in a street car in 1934.

Chocano had defects aplenty and there was almost no limit to his excesses. His motto was: "Poetic Life; Vital Poetry." Although his early poems were democratic, and although he later took the side of the oppressed in Mexico, he was at heart aristocratic and had little of the humanitarian spirit, for he admired only strong men and had almost no sympathy for the weak. A born adventurer, he was always in rebellion, but more often against the law than against men. His excuse for associating himself with tyrants was that they were either opposing the plutocracies or defying Yankee imperialism; his real motive was probably his desperate need of funds. He complained in his *Memoirs* that he could never devote himself exclusively to his literary work because he lacked economic security. His writings had to be "improvised." "My poems," he said, "must be considered as rapid notes which I have jotted down on the margin of my life." [20] He claims to have had at least one virtue besides his poetic talent; he never drank. It seems a great pity, for intoxication might have served as an excuse for some of his wickedness. But he was a great poet; Latin America had few who excelled him in his day. Darío so admired him that he often refused to drink in his presence and wrote a laudatory poetic introduction to his *Soul of America;* and José Enrique Rodó, before he had any evidence that Chocano's talent would frequently be sold to the highest bidder, hailed him as a singer who united "the proud audacity of inspiration with sculptural firmness of form" and proposed "to return to poetry its arms of combat and its civilizing mission." [21]

"I am the singer of autochthonous and aboriginal America," Chocano wrote in one of his sonnets; "my lyre possesses a soul, my song an ideal. . . . When I feel myself an Inca, I render homage to the Sun, which gives me the scepter of its royal power; when I feel myself a Spaniard and evoke the Colonial epoch, my strophes ring out like crystal trumpets. My fancy derives from Moorish ancestry; . . . the two races mingle with an epic rumble. The blood is Spanish but the pulse is Incaic. . . . " [22] He pastured his winged Pegasus in Inca meadows and rode him in majestic flights over the Andes, over the American Isthmus, over mighty rivers and dense jungles, over the Straits of Magellan. He spurred him into the years ahead and returned with visions of an America united and rejuvenated through the digging of the Panama Canal and the marriage of the Anglo-Saxon Adam and the Latin Eve. Sometimes he led his steed gently through fields sprinkled with orchids or woods filled with magnolias. There was hardly anything possessing beauty or grandeur that he did not portray. He was a master of apt and striking phrases. Castilian was the "language of Utopia land." The heterogeneous peoples of Latin America were "mad pranks of the sun." Schopenhauer he described as "an Attila" flaying God "in the name of nothingness" and Nietzsche as the "Don Quixote of evils." He reminded the lethargic Latins that their ancestors were not driven from Eden because they toiled; work was not to blame for Paradise lost, but the only means of returning to enjoy it. Observe the flashing brilliance of this little gem on archaeology:

> Searching 'mid Eastern ruins, groping slow,
> When some explorer in our modern days
> His hand upon a hidden treasure lays—
> Gold idols heathens worshipped long ago—
> Then with what eager interest aglow
> The spirit of the Present backward strays
> To that far age when priests raised hymns of praise
> To monstrous gods deformed with foreheads low!
>
> When our age too is dead, from tomb to tomb
> Some new explorer, groping in the gloom,
> Will search for what the ruins may afford.
> And what horror, how strange his thoughts will be
> When shining amid the ruins he shall see,
> As the rarest and most precious jewel, a sword!

Note how he infuses the epic spirit into this sonnet on the magnolia:

> Deep in the forest, full of song and fragrance,
> Blooms the magnolia, delicate and light,
> Like snowy wool among the thorns entangled
> Or, on the quiet lake, a foam-like white.
>
> Its vase is worthy of a Grecian maker,
> A marble wonder of the classic days. . . .

Or how he reveals the rebelliousness that he fain would chasten in these verses on the orchids:

> Freaks of bright crystal, airy beauties fair,
> Whose enigmatic forms amaze the eye—
> Crowns fit to deck Apollo's brows on high,
> Adornments meet for halls of splendor rare!
> They spring from knots in tree-trunks, rising there
> In sweet gradation; winding wondrously,
> They twist their serpent stems, and far and nigh
> Hang overhead like wingless birds in air.
>
> Lonely, like pensive heads, all fetterless,
> Lofty and free they bloom; by no dull chain
> Their flowers to any tyrant root are bound;
> Because they too, at war with pettiness,
> Desire to live like souls that know no stain,
> Without one touch of contact with the ground.[23]

Finally, note how his imagination penetrates and soars in *The Song of the Future* and *The Epic of the Pacific:* The long quest for the opening connecting Balboa's sea with the sea of Columbus and Cabral will soon be ended. Magellan will weep because his strait has become useless. The passage to Cipango will be found at last. Russia and Japan have had their war. The United States shortened it by mediating the peace. "The decisive triumph of the yellow Court was not good for the land of the North, and even less was the formidable dominion of the Czars over eagerly sought lands and coveted seas." In the gigantic combat of the coming years the big nations would become exhausted, and "young, free and fecund, the Land of the Amazon" would emerge as the "Center of the World." "The United States, like a bronze ring pressing against a spike, tortures Latin America with a [giant] foot [on the Isthmus], but if Latin America desires to be free it must imitate first and equal afterwards. Let us imitate . . . the creaking strophes that move in the North with the grace of a train whose rapidly gyrating wheels drop rhymed verses as they measure the rails." Let the sense of fear be lulled by confidence that salvation lies in hard work. "Let none grieve about future conquests: our forests know no better race; our Andes know not what it is to be white; our rivers disdain the valor of a Saxon; . . . on the day another race dares" to conquer "our countries, it will utter a cry of horror, for miasma and fever, reptile and swamp will sink it into the earth, under the fire of the Sun. It will not be the race with the blond hair that will finally rend the Isthmus." It will be the black-headed workers—the race of the Pyramids, the race that gave its blood in the Roman Circus and its sweat to the Suez Canal—that will seethe in gloomy huddles in the breaches to open the immense channel; and when it is finally finished it will benefit the Latin race more than the Anglo-Saxon.[24]

JOSÉ ASUNCIÓN SILVA OF COLOMBIA

José Asunción Silva (1865–96), one of Colombia's best-loved poets of the recent epoch (though like Nájera he died shortly before 1900), might have ranked with Gutiérrez Nájera, Nervo, Darío, and Chocano if he had not died so young. He was a precursor of that great literary movement of which they were the leading exponents.

Born of wealthy and aristocratic parents in Bogotá, a city of fanaticism and misery, he began at an early age to suffer the misfortunes of country and family. During his short life, it will be recalled, Colombia was harried by three general civil wars and numerous local uprisings. The Silva fortune was destroyed; José's father died and left him to support the family and pay off its debts; his favorite sister was claimed by death; several of his poems were lost in manuscript in a vessel that was wrecked off the Colombian coast on its way to France where they were to be published. In a fit of melancholy, apparently after days of debauchery in which he tried to assuage his grief and frustration, Silva wrote an autobiographical sketch as he moved toward the verge of insanity: "An intellectual cultivation undertaken without method and with foolish pretensions to universalism, an intellectual cultivation that ended in complete lack of faith, in the mockery of all human effort, in the desire to taste all experiences of life. . . . I am thine; thou art mine. I am madness. . . . Thus died Baudelaire . . . ; thus died Maupassant. . . . Then why should you not die thus, poor degenerate who abused everything, who dreamed of ruling over art, of mastering all science, all knowledge, and of draining all glasses into which Life pours its supreme intoxication?" [25] Tortured by acute sensitiveness, misunderstood, maligned, persecuted, battered by the hammer-blows of fate, Silva fired a pistol into his heart at the age of thirty-one.

Obsessed by death, seeking solace from his woes in the happy memories of his childhood, he suffered, he dreamed, and he sang— sang with a music and a lyric quality new in the Spanish language. Fascinated by the fairy tales of Grimm and Andersen, he predicted that they would be more enduring than the wisdom of the philosophers. Childhood he described as a "fair valley of blessed calm and coolness, where the sun's ray that scorches the rest of life is gentle." "How saintly," he exclaimed, "are your pure innocence and your fleeting, transitory joys; how sweet in the hours of bitterness to look to the past and invoke your memories." Alluding to the futility of philosophy, he declared that he suffered from a disease that attacked few men and rarely attacked women at all: *Thought,* which was the main cause of his "grave and subtle melancholy." Fully aware of Bolívar's great tragedy, he wrote a poem to the Liberator's statue in which he dwelt upon the ingratitude of the people whom the great warrior had freed from the Spanish yoke. He probed the depths of pessimism in a poem on Lazarus in which he has that famous Biblical character, four days after his resurrection, wandering amid the tombs in solitary grief, envying the dead.

Now and then Silva managed to strike a cheerful note, as, for instance, in the *Serenade:*

> The street is deserted, the night is cold,
> The moon glides, veiled, amid cloud-banks dun;
> The lattice above is tightly closed,
> And the notes ring clearly, one by one,
> Under his fingers light and strong,

While the voice that sings tells tender things,
As the player strikes on his sweet guitar
The fragile strings. . . .
The street is deserted, the night is cold;
The moon shines out from the clouds aloft;
The lattice above is opened now,
And the notes are growing more low, more soft.
The singer with fingers light and strong
Clings to the ancient window's bar,
And a moan is heard from the fragile strings
Of the sweet guitar.

He attached swift wings to his fancy in a poem on the stars:

Stars that in the shadowy darkness
Of the vast and the unknown
Seem like pallid drifts of incense
Through the empty spaces blown! . . .

Stars that in unknown abysses
With vague brightness overflow!
Constellations that the Magi
Worshipped, long and long ago!

Far-off whorls in millions, blossoms
Of fantastic flowers and bright!
Shining isles in the unsounded,
Shoreless oceans of the night!

Stars, ye thoughtful, pensive splendors!
Eyes that flickering glory shed!
If ye live, why are ye silent?
Wherefore shine, if ye are dead?

So the poet returned to his obsession even while addressing the stars. One of his longest poems is entitled *Day of the Dead*. It resembles Poe's *The Bells*. On this day all the bells are planging and clanging, but one bell rings out above the chorus in discordant irony and mocking laughter. It is the bell on the clock tower that keeps on marking the minutes and hours of endless time that dims the memory of all but the fortunate few and wafts the millions into oblivion: "One bell complains and another weeps; this one has the voice of an old woman, and that one of a girl who is praying. The largest bells . . . sound with the voice of deep disdain; but the bell that tells the time laughs, it does not mourn. . . . It is the voice of the century, amid a chorus of monks, and with its notes it laughs skeptically and mocks the bell that laments, the bell that entreats, and everything that chorus commemorates. . . . Up there it rings, rhythmical and sonorous . . . ; after the sadness, the cries of grief, the words of sorrow, the touching

tears, it marks in just the same way the moment when . . . the thought
of the dead . . . vanished, six months later—or ten. And today, the
day of the dead, today when sadness hovers in the gray mists, while the
drizzle falls drop by drop and stupefies the nerves with its melancholy,
and wraps the gloomy city in its mantle, this bell that has marked the
day and the hour when to each dismal and empty house, after a short
period of mourning, gladness returned; . . . that has marked the hour
of the dance when, after just a year, the girl whose mother sleeps in
the cemetery, forgotten and alone, tried on for the first time a bright
dress . . . ; this bell that marked the hour when the widower talked
of suicide and asked for poison . . . and soon marked the hour when
. . . he went to the same church with another bride, to be joined in
holy bonds . . . it . . . keeps on marking in the same way, with the
same enthusiasm and the same disdain, the flight of time which blots
out everything! And this . . . is the note of irony that vibrates in the
concert raised by the bells of bronze when they toll for the dead—for
all those who have been. It is . . . the voice . . . which with child-
like accents, indifferent to good and evil, measures the base hour equally
with the sublime and fatal hour and resounds in the sad, dark heights
without having in its clear, rhythmic and sonorous playing the intensely sad, dejected, and wavering accents of that mysterious chorus
rung by the bells—the mournful bells that speak to the living of the
dead!" [26]

RODÓ, URUGUAY'S MASTER OF PROSE

José Enrique Rodó (1872–1917), one of the greatest prose writers of
the Spanish world, may serve as an appropriate transition from the
poets to the *pensadores,* social critics, and novelists whose works
will be dealt with in the following chapter. Like these, he wrote with
a social purpose; but, like the poets, he also was motivated by a profound interest in the development of personality, his own as well as
that of the Spanish American youth.

A native of Montevideo, the youngest child of a family of considerable
means and high social position, he received a good education, obtaining a degree from the National University and teaching literature there
for a time. His literary career was not interfered with by the poverty
of which Nervo and Chocano complained and which caused both
Chocano and Darío to fawn upon tyrants for a living. His only distraction was politics, to which he devoted less than a third of his life, serving in the national Chamber of Deputies for nine years. He never married or marred his personal life by illegitimate adventures in love. He
was a man of fine poise and balance who followed the classic principles

of moderation and the golden mean. He not only preached the gospel of high ideals; he practiced the precepts he preached.

His best works were a protest against materialism and the increasing tendency toward specialization that threatened to fetter the individual and prevent him from seeing human life and destiny as a whole. Because he used the United States as an example and a warning in an essay entitled *Ariel,* which he published at a period (1900) when the influence and power of the Yankees was beginning to be feared in lands to the south, he leaped suddenly into fame. He prefaced his criticism of the United States by a tribute to the Anglo-Saxon republic for translating freedom into reality, for illustrating the virtues of hard work, for championing religious liberty and public education, and for the great skill displayed in the development of its material resources; but mainly because the Latin Americans were suffering from fear and a feeling of inferiority, they overlooked his preface and found compensation for frustration in politics and inefficiency in economics in the assumption of greater Latin devotion to things of the mind and the spirit. This was one of the passages that appealed to their sentiments and administered to their self-satisfaction: "It [the United States] lives for the immediate reality, and through it subordinates all its activity to the egotism of personal and collective well-being. Of the sum of the elements of its riches and its powers, one might say . . . it is a heap of wood which it has been impossible to ignite." The United States seemed to lack the poetic instinct; even its religion, Rodó suggested, would be abandoned or reduced to "an auxiliary force of penal legislation" if ever it became "possible to give to utilitarian morals that religious power with which Stuart Mill was so desirous of endowing it."

Such sentences as the following, Latin American readers passed over rapidly: [27] "The will is the chisel that has sculptured this people out of solid rock. Its salient characteristics are two manifestations of the power of the will: originality and audacity. Its entire history is the manifestation of a virile activity. Its representative personage is named *I will,* like the superman of Nietzsche. If anything rescues it collectively from vulgarity, it is that extraordinary exemplification of energy which carries it everywhere and with which it imprints a certain character of epic grandeur even upon the struggle of interests and material life. . . . But please remember that when I . . . deny to their utilitarianism the right to impose itself . . . as mould or model, I do not in the least assert that its labors are wasted even in relation to those things which we may call soul-interests. . . . That which this people of Cyclops have achieved for the direct purpose of material advantage, with all their sense for what is useful and their admirable faculty of mechanical invention, will be converted by other peoples, or later, even by themselves, to a wealth of material for the higher selection."

Rodó published two other important books and left some manuscripts that were published after his death, but none of his works ever achieved the popularity of his *Ariel,* which went through eight editions by 1910 and twice as many within twenty years after his death. This little essay of less than 150 pages sounded a note that thrilled the Spanish world at an epoch when it was in desperate search for escape from its pessimism.

José Batlle was coming rapidly to the front as a political leader in Uruguay at the time Rodó was most active in politics; and Rodó followed Batlle for several years but finally ended his political career by breaking with the Uruguayan reformer in 1913. A believer in "gradualism," Rodó considered Batlle too impetuous. The great Uruguayan literary master was more moderate than Batlle in his attitude toward the Roman Catholic Church and the industrialists. He was willing to accept the eight-hour day for certain types of work, but he was opposed to its universal and rigid application. Nor could he accept democracy without certain reservations. He contended that nations should be guided and governed by their superior personalities and that a way must be found to teach the people to distinguish between their great men and the demagogues who were always ready to promise everything calculated to gratify mass appetites and whims. His objective was a fusion of Christianity and Greek ideals. "From the spirit of Christianity is born . . . the feeling of equality, vitiated by a certain ascetic scorn for spiritual selection and culture. From the heritage of classic civilizations is born the feeling for order, for hierarchy, and almost a religious respect for genius, vitiated by a certain aristocratic disdain for the humble and the weak." He hoped the future might bring the two together. Democracy without respect for hallowed traditions and personal genius would lead "fatally" to "mediocrity." [28]

In international politics Rodó advocated Pan-Hispanism and Latin-American solidarity without becoming a "Yankeephobe." But the primary interest of his life was personal and cultural rather than political. He was a seeker after ideals for himself and the select spirits of his day. He dwelt at length on the problem of vocation in an age of specialization. He recognized that professional and technical skills were necessary as means of livelihood; but he contended that man's highest vocation was the development of his entire personality by constant inner probings and eternal self-renewal. He was not a profound philosopher; in fact, he did not seek so much to discover new truths as to set forth new ideals and inculcate a love of truth. He attempted to substitute an optimistic idealism for pessimism and materialism.[29]

CHAPTER XXXII

Pensadores and Social Critics

The works of most of the intellectuals to be discussed in this chapter are noted for their literary style. Failure to include them with the literary masters should not be interpreted as a reflection upon their literary ability, nor should it be assumed that the writers dealt with in the previous chapter were not thinkers and social critics. The categories set up here are not rigid; they have been adopted for convenience and emphasis, and it should hardly be necessary to repeat that the Latin-American intelligentsia of the recent period embraced many more able writers than can be examined in these pages.

Among the renowned Latin-American *pensadores* of the recent epoch were Varona, Caso, and Ingenieros. They do not rank with the Occident's greatest philosophers; but they were familiar with the great philosophers' ideas and systems, and they produced works that have the merit of originality in both thought and expression.[1]

VARONA OF CUBA

Enrique José Varona (1849–1933) was a native of Camagüey, Cuba, and the son of fairly prosperous parents who probably left him a small inheritance. At any rate, he was able to devote all of his time to study, teaching, philosophy, literature, and politics, and he lived until past his eighty-fifth year. For half a century he taught philosophy at the University of Havana, and for an even longer period he contributed articles to the Cuban newspapers. He bore the exalted title of *"Maestro"* and no other Cuban outranked him in intellectual prestige.

He began to publish lectures, articles, and monographs at the age of twenty-four and became well known throughout his island before he reached forty-five. His support of Cuban autonomy and independence added to his fame. He served as secretary of education under General Leonard Wood, was one of the organizers of the Conservative party as well as its president for a time, and was also vice-president of the republic for four years (1913–17). He then retired from politics in disgust at the selfishness, greed, and dishonesty of the politicians (and perhaps because his vigorous criticism of the United States displeased the Washington authorities, whose influence in Cuba was very great before the abandonment of the Platt Amendment). Always a skeptic in a Roman Catholic country, he became profoundly pessimistic toward the end of his life. Machado's police shot down two students who formed part of a parade that was marching through the streets of Havana to his home in September, 1930, to honor him on the fiftieth anniversary of his teaching, a tragedy which was followed by the closing of the university, the termination of Varona's professorship, and three years of practical silence; but Varona lived long enough to witness the overthrow of the despot. The publication of his complete works was begun in 1937, but was discontinued for some reason—perhaps because of his utilitarianism and pessimism—the next year.

An evolutionist and an advocate of a philosophy grounded in science, Varona was opposed to metaphysics and saw in religion a consolation based upon blind faith rather than a system of truth. Sympathetic with Rousseau, he followed the radical Frenchman's ideas in education and preferred example to precept. The history of thousands of years of effort by "sacerdotes, prophets, moralists, mandarins, magistrates, and tribunes" but proved his thesis, he declared. "What works upon the conscience is the action that is seen repeated and is repeated. . . . Each individual imitates another whom he admires; each class the one above. Education descends from the top to those below." [2] Varona was empirical in logic, physiological and sensualist in psychology, and individualist and relativist in ethics. He did not believe that any significant segment of history could ever be complete or accurate. The documents of the distant past were too fragmentary, those of modern times too bewildering in their hypocrisy and abundance, and the historian could never avoid injecting his own views into his narrative. Since sociology must have imperfect history as a handmaiden, sociology could never become a science; and, since all sound philosophies must be based upon social experience and accurate social data, Varona confronted an impasse in his own specialty. The older he grew the more convinced he became that man could know very little for certain.

There were some contradictions in his thought. Believing at first in human perfectibility, he soon modified his views. In 1896, putting himself in the place of the obelisk in New York's Central Park, he imagined its reflections on history: "I have seen millions of men in thousands of years; I have seen them change their clothes, their dwellings, their gestures, their language, their ideas. I have not seen them change their appetites or their passions." Yet he wrote eight years later: "The human obeys the inflexible law of change. All is transitory. . . . Nothing persists, not even ideas. . . . Not even in their passions are men of different epochs the same." [3] In the last days of his life, however, Varona was far from accepting the view that mankind was moving toward perfection.

He was a striking illustration of the fact that some agnostics are capable of exemplary personal conduct. To the admonition that the universe was Christian and that he was a mere atom, he replied that he did not rotate in Christianity's orbit. He commented on Spinoza's intoxication with God with the laconic remark that he, himself, would continue to abstain. Yet he taught that men should not injure their fellow beings, that they should co-operate with one another, and that benevolence is a major virtue; and he was not only a sincere humanitarian in word and action, but an honest and honorable patriot. If he withdrew from active politics in 1917, it was because he felt that further participation was futile; he continued to advocate political reform through the press.

Deprived of the opportunity to improve political practices by example, he had to depend upon precept. But he had been teaching his people for so many years that he had become expert in handing down preachments. As early as 1895 he had declared that a lying press encouraged a lying spirit. "I love liberty," he said, "because it teaches a man to be a man . . . to have a heart that rises to the level of his thought, to have the courage to call the good, good and the bad, bad. To deceive the people by giving them the false for the true is worse than to poison their bread and water; it infects their moral atmosphere." He scolded his fellow-citizens for their love of ostentation and their tendency to live beyond their means, for their addiction to gambling and their aversion to mercantile life. Urging that laws should always be simple and clear, he denounced the legislators for their verbosity, and remarked further that laws were never any better than the men who applied them and that it was useless to change the form of institutions before men's hearts were changed. "Equality, before being written into the law, should be written in the conscience." [4]

One hardly knows whether to describe Varona as a conservative aristocrat or a realist. He believed in government of the people, for the people, by the best of the people and declared that a nation which habitually confided its destiny to mediocrities was headed for suicide. Although the Cuban constitution of 1901 had granted the right to vote and hold office to every adult male, Varona was opposed to universal suffrage because too many Cubans were indigent and illiterate. With superb irony, he described his countrymen (and perhaps incidentally the citizens of other little Latin-American republics as well) in a letter to Plutarch [5] in which he asked that great biographer of ancient heroes to grant him a favor. "I live in an island of which you have not heard. . . . This island is famous for its fertility; and although it is not thickly settled, its inhabitants make up for lack of quantity by an excess of quality. We are few, but we are all illustrious. Our history is not mere history, but an epic. Our deeds are not deeds, but exploits. . . . So many supermen so close together feel hampered, jostle one another, and in a way nullify one another. . . . Our common grandeur causes monotony. If in some manner something is not introduced among us to form a contrast, we are going to die of hypertrophy. . . . We desire, good Plutarch, laborious men who do not proclaim their industry to all the winds as a sublime virtue; men who cultivate their fields and do not feel that they should receive public compensation for it, who love their country and do not assume that a sentiment so natural merits statues to themselves; . . . men who serve the republic with zeal and feel sufficiently compensated by the general prosperity . . ."

Varona resented the intervention of the United States in Cuba but admitted that Cuban politicians were largely to blame. "They are concerned with nothing more than to make the best capital of the moment, at the cost of the country, destined beforehand to fill the role of propitiatory victim. But what with greatest reason ought to cause us indignation is to hear them talk only of the good of the country, the honor of the country, the liberty of the country . . ." Insurrectionists had discovered the Cuban "heel of Achilles" in their ability to force intervention by a threat to destroy foreign property. The arbiters sent to the island by the Washington authorities in 1906 were not sent there to promote democracy, Varona declared, but to protect foreign capital. "This capital, these four hundred millions belonging to Americans, Englishmen, Spaniards, and Germans, employed in the sugar centrals, the tobacco lands, the tobacco factories, the railways, and the shipping enterprises, are . . . what has brought the squadron anchored in our port." Cuba was becoming a "factory . . . exploited by foreign" investors.[6]

Without being an economic determinist, Varona dreaded the power of corporate capitalism and doubted that it could be controlled in the best interest of human culture. He feared that it would either destroy the freedom of all but a favored few, or else provoke a universal hurricane that would end in the destruction of both private capital and individual liberty by an omnipotent state under the guise of socialism, communism, or fascism. He was a nineteenth-century liberal.

⁂ MEXICO'S CASO

Antonio Caso (1883–1946), Mexico's most distinguished *pensador,* differs from Varona mainly in three important respects: in his religious faith, his almost complete concentration on philosophy, and his vigorous search for values. The two were similar in their appreciation of art, history, and science as materials which the philosopher must use; in their concern for education; in their readiness to point out the faults of the Latin Americans; in their aristocratic leanings; and in their attitude toward the United States.

Caso was an orthodox Roman Catholic who attacked Positivism and the "excesses" of intellectualism and tried to construct a "philosophy of life, intuition, and action." He believed that man's ideals could be satisfied only by positing an ideal person to synthesize his being and his aspirations, and he called that ideal person God. He thought that man should be guided by intuitions and sentiments as well as by reason and preached the gospel of Christian charity. Christianity, he contended, did not exalt weakness. The Christian was a strong soul who loved the weak, but only to help the weak grow strong. The virtuous man is always the strong man; there are no weak virtues. The highest virtue is enthusiasm and the worst vice is laziness.

Caso scolded the Hispanic Americans for talking about ideals which they either did not really have or failed to apply, for not putting their hearts into cultural enterprises or humanitarian labors, for failing to compel their rulers to practice liberal, constitutional government, for letting justice remain in the stratosphere, for not taking the task of education seriously, and for their general lethargy. Regarding his own country specifically, he said in 1924: [7] "When Mexico shall have become a nation of good workers, she will have been saved forever; . . . she will belong to herself."

He dreaded the influence of the United States in Latin America and called upon the nations of the region to consider themselves as a single fatherland, "holy and invincible." He complained that the motion pictures of Hollywood were slandering the Latins and that the Latin Americans' sources of wealth, particularly in Mexico, were not in their own hands. Only the worst of all industries—politics, civil war, and bureaucracy—were left to the natives. In the 1940's, however, partly as the result of the Good Neighbor Policy, no doubt, he wrote that both morally and economically the Anglo-Saxon peoples were the "best endowed in the world." [8]

Revolting against Comte and the utilitarians and pragmatists, Caso rejected the thesis of universal progress, but thought progress was possible in some societies and some fields of endeavor. Like many scholars who write little history, he was more concerned than the historians themselves with its definition. He declared that there are no laws of history and that a search for them is futile. "Collective facts are not history. The masses are only the substratum of history. History is never the science of the general." The writing of history is "an act of creative imitation . . . an intuition of what was." It is not an invention like art, nor an abstract synthesis like science, nor an intuition of universal principles like philosophy. But philosophy must be based upon history because it is primarily a search for values, for the good, the beautiful, the true, the holy, and the useful, which have value mainly in relation to particular societies and circumstances.[9]

On the origin of value patterns, Caso's position does not seem to be clearly defined. He speaks of eternal values, of values created by individuals, and of values created by societies. Perhaps he thought they had this threefold origin: God, individuals, and societies. He says that man is "the medium between eternal values and their historic realization," but that the genius does more than sum up in his own person the values of his time or his nation; he gives to history more than he has gotten from the society in which he is born. Progress, Caso contended, was largely the result of the impact of great individuals. Their lives are the most significant phenomena of history; they are the heroic wise men, the saintly philosophers, the historians that are fundamentally poets, and, in recent times, the scientists and inventors. "Mexico stands out for its failure to understand the nature and functions of universities, for its neglect of the aristocracy of science and its accompanying enthusiasm for . . . popular education." [10] There is no greater social wisdom than the wisdom which accords the right of absolute freedom of thought, for liberty of thought has created among other things the marvels of science, the foundation of human progress. "Science has made the primitive horde into the modern city, and will remake present society in ways we cannot imagine." [11] Essentially an aristocrat, Caso wished to fuse the ideals of Christianity with the aristocratic ideal of classical times, or the mysticism of the East with the rationalism of the West.

He contrasted the importance of *being* and *having* and lamented that modern civilization had glorified the second while permitting the first to fall into obscurity, subordinating the man that *is* to the man that *has*. The great disease of modern Western culture, he declared, was lack of respect for the individual. There was entirely too much talk of "masses" and "biological entities." The fundamental bases of respect for personality are political and religious freedom and private property; and standing out above the deified state is the spirit of man, manifesting itself in religion, art, science, philosophy, morality, and law. Yet, in writing of liberty, law, and authority, Caso not only admitted that they must be combined so as to avoid anarchy on the one hand and tyranny on the other but contended that both liberty and democracy were means, and not ends to which culture should be subordinated. Government should strive to effect this combination of liberty, law, and authority and at the same time distinguish between objectives and instrumentalities.

A moderate conservative as well as a mystic, Caso revealed a reverence for historical experience and tradition. Since the past is always a part of the present, a too violent break with it disrupts culture and causes confusion. The ideal procedure is to modify the past without destroying it, making use of it as the foundation for further progress.

Mainly because of his idealism, optimism, and orthodox religious position, Caso became a continental figure. His works were more widely read in the neighboring countries than were the writings of Varona; but the Mexican *pensador* lacked the Cuban's pungent phrases, humor, and irony. He was an academician rather than a journalist and an active participant in politics. His works on philosophy and related themes fill some twenty-five volumes, which must be read if his evangelical fervor and sincerity are to be properly appreciated. He did not attempt to construct a new system; he preferred to deal with a few major philosophical and ethical problems.

ARGENTINA'S INGENIEROS

José Ingenieros (1877–1925) of Argentina was for at least twenty years the favorite author of Latin-American youth and one of the best known modern writers in the Spanish world. Physician, criminologist, and psychologist, he was among the first of the Latin scientists of America to win recognition in Europe; but his reputation on his side of the Atlantic rested mainly upon his writings on philosophy and ethics.

The son of Italian immigrant parents of very small means, he nevertheless managed to obtain three or four college and professional degrees before he reached the age of twenty-four and to secure various government and university posts afterwards. His career as a publicist began as a student with articles in literary and scientific journals. In 1905 he was sent as an official delegate to an international congress on psychology in Rome, and he managed to spend almost two years in Europe before he returned to Buenos Aires to resume his teaching and help to found the Institute of Criminology. In 1911 he went back across the Atlantic to study in France and Germany in order to prepare himself for a shift from medicine and psychology to philosophy and ethics. With the exception of brief sojourns in the United States and Mexico, he spent the rest of his short life in Argentina. Although he had barely reached forty-eight at the time of his death from meningitis, his collected works fill twenty-three volumes.

A disciple of Darwin and Spencer, Ingenieros liked to dwell upon evolution and survival, to investigate individual and social pathology, and to utilize science as a weapon to destroy outmoded customs and superstitions. He was an interesting combination of cynic and idealist. The same man who in earlier years proclaimed that there were no rights without strength to enforce them, and no laws that were not imposed upon the weak and unwary by the strong and the astute, later became a moralist who declared that ideals were the prime essential of progress and a philosopher who believed that science could furnish both truth and ideals. With his immense enthusiasm for science, he might have been expected to turn his back on metaphysics; yet in his later years he was willing to entertain the hypotheses of metaphysics as well as those of science. With definite socialistic leanings during most of his life and a member of the Socialist party for a time, he refused to accept the Marxist dogma without important modifications and had profound misgivings regarding any sort of bureaucracy. He wrote in 1908 that imperialism was inevitable and that the sensible procedure would be for the weaker and retarded peoples to submit without a struggle to the stronger and more highly developed powers; but in the 1920's he was busy organizing a Latin-American union against imperialism.

Whatever the minor inconsistencies in his thought and action, however, his approach to the problems of life and civilization was always the same. He viewed everything in the light of evolution and survival and demanded that every custom, belief, and law be submitted to the test of experiment. He was always searching for the moving forces in individuals and societies, and he always hoped to find them in geography, biology, psychology, and economics. Iconoclast and idealist, he demolished in order to construct on the foundations of truth and justice. His most cynical writings always concluded with idealistic appeals.

Everything that Ingenieros ever wrote was replete with original ideas and brilliant suggestions. His most widely read works are *Deception in the Struggle for Existence* (1903), *Argentine Sociology* (1908), *The Mediocre Man* (1913), *Toward a Morality without Dogmas* (1917), *Propositions Relative to the Future of Philosophy* (1918), a long treatise on the *Evolution of Argentine Ideas* (1918), and *Moral Forces* (1918). In the closely related fields of sociology, psychology, and philosophy there are no works in the Spanish language that can be read with more profit.

A few quotations will illustrate his style and thought. Rejecting the Marxist theory of the class conflict as too simple and absolute, he wrote: "Economic activity within a particular country creates *various* interests, those of the landlords, the industrialists, the merchants, and the speculators, and the correspondingly diverse interests of the industrial workers, the agricultural laborers, the middle men, and the little proprietors. . . . The antagonism or the harmony of interests is not simple. There are collective interests which are common to all humanity, to an entire race, to a nation, to a class, to a sex, to a guild or labor union, or to a family." [12]

Pointing out that materialists as well as so-called idealists may have ideals, since ideals are merely visions of a better way of life, he declared: "There are as many idealisms as ideals and as many idealists as there are men apt to envisage perfection and shape their lives accordingly. A monopoly of ideals ought not to be conceded to those who claim it in the name of philosophical schools, moral systems, religious creeds, the fanaticism of sects, and the dogma of esthetics. Idealism is not the exclusive privilege of spiritualistic doctrines which seek to make materialism odious by contrast. . . . As long as there are hearts that pant for perfection, they will be moved by everything which reveals faith in an ideal: by the song of the poets, the valor of the heroes, the virtue of the saints, the precepts of the wise, the philosophy of the *pensadores*." The mediocre man has many traits that are far from admirable, but his worst defect is his lack of ideals, his readiness to become enslaved to the "contingencies of the immediately practical, renouncing the possibility of moral perfection." [13] Speaking from the heights to the admiring youth shortly before his death, Ingenieros declared that "the road to perfection is to live as if your ideals were a reality . . . ; sainthood is of this world, and those who enter into it so live that their names are passed down as examples of the most perfect humanity. . . . Every hour, every minute should be used wisely so as to extract from it as much as possible, whether in work or pleasure." [14] Most of his life exemplified the advice he gave in his departing message. The young men of Latin America, from Argentine to Mexico and Cuba, almost deified him.

A SAMPLE OF LATIN AMERICA'S SOCIAL CRITICS

Much of Latin America's recent fiction has been concerned with the ailments and miseries of the lower classes. Its remote background may be found in the works of Matto de Turner, Blest Gana, Martín Palma, and Eusebio Lillo, all mentioned in Chapter XXI. The immediate precursors of the contemporary writers of fiction were the social critics and novelists of the late nineteenth and early twentieth centuries.

Manuel González Prada (1848–1918), a native of Peru, began his assault upon the Peruvian politicians and clergy in the late 1880's, but his most violent blows were delivered later. Born into an aristocratic family and educated in the University of San Marcos, he eventually developed a deep sympathy for the Peruvian Indians and all his nation's underprivileged, advocated an alliance between Peru's intellectuals and its masses, and became the spiritual father of the Aprista party later headed by Víctor Raul Haya de la Torre. The following bitter sentences from an article he published in 1906 in a labor magazine, *The Parias,* are typical of his blunt and vigorous prose: "There are two great lies in Peru: the republic and Christianity. We talk of civil rights . . . and the majority of Peruvians have no security in either liberty or life. We talk about Christian charity . . . and passively witness the crucifixion of a race. Our Catholicism is a paganism . . . without philosophic grandeur or artistic magnificence; our form of government should be called a prolongation of the Conquest and the Viceroyalty." [15] He flayed the politicians (Piérola, Pardo, Benavides, and several others) and managed to keep out of jail; but some of his excoriations were not published until after his death. His language was obviously unrestrained, but he felt his mission could not be carried out otherwise. "Leprosy is not cured by hiding it under a white glove," he said. He believed in "propaganda and attack." [16]

Francisco Bulnes (1853–1924), Mexican engineer, educator, congressman, and publicist and member of the small *científico* group that surrounded Díaz during the later years of that dictator's rule, was pessimistic regarding the future of a good part of Latin America. Having little respect for its lower classes, he looked upon immigration as holding out the best promise of redemption but felt that only Mexico and the Temperate Zone countries of South America could attract immigrants in any significant numbers. For the Indians he saw no remedy; he expected the majority of them to be exterminated or otherwise disappear. The future of the mestizos he considered brighter, provided they could escape from the demon of alcohol and be given an opportunity to follow the example of Caucasians with the instinct of workmanship.

Bulnes also dwelt upon the evil effects of the Hispanic heritage and disclosed a hostility hardly less vehement than González Prada's toward the Roman Catholic Church. The Spaniards, said Bulnes, not only introduced wheat into America, and the use of iron and the domestic animals indispensable for civilization; they also introduced *aguardiente* (a potent drink), "licentious and voracious friars, ignorance and super-stition, a religion full of hatred," and a militant patriotism that dis-regarded the truth; and, instead of employing the Indians to construct vast irrigation works so badly needed, they forced the natives to build thousands of churches and convents. Spain had been ruined by an overdose of patriotism of the military variety, and Latin America was suffering from the same poison. The Latins of the New World were also suffering from too much emphasis on estheticism. "The great Latin delusion is the belief that art is the highest, almost the only, object of national life." What the countries of the region needed was a practical education and a peacetime patriotism that emphasized hard work, truth, justice, foresight, and co-operation. Until the Latin Ameri-cans acquired greater wisdom and better habits, the best governments for them were liberal dictatorships with educational policies. Bulnes concluded his most famous book, published in 1899, with this observa-tion: "Europe and the United States . . . are not the real enemies of the Latin peoples of America; there are no more terrible enemies of our welfare and independence than ourselves: . . . our tradition, our history, our morbid inheritance, our alcoholism, and our education contrary to the development of character." [17]

Carlos Octavio Bunge (1875–1918), an Argentine whose most widely read volume, *Our America,* came off the press in 1903, prac-tically ignored the church but in most other respects presented the same diagnosis of the region's ills as that offered by Bulnes; for Bunge wrote of the Spanish heritage of arrogance, ostentation, and disdain for work; of the Indian's fatalism and passion for vengeance; of the Negro's servility and infatuation; of the mulatto's petulance, overweening ambi-tion, instability, and dishonesty; and of the mestizo's rapacity, apathy, and fatalistic spirit. Viewing the Spanish Americans as a group, he concluded that they had three fundamental traits which tended to retard their progress: laziness, sadness, and arrogance; and he could prescribe no remedy except hard work, immigration, and progressive dictatorships like the Díaz dictatorship in Mexico. "The concept . . . of the republic . . . is eminently European"; but the Spain of the Conquest was not European. Spain and Portugal had been "de-Euro-peanized" by the invasions of the Moslems from Africa; and, of course, the other races in Latin America were not European, but Oriental and African. "Two criteria are possible in judging the Hispanic American *cacique* [*caudillo*]: The European and the creole. Judged according to the European, the republican, criterion, he is always an odious despot. Judged by the creole, he may be beneficent or ma-lign. . . ." [18] And Bunge devoted the last three chapters of his little volume to rather sympathetic sketches of Rosas, García Moreno, and Díaz, suggesting that they were men well suited to their time and environment.

Alcides Argüedas (1879–1946), a Bolivian who made a clinical inspection of his country and published his findings in Barcelona in 1909, under the title *Sick People,* was even more pessimistic.[19] He dwelt upon the appalling geographical handicaps that confronted his people: the lofty inter-Andine plateaus where men shivered under the eternal blasts of bleak winds that prevented the growth of all but the hardiest crops; the plains of the southeast where rainfall was not distributed so as to favor flourishing agriculture; the rain-soaked Amazonian jungle in the northeast; the immense problems of transportation, of regionalism, provincialism, and perpetual feuds, and the consequent lack of common interests and ideals making for national unity. He not only portrayed the degradation of the Indians in blackest colors but described in detail the vices of the cholos (mestizos) and the little group of whites, dwelling upon their physical lethargy, arrogance, rapacity, verbosity, and mania for government and army posts. Not even the clergy escaped his denunciation for their heartless abuses of the Indians' ignorance and superstition and their indifference to the welfare of the natives. He declared that the Indians and the cholos, if not also some of the whites, were threatened by complete physical decadence as the result of alcoholism and other excesses caused in part by the climate and in part by social stratification and misery. More than half of Bolivia's children, he declared, were born out of wedlock, and many of the illegitimates grew up as waifs and criminals. Of a population of more than 1,744,000 in 1905, less than 220,000 were literate. National wealth was pitifully small. In spite of high import duties and heavy taxes on consumption, national revenues were hardly more than 4,000,-000 bolivianos ($1,600,000) in 1895 and less than 8,000,000 ($3,200,-000) in 1905. Methods of production were most primitive. The whites and the cholos made their living from government employment and by exploiting the Indians, who were fettered by the "routine" of the centuries and hostile to new methods. The only remedies Argüedas could think of for these maladies were practical and moral education and immigration, and he did not expect Caucasian immigrants to be attracted by Bolivia's high plateaus and lowland jungles.

Bulnes, Bunge, and Arguedas represented the lowest depths of racial pessimism. Other writers of the time were more optimistic regarding the innate capacity of the Hispanic, primitive, and mixed peoples of the region.

A Brazilian writer, José do Manoel Bomfím (1868–1932), in a

volume entitled *Latin America* published in Rio de Janeiro in 1905, dwelt upon the evil heritage from Spain and Portugal and the miserable state of the Indian, Negro, and hybrid races, but refused to admit permanent racial inferiority. What the people of Latin America needed, he declared, was sanitation, medical attention, a better diet, education, and economic opportunities.

Enrique Pérez (1874–1921?), a Colombian businessman and journalist and a member of a distinguished Liberal family, attributed the political disorders and economic backwardness of Latin America to two main causes: "We believe that the ignorance of our masses, aggravated by the neglect of our governments, is at least 50 per cent responsible for the fact that we have not been able during a century of our national life to resolve our political and economic problems. The other 50 per cent of the responsibility rests upon the vices rooted in the colonial regime." [20] The nations of the region were suffering from the maladies of ignorance, intolerance, authoritarianism, *personalismo,* or *caudillaje* (based upon the instincts of the horde), rule by mediocrities, and empleomania.

The remedy Pérez prescribed was a sane and practical education— mental, physical, and moral—an education for the lower as well as the upper and the middle classes. Training in theology and esthetics was not enough, nor should encyclopedists be the main objective. Men of "action and will" were needed, "men apt for the agricultural, commercial, industrial, and civic contests of the future." "To improve the social condition of the people is to improve the quality and number of our representative men" and enable the multitude to resist the appeals of the demagogue and the insurgent. "The promoters of revolution . . . are the only ones who know why they go to war. . . . The rural people, the enormous illiterate mass, the cannon fodder, does not know or understand." "Let us give much more, very much more, thought to the education of the lower classes of our people. Let us not forget that in the epoch of the wars against Spain the sons of the people bore upon their backs the mark of three centuries of oppression and upon their countenances the seal of complete ignorance. And let us admit that from independence down to this day we have done nothing for these unfortunate slaves of ignorance. . . . The Indians who had been the vassals of Spain before the epoch of independence have continued . . . to give their blood and their lives to the governments and the *caudillos.* Accustomed from time immemorial to look upon the directing classes as natural lords and masters, they have continued to live under the most odious of all servitudes, that of ignorance." No one had taken the trouble even to teach them to read, or to appreciate the facts that liberty is based upon law, that peace is founded upon justice, and that independence cannot exist without education. "Intertropical America will not be emancipated from the tyranny of its *caudillos* as long as the illiterate masses are not taught the duties of citizenship and the more intelligent citizens are befuddled by that sophistic peace which has repression for its norm and the voice of the *caudillo* as its oracle." [21]

Since this industrious search for diseases and remedies was activated in part by the pessimism and fear occasioned by the defeat of Spain by the United States in 1898 and by the "Yankee imperialism" that followed, it is but natural that intense uneasiness and depression should have been felt in Central America, situated not far away from the "Colossus."

One of the most penetrating social and political investigations of the period was made by Salvador Mendieta (1879–1955), a native of Nicaragua who lived for several years in the other Central American countries. A student in Guatemala during the Spanish-American War, Mendieta not only began to feel a deep sympathy for Spain but to develop a profound apprehensiveness regarding the future of Middle America, and he set out to investigate its problems with the view of publishing a major work on the subject. His studies—in jail and out of jail, in exile and at home in Nicaragua—extended over almost a quarter of a century, and their publication was delayed still longer by lack of funds and restrictions upon the freedom of the press. His first book was printed in León, Nicaragua, in 1903; his second in San José, Costa Rica, in 1905; his third in Barcelona, Spain, in 1910; and his fourth in Managua, Nicaragua, in 1916; but it was not until 1934 that he found a publisher (in Spain) for his major studies, which included a new edition of his third work and four other volumes besides.[22]

Mendieta concentrated upon two major themes: the causes and the cure of Central America's disorders and retarded development. He dealt at length with the faults of the Middle Americans without overlooking their virtues. He listed and described both their bad and their good traits, refused to accept the thesis of racial inferiority, and never allowed himself to succumb to pessimism. Planter, lawyer, and merchant as well as writer and educator, he held few government posts because he found it difficult to tolerate the petty dictators of the region, but he taught for brief periods in the academies and served in the early 1940's as rector of two different institutions that described themselves as universities. His method of investigation was probably suggested by Bunge's *Our America,* which he occasionally mentioned in his writings.

His major work was *La enfermedad de Centro-América* (*"The Sickness of Central America"*) which consisted of three volumes with the following subtitles: *"The Patient and the Symptoms of his Disease"; "Diagnosis and Origins of the Disease";* and *"Therapeutics."* A more thorough sociological study of the region would be difficult to find, and his prescriptions were set down in sane and elaborate detail.

According to Mendieta's diagnosis, the Central Americans were suffering from laziness, physical debility, lack of initiative and self-control, parasitism, meager foresight, carelessness in the contraction and payment of debts, fickleness, egotism, a national and regional inferiority complex, deficiency of moral courage (which expressed itself in lying and other misdemeanors), cynicism and mutual distrust, lack of public spirit, and general unwillingness to co-operate. Over against this long list of defects, he placed a number of virtues: A lively intelligence, easy assimilation (by which he meant a readiness to adopt the ways and methods of foreigners), charity and generosity, physical valor, and a combativeness that signified an independence of spirit and a persistence in the pursuit of objectives.

The origin of the disease—or rather of the complication of diseases—he ascribed, with ample illustrations, to diversity in race and culture, colonial traditions or heritage, and the numerous civil wars of the early National period. The remedies he prescribed were two: first, education—physical, moral, intellectual, and civic; education in the home as well as in the schools and colleges; adult education as well as education for the children and the youth—and second, the unification of Central America, which would provide wider markets, reduce the cost of lawmaking and public administration, and make available the revenues required to carry out his educational program.

Few writers have had a clearer conception of the ills of any part of Latin America or of the remedies that needed to be applied. But the patients refused to take the medicine, especially the potion labelled "unification." Costa Rica, however, was always a more reasonable patient than the other four countries north of Panama, and Mendieta did not fail to point out repeatedly that this little republic was in better health than the rest, although he lamented the refusal of its leaders to assuage their nationalistic fever by a dose of regional loyalty.

Mendieta cannot be classed with the literary masters. He is a bit repetitious, and he uses many local words and expressions difficult to find in the grammars and dictionaries. But he presents a great wealth of detail and some interesting facts or interpretations on almost every page. He also writes with evident sincerity and common sense, and occasionally he pens some striking sentences.

He began his *La enfermedad* by regretting that Central Americans were more interested in reading about every other part of the world, even Japan, Russia, and Manchuria, than in the study of their own region, and expressed the hope that just as charity should begin at home, so some day his compatriots would concede that an investigation of the problems of the globe should begin with those nearest at hand. At any rate, he was determined, he said, to apply the maxim about charity to his own intellectual activities. The despots of Nicaragua and Guatemala had persecuted him, but he did not intend to spend his time denouncing Zelaya and Estrada Cabrera, for he felt that it was much more profitable to examine the "corrupted blood" than the "ulcers" that were its consequence. Of Middle America's vicious political circle, he wrote: "The governments say they oppress in order to prevent revolutions and the insurgents say they revolt in order to liberate the people from the oppression of the governments." [23] He doubted the sincerity of both the despots and the insurgents; but remarked that underground opposition was perpetual. He portrayed the military cruelties of the epoch in darkest colors. "They do not eat the prisoners," he said, "but they assassinate them. The current practice is to grant no quarter." [24] Alluding to padded payrolls and the idle bureaucracy, he declared that the only busy day in Central America was pay day. He described the farce of "reluctant" *continuismo* with ironic humor. In every city, town, and village of Nicaragua and Guatemala the minions of the tyrants formed a legion of "unconditional friends of the government" and "compelled" Zelaya and Estrada Cabrera, "most ardent lovers" of their respective countries, to "occupy the hard armchair" of the presidency a little longer.[25]

Such illustrations might be expanded almost indefinitely, but Mendieta's *La enfermedad* must be read in order to be fully appreciated. The second volume of this work presents an excellent description of both the racial composition of these countries and the institutional abuses of the long Colonial epoch. The third reveals the author's zeal for public education, his familiarity with educational conditions, his clear vision of what needed to be done, and the methods he proposed to adopt.

Mendieta's works on the unification movement contains important historical documents and sketches. They deal with what seems to be a "lost cause," but that does not greatly diminish their interest or value. If his dream should ever become a reality he would no doubt take his place along with Morazán, Barrios, and others in Middle America's pantheon of heroes. The fervor and tenacity of the man are impressive.

፠ SOME OUTSTANDING NOVELISTS

Before 1910 Latin-American fiction was comparatively insignificant. Few novels had been produced "whose charm or literary interest had been sufficiently great to arouse comment, inspire translations, or even induce reading beyond the confines of the country which gave them birth." [26] By the middle of the twentieth century the novel had become Latin America's most important literary expression, and the novelists of the region, for their vigor, their mastery of style, and their originality, had taken their place alongside "their most distinguished fellow craftsmen in the modern world." [27]

The fiction writers of the recent epoch may be classified roughly in four groups: (1) the "escapists" interested in purely esthetic literature who usually deal with distant lands and historical themes; (2) the psychological and philosophical novelists who probe the emotions, doubts, and passions of the world within; (3) the novelists of the city; and (4) the novelists of rural life and of hostile tropical nature. The novelists of the fourth class wrote vigorously of the oppression of the Indians and other rural workers; those of the third dealt with the squalor and shame of urban life—its brothels, its tenements, its underpaid workers, its corrupt politicians, its social and cultural cleavages, its prejudices of race, class, and religion. Although the novels of the first and second groups often surpass those of the third and fourth in literary merit, the urban and rural novels have far more social significance, and these are the works of fiction which seem to deserve consideration in the present narrative. Readers interested in the others may consult Spell, Torres-Ríoseco,[28] and Goldberg.[29]

Carlos Loveira (1882–1928), a Cuban of Spanish descent, grew up as an orphan on the streets of New York, working in hotels and at whatever other tasks he could find. Later, he became a locomotive engineer and followed his trade in Costa Rica, Panama, and Cuba. During the last decade of his life, he published five novels: *The Immoral* (1919), *Generals and Doctors* (1920), *The Blind* (1922), *The Last Lesson* (1924), and *Juan the Creole* (1927). He was a social critic and a propagandist who championed labor and all the underprivileged. His style is journalistic and his themes are mainly autobiographical. He flayed the politicians, lawyers, physicians, army officers, and Cuban and foreign capitalists, revolted against social restraints, and favored divorce if not even free love. The leading character in *Juan the Creole,* generally considered his best book, endures a life of hunger and misery in the slums of Havana, but finally builds up enough political influence to become a member of congress and extract sufficient profits from politics to buy a fine house and luxurious automobiles.

Mariano Azuela (1873–1954), the novelist of the twentieth-century Mexican revolution, is an amazingly prolific writer. His some eighteen novels and novelettes cover a period of more than three decades of Mexican history, from the last years of the Díaz regime until near the end of the Cárdenas administration late in 1940. The scenes of some of his works are laid in Mexico City, but they portray in the main the life of the people in the provincial towns and the neighboring haciendas. Known as the novelist of the Mexican proletariat because his sympathies are always with the lower classes, Azuela deals with characters from all strata of his nation; and while he uses his biting satire and mordant humor to flagellate the middle and upper layers, he does not idealize the masses. His most famous novel is *The Underdogs* (1915), which has been translated into every important living language. Born of a family of small means in Lagos de Moreno, Jalisco, he studied medicine, began the practice of his profession in his small home town shortly before 1900, and served as mayor for a few months during the Madero period. Later he became a physician in the *Villista* forces and fled to El Paso, Texas, in 1915 after Villa's severe defeat by Carranza. It was in a newspaper called *El Paso del Norte* in that border town that his *Underdogs* first appeared (as a serial). The next year he moved to Mexico City, where he continued his dual role as physician and writer of fiction. He portrayed the long revolution in all of its aspects. "As an ominous cloud, he had seen it approach; in the midst of the hurricane, he perceived only destruction; and when the sky had cleared, he found that little of its gigantic force had been expended for the betterment of those who most needed help—the Indian and the downtrodden masses of Mexico. In his eyes, their problems still remained unsolved." [30] Perhaps he exaggerated his pessimism somewhat in the hope of hastening the progress of reform.

Rómulo Gallegos (1884–   ), a Venezuelan already mentioned in these pages as president of his country for approximately a year in the late 1940's, spent more than a decade as teacher and educational administrator before he began to write fiction. He lived in Spain as a voluntary exile during the latter part of the Gómez dictatorship and published in Barcelona three of his most famous novels: *Doña Bárbara* (1929), *The Ballad Singer* (1931), and *Canaima* (1935). Although his first novel dealt with city life and the lack of persistence and realism in Venezuela, his second with life in a mountain village, and a later work with the race wars of the period intervening between the overthrow of Páez in 1846 and the rise of Guzmán Blanco twenty years later, Gallegos is most noted for his fiction depicting the semibarbarous conditions on the Venezuelan llanos and in the selvas (forests) beyond the Orinoco where the natives were forced by adventurers to collect rubber (balata) for the world market before it was flooded with plantation rubber from the Orient. All of his novels reveal a deep sympathy for the lower classes and a desire to eliminate color prejudice. He seems to be an advocate of racial amalgamation; at any rate, his whites usually marry men and women of darker hue. *Doña Bárbara,* his masterpiece, went through twenty editions within a decade.

José Eustasio Rivera (1889–1928) was born in the town of Neiva, Colombia. His fame as a novelist—he was also a lawyer and a poet—rests on a single work, a remarkable piece of jungle fiction, *The Vortex* (1924), which exposes the ruthless exploitation of the natives along the Orinoco and Amazon tributaries by the rubber barons. Government commissions afforded him an opportunity to study at first hand the great rivers and forests and the human types he later described with such skill in his novel. *The Vortex* is at the same time romantic, sociological, and poetic, perhaps Spanish America's greatest piece of fiction dealing with the jungle tropics. Rivera might have produced even superior novels if he had lived longer. Weakened by tropical disease, he died of pneumonia in New York soon after he arrived to publish a new edition of his *Vortex* and enjoy a literary triumph.

Jorge Icaza (1906–   ), champion of Ecuador's downtrodden Indians, published his first volume of fiction, a collection of short stories called *Mountain Soil,* at the age of twenty-seven, and followed it with three other novels during the next five years: *Huasipungo* (1934), *In the Streets* (1936), and *Half-Breeds* (1938). After attending a Jesuit college in Quito, he began the study of medicine, but the death of his father compelled him to discontinue his professional training and earn his living. He had to work at various unpleasant tasks before he finally secured employment in the national theater, where he translated French plays and produced some of his own, one of which caused such a furor that the petty tyrants of the period closed the theater. It was shortly afterward that he began to write his novels. His aims are political and social rather than esthetic. He personalizes the Indians en masse and portrays all of the whites and mixed breeds as their oppressors, stealing their lands, depriving them of water rights, burning their villages and rural hovels, assassinating their leaders, and reducing them to peonage; all is "violent, bestial, bloody, black as nightmare." [31]

Ciro Alegría (1909–   ), Peru's leading novelist of the recent period, a member of the Aprista party, also dwells upon the oppressions of the Indians, but does not so completely subordinate his art to propaganda. Between 1935 and 1941, he published three *Indianista* works of fiction, all in Santiago, Chile, where he appears to have been residing in exile during most of the period, having been expelled from his native land, after months in prison, by the Peruvian dictator Oscar Benavides: *The Golden Serpent* (1935), *Hungry Dogs* (1939), and *Broad and Alien is the World* (1941). The first of the three has the upper Amazon (here called Marañón) as its setting, and the Indian village located there has a terrific struggle with tropical floods and jungle but no serious difficulties with the whites. The other two depict the contests of the natives with both cruel men and a hostile physical environment in which the Indians are scattered, enslaved, and destroyed. "It is not enough for the novelist to express sympathy or even violent fury at the suffering and exploitation of the Indian"; he also discloses deep appreciation for "the picturesque folkways and the ancient traditions and values of American aboriginal life." [32]

Although Chile produced a few novelists and short-story writers who utilized rural themes and described conditions on the country estates or in the coal mines, its most outstanding novelists of the recent period have preferred to portray life in the cities. Among them, Joaquín Edwards Bello (1888–   ), whose aristocratic ancestors include wealthy Englishmen and the renowned Andrés Bello, holds a prominent place. In five works of fiction published between 1910 and 1931—*Useless* (1910), *The Monster* (1912), *Esmeraldo's Cradle* (1918), *The Roto* (1920), and *Valparaiso, the Windy City* (1931)—he presents realistic and vivid, if somewhat caricatured descriptions of life in Chile's leading cities, their banks, mercantile firms, churches, boarding houses, brothels, and gambling dens. The Chilean *roto* is the man of the lowest class in the urban centers as well as the rural peon, and Edwards Bello, although an aristocrat, continuously sets forth the city *roto*'s miserable existence and degeneracy, while at the same time frequently dashing off portraits of high society with superficial strokes that berate its members for their idleness, laziness, vanity, immorality, and indifference to the welfare of the Chilean masses.

Literature in Uruguay and Argentina of the recent epoch is distinguished by the perfection of Gaucho fiction. Some writers described cowboy life and character realistically; others infused their works with nostalgic idealizations. Among the former may be mentioned the Uruguayans Eduardo Acevedo Díaz (1851–1924) and Javier de Viana (1872–1925) and the Irish Argentine Benito Lynch (1885–1954). Acevedo Díaz's masterpiece, *Soledad* (1894), portrays an untamed landscape and the brutality and violence of elemental characters. Viana, in two volumes of short stories—*Yuyos* (1912) and *Dry Wood* (1913) —and in two earlier novelettes—*Campo* (1896) and *Guri* (1898)— correctly suggests that the Uruguayan cowboys have been transformed by the coming of the immigrants and the inroads of agricultural progress from picturesque nomads to agricultural laborers or bandits. Poverty, disease, and drink have destroyed their former robust qualities and reduced them to the lowest ranks of rural workers. Lynch portrays the Argentine pampa Gauchos bereft of their heroic trappings, describing them as unlettered countrymen who express themselves in few words and in explosive acts of cruelty and violence, and who have been reduced to the lowest level of society by the competition of European labor and the advance of the farm frontier. Lynch's best novels—*The Carrion Hawks of Florida* (1916), *Raquela* (1918), *The Englishman of the Bones* (1924), and *The Romance of a Gaucho* (1930)—are an attempt to paint these vanishing figures and their environment as they really were. But Ricardo Güiraldes (1886–1927) in his most renowned work, *Don Segundo Sombra* (1926), has portrayed at least one Gaucho as a knight of the ideal of simple manliness and freedom, and that is probably the portrait that will linger forever in the minds of most Argentinos as they confront the complex problems of the present and the future.

Argentina's best known novelist of town and city life is Manuel Gálvez (1882–1956), lawyer, educator, essayist, literary critic, and propagandist, as well as a writer of fiction. Enormously prolific, he published ten novels on this general theme between 1914 and 1930. Perhaps the best of them are *The Normal School Teacher* (1914), in which he describes the vulgar and monotonous life of La Rioja and the tragic love affair of one of the women of the staff; *The Metaphysical Malady* (1916), in which he portrays the desperate struggle, failure, and death of a literary man in Buenos Aires; *The Shadow of the Convent* (1917), in which he describes the bitter struggle between a narrow clericalism and a rising liberalism in drowsy Córdoba; and *Nacha Regules* (1919), a novel of protest against the corrupting forces in Buenos Aires which debased and debauched the lives of upper and lower classes alike. "No phenomenon seems to escape the interest of this writer; he gives copious data on such problems as marriage, divorce, free love, corruption in education and politics, the death-hold of capitalism upon society, and the despair of the masses in its grip. In his pages, the reader finds himself in the salons of Argentine society; in the waiting rooms of Ministers of State; in the offices of school directors; in the country mansions of landowners; in cloisters; and even in the gloomy recesses of meat-packing houses, jails, [dens of vice], and fishermen's hovels." [33]

The main purpose of the Brazilian novelists of the twentieth century seems to be to portray realistically social and economic, if not political, conditions with the hope of improving them. This was also the apparent purpose of most of the Brazilian novelists of the late nineteenth century; but one of them, Machado Assís, already mentioned at the end of Chapter XXI, was a rather cynical artist who did not cringe at evil or rejoice at the good. Aluízio Azevedo (1857–1913), in a series of five novels published between 1881 and 1890, faithfully portrayed Brazilian society and its social problems; Graça Aranha (1861–1931) dealt with immigration and miscegenation in his *Canaan* (1901) and included excellent descriptions of native landscapes and customs; Henrique M. Coelho Netto (1864–1934) centered his attention on the sufferings of the frontiersmen and the exploitation of the Negro serfs in two works published between 1896 and 1914.

Among more recent Brazilian novelists, four deserve special mention. Afranio Peixoto (1876–1947) describes the social and psychological position of the Negroes and half-breeds on the plantations and in the rural villages of his country in *Maria Bonita* (1914), *Fruit of the Forest* (1920), and *Sinházina* (1929). José Lins do Rego (1901–   ), in a series of eight novels published between 1932 and 1939, portrays plantation life in the northeast, describing the sugar mills, the field hands, the habits and customs of the people, and their passions, conflicts, and poverty. Jorge Amado (1912–   ) describes both city and rural life in the state of Bahía in a series of six works of fiction published during the 1930's and presents skilful propaganda for amelioration of the underprivileged. Meantime Enrico Veríssimo (1905–   ), in five novels, was dwelling upon the metropolitan scene with the same objective, among others, in view.

If the major ills of Latin America were not remedied during the first half of the twentieth century, it was not because its *pensadores,* social critics, and novelists failed to describe the diseases and the symptoms and suggest possible remedies. That these years were a period of greater awareness of the underdogs and of some effort to improve their lot may indicate that such writers did not work in vain and that the Latin countries of America were beginning to create at home the dynamics of their intellectual, social, and economic life. Whatever the influence of these literary men may have been, they must be taken into consideration in appraising the ideals and achievements of Latin-American civilization. Although the region generally was "backward" in some phases of its culture, the literary output of several of the republics was little short of remarkable. Most of their ablest writers, however, were either pure Caucasians or whites with only a slight admixture of Indian or Negro blood. The mixed and primitive peoples were still largely excluded from full participation in higher cultural activities.[34]

CHAPTER XXXIII

Latin America in World Politics

✦ INCREASING INVOLVEMENT

The role of the Latin-American nations in world politics, after 1900 as earlier, was largely passive. Such influence as they were able to exert upon the great powers resulted mainly from their markets, their material resources, and whatever capacity they possessed to play one rival against another or appeal to humanitarian sentiments and moral principles.[1]

A combination of Europe's strife, British policy and sea power, and the Monroe Doctrine prevented them from becoming an actual battleground of power politics; but several of the Caribbean countries suffered a curtailment of their sovereignty for a few years, and the whole Latin-American region became a center of vigorous rivalry among the big industrial nations for trade, investment opportunities, and political and cultural influence. Courted now as well as coerced, the American Latins were propagandized—first by France and Spain and then by nearly all of the great competitors—until they must have been "punch-drunk on propaganda" for months at a time. Efforts were made, particularly by Spain, Germany, and Italy, to keep their nationals and former nationals residing in the region loyal to the mother countries and use them for propaganda purposes; and to the extent that they succeeded (Germany being more successful perhaps than the others), they introduced another element of discord into national political conditions already conspicuous for lack of harmony.

The Latin nations of America were ignored for many years by the planners of world assemblies. Only Mexico and Brazil received invitations to participate in the first peace conference at The Hague (1899), and Brazil failed to send delegates. Thanks mainly to the United States, however, they were all asked to send representatives to the peace assembly of 1907, and eighteen of the twenty countries took part in that conference.

Lacking material force to protect themselves, they had the appreciation of all weak states for such bulwarks as a peace conference might erect against the stronger powers, and their delegations acted accordingly, supporting practically every proposal for reducing the brutality of international war and for pacific settlement of international disputes. They were particularly interested in limiting the employment of force in the collection of spoliation claims and contract debts, a problem upon which the joint coercion of Venezuela by Great Britain, Germany, and Italy in 1902–3 had focused world attention; but the convention finally adopted at The Hague on that subject was not entirely satisfactory to them. Its most important provisions were as follows:

"The contracting powers agree not to have recourse to armed force for the recovery of contract debts claimed from the Government of one country by the Government of another . . . as being due to its nationals. This understanding is, however, not applicable when the debtor State refuses or neglects to reply to an offer of arbitration, or, after having accepted the offer, prevents any *compromis* from being agreed on, or after the arbitration, fails to submit to the award."

Objecting to this agreement because it did not go far enough in protecting weak and disorderly debtor countries against the coercion of the stronger powers in behalf of the pecuniary claims of their nationals, the Venezuelan delegation refused to sign it; and most of the other Latin-American representatives signed with reservations, those of Brazil alone affixing their signatures without complaint. But while the majority of the Latin Americans were dissatisfied with their achievement on one of the major issues of the conference, they had been offered a great forum in which to air their views and given an opportunity to participate actively for the first time in the broad arena of world politics.[2]

Seven years later they were pulled and tugged by World War I. The influence of France, England, and eventually Italy and the United States pulled them in one direction; Germany and Spain tugged them in another; for while Spain was officially neutral during the struggle, its major propaganda forces operated in behalf of Germany. The Allies might have had a decided advantage over the Central Powers in Latin America if France had not helped Spain during previous decades to undermine the influence of the United States by bitter criticisms of its Latin-American policy, which was offensive enough to many of the Latin-American neighbors without its being misrepresented by the French and Spanish propaganda. The Pan-American movement, revived in the late 1880's under the leadership of the United States, had failed to win Latin-American friendship because of the American intervention policy and its denunciation by European rivals.

✠ THE PAN-HISPANIC MOVEMENT

A Pan-Hispanic movement had been inaugurated in Spain in the early 1890's by a congress convoked to celebrate the fourth centenary of the discovery of America and by the founding of the Ibero-American Union; and the Spanish-American War, together with the interventionist policy of the United States that followed it, had given *Hispanismo* a decidedly anti-Yankee tinge. This became quite evident in the writings of José F. Gómez [3] and Ricardo Beltrán y Rózpide.[4]

Gómez, writing in 1897, advocated a customs union as the first step in the formation of a more solid combination between Spain and the peoples of Spanish origin in America. The following passage summarizes his objectives: "If we know how to take advantage of the situation, our country may yet become the polar star of a Latin confederation on that continent against the Saxon preponderance represented by this Anglo-American Colossus . . . and we may advance firmly and serenely to a league of race, draw the former possessions of the mother country together in the interest of all, and give potency, unity, and fire to the idea of solidarity among the peoples who pray, make laws, and converse in the beautiful language of Castile."

Beltrán y Rózpide, who published his work a decade later, was intensely hostile toward the United States, painting its policy in the Western Hemisphere in blackest colors and dwelling on the "Yankee Peril" in the hope of promoting a confederation of the Hispanic republics. His ultimate aim was a profitable bulwark for Spain, which he expected to be accorded the *"Presidencia de Honor"* in a grand alliance of the Hispanic peoples.

"Yankeephobia" was even more evident in the Spanish newspapers. The following illustrations will indicate their severity. *Correo Español* declared in July, 1898: "When Spain has been driven from the continent she created, the possessions of other nations still holding colonies there will soon be disposed of. The dreams of the North American politicians will be realized. Mexico, already mutilated by the amputation of Texas and California, will fall an easy prey. Venezuela will next fall under the talons of the American vulture. Brazil, Chile, Argentina, and other American republics would be succulent food. . . . It is not only the Antilles that are threatened; the nations of Central and South America will also disappear before an . . . invasion more terrible than that of the Vandals and the Goths." There was only one way to avoid the immense peril. "The Spanish-Americans must, in union with the mother country, fight for their land, for their religion, and for their race." [5]

This article, written with the fervor of a war psychosis, was only a little more extreme than many that followed. Three years later, for example, *España Moderna* exhorted Europe to save itself and the "virgin South American continent from the barbaric Yankees"; [6] and in 1910 it was still shouting about the "Yankee Peril," declaring that Latin America was on the verge of being "gobbled up," and urging that the region, or at least a good part of it, must be saved by means of an alliance based upon "traditions of race and the language of Castile." [7]

Similar sentiments were expressed by some of the professors in the Spanish universities. Vicente Gay of the University of Valladolid, for instance, declared that Spain must rescue the Latin Americans from the ruthless intrigues of the United States. "We should insist upon the common blood of Spain and South America," he urged, "and encourage trade and intercourse." "Spain is the Rome of the West and the fountain of its greatness. In Spain should be recognized the Pantheon of American heroes. . . . It is necessary to bear this in mind if we would cultivate the Ibero-American spirit which must prove the salvation of Latin America." [8]

An able group of Spaniards rallied around the ideal of Hispano-American friendship and called themselves "Americanists." The Spanish government took up the cue as early as 1900 and assembled a social and economic congress of all the Hispanic peoples in Madrid. The Spanish minister of state declared at this time that the "social and economic future" of his country depended to a large extent upon the fostering of "those racial sympathies" that Spain enjoyed in America, and that the day had arrived to cultivate the spiritual affections of Spaniards overseas and prepare for vigorous competition in their markets.

This conference was soon followed by several others. In 1908 the countries of Spanish America took part in the celebration of the centenary of the Spanish uprising against Napoleon; two years later a Hispano-American assembly was held in Barcelona; in 1912 another conference of the Hispanic peoples was called together to celebrate the centenary of the meeting of the Cortes in Cádiz; and in 1914 a Historical and Geographical Congress was held in Seville to commemorate the four hundredth anniversary of the discovery of the Pacific Ocean.

Meantime the Spanish government was sending out official agents to take part in the celebration of the centenaries of independence in Spanish America, and Spanish intellectuals, politicians, and merchants were founding numerous organizations, some of them subsidized by the monarchy, for the purpose of promoting trade and cultivating the friendship of their American kinsmen. Among such organizations were the *Casa de América* and a "Center" for the promotion of Hispano-American friendship in Barcelona; the Hispanic-American Royal Academy of Arts and Sciences at Cádiz; the Center of Americanist Studies in Seville; and three or four "Academies," "Institutes," and "Centers" in Madrid; and while all these and many more were being established, a number of the universities were creating professorships devoted to the teaching of American history, law, and politics and several journals and publishing enterprises were being founded for the purpose of distributing literature on Spanish America in the former mother country.

Individuals connected with these enterprises soon carried their propaganda across the Atlantic. Prominent Spaniards made frequent journeys to Latin America; professorial and student interchanges were arranged; Spanish immigrants overseas were organized and encouraged to participate in the celebration of *Fiestas de la Raza* (Racial Holidays); [9] and the old and dignified Spanish Academies—those of Languages, of History, and of Sciences, for example—established branches, correspondents, and exchanges in and with the Spanish American countries.

Of the various cultural missions to Latin America, the one by the distinguished Spanish historian Rafael Altamira, who represented the University of Oviedo, deserves special mention because of the prestige of the visitor, the eloquent statement of Pan-Hispanic ideals issued by the university authorities, and Altamira's cordial reception almost everywhere. The University of Oviedo's "Address to the Spaniards and Brothers of America" stated the purpose of the mission as follows: [10]

On the noble eve of the Centenary of the Independence of America the University of Oviedo . . . desires that the affectionate voice of Spain pronounce a benediction upon her emancipated daughters; it desires to unite its song to the chorus . . . in commemoration of that memorable date when, eager for life, they left their paternal home; it desires above all to bear to these puissant nationalities vigorous shoots of our spirit in order to plant them in the fertile lands bathed by the Gulf, enriched by the Río de la Plata, and shaded by the lofty Andes; it desires to send to America flames of our fire in order that our souls may be welded into one, and the people forming the Great Iberia on both sides of the sea having thus been united, we shall be able to fulfill the high civilizing mission which destiny has confided to us.

Space does not permit an analysis of the Spanish American response to these appeals to race, language, and religion. But the sources of information, both official and private, indicate that the Spaniards succeeded in obliterating the unpleasant memories and grievances of the past and restoring the affections of many of the leaders of the region for the mother country, while intensifying suspicion and hostility toward the United States.[11]

🖐️ FRENCH CRITICISMS OF THE LATIN-AMERICAN POLICY OF THE UNITED STATES

French criticisms of the American policy of the United States were probably more damaging than those of the Spaniards, some of whom were not pleased by the Pan-Latin note sounded by the French writers. French prestige, although injured for a time by the Napoleonic intervention in Mexico, stood higher than that of any other foreign nation.

Frenchmen felt a close racial and cultural affinity for the Latins of America. This sentiment, as already noted in Chapter XXIV, was one of the motives back of Louis Napoleon's quixotic Mexican expedition, and it was one of the most persistent influences molding French attitude. An article published in the *Revue de Deux Mondes* in 1893,[12] to go back no further, pointed out that French political, scientific, and cultural ideas were in the ascendant in Mexico. Díaz' administrative system was modeled after that of France; Mexico's civil code was almost a literal reproduction of the *Code Napoleon;* and cultured Mexicans were not only reading more French than Spanish books but were sending their sons and daughters to Paris to complete their education. This filled the journalist with pride; and after warning the nations of Latin America, especially those with large Indian populations, that too intimate association with the Anglo-Saxons might mean their extermination, he expressed the hope that Frenchmen and the French government would assist the Latin nationalities in America to defend themselves.

It was not long until a host of French writers were calling upon the Latins of Europe to rescue their overseas kinsmen from the "imperialism" of the United States. One of them remarked in 1902: "The nations of Central and South America must be ranked among the Latin peoples. A positive alliance . . . would be difficult perhaps, because it would arouse the suspicion of the United States. But at any rate a cordial understanding is needed, a growing intimacy . . . between the Latin peoples of Europe and those of America." [13] Writing in 1909, another predicted that his generation might live to see the major part of Latin America under the control of the United States. Rome would then be transferred to the New World, he said, and Paris would become another Athens entering "the melancholy shades of the past." [14]

The critical utterances of Frenchmen were also activated in part by imperial defense. They feared that the "rising tide of American imperialism" might submerge the French Antilles and French Guiana, remnants of an empire that reminded them of a glorious past. This danger was envisaged in 1890 in connection with the revival of Pan-Americanism. The vigorous stand taken by the United States with reference to the Anglo-Venezuelan boundary dispute five years later caused further anxiety, and French journalists contended that the Washington government was following a definite policy of shutting Europe out of the Western Hemisphere. This anxiety had become so evident by 1898 that the German Emperor suggested that the French government might be persuaded on this basis alone to join a concert against the United States. It proved impossible, however, for the major European powers to effect a concert to prevent the Spanish-American War and the subsequent acquisition of colonies and protectorates by the United States.

The Spanish-American War and the expansion of the United States into the Pacific area furnished Frenchmen another opportunity to express their apprehensions. Pointing out that the Monroe Doctrine contained a pledge not to disturb Europe's American colonies, Maurice de Beaumarchais declared that "in the Cuban affair" the doctrine had been openly violated both in its text and in its spirit.[15] Hector Petín went further and complained that at the very time the political leaders of the United States were asserting most vociferously their pretensions to a paramount interest in the Western Hemisphere as an exclusive field for their exploitation, they were aggressively demanding equal rights with other nations all around the world. European governments asking themselves where the Yankee choice would lie when confronted by the dilemma of choosing between the Monroe Doctrine and world empire were soon astounded by what happened; the Yankees overlooked the dilemma and chose both! [16]

Another factor that shaped French attitude—not to mention the hostility which some Frenchmen may have felt because of American opposition to Napoleon's Mexican invasion and to the canal enterprise of Ferdinand de Lesseps in Panama—was a sort of melancholy envy produced by the fact that the United States was profiting by the failures of France. Frenchmen could not help recalling, for instance, that the fertile Mississippi Valley, the great treasure-house of the United States, once belonged to their country and, moreover, that its products were flooding into the world markets to compete with those of France. This attitude, as already observed in Chapter XXIV, comes out clearly in an essay published by Comte d'Haussonville in 1905.

Probably more important than any other motive for French attacks upon the Latin-American policy of the United States was the economic motive. It has already been mentioned as a motive for Napoleon's

Mexican enterprise. The United States was by no means France's sole competitor in the Latin-American markets; British and German competition was also formidable. But Yankee initiative and shrewdness were dreaded, and the French press dwelt upon American commercial designs. The Monroe Doctrine was declared to be primarily a commercial doctrine, and the Pan-American movement was decried as a scheme to erect a Chinese Wall between Europe and the three Americas. Perhaps two examples will suffice at this point to illustrate this phase of their propaganda. It was contended in 1890 that James G. Blaine was planning to prevent both political and economic relationships between Europe and America and that the Republican party had resolved "to prohibit all importation from Europe into the New World"; [17] and a French writer declared in 1893 that the Monroe Doctrine signified the economic hegemony of the United States in the Americas, for "in our day . . . economic interests tend always to dominate political." [18]

Such were the attitudes and motivations of the French press in its assaults upon the Latin-American policy of the United States. It is not unlikely that the French government sometimes felt the impulse to act in accord with such sentiments. But whatever official feeling may have been, French official policy was cautious and mild. Two important considerations had to be weighed carefully in dealing with the subject: Europe's delicate power balance and the sensitiveness of the United States with respect to European intervention in American affairs. The Napoleonic fiasco in Mexico was an impressive lesson on both counts. The French government rejected two offers of a naval base and a protectorate made in the 1880's by the despots of Haiti, disavowed any connection with De Lessep's canal enterprise in Panama and refused to give his company financial support, and promptly submitted its Guiana boundary dispute with Brazil to arbitration after the United States invoked the Monroe Doctrine against England in the British boundary dispute with Venezuela. The French government also used its navy less vigorously in protecting French interests in Latin America than did some of the other European powers, as pointed out in another connection. It took no part in the joint naval action by Germany, England, and Italy against Venezuela in 1902–3 and conferred with the United States politely and patiently with reference to claims settlements with the Dominican Republic in 1904 and with Haiti in 1914–15. Practically the only instances of the use of force after the middle 1880's were the coercion of the Dominican Republic in 1893 and the landing of a small naval detachment in Haiti in 1915. Even after the Theodore Roosevelt administration signified its assent to drastic measures in dealing with Castro in 1905 in order to compel him to reach a settlement with a French cable company, the French government was reluctant to take action and finally adjusted the matter without employing the naval arm.

Because of the tense situation in Europe, if for no other reason, France appeared to be a giantess with her hands fettered—but with tongue sharpened by the manacles that bound them. Pan-Americanism and the Monroe Doctrine were denounced as cloaks for monopoly and haughty imperialism. Latins in America were warned that they should cease fighting among themselves, unite, foster their economic connections with Europe, and lend a willing ear to Pan-Hispanism and Pan-Latinism. "Washington aspires to become the capital of an enormous empire comprising, with the exception of Canada, the whole of the New World," declared Maurice de Waleffe.[19] The United States was planning to bring under its imperial sway every Latin-American country that might conceivably affect its control over the Panama Canal, summarized the contention of Angel Marvaud.[20] *Journal des Débats* addressed this explicit advice to Latin Americans: "If you want *rapprochement* . . . look to your mother Spain rather than to the great invading republic of the North." [21] "The simplest foresight imposes upon Latin America . . . three conditions for the maintenance of independence," warned *Economiste français:* "Order and good government, peace among the various sister republics, and close economic . . . relations with Europe, from whom she has nothing to fear." [22] And even some distinguished French scholars joined the fray. Paul Leroy-Beaulieu urged the Latin-American nations to avoid encouraging the invocation of the Monroe Doctrine. "Neither Mexico, nor the states of Central America, nor those of South America," he assured, "have anything to fear from the European powers. It is less certain that the government in Washington will always observe . . . a discretion equally absolute." [23] Alexandre Merignhac expressed the hope that the Latin nations of America would seek the aid of Europe against the pseudo-benevolent and self-appointed intervention of the United States.[24]

EUROPEAN PROPAGANDA AND LATIN-AMERICAN ATTITUDE DURING WORLD WAR I

This Spanish and French propaganda has been analyzed at some length because it undoubtedly influenced the attitude of Latin-American leaders during World War I. Only eight of the countries declared war against Germany and half of these were quasi-protectorates of the United States, while three of the others—Costa Rica, Guatemala, and Honduras—were small Caribbean countries either dominated by the financial influence of the United States and Great Britain or actuated by peculiar motives of their own. Only Brazil made its choice with comparative freedom. If five other republics went half way and broke relations with Germany, one member of this group, the Dominican Republic, was also a protectorate, and the favorable alignment represented by this five and by the eight belligerents must be balanced against the neutrality of seven of the twenty republics—a group that included not merely Argentina, Chile, and Paraguay, but Venezuela, Colombia, and El Salvador in the Caribbean danger zone and Mexico on the southern flank of the United States—and against pro-German sentiments in some of the neutral states. The governments of three of the seven republics described as neutral were accused of being decidedly pro-German, and one of the three, that of Mexico, undoubtedly was.

More important than official attitudes, however, were the foods and strategic materials furnished by the Latin-American countries. These they supplied to the Allies in abundance, since the seas were controlled by England and the United States; but only Brazil and Cuba offered military aid, which was all but negligible because of conditions largely outside their control.

LATIN AMERICA AND THE LEAGUE OF NATIONS

The majority of the countries of the region, neutrals and belligerents, took part in the peace conference at Versailles, and ten of them became charter members of the League of Nations, which practically all of the twenty republics eventually joined, although some were far less enthusiastic and active participants than others. It was not that Latin Americans for the most part did not believe in the general principles upon which the League was based; it was rather that they objected to its failure to recognize the legal equality of states and doubted the sincerity of some of the great powers. Multilateral diplomacy, arbitration, and judicial settlement of disputes were distinctly to their advantage in dealing with the more powerful nations of the world, and the League not only gave promise of protecting them from the United States but offered them an excellent opportunity to express their grievances against the big neighbor that had refused to join the world organization which its distinguished chief executive had sponsored. As a matter of fact, the representatives of the leading European powers in the League made special efforts to attach the Latin Americans to it, electing or appointing them to many important positions, establishing a special Liaison Bureau, sending the League Secretariat on a visit to Latin America, and compiling and publishing two volumes on the social legislation of the region.

It must be admitted, however, that the League of Nations took little part in the settlement of Latin-American disputes. It refused to deal with the Tacna-Arica problem, which had long prevented friendly relations between Chile on the one hand and Peru and Bolivia on the other; it also failed to deal with a boundary dispute between Panama and Costa Rica; and its efforts to settle the Chaco dispute between Bolivia and Paraguay proved futile. For these shortcomings the Latin-American countries and the United States were partially to blame. The Washington authorities were opposed to the League's operations in America and hoped to have American problems solved by Americans rather than by diplomats from the outside. Chile objected to the League's interference in the Tacna-Arica question, and Bolivia and Paraguay attempted to play the League and the United States against each other.

LATER SPANISH PROPAGANDA

Spain's propaganda for *Hispanismo* and against the United States was not interrupted by the war; French propaganda was soon resumed; and it was not long until Italy, Germany, and England (rather *sub rosa*) joined in the general criticism and attack. In spite of—and sometimes because of—the large stream of capital that flowed from the United States into the neighboring countries, resentment against the *"Yanquis"* rose to a high pitch during the 1920's. Suspicion and hostility, fomented not merely by the propaganda of rivals but also by "dollar diplomacy" and the intervention policy of the Harding and Coolidge administrations, pervaded almost the entire region except Brazil.[25]

Spanish interest in Spaniards overseas was actually intensified by the global conflict, and enthusiasm for Pan-Hispanism continued thereafter without abatement. Space does not permit an analysis of the various activities or the literature. For the period of the 1920's it must suffice to mention the titles of a few books which stressed the anti-Yankee phase of the movement. Luís Araquistaín published *The Yankee Peril* in 1921 and *The Antillean Agony* in 1928.[26] Both were violent diatribes. Camillo Barcia's *North American Post-War Foreign Policy* came off the press in 1924 and his *Petroleum Imperialism and World Peace* appeared the next year.[27] Alberto Ghiraldo's *Barbarous Yankee-land* was published in 1929.[28] Four of these works and the second edition of Araquistaín's *Yankee Peril* were issued after the beginning of the Primo de Rivera dictatorship in Spain and probably had to be passed upon by the government censors. At any rate, Primo revealed his deep interest in Pan-Hispanism by official approval of many activities to promote it.

With the arrival of the *Falange Español* and the Francisco Franco dictatorship, the movement entered a new phase. Pan-Hispanism, or

Hispanismo, as it was usually called, became *Hispanidad.* The difference was considerable. The first was mainly liberal and rarely politically aggressive despite the extreme utterances of some of its champions. The second was reactionary and frankly imperialistic. The first stressed race, culture, and commerce and was, on the whole, defensive and rather pacific. The second emphasized not only race and culture but religion, military glory, and the grandeur of empire and was uniformly violent in its hostility toward the United States, whereas Altamira and other scholars of his type had tended to tone down the extravagant pronouncements of such champions of *Hispanismo* as Araquistaín, Barcia, and Ghiraldo. *Hispanismo* was generally not unfriendly toward democracy and freedom. *Hispanidad* lauded Fascism and denounced, berated, and ridiculed the whole democratic system. To what extent the utterances of its proponents were exaggerated in order to appease the Nazis and avoid conquest by Germany it is impossible to say, but there is little doubt that its devotees were mostly fanatics.[29]

"Spain has always been Catholic in spirit," declared Joaquín Arraras. "Franco, moreover, is a religious man. . . . Religion gives character to Spanish civilization and culture." "Spain is the true heir of Catholic Europe," contended José Permartín. "The other nations have been only planets and satellites receiving indirect light, dim and reflected, from the Church, depository of Truth." Spain, which had always defended Europe against paganism, was now shielding it against Communism, which "is nothing but the last consequences of the Reformation and Cartesian Rationalism." Spain must continue the fight, endowing "Western Civilization with Model Institutions" and sharing the "immortal spirit" of her "Catholic Culture" with the "young nations of Hispanic America." *Hispanidad's* mission must be "to expand our great Hispanic, Latin Christian culture and our political grand-mastership . . . over those American countries of Hispano-Iberian soul and language."

The *Falange Español* announced its will to empire as early as 1936. Regarding the Latin-American nations, it declared its intention to "tighten the links of culture, economic interest, and power." "Spain claims to be the spiritual axle of the Spanish World." [30] Franco exhorted his followers early in 1939 to recall those early *"Conquistadores* who had spread throughout the world the faith and will of the nation." "We should have a will to empire," he declared. On March 24, 1940, he is said to have written this sentence in the guest book of the Archive of the Indies: "Before the relics of our Empire, with the promise of another." The *Falange Exterior* was organized in 1938 and the Council of *Hispanidad* two years later.

Latin America was now subjected to more intense propaganda than ever before. Newspapers were founded or subsidized and radio programs inaugurated throughout the region. Organizers and secret agents were dispatched to practically every country. "Our missionary labor has begun," proclaimed one of the *Falangista* journals. "Spanish America again turns its eyes to us and again on the other side of the Atlantic there are bent knees for the triumph of Franco. The race once more has heard the voice of God, and *Hispanidad,* aware of its mission, is again on the march. . . . It is the work of the *Falange* to unify . . . in their souls the pride of our old glory; and to . . . shout to the world that our jurisprudence, our industry, and our spiritual influence have the right to hegemony over a third of the earth. . . ." [31]

Of course, this mission could not be achieved without vociferous denunciation of the United States. A *Falange* propaganda sheet in Mexico declared that the United States was "driven by a thirst for dominating other people." "Still unsatisfied" with its vast continental territory and its outlying empire, it "now wants control of all the countries of Latin America, rightful sons of Spain." [32] *Voz de España,* San Sebastián, Spain, contained this friendly comment on December 7, 1938: "With a cynicism that breaks all world records . . . the United States, through the voice of that man they call the First Citizen of the World, have constituted themselves the defenders of the moral values of the Occident. . . . The country of divorce, of Lynch Law, of Four Hundred sects, of universities where a doctorate of philosophy may be bought for a bagatelle . . . the country of gangsters, of thieving mayors . . . of birth control, the country where dogs are protected and Negroes persecuted! Is this the country that can defend the culture and values of the Occident?"

🐚 BITTER FRENCH COMMENTS OF THE 1920's

Desperate as France's plight was during World War I, Frenchmen managed to make surveys of the economic interests, the cultural influence, and the prestige of France in Latin America. The war and its aftermath reduced their investments and hampered their trade; but there were not a few French enthusiasts who were determined to recoup their nation's losses. Among them were some still under the spell of Pan-Latinism who were prompt to renew the French denunciation of the policies and activities of the United States and its business interests.

The post-bellum era had scarcely begun when a French journalist named Lafon declared [33] that one of the "inevitable consequences of the European war" would be a "most terrible competition in Latin America," a competition that would not be limited to commerce but would "extend itself to all fields of human activity." "There will be a political, financial, industrial, and intellectual contest," he warned. "It is necessary to prepare for it." Taking up again the old refrains of Pan-Latinism and resentment toward the United States, he continued: "There are two competitors, Europe and the United States. The United States displays the Monroe Doctrine to exclude, if possible, from the southern markets European capital and production. But the South prefers her liberty to purely geographical union. Her points of contact with North America are few. Neither language nor race, nor customs, nor religion are included. She will gain little if she enters the orbit of the United States, but on the contrary will lose much." Insisting that "Latinity" was not a "vague and literary phrase" but a real force "in many economic and political problems," Lafon declared that European immigrants were the most active elements in these countries, that they had maintained close ties with their several fatherlands, and that while their descendants called themselves the "sons" of their adopted countries, those from Latin Europe had no disposition to deny that they were Latins. Moreover: "The Latin republics of America feel their affinity of race for the Latins of Europe." The article ended with this practical advice: "We must prepare promptly an army of young men for this new struggle. . . . Only thus shall we be able to conquer the place which the Latins deserve."

More hostile in tone was *Le Correspondent*. It published an article in 1921 which accused the United States of preventing Costa Rica and Nicaragua from joining the movement to restore the old Central American union; and two years later it repeated the charge, adding that the objective of the United States was the domination of the little republics of the region, and bitterly denounced the postwar policy of the Washington government with respect to Mexico and all the Caribbean countries.[34]

The year 1923 offered two tempting occasions for violent French criticism of the Latin-American policy of the United States: the centennial of the Monroe Doctrine and the Pan-American Conference at Santiago, Chile. Pierre Arthuys opened the discussion with a bitter article [35] on "dollar diplomacy," and other French journalists soon joined in the barrage.

Arthuys charged that the United States was attempting to reduce its neighbors to "economic fiefs, through the agencies of trusts, financial control, loans, and political intervention," and admitted that it might succeed in its nefarious efforts. "Europe is financially pauperized and politically insolvent. Latin America cannot maintain itself and make progress without foreign aid. Its needs play directly into the hands of the Yankee graspers for power. Wall Street lends money freely because it gives them the key to the door of every one of these countries."

"Your Yankee," continued Arthuys, "is a hard-headed, practical man, keenly alive to his own interests. So he insists that customs duties shall be pledged—or city revenues in case of a municipality—as security for what he lends. He likes still better to place a man of his own in charge of the customs-houses, or even of the nation's treasury," thus controlling the "funds that pay the salaries of presidents, cabinets, and the civil service." Such action meant not only curtailment of sovereignty but almost complete domination. "Administering the customs, standing guard over the goods that leave the country and the goods that enter it, the Americans are indeed economic masters. They can easily show favor to their own products and discriminate against those of foreign countries. Whenever they get control, they boycott our manufactures, for the United States recognizes no friends when it comes to business."

Having revealed the main basis of his animosity in this last sentence, Arthuys opened up his biggest guns and accused American business interests of fomenting revolutions. "American money has played a part in many such disturbances and has thereby created excuses for intervention and eventual subjugation. Most Mexican revolutions have been fomented by Yankee intrigue. The Republic of Panama . . . owes its existence to a revolution supported by Americans. The civil dissensions in Nicaragua, followed by . . . military occupation, the seizure of Santo Domingo, the practical absorption of Haiti, the dictation to Cuba that makes it a virtual vassal of the United States, all accord with the fundamental policy of a country that represents itself to Europe as a champion of political liberty."

Unable to conclude his article without attacking the Monroe Doctrine, Arthuys disposed of it with fierce brevity, describing it as a "hypocritical charter of North American monopoly" that functioned as a "cover for Yankee imperialism" and prevented "France from exercising her . . . rights in America," and climaxing his assault with this tirade: "It makes no difference whether Democrats or Republicans are in power in Washington. . . . For they do not represent two parties, but two plutocracies. . . . For the American government now rests upon a monarchy of gold and an aristocracy of finance. It is the prototype of that quantitative civilization that is striving to erect a new form of feudalism in the modern world."

After this opening diatribe the attacks of other Frenchmen, bitter as they were, seem rather restrained, and they need not be analyzed at length. *Le Temps* emphasized Latin-American distrust of the United States, which was refusing to assume any responsibility for world organization while seeking to extend its "political control over Mexico, Central America, and the Antilles," and predicted that the American delegates at Santiago would bind Latin America more firmly to the League of Nations by their efforts to prevent the conference from "doing anything which goes against their imperialistic interpretation of the Monroe Doctrine." *La Liberté,* speaking scornfully of loans with "Draconian guaranties," jubilantly proclaimed that Pan-Americanism was "stuck on a reef." The United States was confronting strong opposition in the practical application of its "badly camouflaged imperialism." Then the Pan-Latin note: "Latin Americans have not forgotten that they are Latin. They know Latin Culture has nourished them, and that even at the origin of their independent life it was the technicians and financiers of Europe who supported and aided them." [36] Louis Guilaine, in two articles published in *L'Europe nouvelle,*[37] declared that the Monroe Doctrine had become the foundation for an offensive which tended to evict Europe from the American continent and subject Latin America to Yankee control and tutelage. The United States was sitting in judgment upon the morality of the Latin governments in America, but who would judge the morals of the United States? He hoped and believed that the nations of Latin America were determined to repudiate "all imperialism and all hegemony" and seek an equilibrium in American Latinism and *rapprochement* with Europe.

French writers continued their denunciation until the United States revealed by its actions that it was receding from its "imperialism" and until conditions in Europe clearly presaged another global war. In early 1927, for instance, the Paris newspapers made a vigorous attack on the Mexican and Nicaraguan policies of the Washington government. An Associated Press dispatch sent out from the French capital on January 7 stated that the condemnation was universal, newspapers of all parties and all classes joining in the general tirade. One of the dailies headed its attack with the cynical phrase, "For Christ and petroleum," and the radical *Humanité* even went so far as to assert that Yankee imperialism in 1927 was becoming more dreadful than the German imperialism of a decade before. The denunciation was so severe that the French government felt obliged to announce that it had "nothing in common" with the newspaper attacks.[38]

⚜ AN EPOCH OF COMPARATIVE HARMONY IN INTER-AMERICAN RELATIONS

Such were the half-truths, exaggerations, and inventions of the Spanish and French journalists, printed in the languages that Latin Americans could most easily read and in the journals they were most likely to peruse. Other rivals of the United States engaged in similar denunciation and misrepresentation either covertly or openly. They also attacked one another, of course; but the United States was the main target because it was the main competitor. The major effects were to make a rather aggressive policy seem worse than it was, to deepen suspicion and increase resentment throughout Spanish America against the leading American republic, and eventually, with the aid of the anti-imperialists in the United States, to cause a change of front in Washington.

It had been difficult for the people of the United States to follow the path of empire without pangs of conscience. Since the beginning of the "new imperialism" in the last quarter of the nineteenth century its proponents had confronted strong domestic opposition. Wilson and Bryan had suggested a change in objectives, if not in practice, and a halting recession from imperialism began before the end of the 1920's. Even Calvin Coolidge became somewhat more conciliatory in dealing with Latin America during the last years of his administration, and Herbert Hoover, who made a tour of inspection in the countries to the south before taking up the duties of his high office, effected several modifications in Republican procedure.

Such changes as occurred between 1924 and early 1933, however, were carried out piecemeal and almost surreptitiously. There was no frank announcement of the new orientation, and the government seemed to act reluctantly under the pressure of strong opposition in the United States, Latin America, and a good part of the Western World. It remained for Franklin D. Roosevelt, who had been denouncing hallowed Republican practices since 1928, to proclaim the new policy from the housetop, name it the Good Neighbor Policy, and speed up the recession with a happy flair. As noted elsewhere in this volume, the five protectorates were abandoned by the early 1940's and intervention in the domestic affairs of the Latin-American republics ceased.

The rise of communism, fascism, and the nazi movement in Europe probably had nothing to do with the change of front; but the new policy was inaugurated and carried to completion at the precise period when it could become most useful in counteracting totalitarian propaganda. Most of the Latin Americans were soon so thoroughly convinced of the sincerity of their big neighbor that the propaganda lines of earlier years lost their appeal. Hitler, Mussolini, Franco, and their agents could no longer persuade the American Latins that the United States was the only threat to their progress and security.

Most of the Latin nations of the New World collaborated with the United States from the outbreak of the second global war, and when the "Colossus" was attacked and involved in the gigantic conflict, all except Chile and Argentina were prompt to follow the maxim that an attack on one American nation is tantamount to an attack on them all. There was plenty of uneasiness in the United States with respect to totalitarian agents south of the Rio Grande, an uneasiness deliberately played upon by some of the journalists of the war period; but it turned out that the Latin-American leaders were able to distinguish friend from foe. All the propaganda and chicanery of the Axis powers proved futile, save in Argentina and possibly Chile, where other considerations were probably decisive in the reluctance of these two republics to go along with the rest.

By the end of January, 1942, nine of the Latin-American governments had declared war on Germany, Italy, and Japan and nine others had severed relations with them; and the war declaration became unanimous before the end of the global conflict. The republics to the south were therefore entitled to participate in the San Francisco Conference of early 1945, which all of them did. Their major contribution to the Charter of the United Nations, of which all immediately became members, was their insistence on the preservation of the right to utilize regional organizations for security purposes. This was a striking expression of their devotion to the Pan-American movement, which had not appealed to them strongly until the United States receded from its interventionist policy, relaxed its pressure in behalf of the economic interests of its nationals, and disclosed a more genuine devotion to cultural relations and the general welfare of its neighbors. A regional defense pact was signed in Rio de Janeiro in 1947 and the Pan American Union became the Organization of the American States the following year.

As the Latin-American countries entered the post-war era, two international problems occupied the minds of their leaders: expansion of foreign investment and the involvement of their nations in the perilous contest between Soviet Russia and the Western powers, particularly the United States. The problems were very closely connected, but the second was fundamental. If "containment of communism" continued to require immense outlays for Europe and other parts of the Old World by the only nation that had much available capital to invest abroad, the Latin Americans would be compelled to shift largely for themselves except in the production of minerals and metals.[39] If the containment policy should lead to war, they would certainly be deeply involved in one way or another. They might avoid military combat as all but two of them had avoided it in World War I and all but three in World War II; but their economies would be profoundly affected by the immense demand for foods and strategic materials and by scarcities in manufactured products, especially capital goods for the continued expansion of their factories.

In face of the contest between a dual alignment of the great powers in the atomic age they were more helpless than ever. Membership in the United Nations had little significance for them; there seemed to be nothing that they could do to relieve the bipolar tension. Like most other small countries, they were in some respects satellites and victims. But there was no question about the orbit in which they revolved. They were a part of the constellation of the West. There were some Communists in their midst, but the Communists had never been a serious threat in the past and were not likely to become a serious threat in the future, provided the Latin-American leaders could find the will and the way to improve levels of living, enlighten their people, and provide wider outlets for their energies and talents. The major domestic peril at mid-century seemed to be the twin dangers of extreme radicalism and Bourbon reaction. By means of technical and economic aid, perhaps the United States, directly and through the United Nations and its affiliated agencies, could make a major contribution to the economic progress of these neighboring nations. To instill a spirit of democracy and progressivism into some of their despotic and conservative leaders and of patient restraint into their peoples probably would be more difficult in the face of extreme national sensitivities. As the sixth decade of the twentieth century approached its end, several despots were assassinated or driven from power. As of May, 1958, only the Dominican Republic, Cuba, Nicaragua, and Paraguay were dominated by dictators. But many Latin Americans were worried about access to the markets and the government finances of their big neighbor to the north.

CHAPTER XXXIV

Latin-American Civilization at Mid-Century

SALIENT CHARACTERISTICS AND PATTERNS OF VALUE

Latin America of the mid-twentieth century was by no means uniform. In fact, it never had been uniform. But the diversity was now more evident than before. Some of the twenty nations comprising the region had made more rapid material and cultural progress than others. The Temperate Zone nations had forged ahead of the tropical nations, and the rate of development among these had also differed. Racial components were not universally the same and tended toward greater variation as some republics became less Caucasian and others, by virtue of immigration, became far more so. There were also marked differences between the various sections of the same countries, especially between the littoral and the deep interior and between the urban and the rural areas. But resemblances were more striking than differences, so that is was still possible to speak of a Latin-American civilization without straining the imagination or seriously departing from realities.

The Latin American was usually an individualist. He loathed standardization. He did not like the restraints of organization and teamwork. He had no great eagerness to carry on business by means of big corporations like those so prevalent in the United States and Western Europe. He was likely to expect the government to take charge of enterprises when they seemed too big for business partnerships composed of small associations of kinsmen and personal friends (although both native corporations—the sons of immigrants figuring largely here—and the stock market had made their appearance in some of the larger republics). He looked upon government mainly as a personal matter and preferred to have it run by self-confident, energetic, and dramatic leaders; issues were incarnated in the personages who championed them.

The Latin American was dignified. He stressed ceremony and etiquette. He liked to say pleasant things and shower his companions and acquaintances with compliments in the manner of the lords and knights of the Age of Chivalry. He did not relish much informality or familiarity. He disapproved of knuckle-cracking handshakes and boisterous backslapping, and rarely engaged in hilarious laughter. He disliked clowning, rough humor, and practical jokes. He danced gravely, drank quietly and with moderation, and accorded his friends and associates a deference which he expected to be reciprocated.

The Latin American was usually polite and accommodating. He lifted his hat when meeting friends and acquaintances, men as well as women, offered to let others precede him in entering doors, elevators, trains, and steamers, and was prompt to assist a stranger who had lost his way or seemed to be in distress for any other reason.

The Latin American rarely appeared to be in a great hurry. He took time for polite inquiries about the members of the families of those whom he met in the course of business or pleasure, for congratulation or commiseration, and for conversation on the topics of the day.

These were the most obvious Latin-American traits. They were especially characteristic of the members of the upper class, but they tended to reach down to the bottom layers of society. There was much kindness and gentility in these countries despite their rough and violent politics. Variations from type, in dress, mode of living, or other respects, were tolerated as expressions of personal taste never to be lightly condemned.

Family ties were strong, particularly in the upper and the small middle class. Although tending to decrease in size, families were still generally large, and each member was likely to feel a keen sense of obligation for every other member. Agricultural, pastoral, and business enterprises of all sorts were still mainly family enterprises upon which parents, children, and grandchildren depended for their livings. Even government and public administration were often family affairs; nepotism was widespread.

Although considerable progress had been made in the equalization of the sexes, women still occupied what would generally be described as a very subordinate place in the social order. They were not very active in business or public affairs. Some middle-class women worked in offices or mercantile establishments, and the women of both the upper-middle and the wealthy classes belonged to charity organizations and occasionally joined the professions or took part in politics; but the male members of the aristocracies, who still largely determined the value patterns, preferred to keep their women in seclusion, clinging to the traditional view that the ordained place for the "weaker sex" was in the home or the convent. More and more schoolteachers were required, however, and more and more women were entering the lower ranks of the teaching profession, where they sometimes taught classes of boys as well as girls, although the sexes usually were segregated in different rooms or sent to separate schools. The women of the lower classes had always been compelled to work, of course, both in the fields and in the household industries, and had filled the market places for centuries; but in recent years they were also entering the factories and the less remunerative occupations in the business life of the towns and cities.

Strange as it may seem, Latin-American society was stable in spite of its turbulent politics. The people of the region were not uprooted and unanchored as they were in the highly industrialized countries where political conditions were usually more tranquil. Homes, estates, and business establishments remained in the same families for generations. Relatives (when some were not in exile) lived close together, often in the same large dwelling or in adjacent apartments, with numerous servants (the household servant group, in the cities and towns and on the big rural estates, composed a surprisingly large percentage of the total population). Family members, including all the in-laws and the first, second, and third cousins, saw each other frequently and not merely at weddings and funerals. Latin-American civilization had not yet fully emerged from the patriarchal stage.

Latin America continued to be overwhelmingly Catholic notwithstanding the many conflicts between Church and State. The people of some countries were more ardently devoted to their religion and its institutions than the people of others; relations between Church and State varied from republic to republic, some having affected a complete separation while others still granted subsidies to the church in return for state supervision, or exercised supervision as in Mexico even without granting subsidies. The wealth and influence of the church were by no means equal in the twenty republics, but nowhere had non-Catholic creeds made marked progress. They were now tolerated in all the countries, and not merely tolerated but welcomed and officially encouraged in some; yet Roman Catholicism continued to hold sway in spite of growing skepticism and religious indifference in some male intellectual circles. Its hold on the common people and the women of all classes was especially strong; so evident, in fact, that political leaders hesitated until very recently to grant women suffrage, fearing that the step might result in a vast increase of the temporal power of the ecclesiastical organization. Cathedrals, churches, and monasteries, many of them built in Colonial days but not a few during the national period, were probably more numerous and only a little less beautiful and impressive than in medieval Europe. This was especially true in the towns and cities, where the clanging of church bells was almost continuous.

Latin-American civilization was still aristocratic and humanistic rather than democratic and scientific, speculative rather than experimental, literary and artistic rather than technological. Latin Americans preferred opera houses to factories, society and politics to business. Their poetry, essays, and novels were likely to have more merit than their works on history and economics; and notwithstanding their achievements in mining, engineering, architecture, and medicine, they seemed to have more talent for painting, sculpture, and music than for the practical arts and industries. Their fondness for leisure persisted; most members of the upper class and of the one next below would suffer great poverty rather than work with their hands. They were not, and never had been, the kind of men that cleared away the forests and built log cabins in the wilderness. All societies tend to develop a repugance to manual toil; but for centuries Latin Americans had felt it. Traditions brought over from Spain and Portugal of the military crusading period had been reinforced by the presence of cheap labor, Indian, mestizo, Negro, mulatto, and indigent immigrant. Nor was leisure to be spent in physical exercise or sports, unless the witnessing of horse-races or bull-fights could be thus described. Physical training and vigorous games like football and baseball had only recently been taken up by the youth, who usually occupied themselves, when not in class or engaged in study, with dinners, dances, and love-making or with student and other politics. In short, most Latin Americans had more capacity for the enjoyment of their environment than for its mastery. As a general rule, they had lacked, and they still lacked, efficiency in the development of their material resources and enthusiasm for commercial and industrial enterprise. Money was spent on consumption, conspicuous or otherwise; it was not hoarded or invested to the extent that prevailed in the United States, for instance, or France. Much of it was spent on fine clothes, furniture, banquets, the cinema and the opera, and short excursions to resorts or long voyages abroad. What was left was invested mainly in real estate or mines, although interest in mercantile firms and manufacturing plants was increasing, particularly in countries that had received large groups of immigrants.

Because of their disorderly politics and their failure to make fuller use of their resources, the Latin-American countries were still generally classed among the more "backward" nations. They themselves would prefer—at least until a decade or so ago—to be considered as merely different, if not even superior. They often denounced the "efficient" nations for their materialism and expatiated on the importance of the intellectual and the spiritual. Their viewpoint is not unworthy of consideration; but the stresses and strains of power politics were making drab and hard-driving efficiency the price of survival.

The population of Latin America, as already noted, had greatly expanded since independence, and especially since the 1880's. The population at independence more than doubled by 1885, multiplied itself by three and a half during the next sixty years, and was approaching 160,000,000 by the early 1950's. The birth rate was extraordinarily high everywhere except in the upper layers of the big cities. But the death rate still remained high also. Sanitation and public health were not by any means receiving sufficient attention. Disease was widespread in spite of recent advances in medicine and sanitation and the support and stimulus given by the Rockefeller Foundation and the United States government to campaigns against yellow fever, hookworm, malaria, and other maladies. Medical care was inadequate or wholly lacking in many regions and among the poor everywhere. Contagions and epidemics continued to levy heavy tolls both in life and in reduced efficiency among those who survived their assaults. The diet of many millions was deficient, not only because of poverty but also because of ignorance of food values. *Pulque, chicha,* rum*, aguardiente,* and wine were more widely consumed than milk, and were often cheaper; and milk was seldom preferred where coffee, Paraguayan tea, or other beverages could be had.

With the exception of two or three countries and some regions in a few others, the Latin-American nations had been slow to adopt mechanical devices. In many sections agricultural implements, in particular, were still primitive. Farmers were just beginning to learn to plow. Railroads and highways for the use of automotive vehicles were still inadequate almost everywhere; and while air transport had been introduced into every republic, rates were far too high for much use of airplanes by the great mass of the people. Telephones were still confined mainly to the wealthier homes of the towns and cities. The vast majority of dwellings, whether in city, town, or country, contained neither toilet facilities nor bathrooms, neither refrigerators nor radios. There were fewer automobiles and trucks in all Latin America than in Canada. The mass of the people did not own any vehicles except oxcarts or wagons, and millions did not possess these, or even beasts of burden. They not only walked long distances but carried heavy loads on their backs or heads. Men, women, and children, from Haiti and

Mexico to Bolivia and Paraguay, could be seen plodding the roads to market or the city streets with the burdens of burros or oxen. In many sections pack animals prodded by barefoot peons still trudged along the mountain trails with baggage and freight that should have been transported by trucks or railroads. In some ports and railway depots human drudges were still unloading boats and freight cars by hand in the tropical heat.

The percentage of illiteracy remained high in most of the twenty republics. It ranged from 15 to 25 per cent in Argentina (much higher in the back country), Uruguay, and Costa Rica, to 80 or 85 in Bolivia, Paraguay, Guatemala, and Haiti, and in Latin America as a whole less than half the inhabitants above the age of eight years were able to read and write. Although the governments of the various nations had long ago accepted the principle of state responsibility for the education of the people, and although primary education was both free of tuition and compulsory according to the law in practically every country, hardly anywhere were the schools sufficient to accommodate the school-age population. The primary schools were badly equipped in the majority of the republics, not a few being housed in leased buildings not adapted to educational purposes. Teachers, as a rule, were poorly paid and ill prepared, many of them mere political appointees. Low-paid and inefficient primary teachers were not confined to Latin America, of course; but with the exception of a few of the Latin-American countries and some parts of others the situation was far worse than in the United States, Canada, or some of the leading nations of Western Europe.

Secondary schools and institutions of higher learning were much better, as might be expected, in oligarchic countries. Practically every republic, no matter how small, had at least one educational plant described as a university, and countries such as Chile, Peru, Colombia, Brazil, and Argentina had from three to six or eight, besides a number of professional and technical schools.

The public library movement had not made much headway even in the larger and more progressive republics. Libraries were confined largely to the colleges and universities and to the capitals and a few other cities. Some of the best collections were private collections in the homes of the aristocrats.

In short, as suggested more than once in these pages in connection with the national histories of the several countries, the level of living for the overwhelming majority of the Latin Americans was still very low. The common people of Uruguay, Costa Rica, a good part of Argentina, and some sections of three or four other countries were the only exceptions. Wealth was highly concentrated everywhere save in Haiti (where there was little wealth to concentrate), in Costa Rica and Uruguay, and possibly in Colombia and El Salvador. Big estates were the rule except in the countries mentioned, in parts of Brazil, and in Mexico, where there were still close to 9,000 latifundia. Wages were close to the subsistence level in most of the republics, although Costa Rica, Uruguay, urban Argentina, and some parts of other republics, especially in the major industrial centers and in most of the foreign enterprises, must again be excepted. The great mass of the people rarely owned any real estate or lived in other than cramped and desolate quarters, where they had few of the conveniences or comforts of civilized life. Millions were shoeless, and while not suffering from the cold, since Latin America had a lot of barefoot weather, they were exposed to many kinds of insects, germs, and infections. Better levels and standards of living could be attained only by arousing latent desires and ambitions through improvements in education and health, by a more general utilization of technology, and by a wider distribution of wealth.

Latin America's economy was still mainly a raw-material economy. Its inhabitants, for the most part, obtained their livelihood and wealth from farms, ranches, mines, and forests. The output of manufacturing establishments was still comparatively insignificant in most countries, and manufactured goods, whether produced in the household or the factory, were sold almost entirely in the domestic markets. Although the industrial revolution was well under way in such republics as Argentina, Uruguay, Brazil, Chile, Colombia, and Mexico, the region had comparatively few heavy industries and continued to import more manufactured commodities than were produced at home. Few of the countries were able to construct ocean liners or war vessels, transport or bombing planes, locomotives or automobiles (although some airplanes and autos were assembled), dynamos or other heavy electrical equipment, threshing machines or reapers, complicated machinery for mines and factories, steel rails or passenger coaches, structural steel for bridges and skyscrapers, or machine tools of any kind. For all of these basic commodities of the Machine Age they must depend largely upon foreign producers. Many of their biggest and best manufacturing plants were either owned or managed by aliens. Their most efficient agricultural enterprises were still producing mainly for foreign markets. Little effort had been made to improve methods in those producing for home consumption. Establishments engaged in processing meat and sugar were usually in foreign hands, and so were the big organizations extracting metals and minerals, excepting petroleum in Mexico and Argentina, and in Brazil, Bolivia, and Chile, where the oil industry was only at its beginning. The Peruvian government, however, owned one petroleum enterprise, and the Colombian government was entering the industry. The banana business was owned or controlled by alien capitalists, who usually dominated also a good part of the coffee industry, by one means or another.

⚡ MAJOR CAUSES OF RETARDATION

The predominantly raw-material and rural economy of Latin America largely accounted for the character of its civilization. All such civilizations have been comparatively poor. To provide educational, health, and other services for people scattered over hundreds of thousands of square miles of countryside or living in hundreds of small towns and villages was an expensive and difficult task.

The attitude of the upper classes toward manual labor, large-scale business organization, civic improvements (anywhere except in the leading towns and cities where most of them lived), and the welfare of the masses was another important factor. It meant that many of the more intelligent and talented groups in most of the countries failed to devote themselves energetically either to increasing the national wealth or to improving the economic efficiency of the millions who composed the lower classes.

This was undoubtedly one of the important reasons why the Latin-American countries continued to be primary producers. Other significant factors must not be overlooked, however. In the first place, it must be remembered that they got a late start in the movement toward mechanization and industrialization, that outside pressures for foods and crude materials were tremendous, and that local manufacturing industries faced strong competition from the more highly developed nations even in spite of the tariffs, which the landed aristocracies usually opposed except for revenue purposes. More important still were such factors as physical environment, racial composition, colonial heritage, and the long and bloody struggle for independence. Failure to recall these would be to ignore the most important influences accounting for the "backwardness" of the region and do the Latin Americans grave injustice.

It should not be forgotten that the majority of the countries are situated in the tropics, where their inhabitants have had to confront the handicaps of tropical insects, reptiles, and disease, constant debilitating heat in most regions, tropical floods in others, and large stretches of jungle or desert difficult to master for economic purposes. In fact, nearly a third of Latin America is choked with dense forests and luxuriant undergrowth; almost another third consists of giant mountains, some of which suggest a conspiracy between the Creator and Orville Wright, while other vast stretches are arid or semiarid; and more than half of the area has tempting siesta weather. It is true that there are many elevated tropical sections with pleasant and even invigorating climates the year round; but much of tropical Latin America does not rise high above the sea and is exposed to humid heat. It will be recalled that of the twenty countries only Uruguay, most of Argentina and Chile, and parts of Paraguay, Brazil, and Mexico are situated in the Temperate Zones.

Much of the region is likewise in the earthquake and volcanic zone where life and property can never be safe. Numerous settlements had been destroyed repeatedly, and such calamities may have nurtured superstition or tended to create an improvident and listless fatalism.

It is necessary to recall also that three-fourths of the nations are too small to provide markets for large-scale and more efficient manufacturing plants, that nearly all of them lack either iron ore or good coking coal for smelting it, and that many of the regions best adapted to habitation are situated in the interior highlands, with mountains, jungle, and steaming heat between them and the seacoasts. Occupation of Latin America had not been characterized, in general, by a progressive and vigorous advance from the coast toward the interior. There were no frontier movements in these countries of the type that so profoundly influenced society and politics in the United States—no great areas of fertile lands in agreeable climates to be occupied with comparative ease by small farmers moving into them in successive waves and thus giving increased mobility, creative activity, renewed vitality, and greater democracy to Latin-American life. In regions where such a frontier movement might have taken place, as in northern Mexico, southern Chile, western Argentina, southern Brazil, southeastern Colombia, or central Venezuela, scarcity of water, unfavorable seasonal distribution of rainfall or too much of it, debilitating climates, mountain barriers or immense distances separating the frontier regions from the leading markets, or agrarian policies that permitted extreme concentration of ownership usually made impossible a frontier development like that which occurred in the United States.

Such physical handicaps and undemocratic land policies were very important factors in retarding Latin America's economic progress. They were by no means offset by rich soils and an abundance of minerals, metals, and forests.

Racial composition should also be brought back into the general perspective. The region probably contained some 20,000,000 semi-civilized Indians and several millions more of the nomadic or largely

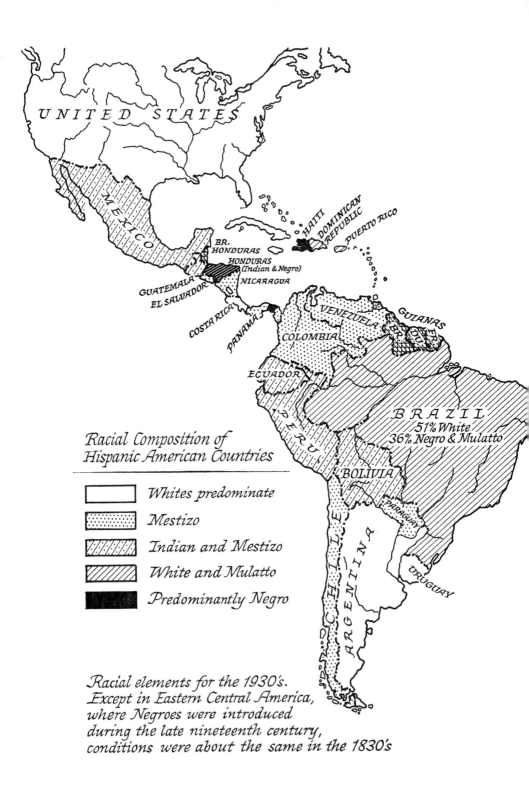

UNITED STATES

MEXICO

BR. HONDURAS
HONDURAS
(Indian & Negro)
GUATEMALA
EL SALVADOR   NICARAGUA

COSTA RICA

PANAMA

HAITI
DOMINICAN
REPUBLIC
PUERTO RICO

VENEZUELA   GUIANAS

COLOMBIA

ECUADOR

PERU

BRAZIL
51% White
36% Negro & Mulatto

BOLIVIA

PARAGUAY

CHILE

ARGENTINA

URUGUAY

Racial Composition of
Hispanic American Countries

Whites predominate

Mestizo

Indian and Mestizo

White and Mulatto

Predominantly Negro

Racial elements for the 1930's.
Except in Eastern Central America,
where Negroes were introduced
during the late nineteenth century,
conditions were about the same in the 1830's

MAP 14

nomadic type familiar in the United States at the time the Europeans began its conquest. Millions were exterminated during the ensuing decades, but millions also survived and their descendants became humble citizens of the new republics. There were around 8,000,000 Indians and some 5,000,000 to 6,000,000 mestizos in Latin America in the 1820's. There were also more than 3,500,000 Negroes and another 1,000,000 mulattoes. The white population, in contrast, numbered only approximately 4,000,000 and was very unevenly distributed, so that at the beginning of the National period the primitive and mixed peoples not only outnumbered the whites in the region as a whole but far outnumbered them in practically every country save Uruguay, Costa Rica, and possibly Chile and Argentina. And they still outnumbered the Caucasians two or three to one in Latin America as a whole in the 1950's, although they had practically disappeared in Costa Rica, Uruguay, Argentina, Chile, and southern Brazil, where recent European immigrants had greatly expanded the Caucasian components of the population. Negroes and mixtures of African and other races formed a large percentage of the inhabitants in the Caribbean island republics, in Panama and all the banana belts of Central America, in Colombia, Venezuela, and Ecuador, and in the tropical regions of Brazil. The majority of the Indians and mestizos were still living in the highlands stretching from Mexico to Bolivia, where the denser native settlements were found by the conquering Spaniards, and in Paraguay, which had been the scene of the Jesuit missions. They accounted for the bulk of the inhabitants in Mexico and Central America, excepting Costa Rica and Panama, in the Andean republics of Ecuador, Peru, and Bolivia, in the Paraguayan plains and hills beyond, and perhaps also in Venezuela. The pure Indians alone were probably more numerous than all other elements combined in Mexico, Guatemala, Peru, and Bolivia. Most of the inhabitants of both the lowland and the highland tropics belonged to the primitive and mixed peoples. The rate of progress in the region should be considered in the light of its racial composition as well as its geography.

These primitive and mixed races, whatever their ultimate capacity or destiny, greatly depressed the general cultural level. Man's advance from barbarism to what writers have been pleased to call civilization has been a very slow process, and the Indians and Negroes, particularly the latter, started very late. The upper classes in Latin America were too little concerned about the progress of their humbler fellow citizens; but even if the dominant groups in each country had taken greater interest in them, one may seriously doubt whether they could have been lifted to a very much higher plane of living within so short a period.

The association and mixture of such races and cultures was accompanied by confusion and misunderstanding; the presence of the primitive peoples and their mixed offspring contributed to upper-class lethargy and made agreement on ideals, objectives, political personnel, and methods more difficult to reach.

The heritage from Spain and Portugal was a further handicap, if one assumes that the goals of Latin America were, and would continue to be, democratic government, prosperity based upon skill in the applied sciences, and "freedom from want" for all the people. The main elements in this heritage, it will be remembered, were a class system; a wealthy, powerful, and intolerant church, especially in Spanish America; corrupt and tyrannical administrative habits which deprived the colonials of experience in public affairs and left them without correct standards; a poor and illiterate mass at the base of the social pyramid; and only a tiny middle class between this mass and the colonial authorities and wealthy creoles above. The dawn of the era of science, technology, and democracy in the United States and Western Europe reflected its first rays upon a Latin America still lingering in the Middle Ages. When finally introduced, the new processes and techniques were brought in mainly by foreigners, who continued to own and control or operate them for nearly a century after their arrival and for many years made no special effort to transfer them to the the Latin Americans.

Finally, the long and destructive wars for independence must again be taken into account. Only Central America, Paraguay, and Brazil escaped them. The struggle dragged on elsewhere for ten or fifteen years, as compared with six in the English colonies which became the United States. The Spanish Americans had to borrow many millions and resort to widespread confiscation in order to finance their emancipation; and at the end of their struggle for independence the new nations were deeply in debt, physically and economically depleted, without much experience in public administration, almost barren of civic leadership, and under the domination of militarism, which held them in subjection for two or three generations—longer in many instances. Force was exalted above enlightenment, persuasion, and consent. The masses were either drafted into armies employed in the bitter contests for power or seduced by promises which hardly anybody intended to keep. Little Haiti was compelled by France to acknowledge a debt of 60,000,000 francs in order to secure French recognition of its independence, and the new Brazilian government felt obliged not only to pay Portugal a large sum for recognition but also to grant special commercial concessions to the British government in compensation for its influence at Lisbon.

HOPE FOR A BRIGHTER FUTURE

Such were the heavy handicaps the Latin Americans confronted, and such, in broad terms, was the character of their civilization in the middle of the twentieth century. Perhaps the culture of the upper classes should be given a little more emphasis before concluding this discussion.

The Latin American nations had produced, and were still producing, a number of excellent poets, essayists, journalists, and novelists, some able historians and international lawyers, a few distinguished anthropologists and sociologists, and several writers whom they ranked as *pensadores*. They had made, according to reliable critics, notable achievements in painting, in architecture, and perhaps in music and other forms of art; and while they had produced few outstanding scientists or inventors, they had attained a measure of distinction in engineering and medicine, Doctors Carlos Finlay of Cuba and Oswaldo Cruz of Brazil being among the earliest of the well-known physicians.

But only a very small fraction of the people had been given an opportunity to develop their talents. In a very real sense, Latin America's civilization was a dual civilization. The culture of the aristocracy and the small upper-middle class was quite different from the culture of the masses, although, of course, there had been considerable diffusion, especially from the top, and the two would probably amalgamate eventually. Miscegenation continued at a rapid pace, much of it without matrimony. It was not unusual for the men of higher classes to have mistresses from the lower ranks and a number of illegitimate children.

The realization that a blending of races and cultures was probably inevitable may have been one reason for a recent change in attitude on the part of the oligarchies in the countries inhabited largely by the primitive and mixed races. It is certain that the oligarchies had begun to reveal either a keener sense of responsibility for their less fortunate compatriots or a greater tact in dealing with them. They had disclosed some consideration for the masses, of course, even during the early National period, in connection with Negro slavery and Indian tributes; but this was largely a political maneuver in most cases. The humanitarian phase of African emancipation occurred later, and mainly in Brazil. Compulsory labor for trifling wages, and other forms of exploitation as well, long prevailed; debt peonage did not disappear until well after 1900 and perhaps still existed in some more or less obscure sections as late as 1950. But a definite change in outlook and disposition became quite evident during the early decades of the twentieth century. Some of the Latin-American leaders—those of Mexico, Uruguay, and

Chile may be recalled in this connection—discovered the "forgotten man" before Franklin D. Roosevelt declared his devotion to him in the United States. Slowly, in all the republics, national and local governments assumed greater responsibility for the health and education of the common people. The claims of labor were recognized and sometimes respected; wages and working conditions improved (although continuous inflation threatened to obliterate the gains); land was given to the landless in Mexico; major or minor agrarian reforms were discussed or initiated in Guatemala, Bolivia, and other republics; agencies, often rather ineffective, were set up to look after the needs and interests of the Indians in most of the Indian countries. Tax systems were also revised with the view of placing more of the burden on the wealthier classes. Income and inheritance taxes began to supplement the revenue from tariffs and excise taxes, and levies were beginning to be made on real estate, which had remained all but exempt from taxation for centuries. Price controls, although seldom well administered, were applied with special regard for the necessities of the lower classes. The general-welfare concept seemed to be taking the place of the trophy concept of government; but the hunger for government employment had not abated.

Meantime world depressions and global wars had helped to quicken the pace of manufacturing—the first by depressing prices for food and raw materials and the second by creating scarcities in manufactured goods, which had to be coped with in spite of increasing demands for beef, wheat, minerals, metals, and other crude materials to feed the armies and the war machines—and progress in manufacturing was developing the skills of the people. The region was becoming industrialized in spite of every impediment. A surprising amount of manufactured products could be turned out even where there were almost no blast furnaces.

Few observers who viewed the Latin-American nations at mid-century in the light of the handicaps they had confronted were likely to be wholly pessimistic regarding their future. The Latin peoples of America seemed destined to achieve a happy blend of humanism and science, of race and culture, of art and efficiency, of the spiritual and the material, unless their way of life should be violently interrupted or contorted by aggression from the outside.

None of the nations of the Western world, large or small, has been indifferent to this vast region. As noted in an earlier chapter, the Latin countries of America were looked upon from the beginning as outlets for surplus capital, goods, and populations and as sources for food and crude materials. Later chapters have indicated that this concept of their place in Western civilization had not appreciably changed. They also revealed that competition among the industrialized nations for these outlets and resources became more intense after the 1820's and that some of the Latin nations of Europe infused a considerable measure of sentiment into their investment and traffic. The Latin Americans were coaxed, courted, and coerced, and finally involved in the global wars (although only two or three of them took any part in actual military combat); but their domestic political affairs were less dominated by outside powers at mid-century than at any time since independence.

Although other regions of the world deemed to be in greater peril have received more bountiful assistance than has Latin America during the past decade, the competition between the Communist world and the world free from Communist domination might eventually result in benefits to Latin America in the form of technical and economic aid and private investment under a more thoughtful and benevolent management than in former times. What would happen if bipolar tensions were relaxed is difficult to predict; but the United States, at least, has indicated through the pronouncement of its highest officials that a considerable portion of any savings made possible by the reduction of military forces and armaments would be devoted to the promotion of economic progress in the underdeveloped countries. All things considered, it did not seem hazardous to predict that Latin America's future might turn out to be brighter than its past. As the inhabitants of the vast region entered the second half of the twentieth century, the major defects of Latin-American civilization were inefficiency and lack of diversity in production, intolerance in politics, and inadequate social mobility.

NOTES

NOTE TO CHAPTER I

1. These are the eight capitals referred to: Guatemala City, Tegucigalpa, San Salvador, San José, Caracas, Bogotá, Quito, La Paz. In altitude, they range from 3,000 to nearly 13,000 feet above sea level.

NOTES TO CHAPTER III

1. Carl Becker, *Beginnings of the American People* (New York, 1915), p. 4.
2. H. G. Wells, *The Outline of History* (New York, 1923), p. 677.
3. I. B. Richman, *The Spanish Conquerors* (New Haven, 1919), p. 5.
4. Vicente Yáñez Pinzón explored the northern and eastern coasts of South America a few weeks before Cabral arrived, but Pinzón was influenced by the voyage of Columbus; and so was John Cabot, who visited the coast of North America in 1497.
5. Quoted by H. D. Sedgwick in his *Short History of Spain* (New York, 1925), p. 126.
6. *Ibid.*, pp. 127–29.
7. *Ibid.*, pp. 153–54.

NOTES TO CHAPTER IV

1. The subjugation of the Pueblos was begun in 1598, and the Spanish town of Santa Fé was founded in 1610.
2. Bernal Díaz del Castillo, who was a participant and eyewitness, has written a most interesting account of the discovery and conquest of the Aztec confederation.
3. Herbert I. Priestley, *The Coming of the White Man* (New York, 1927), pp. 11–12.
4. In fact, one of Columbus's titles was viceroy, but the Columbus family soon lost the title, and it did not appear again until 1535.
5. Their distribution and the dates of their establishment were as follows: Santo Domingo, Española, 1511; Mexico City, New Spain, 1527; Panama, 1535; Lima, 1542; Guatemala City, 1543; Guadalajara, New Spain, 1548; Bogotá, New Granada, 1549; La Plata, later called Chuquisaca, in Charcas, or modern Bolivia, 1559; and Quito, which eventually became Ecuador, 1563.
6. Havana, Santo Domingo, Mexico City, San Salvador, Guatemala City, Panama, Caracas, Bogotá, Quito, Lima, Santiago, La Paz, Asunción, Buenos Aires.
7. Among those not yet in existence in 1600 were San Francisco, Los Angeles, San Antonio, Managua (Nicaragua), Barranquilla and Medellín (Colombia), Rosario (Argentina), and Montevideo.

8. *Op. cit.,* pp. 96–97. The land grants ran from 100 to 500 acres, with much more for the leader. The crown rarely sold any land during the early Colonial period.

9. Primary schools were mostly in charge of the clergy, who also founded scores of academies (*colegios*) by 1600, and with royal aid, established a few universities, those in Mexico City, Lima, and Santo Domingo being the most important. But nearly all of these educational institutions were mainly for the instruction of pupils and students of Spanish blood.

10. The Spaniards had transferred to America during the course of the century specimens of all their cereals, fruits, vegetables, and domestic animals. But most of the Indians, for security reasons, were forbidden to ride horseback—or possess firearms.

11. These were Santo Domingo, New Spain, Peru, New Granada, and Charcas, named in the order of their establishment.

12. Las Casas and probably other members of the clergy even went so far as to advocate Negro slavery as a means of lightening the burdens of the Indians; but Las Casas, at least, later felt that this was a mistake.

13. A few vessels were allowed to stop in the ports of Venezuela and Guatemala, but the port of Buenos Aires was closed except to an occasional "register" ship.

14. The destruction of the Spanish Armada by the English navy in 1588 will be recalled.

15. It is likely that some women above 18 years of age also had to pay this odious assessment.

NOTE TO CHAPTER V

1. The captaincies extended from the mouth of the Amazon to the modern state of Santa Catarina, and eventually there seems to have been thirteen, as indicated on the map. As the crown gradually purchased the rights of the grantees, the captaincies became colonial provinces, ruled by royal officials with the title of governor or captain.

NOTES TO CHAPTER VI

1. Between 1580 and 1700 there were forty-seven years during which no Spanish fleet cleared for the American colonies.

2. In Venezuela there was a range of mountains not far from the coast.

3. The basins of the Amazon, the Orinoco, and the Magdalena did not attract settlers from the mountain areas thickly populated by the native races. The settlers in the plateau regions of Venezuela and Colombia were far away from the sweltering banks of the Orinoco. It was 3,000 miles from the centers of Spanish settlement in Peru to the mouth of the Amazon, and the Spaniards of the plateau of Cundinamarca (New Granada) had nearly 100 miles betwen them and the Magdalena— which was not really well adapted to navigation—and yet another 500 miles of this river before they emerged at Cartagena or Barranquilla.

4. Most of the important towns of Spanish America were gravely injured

by earthquakes and volcanoes, many of them several times, during the Colonial period.

5. This and the following quotation are from Haring, *Trade and Navigation between Spain and the Indies* (Cambridge, Mass., 1918), pp. 113, 115.

6. In addition, Englishmen, Frenchmen, and Dutchmen established themselves in the Guianas soon after 1600; England seized Jamaica in 1655, and France occupied western Española shortly before 1700.

7. So writes Haring; but the point should not be pressed too far. The colonists often resisted the invaders and thus developed a spirit of unity and self-confidence which contributed to the independence impulse of a later era.

8. Bolton, "The Mission as a Frontier Institution . . ." in *American Historical Review*, XXIII (1917): 45.

9. *Travels* (Bohn ed.), I: 297.

10. By 1700 there were in Sinaloa only 600 families of pure Spanish blood, but many more half-caste Christians, and around 1,200 Spaniards and mestizos in San Felipe alone. In Sonora the people of Spanish or mixed blood numbered about 500 at that time. In Chihuahua, Parral was founded in 1631–32, and the civilian population had reached Janos and Casas Grandes by 1680. After a bloody Pueblo revolt in New Mexico (1680 and after), El Paso and Santa Cruz de la Cañada were established. Monclova, Coahuila, was founded in 1674.

11. In 1637, after conquering the bellicose Indians of the region, Juan de Urpín founded Barcelona and Nueva Tarragona near the northeast coast of Venezuela. In the same year Santo Tomé, after having been burnt by Sir Walter Raleigh in 1619 and refounded, was moved to another site near the junction of the Orinoco and the Caroni. In Bolívar's day it was located still farther up the river and bore the name of Angostura. Several towns grew up around the missions established along the friars' line of advance toward the llanos of central Venezuela. The most important settlements founded in New Granada during the century were Quibdó in the Atrato Valley, Barranquilla (1629), Medellín (1675), which became a thriving mining center, and Socorro (1681).

12. The mining town of Oruro, northeast of Potosí, was erected in 1604; and the celebrated silver mines of Cerro de Pasco began to be worked about 1630.

13. The new settlements were Rere and Talca, both founded in 1695.

14. The properties of quinine, which is made from cinchona bark, were discovered by the Spaniards about 1638, although the Indians had long known some of its virtues.

15. Don Carlos Sigüenza y Góngora.

16. Irvin A. Leonard, *Góngora* (Berkeley, 1929), p. 183. At the opening of this century the greatest poet of colonial Chile wrote some works of real merit, and before its end a poetic genius saw the light in Mexico. The name of the Chilean was Pedro de Ona; the genius of New Spain was Juana Ines de Santa Cruz, a woman whose collected works fill three volumes. One of the best poems of the century was written by Father Matías de Bocanegra. A few histories which possessed some merit also

appeared, and Juan de Solórzano Pereira's valuable work on law and government in the Spanish colonies (*Política indiana*) was published shortly before the middle of the century.

NOTES TO CHAPTER VII

1. Apparently Calvo made some allowance for contraband in the figures for importations into the colonies.
2. Debt peonage, a common form of servitude during the nineteenth century, was gradually taking the place of the old system of compulsory labor.
3. W. W. Pierson, *The Intendencia of Cuba* (Chapel Hill, N.C., 1927), p. 89.
4. From Javier F. Brabo, *Expulsión de los Jesuitas* (Madrid, 1897), I take the following figures: number of Jesuits in America at the time of their expulsion, 2,260; number of Indians in their different missions, 717,000; number of colleges, residences, and missions, 191; incomplete estimate of the value of Jesuit property seized in Spain and America, 71,483,917 pesos duros. Except in Paraguay, where the enumeration appears to be incomplete, Brabo's list contains only the mission centers, not each separate mission. If these had been included, the number of establishments would have approached 300.
5. In California several of the mission buildings have been restored.
6. Quoted by Bernard Moses in his *Spanish Dependencies in South America* (New York, 1914), II: 398–99.
7. There was a *colegio* in every important town and city, but it seldom amounted to more than a sort of grammar school.
8. Professor John Tate Lanning, who has made a special study of institutions of higher learning in Colonial Spanish America, informs me that there were at least twenty universities in 1800. The three best were in Mexico, Lima, and Chuquisaca. See his *Academic Culture in the Spanish Colonies* (New York, 1940).
9. Víctor Belaunde, in *The Hispanic American Historical Review,* IX (1929): 145. The viceroyalties and captaincies general and some of the *audiencias* were referred to as "kingdoms."

NOTES TO CHAPTER VIII

1. Ronald de Carvalho, *Pequena Historia de Literatura Brasileira* (Rio de Janeiro, 1919), p. 127.
2. *Op. cit.,* pp. 13–14.
3. João Ribeiro, *Historia do Brasil* (Rio de Janeiro, 1914), p. 195; see the following pages for a description of despotism and peculation.
4. John Armitage, *The History of Brazil* (London, 1836), II, 161 ff.
5. Da Cunha de Azevedo Coutinho, *An Essay on the Brazils* (Eng. ed., London, 1807), pp. 43–45.
6. Andrew Grant, *History of Brazil* (London, 1809), p. 116.
7. Samuel Putnam, in his *Marvelous Journey* (New York, 1948), pp. 3–95, surveys the writings of the Colonial period.

8. As translated by Isaac Goldberg, in his *Brazilian Literature* (New York, 1922), p. 49.

NOTES TO CHAPTER IX

1. *Latin America* (London, 1913), pp. 84–85. But hatred of the Inquisition and the colonial authorities did not extend to all classes and cas.es in Spanish America. Many were loyal at the beginning of the movement and some remained loyal until the end.
2. Víctor Belaunde, "The Centennial of South American Independence," in *Rice Institute Pamphlets* (Houston, Texas, 1923), X, 239–41. Perhaps brutal would have been a more appropriate word than "primitive." But are not all wars brutal?
3. This is the area to which the term is customarily applied; perhaps Aranda meant to include all Spanish South America save Peru.

NOTES TO CHAPTER X

1. It was a simple, sincere, and touching tribute: "Here lies Remedios Escalada, the wife and friend of General San Martín." He made no effort to bring his daughter up as a great lady. He only wished to "make her a tender mother and a good spouse."
2. The substance of the declaration, known as the *Grito de Ypiranga,* made by Pedro while standing on the banks of the Ypiranga River is contained in the following quotation: "Comrades, the Cortes of Portugal wishes to reduce Brazil to slavery; we must declare forthwith her independence. . . . Independence or death!"
3. Brazil had annexed the small section of Spanish America lying east of the Plata Estuary in 1820, giving it the name of Cisplatine Province the next year. The people of the area had already won their independence from Spain, but they did not gain their independence from Brazil until 1828.

NOTES TO CHAPTER XI

1. Bernard Moses, *The Intellectual Background of the Revolution in South America* (New York, 1926), p. 40.
2. William R. Manning, *Diplomatic Correspondence of the United States Concerning the Independence of the Latin-American Nations* (Washington, D.C., 1926), III: 1478.
3. Canning's memorandum of the conference is printed in C. K. Webster, *Britain and the Independence of Latin America* (London, 1938), II: 115–20.

NOTES TO CHAPTER XII

1. No single compilation contains all of the Latin-American constitutions of the early National period. One of the most convenient and satisfactory works on the subject is Justo Arosemena's *Constituciones políticas*

de la América meridional (2 vols., Havre, 1870; 2nd ed., Paris, 1878).

2. There is no satisfactory work dealing with the abolition of Negro slavery in Latin America as a whole; but see *Hispanic American Historical Review,* XIII (1923): 151–96, and XXIV (1944): 363–431, 547–59. Frank Tannenbaum's *Slave and Citizen* (New York, 1947), while stimulating and satisfactory in many respects, lacks concrete detail on the subject of emancipation. The Negro slaves in Haiti emancipated themselves shortly before 1800.

3. J. Lloyd Mecham's *Church and State in Latin America* (Chapel Hill, N.C., 1934) is an excellent survey of this problem.

NOTES TO CHAPTER XIII

1. Earlier civil strife was confined mainly to the townsmen and the peasants of the adjacent countrysides, but during the civil war of the 1860's the *cacos* and *piquets* were summoned from the foothills and mountains. In later years the *cacos* acquired a taste for the spoils of revolution and became the mercenaries of Haitian military politics.

2. At any rate, Canal felt that his situation was hopeless. Salomon, the victor in the election, was crowding him, fearing that the defeated candidate would stage a successful revolution before Canal's term ended.

NOTES TO CHAPTER XIV

1. William Spence Robertson's *Iturbide of Mexico* (Durham, 1952) is the best biography of Mexico's first monarch.

2. See Thomas Ewing Cotner, *The Military and Political Career of José Joaquín de Herrera* (Austin, 1949).

3. Juárez died in office in 1872. For a moving idealization, see Leonardo S. Viramonte, *Biografía popular del Benemérito de América, Benito Juárez* (Mexico, 1906). This was published, it will be observed, on the hundredth anniversary of the hero's birth.

4. Roeder, *Juárez and His Mexico* (New York, 1947), pp. 127–29.

5. *Ibid.,* pp. 135–36.

6. *Ibid.,* pp. 700–702.

7. French intervention will be discussed in another connection. Ferdinand Maximilian, a member of the Hapsburg royal family supported by Louis Napoleon, and Mexico's second monarch, theoretically became emperor in June, 1864; but his empire never extended over the whole of Mexico or enjoyed a day of peace. Too liberal for the Conservatives and hated by the Liberals, he was finally deposed and shot in July, 1867.

8. Quoted in James Creelman's, *Díaz, Master of Mexico* (New York, 1916), p. 419. See José F. Godoy's *Porfirio Díaz, . . . Master Builder of a Great Commonwealth* (New York, 1910), for still more extravagant laudation; it includes nearly 200 pages of quotations from "prominent men" in the United States—politicians, diplomats, bureaucrats, and others—as well as from a few Canadians and Englishmen.

NOTES TO CHAPTER XVI

1. No satisfactory history of Greater Colombia has been written. The most recent effort was made by the late Joaquín Tamayo, who published his *La Gran Colombia* in Bogotá in 1941. Gerhard Masur's *Simón Bolívar* (Albuquerque, 1948) is probably the best biography of the Liberator. Biographies of the other great captains, excepting Flores, can be found in almost any big library. Most of them are in Spanish, but Guillermo Sherwell gives a good account of Sucre's career in English (Washington, D.C., 1924) and there are two or three fairly satisfactory biographies of San Martín in English, the most recent of them being a translation of Ricardo Rojas's too laudatory *El Santo de la espada* (Buenos Aires, 1939). The most complete work, although likewise too laudatory, is José P. Otero's *Historia del Libertador Don José de San Martín*, 4 vols. (Buenos Aires, 1932). Those who can read Spanish will be delighted with Vicente Lecuna's *Cartas del Libertador* (10 vols.; Caracas, 1929–30) and Daniel F. O'Leary's *Cartas de Sucre al Libertador*, 2 vols. (Madrid, 1919).
2. Vicente Lecuna, *Cartas del Libertador*, I: 35–41. J. A. Cova, in his *Ideario político* (Caracas, 1940), has brought together the documents containing Bolívar's basic political ideas.
3. Quoted from Bolívar's *Mirada sobre América española*, published in Quito in late 1829.
4. There are some doubts about the authenticity of this story.

NOTES TO CHAPTER XVII

1. Historians seldom discuss South America as a unit, but the following works are pertinent and useful: Thomas C. Dawson, *The South American Republics* (New York, 1904); Charles Edmund Akers, *A History of South America* (3rd ed.; New York, 1930); A. Curtis Wilgus, ed., *South American Dictators* (Washington, D.C., 1937). Tom B. Jones, in his *South America Rediscovered* (Minneapolis, 1949), gives a stimulating summary of the views of foreign observers.
2. This quotation from Núñez and the one following are taken from my translations in Wilgus, *South American Dictators*, pp. 379–80.

NOTE TO CHAPTER XVIII

1. No satisfactory work on Bolivia's national history has appeared in English. The best surveys in Spanish are: Alcides Arguedas, *Historia General de Bolivia* (La Paz, 1922), and Enrique Finot, *Nueva Historia de Bolivia* (Buenos Aires, 1946). Neither work, however, contains an adequate bibliography. For sketches of Santa Cruz and Melgarejo, see N. A. N. Cleven's essays in Wilgus, *South American Dictators*, pp. 289–347. Consult also Alfonso Crespo's *Santa Cruz* (Mexico City, 1944).

NOTES TO CHAPTER XIX

1. Bolivia, subordinated to the viceroyalty of Peru for two centuries before it was made a part of the new viceroyalty of Río de la Plata, continued to face toward its Pacific outlets. The armies which liberated it from Spain advanced from the Peruvian base and not from the Río de la Plata, although some futile expeditions were made from the Plata area.
2. *The Purple Land* (London, 1904 ed.), pp. 334–35.
3. Thomas Carlyle, who evidently knew little about Francia, defended his "reign of rigour" and placed him among his "heroes" in his *Critical and Miscellaneous Essays* (London, 1872), Vol. VII.

NOTES TO CHAPTER XX

1. Dom Pedro also received lavish praise in the United States, where monarchs were generally not much esteemed. See my article in *The Southwestern Political Science Quarterly*, III (Austin, 1922): 1–15.
2. As quoted in Mary W. Williams, *Dom Pedro the Magnanimous* (Chapel Hill, N.C., 1937), p. 142.
3. The rebellion of Maciel, known to his followers as "The Counselor," was attributed in part to the influence of the monarchists.

NOTES TO CHAPTER XXI

1. *South America: Observations and Impressions* (rev. ed.; New York, 1916), p. 522.
2. *Latin America: Its Rise and Progress* (London, 1913), pp. 269–70.
3. *Latin America,* p. 236.
4. Without neglecting the sources, namely, the works of the Latin-American writers mentioned in this chapter, I have relied heavily upon the following surveys, which provide good starting points for those interested in probing the subject further: Arturo Torres-Ríoseco, *The Epic of Latin American Literature* (New York, 1942); Alfred Coester, *The Literary History of Spanish America* (New York, 1919), which contains a good many erroneous dates and is weak on political background; E. Herman Hespelt, ed., *An Outline History of Spanish American Literature* (New York, 1941); Isaac Goldberg, *Brazilian Literature* (New York, 1922), rather dogmatic and unsatisfactory in biographical details, but an able analysis; Samuel Putnam's short chapter on Brazilian literature in a collaborative volume, *Brazil,* edited by Lawrence F. Hill (Berkeley, 1947); and William R. Crawford, *A Century of Latin-American Thought* (Cambridge, Mass., 1944).
5. Coester, *Lit. History,* pp. 277–78. I quote only extracts from Coester's translation.
6. The quotation is from Coester's version, *Lit. History,* p. 229.
7. Crawford, *Century,* p. 71, whose translation I have followed.

8. Torres-Ríoseco, *Epic,* p. 140. The English version is Torres-Ríoseco's; the poem consists of several stanzas.
9. *Ibid.,* p. 150; Torres-Ríoseco's translation again.
10. Some portions of these have been translated into English by Stuart E. Grummon and edited, with introduction and notes, by Allison W. Bunkley under the title of *A Sarmiento Anthology* (Princeton, 1948). Mrs. Horace Mann's English edition of *Facundo,* which also contained a biographical sketch of the Argentine writer, was published in New York in 1868, and is now not easy to find in the book markets.
11. The quotations translated in this paragraph are mainly from Alberdi's *Bases,* edited and published recently, though undated, in Buenos Aires by Alberto Palcos. Crawford quotes a few passages which I have not been able to locate in any edition of this famous treatise.
12. Alberto Palcos, ed., *Juan Bautista Alberdi: Autobiographía—La Evolución de su Pensamiento* (Buenos Aires, n.d.), pp. 208–48.
13. Goldberg, *Brazilian Literature,* p. 138.
14. *Ibid.,* p. 139. In these two quotations from Castro Alves I have followed Goldberg's English version rather closely.

NOTES TO CHAPTER XXII

1. Dexter Perkins, in his *Monroe Doctrine, 1826–1867* (Baltimore, 1933), presents an elaborate discussion of most of the topics dealt with in this section.
2. For a full account of this contest, see J. Fred Rippy, *The Caribbean Danger Zone* (New York, 1940), Chs. IV–VI.
3. By far the best general work on this subject is *International Migrations,* 2 vols. (New York, 1929, 1931), edited by Walter F. Willcox.
4. A comparative account of this American contribution is given by J. Fred Rippy, *Latin America and the Industrial Age* (rev. ed.; New York, 1947).
5. For a fuller account of these flotations, consult J. Fred Rippy, "Latin America and the British Investment 'Boom' of the 1820's," *Journal of Modern History,* XIX (1947): 122–29.
6. Consult my articles on this subject in *Inter-American Economic Affairs,* volume 2 and following, running through the years 1948–54.
7. The ablest exponent of the Latin-American view is Carlos Calvo of Argentina, who published *Derecho internacional* in two volumes (Paris, 1868). His work soon became famous and appeared in three different French editions, the last of them in six volumes (Paris, 1896). Rafael F. Seijas, a Venezuelan who passionately approved all that Calvo wrote and ardently championed what became widely known as the Calvo Doctrine, set forth his contentions and the abuses and alleged abuses to which the Latin-American nations were subjected in six large tomes (Caracas, 1884–85). For an understanding of the Latin-American attitude on this most important phase of their foreign relations, it would be well to peruse these elaborate treatises. The title of Seijas's work is *El derecho internacional Hispano-americano.*

8. John F. Cady, in his *Foreign Intervention in the Río de la Plata* (Philadelphia, 1929), deals exhaustively with this episode.

9. For more details on the Panama Riot and the efforts to exact indemnity, see J. Fred Rippy, *The Capitalists and Colombia* (New York, 1931), pp. 64–77.

10. On this important and much discussed episode, Daniel Dawson's *Mexican Adventure* (London, 1935) and the volume by Perkins on the Monroe Doctrine, already referred to, are strongly recommended.

11. I have translated this famous letter from a copy of the French original found in Genaro García's *Documentos inéditos,* XIV (Mexico City, 1906), 13–15. A defective English version of this letter was published in *Senate Executive Documents* No. 11, 38 Congress, 2 Session, Serial 1209, pp. 272–73.

12. Seijas dwells at great length and furiously on this long period of storm and stress for Venezuela. See especially the third volume of his treatise cited in note 7, above.

13. For a detailed examination of the antecedents of the Roosevelt "corollary," see J. Fred Rippy, *Caribbean Danger Zone,* Chap. III.

NOTES TO CHAPTER XXIII

1. These and subsequent quotations from the British foreign secretary are from Harold Temperley's "The Later American Policy of George Canning," *American Historical Review,* XI (1906): 779–97.

2. W. R. Manning, *Early Diplomatic Relations Between the United States and Mexico* (Baltimore, 1916), p. 48.

3. *The International American Conference* (Washington, D.C., 1890), IV: 113 ff. President Adams in his message regarding the Congress contended that the adoption of its maritime and commercial policy would "redound to" the "honor" of the United States and "drain the fountain of many a future sanguinary war."

4. Quoted by J. B. Lockey, in his *Pan Americanism: Its Beginnings* (New York, 1921), pp. 420–21.

5. Their commercial treaties were contradictory: those signed with England tended to accept the British view; those negotiated with the United States accepted its contentions. The Declaration of Paris (1856) embodied most of the principles advocated by the United States but outlawed privateers, and mainly for that reason, the United States rejected the declaration, while most of the Latin-American countries registered their reluctant adherence.

6. Quoted by Harold Temperley, in *The American Historical Review,* XI (1906): 781–82.

7. These and other statements are quoted in *Littell's Living Age,* 2d Series, XIV (1856): 312 *passim.*

8. Lettsom to Clarendon, No. 63, Foreign Office, London, 50, vol. 310.

9. Dallas to Cass, No. 99, Dispatches from Great Britain, vol. 71, State Department Archives, Washington, D.C.

10. George W. Mathew to Lord Russell, No. 85, December 29, 1860, Foreign Office 50, vol. 344. The United States legation in Mexico may

have issued the protest without instruction to do so by its superiors.

11. J. B. Moore, ed., *The Works of James Buchanan* (New York, 1910), X: 115.

12. The par value of British investments in Latin America exceeded £425,-700,000 by the end of 1890 and fell only a little short of £538,000,000 at the close of the year 1900, with more than half of the total in the latter year in southern South America, with hardly more than £65,-000,000 in Mexico, slightly above £32,000,000 in Cuba, much less in Central America, and almost no investments in Haiti and the Dominican Republic. Investments of citizens of the United States in Latin America in 1900 amounted to less than $360,000,000, with most of the capital in Mexico and the Caribbean countries. The par value of French capital invested in the region at the end of the century was in the neighborhood of $600,000,000, most of it in southern South America, Colombia (Panama Canal Company), and Mexico. Investments of other European countries were quite small at this time, but German investments were rapidly increasing.

13. Blaine thought that British capital was backing Chile in her "Nitrate War" (1879–83) in the hope of exploiting that commodity after Chile got possession of the nitrate deposits. The United States made no protests against British employment of naval forces against various Latin-American countries to redress injuries to persons and property, although such coercive action caused some irritation and uneasiness. Shortly before the Civil War, the United States became intensely interested in the navigation of South American rivers, especially the Amazon.

14. Robert McElroy, *Grover Cleveland* (New York, 1923), II, 178.

15. The correspondence regarding the dispute is published in *Foreign Relations of the United States* (1895), I: 558 ff.

NOTES TO CHAPTER XXIV

1. Relations with Portugal were insignificant except for Brazil, which received numerous Portuguese immigrants and some Portuguese capital.

2. Robert B. Foerster, *The Italian Emigration of our Times* (Cambridge, Mass., 1919), pp. 476–78.

3. As quoted by M. Barral-Montferrat in his *De Monroe à Roosevelt* (Paris, 1907), Introduction.

4. A. Merignac, *Revue du droit public*, V (1896): 202 ff.

5. Gabriel Couillault, *Le Monde économique*, Jan., 1896, pp. 7–8. This boundary dispute was settled by arbitration in 1899–1900.

NOTES TO CHAPTER XXV

1. Foreign companies objected to the "nationalization" of the nitrate deposits of Tarapacá. Holders of Peruvian bonds were offended by Peruvian defalcations. Both groups were in touch with Chilean officials.

2. Matías Romero to the Mexican minister of foreign affairs, printed in

> *Archivo Histórico Diplomático Mexicano,* no. 19 (Mexico, D.F., 1926): p. 202.

3. *Minutes of the International American Conference* (Washington, D.C., 1890): p. 107.

4. *Ibid.,* p. 811.

NOTES TO CHAPTER XXVI

1. See George Wythe, *An Outline of Latin-American Economic Development* (New York, 1946); Seymour E. Harris, ed., *Economic Problems of Latin America* (New York, 1944); and J. Fred Rippy, *Latin America and the Industrial Age.*

2. In a recent series of articles too numerous to cite in detail I have dealt with foreign investments in Latin America. They appeared in the following journals during the years 1947–50: *Journal of Modern History; Journal of Business; Journal of Political Economy; Inter-American Economic Affairs; Pacific Historical Review;* and *Hispanic American Historical Review. Journal of Business,* XIV (Chicago, Oct., 1941): 345–55, gives a summary of the scandals accompanying the sale of Latin-American bonds in the United States during the 1920's, with specific references to the Senate hearings. See also Rippy, *South America and Hemisphere Defense* (Baton Rouge, La., 1941), pp. 82–99, and Rippy, *The Caribbean Danger Zone,* pp. 229–40.

3. For a full discussion of this subject, consult J. Fred Rippy, *The Caribbean Danger Zone.* The same author, in collaboration with Clyde E. Hewitt, has dealt with the prevention of Castro's return to Venezuela in *The American Historical Review,* LV (1949): 36–53. See also Alexander de Conde, *Herbert Hoover's Latin-American Policy* (Stanford, 1951), and Edward O. Guerrant, *Roosevelt's Good Neighbor Policy* (Albuquerque, 1950).

4. See Rippy, *The Caribbean Danger Zone,* and Dexter Perkins, *Hands Off: The Monroe Doctrine* (Boston, 1941).

5. A series of pamphlets published by the United States Tariff Commission on *Economic Controls and Commercial Policy* in the various Latin-American republics (Washington, D.C., 1945–47) throws a flood of light on this new economic nationalism.

NOTES TO CHAPTER XXVII

1. Approximately half of the some 13,000,000 immigrants who arrived in Latin America between 1825 and 1956 entered the region during the period following 1900, and mainly during the first forty years of the new century. The par value of British capital invested in the region rose to a peak of £1,211,000,000 in 1928. Investments of citizens of the United States exceeded $5,201,000,000 by the end of 1930. French capital expanded to $1,675,000,000 in 1913 and then shrank to some $454,000.000 by the end of 1938. German investments, which amounted to approximately $677,000,000 in 1918, were partly con-

fiscated during the next few years, but soon expanded again, reaching some $969,000,000 in 1940. Capital invested by residents of other countries—the Dutch Netherlands, Belgium, Switzerland, Italy, Spain, Portugal, Sweden—was much smaller; but the total from all foreign countries must have amounted to no less than $12,000,000,000 by the end of 1929. The major recipients were Argentina, Brazil, Uruguay, Chile, Peru, Colombia, Venezuela, Mexico, and Cuba, but all the countries—even Paraguay and the small republics in Central America and the Caribbean islands—received some foreign capital.

2. With few exceptions, the state of the economies of the Latin-American countries is likely to be revealed by exports, which are usually more valuable than imports, since exports must service foreign debts as well as pay for imports. Production for export is normally more efficient than production for home consumption. A very convenient source for statistics on international trade is *Foreign Commerce Yearbook,* published by the United States Department of Commerce since 1922; earlier numbers have the shorter title of *Commerce Yearbook.*

3. Charles E. Chapman, *History of the Cuban Republic* (New York, 1927), p. 28.

4. Puerto Rico was also detached from Spain in 1898 and annexed to the United States as a war indemnity; but since it did not become an independent nation, its history will not be dealt with here.

NOTES TO CHAPTER XXVIII

1. Herbert I. Priestley, in *Proceedings of the Pacific Coast Branch of the American Historical Association* (1927), p. 110.

2. *Extremos de América* (Mexico City, 1949), pp. 17–18.

3. "Rise and Fall of Mexico's Revolution," in *The Nation* (New York), Oct. 22, 1949, p. 396.

4. Leopoldo Peniche Vallado, *Crítica y análisis de la revolución mexicana* (Mérida, 1948), p. 18.

5. Dana Munro, *The Five Republics of Central America* (New York, 1918), p. 53.

NOTES TO CHAPTER XXIX

1. Jesús M. Henao and Gerardo Arrubla, *History of Colombia* (Chapel Hill, N.C., 1938), p. 519.

2. Germán Arciniegas, *The State of Latin America* (New York, 1952), p. 155.

3. *Ibid.,* p. 95.

4. *Ibid.,* p. 105.

5. *Problems of Democracy in Latin America* (Chapel Hill, N.C., 1955), pp. 20–21.

6. As quoted by Arciniegas, *op. cit.,* pp. 84–85.

NOTES TO CHAPTER XXX

1. Two of them were presidents: Luís Batlle Berres (1947–51), nephew of the late José Batlle, and Andrés Martínez Trueba (1951–52).
2. Russell H. Fitzgibbon, in his *Uruguay, Portrait of a Democracy* (New Brunswick, N.J., 1954), deals with the neglect of the Uruguayan countryside under the heading "Capital against Campo." He points out that an agrarian problem is developing in spite of efforts to widen land-ownership. He also includes a chapter giving an account of the educational work in the 1870's of Pedro Varela, Uruguay's Domingo F. Sarmiento and Horace Mann.
3. *Paraguay: An Informal History* (Norman, Okla., 1949), p. 353.
4. C. H. Haring, in *Foreign Affairs,* IX (1931): 292.
5. It is possible that Perón did not deliberately deceive the masses, although this seems doubtful. He had certainly been more successful in promoting his own interests than in serving theirs.

NOTES TO CHAPTER XXXI

1. Most of these heroes have been mentioned in connection with the national histories of the various countries. Peru's Hipólito Unánue, Ecuador's Eugenio Espejo, and Brazil's José Bonifácio were scientists; Cuba's José Martí was a distinguished literary man.
2. A number of them are listed by A. Curtis Wilgus in his *Histories and Historians of Latin America* (New York, 1942).
3. For fuller information on the writers discussed in this chapter, consult: Isaac Goldberg's *Studies in Spanish-American Literature* (New York, 1920) and *Brazilian Literature;* Coester's *Literary History of Spanish America;* Torres-Ríoseco's *Epic of Latin-American Literature; An Outline History of Spanish-American Literature,* edited by Hespelt; and Samuel Putnam's *Marvellous Journey* as well as his chapter on Brazilian writers in *Brazil,* edited by Hill. All except the first have been listed in Chapter X, note 4.

   I have relied heavily upon these works, but I have also read and appreciated the writings of the great masters I have attempted to discuss. The six dealt with in this chapter happen to belong to the "Modernist School," but I have avoided the refinements of classification.
4. This quotation and the three preceding ones are taken from Goldberg's *Studies in Spanish-American Literature,* pp. 50, 51, 89, 113.
5. Coester, *Lit. History,* p. 427.
6. Editorial Trópico. Fifty-seven volumes had appeared by 1945. The most complete account of his life and works is Andrés Iduarte's, *Martí, Escritor* (Mexico City, 1945).
7. Goldberg, *Studies,* p. 27.
8. *Ibid.,* pp. 38, 360.
9. *Ibid.,* pp. 39–40, 360.
10. Alice Stone Blackwell, *Some Spanish-American Poets* (New York,

1929), pp. 2–4. There are eight lines instead of four in each stanza; I have quoted only a part of Miss Blackwell's translation of the poem.

11. As quoted by Goldberg in *Studies,* pp. 76–77.

12. Torres-Ríoseco, *Epic,* p. 102.

13. Goldberg, *Studies,* pp. 78–80. Miss Blackwell's collection includes sixteen of Nervo's poems.

14. *Ibid.,* p. 182.

15. *Ibid.,* pp. 106–363.

16. *Ibid.,* pp. 156, 365–66.

17. *Ibid.,* p. 158; Coester, *Lit. History,* pp. 464–65. Darío's *Salutation to the Eagle,* written a few years later, was friendly and envisaged a fruitful collaboration between Latin and Anglo-Saxon America.

18. Coester, *Lit. History,* pp. 461–62.

19. *Memorias: Las mil y una aventuras* (Santiago de Chile, 1940), p. 8.

20. *Memorias,* p. 14.

21. Goldberg, *Studies,* p. 280.

22. *Memorias,* p. 291.

23. I have taken these three poems from Miss Blackwell's collection cited in note 10, but have ventured to give my own version of the last three lines of the first poem.

24. José Santos Chocano, *Poesias escogidas* (Paris, 1938), pp. 61–65.

25. Goldberg, *Studies,* pp. 62–63; Carlos García-Prada, *José Asunción Silva: Prosas y versos* (Mexico, D.F., 1942), pp. 32–34.

26. Blackwell, *Some . . . Poets,* pp. 402–11. Miss Blackwell publishes these three poems in both Spanish and English. I have followed her translations rather closely, but have omitted parts of them. A complete edition of Silva's poems (Poesías) was published in Santiago in 1923. His autobiographical novel, *De sobremesa,* was published in Bogotá in 1925. See also García-Prada's volume cited in note 25 above.

27. Rodó, *Ariel,* F. J. Stimson translation (Boston, 1922), pp. 121–26.

28. *Ibid.,* pp. 61–62, *passim.*

29. For the Brazilian literary masters of the recent epoch, see Goldberg's *Brazilian Literature,* especially the chapters in which he discusses the works of Machado de Assís, Olavo Bilac, and Euclydes da Cunha.

NOTES TO CHAPTER XXXII

1. See Crawford's *A Century of Latin-American Thought,* mentioned in Chapter XXI, note 4. I have read most of the published works of these three men and tried to make my own summaries of their thought. In most cases, the quotations are my translations from the original Spanish. I have not considered it necessary to list all of their works, but they can be found by consulting the citations I have given.

2. *Desde mi belvedere* (Habana, 1938), pp. 83–84.

3. *Ibid.,* pp. 63–65, 202–3.

4. *Ibid.,* pp. 48, 127.

5. *Ibid.,* pp. 187–88.

6. Chapman, *History of the Cuban Republic,* pp. 203, 216; Varela, *El talón de aquiles* (Habana, 1906).

7. *Caso. Prologo y seleccion de Eduardo García Máynez* (Mexico City, 1943), p. 88.
8. *El peligro de hombre* (Mexico City, 1943), p. 30.
9. Crawford, *Century,* p. 282; *Caso,* . . . *selección,* p. 77.
10. *Ibid.,* p. 283, quoting Caso.
11. *Ibid.,* p. 288, quoting from Caso's *La persona humana y el estado totalitario* (Mexico City, 1941).
12. *Sociología argentina* (2d ed.; Madrid, 1913), pp. 102–3.
13. *El hombre mediocre* (Buenos Aires, n.d.), pp. 35, 37, 276.
14. As quoted by Crawford, *Century,* p. 140.
15. *Prosa menuda* (Buenos Aires, 1941), p. 156.
16. *Pájinas libres* (Lima, 1946), p. 168. The first edition of this work was published in Paris in 1894. A posthumous volume entitled *Propaganda y ataque* was published in Buenos Aires in 1938. Among his other works are *Horas de Lucha* (Lima, 1908), *Bajo el aprobrio* (Paris, 1933), and *Figuras y figurones* (Paris, 1938). González Prada was also a gifted poet.
17. *El porvenir de las naciones hispano-americanos ante las conquistas de Europa y los Estados Unidos* (Mexico, 1899), pp. 17, 30–31, 85, 106–9, 281–82. See also Bulnes's *Las grandes mentiras de nuestra historia* (Mexico, 1904) and *Los grandes problemas de México* (Mexico, 1926).
18. *Nuestra América* (Barcelona, 1903), pp. 136, 180. In the definitive edition of this work, published after his death (Madrid, 1926), Bunge modified his earlier views, giving more emphasis to physical and social environment and less to the thesis of innate racial inferiority.
19. The third edition of Arguedas's book (Santiago, 1937) was more optimistic. The cholos and whites had now begun to reveal more interest in production and other business enterprises and greater awareness of their responsibility for the improvement of the condition of the Indians, and national wealth had increased.
20. *Vicios políticos de América* (Paris, n.d.), p. 91. The volume was probably written in 1910 or earlier.
21. *Ibid.,* pp. 9–11, 28, 31–32, 80, 220–22.
22. These works, in the order mentioned in the text, were: (1) *Paginas del Unión;* (2) *La nacionalidad y el Partido Unionista centroamericana;* (3) *La enfermedad de Centro-América; el sujecto y los síntomas de su dolencia;* (4) *Tratado de educación cívica centroamericana;* (5) *La enfermedad de Centro-América,* 3 vols.; (6) *Alrededor del problema unionista de Centro-América,* 2 vols. Numbers 3, 5, and 6 were published in Barcelona, 1910 and 1934.
23. *La enfermedad de Centro-América,* I: 263.
24. *Ibid.,* I: 265.
25. *Ibid.,* I: 181.
26. Jefferson Rea Spell, *Contemporary Spanish-American Fiction* (Chapel Hill, N.C., 1943), p. 3.
27. Torres-Ríoseco, *The Epic of Latin-American Literature,* p. 168.
28. *Novelistas contemporaneos de América* (Santiago de Chile, 1939) and *Grandes novelistas de la América Hispana,* 2 vols. (Berkeley, 1949),

29. *Brazilian Literature*. See also E. Herman Hespelt, *An Outline History of Spanish American Literature*.
30. Spell, . . . *Fiction*, p. 100.
31. Torres-Ríoseco, *Epic*, p. 189.
32. *Ibid.*, p. 191.
33. *Ibid.*, p. 175.
34. Some of the works of these novelists have been translated into English. See the volumes by Hespelt and Spell mentioned in this chapter for those that have; and see also *The Inter-American Quarterly*, III (July, 1941): 55–71, for a longer list.

NOTES TO CHAPTER XXXIII

1. The pioneer work on the subject of this Chapter is my *Latin America in World Politics* (1st ed., New York, 1928; 3rd ed., 1938).
2. James Brown Scott, ed., *Proceedings of The Hague Peace Conferences,* 3 vols. (New York, 1921–22); William I. Hull, "The United States and Latin America at The Hague," *International Conciliation* (Boston), No. 44, July, 1911.
3. *La solidaridad latina en América* (Habana, 1897, pamphlet, 22 pp.).
4. *Los pueblos hispanoamericanos en el siglo XX* (Madrid, 1907).
5. As quoted in *Literary Digest*, XVII (1898): 113.
6. As quoted in *Lit. Digest*, XXIII (1901): 51.
7. *Lit. Digest*, XL (1910): 866–67.
8. *Lit. Digest*, XLIII (1911): 198.
9. The *fiestas* were held on October 12, "Columbus Day," which was more often called "Día de la Raza."
10. Rafael Altamira y Crevea, *Mi Viaje a América* (Madrid, 1911), p. 11.
11. See Chapters XXXI and XXXII above, for the attitude of some of the Latin-American writers.
12. Vol. CXVI (1893): 366–68.
13. As quoted in *Lit. Digest*, XXV (1902): 530.
14. Maurice de Waleffe, *Les Paradis de l'Amérique Centrale* (Paris, 1909), pp. 303–4.
15. *La Doctrine de Monroe* (Paris, 1898), pp. 55–56, 145.
16. *Les États-Unis et la Doctrine de Monroe* (Paris, 1900), pp. 433–36.
17. *La nouvelle revue*, Sept. 1890. Translation in *Lit. Digest*, I: 590.
18. *Revue des deux mondes*, CXVI (March 15, 1893): 363.
19. *Les Paradis*, p. 3.
20. *Revue politique et parlementaire*, LXXIX (Feb., 1914): 245 ff.
21. As quoted in *Lit. Digest*, XXIII (July 13, 1901): 51–52.
22. *Lit. Digest*, XXIV (June 14, 1902): 814.
23. *L'Economiste français*, II (1894): 797–99.
24. *Revue du droit public*, V (Feb., 1896): 201–78.
25. See Clarence H. Haring, *South America Looks at the United States* (New York, 1928), on the "anti-Yankee" propaganda of the 1920's.
26. Both published in Madrid.
27. Both published in Valladolid.
28. Published in Madrid.

29. Bailey W. Diffie has summarized this phase of the movement in his "Ideology of *Hispanidad," Hispanic American Historical Review,* XXIII (1943): 457–82. Unless otherwise indicated, the quotations in this section are taken from this article.

30. Allan Chase, *Falange* (New York, 1943), p. 14.

31. Chase, *Falange,* p. 227.

32. *Ibid.,* p. 162.

33. G. Lafon in *Revue Minerva,* as quoted by Samuel Guy Inman, *Problems in Pan Americanism* (New York, 1929), pp. 240–41.

34. CCXLIX (1921): 1080 ff.; CCLIV (1923): 609 ff.

35. *La revue universelle,* XII (Jan. 15, 1923): 219–30, as quoted in *Living Age,* CCCXVI (March 10, 1923): 571–76.

36. *New York Times,* March 7, 1923, quoted these two journals.

37. March 31, 1923, 391–93; June 2, 1923, 688–89.

38. *New York Times,* June 8, 1927.

39. *Point Four,* a small volume published by the U.S. State Department in 1950, points out that the stream of private capital flowing into direct investment in Latin America had not dried up (see pp. 57–58). The net total for 1945 was $140,400,000; for 1946 the net aggregate was $55,700,000 and for 1947 it was $407,700,000. More than two-thirds of the total for the three years was invested in petroleum, however. In addition to these private direct investments, considerable grants and credits were extended by the United States government. During the middle of the 1950's the flow of capital from the United States to Latin America increased. Large sales of agricultural commodities in exchange for Latin-American local currencies as well as liberal grants of such commodities began late in 1954.

TABLE 1

Expansion and Contraction of Latin America's Foreign Trade
(*in millions of dollars*)

Year	Imports	Exports	Total
1910	1,098.1	1,308.6	2,406.7
1920	2,884.6	3,490.7	6,375.3
1922	1,616.4	2,108.1	3,724.5
1928	2,393.6	3,029.7	5,423.3
1932	610.4	1,030.4	1,640.8
1939	1,346.5	1,858.5	3,205.0
1946	3,532.1	5,993.9	9,526.0
1951	7,287.4	7,311.3	14,598.7

Share of Leading Countries in Latin America's Foreign Trade
(*in per cent*)

Year	Latin America's Imports				Latin America's Exports			
	U.S.	U.K.	Germany	France	U.S.	U.K.	Germany	France
1910	23.5	26.0	15.6	8.4	34.5	20.9	11.1	8.4
1920	50.1	17.9	3.4	4.8	47.7	16.7	1.8	5.9
1928	37.7	16.3	10.9	5.9	34.4	19.2	9.8	5.3
1932	32.3	16.3	9.4	4.9	29.4	19.4	7.2	6.7
1939	40.6	10.1	13.3	3.4	35.2	15.6	6.3	3.8
1941	62.4	7.8	0.5	0.1	54.0	13.1	0.3	0.1
1946	59.2	6.2	—	—	40.2	12.2	—	—
1951	54.5	7.2	6.2	2.6	52.1	12.8	4.6	2.9

Compiled from the Pan American Union's *Foreign Trade Series* and from *Foreign Commerce Yearbook*, published by the U.S. Department of Commerce, and from George Wythe, *An Outline of Latin American Economic Development* (New York, 1946), p. 237.

TABLE 2

British Investments in Latin America
(*in millions of pounds*)

Country	1890	1900	1913	1928
Argentina	157.0	206.9	357.7	420.4
Brazil	68.7	90.6	223.9	285.7
Chile	24.4	38.6	63.9	76.9
Colombia	5.4	6.1	6.7	7.5
Cuba	26.8	32.1	44.4	43.8
Mexico	59.9	65.4	159.0	199.0
Peru	19.1	22.0	25.7	26.2
Uruguay	27.7	35.8	46.1	41.1
Venezuela	9.8	8.5	7.9	26.4
Other Countries	16.6	20.5	30.0	42.2
Undistributed	10.3	11.4	33.8	41.8
Totals	425.7	537.9	999.1	1,211.0
Government bonds	194.4	229.2	316.4	343.8
Railways	146.9	198.3	457.8	491.0
Mines	23.3	12.3	22.2	22.4
Commercial banks	3.6	7.8	18.5	9.2
Chilean nitrate	5.4	9.2	28.0	12.5

Compiled from the *Stock Exchange Year-Book* (London) for the years 1890–1929 and *South American Journal* for the same period. I have dealt fully with British investments in Latin America in a series of articles published in *Inter-American Economic Affairs* (Washington, D.C.), 1949–54. British investments in the region reached their peak in 1928. (I think the figures for that year are too high.) The British investment in Latin America, owing mainly to sales to private interests in the United States and to Latin-American governments, had shrunk to less than £500 million by the end of 1950.

TABLE 3

Private Investments of Citizens of the United States in
Latin America (*in millions of dollars*)

Country	1914	1930	1943	1950 *
Argentina	36.0	807.8	497.5	355.6
Bolivia	11.0	116.0	24.0	10.8
Brazil	28.0	557.0	334.7	644.2
Chile	180.5	700.9	388.1	540.1
Colombia	21.5	301.7	178.9	193.4
Costa Rica	24.0	32.6	36.7	60.0
Cuba	265.0	1,066.6	590.5	642.4
Dominican Republic	16.0	87.2	80.5	105.7
Ecuador	9.0	11.8	13.3	14.2
El Salvador	7.0	34.7	20.4	18.5
Guatemala	36.5	75.1	93.0	105.9
Haiti	11.5	28.5	17.7	12.7
Honduras	10.0	71.7	42.2	61.9
Mexico	853.5	709.8	422.2	414.5
Nicaragua	4.5	13.0	13.5	9.0
Panama	13.5	46.5	154.4	348.0
Paraguay	5.5	12.6	10.0	
Peru	62.5	200.1	88.8	144.5
Uruguay	5.5	81.1	19.3	61.0 §
Venezuela	8.0	247.2	398.6	993.0
Totals	1,609.0	5,201.9	3,424.3	4,735.4
Government bonds	353.6	1,589.9	175.6 †	—
Rys., Pub. Utils.	175.7	887.1 ‡	869.9	1,041.5
Mining, Smelting	449.0	732.1 ‡	396.0	628.4
Petroleum	130.0	616.8 ‡	559.7	1,407.8
Agriculture	238.5	807.9 ‡	275.3	519.6
Manufacturing	37.0	231.0 ‡	332.3	779.8
Trading	32.0	119.2	138.4	242.5

Compiled from the publications of the U.S. Department of Commerce and the
U.S. Treasury Department (1943). See especially: *Census of American-Owned
Assets in Foreign Countries,* published by the Treasury Department in 1947;
Direct Private Foreign Investments of the United States, Census of 1950, pub-
lished by the Commerce Department in 1953; and J. Fred Rippy, "Investments of
Citizens of the United States in Latin America," in *Journal of Business,* XXII
(Jan., 1949), 17–29.

* Does not include government bonds and other portfolio investments. These
  would raise the total for 1950 to around $6 billion.
† This is the much-depreciated market value of the bonds; the par value was
  $463.3 million.
‡ These figures are for 1929; those for 1930 are not available.
§ Uruguay and Paraguay.

TABLE 4

French and German Investments in Latin America
(*in millions of dollars*)

Country	French Capital			German Capital	
	1902	*1913*	*1938*	*1918*	*1940*
Argentina	184.6	400.0	160.0	250.0	540.0
Bolivia	14.0	20.0	5.4	5.0	8.0
Brazil	139.2	700.0	134.2	150.0	200.0
Chile	45.2	42.4	17.2	75.0	85.0
Colombia	49.2	3.0	3.6	2.0	5.0
Ecuador	1.0	3.0	2.8	4.0	5.0
Mexico	60.0	400.0	91.0	105.0	35.0
Paraguay	0.2	8.0	7.0	2.0	3.0
Peru	21.4	10.0	5.0	21.0	25.0
Uruguay	59.4	40.0	12.4	2.5	4.0
Venezuela	26.0	10.0	1.2	20.0	3.0
Other Countries *	50.3	38.6	14.8	40.5	56.0
Totals	650.5	1,675.0	453.6	677.0	969.0

Sources used in arriving at these statistics, which are largely approximations, are the following articles: J. Fred Rippy, "French Investments in Latin America," in *Inter-American Economic Affairs,* II (Autumn, 1948), 53–71, and "German Investments in Latin America," in *Journal of Business,* XXI (April, 1948), 63–73. French capital was invested mainly in government securities, mining, banking, real estate, and railways. German capital was largely in manufacturing, banking, and real estate. German investments were confiscated during World War II; French investments were sold to Latin Americans and others.

* Among these countries, French investments were largest in Cuba, Haiti, and Costa Rica while German investments were largest in Guatemala, where the total was some $35 million in 1918 and $50 million in 1940, mostly in coffee *fincas* in both years.

TABLE 5

Latin America: Population, Transportation, Communications

Country	Population 1950	Railways 1952	All-Weather Roads 1952	Motor Vehicles 1952	Tele-phones 1952	Radio Receivers 1952
	(*Thousands*)	(*Miles*)	(*Miles*)			(*Thousands*)
Argentina	17,160.4	27,292	19,800	367,246	852,327	1,500
Bolivia	3,019.0	1,456	620	13,550	10,535	150
Brazil	52,645.5	22,171	44,700	564,381	591,700	781
Chile	5,860.2	6,161	12,000	83,128	137,700	550
Colombia	11,259.7	1,847	900	83,800	97,864	500
Costa Rica	812.1	500	1,000	8,763	9,938	23
Cuba	5,426.8	3,038	2,158	150,086	131,405	700
Dom. Repub.	2,121.1	786	1,460	10,382	7,360	35
Ecuador	3,202.8	731	1,450	16,150	9,000	50
El Salvador	1,856.9	375	1,200	11,143	8,100	21
Guatemala	2,787.0	736	6,770	16,845	5,575	31
Haiti	3,112.0	254	720	7,112	3,809	4
Honduras	1,368.6	920	768	3,970	2,451	25
Mexico	25,791.0	15,138	30,000	369,941	299,327	1,220
Nicaragua	1,057.0	252	820	4,973	3,522	16
Panama	805.3	231	1,025	14,600	13,107	81
Paraguay	1,405.6	706	460	4,500	5,316	35
Peru	8,404.9	2,375	8,000	72,000	51,407	500
Uruguay	2,366.4	1,868	6,320	85,800	95,080	362
Venezuela	4,985.7	584	5,780	153,706	74,494	200
Totals	155,448.1	87,421	145,951	2,041,076	2,410,017	6,784

Source: U.S. Department of Commerce. The population figures for Argentina, Chile and Cuba are estimates. Those for the other countries are based upon the censuses for 1950. Railway mileage includes industrial railways, which expand the mileage considerably in such countries as Costa Rica, Cuba, Guatemala, Honduras, and Paraguay. The figures for highways are mostly estimates, as the rounded sums indicate. In some cases this is also true of the number of motor vehicles; I doubt that Haiti has more motor vehicles than Honduras or Nicaragua. Figures for motor vehicles and radio receivers in Panama include the Canal Zone. For comparative purposes the following statistics for the United States and Canada for the years indicated in the table should be of interest: with a population of approximately 151,677,000 in 1950, in the year 1952 the United States had over 235,000 miles of railway, nearly 2,000,000 miles of all-weather roads, some 52,000,000 motor vehicles, approximately 45.636,000 telephones, and around 105,000,000 radio receiving sets; with a population of 13,712,000 in 1950, Canada had in 1952 50,000 miles of railways, over 150,000 miles of all-weather roads, nearly 3,000,000 motor vehicles, more than 3,100,000 telephones, and 2,314,000 radio receivers.

TABLE 6

Latin America, 1952: Income, Education, Physicians, Medical Statistics

Country	Income per cap.	Illiteracy per cent	Inhabitants per Physician	Birth Rate per 1000	Death Rate per 1000	Infant Mortality per 1000
Argentina	$308	16	880	24.9	8.8	66.5
Bolivia	96	84	4,740	38.0	17.1	126.0
Brazil	218	56	2,650	39.5	16.2	118.5
Chile	215	37	1,760	33.6	13.8	133.6
Colombia	240	48	2,800	37.1	14.2	110.7
Costa Rica	145	18	3,200	54.8	11.6	80.2
Cuba	305	22	1,600	29.1	8.5	55.0
Dom. Repub.	168	58	2,780	42.2	10.5	78.0
Ecuador	88	57	3,900	46.5	16.5	115.2
El Salvador	180	57	5,070	48.7	16.3	85.4
Guatemala	166	80	5,800	52.4	19.6	75.1
Haiti	65	85	9,940	48.1	20.1	80.4
Honduras	128	72	6,500	41.1	13.7	64.3
Mexico	175	54	2,060	43.9	14.9	99.7
Nicaragua	140	70	2,350	42.4	11.4	82.1
Panama	296	38	3,240	33.1	8.1	51.2
Paraguay	73	79	2,480	24.5	9.2	75.8
Peru	100	62	4,500	25.9	10.1	104.6
Uruguay	305	16	1,100	21.8	7.8	65.7
Venezuela	425	60	1,900	43.7	10.8	79.4
U.S.A.	$1,594	3	740	24.5	9.6	28.5

Sources: United Nations, the Columbus Memorial Library of the Pan American Union, and the United States Department of Commerce. In some cases they are mere estimates. The income figure for Venezuela is probably distorted by receipts from the petroleum industry. The figures for illiteracy represent the percentage of individuals 14 years of age and more who were unable to read and write. The birth rates for Paraguay and Peru seem too low, and so do the death rates for Cuba, the Dominican Republic, Nicaragua, Panama, and Paraguay.

TABLE 7

Aid to Latin America by the U.S. Government, July 1, 1945–December 31, 1955
(*in thousands of dollars*)

Country	Grants	Loans and Credits	Total
Argentina	198	101,675	101,873
Bolivia	42,554	39,912	82,466
Brazil	23,707	599,692	623,399
Chile	10,504	121,746	132,250
Colombia	7,166	61,045	68,211
Costa Rica	13,899	3,857	17,756
Cuba	1,437	26,490	27,927
Dominican Republic	2,005	none	2,005
Ecuador	8,514	26,500	35,014
El Salvador	5,026	576	5,602
Guatemala	22,311	494	22,805
Haiti	11,719	20,408	32,127
Honduras	6,005	223	6,228
Mexico	105.311	229,144	334,455
Nicaragua	10,530	600	11,130
Panama	9,113	4,000	13,113
Paraguay	8,273	825	9,098
Peru	14,940	27,620	42,560
Uruguay	1,944	11,554	13,498
Venezuela	2,152	13,301	15,453
Unspecified	300,109	6,069	306,178
Totals	607,469	1,295,733	1,903,202

Compiled from *Foreign Grants and Credits by the United States Government: December 1955 Quarter,* tables 3 and 6, U.S. Department of Commerce, Office of Business Economics. Grants to the Inter-American Highway (extending from the southern boundary of Mexico to the Panama Canal) are not listed here, nor are the indirect contributions made through the United Nations and its affiliated organizations. By June, 1957, the total aid had risen to $2,336,018,000: grants, $848,250,000; credits utilized, $1,487,768,000.

SUGGESTED READINGS

🐛 THE COLONIAL PERIOD

I. GENERAL WORKS

1. Guides

Keniston, R. H. *List of Works for the Study of Hispanic American History*. New York, 1920.

Manchester, Alan K. *Descriptive Bibliography of the Brazilian Section of the Duke University Library*. Durham, N.C., 1933.

Sanchez, Alonso B. *Fuentes de la historia española e hispano-americans*. 3 vols., Madrid, 1952.

Spain and Spanish America in the Libraries of the University of California. 2 vols., Berkeley, 1928–30.

Wilgus, A. Curtis. *Histories and Historians of Hispanic America*. Washington, D.C., 1937.

2. General Histories and Periodicals

Barros Arana, Diego. *Historia de América*. 2 vols., Santiago, Chile, 1908.

Carrancá y Trujillo, Raúl. *La evolución política de Iberoamérica*. Madrid, 1925.

Cleven, Nels A. N. *Readings in Hispanic American History*. Boston, 1927.

Diffie, Bailey C. *Latin American Civilization: Colonial Period*. Harrisburg, Penn., 1947.

Galíndez, Jesús de. *Iberoamérica*. New York, 1954.

García Calderón, Francisco. *Latin America; Its Rise and Progress*. London, 1913.

Herring, Hubert. *A History of Latin America*. New York, 1955.

Hispanic American Historical Review. Quarterly, Durham, N.C., 1918—.

Hispanic American Report. Monthly, Stanford University, Calif., 1948—.

Inter-American Economic Affairs. Quarterly, Washington, D.C., 1947—.

Keen, Benjamin. *Readings in Latin-American Civilization*. Boston, 1955.

Serrano y Sanz, Manuel. *Compendio de la historia de América*. 2 vols., Barcelona, 1917.

Thomas, Alfred B. *Latin America*. New York, 1956.

II. PHYSICAL ENVIRONMENT

Bain, Howard F., and Read, T. T. *Ores and Industry in South America*. New York, 1934.

James, Preston E. *Latin America.* New York, 1950.
Miller, Benjamin, and Singewald, J. T. *The Mineral Deposits of South America.* New York, 1919.

III.   OLD-WORLD BACKGROUND

Chapman, Charles E. *History of Spain.* New York, 1918.
Cheyney, Edward P. *European Background of American History.* New York, 1904.
————. *The Dawn of a New Era.* New York, 1936.
Emerton, Ephraim. *The Beginnings of Modern Europe.* New York, 1917.
Gillespie, J. E. *History of Geographical Discovery.* New York, 1933.
Livermore, H. V. *Portugal and Brazil.* Oxford, 1953.
Nowell, Charles E. *A History of Portugal.* New York, 1952.
Prestage, Edgar. *The Portuguese Pioneers.* New York, 1934.
Robinson, James H., Breasted, J. H., and Smith, E. T., *History of Civilization: Earlier Ages.* New York, 1937.
Sedwick, Henry D. *A Short History of Spain.* Boston, 1925.

IV.   THE FIRST AMERICANS

Church, George E. *Indians of South America.* London, 1912.
Embree, Edwin R. *Indians of the Americas.* Boston, 1939.
Kroeber, A. L. *Anthropology.* New York, 1923.
Macgowan, Kenneth. *Early Man in the New World.* New York, 1950.
Means, Philip A. *Ancient Civilizations of the Andes.* New York, 1928.
Morley, Sylvanus G. *The Ancient Maya.* Stanford University, Calif., 1947.
Steward, J. H. (ed.). *Handbook of South American Indians.* 6 vols., Washington, D.C., 1946–50.
Thompson, J. Eric. *Mexico Before Cortés.* New York, 1933.
————. *The Rise and Fall of the Maya Civilization.* Norman, Okla., 1954.
Wissler, Clark. *The American Indian.* New York, 1922.

V.   CONQUEST AND COLONIZATION

1. The Sixteenth Century
Aiton, Arthur. *Antonio Mendoza.* Durham, N.C., 1927.
Bishop, Morris. *The Odyssey of Cabeza de Vaca.* New York, 1933.
Bourne, Edward G. *Spain in America.* New York, 1908.
Collis, Maurice. *Cortes and Montezuma.* New York, 1955.
Descola, Jean. *The Conquistadors.* New York, 1957.
Díaz del Castillo, Bernal. *The Discovery and Conquest of Mexico.* New York, 1956.
Grahame, Robert B. C. *The Conquest of New Granada.* New York, 1922.
————. *The Conquest of the River Plate.* New York, 1924.
————. *Pedro de Valdivia.* London, 1926.
Hamilton, Earl J. *American Treasure and the Price Revolution in Spain.* Cambridge, Mass., 1934.

Hanke, Lewis. *The Spanish Struggle for Justice in the Conquest of America.* Philadelphia, 1949.

Haring, Clarence H. *Trade and Navigation Between Spain and the West Indies. . . .* Cambridge, Mass., 1928.

Kelly, John E. *Pedro de Alvarado.* Princeton, N.J., 1932.

Kirkpatrick, F. A. *The Spanish Conquistadores.* London, 1934.

Markham, Clements R. *The Conquest of New Granada.* London, 1912.

May, Stella B. *The Conqueror's Lady* [consort of Valdivia], New York, 1930.

Maynard, Theodore. *De Soto and the Conquistadores.* New York, 1930.

Means, Philip A. *History of the Spanish Conquest of Yucatán . . .* Cambridge, Mass., 1917.

———. *The Fall of the Inca Empire.* New York, 1932.

Morison, Samuel E. *Admiral of the Ocean Sea* [Columbus]. Boston, 1942.

Prescott, William H. *The Conquest of Mexico.* Many editions.

———. *The Conquest of Peru.* Many editions.

Priestley, Herbert I. *The Coming of the White Man.* New York, 1927.

Richman, Irving B. *The Spanish Conquerors.* New Haven, 1919.

Simpson, Leslie B. *The Encomienda in New Spain.* Berkeley, 1950.

Wood, William. *Elizabethan Sea-Dogs.* New Haven, 1921.

Zimmerman, A. F. *Francisco de Toledo.* Caldwell, Idaho, 1938.

2. Spanish America, 1600–1800

Bolton, Herbert E. *The Spanish Borderlands.* New Haven, 1921.

———. *Outpost of Empire.* New York, 1931.

———. *Rim of Christendom.* New York, 1936.

Cunningham, Charles A. *The Audiencia in the Spanish Colonies.* Berkeley, Calif., 1919.

Fisher, Lilian E. *Viceregal Administration in the Spanish Colonies.* Berkeley, Calif., 1926.

———. *The Intendent System in Spanish America.* Berkeley, Calif., 1939.

Gage, Thomas A. *A New Survey of the West Indies.* New York, 1929.

Haring, Clarence H. *Buccaneers in the West Indies . . .* New York, 1910.

———. *The Spanish Empire in America.* New York, 1947.

Humboldt, Alex. von. *Political Essay on the Kingdom of New Spain.* Many editions.

———. *Travels in Equinoctial America.* Many editions.

Juan, Jorge, and Ulloa, Antonio. *A Voyage to South America.* 2 vols., London, 1806.

Keller, A. G. *Colonization.* New York, 1908.

Lanning, John Tate. *Academic Culture in the Spanish Colonies.* New York, 1940.

———. *The University in the Kingdom of Guatemala.* Ithaca, N.Y., 1955.

———. *The Eighteenth-Century Enlightenment in the University of San Carlos de Guatemala.* Ithaca, N.Y., 1956.

Lea, Henry C. *The Inquisition in the Spanish Colonies.* New York, 1922.

Leonard, Irving A. *Sigüenza y Gongóra* . . . Berkeley, 1929.

———. *Books of the Brave.* Cambridge, Mass., 1949.

Means, Philip A. *The Spanish Main* . . . New York, 1935.

Moses, Bernard. *The Spanish Dependencies in South America.* 2 vols., New York, 1914.

———. *Spain's Declining Power in South America.* Berkeley, 1919.

———. *Spanish Colonial Literature.* New York, 1922.

Parry, John. *The Sale of Public Offices in the Indies* . . . Berkeley, 1952.

Pons, F. R. J. de. *Travels in South America.* 2 vols., London, 1807.

Rippy, J. Fred, and Nelson, J. T. *Crusaders of the Jungle.* Chapel Hill, N.C., 1936.

Watson, R. G. *Spanish and Portuguese South America.* 2 vols., London, 1884.

3. Colonial Brazil

Armitage, John. *The History of Brazil.* 2 vols., London, 1836.

Da Cunha de Azevedo Coutinho. *An Essay on the Brazils.* London, 1807.

Dawson, Thos. C. *The South American Republics.* 2 vols., New York, 1904. See Vol. I.

Grant, Andrew. *History of Brazil.* London, 1909.

Koster, Henry. *Travels in Brazil.* 2 vols., London, 1817.

Mawe, John. *Travels in the Interior of Brazil.* London, 1812.

Southey, Robert. *History of Brazil.* 3 vols., London, 1817–22.

Varnhagen, Francisco A. de. *Historia geral do Brasil.* 5 vols., São Paulo, Brazil, 1927–30.

VI. THE WARS OF INDEPENDENCE

Angell, Hildegarde. *Simón Bolívar.* New York, 1930.

Armitage, John. *History of Brazil.* 2 vols., London, 1836.

Caruso, John A. *The Liberators of Mexico.* New York, 1954.

Grahame, Robt. B. C. *José Antonio Páez.* London, 1929.

Hasbrouck, Alfred. *Foreign Legionaries in the Liberation of Spanish South America.* New York, 1928.

Masur, Gerhard. *Simón Bolívar.* Albuquerque, N.M., 1948.

Mitre Bartolomé. *The Emancipation of South America.* London, 1893.

Moses, Bernard. *The Intellectual Background of the Revolution in South America.* New York, 1926.

Perkins, Dexter. *Hands Off: The Monroe Doctrine.* Boston, 1941.

Robertson, W. S. *Rise of the Spanish-American Republics as Told in the Lives of their Liberators.* New York, 1918.

———. *Life of Miranda.* 2 vols., Chapel Hill, N.C., 1929.

———. *France and Latin-American Independence.* Baltimore, Md., 1939.

———. *Iturbide of Mexico.* Durham, N.C., 1952.

Schoellkopf, Anna. *José de San Martín.* New York, 1924.

Sherwell, Guillermo A. *Antonio José de Sucre.* Washington, D.C., 1924.

575

Stoddard, T. L. *The French Revolution in Santo Domingo.* New York, 1914.

Walsh, R. *Notices of Brazil.* 2 vols., London, 1830.

Webster, C. K. *Britain and the Independence of Latin America.* 2 vols., New York, 1938.

Whitaker, Arthur P. *The United States and the Independence of Latin America.* Baltimore, Md., 1941.

Ybarra, T. R. *Bolívar, Passionate Warrior.* New York, 1929.

ℵ THE NATIONAL PERIOD

I. GENERAL WORKS

1. Guides (consult the references for the Colonial Period)

2. General and Special Works (see also the works listed under section 2 for the Colonial Period)

Akers, C. E. *A History of South America.* New York, 1930.

Arciniegas, Germán. *The State of Latin America.* New York, 1952.

Dawson, T. C. *The South American Republics.* 2 vols., New York, 1904.

Gunther, John. *Inside Latin America.* New York, 1941.

Herring, Hubert. *Good Neighbors.* New Haven, Conn., 1941.

Jones, Tom B. *South America Rediscovered.* Minneapolis, Minn., 1949.

Mecham, J. Lloyd. *Church and State in Latin America.* Chapel Hill, N.C., 1932.

Munro, Dana G. *The Five Republics of Central America.* New York, 1918.

Plaza, Galo. *Problems of Democracy in Latin America.* Chapel Hill, N.C., 1955.

Stephens, John L. *Incidents of Travel in Central America . . .* 2 vols., New Brunswick, N.J., 1949.

Villacorta, J. A. *Cursa de la historia de la América Central.* Guatemala City, 1928.

Wilgus, A. Curtis (ed.). *Argentina, Chile, and Brazil since Independence.* Washington, D.C., 1935.

———. *South American Dictators.* Washington, D.C., 1937.

II. THE SOUTH AMERICAN COUNTRIES

1. Argentina

Alexander, R. I. *The Perón Era.* New York, 1951.

Blanksten, George I. *Perón's Argentina.* Chicago, 1953.

Gandía, Enrique de. *Historia de la República Argentina . . .* Buenos Aires, 1940.

Jefferson, Mark. *Peopling the Argentine Pampa.* New York, 1926.

Kirkpatrick, F. A. *A History of the Argentine Republic.* Cambridge, Eng., 1931.

Rennie, Ysabel F. *The Argentine Republic.* New York, 1944.

2. Bolivia

Argüedas, Alcides. *Historia general de Bolivia.* La Paz, Bolivia, 1922.
Leonard, Olen E. *Bolivia: Land, People, and Institutions.* Washington, D.C., 1952.

3. Brazil

Calogeras, João F. *A History of Brazil.* Chapel Hill, N.C., 1939.
Hill, Lawrence F. (ed.). *Brazil.* Berkeley, Calif., 1947.
Nash, Roy. *The Conquest of Brazil.* New York, 1926.
Williams, Mary W. *Dom Pedro the Magnanimous.* Chapel Hill, N.C., 1937.

4. Chile

Edwards, Agustín. *My Native Land.* London, 1928.
Galdames, Luís. *A History of Chile.* Chapel Hill, N.C., 1941.
McBride, George M. *Chile: Land and Society.* New York, 1936.
Stevenson, John R. *The Chilean Popular Front.* Philadelphia, 1942.

5. Colombia

Eder, Phanor, J. *Colombia,* New York, 1913.
Gibson, William M. *The Constitutions of Colombia.* Durham, N.C., 1948.
Henao, Jesús M. and Arrubla, G., *A History of Colombia.* Chapel Hill, N.C., 1938.
Romoli, Kathleen. *Colombia, Gateway to South America.* New York, 1941.

6. Ecuador

Blanksten, George I. *Ecuador: Constitutions and Caudillos.* Berkeley, Calif., 1951.
Franklin, Albert. *Ecuador.* New York, 1943.
Linke, Lilo. *Ecuador, Country of Contrasts.* London, 1954.
Pattee, Richard. *Gabriel García Moreno* . . . Quito, Ecuador, 1941.

7. Paraguay

Pendle, George. *Paraguay, A Riverside Nation.* London, 1954.
Warren, Harris G. *Paraguay, An Informal History.* Norman, Okla., 1949.

8. Peru

Basadre, Jorge. *Historia de la República del Perú.* 2 vols., Lima, Peru, 1949.
Enoch, C. R. *Peru.* London, 1935.
Kantor, Harry. *The Ideology and Program of the Peruvian Aprista Movement.* Berkeley, Calif., 1953.

9. Uruguay

Fitzgibbon, Russell H. *Uruguay, Portrait of a Democracy.* New Brunswick, N.J., 1954.
Hanson, Simon G. *Utopia in Uruguay.* New York, 1938.

Pendle, George. *Uruguay, South America's First Welfare State*. London, 1952.

10. Venezuela

Gil Fortoul, José. *Historia constitucional de Venezuela*. 2 vols., Caracas, Venezuela, 1942.
Marshland, W. D., and H. L. *Venezuela Through Its History*. New York, 1954.
Rourke, Thomas. *Gómez, Tyrant of the Andes*. New York, 1948.
Wise, George S. *Caudillo: A Portrait of Antonio Guzmán Blanco*. New York, 1951.

III. REPUBLICS OF NORTHERN LATIN AMERICA

1. Costa Rica

Jones, Chester L. *Costa Rica* . . . Madison, Wis., 1935.

2. Cuba

Chapman, C. E. *A History of the Cuban Republic*. New York, 1927.
Chester, Edmund A. *A Sergeant Named Batista*. New York, 1954.
Nelson, Lowery. *Rural Cuba*. Minneapolis, Minn., 1950.
Strode, Hudson. *The Pageant of Cuba*. New York, 1934.

3. Dominican Republic

Hicks, Albert C. *Blood in the Streets; The Life and Rule of Trujillo*. New York, 1946.
Welles, Sumner. *Naboth's Vineyard* . . . 2 vols., New York, 1928.

4. Guatemala

Holleran, Mary P. *Church and State in Guatemala*. New York, 1949.
Jones, Chester L. *Guatemala, Past and Present*. Minneapolis, Minn., 1940.

5. Haiti

Leyburn, J. G. *The Haitian People*. New Haven, 1941.
Rodman, Selden. *Haiti: The Black Republic*. New York, 1954.

6. Honduras

Stokes, William S. *Honduras* . . . Madison, Wis., 1950.

7. Mexico

Beals, Carlton. *Porfirio Díaz*. Philadelphia, 1932.
Callcott, Winfred H. *Santa Anna* . . . Norman, Okla., 1936.
Hannay, David. *Porfirio Díaz*. London, 1917.
Parkes, Henry B. *A History of Mexico*. New York, 1938.
Priestley, Herbert I. *The Mexican Nation*. New York, 1923.
Roeder, Ralph. *Juárez and His Mexico*. 2 vols., New York, 1947.
Tannenbaum, Frank. *Mexico: The Struggle for Peace and Bread*. New York, 1950.
Townsend, William C. *Lázaro Cárdenas*. Ann Arbor, Mich., 1952.
Whetten, Nathan. *Rural Mexico*. Chicago, 1948.

8. *Panama*

Biesanz, John and Mavis. *The People of Panama.* New York, 1955.

IV. ECONOMIC DEVELOPMENT

Gordon, Wendell C. *The Economy of Latin America.* New York, 1950.
Hanson, Simon G. *Economic Development of Latin America.* Washington, D.C., 1950.
Kepner, C. D. and Soothill, J. H. *The Banana Empire.* New York, 1935.
Lieuwen, Edwin. *Petroleum in Venezuela.* Berkeley, Calif., 1954.
Rippy, J. Fred. *Latin America and the Industrial Age.* New York, 1947.
Stewart, Watt. *Henry Meiggs, Yankee Pizarro.* Durham, N.C., 1946.
————. *Chinese Bondage in Peru.* Durham, N.C., 1951.
Wythe, George. *An Outline of Latin-American Economic Development.* New York, 1946.
————. *Industry in Latin America.* New York, 1949.

V. THE "HIGHER CULTURE"

Blackwell, Alice S. *Some Spanish-American Poets.* New York, 1929.
Botsford, Florence. *Songs of the Americas.* New York, 1940.
Coester, Alfred. *The Literary History of Spanish America.* New York, 1916.
Crawford, Rex. *A Century of Latin-American Thought.* Cambridge, Mass., 1944.
Ellison, Fred P. *Brazil's New Novel.* Berkeley, Calif., 1954.
Goldberg, Isaac. *Studies in Spanish-American Literature.* New York, 1920.
————. *Brazilian Literature.* New York, 1922.
Putnam, Samuel. *Marvelous Journey: A Survey of . . . Brazilian Literature.* New York, 1948.
Romanell, Patrick. *Making of the Mexican Mind.* Lincoln, Nebr., 1952.
Sánchez Reulet, Aníbal. *Contemporary Latin-American Philosophy.* Albuquerque, N.M., 1954.
Spell, Jefferson R. *Contemporary Spanish-American Fiction.* Chapel Hill, N.C., 1943.
Torres-Ríoseco, Arturo. *The Epic of Spanish-American Literature.* New York, 1942.

VI. INTERNATIONAL RELATIONS

Beale, Howard K. *Theodore Roosevelt and the Rise of America to World Power.* Baltimore, Md., 1956.
Bemis, Samuel F. *The Latin American Policy of the United States.* New York, 1943.
Box, Pelham. *Origins of the Paraguayan War.* Urbana, Ill., 1927.
Cady, John F. *Foreign Intervention in the Río de la Plata . . .* Philadelphia, 1929.
Dávila, Carlos. *We of the Americas.* New York, 1949.
Dawson, Daniel. *The Mexican Venture* [French Intervention]. London, 1915.

De Conde, Alexander. *Herbert Hoover's Latin American Policy*. Stanford University, Calif., 1951.

Ferrera, Orestes. *The Last Spanish War* [1898]. New York, 1937.

Fitzgibbon, Russell. *Cuba and the United States*. Menasha, Wis., 1935.

Guerrant, Edward O. *Roosevelt's Good Neighbor Policy*. Albuquerque, N.M., 1950.

Hill, Lawrence F. *The United States and Brazil*. Durham, N.C., 1932.

Kelchner, Warren H. *Latin-American Relations with the League of Nations*. Boston, 1930.

McCain, William D. *The United States and the Republic of Panama*. Durham, N.C., 1937.

Manchester, Alan K. *British Pre-eminence in Brazil* . . . Chapel Hill, N.C., 1933.

Martin, Percy A. *Latin America and the World War*. Baltimore, Md., 1925.

Parks, E. Taylor. *Colombia and the United States*. Durham, N.C., 1934.

Perkins, Dexter. *Hands Off: The Monroe Doctrine*. Boston, 1941.

Rippy, J. Fred. *Rivalry of the United States and Great Britain Over Latin America*. Baltimore, Md., 1929.

————. *The United States and Mexico*. New York, 1931.

————. *Latin America in World Politics*. New York, 1938.

————. *The Caribbean Danger Zone*. New York, 1940.

Robertson, W. S. *France and Latin-American Independence*. Baltimore, Md., 1939.

Scott, James Brown. *The International Conferences of the American States*. New York, 1931.

Smith, Justin H. *The Annexation of Texas*. New York, 1919.

————. *The War With Mexico*. 2 vols., New York, 1919.

Stuart, Graham H. *Latin America and the United States*. New York, 1955.

Temperley, Harold V. *The Foreign Policy of Canning*. London, 1925.

Webster, C. K. *Britain and the Independence of Latin America*. 2 vols., New York, 1938.

Whitaker, Arthur P. *The United States and the Independence of Latin America*. Baltimore, Md., 1941.

————. *The Western Hemisphere Idea: Its Rise and Decline*. Ithaca, N.Y., 1954.

INDEX